Agrarian Change and Crisis in Europe, 1200–1500

Routledge Research in Medieval Studies

1 **Agrarian Change and Crisis in Europe, 1200–1500**
Edited by Harry Kitsikopoulos

Agrarian Change and Crisis in Europe, 1200–1500

Edited by Harry Kitsikopoulos

Routledge
Taylor & Francis Group
NEW YORK LONDON

First published 2012
by Routledge
270 Madison Avenue, New York, NY 10016

Simultaneously published in the UK
by Routledge
2 Park Square, Milton Park, Abingdon, Oxon OX14 4RN

Routledge is an imprint of the Taylor & Francis Group, an informa business

Typeset in Sabon by IBT Global.
Printed and bound in the United States of America on acid-free paper by IBT Global.

Library of Congress Cataloging-in-Publication Data

Agrarian change and crisis in Europe, 1200–1500 / edited by Harry Kitsikopoulos.
p. cm. — (Routledge research in medieval studies ; 1)
Includes bibliographical references and index.
1. Agriculture—Economic aspects—Europe—History—To 1500. 2. Agriculture—Social aspects—Europe—History—To 1500. 3. Social change—Europe—History—To 1500. 4. Crises—Europe—History—To 1500. 5. Europe—Economic conditions—To 1492. 6. Europe—Social conditions—To 1492. 7. Europe—Rural conditions. I. Kitsikopoulos, Harry.
HD1917.A325 2011
338.1094'0902—dc22
2011004621

ISBN13: 978-0-415-89578-1 (hbk)
ISBN13: 978-0-203-12823-7 (ebk)

To my parents

Contents

Figures

Tables

1 Introduction

Harry Kitsikopoulos

The essays in this volume address one of the classic subjects on economic history: the process of aggregate economic growth and the crisis that engulfed the European continent during the late Middle Ages. This was not an ordinary crisis. During the period 1200–1500 Europe witnessed wars, endemic episodes of famine, the culmination of a long-drawn process of declining temperatures, and a wave of plague epidemics which amounted to one of its worst health crisis, rivaled only by the Justinian plague in the sixth century. The combined effect of these challenges was to call into question the property rights and institutions which determined the production of goods and services and the distribution of wealth; in other words, this was a crisis which opened the possibility of fundamental systemic change, one of the rarest events in human history. Change did take place by 1500 but the outcomes that came about across different countries and regions were very diverse and often ambivalent in the sense that institutional arrangements shifted but were still in a state of flux.

This is not an easy story to tell given the scarcity of surviving sources and it is even more difficult to synthesize it at a high level of abstraction in order to make sense of it given the diversity of experiences across the continent. A limited number of commonalities do exist, the most noticeable being the universal population growth which took place during the thirteenth century. The various countries, however, started the period with very different population densities and thus by 1300 some of them (England, France, Italy, Byzantium) found themselves being heavily populated and highly urbanized, whereas others lagged behind in either one or both respects (Spain, Scandinavia, Russia, Central Europe). These developments raised the need for greater food supplies. Producers responded by utilizing various elements of the existing technological package with particular choices being determined by differences in climate, ecological profiles, and land/labor ratios. But the particular technological package was a mature one in the sense that it, by and large, was not infused with new inventions and hence it makes more sense to be preoccupied with the diffusion of existing techniques. Nevertheless, it was a package that, at its best, had the capacity to lead to exceptional levels of productivity. The latter was realized in a few regions; but, by and large, productivity levels in late medieval Europe reveal a very wide spectrum with most regions being classified towards the middle or low end of it.

Did Europeans raise their food supplies by 1300 sufficiently enough to match the demographic upswing? If not, this calls into question the very viability of the feudal system and opens the door to a debate on crisis based on endogenous factors. Plain intuition would suggest that such debate would be pertinent only to those countries which achieved the highest levels of population growth by that time but not to others. The issue of a systemic crisis has proven to be one of the most intractable aspects of this debate, leading many historians to seek the roots of the medieval economic crisis in a pair of exogenous factors: the decline of temperatures which culminated in a reduction of yields as well as famines by the beginning of the fourteenth century and, even more so, the shock brought by the series of plague epidemics whose impact reverberated through the next century.

The issues outlined so far are mainly empirical and the reason consensus on them is still eluding us has to do with major gaps that exist in the available evidence. The last issue pertinent to this debate is equally difficult to tackle: should the events of this period be explicated through the narrative of conventional historians or is it preferable to adopt the logic of models often used by economic historians? The latter methodology has dominated the debate on the feudal crisis despite the fact that it has both virtues and drawbacks. On the one hand, formal models offer a convenient 'manual of instructions' of how to choose from a multitude of facts and how to classify and interpret them; on the other hand, models are often restrictive in terms of the number of variables they incorporate and hence, in an effort to simplify the reality of human experience, may end up doing injustice to its complexity.

The aforementioned questions have sparked a fierce exchange among historians, particularly in the context of the Brenner debate which started in the pages of *Past and Present* in 1976 and culminated in a collection of essays in 1987.[1] The Brenner debate induced scholarship in the context of individual European countries, in some cases initiating such a dialogue for the first time, in others forcing the re-examination of views which predated this debate. The review of the literature that follows focuses on scholars who have offered holistic and comprehensive theoretical paradigms at the expense of others who have contributed partial theoretical interpretations and/or have generated empirical evidence buttressing a particular theory; the latter type of contributions, however, are cited in the context of individual chapters.

Since the theories of classical economists offered the inspiration for many of the key interpretations, it makes sense to make a reference to them, beginning with the Ricardian theory of rent. The Ricardian model portrays land as a non-reproducible factor containing a wide variety of plots with different levels of fertility determined by soil conditions and locational characteristics. Capital and labor are the variable inputs, the former embodying technology with inertial characteristics. Population growth functions as the dynamic element providing the momentum of historical change. The need to raise food supplies prompts two types of responses: either injecting additional quantities of labor and capital to already utilized plots (the intensive margin of cultivation) or leading to the reclamation of progressively less fertile plots (the extensive margin). Either way, marginal product declines whereas marginal cost and prices move up. Rent is not a component of price since the latter is determined at the margin but rent is generated in plots of higher fertility compared to the margin and is equal to the output differential between them; rent as social revenue keeps expanding throughout the process. As more marginal plots are brought into cultivation the productivity differential between them and more fertile plots widens and translates into growing rental income for landowners, assuming the presence of purely competitive markets. The Ricardian logic is mechanistic, teleological, highly pessimistic, and evokes the specter of a Malthusian 'positive check' as the most likely way out of this gloomy scenario. It is a theory which reveals tension among social classes, but class relations are irrelevant in terms of determining outcomes because even if landlords did not exist as a class the evolution of productivity, costs, and prices would remain identical.[2]

Ideas influenced by the Ricardian framework were expressed by several early historians but it was Postan who formulated one of the first comprehensive applications of this theory to the pre-plague English economy and became its most influential proponent by being one of the main participants in the Brenner debate.[3] Postan, through his own research and that of his pupils and collaborators, established a causal relationship between the robust population growth of the thirteenth century and the responses it prompted, taking the form of extensive land reclamation and extending the margins of arable husbandry at the expense of grazing grounds since the former provides more calorific output than the latter; consequently, the increasing utilization of more marginal land and the shrinking numbers of livestock and manure supplies led to declining yields. The second option described in the Ricardian model, greater intensification through capital formation, was not particularly noticeable due to the absence of major technological innovations and on the basis of prevailing cultural values among the class of landlords which favored the possession of land, functioning as a status symbol, as opposed to investment spending; landownership translated to raising a standing army, seeking salvation through land endowments, and attracting alliances with other members of the baronial class through marriage arrangements. There is no doubt that English feudalism was in a state of crisis by the end of the century, reflected in rising product prices, in the exorbitant rents charged for leaseholds and tenancies-at-will as well as high entry fines relating to free and customary holdings and, most dramatically, in the heavy mortality of the 1315–17 famines. Ultimately, however, the crisis was resolved by the wave of plague epidemics which reversed the movement of key economic variables. Postan's allegiance to the Ricardian logic was also reflected in his unwillingness to treat the feudal class structure as a relevant factor. In fact, when this stance drew sharp criticism by Marxist historians (see below), Hatcher (his main collaborator) argued that, unlike a capitalist economy in which rents are allowed to adjust upwards, customary law blocked in many cases the free functioning of market forces to the benefit of peasants.[4]

Marx's theory of historical materialism offered another theoretical framework centered around the notion of a dialectical interpretation of historical change which is driven by class conflict over the distribution of wealth. It is this conflict in the context of the relations of production which determines the nature and degree to which skills and technology can develop and, therefore, the long-term viability of a mode of production. At some point, the former becomes a fetter to the latter, ushering a period of crisis which functions as the preamble to a transitioning into a different socioeconomic formation. There is a considerable degree of determinism in Marx's account, allowing a very limited role to human volition as long as the relations and forces of production go through their symbiotic phase. It is only with the onset of the crisis that human will becomes instrumental, acting as a midwife, to use Marx's analogy, in speeding up the transition to a new system.

The Marxist tradition had established a longstanding interest in the feudal crisis as part of its interest in the transition from feudalism to capitalism.[5] But it was in the context of the Brenner debate that it transcended the stage of its members having a dialogue largely among themselves to the point of confronting the dominant mainstream approach. At the center of Brenner's argument was the statement that "the problem . . . was not, as Postan and Hatcher contend, the 'insufficient supply of new technological possibilities,' but rather the feudal economy's inability to *make use* of possibilities which existed."[6] In other words, granted the absence of technological innovations during the pre-plague period, what prevented the more widespread diffusion of already existing techniques carried through a more extensive capital formation? Postan's and Hatcher's emphasis on the cultural values of the ruling class did not seem particularly convincing. The explanation lies in the very class relations of feudal society which established seigneurial prerogatives based on political and military compulsion evident, to provide just one illustration, in the fact that the total obligations of serfs were significantly higher than those of free peasants. Access to such prerogatives, which often generated the bulk of the ruling elite's revenues, diminished incentives towards investment; the problem was compounded by extravagant levels of consumption which siphoned away from productive uses a substantial portion of their revenues. At the same time, the feudal extraction mechanism drained resources away from peasant holdings, thus limiting also their capability towards productive investment. It follows that it was the nature of the feudal class relations that explains the failure to increase output through the intensive margin of cultivation, despite the fact that this is a distinct option in the Ricardian model; "feudal development tended to take inward-looking forms—forms of redistribution of wealth, rather than its creation."[7] In the end, Brenner found himself in agreement with Postan on the presence of a structural crisis but argued that the type of forces discussed by the latter were of limited relevance, only to the extent they were "refracted through the prism of changing social-property relations and fluctuating balance of class forces." Such property relations "once established, tend to impose rather strict limits and possibilities, indeed rather specific long-term patterns, on a society's economic development . . . as a rule, they are not shaped by, or alterable in terms of changes in demographic or commercial trends."[8] The resolution of the feudal crisis during the post-plague period took the form of multiple class conflicts, often violent, across Europe with outcomes being determined based on the relative strength of the opposing forces.

The New Institutional Economics (NIE) of D. C. North and his followers found itself in agreement with several aspects of Brenner's analysis in light of the school's core belief that "institutions . . . are the underlying determinant of the long-run performance of the economy."[9] According to North, institutional arrangements can be conveniently analyzed by utilizing the concept of equilibrium. The presence of equilibrium implies that the contractual arrangements among economic agents and their relative bargaining power does not render worthwhile any restructuring. That is not to imply that every agent is perfectly content with the existing arrangements, rather that the relative costs and benefits of change do not render the latter a worthy goal. Nor does the presence of equilibrium necessarily imply the existence of efficient outcomes. "The increasing returns characteristic of an initial set of institutions that provide disincentives to productive activity will create organizations and interest groups with a stake in the existing constraints. They will shape the polity in their interests. Such institutions provide incentives that may encourage military domination of the polity and economy, religious fanaticism, or plain, simple redistributive organizations, but they provide few rewards from increases in the stock and dissemination of economically useful knowledge."[10]

A radical shift in relative prices may act as an inducement mechanism leading the party which stands to derive benefits from change to seek a redefinition of existing rules, but often these revised rules can come about only within the context of an institutional restructuring. If and when the latter becomes a reality, rules, customs, and traditions are either ignored or altered. But it is important to emphasize that change does not follow uniform pathways, outcomes being conditioned by the relative bargaining power of the conflicting groups and the form of organizations that have evolved in the context of the existing institutional structure. Thus, according to North, historical change is evolutionary and contains a certain degree of indeterminacy which prevents convergence of outcomes when comparing societies that may be facing similar challenges. Applied to the case of feudalism, the radical change of the land/labor ratio following the Black Death led to weakening seigneurial power and the gradual ascendancy of contractual tenures in place of customary ones. This process led to fundamental change overtime as a result of myriads of separate agreements between lords and serfs. But these outcomes were most prevalent in large parts of Western Europe, the eastern part of the continent following a radically different trajectory.[11]

North's theoretical paradigm has been refined, as applied to the late Middle Ages, particularly by two eminent economic historians, S. R. Epstein and Bas van Bavel, both being very keen to stress in their work that the analysis of regional contrasts is key to appreciating how different institutions and balance of power configurations may lead to different outcomes in the context of societies faced by a similar set of circumstances. According to Epstein, the post-plague population decline and the retreat of cultivation from marginal lands led to reducing the cost of labor in these particular regions and thus creating the opportunity for more labor intensive and specialized manufacturing and agricultural activities. But for such activities to flourish and specialization to be irreversible certain conditions had to be present. First, there had to be a growth of aggregate demand for such products through the redistribution of wealth in favor of lower-middle class strata of the population, such redistribution being the outcome of acute social conflicts. But the degree to which these redistributional effects were realized depended on the flexibility (or lack thereof) of institutional arrangements such as "the character of the state, the nature of urban power, the structure of relations of production and of the markets." In regions where institutions proved to be flexible the redistribution of wealth did take place raising aggregate demand for non-staple agricultural and manufactured goods, specialization, and market expansion.[12]

The close ties between Marxist interpretations and NIE ought to be apparent. North openly acknowledged Marx's pioneering role in delving into the role of institutions and in referring to Marxist models of historical change commented that to the extent they "convincingly relate institutions to incentives to choices to outcomes they are consistent with the argument of this study. And because much of human economic history is a story of humans with unequal bargaining strength maximizing their own well-being, it would be amazing if such maximizing activity were not frequently at the expense of others."[13] But there are also subtle but important distinctions in these two methodologies. In Epstein's argument the Marxist emphasis on the 'relations of production' becomes simply one of the conditioning factors of growth, in fact largely determined by the wider institutional context. While Marxists focused on the role of lords in stifling productive efficiency, Epstein's analysis encompassed a wider net of institutions such as the role of urban jurisdictions which could be as feudal as lords; the difference between the two is that while the latter sought to divert resources from the sphere of production, the former interfered in the sphere of distribution. Another important difference between the two models is that while for Marxists the contours and determinants of technological change are key elements in understanding growth patterns, for Epstein the role of institutions is far more important. The slow progression of technological developments could have only a limited role in reducing transaction costs, as opposed to institutional changes which had far greater potential in this regard (e.g., through the removal of tolls) in the context of economies characterized by high transportation costs regarding low value and, in most cases, bulky goods.

Adam Smith's theory of economic growth, with its emphasis on the extent of the market (defined by population densities and urbanization rates) as the prime determinant of productivity and output growth via its positive effects on the division of labor and technological innovation, was the inspiration for a final interpretation. Various accounts of this approach appeared even prior to the Brenner debate but the most sophisticated version of it was formulated by Campbell, whose empirical work spans three decades, though his theoretical model started taking shape during the last 15–20 years; despite the fact that it offers an account distinct to the English experience, it is worth discussing because it has gained quite a few sympathetic ears among other English medievalists and its methodology shows signs of growing popularity across national borders.[14] It is an interpretation which marks a radical departure from previous ones by underplaying the role of institutional factors, places its emphasis on the impact of market forces and, most strikingly, it denies the presence of an endogenous crisis.

Campbell cites the existence of certain supply side constraints having a negative impact on overall economic growth; specifically, the presence of institutional rigidities emanating from the lack of universal private property rights. The presence of inflexible arrangements in the context of common fields, pastures, and wastes precluded more efficient alternatives in the form of enclosed fields that would have brought a more rational managerial regime with higher inputs of labor and capital. Nevertheless, such arrangements, along with instances of managerial conservatism and substantial reliance on customary labor (whose productivity was lower compared to wage labor), were features that "had as much *if not more* to do with limitations of demand as with the shortcoming of supply."[15]

It is mainly on demand factors we have to look at to understand the dynamics of the pre-plague economy. Focusing his attention on evidence drawn from demesnes, Campbell argues that England made noticeable progress by c. 1300 in developing a commercial economy with a fairly sophisticated trading network. Consumption needs were bound to influence production decisions on the part of estates but "market exchange was plainly already the greater influence upon production." The reason for this conspicuous market orientation on the part of landlords was the need for cash to buy a variety of consumption goods that became available with the expansion of regional and international trade, and to pay taxes due to the growing appetite of the Crown for such revenues.[16]

Campbell not only attributes a sense of commercial orientation to feudal lords but takes a (very bold) step further by arguing that "the market via its influence upon economic rent" largely determined major production decisions such as the spatial distribution of field systems and crops, as well as the level of productive intensity. It was the German economist Johann von Thünen who first came up with the concept of economic rent in outlining an idealized pattern of agricultural production in the context of a nineteenth-century capitalist economy. To Campbell this theoretical framework offered a useful tool in explaining production decisions among estates in the London region given the demand for foodstuffs emanating from the metropolis. Farm specialization and division of labor, two major instruments of increasing productivity, were some of the benefits tied to this commercial orientation.[17] It follows that "commercialization was not merely an aspect of growth, it helped to make expansion possible in the first place."[18]

Nevertheless, Campbell is willing to go only so far in terms of his optimism. The aforementioned supply side constraints and, most importantly, the relatively small size of London and other urban centers imposed limitations in terms of the intensity of production and the clarity at which the Thünenesque scenario was applied. The difference between London in the fourteenth compared to the seventeenth century was the size of its population, being less than a fifth of its size in the former time compared to the latter. The limited size of the capital meant that it could not raise the level of economic rent over a wider area and thus drive the English economy into more sustained economic growth. It is important to note that it was not the lack of adequate technologies that presented a problem since they were essentially the same in both the medieval and early modern periods. All in all, this Smithian scenario was in the process of being unfolded by c. 1300 and despite the presence of strains, the level of production was on a par with the growth of population leaving grain output per capita virtually the same. But strains do not amount to a crisis. In fact, Campbell's analysis implies that if this scenario kept unfolding, market forces would have eventually eroded the institutional rigidities on the supply side.[19]

A crisis did emerge but it was due to an exogenous factor. Campbell refers to the evidence from the early fourteenth century of a spell of abnormally bad weather with very low temperatures, harvest failures, and a series of devastating epidemics affecting cattle and sheep. These environmental and biological factors, commencing with the poor harvest of 1314, and continuing with harvest failures (1315–17) and livestock diseases, dragged until the 1350s and beyond; these events not only dealt a devastating blow on demography and economic conditions but they may have also triggered the spread of the bacteria associated with the great plague. These events "were separate manifestations of the same prolonged episode of environmental disturbance" and ended up being "the most difficult and hazardous episode in the annals of English agriculture."[20] In the end, it was bad weather and microbes that brought about the crisis of English feudalism.

French historiography is the only tradition that has succeeded in rivaling, but not quite matching, the English literature on the feudal crisis debate.[21] The 'total history' approach of the *Annales* school has dominated the debate with most of its members playing an active role in promoting Postan's line of argument based on the French evidence on prices and wages. But this was not a tradition which simply echoed others' interpretations. Le Roy Ladurie's work, centered in the early modern period but often extending back to the Middle Ages, revealed long-term cycles whose ebbs were characterized by fragmentation of property among peasants and declining living standards conditioned by "regulating mechanisms which . . . spring from the movement of population and from the phenomena analyzed by Ricardo and Malthus."[22] But, even more so than Postan, he believed "that history must give more and more room to specifically epidemic and, therefore, one might say, 'biological' factors in order to explain instances of Neo-Malthusian 'blockages' in the fourteenth" century.[23] In other words, feudalism was crippled by the upswing of the demographic cycle but its demise was brought by microbes, an account repeated three decades later by Campbell in the context of a far more optimistic narrative.

But it was the work of another French historian, Guy Bois, which made one of the most influential contributions to this debate by combining a solid record on empirical work and a non-dogmatic adherence to the Marxist model, allowing him to be appreciative of certain elements of the Neo-Malthusian argument. Brenner's version of Marxism, according to Bois, amounted to a "voluntarist vision of history" by refusing to acknowledge that the resolution of particular class conflicts was contingent upon the impact of the demographic cycle on economic variables. "By what strange perversion of Marxism it is possible to refuse to take such firm data into account on the absurd pretext that another theoretical construction rests upon it? . . . Postan or Le Roy Ladurie should not be criticized for giving too much importance to the demographic factor. They should on the contrary be criticized for stopping themselves mid-stream and for not integrating the demographic factor into the all-embracing whole that is the socio-economic system."[24] In other words, in order to be able to describe in concrete terms the point of crisis between the relations and forces of production, when class struggle becomes relevant for the resolution of the crisis, one has to take into account the prevailing demographic-economic configurations. Bois' version of Marxist analysis finds sympathetic ears in two contributions to this volume, by Myrdal and Kitsikopoulos (who also finds substantial merit to the NIE argument), applied to the cases of Scandinavia and England respectively.

In contrast to these two longstanding traditions, the 'Smithian' model hardly found any proponents. There were several empirical studies such as

Moriceau's which focused on the large farms in Île de France essentially depicting them as large capitalist enterprises, as well as Morineau's claim that productivity in the later Middle Ages rivaled the levels achieved in the eighteenth century but these efforts have not been incorporated into a coherent theoretical model. A sole exception is Grantham's work which views urbanization rates as the driving force of productivity and output growth, at the same time adopting an optimistic perspective on the ability of the pre-plague French economy in coping with demographic growth.[25]

The historiography of the Italian case amounted also to a duel but with different polar opposites. Prior to the 1950s there was a mainstream approach portraying the Italian economy of the high Middle Ages as the first one in Europe to adopt a widespread range of capitalist features: a rational business mentality, modern forms of accountancy, a widespread culture of profit, and a vibrant and modern urban sector fostering a wide array of artisan production. In the 1950s and 60s this mainstream approach was represented by some scholars of international reputation (e.g., Cipolla, Lopez, Miskimin) who had firm interests in Italy but whose writings adopted a global perspective encompassing the entire European economy and its ties with the outside world. Lopez's work is particularly interesting in that it lays out an argument that is virtually identical to the one advanced later on by Campbell.[26] The manner in which the different elements of his argument come together resembles a domino effect. The starting point is the population growth and higher urbanization rates that came about between the tenth and fourteenth centuries. The need to increase food supplies was met with greater farm specialization and, in the absence of innovations, with the diffusion of earlier technologies. Surpluses expanded, and aided by transportation improvements, this chain of events produced a veritable commercial revolution. Underdeveloped regions were drawn into a web of progress and in the end the entire social structure, culture, and lifestyles were transformed. Lopez acknowledged the high population densities in parts of England, France, and Italy, speculating that marginal lands may have come into cultivation. But he quickly added that one cannot conclude that Europe overstepped the boundaries dictated by the productive capacity of its agriculture in light of the fact that people were accustomed to abysmally low living standards. Lopez's commercial revolution had more than economic repercussions; it brought fundamental institutional changes as well. The rise of a money economy led to the commutation of labor services and rents in kind, leading to blurring the lines between serfs and free peasants and eroding the traditional ties with their masters because at that point neither party regarded such ties as particularly beneficial to them. In the end, not only lords but also peasants were drawn into the market networks, disposing their surpluses and taking advantage of commercial opportunities. Lopez did qualify these statements by pointing out that the debasement of coinage led some lords to reintroduce older forms of rent or demand new ones; and there was always the risk of population growing too rapidly, without being absorbed fast enough by towns or through migratory flows. But these comments took more the form of passing references doing little to alter the grand picture of glorious progress.

The mainstream approach met a serious challenge by Italy's formidable leftist tradition beginning in the 1950s following the publication of Gramsci's prison notes. Gramsci's *Quaderni del carcere* did not deal particularly with this debate but made references to 'feudal remains' (*residui feudali*), a notion that was explored by a number of Marxist historians to mean the political influence of landed interests and use of their power both in the countryside and urban centers expressed through non-contractual relationships. This group of historians argued that the presence of such 'feudal remains' was previously underestimated and that they were responsible for Italy's late appearance of modern growth and industrialization in relation to latecomers, such as England, and despite being the first feudal economy to introduce capitalist elements. The newest arguments succeeded in changing the debate's tone: urban Italy still seemed bright, but the new focus on the countryside revealed a gloomier picture.[27] The sense of gloominess, however, remained Marxist as opposed to Neo-Malthusian. In light of it, Malanima's contribution to this volume is particularly interesting in that it reveals Ricardian patterns in the Italian economy of this period by using a thoroughly neoclassical narrative and use of cliometric tools in analyzing existing data. In addition to the Marxist reaction, the methodology of NIE was used by Epstein in pointing out and explaining regional differences in growth patterns based on variations in institutional configurations.[28]

While many scholars studying medieval England, France, and Italy have often played an active role in shaping theoretical debates, experts on Byzantium, Iberia, and Scandinavia were mostly preoccupied with adopting particular streams within the debate to fit best the evidence at hand or were inspired by such debates taking place outside their academic milieu in guiding their empirical research. In the case of Byzantium, Lefort has proposed what appears to be a classic Malthusian scenario with continuing population growth and encroachment upon marginal lands through the great plague resulting in declining productivity and living standards. On the other hand, Laiou has argued that overpopulation characterized only some areas of Macedonia (which is the only documented part of the empire) and that land reclamation was still an option through the first half of the fourteenth century. Her explanation, instead, has been formulated outside the standard models: the decline of Byzantium started in the thirteenth century with the growing dominance of its trade network by Italian merchants which resulted in the decay of various sectors of handicraft production through cheaper imports; and it reached a crisis point by the beginning of the next century due to the combination of civil wars, the Catalan raids, and opportunistic policies on the part of landlords absorbing the lands of peasants who were in economic distress.[29]

The duopoly Laiou-Lefort observed in the literature on Byzantium is transformed to a multiplicity of contributions on the Iberian Middle Ages but with only faint traces when it comes to theoretical debates. Postan's works and the volume of essays comprising the Brenner debate, though known earlier, were translated in the 1980s. The usefulness of the Neo-Malthusian logic was taken for granted particularly as applied to the most heavily populated parts of the peninsula (e.g., north Castile) but it was a group of Marxist historians (Valdeón being the first one, followed by Moreta, Vaca, Barrios, Casado, and Yun) which made the most noticeable contributions since the 1970s. On the other hand, the Commercialist model seems to have inspired a couple of empirical works but no explicit adherence to it at a theoretical level.[30] Overall, Spanish historians have abstained from engaging in an open theoretical debate, using particular views more as guiding principles towards empirical work; one possible explanation is that the majority of the participants were conventional historians, as opposed to economic historians, and therefore less keen to define their work within the parameters of a particular model (though Marxist historians were somewhat more explicit than others).

But it was Scandinavian historians that have exhibited the least appetite for theoretical debates, the general consensus being that the causes of the region's crisis were straightforward: with the possible exception of the plains in Southern Scandinavia (especially in Denmark) the scenario of a Malthusian 'full world' did not apply and, given low population densities and urbanization rates, the Commercialist model was even more irrelevant. It was left to the Black Death to function as the sole explanation of the crisis channeling academic brain power towards empirical work to quantify the impact of the disaster by measuring the extent of deserted villages. Methodological disputes over the sort of evidence which constitutes firm proof of desertions became the focus of studies, in the end concluding that three-quarters of the farms were abandoned in Norway in the wake of the epidemics, the figures being lower in Denmark and Sweden.[31] In light of the absence of theoretical modeling, Myrdal's chapter in this volume is of particular interest because it contributes one of the few attempts in outlining a coherent theoretical framework.

The historiographies on the late Middle Ages in Central and Eastern Europe have been left for last due to the uniqueness of the demographic and economic developments in these countries compared to westerns parts of the continent and the skewing of scholarship under the influence of official Marxist positions. The lack of Malthusian constraints in these regions rendered the debate of a structural crisis a moot issue and reduced the significance of the fourteenth century as a turning point, thereby shifting attention to events such as the Mongol conquests of the thirteenth century in Russia and the Hussite wars of the fifteenth century. Marxist scholarship produced in these countries adopted a 'mode of production' approach focusing on defining the essential features of feudalism. Soviet scholarship tended to trace the origins of feudalism back to the early Rus' phase lasting through the nineteenth century whereas its Central European counterpart, indicative in the writings of Topolski, focused on the fourteenth and fifteenth centuries as the transition phase to a feudal regime with the introduction of servility prompted by the decline of rent revenues which threatened the lifestyles and political ambitions of local elites. The grip of official ideology on produced scholarship became less tight from the 1960s onward but did not necessarily lead to the adoption of well-constructed alternative models. Empirically oriented studies on Russia pointed to changes in farming methods (e.g., from slash-and-burn to three-field systems) leading to greater intensification but the presence of low population densities and the devastation of cities by the Mongol invasions (with the exception of Novgorod) could not support either a Neo-Malthusian or a Commercialist approach to Russian developments. Central European historians (e.g., Malowist, Samsonowicz, Dygo) were more active exploring mechanisms of development and sources of retardation by focusing on the role of towns, long-distance trade, mining, and the restructuring of supply in Central Europe in response to demand patterns emanating further west, thereby giving the appearance of adopting a 'market forces' approach. But such scholarship has not led to well-constructed Commercialist models both due to the insufficiency of data but also because of reluctance to adopt theoretical models reacting to the rigidity and coerciveness of Marxist viewpoints.[32]

In the end, the debates that have taken place over the last four decades have produced clashing viewpoints not only across but also within intellectual traditions: Neo-Malthusian arguments favoring the idea of a systemic crisis and others which, without denying the presence of the latter, elevate the exogenous impact of the plagues into more prominence; Marxist accounts which point to class conflict as the culprit of the feudal crisis but diverge on whether the impact of key demographic and economic variables should be incorporated into the narrative; NIE interpretations which, after facing severe criticism by Marxist historians, became more sympathetic to the role of power relationships in shaping regional differences in patterns of economic growth; and a Commercialist approach which since its inception has consistently denied the notion of a systemic crisis glorifying the achievements of the commercial expansion. The appearance of NIE and the revival of the Commercialist approach are testaments to the considerable interest the crisis of feudalism still commands among historians.

The Brenner debate had an effect equivalent to throwing a heavy pebble on the still waters of a pond. It created a veritable splash followed by a ripple effect whose reverberations still go on, evident by a fairly recent publication which examines the economic transformation of the Low Countries in light of this debate.[33] Differences of interpretation are not likely to be settled any time soon. Large gaps in the evidence coupled with ideological biases and the entrenched rigidity that emerges once one's reputation is built through adherence to a particular viewpoint make this debate unlike the neat succession of Kuhnian paradigms. And some may even question the usefulness of approaching the late Middle Ages through the prism of models or theoretical paradigms; the strength of scholarship shown in the chapters of this volume by Martin, Myśliwski, Rodríguez, and Smyrlis render this viewpoint worth pondering.

The conception of essays originated as an idea because, in the editor's view, this volume may find a useful niche in these debates. The contributions to the Brenner debate placed emphasis on theoretical modeling and drew evidence from only four countries, whereas a more recent publication took the same approach but focused exclusively on England.[34] Other collections of essays combined theory and evidence but subsumed the feudal crisis in the wider debate of the transition from feudalism to capitalism, focusing on a narrow geographical area;[35] while others dealt also with part of the continent examining topics such as farming and technology but did not place these subjects in a wider theoretical framework.[36] The scholars involved in these publications are among the leading figures in this academic field but it was felt that those interested in such topics would benefit from a collection of essays that provided a more balanced summary of theory and evidence, viewed the feudal crisis as a monumental event on its own and not as part of the wider debate of the transition from feudalism to capitalism, and adopted a more holistic overview of the European experience including regions that were perceived up until now as too 'exotic' to be included in these discussions (Byzantium).

The most important contribution of the various essays in this volume is the empirical synthesis they provide on a host of economic, demographic, and technological developments which characterized the period 1200–1500; by doing so in relation to eight countries or wider regions, covering most of Europe, they provide a basis on which the formulation of theoretical generalizations can be constructed. The reader will notice that while the range of covered topics is broad in all essays, the depth of analysis on some of them is often different. Part of the explanation, a very important one, stems from the unevenness that exists in relation to surviving sources; while the English record is unparalleled, continental Europe is much less endowed in this regard. But it also has to do with implicit normative preferences on the part of authors in terms of what type of evidence is more relevant in constructing particular historical narratives; for instance, the role of class relations and feudal institutions are likely to receive less systematic treatment in the accounts of mainstream historians, as opposed to those inspired by the Marxist argument. The same normative preferences, along with differences in academic training, influence the treatment given to the question of crisis, that is, whether it was structural as opposed to stemming from exogenous, non-economic, factors. The role of an editor is particularly challenging in this regard. On the one hand, it is important not to allow his colleagues to behave as free-range chickens in order to avoid a narrative with disjointed parts. On the other hand, demanding strict conformity to a predetermined list of topics that ought to be covered to one degree or another would not have done justice to the multiplicity of methodologies which have been developed in telling the story of the late Middle Ages. In the end, it is hoped the right balance has been struck.

That is not to say that this volume is free of drawbacks and limitations: the important case of Germany is absent and the experience of the Low Countries is summarized in the concluding essay but lacks a separate chapter; perhaps, most importantly, in its effort to balance the presentation of both theory and evidence it occasionally sacrifices analytical depth in either of these regards. But it is hoped that its comparative approach will raise the interest of novices to the subject and offer fresh insights to more advanced scholars. The volume itself is meant to function only as a springboard, with the extensive bibliography leading to a more systematic study of this subject.

The idea of this collaborative effort was born in the fall of 2006 and got a boost in the following summer through the award of a fellowship by NYU's Office of Global Programs, which was later supplemented by funds from the school's Economics department, the Program in European Studies, and the Office of the Associate Dean, FAS. It culminated in a symposium which took place in the idyllic environment of NYU's Villa La Pietra, tucked in the hills overlooking Florence in May 2008, and came to its conclusion through a series of revisions of the presented papers.[37] It is important to stress that in choosing the panel of participants the only litmus test used was their abilities to carry their tasks successfully, i.e., the issues of the type of academic training and adherence to particular viewpoints played no role in the selection process.

There are several individuals that played a key role in ensuring the success of this project. On the funding side, I would like to acknowledge the generous support of Yaw Nyarko, Jonathan Lipman, Katherine Fleming, and Ennio Stachetti. Scott Hughes (in New York) and Angela Santella (in Florence), along with the rest of the staff of the villa, provided impeccable logistical support. John Langdon, Piotr Górecki, Per Lagerås, Bjørn Poulsen, and anonymous referees improved significantly the content and style of individual papers, whereas Markus Cerman provided advise in areas too numerous to mention. Catherine Glover worked her magic in copyediting three essays before the project was submitted to the publisher. Once it got to the latter, Laura Stearns provided superb editorial guidance and Stacy Noto impeccable support in dealing with myriads of tedious logistical issues. Most importantly, I would like to thank all the contributors to this volume for putting up with my endless nagging on revisions and meeting deadlines. The role of Kostis Smyrlis was particularly important, in fact, indispensable. Kostis not only contributed a chapter to this volume but also acted as the co-organizer of the symposium. To all these individuals I extend my sincere gratitude.

Riverdale, November 2010

APPENDIX 1.1: THE RICARDIAN THEORY OF RENT

The Ricardian theory of rent seeks to outline the long-run developments regarding the shares of profits, wages, and rents comprising national income. It focuses on agriculture, although long-run outcomes in this sector have spillover effects for the entire economy, and presupposes the existence of three major classes: absentee landowners, capitalist farmers renting land from the former and managing the production process, and wage workers.

There are four critical assumptions to the theory: 1. Acceptance of one of the main premises of the Malthusian theory of population, i.e., that the growth rate of population is often higher than that of food supplies. 2. Land is comprised of plots which can be arranged along a spectrum based on different fertility levels, implying diminishing returns as we extend production. That is, successive applications of capital and labor either on the same plot or in more marginal plots will lead to smaller marginal products and retardation in the growth of total product. 3. Perfectly competitive markets. 4. Rational economic actors motivated by self-interest. The last two assumptions imply that resources, particularly capital, can flow freely within and across sectors leading to the equalization of profit rates.

Let us look at the agricultural sector of a fictional economy whose land can be classified into three large categories based on its quality (A, B, and C) and in which the three major sources of income are expressed in terms of grain units (quarters). If we presume that this country is still at the initial stage of its settlement having low population densities, let us call this Scenario One, only some plots of the highest fertility will be utilized (Land A). If output (Qa) and wages (Wa) are 100 and 70 quarters respectively, the remaining 30 quarters would comprise capitalist profits (Pa) with rents (Ra) being zero. Landowners would fail to collect rent since they are still

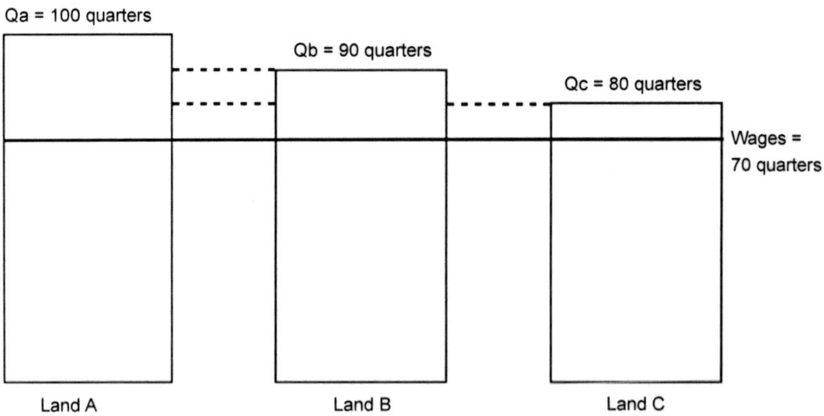

Figure 1.1 An illustration of the Ricardian theory of rent.

unoccupied plots within category A giving the option to capitalist farmers to move, if so pressed; a landowner would still benefit by allowing capitalist farmers to cultivate his land since uncultivated land may deteriorate in fertility without weeding and fertilizing.

If we jump now several decades ahead (Scenario Two), let us assume that all plots within Land A are fully utilized forcing production to spill over into Land B whose output per plot is 90 quarters. Given wages equal to 70 quarters in Land B, capitalist profit will be 20 quarters and rents equal to zero, the rationale being the same, i.e., landowners will not be successful in claiming rent since there are still unoccupied plots within Land B. But an event of historic importance is about to take place in Land A. For the first time in the history of the country landowners will face their capitalist farmers and demand rent equal to 10 quarters. Capitalist farmers in Land A would have no choice but to pay rent since the alternative of moving to plots of Land B would leave them with the same profit of 20 quarters.

Pushing this story even further into the future (Scenario Three), let us assume that plots of Land B are now fully utilized and thus cultivation spills over to plots of Land C. The output of 80 quarters in the latter will be split between wages and capitalist profits, being 70 and 10 quarters respectively, rental income being absent for the same reason as in the previous two scenarios. Following the exact same logic, landowners in Land A will increase rent from 10 to 20 quarters and those of Land B would demand for the first time, and get, rent equal to 10 quarters, capitalist farmers in both cases paying these amounts since moving to some empty plots of Land C would leave them with the same profit.

These three scenarios, summarized in Table 1.1, reveal that rental income comes up due to the growing scarcity of land and the law of diminishing returns, that its level correlates positively with the fertility of soil, and that its size in a particular plot is equal to the output differential between this plot and others in the most marginal category of land. The exact same results are derived if we tell the story from the point of view of the intensive margin of cultivation, i.e., when successive doses of labor and capital are applied to previously cultivated plots of land, each successive dose resulting in diminishing returns in terms of output.

Table 1.1 The Distribution of Output among Various Income Shares in the Ricardian Theory of Rent

Scenario One	*Scenario Two*		*Scenario Three*		
Qa = 100	Qb = 90	Qa = 100	Qc = 80	Qb = 90	Qa = 100
Wa = 70	Wb = 70	Wa = 70	Wc = 70	Wb = 70	Wa = 70
Pa = 30	Pb = 20	Pa = 20	Pc = 10	Pb = 10	Pa = 10
Ra = 0	Rb = 0	Ra = 10	Rc = 0	Rb = 10	Ra = 20

Another way of looking at the Ricardian theory of rent is by introducing money in this fictional economy and focusing on the evolution of marginal cost. If we assume that each dose of labor and replacement capital costs a capitalist farmer $100 then cost per quarter of grain in Land A is equal to $1 ($100/100 quarters). When plots in Land B are taken up for cultivation unit cost at the margin becomes $1.11 ($100/90 quarters) and when cultivation spills over to Land C unit cost rises to $1.25 ($100/80 quarters).

There are two major conclusions deriving from the Ricardian theory of rent. First, rent is not one of the determinants of market prices since the latter is equal to marginal cost in purely competitive markets and there is no rent at the margin. Second, Ricardo argues that the reason the cost and prices of grains rise over time is not because rents keep rising, in fact, the opposite is the case. Higher costs and prices ensue because of the law of diminishing returns allowing landowners in Land A and B to take advantage of the situation by claiming rents. It follows that even if landowners were eliminated from the face of the earth grain prices would still rise, although rents would be transformed into profits for the capitalist farmers.

NOTES

1. T. H. Aston and C. H. E. Philpin, eds., *The Brenner Debate: Agrarian Class Structure and Economic Development in Pre-industrial Europe* (Cambridge: Cambridge University Press, 1985). All references to the debate's contributions refer to this volume.
2. David Ricardo, *On the Principles of Political Economy and Taxation*, ed. Piero Sraffa (Cambridge: Cambridge University Press, 1983), esp. 67–84; see also Robert Thomas Malthus, *First Essay on Population* (London: Macmillan, 1926). The reader who is not familiar with the Ricardian theory of rent may wish to consult the appendix of this chapter.
3. Earlier works included William Denton, *England in the Fifteenth Century* (London: G. Bell and Sons, 1888), Baron Ernle (formerly R. Prothero), *English Farming, Past and Present* (London: Heinemann 1961); and, especially, Wilhelm Abel, *Agricultural Fluctuations in Europe: From the Thirteenth to the Twentieth Centuries,* trans. Olive Ordish (London: Methuen & Co, 1980). Abel's work, spanning a period of six to seven centuries and covering large parts of the continent, was an ambitious attempt to synthesize the empirical evidence regarding key macroeconomic variables such as the positive relationship between population and grain price movements and the inverse relationship between the former and wages. In contrasting Abel and Postan, it is true that the former's work had a stronger empirical basis and geographical scope; on the other hand, Postan's key publications on the subject had a more explicit theoretical tone.
4. The best representation of Postan's argument is M. M. Postan, "Medieval agrarian society in its prime: England," in *The Cambridge Economic History of Europe*, vol. 1, *The Agrarian Life of the Middle Ages*, ed. M. M. Postan (Cambridge: Cambridge University Press, 1966); and M. M. Postan, *The Medieval Economy and Society: An Economic History of Britain in the Middle Ages* (Harmondsworth: Penguin, 1975); see also M. M. Postan, *Essays on Medieval Agriculture and General Problems of the*

Medieval Economy (Cambridge: Cambridge University Press, 1973). His contribution to the Brenner debate (with Hatcher as his co-author) was M. M. Postan and J. Hatcher, "Population and Class Relations in Feudal Society," in *The Brenner Debate*, eds. Aston and Philpin. See also J. Hatcher, "English Serfdom and Villeinage: Towards a Reassessment," *Past and Present* 90 (1981).

5. See, for instance, Maurice Dobb, *Studies in the Development of Capitalism* (New York: International Publishers, 1984) esp. 33–82.
6. Robert Brenner, "The Agrarian Roots of European Capitalism," eds. T. H. Aston and C. H. E. Philpin, *The Brenner Debate*, 233 (emphasis in original).
7. Ibid., 237 (emphasis in original). The credibility of Brenner's argument was boosted by the publication, a few years prior to the debate, of a couple of studies showing exceptional levels of productivity among estates which lacked strong seigneurial prerogatives; Eleanor Searle, *Lordship and Community: Battle Abbey and its Banlieu, 1066–1538* (Toronto: Pontifical Institute of Medieval Studies, 1974) was particularly relevant in this regard.
8. Robert Brenner, "Agrarian Class Structure and Economic Development in Pre-industrial Europe," eds. T. H. Aston and C. H. E. Philpin, *The Brenner Debate*, 12; idem, "The Agrarian Roots," 218.
9. Douglass C. North, *Institutions, Institutional Change and Economic Performance* (Cambridge: Cambridge University Press, 1990), 107.
10. Ibid., 99.
11. Ibid., 83–91, 101.
12. S. R. Epstein, "Cities, Regions and the Late Medieval Crisis: Sicily and Tuscany Compared," *Past and Present* 130 (1991), quote from p. 10.
13. North, *Institutions, Institutional Change and Economic Performance*, 134. Van Bavel also acknowledged the useful contributions made by Brenner in pointing out regional differences in social property systems, adding that Marxist and NIE models offer a firmer theoretical basis for explaining historical processes; Bas van Bavel, *Manors and Markets: Economy and Society in the Low Countries, 500–1600* (Oxford: Oxford University Press, 2010), 6, see also pp. 387–409.
14. Arguments similar to Campbell's positions, albeit without his empirical rigor, were formulated earlier by such historians as Pirenne and Lopez (see below).
15. B. M. S. Campbell, *English Seigniorial Agriculture, 1250–1450* (Cambridge: Cambridge University Press, 2000), 414, 424; the quote, with emphasis added, is from the latter page.
16. Ibid., 203.
17. Ibid.; see also B. M. S. Campbell, et al., *A Medieval Capital and its Grain Supply: Agrarian Production and Distribution in the London Region c. 1300* (Historical Geography Research Series 30, n.p., 1993). For a theoretical exposition of von Thünen's model, see Harry Kitsikopoulos, "Manorial Estates as Business Firms: The Relevance of Economic Rent in Determining Crop Choices in London's Hinterland c. 1300," *Agricultural History Review* 56 (2008): 145–148.
18. R. Britnell and B. M. S. Campbell, "Introduction," in *A Commercializing Economy: England 1086 to c. 1300*, eds. R. Britnell and B. M. S. Campbell (Manchester: Manchester University Press, 1995), 4.
19. Campbell, *English Seigniorial Agriculture, 1250–1450*, 427–429.
20. Ibid., 22–23; quotes from the latter page. See also B. M. S. Campbell, "Nature as Historical Protagonist: Environment and Society in Pre-industrial England," *Economic History Review* 63, 2 (2010).

21. The review of the different national debates that follows relies heavily on information and comments provided by the various contributors to this volume to whom I am extraordinarily indebted. It is not meant to be a thorough review of arguments and personalities involved but a rough sketch of particular traditions.
22. E. Le Roy Ladurie and Joseph Goy, *Tithe and Agrarian History from the Fourteenth to the Nineteenth Century: An Essay in Comparative History* (Cambridge: Cambridge University Press, 1982), 77–78.
23. E. Le Roy Ladurie, "A Reply to Brenner," in *The Brenner Debate*, eds. T. H. Aston and C. H. E. Philpin, 103; see also E. Le Roy Ladurie, "L'Histoire Immobile," *Annales Économies, Sociétés, Civilisations* 29 (1974).
24. G. Bois, "Against the Neo-Malthusian Orthodoxy," in *The Brenner Debate*, eds. T. H. Aston and C. H. E. Philpin, 116–117.
25. In this sense his contribution to this volume is of particular interest; see also George Grantham, "*Contra* Ricardo: On the Macroeconomics of Preindustrial Economies," *European Review of Economic History* 3 (1999). References and discussion of the relevant empirical studies can be found in Grantham's chapter below.
26. One of Lopez's representative works is R. Lopez, *The Commercial Revolution of the Middle Ages, 950–1350* (Englewood Cliffs, N.J: Prentice-Hall, 1971). For the arguments made by Cipolla and Miskimin, see Malanima's chapter in this volume.
27. Emilio Sereni, *Storia del Paesaggio Agrario Italiano* (Bari: Laterza, 1974); Ruggiero Romano, *Tra Due Crisi: L' Italia del Rinascimento* (Torino: Einaudi, 1971).
28. Epstein, "Cities, Regions and the Late Medieval Crisis: Sicily and Tuscany Compared."
29. For a more analytical treatment of these themes and relevant citations, see Smyrlis' contribution to this volume.
30. Citations of the representative works of these historians can be found in Rodriguez's contribution to this volume.
31. Some of this research is summarized in Svend Gissel et al., *Desertion and Land Colonization in the Nordic Countries c. 1300–1600: Comparative Report from the Scandinavian Research Project on Deserted Farms and Villages* (Stockholm: Almqvist & Wiksell International, 1981).
32. A good summary of the debates on Russian feudalism can be found in the introduction of R. Hellie, *Enserfment and Military Change in Muscovy* (Chicago: Chicago University Press, 1971) whereas a refutation of Marxist positions can be found in George Vernadsky, "Feudalism in Russia," *Speculum* 14 (1939). On the publications of the aforementioned Central European historians, see Mysliwski's contribution to this volume.
33. P. Hoppenbrowers and Jan Luiten van Zanden, eds., *Peasants into Farmers? The Transformation of Rural Economy and Society in the Low Countries (Middle Ages–19th Century) in Light of the Brenner Debate* (Turnhout: Brepols, 1971)
34. J. Hatcher and M. Bailey, *Modelling the Middle Ages: The History and Theory of England's Economic Development* (Oxford: Oxford University Press, 2001).
35. See note 33.
36. G. Astill and J. L. Langdon, eds., *Medieval Farming and Technology: The Impact of Agricultural Change in North-west Europe in the Middle Ages* (Leiden: Brill, 1997).
37. Janet Martin joined the group fairly late and thus was unable to attend the Florence meeting.

BIBLIOGRAPHY

Abel, W. *Agricultural Fluctuations in Europe: From the Thirteenth to the Twentieth Centuries*, transl. Olive Ordish. London: Methuen & Co, 1980.

Astill, G., and J. L. Langdon, eds. *Medieval Farming and Technology: The Impact of Agricultural Change in North-west Europe in the Middle Ages*. Leiden: Brill, 1997.

Aston, T. H., and C. H. E. Philpin, eds. *The Brenner Debate: Agrarian Class Structure and Economic Development in Pre-industrial Europe*. Cambridge: Cambridge University Press, 1985.

Bois, G. "Against the Neo-Malthusian Orthodoxy," in *The Brenner Debate: Agrarian Class Structure and Economic Development in Pre-industrial Europe*, edited by T. H. Aston and C. H. E. Philpin, 107–118. Cambridge: Cambridge University Press, 1985.

Brenner, R. "The Agrarian Roots of European Capitalism," in *The Brenner Debate: Agrarian Class Structure and Economic Development in Pre-industrial Europe*, edited by T. H. Aston and C. H. E. Philpin, 213–327. Cambridge: Cambridge University Press, 1985.

Brenner, R. "Agrarian Class Structure and Economic Development in Pre-industrial Europe," in *The Brenner Debate: Agrarian Class Structure and Economic Development in Pre-industrial Europe*, edited by T. H. Aston and C. H. E. Philpin, 10–63. Cambridge: Cambridge University Press, 1985.

Britnell, R., and B. M. S. Campbell. "Introduction," in *A Commercialising Economy: England 1086 to c. 1300*, edited by R. Britnell and B. M. S. Campbell, 1–6. Manchester: Manchester University Press, 1995.

Britnell, R., and B. M. S. Campbell, eds. *A Commercialising Economy: England 1086 to c. 1300*. Manchester: Manchester University Press, 1995.

Campbell, B. M. S. *English Seigniorial Agriculture, 1250–1450*. Cambridge: Cambridge University Press, 2000.

Campbell, B. M. S. "Nature as Historical Protagonist: Environment and Society in Pre-industrial England." *Economic History Review* 63, 2 (2010): 281–314.

Campbell, B. M. S., J. A. Galloway, D. J. Keene, and M. Murphy. *A Medieval Capital and its Grain Supply: Agrarian Production and Distribution in the London Region c. 1300*. Historical Geography Research Series 30, n.p., 1993.

Denton, W. *England in the Fifteenth Century*. London: G. Bell and Sons, 1888.

Dobb, M. *Studies in the Development of Capitalism*. New York: International Publishers, 1984.

Epstein, S. R. "Cities, Regions and the Late Medieval Crisis: Sicily and Tuscany Compared." *Past and Present* 130 (1991): 3–50.

Ernle, Baron (formerly R. Prothero). *English Farming, Past and Present*. London: Heinemann, 1961.

Gissel, S., E. Jutikkala, E. Österberg, J. Sandnes, B. Teitsson. *Desertion and Land Colonization in the Nordic Countries c. 1300–1600: Comparative Report from the Scandinavian Research Project on Deserted Farms and Villages*. Stockholm: Almqvist & Wiksell International, 1981.

Grantham, G. "*Contra* Ricardo: On the Macroeconomics of Pre-industrial Economies." *European Review of Economic History* 3 (1999): 199–233.

Hatcher, J. "English Serfdom and Villeinage: Towards a Reassessment." *Past and Present* 90 (1981): 3–39.

Hatcher, J., and M. Bailey. *Modelling the Middle Ages: The History and Theory of England's Economic Development*. Oxford: Oxford University Press, 2001.

Hellie, R. *Enserfment and Military Change in Muscovy*. Chicago: Chicago University Press, 1971.
Hoppenbrowers, P., and J. Luiten van Zanden. *Peasants into Farmers? The Transformation of Rural Economy and Society in the Low Countries (Middle Ages–19th century) in Light of the Brenner Debate*. Turnhout: Brepols, 2001.
Kitsikopoulos, H. "Manorial Estates as Business Firms: The Relevance of Economic Rent in Determining Crop Choices in London's Hinterland c. 1300." *Agricultural History Review* 56 (2008): 142–166.
Le Roy Ladurie, E. "L' Histoire Immobile." *Annales Économies, Sociétés, Civilisations* 29 (1974): 673–692.
Le Roy Ladurie, E. "A Reply to Brenner," in *The Brenner Debate: Agrarian Class Structure and Economic Development in Pre-industrial Europe*, edited by T. H. Aston and C. H. E. Philpin, 101–106. Cambridge: Cambridge University Press, 1985.
Le Roy Ladurie, E., and J. Goy. *Tithe and Agrarian History from the Fourteenth to the Nineteenth Century: An Essay in Comparative History*. Cambridge: Cambridge University Press, 1982.
Lopez, R. *The Commercial Revolution of the Middle Ages, 950–1350*. Englewood Cliffs, NJ: Prentice-Hall, 1971.
Malthus, R. T. *First Essay on Population*. London: Macmillan, 1926.
North, D. C. *Institutions, Institutional Change and Economic Performance*. Cambridge: Cambridge University Press, 1990.
Postan, M. M., ed. *The Cambridge Economic History of Europe*, vol. 1, *The Agrarian Life of the Middle Ages*, 2nd edition. Cambridge: Cambridge University Press, 1966.
Postan, M. M. "Medieval Agrarian Society in its Prime: England." in *The Cambridge Economic History of Europe*, vol. 1, *The Agrarian Life of the Middle Ages*, edited by M. M. Postan, 549–632. Cambridge: Cambridge University Press, 1966.
Postan, M. M, *Essays on Medieval Agriculture and General Problems of the Medieval Economy*. Cambridge: Cambridge University Press, 1973.
Postan, M. M. *The Medieval Economy and Society: An Economic History of Britain in the Middle Ages*. Harmondsworth: Penguin, 1975.
Postan, M. M., and J. Hatcher. "Population and Class Relations in Feudal Society," in *The Brenner Debate: Agrarian Class Structure and Economic Development in Pre-industrial Europe*, edited by T. H. Aston and C. H. E. Philpin, 64–78. Cambridge: Cambridge University Press, 1985.
Ricardo, D. *On the Principles of Political Economy and Taxation*, edited by Piero Sraffa. Cambridge: Cambridge University Press, 1983.
Romano, R. *Tra Due Crisi: L' Italia del Rinascimento*. Torino: Einaudi, 1971.
Searle, E. *Lordship and Community: Battle Abbey and its Banlieu, 1066–1538*. Toronto: Pontifical Institute of Medieval Studies, 1974.
Sereni, E. *Storia Del Paesaggio Agrario Italiano*, 2nd edition. Bari: Laterza, 1974.
van Bavel, B. *Manors and Markets: Economy and Society in the Low Countries, 500–1600*. Oxford: Oxford University Press, 2010.
Vernadsky, G. "Feudalism in Russia." *Speculum* 14 (1939): 300–323.

2 England

Harry Kitsikopoulos

SOURCES OF EVIDENCE

The available documentation regarding the economy of late feudal England is unparalleled in the context of the European continent. Regarding the seigneurial sector, the most comprehensive and systematic source of information are manorial accounts, composed each year by reeves and bailiffs of individual manors. Such accounts reveal various types of husbandry practices, the financial standing of manors in terms of receipts and expenses, and sometimes the amount of labor services due by customary tenants and the use made of them.

The earliest individual accounts date back to 1208–09 and come from ecclesiastical properties of the bishop of Winchester while others from East Anglia follow shortly thereafter. During the second half of the thirteenth century two important developments take place: the number of such accounts multiplies and expands down the seigneurial ladder to minor estate owners, and their content becomes more detailed. The degree of detail is enhanced through the second half of the fourteenth century but their frequency diminishes beginning in the 1380s with the leasing of demesnes. Numerical decline reaches the point of sparseness by the fifteenth century with lay estates being the first ones to abandon the practice, as opposed to a few ecclesiastical properties that held on to it until the end of the century.

The overall number of surviving accounts reaches tens of thousands. Impressive as their numbers and diversity of information they provide may be, their geographical distribution is quite uneven with the central, eastern, and southern regions providing most of the material, as opposed to the extreme northwest and southwest where direct demesnial management was infrequent and thus surviving records are fewer. Another serious imbalance stems from the fact that the majority of surviving accounts pertains to large ecclesiastical landlords despite the fact that, according to one estimate, they controlled only 29 percent of annual income from landed property in 1300, in contrast to 66 percent by lay lords, with the remaining 5 percent going to the crown;[1] consequently, lay lords, particularly those with a single manor or two, are under represented. Such bias, if not pointed out, has the potential of creating false impressions in several respects. To cite one example, ecclesiastical estates were more endowed with villein land and, therefore, the cultivation of their demesnes relied more heavily on the performance of labor services.

This drawback is compensated by a second major source of information, manorial extents, particularly those under the rubric of the *Inquisitiones Post Mortem* (IPMs) which were drawn on behalf of the crown upon the death of its tenants-in-chief. Extents fill the gap of the accounts since they refer exclusively to lay lords, from the very large ones down to those of a humble status. The chronology of the IPMs parallels that of accounts; nevertheless, their main drawback is that they do not rise to the same degree of reliability nor do they descend to the same level of analytical detail, particularly in jurisdictions north of the Trent.

Given their chronological and geographical dispersion, and despite the noted biases, accounts and extents provide the bulk of documentation of the seigneurial sector. They have been supplemented often by other scarcer sources such as charters, deeds, leases, inventories, local tax assessments, and central estate accounts which record the quantities of products finding their way to a central household as well as capital expenditures.

In contrast to the seigneurial sector, peasant holdings lack such thorough documentation; in fact, most of the existing evidence comes from documents drawn either by manorial estates or the central government. The best information we have refers to holding sizes and the various rental obligations of free and customary tenants, the evidence stemming from manorial custumals and surveys, the IPMs, the Hundred Rolls of 1279–80 (the most extensive survey of holding sizes for both freemen and villeins), manorial surveys drawn on an estate basis, and manorial court rolls which, among other things, record the transfer of holdings and thus provide a more dynamic picture of the land market complementing the snapshot impression given by other sources. Some documentation also exists, from tithe data, regarding the type of crops grown.[2] The number and type of animals held by peasants is revealed from local assessments of peasant taxable wealth ('lay subsidies'), manorial by-laws referring to stints (specifying the number of animals per tenant allowed in grazing grounds), and heriot records (surrendering the best animal once a tenant died or vacated his holding). Some of these sources (e.g., lay subsidies), however, should be treated with caution due to evasion and the fact that they exclude a substantial portion of poor peasants.

Regarding other aspects of social and economic life, documentation becomes sparse or non-existent. Some court records and leases between peasants refer to the use of common marlpits by customary tenants and the stipulation of clauses referring to the frequency of liming; food items given to harvest workers can provide important clues about the changing composition of diets when viewed from a long-run perspective; some serf lists and wills reveal the size of families whereas inventories refer to common household items; finally, archeological excavations have revealed aspects of everyday life such as the finding of a large number of spindle whorls indicating that spinning with a distaff was a common activity among female members of the household.

Despite the ingenuity exhibited by historians in squeezing the most out of these sources, significant gaps remain regarding the consumption and investment aspects of the peasant sector. For example, we do not know enough about peasant diets, the level of spending on consumption goods drawn from the market, the extent of employment opportunities, the full extent of capital spending and, perhaps most importantly, the level of yields of crops and animal products. Nevertheless, efforts have been made to reconstruct the economic aspects of peasant households by filling the gaps through the utilization of manorial sources.[3]

ORGANIZATION OF AGRICULTURAL PRODUCTION

The manor, sometimes (to be precise, rarely) conterminous with the village, was the most basic constituent element of English feudalism. Manors were held under three types of ownership (crown, lay, and ecclesiastical lords), the distribution of ownership itself being unequal.[4] The greatest of estates owned dozens of manors with thousands of acres. At the peak of the pyramid, the most impressive sizes were reached by lay lords such as the holdings of Gilbert de Clare, earl of Gloucester and Hertford, who owned 160 manors comprising 18,800 acres during the decades prior to the Black Death. Although these figures are impressive they are far from typical. A national IPM sample of 1,511 lay lords (1300–49) reveals that 80 percent of them held less than 500 acres, with the average lay lord holding three manors generating an annual revenue of £16–17. At the bottom of the scale there were members of this class holding a single manor. A similar picture is reproduced among ecclesiastical estates. The Winchester bishopric controlled 60 manors totaling 13,000 acres by the middle of the thirteenth century; by the beginning of the next century the land assets of the abbot and convent of Westminster reached 14,500 acres. At the bottom of this group were rectors with a single manor.

Lords, however, did not engage in a direct cultivation of their land in its entirety. Working with data from the Hundred Rolls (1279) drawn from six counties, Kosminsky concluded that the proportion of arable land under demesnial cultivation was 32 percent. But, given the geographical concentration of the Hundred Rolls in the heavily manorialized belt of central England, Campbell has argued that the figure for the country as a whole must have been lower, possibly as low as a fifth of total arable land.[5] It is not clear whether the radical downgrading of the share of demesnial agriculture by Campbell is justified. Nevertheless, he has produced more robust data when it comes to the size of a typical demesne during the pre-plague period. He estimates this size to have been 200 arable acres when both lay and ecclesiastical estates are included but, given the fact that the latter tended to be larger and over represented in the evidence, the actual figure was bound to be smaller; an IPM sample including only lay estates produces an average of 151 acres.[6] Demesnial exploitation witnessed a drastic reduction after the Black Death and, according to one estimate, shrank down to 5–10 percent of all land by 1500.[7]

Demesnes were run mainly through the utilization of hired labor, with labor services provided by villeins contributing only 8 percent of demesnial labor inputs c. 1300.[8] According to Hatcher, about a third of villein households performed regular week-work, with services relating to harvest being the ones lords held onto most tenaciously given the peak demand for labor in that season. The remaining villein households owed the less irksome boon-works and, therefore, during the pre-plague period labor services accounted for a minor part of seigneurial output and total agricultural production.[9]

If the estimates on the amount of labor services is close to reality, their significance is inversely related to the distribution of land between free and villein peasants. According to Kosminsky's analysis of the Hundred Rolls, 40 percent of the arable land was in villein hands, whereas 28 percent were free holdings; in other words, villeins cultivated about three-fifths of the land rented by landlords. Once again, the proportion of unfree households and of the land they held in the country as a whole is unclear. There have been arguments that the proportion of free vs. unfree tenants/land was more balanced throughout the country given the more sporadic nature of villeinage in northern and western counties and in places like Kent; on the other hand, in counties south of the area covered by the Hundred Rolls, villeinage exhibited some of its strongest manifestations. All in all, irrespective of tenurial arrangements, the number of peasant farms has been estimated by Dyer to have been about one million c. 1300.[10]

Peasant holdings and demesnes could be cultivated under similar arrangements and practices or they could function as autonomous units depending on the field system that was adopted. The choice of field system was of paramount importance because it mattered (on par with the relative portions of cropping vs. pastures, and the size of animal stock) how well these two types of husbandry complemented each other to their mutual benefit through the efficient utilization of manure and thus of nitrogen. There was a multitude of field arrangements but two main types can be discerned: common fields with an intermixture of holdings which usually practiced two- or three-course rotations; and arrangements based on consolidated holdings and demesnes, often practicing flexible rotations in the context of convertible husbandry or the mixed variation of infields-outfields. Convertible husbandry was a more efficient option given the fact that the grazing portion of the land (leys) was integrated within the cropping routine, as opposed to classic versions of common fields where the permanent division of arable land and pastures led to a waste of manure supplies.[11]

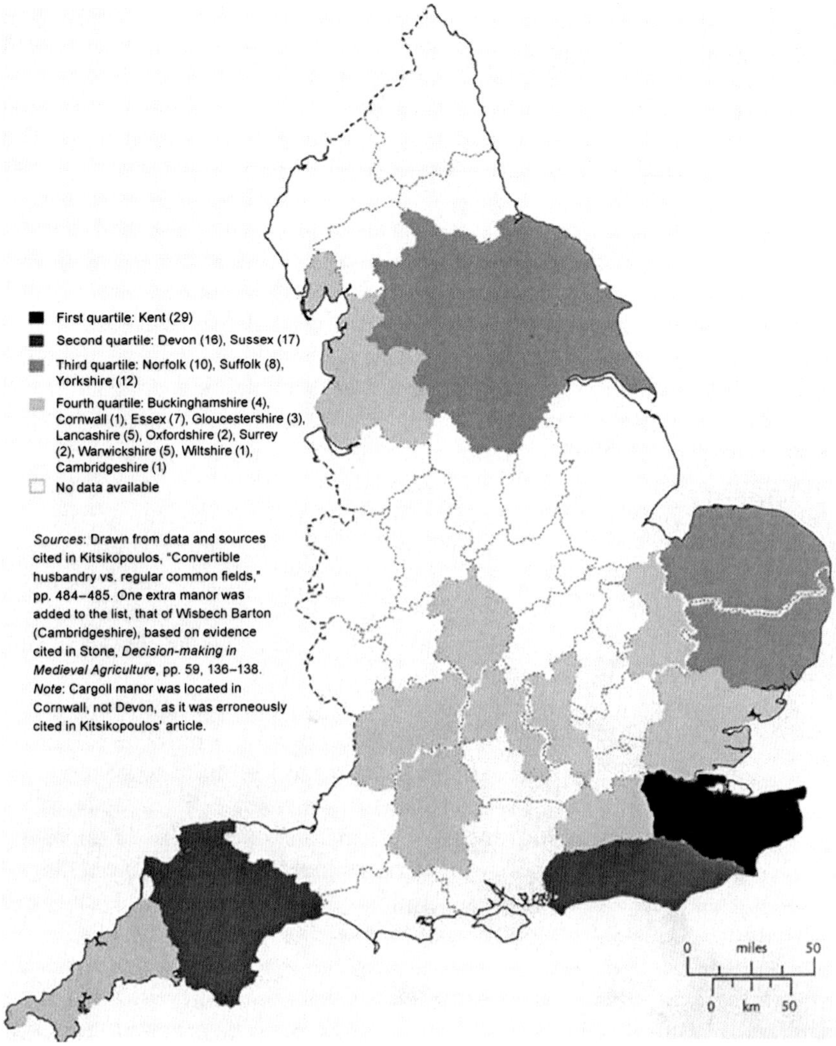

Figure 2.1 The regional diffusion of convertible husbandry (and other flexible rotations) in England, pre- and post-plague periods.

Nevertheless, flexible rotations remained an exception throughout this period. Figure 2.1 divides several counties into quartiles based on the number of manors practicing convertible husbandry or variations of it (e.g., infield-outfield) during the period 1200–1500. Given the total number of 123 documented cases, the heaviest concentration was in the southeastern coastline and the southwestern peninsula; Kent alone accounted for a quarter of the total and when we add Sussex and Devon the proportion rises to half. An intermediate layer forms in East Anglia and northern counties, whereas a very sporadic distribution appears in the Home Counties and parts of the Midlands.[12]

A brief reference to the historical evolution of field systems will help explain their regional diffusion. The record is fraught with gaps but, according to one interpretation, the original organizational matrix during the early Middle Ages was the infield-outfield type, with regular cultivation in the infield and occasional in the outfields.[13] As population grew, particularly between the Domesday Book and the Black Death, there was increased pressure to expand the tilled area given the fact that crops provide more calories per acre compared to animal husbandry. In the southern and eastern parts of the country, where these pressures and the manorial element were the strongest, seigneurial authority came to impose a rigid form of common and subdivided fields in an effort to rationalize the use of grazing grounds and the utilization of manure. For reasons which are still debated, a few parts of this region (most notably Norfolk, Kent, and Sussex) deviated from this scenario by retaining a high degree of flexibility and individualistic practices, often in the context of convertible husbandry. The third and final category pertains to northern and western counties where poorer environmental conditions were less inviting to population growth and the seigneurial element; signs of evolving towards the rigid arrangements of the south and east started coming into play but fields still retained, by and large, their irregular character and thus allowed the accommodation of flexible systems.[14]

Environmental and social conditions, along with demographic and commercial factors (see below), converged in determining not only the choice of field systems but also the degree of intensity practiced in their context. In terms of this criterion and based on demesnial evidence, Campbell distinguished three tiers. The first group, comprising just over a fifth of the total, exhibited high degrees of intensity in the context of irregular field systems; its constituent demesnes were located mainly in Kent and Norfolk, with some notable outliers in the London region, Sussex, and the Isle of Wight. Some Norfolk demesnes, for instance, were able to achieve high levels of intensity by placing great emphasis on spring-sown crops, particularly barley, thus utilizing land for only a brief period during the year; high proportions of the cropped area were also dedicated to legumes. These practices allowed them to crop consecutively for up to five to six years without any fallowing. Favorable edaphic conditions, high population densities, and strong commercial opportunities were the combined features of these areas.[15]

At the other extreme there was a second group comprising over 40 percent of demesnes following the traditional routine of common fields and two-course rotations and thus adopting a low level of intensity. This type of demesnes was spread widely throughout the country, in the north and west, and the London region but also in more landlocked areas to the north and south of this region. It is important to note that edaphic conditions across this group were largely unfavorable (e.g., heavy soils in lowland areas) but there was a diverse experience in terms of demographic and commercial factors.

Finally, there was a third group, comprising 35 percent of the total, which was located in the very same areas, particularly in the light soils of the south and east, exhibiting intermediate levels of intensity and flexibility in terms of crop rotations.[16]

Overall, "early fourteenth century England remained a country more extensive than intensive and more conservative than innovative in its demesne cropping systems."[17] Campbell notes that the wide gap, in terms of cropping intensity, which existed prior to the Black Death became more narrow after the epidemic with demesnes at the top tier scaling down but also those at the bottom moving up, perhaps due to the withdrawal of land from the most marginal fields. The result was more crowding around the intermediate tier but, overall, there was a lower level of intensity compared to the pre-plague period. The same conclusion applies to demesnes following convertible husbandry. Before the Black Death about half of the arable land, on average, was under crops, the remaining being regular fallows and leys. After the epidemic the proportion of the cropped area went down to a quarter of all arable land.[18]

As noted earlier, field systems functioned as organizational matrices with two cells, so to speak, arable and pastoral husbandries. Tithe data, lay subsidies, and other manorial records do provide some information on peasant holdings but the evidence refers mainly to the management of demesnes. To the extent, however, that peasant farms and demesnes shared the same ecological profiles there were bound to be similarities, although differences in financial endowments and diets also had an impact.[19]

Based on a large sample of lay manors drawn from the IPMs (1300–49), two-thirds of the land was arable and the remaining pasturage; it should be stressed, however, that these figures mask wide variations between north and south. Within the arable sector, grains dominated the cropping routine with wheat being the dominant crop (32 percent of total sown area), followed by oats (30 percent), barley (17 percent), rye and grain mixtures with 6–7 percent each, whereas legumes counted for less than 10 percent.[20] Vegetables and fruits were grown in gardens and orchards, outside the matrix of field systems. Within the pastoral sector horses, cattle, sheep, and pigs would be kept and provided with feed either through the output of mowable grasslands (comprising about 60 percent of pasturage) or by grazing rough pastures, woodlands, fenlands, etc. Pasturage was becoming increasingly scarce as we approach the Black Death, resulting in values per acre four to five times higher compared to the value of arable land.[21]

The radical changes in the relative prices of land and labor due to the Black Death and the consequent shifts in diets brought some drastic realignments on the relative extent of arable and pasture lands and the internal composition of the former. Manorial officials explored different options such as leasing land to tenants, as well as replacing grains with legumes to be used as fodder and a greater emphasis on pastoral husbandry. At the beginning of the fourteenth century bread grains, brewing grains, and pottage/fodder crops were grown in demesnes in a ratio of 41:18:41. A century later these figures changed to 35:28:38; that is, less land was devoted to bread grains, much more to brewing grains, whereas the slight reduction in the share of pottage/fodder crops masks an internal shift from human to animal consumption. These trends become more evident when we consider that by the end of the fourteenth century demesnes had, on average, 25 percent less land under crops and, consequently, livestock units rose by an equivalent proportion.[22] The trend from corn to horn was particularly pronounced in the south, diminishing as we move towards the north. A reflection of these trends is the relative proportions of arable and pastoral revenues referring to a large sample of manors from the London region. Excluding products consumed by the manorial household and used as seed and fodder, and treating intermanorial transfers as sales, this sample shows that c. 1300 crops generated a sales revenue that stood in a ratio of almost 2:1 compared to revenues from animals and their products. In contrast, by the end of the century sales from pastoral husbandry exceeded those from the arable sector.[23]

Before moving on it is useful to assert, in the form of a summary, that English manorialism found its classic manifestation in the eastern and southern parts of the country combining the presence of large numbers of unfree tenants, heavier overall obligations and labor services in particular, and rigid field systems emphasizing arable cultivation and operating at low to modest levels of intensity; but parts of the three coastal counties of Norfolk, Kent, and Sussex functioned as exceptions to this norm having the exact opposite characteristics (notwithstanding arable cropping which was equally pronounced). On the other hand, the rest of the country presented its own unique social and economic profile: weaker manorialism, lower frequency of unfree tenants, lighter obligations and labor services, a fair amount of flexibility in the arrangement of field systems, low levels of intensity, and a greater emphasis on pastoral husbandry. However, the presence of some powerful estates with rigid field formations in these regions leaves the impression that this part of the country was in the process (admittedly slow) of conforming to the image of what was the norm in the south and east. It is important to keep this regional differentiation in mind since it serves well in addressing the question of the presence or absence of a structural crisis, as well as its causes, within English feudalism.

Agricultural Technology and Productivity

By all accounts, there were no major technological breakthroughs during this period. It follows that productivity and output growth hinged on the improvement of existing technologies and, most importantly, on their pace of diffusion; but it is certain that the former was not revolutionary and it is likely that the latter was not particularly dynamic.

Improvements in harnessing techniques and shoeing, better designed plows and carts, and the replacement of horses for oxen are developments that are often referred to in the literature.[24] There was an interactive mechanism in terms of how these developments related to each other. The improvements in the design and speed of plows contributed to the extension of arable land during the pre-plague period and necessitated the cultivation of fodder crops, given the reduction of pastures. These developments favored the utilization of horses which, in turn, led to an increase in the speed and efficiency of plowing. Moreover, the heavier reliance on horses allowed the reduction in the size of plow teams, and thus of the number of replacement draught beasts, as well as greater speed and efficiency in terms of carting goods to the market. Ecological factors and commercial forces were of paramount importance in determining these developments at the regional level; when the confluence of these factors was favorable, as in Norfolk and Kent, a dynamic picture evolved over time. At the national level, during the time of Domesday Book only 10 percent of demesnial draught animals were horses; by the beginning of the fourteenth century this figure doubled and it was even more impressive among peasant holdings (50 percent).

But we ought to keep the right perspective in terms of what these developments signify for the overall productivity of medieval agriculture. A horse was 40 percent more expensive to maintain compared to an ox but the greater speed and efficiency brought by the former allowed the reduction in the size of plow teams; a team of four horses cost less to maintain than a team of eight oxen.[25] Moreover, the utilization of horses saved time both in terms of plowing and transporting goods to the market. If these savings in labor time resulted in higher capital formation and injection of labor inputs in other activities there were bound to have a beneficial effect. But it is uncertain whether these benefits materialized and, even if they did, whether they were of more than marginal importance.

The challenge faced, particularly by pre-plague England, was the greater utilization of techniques that contributed more directly to land, as opposed to labor, productivity (labor inputs were plentiful after all); in this sense the utilization of marl/lime and manure were of paramount importance. The use of the former two conditioners in demesnes and the rental of marlpits to tenants are well-documented for the pre-plague period, as well as the drastic reduction that took place after the epidemic due to the exorbitant labor cost of these activities.[26] But we do not possess aggregate data regarding the extent of such practices.

On the other hand, the *availability* of manure is reflected on stocking densities, expressed as livestock units per 100 grain acres. This index did improve during the century leading to the Black Death because, while the size of livestock units remained stable, the size of grain acreage started retreating as we approach the great epidemic.[27] There is a more modest improvement in the latter part of the fourteenth century but a more radical one during the fifteenth century when the drastic shift towards pastoral husbandry took place. Are we to conclude then that, in terms of this important factor, medieval agriculture was scoring continuous improvements during this period? The answer is not as obvious as it seems. The spreading of manure is a labor intensive activity and hence it may have retreated after the Black Death, as it was the case in the 1410s at Wisbech Barton whose officials chose not to utilize manure despite an increase in livestock units.[28] But, most importantly, the efficient recycling of manure hinged on the choice of field systems. As an illustration, stocking densities in eastern Norfolk were below the national average, as opposed to the manors of the Winchester bishopric whose figure stood above it; nevertheless, the productivity performance of the two was precisely the reverse. This example highlights that the integration of the two types of husbandry was as important, if not more so, as the absolute size of herds and flocks; in other words, availability of manure does not translate necessarily to its efficient utilization. All in all, in the absence of major technological breakthroughs, organizational changes reflected in the diffusion of efficient field systems offered the greatest potential of elevating medieval agricultural productivity. But, as noted in the previous section, field systems remained more conservative than innovative during this period.

The less than ideal organizational and technological choices made in this period are clearly reflected on land productivity figures. Viewed from a regional perspective, low to modest yields remained the norm within the southern and eastern parts of the country, the main notable exceptions being manors near the coastlines of Norfolk, Kent, and Sussex (as well as in northern Northamptonshire and sporadic instances in the Thames valley) where yields per acre (net of seed) of the three main grains (wheat, barley, oats) sometimes reached the range of 20–24 bushels. This level of productivity was on a par with the best results obtained in the exceptionally productive areas of Artois and parts of Flanders. Yields per seed and per acre were sometimes impressive in northern and western counties, particularly in Devon and Cornwall; nevertheless, the (by and large) poorer soils of these counties meant that the non-cropped portions of the arable were considerable at the expense of total land productivity.[29]

Table 2.1 Yields per Acre, Net of Seed, and Revenues in Common Fields and (Convertible Husbandry) Demesnes, in Bushels and Shillings

	Wheat	*Barley*	*Oats*	*Rye*	*Legumes*	*Net output, composite acre*	*Revenues, composite acre*
Pre-plague period	7.7 (6.5)	13.0 (9.1)	8.0 (6.5)	10.9 (8.2)	7.4 (4.9)	8.82 (6.93)	4.39 (3.37)
Post-plague period	8.5 (7.8)	11.4 (10.9)	8.4 (12.0)	7.4 (8.4)	7.4 (4.5)	8.91 (9.45)	4.54 (4.36)

Source: Kitsikopoulos, "Convertible Husbandry vs. Regular Common Fields," 466 (Table 1), 474 (Table 5).

The same sense of mediocre performance is revealed in Table 2.1 where yields are seen in the context of field systems drawing data from a large number of demesnes. In common field demesnes the level of yields (net of seed) for wheat and oats was around eight bushels per acre, 12 bushels for barley, nine bushels for rye, and a little over seven for legumes. Creating a composite acre by weighting the proportions dedicated to each crop results in a net output slightly short of nine bushels, both for the pre- and post-plague periods. These disappointing figures have been explained on the basis of low and static levels of nitrogen retention due to the permanent division of arable land and pastures in the context of common fields.[30]

But the surprising element in the figures of Table 2.1 is the even worse level of productivity among demesnes following variations of convertible husbandry, a system in which arable and pastoral activities were well-integrated with each other; the net output of a composite acre was slightly below seven bushels during the pre-plague period, but rising to well over nine after the epidemic. According to one explanation, the abysmally low pre-plague yield levels of convertible husbandry were due to poor edaphic conditions characterizing the majority of manors that practiced it (mainly located on light soils), a problem that was compounded by the somewhat high proportion of the land dedicated to cropping (50 percent). The latter problem was resolved in the post-plague period with the drastic reduction of cropping down to a quarter of the entire arable area, a reduction that was proportionally double the one recorded in common fields. On the other hand, the problem of poor edaphic conditions was not resolved since the practice of convertible husbandry remained exceptional throughout this period. However, it has been argued that if convertible husbandry was the norm (i.e., adopted in lands of higher fertility throughout the country), English yields (net of seed) could have been raised to the level of 10–15 bushels per acre, a level that would have been more competitive with the norm of the exceptional continental regions.[31]

Data on peasant yields are virtually non-existent. The few instances that do exist come from inventories of departed peasants who left their crops to be harvested by manorial officials. Stone has speculated that peasant yields may well have been higher than demesnial ones attributing it both to higher labor inputs and more zealously performed. There are a few isolated instances to support this optimism.[32] But let us not forget that peasants were less well-endowed with capital resources (especially animals and manure); hence, it is unlikely that peasant yields were, all in all, very different from those in demesnes.

Finally, manorial documents and expectations expressed in agricultural treatises provide us with a reasonable amount of information on labor productivity. Two important trends emerge: first, a significant gap appears in the productivity of customary tenants who performed labor services in the demesne, in contrast to the more efficient workers who received wages;[33] second, the ebbs and flows of labor productivity conform to the logic of the Ricardian model with declines in the level of labor productivity during the phase of agricultural intensification in the pre-plague period and the reverse scenario after the epidemic.[34]

DEMOGRAPHY, URBANIZATION, AND COMMERCE

Regardless of whether a historian wishes to view population as a strategic factor in shaping economic trends, the ebbs and flows of demographic movements simply cannot be ignored. Precise figures are (and always will be) lacking, but micro studies at the level of manors and the fluctuations of prices and wages offer a clear picture when it comes to overall trends. By working with some data produced by D. L. Farmer, Campbell has identified four phases during the period 1208–1466.[35]

The first phase extends from the beginning of the thirteenth century until the famines of 1315–22. During this period prices increased whereas real wages declined to the point that by the 1270s they stood at 50 percent less compared to the beginning of the century and remained at that low level until the end of the period. While a significant increase in the money supply contributed to the rise in prices, population growth seems to have been the main driving force. As an illustration, in the Somerset manor of Taunton the number of resident adult males increased by 228 percent during the period 1212–1312. Landlords, having to sell substantial surpluses and pay for labor, were the major beneficiaries; on the other hand, peasants were driven to greater self-sufficiency, assuming they could afford it, and scaled down their diets towards more grains and away from meat and ale.

The second phase extends from the famines of 1315–22 until the Black Death. The famines reduced population by 10–15 percent driving prices down and leading to an increase of real wages, although a reduction in the money supply contributed to these trends.

The third phase is ushered with the Black Death, which reduced the population by between a quarter and a half with further tolls taken by successive epidemics, and lasted until the 1370s. In addition to high mortality, fertility may have declined due to improved employment opportunities that may have delayed marriage, and the desire to have fewer children within marriage due to a reluctance to bring them into a disease ridden environment. The impact of these events was the reverse on prices and wages compared to the earlier famines since it was not simply a matter of curbed demand but of having a structural blow to the economy, particularly on the supply side. As a result prices soared and, in conjunction with restrictions imposed by the government on nominal wages, led to a decline of real wages. In Bridbury's words, this was an 'Indian summer' for seigneurial agriculture.

The final phase begins in the last quarter of the fourteenth century with the lower demand adjusting to the collapsed supply and thereby leading to a relative stabilization of prices for the next 100 years. At the same time, the Peasants' Revolt of 1381 brought a de facto annulment of the restrictions on nominal wages which led to an increase of real wages. Hence the resort to more extensive forms of husbandry, the shift towards pastoral activities and, ultimately, the retreat of seigneurial agriculture to the benefit of the peasant sector which found itself with more land, a lighter load in terms of seigneurial obligations, and a gradual transformation of tenures from customary to contractual ones.

The growth of population during the pre-plague period had a greater impact on the urban segment, increasing its share from a tenth of the total (1086) to about 15–20 percent by c. 1300. Assuming, a total population of 4.25 mil., as Campbell does, the urban element accounted for c. 0.7 mil., contributing one-fifth of the total national income of £4.7–5.0 mil. The southern and eastern counties were not only the most densely populated but also the most urbanized part of the country. London was at the peak of the urban pyramid with about 70,000 souls and there were another 13 or so towns with a population of at least 10,000 each.[36]

The dependence of towns, however, on their agrarian hinterlands was stronger, rather than the other way around, both because a substantial portion of raw materials utilized by craftsmen and artisans were provided by agriculture (e.g., wool, hemp, tallow, hides, etc.) but also, and most importantly, because the very survival of urban residents hinged on drawing goods from the countryside. The most comprehensive study regarding the degree of commercialization of seigneurial agriculture has been undertaken for ten counties surrounding London and it has been shown that the percentage of grain output finding its way to the market, excluding intermanorial transfers since "these are not true sales," was 38 percent c. 1300 while gross income per 100 sown acres stood at £8.8.[37] Crop sales accounted for two-thirds of total agricultural sales income, the remaining revenues coming from animals and their products. It is likely that peasants were also forced to engage in market sales drawing cash revenue to be used for the purchase of consumption and capital goods they could not produce but, in their case, their low level of animal resources meant that crops played a more prominent role in their market transactions.

The aforementioned statistics, along with the sheer proliferation of markets and fairs during the thirteenth century, have been used to buttress the argument that a strong commercial network developed around urban centers, as well as along interregional terms. However, the poor transportation infrastructure rendered difficult travel for long distances and thus tended to create a fragmentation and lack of integration of the commercial network; hence, it was important to have a high density of markets and fairs. But their sheer number does not mean that each one of them flourished: "40 per cent of markets and 54 per cent of fairs were valued at less than £1" during the first half of the fourteenth century.[38]

But whatever role urbanization played in boosting trade during the pre-plague period, there is no doubt that its significance diminished after the epidemics, at least in terms of its impact on the seigneurial sector.[39] The proportion of grain output sold from manors in the London region during the last quarter of the fourteenth century remained remarkably stable (37 percent) but, given the retreat of arable cultivation and the decline of grain prices, gross income per 100 sown acres fell to £8.1; over the course of the century the share of the arable sector in terms of agricultural sales income was reduced from two-thirds to about half of the total. By the end of the fifteenth century the impact of the urban sector was likely to have been substantially weaker given London's population decline by one-third compared to its pre-plague size and the fact that only five towns had populations exceeding 10,000.

STANDARDS OF LIVING

The previously outlined economic trends impacted the material standards of living of peasants and seigneurial households in radically different ways before and after the Black Death. Economic conditions were particularly favorable to landlords before the epidemic. In an era of mostly high product prices and low labor costs, direct involvement in production meant that "unless mismanaged, demesne lands . . . mostly gave good value."[40] Access to labor services would add to profitability on the production side because the documented inefficiency of servile labor was more than counterbalanced by its low compensation and therefore was likely to result in lower unit labor costs. But high as the profitability of demesnial lands may have been, revenues relating to the sale of produce generated less than a third of total seigneurial revenues (30 percent), based on a large sample of manors analyzed by Campbell.[41] The most prominent source of revenue was the appropriation of various rents (accounting for 37 percent), whereas tithes and banalities (relating to certain seigneurial prerogatives such as court profits, and monopolies of mills, market fairs, and boroughs) generated 20 and 13 percent respectively of total revenues. Simply put, the ownership of land and the prerogatives attached to it paid better than the management of it.

Lifestyles reflected the benefits of social and economic privilege. Dyer, among others, has documented extravagant levels of expenditure, although varying based on the size of retained servants (from a couple to several dozen in the case of high nobility), the number of guests visiting periodically during the year, and the degree of travel of the lord and his companions from manor to manor in the process "eating the estate produce or using up the accumulated cash from rents."[42] The most prominent cost of such lifestyles were the amounts spent on food which would count for between a quarter and half of a household's budget, although even more extravagant levels have been recorded. The largest amounts were spent on meat, followed by bread, ale, and wine, with the list extending down to fish, spices, dairy produce, etc. In addition to food, the purchase of clothes and the raising of expensive horses also drew fairly high levels of spending.

For the sake of having a balanced view, however, it is important to recall that the typical lay landlord of the pre-plague period would generate an annual revenue of £16–17, an amount enough to ensure considerable comfort but not enough to support foolish extravagance and, according to Dyer, the same principle applied higher up in the social ladder: "The aristocracy seem . . . to have been influenced by ideas about consumption that put emphasis on largesse, tempered always by a practical restraint and occasional moral qualms. The ideal was a lord who used his wealth, neither running foolishly into debt, nor hoarding in a miserly fashion. In modern economic terms, they were expected to live up to their income."[43]

Guided by such principles of balance and moderation would prove particularly fruitful after the epidemic at a time of falling revenues drawn from tenants and the declining profitability of demesnes which could be dealt with only by having access to labor services and by cutting drastically some of the most expensive types of capital cost, particularly marling.[44] But even if prudence were more likely to prevail during this period, the inertia towards indulgence was still powerful. One illustration is particularly illuminating. When the monks of Bury St. Edmunds fell into financial straights in the 1430s, Abbot William Curteys decided to impose some discipline regarding the food budget; in this context, he specified that the cost of feeding a monk should be 2s6d per week. This weekly allowance would have been sufficient to cover the grain needs of a member of a low- to middle-income level peasant family for half of the year.[45] It is worth repeating that this allowance was imposed once greater economy was deemed necessary.

Material standards of living for peasant families followed the exact opposite trajectory. There are no complete data that would allow us to recreate the annual budgets of peasant families but there were several attempts in the past to come up with budgetary models in order to define the minimum size of holding necessary to ensure subsistence. Such exercises involve collating the pieces of fragmentary evidence referring to peasant holdings and supplementing it by making reasonable extrapolations from information gathered from demesnes. The most recent of these attempts defined the minimum threshold of subsistence at 18 arable acres for the pre-plague period.[46] Sufficient data on peasant holdings exist to suggest that about half of the population failed to reach this threshold and, according to Dodds, as much as a quarter of all tenants may have held less than three acres.[47] In fact, existing statistics tend to underestimate the extent of fragmentation regarding peasant holdings because they are drawn from manorial surveys which record only the tenants holding land directly from a lord, as opposed to subtenants; furthermore, there is considerable evidence pointing towards the growing numbers of landless people.

There was no easy way out of this financial predicament. Product markets offered more liabilities than opportunities. Lords demanded from their tenants the payment of a higher proportion of their cash rents between September and December, thus forcing them to sell their surplus crops at a time when supply was abundant and hence prices low. At the same time, it has been documented (e.g., for the Ely manor of Wisbech Barton, Cuxham manor, Westminster

Abbey, and the Clare estates) that manorial officials held back on the sale of crops until January–July and that they sold first the cheapest grains and as late as possible the most valuable ones in order to take advantage of the highest possible prices; buyers during those times were mostly peasants who may have run out of their own supplies.[48] Furthermore, grain prices during the pre-plague period were remarkably unstable, thus failing to function as a signaling mechanism upon which a strategy of product specialization could be based; and the fact that markets were localized meant that even if such strategy were feasible it was bound to result in gluts if pursued by other farmers.

Harvest failures turned peasants' predicament from mere dilemmas to a struggle for survival. While landlords still had surpluses to sell at high prices, peasants faced a considerable reduction in basic necessities and cash revenues; moreover, employment opportunities were scarcer during harvest failures, the latter triggering a depression of economic activity in arable farming and related industries (e.g., milling and brewing). Desperate times induced desperate measures. Briggs' study on credit relations in the midlands concluded that lenders and borrowers often belonged to the same wealth category and that exploitation of weak peasants by their powerful counterparts was fairly rare. He points out, however, that instances of exploitation due to credit burdens were far more common in East Anglia, particularly in periods of adverse economic conditions such as famines and livestock epidemics.[49] Other drastic measures included the sale of animals and there is considerable evidence to prove that small and middling peasants were not well-endowed in this regard. But the most desperate measure was the piecemeal sales of land which further undermined the economic viability of farms; land sales were acts of last resort but flared up during particularly difficult times such as the famines initiated in 1315.[50] During the same time a crime wave has been documented reflected in cases presented to manorial courts, particularly crimes against property (e.g., stealing of grains and animals).[51] By 1327–32 about 70–75 percent (depending on the population estimate we adopt) of rural non-seigneurial households failed to reach the level of 12s in terms of movable wealth and thus deemed too poor to pay tax in the context of lay subsidies.[52]

Given the pessimism of theoretical budget models and the aforementioned evidence, medievalists have expressed a sense of wonderment as to how the lower half of the population made ends meet. Perhaps yields on peasant holdings matched, or even exceeded, demesnial yields particularly in regions of high-performing manors that were also characterized by a large number of smallholders (e.g., East Anglia). Or, perhaps income from outside employment was higher than we think. Langdon and Masschaele, two historians who hold favorable views of the opportunities ushered by the commercial expansion of the thirteenth century, have argued that focusing on the low wage rates is a misleading indicator of peasant welfare; instead, they believe that the tide of commercial expansion lifted total family incomes through increased employment opportunities.[53]

Significant improvements, however, took place in the aftermath of the Black Death.[54] The most important contributory factor was the reduction of seigneurial obligations. As it proved increasingly more difficult to generate profits from arable husbandry, the retreat of estates from cultivation went hand-in-hand with the gradual abandonment of labor services; and the subsequent shrinkage of manorial bureaucracies translated to limiting the ability to extract the most despised manifestations of serfdom such as the heriot and the merchet. Equally important, the ability of tenants to leave their manors and seek either higher wages or lower rent obligations elsewhere, along with the willingness of many landlords to give into such demands, meant that rents declined by as much as 20 percent, beginning in the fifteenth century. The reduction of seigneurial obligations, along with the decline of family sizes (and, therefore, of consumption needs), meant that a middling peasant would increase substantially his savings left over by the end of the year allowing him to pursue one or all of three options; first, the improvement of his living standards through higher levels of consumption. Evidence on the food allowance of workers showing a reduction of the grain component in favor of more meat and ale; the Sumptuary Law of 1363 which sought to define limits (despite the fact it was never enforced) on the value of clothes wore by servants, clearly reflecting the resentment of the elite regarding the gains of those below them; and the construction of more sturdy and comfortable homes (evident by their survival to our days), along with the elaborate furnishings bought, all stand in stark contrast to the gloomy days of the past.[55] The accumulation of land and the building up of animal stock were two other outlets to which savings were channeled. Considerable evidence points to the active pursuit of the last two options, although the process of land accumulation was bound to be discouraged after a certain point due to the high cost of labor.

AN AGGREGATE VIEW

It may be useful to conclude the empirical section of the paper with some aggregate figures produced by Campbell regarding the levels of total arable

Table 2.2 Estimates on the Size of Arable and Grain Areas, Total and Per Capita Grain Output, Population, and Growth Rates Compared to Previous Year (in Parentheses)

Date	*Total arable (mil. acres)*	*Total grain area (mil. acres)*	*Grain output (mil. quarters)*	*Population (millions)*	*Grain output per capita (quarters)*
1086	5.75–6.0	3.29	3.4–3.9	2.0–2.25	1.72
1300	10.5 (+79%)	6.23 (+89%)	7.4 (+103%)	4.0-4.25 (+94%)	1.79
1375	7.9 (-25%)	4.01 (-36%)	4.8 (-35%)	2.25-2.5 (-42%)	2.02

Note: To facilitate a sharper comparison, mean values have been used to calculate percentage changes wherever Campbell cites a range of figures; percentages have been rounded to the nearest figure.

Source: Campbell, *English Seigniorial Agriculture*, 386–410.

acreage, total grain acreage and output, and population for three benchmark years (Table 2.2). Campbell, being fully aware that his calculations are fraught with gaps in the evidence, estimates a population increase of 94 percent between 1086 and 1300, at the peak of England's agricultural performance, while the amount of grain output increased slightly faster (103 percent). The cited figures regarding the increase in the size of arable and grain areas suggest that this increase of grain output came both from increased land reclamation and/or a reduction of fallows (i.e., by pushing the extensive margin of cultivation) but also through an increase in the level of yields which, in theory, is associated with the intensive margin of cultivation. In the end, he argues, grain output per capita remained virtually the same between these two years. This is a highly controversial conclusion and stands in stark contrast with the long-held view that yields probably declined during the thirteenth century and that, overall, grain output did not keep pace with population growth.

On the other hand, the magnitude of trends revealed by Campbell's figures regarding the period 1300–75 appear far more plausible. He suggests a quarter decline in the size of arable land and a more drastic fall in the size of the grain acreage, which is consistent with the widely held belief that farming became more extensive. The decline in the amount of grain output, he suggests, was only marginally lower compared to the decline of the total grain area, which is plausible given the very slight improvement of yields in common field areas and despite the more drastic improvement in demesnes practicing convertible husbandry (see Table 2.1) since the latter remained a distinct minority. Finally, the more drastic decline of population compared to grain output is certainly consistent with the widely held belief that standards of living were in the process of improving significantly during this period.

THE CRISIS AND ITS CAUSES

Was the English agrarian economy in a state of crisis prior to the environmental disturbances of the early fourteenth century, or did it simply face strains with the latter events being the culprit for the crisis? In other words, was population growth coupled with an equivalent increase of productivity up to that point and could further increments in population be accommodated in the absence of these exogenous sources of instability? This is not a moot point, as Campbell has called it, but the most central issue to address in resolving the controversy surrounding the question of crisis.[56]

In reviewing the evidence as to how England responded to the demographic challenge between the Domesday Book and c. 1300, there is no doubt that certain key aspects of a Ricardian/Malthusian scenario unfolded. Namely, in attempting to increase food supplies, both seigneurial estates and peasants attempted to push the extensive margin of cultivation through land reclamation. Nevertheless, there were clear signs that the extent of cultivation was reaching a point of exhaustion by the middle of the thirteenth century, particularly in the more densely populated lowlands.[57] In some cases, like on the estates of the bishops of Worcester and Winchester, such limitations towards expansion became evident even earlier.[58] But the most glaring manifestation of how this process was bound to be self-defeating was the fragmentation of peasant holdings which threw about half of the agrarian non-seigneurial population in a state of subsistence crisis by the time of the Hundred Rolls and at least one-tenth of it into graveyards at the time of the 1310s famines. It is hard to fathom a more dramatic scenario that would convince one to call it a crisis. Escape from this worsening state of poverty was faced with serious obstacles in the midst of a land market of rising values for both arable- and pastureland.

Was this, however, the only type of response on the part of agrarian producers? After all, the Ricardian model envisages the option of increasing output through the intensive margin of cultivation. Such an option would entail an intensification of farming through the injection of more labor and capital inputs, a faster rate of adoption of existing techniques through capital formation and, ultimately, improvements in the level of yields per unit of land. Campbell clearly argues in favor of such a scenario taking place in the period 1086–1300 when he speculates that the growth rate of grain output exceeded the growth rate of the acreage under grains (see Table 2.2) attributing this development to the expansion of urban centers and markets.

However, one is baffled by the fact that the evidence on yields does not support such speculative optimism. Evidence from Norfolk during the second half of the thirteenth century proves that some landlords pushed the intensive margin of cultivation by injecting into production high quantities of labor and capital inputs along with a reduction of fallowing and, in the end, increased both yields per seed and per acre. Nevertheless, Norfolk and some other areas that exhibited the same type of dynamism were atypical. Data referring to yields per seed drawn from a national sample, including the most well-documented estates of the bishops of Winchester, show a decline of this ratio during the thirteenth century.[59] In theory, declining yields per seed may go hand-in-hand with increasing yields per acre assuming an increase of seeding rates in a classic scenario of diminishing returns. But an improvement of yields per acre is highly unlikely given Campbell's admission that English agriculture was "more extensive than intensive." Of course, land productivity may have been raised in the context of peasant holdings but, as noted earlier, there is lack of evidence supporting this view. This assessment becomes even more reasonable in light of the record on technological choices. The rate of adoption of certain practices (e.g., marling) that could raise the level of land (as opposed to labor) productivity has not, or cannot, been systematically quantified. But the utilization of others was clearly deficient, such as the cultivation of legumes in demesnes and the utilization of animal resources, and thus of manure, among peasant holdings. Manorial estates were better endowed in terms of the latter but the absence of radical innovations regarding field systems translated to an inefficient recycling of manure; in fact, the evolution of field systems suggests that they were becoming less, not more, flexible during this period.

The evidence on the evolution of yields and technological choices, admittedly being less than ideal, when viewed in conjunction with the steep rise of prices during the thirteenth century clearly points to the widening scissors between productivity and population growth.[60] In dealing with the predicament of modern less developed countries (LDCs), economics textbooks point out that "an outward shift of the PPF [Production Possibilities Frontier] does not, in itself, guarantee an increase in the standard of living. In the LDCs, the population growth rate is often very high . . . If employment grows more rapidly than the capital stock, then even though the PPF is shifting outward, capital per worker will decline. Unless some other factor-such as technological change-is raising productivity, then living standards will fall."[61] Taking this elementary dictum of economic theory and applying it to pre-plague England leads to a greater sense of pessimism in relation to Campbell's figures summarized in Table 2.2. Even if we assume a static, as opposed to declining, level of yields per acre between Domesday and c. 1300, grain output would have increased in proportion to the total grain area (89 percent), from 3.65 mil. quarters (the mean of Campbell's figures for 1086) to 6.89 mil. quarters in c. 1300. That would translate to a decline of per capita grain output from 1.72 down to 1.67 quarters. This decline may not seem very dramatic in a span of two centuries but we have to bear in mind two important qualifications. First, the decline may have been far more dramatic when we bear in mind that Campbell's population estimate for 1300 (4.0–4.25 mil.) is very low compared to mainstream views, with some historians adopting figures up to six mil.[62] But even if the 1300 population figure was close to Campbell's estimate and the decline of grain output per capita was modest, the latter masks the plausible scenario of a growing inequality of wealth during the thirteenth century, given the declining value of labor, which benefited estate owners at the expense of smallholders. Growing wealth inequality goes a long way in explaining why famines brought such devastating mortality in the 1310s but failed to have a substantial impact after the Black Death when wealth was more equitably distributed.[63] In the end, it is true that exogenous factors dealt the decisive blow to English feudalism; but this admission should not be used to deny that the system resembled a train bound for derailment, sooner or later.

In passing from the question on the existence of a crisis to one of explaining it, one ought to focus on the technological matrix of that economy since the only way to halt the application of the law of diminishing returns, driven by population growth and leading to lower productivity and declining living standards, is either through innovation or the diffusion of already existing techniques. In addressing this issue, the Ricardian framework ceases to be useful. It is true that it operates under the assumption of a near absence of innovations, and pre-plague England conforms to it, but it is on the issue of technological diffusion through capital formation that the model becomes problematic. That is so because it is set in the context of a system (i.e., capitalism) with very different institutions and economic agents than those prevailing in the Middle Ages. It is not surprising then that Postan, in particular, did notice the lack of technological possibilities and the levels of inadequate investment attributing them to the conservatism of landlords and the poverty of peasants but failed to provide convincing explanations for either of them, aside of cultural values and the impact of population on the integrity of holdings.[64]

On the other hand, the argument emphasizing the role of markets as engines of technological/organizational improvements and economic growth is currently witnessing a growing popularity to the point of becoming the mainstream view. Some recent publications have played an instrumental role in this regard. Working with data from the manor of Wisbech Barton, Stone has shown a clear responsiveness of cropping patterns to grain prices, inducing certain sophisticated decisions such as the cultivation of legumes in fields preceding the cropping of commercial grains. He concluded that "medieval reeves were clearly capable of extremely businesslike behaviour and could be highly responsive to changing market conditions."[65] Using tithe data from the Durham region, Dodds argued that peasants were also responsive to changes in grain prices, in fact, even more so than demesnes because the latter may have been constrained by decisions regarding their output mix due to obligations delivering part of the output to central households and making payments to *famuli*. His analysis proves that peasants were not "too stupid to respond to economic incentives."[66]

Aside of the fact that both of these studies rely on evidence from a single parish and that we can point to cases in which manorial production decisions were driven by consumption needs or exhibited a glaring indifference to innovation,[67] they do raise some important issues. The review of the evidence on the diffusion of flexible field systems and the use of high levels of labor and capital inputs (relative to ecological endowments) has shown that regions that performed well had very different levels of exposure to market forces and urbanization rates, from East Anglia and Kent, followed by Sussex, down to parts of the southwestern peninsula.[68] On the other hand, why do we fail to see more instances of innovation within the London region whose "hinterland was more diverse than it was developed and productive" and where the mean value of arable land was 16 percent below the national average (south of the Trent) despite the presence of fertile loams in three-quarters of this area?[69] Stone has expressed an intriguing hypothesis worth pondering about: managerial performance may have been suboptimal in manors close to urban centers because disposal strategies were more plentiful; on the other hand, higher standards may have prevailed in geographically isolated manors given the fact they had less leeway for mistakes. He has also expressed some interesting ideas when looking at the impact of market forces along chronological lines: managerial efficiency went through ebbs and flows, being below optimal levels during the thirteenth century when high product prices and low wages converged in boosting commercial expansion; tightened up around the turn of the century when profit margins were squeezed and royal taxation became heavier; and reached a new low after the Black Death, although by that time economic configurations and peasant discontent rendered the tasks of manorial officials extraordinarily difficult.[70] In the end, it would be unreasonable to deny that a certain segment of the landholding elite was attentive to commercial opportunities. But it does not follow that they always ended up with sophisticated, profit-maximizing, decisions or that this commercial astuteness was widespread enough to make a substantial difference in inducing technological innovation, productivity growth and output expansion; after all, "feudal lords were [not] capitalist entrepreneurs."[71]

But how about Dodds' assessment on the commercial orientation of the peasantry? Did markets drive productivity growth among peasant holdings, accounting for four-fifths of all land, raising yields above demesnial standards, and thus keeping grain output per capita stable in spite of demographic growth, as Campbell has speculated? Dodds' study refers to an area that was historically free of Malthusian constraints, particularly in the late fifteenth century when most of his evidence derives from, thereby referring to holdings that were fairly large; hence, his findings are not surprising. And he clearly stresses that there is still ambiguity on the correlation between holding sizes (and thus marketable surpluses) and the degree of peasants' market orientation, in the end admitting that his findings do not overturn the pessimism of some historians regarding the bleak conditions of the pre-plague decades. One may presume that even less well-endowed peasants, especially further south, exhibited an equally keen commercial orientation in an effort to find cash for the payment of seigneurial dues or to sell expensive grains and then buy cheaper ones for their own consumption. I would argue, however, that medieval markets did not offer the potential of substantial gains to peasants in light of the fact that their obligations to pay the bulk of cash rents in the fall translated to selling in periods of market gluts at low prices. Or, due to laws against forestalling (the practice of intercepting goods destined for the market and buying them with the aim of reselling them at a higher price); these laws, aimed at combating monopolistic situations, should be contrasted with the tolerance towards manorial estates when selling their surplus late in the season in the midst of relative scarcities. Medieval market regulations "were far from expressing a neutral concern for universal welfare . . . The evidence shows unambiguously that market operations were not unaffected by distinctions of power and social status."[72] Commercial astuteness on the part of peasants may have rewarded them with some gains. But as we descend down to the level of smallholders, their limited resources restricted the surpluses they could sell and whatever gains they may have scored were more likely to boost family consumption rather than capital formation.

The main cause of the feudal crisis in England, to state it explicitly, was its institutional structure.[73] What is meant by institutions, however, goes beyond the notion of some supply side constraints (e.g., communal field regulations, lack of labor mobility), which are also noted in mainstream views, to include the role of seigneurial prerogatives in retarding economic growth. The differences in regional patterns of economic growth are particularly useful in addressing the question of causation in regard to crisis. The coastal areas of the southeast and the southwestern peninsula were characterized by a diversity of ecological profiles, population densities, urbanization rates, and market networks. How can we argue then that any of these factors functioned as the prime mover since they were less favorable in some of these instances? In contrast, what all these areas had in common were feudal institutions with decidedly weaker seigneurial prerogatives compared to the norm in many other parts of the country. It is in this sense that we are justified to argue that the nature and strength of feudal property rights functioned as the primary conditioning factor of economic growth during the pre-plague period. That is not to say that population growth and greater urbanization do not offer important inducements to productivity growth, particularly by justifying the adoption of costly techniques (e.g., marling). What is questioned here is the assertion that they functioned as prime movers of economic growth. Market demand simply offers incentives to economic agents who may respond to it in search of profits. Whether they actually do respond is conditioned by a number of supply side factors relating to institutions, property rights, and the distribution of wealth on the basis of non-economic prerogatives; such factors may render producers either hesitant to engage heavily in the market if perceptions of risk are heightened (i.e., poor peasants), or may render others indifferent or only mildly interested in responding to such incentives (i.e., estates relying heavily on seigneurial revenues).

It is important to recall that the bulk of manorial revenues were derived from the role of landlords as property owners and their entitlement to seigneurial prerogatives; while not trivial, revenues through the direct exploitation of the land accounted for less than a third of the total (30 percent).[74] Despite the fact that responding to market opportunities was bound to produce rewards, not being attentive to such opportunities did not rise to the level of seriously penalizing the financial standing of estates, at least not those relying heavily on seigneurial extractions. "For the great landlords the maximization of income often took second place, because they were warriors, churchmen, politicians, and dispensers of hospitality and patronage as well as owners of assets";[75] it follows that landlords did not have to act as profit maximizers. Not every landlord possessed the kind of property rights and seigneurial prerogatives that would allow him to raise large revenues from such sources; managerial astuteness was the only option in their case. It was precisely the presence of these types of landlords in areas of weak manorialism that explains their exceptional performance in raising productivity, although the degree of success was also conditioned by market forces and the type of ecological environments they operated in.[76]

The thesis that variations regarding the strength of feudal institutions conditioned regional differences on innovation and productivity levels among manors is one side of the coin; the effect of these very same institutions on the ability of peasants to engage in capital formation is the other. All but proponents of the Marxist argument (and to some extent of the NIE) have sought to underplay the burden imposed on the peasantry, particularly in light of developments that took place during the thirteenth century. The argument goes that since custom prevented the rise of rents for customary holdings and freeholders, comprising the majority of tenures, at a time that land scarcity was becoming acute, it follows that actual rents were below market values. Campbell goes as far as endorsing the view that it is more justified to talk about the exploitation of lords by their tenants than the other way around. And in addressing the predicament of a large portion of the peasantry, he argues that it was this access to (especially free) holdings with rents below market value that contributed to overpopulation, the fragmentation of holdings, indebtedness and, in the end, widespread poverty.[77] This is a bold statement indeed.

While it is reasonable to argue that seigneurial extractions may not have kept pace in many cases with the rising value of land, and despite the ability of lords to seek other alternatives (e.g., raising entry fines), this argument distorts historical reality by reflecting only a partial view of it. The part that is ignored is the assault on the rights of the peasantry between the eleventh and fourteenth centuries manifested in the subjugation of formerly free tenants into serfdom and the substantial increase of their obligations. Despite the fact that Hatcher was singularly responsible for making the argument of peasant obligations lagging behind land values, nevertheless, he (along with Bailey) and others do note certain changes in common law taking place between the Domesday Book and c. 1300 that we should keep in mind.[78] Prior to 1200 legal distinctions were unclear but around that time lords succeeded in assigning unfree status to those owing labor services or acting as reeves, despite the fact that such features were not considered to be attributes of servility up to that point. Hence, the term "villein" which used to refer to a tenant with a fairly substantial holding ended up, through these legal changes (which also encompassed the exclusion of hitherto free peasants from the protection of royal courts), being synonymous with servility. These developments coincided with the increased interest on the part of landlords in managing their estates and were accompanied by the imposition or re-imposition of labor services, thereby increasing the burden of the unfree. Not to mention that the very concept of serfdom translated to restrictions on basic rights and the most personal aspects of one's life, such as the ability to move, marry, have relationships with the opposite sex, and even penalize the family of a serf at a time of death.

A fundamental flaw of many mainstream historians is to ignore the origins of feudal property rights and to justify their existence on the basis of providing protection and a judicial system to peasants. The historical record is clearly different, pointing out the fact that such property rights were often the fruits of military might, while the judicial system acted as one of the instruments used to provide an appearance of legitimacy to exploitative extraction mechanisms without denying its role in establishing order in other aspects of the economic and social life of the manor (e.g., in handling disputes among peasants). But if the legitimacy of feudal property rights is in question, under what logic is it justified to raise the issue that the revenues they laid claim upon may not have kept pace with the rate of inflation during a particular period of time? Campbell's thesis, in particular, is difficult to justify in light of his own analysis of seigneurial revenues which shows a correlation between the size of an estate and the strength of its seigneurial prerogatives: a significantly higher portion of total revenues were derived from rents and banalities in the case of great landlords compared to their lesser counterparts.[79] Simply put, might had its privileges.

Dodds cites a story that is worth repeating in this context. An auditing of some *famuli* holdings of Westminster Abbey recorded double the level of yields compared to the nearby demesne; on the other hand, analysis of tithe data reveals that other peasants in the same area achieved yields that stood at half the level of demesnial yields. What made the difference is that *famuli* may have had access to capital resources (e.g., tools, manure) from the demesne that their less fortunate counterparts did not. These events were recorded in 1367 but such outcomes were even more likely prior to the Black Death.[80] Here we have a large religious institution which sold a fairly low proportion of its produce (despite having access to large markets), followed poor managerial practices (e.g., low stocking densities, cropping legumes following the fallow) and, in the end, achieved low yields. It is hard to escape the conclusion that its heavy reliance on seigneurial extractions for its revenues drained capital resources away from its peasants, resources which (as the case of *famuli* holdings reveals) could have made a decisive difference in raising output; in other words, seigneurial prerogatives were a zero-sum game.

NOTES

1. The numerical estimates belong to Mayhew and are cited by B. M. S. Campbell, *English Seigniorial Agriculture, 1250–1450* (Cambridge: Cambridge University Press, 2000), 33. For a more detailed account of available sources regarding the seigneurial sector, see Ch. 2. Campbell (and some associates) is solely responsible for the most ambitious aggregation project drawn from data from manorial accounts and the IPMs (see text below).
2. A comprehensive study of tithe data is Ben Dodds, *Peasants and Production in the Medieval Northeast: The Evidence from Tithes, 1270–1536* (Woodbridge, UK and Rochester, NY: Boydell Press, 2007).
3. Regarding the availability of sources and the existing gaps in the evidence, see C. C. Dyer, *Standards of Living in the Later Middle Ages: Social Change*

in England c. 1200–1520 (Cambridge: Cambridge University Press, 1989); Harry Kitsikopoulos, "Standards of Living and Capital Formation in Pre-plague England: A Peasant Budget Model," *Economic History Review* 53 (2000); idem, "The Impact of the Black Death on Peasant Economy in England, 1350–1500," *The Journal of Peasant Studies*, 29 (2002).

4. Campbell, *English Seigniorial Agriculture*, 55, 61–62; C. C. Dyer, "Documentary Evidence: Problems and Enquiries," in *The Countryside of Medieval England*, eds. G. Astill and A. Grant (Oxford and New York: B. Blackwell, 1988), 22. A good introduction to the function and origins of the English manor is Mark Bailey, *The English Manor c. 1200–c. 1500* (Manchester and New York: Manchester University Press, 2002), 1–18; see also pp. 25–37 for the rights and obligations of the different types of tenures; and pp. 21–25, 37ff on the various types of manorial documents and numerous examples of them.
5. Campbell bases his assertion on the relative weakness of the manorial element in northern and western counties, to the fact that tenants were more actively involved in the reclamation of land between the time of the Domesday Book (1086) and the Hundred Rolls (particularly in areas beyond the ones covered by the latter), and the piecemeal leasing of the demesne by the beginning of the fourteenth century. See Campbell, *English Seigniorial Agriculture*, pp. 57–60; E. A. Kosminsky, *Studies in the Agrarian History of England in the Thirteenth Century*, trans. R. Kisch, ed. R. H. Hilton (Oxford: B. Blackwell, 1956), 89.
6. Campbell, *English Seigniorial Agriculture*, 67–68.
7. C. C. Dyer, *An Age of Transition? Economy and Society in England in the Later Middle Ages* (Oxford and New York: Clarendon Press), 110–111.
8. C. C. Dyer, *Making a Living in the Middle Ages: The People of Britain 850–1520* (New Haven and London: Yale University Press, 2002), 133.
9. J. Hatcher, "English Serfdom and Villeinage: Towards a Reassessment," *Past and Present* 90 (1981): 12. Britnell speculates that the proportion of total agricultural production accounted by labor services in the thirteenth century did not exceed 3 percent, with wage labor counting for another 20–25 percent. These proportions most certainly declined with the decay of seigneurial power and shrinking of demesnes after the Black Death; see Richard Britnell, "Commerce and Capitalism in Late Medieval England: Problems of Description and Theory," *Journal of Historical Sociology* 6 (1993): 364.
10. Kosminsky, *Studies,* 89; J. Hatcher and Mark Bailey, *Modelling the Middle Ages: The History and Theory of England's Economic Development* (Oxford and New York: Oxford University Press: 2001), 99; C. C. Dyer, "Documentary Evidence" 21.
11. Harry Kitsikopoulos, "Convertible Husbandry vs. Regular Common Fields: A Model on the Relative Efficiency of Medieval Field Systems," *Journal of Economic History* 64 (2004): 462–463; Campbell, *English Seigniorial Agriculture*, 179.
12. The map is constructed based on a fairly thorough scouring of the secondary literature and thus may reflect biases stemming from the availability of documents and the preferences of researchers. It is plausible, for instance, that the spread of such systems in the southwest (e.g., Cornwall) and the extreme north was even stronger given the absence of extensive demesnial cultivation and thus of surviving documents (see n. 5).
13. Kitsikopoulos, "Convertible Husbandry vs. Regular Common Fields" 484–485; idem, "Urban Demand and Agrarian Productivity in Pre-plague England: Reassessing the Relevancy of von Thünen's Model," *Agricultural History* 77 (2003), 503–511.
14. Campbell and Bartley have produced a number of maps showing the virtual absence of common field arrangements in Kent, Devon, and Cornwall; a very

sporadic one in places like Sussex and Yorkshire (especially in N. and W. Riding); and a more mixed picture in East Anglia and Essex but, even in these areas, there were pockets in which common fields were either absent or there was a minimal degree of regulations. See B. M. S. Campbell and Ken Bartley, *England on the Eve of the Black Death: An Atlas of Lay Lordship, Land and Wealth, 1300–49* (Manchester and New York: Manchester University Press, 2006), 55–68, esp. map 5:3. In large parts of these counties land was cultivated in severalty and it was often enclosed, covering about two mil. acres (a quarter of the total) in the country as a whole c. 1200, according to Dyer; see Dyer, *An Age of Transition?*, 58.

15. Campbell, *English Seigniorial Agriculture*, 177, 179, 273–274, 291–292.
16. Ibid., 273–274.
17. Ibid., 274.
18. Ibid., 275, 301; Kitsikopoulos, "Convertible Husbandry vs. Regular Common Fields," 486–487, 492–493. For an overview of the evidence extending to the lower utilization of capital and labor inputs beginning in the first half of the fourteenth century and becoming more pronounced after the Black Death, see D. Stone, *Decision-making in Medieval Agriculture* (Oxford and New York: Oxford University Press, 2005), 235–253.
19. Campbell, *English Seigniorial Agriculture*, 1.
20. Using tithe records from six manors in Essex, Kent, and Hampshire, Dodds documented close similarities in the type of crops grown in the demesne and peasant holdings, although peasants tended to cultivate somewhat higher quantities of the more valuable crops (e.g., wheat and barley); see Ben Dodds, "Demesne and Tithe: Peasant Agriculture in the Late Middle Ages," *Agricultural History Review* 56 (2008): 128–132.
21. Campbell, *English Seigniorial Agriculture*, 72, 90, 250–251; Dyer, "Documentary Evidence," 19.
22. On the definition and calculation method of livestock units, see Campbell, *English Seigniorial Agriculture*, 104–106.
23. Ibid., 159–160, 171, 180–181, 183–186, 236–237, 247.
24. J. L. Langdon, *Horses, Oxen and Technological Innovation: The Use of Draught Animals in English Farming from 1066–1500* (Cambridge: Cambridge University Press, 1986); Campbell, *English Seigniorial Agriculture*, 15, 122, 129.
25. J. L. Langdon, "The Economics of Horses and Oxen in Medieval England," *Agricultural History Review* 30 (1982).
26. For a summary of the evidence, see Kitsikopoulos, "Convertible Husbandry vs. Regular Common Fields" 471, 476–477, 489–490.
27. Campbell, *English Seigniorial Agriculture*, 173–176.
28. Stone, *Decision-making*, 178–180.
29. Campbell, *English Seigniorial Agriculture*, 309–355; Harry Kitsikopoulos, "Technological Change in Medieval England: A Critique of the Neo-Malthusian Argument," *Proceedings of the American Philosophical Society* 144 (2000): 403–406, 446–449. Yields per acre is an inadequate indicator of both grain and overall agricultural productivity since the extent of fallowing as well as the productivity of non-cereal production and animal husbandry (activities which are less well-documented) are not taken into account.
30. Kitsikopoulos, "Convertible Husbandry vs. Regular Common Fields," 478–483, 494–495.
31. Ibid. A sense of regional variations of land productivity can be gained by looking at the mean unit value of arable land calculated by Campbell from the IPMs (1300–49). In broad terms, it was in the Soke of Peterborough, Norfolk, and Kent where the highest values were recorded, followed by parts

of the East Midlands, Sussex, and spotty areas in the London region. Despite the presence of the metropolis, arable land values around London were not particularly high; in fact, they were 16 percent lower compared to the entire IPM sample covering all areas below the Trent; see Campbell, *English Seigniorial Agriculture*, 350–351, 354. Such figures, however, should be used with caution since arable land values do not reflect only productivity levels but also land scarcity and variations in seigneurial prerogatives.

32. As was the case with a Norfolk farmer who achieved oat yields c. 20 bushels/acre in 1468–9 when the norm in demesnial holdings was c. 14 bushels. See Dyer, *An Age of Transition?*, 207; idem., "Documentary Evidence," 30; Stone, *Decision-making*, 269–272. Karakacili's study on the Ramsey abbey manors, however, noted that "labor inputs on the demesne reflected, at least fairly closely, those used by local farmers in these same regions"; see Eona Karakacili, "English Agrarian Labor Productivity Rates Before the Black Death: A Case Study," *Journal of Economic History* 64 (2004): 35.
33. D. Stone, "The Productivity of Hired and Customary Labour: Evidence from Wisbech Barton in the Fourteenth Century," *Economic History Review* 50 (1997). On the productivity figures of particular activities, see Kitsikopoulos, "Standards of Living and Capital Formation," 255–257.
34. Thornton has shown that in the Somerset manor of Rimpton (Winchester bishopric) a 40 percent increase in the number of days worked per arable acre between c. 1230 and c. 1300 led to a decline of crop yields per labor unit by 37 percent. Conversely, a 22 percent reduction in labor time between c. 1300 and c. 1375 led to a 19 percent increase in crop yields per labor unit, despite the absolute decline of yields; see C. Thornton, "The Determinants of Land Productivity on the Bishop of Winchester's Demesne of Rimpton, 1208 to 1403," in *Land, Labour and Livestock: Historical Studies in European Agricultural Productivity*, eds. B. M. S. Campbell and M. Overton (Manchester and New York: Manchester University Press, 1991), 205 (Table 7.7).
35. Campbell, *English Seigniorial Agriculture*, 4–10; see also Hatcher and Bailey, *Modelling the Middle Ages*, 32, 178. Clark's reconstruction of nominal and real wage series shows roughly similar trends with Campbell's figures. According to Clark, real wages during the years 1290–1319 stood at their lowest point throughout England's pre-modern history but doubled by the mid-fifteenth century compared to early thirteenth century levels; see Gregory Clark, "The Long March of History: Farm Wages, Population, and Economic Growth, England, 1209–1869," *Economic History Review*, 60 (2007). On the causation between wages and employment opportunities particularly for females and how they affected the slow population recovery after the Black Death, see the critical discussion in Mark Bailey, "Demographic Decline in Late Medieval England: Some Thoughts on Recent Research," *Economic History Review*, 49 (1996).
36. Campbell, *English Seigniorial Agriculture*, pp. 20–21, 405; idem, "The Agrarian Problem in the Early Fourteenth Century," *Past and Present* 188 (2005): 16; Hatcher and Bailey, *Modelling the Middle Ages*, 140; Richard Smith, "Human Resources," in *The Countryside of Medieval England*, eds. G. Astill and A. Grant.
37. Campbell, *English Seigniorial Agriculture,* 21, 194–195, 204–205; Kitsikopoulos, "Standards of Living and Capital Formation"
38. Campbell and Bartley, *England on the Eve of the Black Death*, 301; Hatcher and Bailey, *Modelling the Middle Ages*, 152. It can also be argued that Campbell's figures on the proportion of sales somewhat exaggerate the importance of commercial disposal because his calculations are made on the basis of output net of tithe and seed, as opposed to gross output. Calculating the figure

on the basis of gross output net of tithe only, to account for the fact that its commercial potential was considerable, would reduce the proportion of crop sales from 38 to 27 percent.

39. Campbell, *English Seigniorial Agriculture*, 196–198, 205–207, 433, 435.
40. Campbell, "The Agrarian Problem," 20. Campbell, however, has made contradictory statements in this regard; see his *English Seigniorial Agriculture*, 357 where he states that "the margin between profit and loss was . . . a very narrow one."
41. Campbell, "The Agrarian Problem" 18–20.
42. Dyer, *Standards of Living*, 27–108; the quote is from p. 54.
43. Ibid., 91.
44. Kitsikopoulos, "Convertible Husbandry vs. Regular Common Fields," 473–478, esp. Table 7, p. 476.
45. Dyer, *Standards of Living*, 98; Kitsikopoulos, "The Impact of the Black Death."
46. Kitsikopoulos, "Standards of Living and Capital Formation"; Hatcher and Bailey, *Modelling the Middle Ages*, 46.
47. The problem of smallholdings was particularly keen in the most densely parts of the country such as East Anglia; as an illustration, 220 of the 364 tenants in Martham held only one to two acres in 1292. See Ben Dodds, "Output and Productivity: Common Themes and Regional Variations," in *Agriculture and Rural Society After the Black Death: Common Themes and Regional Variations*. eds. B. Dodds and R. Britnell (Hartfield, UK: University of Hertfordshire Press, 2008), 83; Dyer, *Making a Living in the Middle Ages*, 167.
48. Stone, *Decision-making*, 49, 191–192; Dyer, *An Age of Transition?*, 88; Richard Britnell, "Minor Landlords in England and Medieval Agrarian Capitalism," *Past and Present*, 89 (1980): 19–20.
49. Chris Briggs, *Credit and Village Society in Fourteenth-century England* (Oxford: Oxford University Press, 2009); see also Campbell, *English Seigniorial Agriculture*, 2, 366–367.
50. In the Suffolk manor of Redgrave land transfers jumped from no more than 65 prior to 1315 to 188 and 135 in 1316 and 1317 respectively. Sellers were mostly smallholders and buyers mainly substantial peasants, the latter finding the opportunity during the desperate famine years to take advantage of their less fortunate neighbors. See Dyer, *Making a Living in the Middle Ages*, 231.
51. For an example of such manorial records, from the Yorkshire manor of Wakefield, see Bailey, *The English Manor*, 230–234.
52. Campbell, "The Agrarian Problem," 63.
53. See J. L. Langdon and James Masschaele, "Commercial Activity and Population Growth in Medieval England," *Past and Present*, 190 (2006). Such interpretation does fall within the realm of possibility, however, the two authors do not provide solid evidence to support it.
54. Kitsikopoulos, "The Impact of the Black Death"; Hatcher and Bailey, *Modelling the Middle Ages*, 115–116.
55. Dyer, *Making a Living in the Middle Ages*, 283, 356–357; idem, *An Age of Transition?*, 128–157.
56. Campbell, *English Seigniorial Agriculture*, 22.
57. Output expansion through land reclamation was still feasible in some parts of the country. The Tyne Tees (Durham) region, for instance, was still far from reaching its Malthusian limits; see Dodds, *Peasants and Production*.
58. Campbell, *English Seigniorial Agriculture*, 3.
59. Campbell, "Land, Labour, Livestock, and Productivity Trends in English Seigniorial Agriculture, 1208–1450," in *Land, Labour and Livestock*, eds.

Campbell and Overton, 161 (table 6.2), 171 (Table 6.6); B. M. S. Campbell and M. Overton, "A New Perspective on Medieval and Early Modern Agriculture: Six Centuries of Norfolk Farming c. 1250–c. 1850," *Past and Present* 141 (1993): 70 (Table 5); Kitsikopoulos, "Technological Change in Medieval England," 403–404 (esp. Table 1).

60. On the behavior of pre-plague prices, see Campbell, *English Seigniorial Agriculture*, 4–5 (esp. Figure 1.01).
61. Robert E. Hall and Marc Lieberman, *Macroeconomics: Principles and Applications*, 5th ed. (Mason, OH: Thomson South-Western, 2008), 223. It is hard to avoid a comparison between this scenario and what was going on in pre-plague England. As noted earlier, in Rimpton manor an increase of labor inputs during the period 1230–1300 caused a proportional decline of productivity (see n. 34); it is very likely that more studies on this subject will produce similar results.
62. Stone, *Decision-making*, 271–272.
63. For instance, famines also hit during the years 1437–40 but they were not accompanied by any great increase in mortality, except in local pockets which also witnessed recurrent episodes of the plague; see Dyer, *Making a Living in the Middle Ages*, 275.
64. For a more comprehensive critique of the Neo-Malthusian argument, see Harry Kitsikopoulos, "Social and Economic Theory in Medieval Studies," in *Handbook of Medieval Studies: Terms-Methods-Trends*, vol. 2, ed. Albrecht Classen (Berlin and New York: DeGruyter, 2010).
65. Stone, *Decision-making*, 51–58, 62–65; quote from p. 194. Stone also acknowledges the important role of consumption needs and soil conditions on cropping patterns.
66. Dodds, *Peasants and Production*, 132–161; quote from p. 161.
67. Bury St. Edmunds, an estate whose relations with its tenants were notoriously adversarial, engaged in a number of poor decisions such as the consecutive cropping of some fields without fallowing or the cultivation of legumes; these practices led some of its manors to operate at a considerable loss during the fourteenth century. Managerial indifference also characterized royal manors while the king exercised his predatory right to confiscate livestock from estates that fell temporarily under his management. Campbell, *English Seigniorial Agriculture*, 417–421. On demesnial decisions driven by 'satisficing strategies,' see K. Biddick, *The Other Economy: Pastoral Husbandry on a Medieval Estate* (Berkeley and Los Angeles: University of California Press, 1989) and K. Biddick (with C. C. J. H. Bijleveld), "Agrarian Productivity on the Estates of the Bishopric of Winchester in the Early Thirteenth Century: A Managerial Perspective," *Land, Labour and Livestock*, ed. Campbell and Overton.
68. B. M. S. Campbell, "Arable Productivity in Medieval England: Some Evidence from Norfolk," *Journal of Economic History* 43 (1983); P. F. Brandon, "Cereal Yields on the Sussex Estates of Battle Abbey During the Later Middle Ages," *Economic History Review* 25 (1972); M. Mate, "The Agrarian Economy of Southeast England Before the Black Death: Depressed or Buoyant?," in *Before the Black Death: Studies in the 'Crisis' of the Early Fourteenth Century*, ed. B. M. S. Campbell (Manchester and New York: Manchester University Press, 1991); idem, "Farming Practice and Techniques: Kent and Sussex," in *The Agrarian History of England and Wales*, vol. 3, *1348–1500*, ed. E. Miller (Cambridge: Cambridge University Press, 1991).
69. Campbell, et al., *A Medieval Capital and its Grain Supply: Agrarian Production and its Distribution in the London Region c. 1300* (Historical Geography Research Series, n.p. 1993), 22; Campbell, *English Seigniorial Agriculture*, 354; quote from Campbell and Bartley, *England on the Eve of the Black Death*, 345.

70. Stone, *Decision-making*, 189–230. Similar doubts on the role of market forces are raised by Hatcher and Bailey along these lines: if there was a direct causation between population growth, urbanization, and trade, on the one hand, and technological change and productivity growth, on the other, why did agricultural (or at least grain) output per capita increased after the plague when both urbanization and commercial activity were both weaker? See Hatcher and Bailey, *Modelling the Middle Ages*, 169–170, 182. Clark also underplays the role of commercial opportunities in raising aggregate output during the thirteenth century, attributing it instead to population growth in the context of an economy driven largely by Malthusian dynanics; see Clark, "The Long March of History," 126.
71. Quote from Campbell, "The Agrarian Problem," 43.On the issue of the relationship between crop choices and price changes it should be noted that, given differences in production costs of different grains, it follows that profits per unit of crop did not always correlate with crop prices; therefore, if manorial officials chose crops based on their prices, it does not mean necessarily they were maximizing profits. This, and similar issues, are explored in Harry Kitsikopoulos, "Manorial Estates as Business Firms: The Relevance of Economic Rent in Determining Crop Choices in London's Hinterland c. 1300," *Agricultural History Review* 56 (2008); and *idem*, "Urban Demand and Agrarian Productivity."
72. Richard Britnell, "Price Setting in English Borough Markets, 1349–1500," *Canadian Journal of History* 31 (1996): 10–11; quote from p. 15.
73. I have not discussed the role of war in shaping economic conditions because England, unlike parts of the continent, was fortunate in this regard. Scottish raids in the north (lasting through the 1320s) and the war with France had a negative impact beginning in the 1290s; but the raids had a localized character and despite the fact that taxation was particularly burdensome in some years by draining resources to the king, it was not oppressive at the aggregate level. See Dyer, *Making a Living in the Middle Ages*, 255–259; Dodds, *Peasants and Production*, 45–70.
74. Campbell, "The Agrarian Problem," 18–20.
75. Hatcher and Bailey, *Modelling the Middle Ages*, 10.
76. Bailey, more than any other historian, stressed the need to take into account locational characteristics and ecological endowments in judging productivity performances, that is, a producer that was less favored in these two respects should not be evaluated by the same standards compared to producers that were so. See M. Bailey, *A Marginal Economy? East Anglian Breckland in the Later Middle Ages* (Cambridge: Cambridge University Press, 1989); and idem, "The Concept of the Margin in the Medieval English Economy," *Economic History Review* 42 (1989).
77. Campbell, "The Agrarian Problem," 23–24, 69–70; see also Hatcher, "English Serfdom and Villeinage".
78. Hatcher and Bailey, *Modelling the Middle Ages*, 79–89; Dyer, *Making a Living in the Middle Ages*, 140–141.
79. Campbell, "The Agrarian Problem," 19 (Table 3).
80. Dodds, "Output and Productivity," 79–80; see also Campbell, *English Seigniorial Agriculture*, 176, 194–198, 201, 205, 208, 298–299, 370–375.

BIBLIOGRAPHY

Astill, G. and A. Grant, eds. *The Countryside of Medieval England*. Oxford and New York: B. Blackwell, 1988.

Bailey, M. *A Marginal Economy? East Anglian Breckland in the Later Middle Ages*. Cambridge: Cambridge University Press, 1989.

Bailey, M. "The Concept of the Margin in the Medieval English Economy." *Economic History Review* 42 (1989): 1–17.

Bailey, M. "Demographic Decline in Late Medieval England: Some Thoughts on Recent Research." *Economic History Review*, 49 (1996): 1–19

Bailey, M. *The English Manor c. 1200–c. 1500*. Manchester and New York: Manchester University Press, 2002.

Biddick, K. *The Other Economy: Pastoral Husbandry on a Medieval Estate*. Berkeley and Los Angeles: University of California Press, 1989.

Biddick, K. (with C. C. J. H. Bijleveld). "Agrarian Productivity on the Estates of the Bishopric of Winchester in the Early Thirteenth Century: A Managerial Perspective," in *Land, Labour and Livestock: Historical Studies in European Agricultural Productivity*, edited by B. M. S. Campbell and M. Overton, 95–123. Manchester and New York: Manchester University Press, 1991.

Brandon, P. F. "Cereal Yields on the Sussex Estates of Battle Abbey During the Later Middle Ages." *Economic History Review*, 25 (1972): 403–429.

Briggs, C. *Credit and Village Society in Fourteenth-century England*. Oxford: Oxford University Press, 2009.

Britnell, R. "Minor Landlords in England and Medieval Agrarian Capitalism." *Past and Present* 89 (1980): 3–22.

Britnell, R. "Commerce and Capitalism in Late Medieval England: Problems of Description and Theory." *Journal of Historical Sociology* 6 (1993): 359–376.

Britnell, R. "Price-setting in English Borough Markets, 1349–1500." *Canadian Journal of History* 31 (1996): 2–15.

Campbell, B. M. S. "Arable Productivity in Medieval England: Some Evidence from Norfolk." *Journal of Economic History* 43 (1983): 379–404.

Campbell, B. M. S., ed., *Before the Black Death: Studies in the 'Crisis' of the Early Fourteenth Century*. Manchester and New York: Manchester University Press, 1991.

Campbell, B. M. S. "Land, Labour, Livestock, and Productivity Trends in English Seigniorial Agriculture, 1208–1450," in *Land, Labour and Livestock: Historical Studies in European Agricultural Productivity*, edited by B. M. S. Campbell and M. Overton, 144–182. Manchester and New York: Manchester University Press, 1991.

Campbell, B. M. S. *English Seigniorial Agriculture 1250–1450*. Cambridge: Cambridge University Press, 2000.

Campbell, B. M. S. "The Agrarian Problem in the Early Fourteenth Century" *Past and Present* 188 (2005): 3–70.

Campbell, B. M. S. and M. Overton, eds. *Land, Labour and Livestock: Historical Studies in European Agricultural Productivity*. Manchester and New York: Manchester University Press, 1991.

Campbell, B. M. S., and M. Overton. "A New Perspective on Medieval and Early Modern Agriculture: Six Centuries of Norfolk Farming c. 1250–c. 1850." *Past and Present* 141 (1993): 38–105.

Campbell, B. M. S., J. A, Galloway, J. A. Keene, and M. Murphy. *A Medieval Capital and its Grain Supply: Agrarian Production and its Distribution in the London Region c. 1300*. Historical Geography Research Series, n. p., 1993.

Campbell, B. M. S. and K. Bartley. *England on the Eve of the Black Death: An Atlas of Lay Lordship, Land and Wealth, 1300–49*. Manchester and New York: Manchester University Press, 2006.

Clark, G. "The Long March of History: Farm Wages, Population, and Economic Growth, England, 1209–1869." *Economic History Review* 6 (2007): 97–135.

Classen, A., ed. *Handbook of Medieval Studies: Terms-Methods-Trends*. De Gruyter: Berlin and New York, 2010.

Dodds, B. *Peasants and Production in the Medieval Northeast: The Evidence from Tithes, 1270–1536*. Woodbridge, UK and Rochester, NY: The Boydell Press, 2007.

Dodds, B. "Output and Productivity: Common Themes and Regional Variations," in *Agriculture and Rural Society After the Black Death: Common Themes and Regional Variations,* edited by B. Dodds and R. Britnell, 73–88. Hartfield, UK: University of Hertfordshire Press, 2008.

Dodds, B. "Demesne and Tithe: Peasant Agriculture in the Late Middle Ages." *Agricultural History Review* 56 (2008): 123–141.

Dodds, B. and R. Britnell. *Agriculture and Rural Society After the Black Death: Common Themes and Regional Variations.* Hartfield, UK: University of Hertfordshire Press, 2008.

Dyer, C. C. "Documentary Evidence: Problems and Enquiries," in *The Countryside of Medieval England,* edited by G. Astill and A. Grant, 12–35. Oxford and New York: B. Blackwell, 1988.

Dyer, C. C. *Standards of Living in the Later Middle Ages: Social Change in England c. 1200–1520.* Cambridge: Cambridge University Press, 1989.

Dyer, C. C. *Making a Living in the Middle Ages: The People of Britain 850–1520.* New Haven and London: Yale University Press, 2002.

Dyer, C. C. *An Age of Transition? Economy and Society in England in the Later Middle Ages.* Oxford and New York: Clarendon Press, 2005.

Hall, R. E. and M. Lieberman. *Macroeconomics: Principles and Applications,* 5th edition. Mason, OH: Thomson South-Western, 2008.

Hatcher, J. "English Serfdom and Villeinage: Towards a Reassessment." *Past and Present* 90 (1981): 3–39.

Hatcher, J. and M. Bailey. *Modelling the Middle Ages: The History and Theory of England's Economic Development.* Oxford and New York: Oxford University Press, 2001.

Karakacili, E. "English Agrarian Labor Productivity Rates Before the Black Death: A Case Study." *Journal of Economic History* 64 (2004): 24–60.

Kitsikopoulos, H. "Technological Change in Medieval England: A Critique of the Neo-Malthusian Argument." *Proceedings of the American Philosophical Society* 144 (2000): 397–449.

Kitsikopoulos, H. "Standards of Living and Capital Formation in Pre-plague England: A Peasant Budget Model." *Economic History Review* 53 (2000): 237–261.

Kitsikopoulos, H. "The Impact of the Black Death on Peasant Economy in England, 1350–1500." *The Journal of Peasant Studies* 29 (2002): 71–90.

Kitsikopoulos, H. "Urban Demand and Agrarian Productivity in Pre-plague England: Reassessing the Relevancy of von Thunen's Model." *Agricultural History* 77 (2003) 482–522.

Kitsikopoulos, H. "Convertible Husbandry vs. Regular Common Fields: A Model on the Relative Efficiency of Medieval Field Systems." *Journal of Economic History* 64 (2004): 462–499.

Kitsikopoulos, H. "Manorial Estates as Business Firms: The Relevance of Economic Rent in Determining Crop Choices in London's Hinterland c. 1300." *Agricultural History Review* 56 (2008): 142–166.

Kitsikopoulos, H. "Social and Economic Theory in Medieval Studies," in *Handbook of Medieval Studies: Terms-Methods-Trends,* vol. 2, edited by A. Classen, 1,270–1,292. Berlin and New York: De Gruyter, 2010.

Kosminsky, E. A. *Studies in the Agrarian History of England in the Thirteenth Century*, trans. R. Kisch, edited by R. H. Hilton. Oxford: B. Blackwell, 1956.

Langdon, J. L. "The Economics of Horses and Oxen in Medieval England." *Agricultural History Review* 30 (1982): 31–40.

Langdon, J. L. *Horses, Oxen and Technological Innovation: The Use of Draught Animals in English Farming from 1066–1500.* Cambridge: Cambridge University Press, 1986.

Langdon, J. L. and J. Masschaele. "Commercial Activity and Population Growth in Medieval England." *Past and Present* 190 (2006): 35–81.

Mate, M. "The Agrarian Economy of Southeast England Before the Black Death: Depressed or Buoyant?," in *Before the Black Death: Studies in the 'Crisis' of the Early Fourteenth Century*, edited by B. M. S. Campbell, 79–109. Manchester and New York: Manchester University Press, 1991.

Mate, M. "Farming Practice and Techniques: Kent and Sussex," in *The Agrarian History of England and Wales*, vol. 3, *1348–1500*, edited by E. Miller, 268–285. Cambridge: Cambridge University Press, 1991.

Miller, E., ed. *The Agrarian History of England and Wales*, vol. 3, *1348–1500*. Cambridge: Cambridge University Press, 1991.

Smith, R. "Human Resources," in *The Countryside of Medieval England*, edited by G. Astill and A. Grant, 189–212. Oxford and New York: B. Blackwell, 1988.

Stone, D. "The Productivity of Hired and Customary Labour: Evidence from Wisbech Barton in the Fourteenth Century." *Economic History Review* 50 (1997): 640–656.

Stone, D. *Decision-making in Medieval Agriculture*. Oxford and New York: Oxford University Press, 2005.

Thornton, C. "The Determinants of Land Productivity on the Bishop of Winchester's Demesne of Rimpton, 1208 to 1403," in *Land, Labour and Livestock: Historical Studies in European Agricultural Productivity*, edited by B. M. S. Campbell and M. Overton, 183–210. Manchester and New York: Manchester University Press, 1991.

3 France

George Grantham

The agricultural history of late medieval France was shaped by a succession of shocks beginning in the second decade of the fourteenth century which arrested and subsequently reversed two and a half centuries of growth in population, output, and productivity. Shortly after 1300 cooler and wetter weather set in, announcing the onset of a 'little ice age' that caused yields to decline on agriculturally marginal uplands, and in 1348 the first of a series of deadly pestilences descended on the subcontinent. But while the ecological shocks were common to all Europe, a third catastrophe fell disproportionately on the Kingdom of France. For two centuries French monarchy had to defend itself against the pretentions of "over mighty subjects" of whom the king of England was one.[1] Although the misnamed Hundred Years War experienced few ranged battles, the sieges and endemic guerrilla warfare that in intervals of truce were succeeded by the depredations of disbanded soldiers left large parts of the country economically devastated.[2] The chronic civil disturbances and declining population caused markets for farm produce to contract and farming to become less specialized than before the onset of the crisis. Labor became scarce, or more aptly, land became more abundant, and farming became less labor-intensive and less productive. The crisis also altered the distribution of rural income, as falling population led to increased wages and reduced rents, and abandoned holdings reduced the ancient seigniorial dues. Finally, the cost of prolonged warfare to the French monarchy led to the establishment of royal taxation, diverting seigniorial revenue to a rising elite whose income and status derived from service to the state.[3]

Yet when all is said and done, the rural economy's outstanding characteristic was the persistence of its methods of husbandry and the resilience of its institutions of land ownership. The agriculture described by Charles Estienne and Jean Liébaut in the 1560s does not differ in any essential respect from that of the late thirteenth century.[4] As in 1300, the overwhelming majority of individual holdings were small, and although the great grain-growing operations around Paris and on the plains south of Flanders were subdivided, they remained large by any contemporary standard, and were cultivated by farmers whose descendants on the eve of the Revolution would rank among the wealthiest families in France, if not Europe.[5] The forms of land tenure were also stable. The most common tenure was the *censive*, which gave the tenant

Figure 3.1 The main regions of France.

an unimpeachable right to bequeathe, sell, and hypothecate it to third parties. Its only seigniorial obligations were a trivial quitrent (*cens*), a light proportional tax on agricultural output (*champart, terrage*) owed in recognition of the seigneur's *droit éminent*, and a sales tax on the holding when it was sold (*lods et vents*). The holding also escheated to the lord in the event its possessor died without heirs. This form of land holding and the structure of fiefs erected on it survived the crisis basically unaltered. The only notable change in land tenure was the spread of sharecropping (*métayage*) in western and central districts given over to raising livestock. Though momentarily shaken, the seigniorial regime thus survived the crisis, as if encased in a chrysalis of parchment deeds ready to burst forth with the restoration of peace and the recovery of population.

Technological and institutional continuity makes it difficult to precisely identify a 'late medieval crisis' distinct from the general disruptions due to plagues and endemic warfare. The original notion referred to the political crisis of the Hundred Years War between the Valois and the Plantagenets and the civil war between the Orléanists and Burgundians, to which the contracting economy and repeated visitations of the plague served as somber backdrops to the vicissitudes of the French state recounted by contemporary chroniclers.[6] In the years following the Second World War, the concept of the period as one of political crisis was superseded by the notion of an economic crisis based on the negative correlation between population density and real wages.[7] According to this account the crisis was brought on by late thirteenth-century overpopulation, a condition ultimately relieved by the plague. An objection to this oversimplified Malthusian dynamics is that the French population continued to decline through the first half of the fifteenth century, well after the 'surplus' people had been removed. The early 1960s saw the reformulation of the crisis in terms of the declining fortunes of seigneurs and the abandonment of peasant holdings.[8] The seigniorial crisis consisted in the decimation of seigniorial lineages by battle, expropriation, and collapsing revenues. They were replaced by new lineages whose wealth derived in large part from their status as royal servants whose income derived from what Epstein has termed "the feudal tributary system,"[9] so that in the end the structure of ownership remained much as before. Finally, Marxist historian Guy Bois identified a crisis that he argued transformed the "feudal mode of surplus extraction" into an embryonic capitalist one.[10] This contention faintly echoes Bloch's conjecture that the new seigneurs from the worlds of trade and state finance introduced a more commercial spirit to French farming.[11]

From the narrow perspective of agricultural history, each of these formulations of the crisis is flawed. The context of the Hundred Year's war is constitutional history, whose path was unrelated to the history of agricultural practices and productivity; the demographic crisis affected farming more directly, but high levels of productivity before the plague and falling population long after any conceivable stress on natural resources had been relieved makes an argument based on the land constraint problematic. The seigniorial crisis was real, but it affected the identities of seigneurs, not the seigneurie as an institution. As to the Marxist interpretation of a 'feudal' crisis, the high level of agricultural productivity and commercialization of French farming in 1300 puts paid to any simple historical schema based on linear progress toward agricultural capitalism. The notion of a cataclysmic moment in the evolution of France's rural economy is thus hard to credit. From a rural perspective the later Middle Ages are therefore less a turning point than a pause caused by the temporary removal of dynamic factors that had spurred agricultural expansion from the tenth to the thirteenth century. The technological and institutional structures that had emerged by 1300 proved to be remarkably robust. The principal question raised by the late medieval troubles is how those structures responded to the economic and political context of the fourteenth and fifteenth centuries.

THE DEMOGRAPHIC CONTEXT

The conventional view of France's late medieval agrarian history takes its point of departure from population estimates derived from an enumeration of fiscal households carried out in 1328 in the territories subject to royal taxation.[12] According to these estimates, the territory of modern France held approximately 21 million persons, about as many as in 1750.[13] That estimate is so high historians initially rejected it on the grounds that contemporary agricultural practices could not have supported it.[14] It is now generally accepted, and constitutes the main support for the hypothesis that France was overpopulated on the eve of the Black Death.[15]

According to the Malthusian paradigm, rural population density ought to be roughly proportional to soil fertility.[16] A positive correlation between these variables would therefore tend to support the hypothesis of a land-constrained rural economy in 1328. On first view the data seem to bear this proposition out. The most sparsely populated districts of early fourteenth-century France were in mountainous districts like the Alps and the Massif Central, where the density of *feux* ranged between three and six households per km^2. Within these territories, the relatively fertile volcanic soils of western Auvergne exhibited a density of about nine.[17] By contrast, the fertile districts of Normandy, Île de France, and Artois, and the alluvial lowlands of Flanders maintained upwards of 20 households or roughly 90 to 100 inhabitants km^2.[18]

The correspondence between soil type and population density is nevertheless misleading. The fertile grain-producing districts around Paris were in fact thinly populated, the best land being held in large farms that supported a light permanent population and drew workers from neighboring districts for seasonal labor. The region's high population density was mainly due to vineyards lining the hillsides of the rivers that converged on the capital.[19] In the thickly settled valleys of the Seine and its tributaries soil quality was actually mediocre, and was made productive only through massive applications of fertilizer, testimony to what five centuries later the French agronomist Gilbert was to characterize as the triumph of art over nature.[20] The celebrated Flemish crop yields were obtained on notoriously poor soils that owed their productivity to investment in surface drains, manure, and hard work. The most productive fields were not in Flanders proper, but on its margins in Artois and Hainault, where large farms producing grain for the Flemish cloth towns made the highest known yields in Europe.[21] Fertility mattered, but what mattered even more was access to commercial outlets for input-intensive produce.

In 1300 roughly 85 percent of all Frenchmen were either farmers or were engaged in rural crafts related to farming. From the perspective of the Malthusian paradigm, the proportion of cultivators who were not self-sufficient is an index of population stress. Information bearing on this question is thin and scattered, but it suggests that most holdings were too small to keep draft animals (six to eight hectares). In Hainault, a village register compiled in 1265 indicates that 80 percent of tenants possessed less than 4.5 hectares of arable and 60 percent less than two.[22] A register from 1286 listing all the tenants in a village near Quesnoy reveals that 72 percent held less than three hectares; a dozen years later, more than half possessed less than one hectare.[23] The small modal size of holdings survived the fourteenth-century demographic collapse. In 1397 46 percent of holdings in the Châtellanie of Neubourg in Normandy were smaller than 1.5 hectares. Around 1400 half of the farms in the parish of Saint-Nicholas d'Allermont on the plateau east of Rouen possessed less than six hectares of arable.[24] At the other end of the kingdom, 30 percent of holdings in a commune near Tarbes were under two hectares and only 25 percent larger than six.[25] If one defines a self-sufficient farm as a holding with draft animals, only a small proportion of France's rural inhabitants could have survived on their holdings.

The idealized 'yeoman' farm cultivated with a pair of horses or oxen, however, is a misleading benchmark for assessing viability. When cultivated by hand, two hectares was more than enough to sustain a family of five, and manual cultivation of cereals was common.[26] In Flanders, fields were tilled by spading, a practice that survived in much of France well into the nineteenth century.[27] While many were true subsistence farms, most of their tenants probably drew income from the sale of labor-intensive specialty crops, rural industry, and seasonal work on large farms. Near Paris vineyards supported not only a population of winegrowers, but also smallholders who cut vine-props from the woods and built wine barrels. Small holdings were often more a consequence of market opportunity than of fragmentation of larger holdings caused by population growth. Near the greater towns, the sale of milk and garden produce, and opportunities for casual employment and domestic service provided reasonable livings for smallholders as long as the towns prospered.[28] An exceptional document recording all sales of land between 1205 and 1412 in a village near Toulouse reveals a spike in the last two decades of the thirteenth century that has been interpreted as indicating increasing distress on the rural population.[29] Yet the same decades saw construction of four new flour mills and several new bridges, hardly signs of rural immiseration, and in 1275 the ecclesiastical seigneur stipulated that henceforth no new holdings were to be hypothecated to outsiders.[30] Although peasants might have been forced to mortgage or sell their holdings, and there is some evidence for this in times of famine, the odds are that most were capitalizing on its rising value, as happened around Paris.[31] After 1316 when conditions in the village became more difficult, sales of land fell off.

Although most holdings were small, most of the land was cultivated in large units. At Saint-Nicholas d'Allermont, the 50 percent of holdings that were less than six hectares controlled only a sixth of the parish's territory.[32] The inequality was especially pronounced in districts that specialized in cereals for urbanized districts. On the plains east of Paris and in Artois farms held in demesne by ecclesiastical establishments, which are the only ones for which we have an abundant documentation, commonly exceeded 75 hectares and sometimes reached 200–300.[33] At its peak toward the mid-thirteenth century, the Cistercian grange at Vaulerent had more than

380 hectares in farm land.[34] Such large-scale operations were exceptional, but farms of 20–30 hectares were the common suppliers of grain for non-farm consumers, and in the period of rising population and urbanization before the Black Death, farms producing grain for townsmen tended to become larger, not smaller. In the Toulousain village mentioned above, most purchases in the late thirteenth century were by a handful of 'coqs du village' expanding their farms, presumably in response to the growing market in Toulouse.[35]

We will never know exactly how many people were carried away by the plague of 1348/1349, and its visitations in 1361, 1369, 1372, 1382, 1390, and 1400, nor the approximate population of France in the late 1440s when the prolonged decline finally hit bottom, because after 1328 the fiscal authorities rated poor households at fractions of *feux* in order to simplify the accounting, making it impossible to infer the number of people from the number of *feux* recorded in fiscal archives.[36] Given that any estimate must be guesswork, Froissart's opinion that the plague of 1348 carried off "la tierce partie du monde" is a plausible lower bound for magnitude of the decline over the whole period.[37] It was likely much larger.

We are better informed about towns and cities than rural districts. Paris fell from slightly over 200,000 inhabitants in 1330 to around 145,000 in the 1420s, and possibly to 100,000 in the early 1440s.[38] By contrast, Lyon, which was situated away from the fighting and protected by good fortifications and the Duke of Bourbon's neutrality, saw its population grow from 20,000 at the beginning of the fifteenth century to 33,000 at its end. Bordeaux, which remained in English hands until the very end of the Hundred Years War, probably held steady, although the surrounding countryside suffered severe losses due to military activity north and east of the city.[39] Other towns were less fortunate. Toulouse declined from 30,000 in the early 1330s to 19,000 in 1405; Montpellier fell from 35,000 to 17,000,[40] Béziers and Nîmes from 16,000 and 18,000 to 4,000 and 7,000, respectively.[41] The number of *feux* in Albi declined 55 percent between 1346 and 1356; in Millau it fell by 67 percent.[42] Northern towns experienced similar decline. At Angers and Tours population dropped by more than half. The greatest decline occurred in the cloth towns of Flanders and Artois. Arras fell from 30,000 to 10,000, Saint-Omer 35,000 to 13,000, Ypres from 20,000 to 8,000, and Troyes from 25,000 to 17,000. Reims declined from 18,000 in 1315 to 9,000 in 1422.[43] The decline was not uniquely due to pandemics. The capacity of towns to sustain a large population depended critically on the state of markets for their products that were everywhere contracting. The agricultural significance of the urban population lay in the contraction of the most dynamic markets for farm produce. As will be shown below, the most productive parts of French farming were the parts specialized to provision towns. The collapse of urban demand in the second half of the fourteenth century removed the prop that supported the most productive forms of traditional husbandry. It is likely that because the urban population decline was so severe, the overall decline in population probably led to a fall in agricultural labor productivity rather than an increase, as the Malthusian model predicts. We shall see below that the evidence for a rising real wage through the crisis seems to be mixed at best.

The rural population is difficult to track. Fiscal and seigniorial records document a significant decline in the number of households and tenants, but the uneven regional incidence of that documentation and internal migration make it hazardous to generalize. The most severely affected districts were marginal territories burdened with high seigniorial charges imposed at the thirteenth century in the high tide of inner colonization. Emigration emptied them. In other regions people were dislocated by warfare and brigandage. The decline in rural population was thus accompanied by spatial redistribution of the survivors. A few regions nevertheless yield samples large enough to support conjectural estimates of the magnitude of the decline. In Artois, which before the crisis was a prosperous cloth-producing and grain-exporting district, the rural population may have fallen by 43 percent between 1300 and 1460. In western Normandy, where guerrilla warfare raged in the 1420 and 1430s, the population under English occupation dropped 70 percent. The coastal districts of Languedoc and Provence lost 46 percent of their population and the hill country 33 to 36 percent. Population fell 60 percent in the Rhone corridor and 50 percent in the surrounding mountains.[44] A document from a district in the Limousin that was entered into a court proceeding gives the actual number of *feux* in 1480. Comparing that figure with the number of *feux* registered in the État of 1328 indicates that population had fallen 30 percent.[45] Since local recovery had begun two decades earlier, the actual decline to 1450 would have been significantly greater. Taking these scattered indications for what they are worth, an overall decline in rural population on the order of 40 percent over 130 years or roughly four generations does not seem implausible.

THE TECHNOLOGICAL CONTEXT

As noted above, the basic elements of agricultural technology were essentially unchanged. Indeed, except for New World food crops introduced in the sixteenth and seventeenth centuries, the biological *materiel* remained essentially the same through the nineteenth century. Medieval mixed husbandry was heir to the Iron-Age synthesis of arable and pastoral husbandry that arrived with the diffusion of iron-working skills between the ninth and sixth centuries BC, in which livestock supplying traction and manure were maintained through winter on straw and cereals from arable land and hay from meadows. Iron raised the productivity of both sectors: the iron share and spade increased the yield of the arable, while the iron scythes increased the yield of meadow hay to the point where farmers could hold large stocks of animals through winter, and thereby secure a large stock of manure. Toward the beginning of the fifth century BC the synthesis was reinforced by the introduction of cultivated forage legumes from western

Asia.[46] Widely cultivated in the Mediterranean region, by the fourth century AD they may have been diffusing northward.[47] In any event, the elements of intensive mixed husbandry were present in France from an early date.

In the centuries following the collapse of Roman administration, some of that inheritance was lost. Forage legumes went out of cultivation, possibly for lack of demand,[48] while the mechanical harvester (*vallus*) that had been employed to harvest wheat in northern Gaul disappeared forever. The quality of draft animals may also have deteriorated, as osteological evidence suggests a 50 percent decline in their size.[49] The subsequent growth of output and productivity between the tenth and fourteenth century thus probably reflects the return of classical methods of farming rather than agricultural invention.[50] There are nevertheless some novelties. From the middle of the twelfth century farmers on the plains of northern France introduced three-course rotations, and intensified them by sowing vetches and pulses on the fallow course.[51] The displacement of spelt (*Triticum spelta*) by winter wheat (*Triticum aestivum*) as the preferred bread cereal for luxury consumption was another significant development.[52] As a 'naked' variety, winter wheat was easier to transport and mill than spelt, which as a hulled variety was not only voluminous in relation to its nutritional content, but required additional processing to remove the hull. Its advantage was cheaper storage, since threshed wheat had to be repeatedly stirred to inhibit sprouting and un-threshed wheat needed to be kept in large barns. Since the nutritional and bread-making quality of the two varieties is identical, the substitution of wheat for spelt in the twelfth century must have been due to a shift in the balance of advantage toward cheap transport. An obvious reason is growing commercialization of grain production.

Mechanical technology was also stable. By the late twelfth or early thirteenth century, large farms were beginning to employ horses in northern France, but down to the fourteenth century oxen continued to be the most common animal employed in field work.[53] The growth of agricultural specialization and advances in ferrous metallurgy seem to have supported improvements in plows, which became increasingly specialized to particular soils and tasks.[54] In the case of harvest implements, improvements in methods of forging made it possible to produce a scythe capable of making a level cut with less effort. Flemish smiths also invented a short-handed scythe known as the *pik*, employed with a baton to harvest thick stands of grain.[55] Like the use of horses in cultivation, both innovations saved labor.

The massive change in the land/labor ratio after 1348 seems to have had little impact on this technology. With the reduction in demand for cereals and falling prices everywhere, farmers reduced the proportion of arable sown in legumes and reduced the intensity of cultivation, with the result that yields declined. By contrast, the employment of horses in cultivation diffused eastward and northward from the large-scale farming districts in Artois and around Paris. A list of demesne plowing services in a seigneurie on the border of Lorraine and Champagne suggests that by the end of the fifteenth century the use of horses had become general.[56] While the shift from oxen to horses may have been provoked by labor shortage, puny animals hitched together in teams of eight to 12 animals requiring three men to manage suggests other factors at work. There are faint signs in the margins of illuminated manuscripts that by the end of the fifteenth century forage legumes were advancing up the Rhone corridor, possibly in consequence of increasing traffic through the Alpine passes to Italy, where isolated patches of lucerne and red clover may have persisted.[57] Continued contract with the Near East kept open a long-standing avenue for the diffusion into France of novel species of fruit and vegetables from the orient.[58] Yet these changes constituted minor adjustments in traditional husbandry. All in all, the technological constraints on agricultural expansion remained unchanged.

THE INSTITUTIONAL CONTEXT

In 1300 almost all the territory of the Kingdom of France was held in seigneurie, which is to say it owed dues and services to persons or institutions possessing seigniorial rights (*droit éminent*) in it. The nature and origin of these rights will be discussed below. They should not be conflated with the right of occupancy (*droit utile*), which comprised the right to exploit the land and to alienate it. Land held on these terms was known as a tenement *en censive*. A modern analogy is freehold held on condition that the owner pays the municipal property taxes, failing which the town may seize it. In the seigneurie the lord occupied the position of the town.

Superimposed upon this nexus was another layer of property known as the fief. Fiefs were the legal form in which *seigneuries* were possessed. Just as a *censive* owed dues and services to the seigneur, so possession of a *seigneurie* incurred liabilities to the lord of whom the fief was held. Fiefs were originally conditional grants of *seigneuries* in return for the grantee performing certain military, administrative, and political services. The acquisition of a fief thus involved a ceremony of investiture (*foi et hommage*) in which the grantee recognized the suzerain's ultimate ownership by swearing an oath of fidelity and kissing him on the lips. Repeated at each entry, including by inheritance, and at each change of suzerain, it triggered fees that produced revenue for the suzerain.[59] The ceremony had to be performed in person, and failure to appear resulted in possession of the fief reverting to the suzerain. The fief was thus a kind of holding company that supported a hierarchy of such holdings that ranged from fractions of a seigneurie to vast principalities like the Duchy of Normandy.

The land, then, was simultaneously possessed by several classes of person, each of which had a claim on its income. As a working farm, it was managed directly by the owner-occupier, or in the case of land in seigniorial demesne, by tenants holding on a fixed term lease or sharecropping. Subject to any regulation of land use by the village community or stipulations in the lease, the occupier could cultivate the land as he pleased. As a seigneurie, it entitled the possessor to fees and obligations from the occupier to be discussed below.

The income from these dues is what ultimately paid for enfeoffment. Fiefs and seigneuries thus mobilized the agricultural surpluses that maintained the political, military, and religious elite who conducted the public functions of defense, and civil and religious administration. Unlike rental income from sharecrop and leaseholds, however, which adjusted to change in the demand price of land, seigniorial fees were inflexible, more like a tax than a rent. This feature of the seigniorial property regime significantly affected the adjustment to the altered circumstances of the fourteenth and fifteenth centuries, by encouraging the abandonment of properties rather than reductions in their effective rental price.

The origins and nature of the seigniorial regime are hotly contested. The conventional view considers it to have originated in conditional grants of territory by Merovingian and Carolingian kings together with authority to exploit the labor of its inhabitants in exchange for military and public service. In that view, the king transferred the ownership of the land in fief to lords who in turn leased it to cultivators in exchange for labor services on demesne land reserved for their own use.[60] In the alternative interpretation the original grant was not in land, but in rights to income from taxes within a given territory together with coercive authority to ensure their collection.[61] The practical difference is that in the first interpretation, a seigneur owned the land outright, and in principle could change its terms of tenancy at will, whereas in the second, the lord's authority over the land and its inhabitants was derived from a grant originating in the imperial or royal fiscal system and was regulated by jurisprudence protecting the property rights of landowners.[62] In this view, ownership was the source of the peasant's *droit utile,* the seigniorial *droit éminent* resting on a fiscal right to tax the holding.[63] As a practical matter, lords exploited variations in the tax rate on different parcels of land and different classes of individuals by shifting land from low to high-tax categories. Most of the documentation bearing on the civil status of peasants comes from court proceedings in which peasants contested seigniorial attempts at 'revenue enhancement.'

The lightness of *cens* and exemption of low-income inhabitants from the heaviest seigniorial charges supports the fiscal interpretation, though the conventional view of the seigneur as landlord continues to have its stout defenders.[64] The seigneurie acquired its definitive form in the eleventh and twelfth century, when the original fiscal system based on the assessment of nominal districts was replaced by assessments based on real households and farmsteads.[65] The essential charges in this revised system were fixed *cens,* a fixed proportional tax on output (the *champart* or *terrage*), and a tax on land transactions (*lods et vents*).[66] None of the direct taxes was particularly burdensome. The *champart* averaged a seventh to an eighth of the harvest, sometimes as low as one-sixteenth, while the *cens* was usually a payment fixed in the unit of account amounting to 1 or 2 percent of the holding's original purchase price.[67] As a proportion of current sales prices, *lods et vents* was more remunerative but, because it was levied only when the land was sold, irregular. In the long run the lord's most valuable seigniorial right was the right to repossess abandoned holdings, which provided a means of rebuilding estates that even before the crisis had become highly fragmented.

The same cannot be said of the seigniorial *taille* levied in the event the seigneur was held for ransom and on the occasion of knighting his eldest son and daughter's marriage. As an extraordinary subvention—the king employed the identical term for emergency wartime levies—the *taille* was readily abused, and in the course of the thirteenth century peasant communities commuted the liability for a fixed sum (*franchise*). In time the distinction between persons subject to arbitrary tallage and those exempt from it became a marker of social and civil status. For seigneurs the right to arbitrarily tax their subjects could be a significant revenue source, and where it survived was closely guarded.[68]

Eminent rights in land were not the only source of seigniorial revenue and usually not the most important. The disintegration of the French monarchy in the ninth and tenth centuries resulted in devolution of judicial and administrative authority to local officials and landlords, who possessed it in fief like any other seigneurie. Originating in the police power of the state, the *seigneurie banale* comprised rights to levy tolls on bridges, roads, and waterways, to hold a court to prosecute (usually minor) offenses, to demand watch service in wartime, and to monopolize food processing facilities such as grain and flour mills, wine presses, and bread ovens, to which was sometimes the right to license Jews, in effect monopolizing the practice of usury.[69] These powers were distinct from the seigniorial rights in land and usually not co-extensive with them. The *seigneurie foncière* was defined on specific pieces of land, whereas the *seigneurie banale* was defined on specific persons and territory. The inhabitants of a given place could thus have several seigneurs, to each of whom they were liable for specific payments and services. The local abbey held the right to hold court in the Bordelaise village of La Sauve although it possessed no local seigniorial rights in land, tolls, or other seigniorial emoluments.[70] The inhabitants were subject to the abbey's justice, but paid seigneurial fees and owed services and tolls to other seigneurs.

The tangle of seigniorial rights caused by the subdivision and alienation of seigniorial rights emerged at an early date. Not surprisingly, intermingled and overlapping seigneuries generated an interminable stream of legal disputes. A particularly telling example concerns the monopoly of operating ovens possessed by the cathedral chapter of Lyon in several villages situated outside the city. The monopoly was jointly possessed with a certain Louis de Saint-Paul, who in 1481 sold his share to Louis Escot who in turn leased out baking rights to 18 individuals. When the chapter learned of the transaction in 1492, it sued Escot for having violated seigneurie's baking monopoly. The court ruled for the canons and awarded them Escot's rental income from the leases, but refused to order the offending ovens destroyed on the grounds that the canons had forfeited the monopoly by neglect.[71]

In this case at least 21 persons or individuals held a claim in the same seigneurie. Seigneurial property was therefore expensive to maintain, and supported an army of legal practioners constituting the core of France's medieval rural bourgeoisie. Even minor *seigneuries* required the services of receivers, bailiffs, and lawyers to collect fees and maintain rights that were being continually nibbled away by peasants attempting to escape and other lords attempting to appropriate them. In some years, the Duc de La Trémoille spent as much as 10 percent of the gross revenue of his enormous estate on legal expenses.[72]

THE PERSISTENCE OF PEASANT PROPERTY

At the end of the thirteenth century, and probably much earlier, most agricultural land in France was held on terms analogous to English fee simple. The predominance of peasant proprietorship was a distinctive characteristic of French agriculture down to the middle of the twentieth century, and is thought to be a determining factor in France's modern trajectory of industrialization.[73] Marc Bloch conjectured that the reason why French peasants maintained their hold on the land while English peasants lost it was that peasant tenure in France received royal protection, whereas villein tenure in England was adjudicated in manorial courts dominated by lords.[74] This hypothesis constitutes a major element of Brenner's well-known thesis on the agricultural origins of European capitalism.[75] While seductive, the argument does not explain how the limited reach of royal jurisdiction in France prior to the late thirteenth century left French lords with less power over their peasants than English lords subject to the strong hand of the king.[76] The issue turns on how a subject peasantry in France managed to obtain protections that were lacking in England. Bloch conjectured that it came down to custom, which he conceived as an impeding inertial force restricting the lords' ability to exploit their powers.[77] Yet in other places he emphasized the extent of those powers through the first feudal age. Given the basic inequality of rural society in the eleventh and twelfth centuries, the question is how protection of property rights in land came to be extended to tenures and persons of low status.

The main reason seems to have been the web of conflicting interests in seigniorial property. Fiefs, seigneuries, and holdings were divisible and alienable from an early date, probably from the beginning, to judge from the handful of notarial documents surviving from the Merovingian era.[78] By the mid-thirteenth century *censives* could be hypothecated as security for loans; a century later the same was true of fiefs.[79] The unrestricted alienation of rights in real property inevitably led to a tangle of overlapping and competing claims to the same property. An extreme, but possibly not unusual case occurred around Paris in the twelfth and thirteenth centuries when acquisitions of *censives* by religious foundations to round out the great demesne farms resulted in their owing *cens* and even labor services to other seigneurs, since obligations attached to a holding simply passed to its new owner.[80] Complications like these limited the ability of an individual seigneur unilaterally to alter the terms of tenure in his favor. Consider, for example, a third party possessing an annuity (*rente perpetuelle*) constituted by a peasant on his *censive*, perhaps to finance the purchase of another piece of land. As a perpetual (though revocable) alienation of income secured by a hypothecation of the *censive*, the *rente* was legally real property, and thus defendable in court. The owner therefore had not only an interest in but also the means of protecting the *censive* from arbitrary exactions by its seigneur that might reduce its capacity to service the *rente*. By the same logic, a person possessing a *rente* that had been constituted by a seigneur on the security of his seigneurie also had an interest in protecting its income from other potential claimants. The persistence of what amounted to peasant freehold in France was thus largely an unintended byproduct of the fragmentation of rights that produced legal gridlock, protecting the peasants along with the powerful because any infringement of peasant property rights resulted in the infringement of the rights of rentiers and seigneurs with claims on the same property. The cost in litigation expense was high, however, and may have impeded restructuring of holdings into more efficient units.[81]

THE POLITICAL CONTEXT

From the 1340s through the 1480s the French countryside was buffeted by invasion and civil war that fell with particular violence on some of the kingdom's most productive agricultural districts. After two centuries of comparative peace, internal fortifications had fallen into disrepair, which left the countryside defenseless against pointless but destructive raids by English armies and in the interludes of 'peace' pillaging by unemployed soldiers. The main reason for the devastation was the inadequate logistical support and irregular pay of troops operating in the field. An army of 10,000 plus camp followers was a middle-sized town in motion requiring a constant flow of food and fodder. On his march through the Cambrésis in 1339 Edward III devastated a belt of territory 40 to 50 kilometers in width.[82] It was for this reason that, provided it could hold out for two or three months, a fortified town could usually survive a siege. On the other hand, it also meant that medieval war had no 'front lines,' but was fought from strongholds from which garrisons sortied to attack supply trains, merchants, and peasants on their way to market.

That in wartime soldiers could confiscate persons and property in enemy territory was legitimized by the contemporary laws of war.[83] But wars were of limited duration. The real damage occurred when disbanded soldiers roved across the countryside like a plague of locusts.[84] Contemporary chronicles give ample evidence of the destruction. In 1346 the chronicler Jean de Venette reported seeing smoke from burning villages invested by English troops on the outskirts of Paris.[85] Fifteen years later Petrarch wrote of "weed-infested fields" marking the "melancholy vestige of the English passage."[86] A century later Thomas Basin wrote of utter desolation extending from Picardy and Champagne to the Loire, "the peasants having been killed off or fled, and apart from a few rare corners the fields left untilled for years on end."[87] We need not rely on chroniclers to document the extent of destruction. Agents sent by the Hospitalers of Saint-Jean of Jerusalem in 1456 and 1495 to survey the order's vast holdings in the Île de France and Normandy reported back to headquarters in Rhodes that 22 to 75 percent of the farms it possessed had fallen out of cultivation. Manor houses and barns where peasants rendered their dues lay in ruins from repeated pillaging by English and French troops.[88] The most extensive damage seems to have occurred around Paris, where both contending parties had garrisons, in Normandy, where guerrilla warfare raged for decades, and in the region to the east and north of Bordeaux. War and brigandage thus touched some of the most prosperous agricultural districts in France.

The most important long-term consequences of prolonged warfare did not result from the physical destruction, however, but from the fiscal expedients taken by the king to shore up defenses. War was expensive and became more so with the rising cost of fortifications and the new artillery deployed to breach them. The evolution of the tax system to finance the expense lies at the heart of France's pre-revolutionary constitutional history.[89] To understand its agrarian effects, we need briefly to summarize it.

Prior to the reforms of the 1440s, French monarchs did not have an unrestricted right to tax subjects. As a seigneur, the king possessed the feudal right to levy *taille* for his ransom, the knighting of his eldest son, and daughter's dowry, and within limits for the upkeep of his fortresses. As king, however, he could appeal to the country for emergency subsidies raised from towns and the clergy as lump sums and levied in the countryside as a *taille*. Such appeals required the consent of tax-payers and thus involved prolonged negotiations with national and provincial Estates convoked for the purpose. Each subsidy required a new negotiation. In the course of the Hundred Years War a succession of military catastrophes, which included the capture and imprisonment of John II, produced finally a general acquiescence in permanent subvention as the lesser of the many evils that had descended on the nation in its time of troubles. By the 1440s royal taxes ceased to be 'extraordinary,' and although there was no explicit transfer of power from the Estates to the crown, the king had for all purposes assumed sole authority to determine what counted as an 'emergency' for the purpose of levying a tax.[90] In the second half of the fifteenth century, more than two-thirds of the now permanent taxes went to a standing army of 10–12 thousand men at arms and the remainder to pensioning off the king's supporters and potential adversaries.[91]

Fiscal problems also had monetary implications. Given the slow tax collection, compounded by grudging negotiations with national and provincial estates and lack of public credit, the only source of quick money was seigniorage. The right to mint coins and to declare their value in official units of account (*livre tournois*) was a royal monopoly that permitted the king to profit from the difference between the demand price of coins as media of exchange and their supply price in silver or gold. To profit from that right, however, the king had to induce holders to bring their coin and bullion to the mint to be struck into new pieces. The only way to do this was to raise the value of new coins by declaring them to be worth more in *livres tournois* or by reducing the metallic content relative to coins of the same denomination.[92] The initial debasements carried out in 1296 and 1303 by Philip IV to finance military operations in Flanders reduced the silver content of the livre by 25 and 50 percent, respectively. The biggest devaluations occurred between 1337 and 1360 and between 1417 and 1436 when the monarchy suffered severe military defeats. Between 1337 and 1342 the livre was devalued by 80 percent. Restored to its pre-devaluation level in 1348, it fell 98 percent over the next dozen years. Between 1417 and 1421 it lost another 94 percent.[93] Although devaluations were offset by the rising value of silver resulting from a secular fall in the price level, the real value of a nominal *cens* fixed in 1300 at the end of the fifteenth century would have suffered diminution of 75 percent.[94] The implications for seigniorial income are obvious.

Royal taxation and monetary manipulation affected the countryside in different ways. The most important consequence was to divert income originating in seigniorial rights over the peasantry to the king. Drawing revenue from the same source, lords had a strong interest in protecting 'their' peasants from the royal fisc. In 1442 the Bishop of Paris learned of the intention of royal assessors to tax his 'subjects' in Chatenay, and hired a brother of the king's chamberlain to negotiate a lower rate with royal tax officials.[95] Other seigneurs simply refused to allow tax collectors access to their domains. In the end, however, the king succeeded in limiting seigniorial claims on the peasantry. On the fiefs held of the crown, lords had long been prohibited from levying *taille* on their peasants.[96] In 1346 John II ordered castellans oppressing peasants in a seigneurie possessed by the royal Abbey of Solignac to cease taxing 'his' peasants.[97] Other impositions, however, were not so readily forestalled. In the absence of an administration capable of raising and remitting funds to the royal treasury, troops in the field had to scavenge locally for supplies and wages. In the aftermath of Poitiers, Charles V authorized royal garrisons to collect taxes directly from the peasantry, regularizing a practice that had metastasized in the disorder following the defeat.[98] It was common in contested districts where local authorities in connivance with military commanders on both sides conceded the right to collect tax to garrisoned troops, including the right to issue safe-conduct passes to merchants and peasants. This was protection money pure and simple, evident in the terms employed to describe the contracts of concession—*appatis, patis,* and *rançon.*[99] The contracts were treated like property to be sold, and even hypothecated. The rates of extortion were high; failure to pay resulted in reprisals.[100] In 1438 the États des Deux Auvergnes authorized a 20,000-livre levy to bribe the notorious 'routier' Rodrigo de Villandrando not to invade their province.[101] When the monarchy finally 'nationalized' its military in the 1440s by establishing a permanent army paid out of taxes affected to that purpose, the first action was to suppress the private military companies. The income extracted from the rural economy by these devices cannot be measured, but in the districts where they operated, the effect on production and productivity must have been significant. Unlike the seigneurs in the 'first feudal age,' the soldiers to whom taxes had been conceded had little interest in encouraging the prosperity of the districts they held.

For all the push and pull, the effect of royal taxation on the peasantry was probably modest. At the end of the fifteenth century royal taxation probably amounted to no more than three percent of national income, and since the majority of peasants paid no *taille* because they were too poor, the land tax only affected those relatively well-off.[102] The return for that taxation was internal peace and the restoration of conditions supporting agricultural investment and the revival of trade. Monetary manipulation may have been more important. Mention has already been made of the devaluation of payments fixed in nominal units of account, which mainly affected *cens*, since the *champart* was a fixed proportion of the harvest. Lenders and landowners adjusted rapidly to the falling value of money in periods of devaluation. In the 1340s the loans in livestock (*bail à cheptel*) stipulated that any increase in the value of the stock to be shared out at the end of the lease were to be calculated in "money of 1338."[103] Landlords shortened the length of term leases and increasingly demanded the rent to be paid in kind rather than cash. There are also signs of demonetization of bequests.[104] So in the end, the fall in the value of money probably had only modest effects on the distribution of income between lords and peasants. The most important consequences of the wars and disruptions were the implosion of markets for farm produce—already badly diminished by general population decline—and the rising price of long-term capital. In the 1430s and 1440s *rentes* issued at rates of 6–8 percent in 1300 were paying nearly 17 percent when lenders could be found at all. But most agricultural investment was short-term, *rentes* being reserved to endow children, pay inheritances, and with the growth in royal income, purchase offices in the state. The biggest effect of the fiscal revolution was to widen sources of income available to the rural elite.

RESPONSES TO CRISIS: PRICES AND OUTPUT

The trend in prices of agricultural produce paralleled trends in other parts of Western Europe. The thirteenth-century rise in grain prices lasted to about 1370, propelled after 1350 by the growing per capita stock of money. During the following four decades, however, the nominal price of cereals first stagnated and then declined as population and urban demand contracted. Between 1410 and 1440 prices were again pushed up by currency debasements, but subsequently fell in the general deflation resulting from the continuing outflow of bullion to the Far East to 1470.[105] In the final decades of the fifteenth century population growth and the urban recovery seconded by the opening of new mines in Central Europe produced a renewal of the rise in prices that persisted to the early seventeenth century. Prices of animal products followed the same trends, but with smaller amplitude, so that in periods of falling prices, they rose relative to the price of cereals. Nominal wages tracked the general trend in grain prices. They seem to have stabilized between 1370 and 1410, when food prices were falling and then started rising slowly to the 1460s, after which there was a slow decline into the sixteenth century.[106] Overall, the purchasing power of wages was higher in 1460 than in 1330, but one should probably not make too much of this, as only a small proportion of the rural population was supported by wage labour. In any event any improvement tracked by a statistical rise in an index of real wages seems to have been less than elsewhere in Europe. In Central Europe, per capita meat consumption in the early fifteenth-century reached 70 kg per head; the few observations from contemporary France suggest an intake of only 30 to 40 kg.[107] That statistical impression is reinforced by anecdote. Sir John Fortescue, whose father was Captain of Meaux during the English occupation, recalled that ordinary Frenchmen "do not eat flesh except it be the fat of bacon, and *that* in very small Quantities with which they make a soup."[108]

As the demand for cereals fell and labor costs rose, farmers took land out of production, and diminished the amount of cultivation and other inputs on the area remaining under plow. The resulting decline in productivity should be measured against the exceptional levels of the late thirteenth century, when yields on well-managed farms equaled the highest level to be attained in the pre-industrial era. The earliest rental accounts from 1281–82 for the Abbey of Saint-Denis'farm at Gennevilliers on the outskirts of Paris record a yield of 21 to 22 hectoliters per hectare.[109] A few dozen kilometers to the east at Vaulerent, the lease of the farm in 1315 stipulated that the tenants would not owe rent if the yield was below 15 hectoliters, implying expected yields that surely exceeded 20 hectoliters.[110] Even higher yields were in Artois, where in the 1320s farms possessed by the Bishop of Arras normally obtained 25 hectoliters.[111] The highest recorded yields—which have been inferred from the lease of tithes and rents in French Flanders and the adjacent province of Hainault—exceeded 30 hectoliters, and some may have touched the upper bound for traditional varieties of wheat of 35 to 40 hectoliters.[112] Similar instances have been reported from other parts of France where demand supported intensive farming, but the normal yield must have been low, as the mean yield for France in the early fourteenth century cannot have much exceeded the 10 hectolitres per hectare that most historians regard as the contemporary English average.[113] Despite the low national average, however, there are simply too many examples exceeding it by more than 50 percent to suppose that low productivity was imposed by a backward technology.[114]

High yields were a consequence of intensive farming that engaged a large input of labor and capital. Near Arras wheat-fields were plowed four times and fields in French Flanders received up to nine cultivations.[115] Farmers hired workers to screen the threshed grain for the best seeds; they hired professionals to sow them and engaged children to scare off birds once the seed was in the ground; they contracted with teams of women to weed the standing crop.[116] Up to 15 percent of the arable was sown in nitrogen-fixing vetch and pulses to keep a larger stock of animals for manuring the fields. The accounts even suggest investment in floated meadows.[117] Farmers bought straw ties for binding sheaves from specialists and purchased manure from farmers holding large stocks of cattle.[118] At the turn of the fourteenth century they were in the course of replacing small weak horses with heavy powerful ones costing two to three times as much.[119] There were outlays for agricultural equipment and seasonal hands for the harvest. The capital requirements of high-yield farming were high and were often financed by credit.[120] Farming at this level of intensity was costly and could be sustained only where farmers had good outlets for their produce, which inevitably meant a large nearby town.[121]

In a period of contracting population and an imploding urban economy the profitability of medieval high farming collapsed, and with it agricultural productivity. We do not have data for the productivity of labor, but the modest gain, if any, in real wages does not suggest any improvement, and may mask a decline. A continuous series drawn from the tithe taken on a well-defined area in a parish on the border of France and Hainault shows yields falling from 21 hectoliters per hectare in the 1410s to 15 hectoliters in the 1460s.[122] This is possibly a lower bound in districts that experienced high yields before the crisis. In the Cambrésis, where at the beginning of the fourteenth century yields in districts served by good roads into Flanders ranged between 20 and 25 hectoliters, tithes fell 45 percent for wheat and 70 percent for oats.[123] Between the 1320s and the 1370s the tithe receipts of the Abbey of Notre-Dame des Prés in Douai declined from 210 *muids* to 130.[124] Rents from farms possessed by the Abbey of Saint-Denis, which was especially hard hit by military operations around Paris, fell from 18,000 livres in 1342–43 to 7,000 in 1374–75; wheat sales, presumably in Paris, fell from 133 *muids* to four.[125] Between 1315 and 1446, the area under crops at Vaulerent fell 15 percent; output fell 90 percent![126] Vineyards near Paris contracted, and luxury cepages that had been sold throughout Northern Europe were replaced by 'mauvais gamay' suited to an impoverished local clientele.[127] Similar declines in the production of specialized districts can be observed in pastoral regions. Between the 1320s and the early 1400s, rents on pastures in Auvergne fell 60 percent.[128] Specialized districts that had developed in response to specific markets probably bore the brunt of the crisis in demand as those markets contracted.

CRISIS AND RECOVERY

Falling output translated into falling seigneurial income. An inventory taken in 1373 of seigneuries held in Perigord by the order of the Hospital shows a fall in revenue of 87 percent since 1350. Another deposition reported a decline in episcopal revenues from around 16,000 livres at the beginning of the century to barely 1,000 at its end.[129] In Anjou the value of tithes and rents fell 30 percent between 1350/1380 and 1400/1410, and by another 15 percent between 1420 and 1435.[130] An inquest on behalf of the Pope into ecclesiastical properties in Quercy between 1387 and 1395 declared a quarter of the benefices "nulle valeur."[131] Income from *censives* received by the Abbey of Saint-Denis, an index of rates of occupancy, fell from 216 livres in 1342–43 to 87 livres in 1374–75.[132] For it was not merely rents that fell, but also seigneurial fees, which evaporated as peasants abandoned their holdings for better farms, or at least for other farms on better terms. The emptying out of the highland districts was therefore not simply due to their infertility. Colonized during the peak of the medieval boom in the twelfth and thirteenth centuries, holdings carved out of the waste tended to carry higher *cens* relative to their productivity than territories settled at an earlier date.[133] Since the *cens* was a fixed payment, falling demand for land resulted in its abandonment rather than rent reductions. By contrast, rent on leased land seems to have responded—with a lag—to the fall in demand. On farms leased for shares, the proportion of the crop going to landlords shrank from half to a third, a fourth, a sixth, and even to a ninth.[134]

Ecclesiastical establishments and important lay seigneurs could generally weather the storm because of their wealth and privileged access to credit, albeit in somewhat reduced circumstances, and a few actually increased their holdings of land.[135] The small seigneuries that maintained the majority of the old knightly class were not so fortunate. The effect of declining prices for farm produce was most serious for the modest seigneurs drawing income mainly from a small demesne.[136] But all of them suffered from the loss of tenants and seigniorial fees. Adam de Mitry is typical. At the start of the fourteenth century he held of the Abbey of Saint-Denis a fief consisting of a house, a *réserve* of three hectares, and seigneurial dues amounting to five *sous* in cash and 9.4 hectoliters in wheat, barely enough to feed a family of four.[137] In less densely populated districts, seigneuries that covered more territory generated no more revenue. In western Auvergne, the average seigneurie had a radius of 2.3 kilometers, but its income rarely exceeded 100 livres.[138] Fifteenth-century seigneuries in the Sologne often got 20 livres, no more than a well-off peasant holding.[139] The low revenue from the possession of agricultural seigneuries had important implications for the survival of this class, for although 20 livres a year met the expenses of a respectable peasant and 100 livres those of a middling townsman, it was inadequate for seigneurs whose social status mandated that they live 'nobly' and whose military functions required them to maintain horses and armor.[140] Living nobly also meant dying nobly, involving a further expense after death.[141] On top of these recurring expenses, to which were added marriage portions and family settlements, came costs of litigation contesting wills and seigniorial rights. In wartime irregular wages and occasional booty provided some relief, but periods of lay-offs left many seigneurs with no option but to mortgage or sell their property.

The turnover of seigniorial lineages was therefore high. Between 1250 and 1350, the seigneurie of Puynormand passed through the hands of six families, and in the following century it subdivided into several smaller seigneuries.[142] The pattern seems universal. At first, the properties were purchased by other seigniorial families, townsmen preferring to restrict land acquisitions to suburban vineyards and country houses. Lyon's position as a thriving commercial and banking center may have been an exception,[143] but in general the French bourgeoisie appear to have followed the advice of the Limoges merchant Étienne Benoist, who counseled his children and relatives to avoid purchasing land they did not need to provision their household, and to have as little to do as possible with seigneurs, nobles, churchmen, and princes.[144] It was only toward the end of the fifteenth century with the return of prosperity that the small-town bourgeoisie began systematically to accumulate land and seigneuries.

From the perspective of seigneurs, abandoned land returned no *cens*, and empty villages and parishes no tolls or fees. The overriding goal was therefore to resettle the seigneurie. Since an abandoned holding reverted to the seigneur, the crisis inevitably increased the amount of land under direct seigniorial control. Paradoxically, the late fifteenth century seems to have marked the high point of peasant property in pre-Revolutionary France, as seigneurs sold off their land by creating new *censives* on more favorable terms. It was in this spirit that the marginal plots incorporated into the farms near Paris in the twelfth and thirteenth century returned to the peasantry along with pieces of the ancient demesne. The procedure of *accensement* is particularly well-documented for the province of Quercy, where isolation, thin soils, and periodic military incursions led to large-scale desertion of the countryside. To re-people it, seigneurs entered into contracts of *accensement*, giving joint possession to associations of peasants in exchange for their bringing the land into cultivation.[145] The syndicate was exempted from *cens* and other fees for a pre-determined number of years, the seigneur reserving only the tolls and rights of justice. Since the actual farms carved from such territories were farmed and effectively possessed by individual families, the purpose of collective *accensement* seems to have been to simplify seigniorial accounting. In any event, within two or three generations, the complications arising from sale and inheritance resulted in the original *censive* being divided up among the heirs and assigns of the original settlers.[146]

In the more prosperous districts of northern France, landlords offered rebates to induce tenants to restore buildings and return the land to a state of cultivation. The contract between the Hospitaler Commanderie of Reims and Jean Culin is typical. In exchange for a temporary reduction in rent, Culin contracted to reconstruct the buildings within four years and bring 10 arpents of abandoned arable into cultivation within six.[147] The archives of the Paris ecclesiastical establishments contain many similar contracts.[148] Once properties were restored to their original condition, rents were raised to their true value. Contracts of this type continued to be made down to the 1520s, giving the misleading impression of rents rising because of rising population. Much of that increase was simply the expiration of rent rebates previously granted to finance agricultural reconstruction. In some instances, however, one can see a renewal of seigneurial demands on tenants. Some *censives* in Quercy that had been conceded to peasants on especially favorable terms at the beginning of the fifteenth century were judicially 'revised' later in the century on the pretext that the proper legal procedures had not been followed or that the seigneur had been 'deceived' in his negotiations with the purchasers.[149] Some revisions may have been intended to evict squatters, but most were arbitrary alterations of legal contracts made possible by land scarcity.

Another inducement was a long lease. Term leases were commonly six to 12 years, but in the aftermath of the crisis, lords began to offer terms of two to three lives. The danger was that tenants might come to regard the holding as their own property, since in their eyes a long lease at a low rent was indistinguishable from a *censive*, and some went so far as to bequeath it to their children and even to sell the property to third parties. Seigniorial landlords thus had always to be on the watch to prevent property from escaping into the hands of their tenants. In 1511, the lease between farmer Jean Crespières and the convent of Celestins stipulated that Crespière's sons were to quit the holding upon attaining their majority.[150] For most seigneurs, the counsel of prudence was to keep leases short. Even so, on the larger farms, the leases tended to remain in the same family for generations.[151]

Despite high interest rates at the end of the Hundred Years War, there does not seem to have been a shortage of capital to reconstruct farms, although there may have been some difficulty in obtaining finance to reconstruct flour mills, which involved an actual outlay of cash for materials and labor.[152] Rent rebates cost nothing to seigneurs other than a temporary diminution in cash flow, and the work of land-clearing was done by peasants in the off season. Financing investment in livestock seems to have been available through an instrument known as *bail à cheptel*, which was a loan of animals for a share of their product and increase in value. The contract goes back at least to the thirteenth century and was the primary means by which small and large farmers financed their working stock.[153] It provided a comparatively safe investment, or at least one in which the high return compensated the mortality risk for townsmen seeking to place their capital locally.[154] The rapid expansion of sheep farming in the south of France after 1450 owes much to it. Loans could also be obtained on promissory notes. In the Limousin, nobles lent funds to peasants using these instruments, consolidating the arrears in *rentes* constituted on their holding.[155] Thus, in 1460 farmers Guillaume and Bernard Pinquier conceded the usufruct of two vineyards to a local nobleman and a merchant of Figeac to repay a loan of 43 *écus*.[156] It was by such devices that seigneurs in some regions gained control of the land. In any event, once peace was restored, there was enough liquid capital to meet the agricultural demand.

THE RECONSTITUTION OF THE SEIGNEURIE

Squatting was nevertheless an impediment to the reconstruction of the agrarian regime. When uncultivated land reverted to waste, markers defining the boundaries of individual holdings disappeared in the brush, giving peasants ample opportunity to claim the land was theirs.[157] The monks who held the seigneurie of Vaux-de-Cernay discovered that *censitaires* could no longer determine exactly where their property lay.[158] Memory is selective, and many lapses were probably deliberate attempts to profit from the destruction of titles and the disappearance of boundary stones. But whatever the cause, uncertainty as to who possessed the land stood in the way of bringing it back into cultivation. The problem was that seigneurs could not concede a new *censive* for fear the rightful owner might return to reclaim the property once the buildings and land had been restored.[159] Agricultural reconstruction thus required assertion of a clear title defining the boundaries of a holding, without which no tenant was prepared to commit labor and capital to improving it. The law required seigneurs to secure a court judgment for each holding they claimed to be abandoned, a cumbersome and costly procedure that was justified only for important properties. Seigneurs who wanted to evict tenants who refused to pay their *cens* on the grounds that their title was invalid incurred similar costs, which goes far to explain the fifteenth century decline in *cens* per hectare.[160] The solution to the legal conundrum was a royal charter (*ordonnance*) authorizing the seigneur to declare holdings vacant, and giving persons opposing the declaration six months to present their titles, after which the property reverted to the seigneur. The earliest orders of this kind were in issued in Paris by the English regent in the 1420s authorizing the owners of abandoned buildings to reclaim them. They were extended to rural properties in the 1440s by Charles VII and in the following six decades became the normal method of reclaiming abandoned land.[161] The procedure thus broke the legal deadlock over vacant property, and although it was initiated by the seigneur, it was generally supported by peasants, who considered it to be a clarification and protection of their property. That acquiescence signified acceptance of the traditional seigneurie as the institutional framework of landholding that would endure to the Revolution.

The reconstitution of the seigneurie in the later fifteenth century clarified and made more precise rights that in earlier periods were often vague and poorly defined. The instrument of that reconstitution was the *terrier*, which was a notarized record of the rights and obligations attached to particular pieces of land in a seigneurie. The *terrier* was an innovation of the fourteenth century and reflected the emergence of notaries as public officers responsible for authenticating and maintaining deeds, wills, and mortgages. Before 1300, the working documents of a seigneurie were the seigneurial accounts recording dues owing and dues paid by tenants and tenements, which were not legal proof of a property right.[162] Around the middle of the fourteenth century seigneurs began to employ documents of record drawn up by a notary and sworn to by the parties concerned, and in time the formulae of these documents were standardized, lowering their cost. Dressing a *terrier* nevertheless remained expensive, and only wealthy seigneurs could afford the luxury of updating it once a generation.[163] The exercise was usually carried out in periods of relative calm, when tenants could be called to collectively swear to their and the lord's rights.[164] The *terrie*r thus put a legal imprimatur on the seigneurie as the mode of land ownership. The vicissitudes of the fourteenth and fifteenth century had shaken the institution, but did not break it. In the end it emerged stronger than it entered.

French agrarian history in the later Middle Ages is a complex mix of many changes. What is remarkable is how so much stayed the same. The major changes occurred on the edges of the agrarian economy in the decline of the great urban centers and the difficult birth of a centralized monarchy. In 1500 much of France looked very much like it did in 1300. By 1600 that would no longer be true, as subterranean changes in technology and the more apparent rebirth of the cities and the state made themselves felt in the countryside. The *terrier* survived to the eighteenth century, when a new generation of legal specialists would deploy their ingenuity to recover long-lost dues in what has come to be known as the 'seigneurial reaction.' By that time, however, the seigneurie was an anachronism. As to the rural economy in the fourteenth and fifteenth century, *plus ça change, plus c'est la même chose.*

NOTES

1. Édouard Perroy, *The Hundred Years War*, trans. W. B. Well (New York: Capricorn Books, 1965).
2. Nicholas Wright, *Knights and Peasants: The Hundred Years War in the French Countryside* (Woodbridge, UK: Boydell Press, 1998).
3. David Potter, *A History of France, 1460–1560: The Emergence of a Nation-State* (New York: St. Martin's Press, 1995).
4. Charles Estienne and Jean Liébaut, *L'Agriculture et la Maison Rustique* (Paris: 1578 [1567]), http://gallica.bnf.fr/ark:/12148/bpt6k52718g.

5. Jean-Marc Moriceau, *Les Fermiers de l'Île de France* (Paris: Fayard, 1994).
6. Jean Froissart, *Chroniques,* ed. Siméon Luce (Paris: J. Renouard, 1869–1957); Alexandre Tuetey, ed., *Journal d'un Bourgeois de Paris, 1405–1449* (Genève: Slatkine Reprints, 1975 [1881]); Thomas Basin, *Histoire de Charles VII,* ed. Charles Samaran (Paris: Les Belles Lettres, 1933).
7. The seminal article is by Édouard Perroy, "À l'Origine d'une Économie Contractée: les Crises du XIVe Siècle," *Annales, Économies, Sociétés, Civilisations* 4 (1949): 167–182.
8. Isabelle Guérin, *La Vie Rurale en Sologne au XIVe et XVe Siècles* (Paris: SEVPEN, 1960); Robert Boutruche, *La Crise d'une Société. Seigneurs et Paysans du Bordelais pendant la Guerre de Cent Ans* (Paris: Les Belles Lettres, 1963); Guy Fourquin, *Les Campagnes de la Région Parisienne à la Fin du Moyen Âge* (Paris: Presses Universitaires de France, 1964); Marie-Thérèse Lorcin, *Les Campagnes de la Région Lyonnaise au XIVe et XVe Siècles* (Lyon: Bosc, 1974); Jean Lartigaut, *Les Campagnes du Quercy après la Guerre de Cent Ans (vers 1440–vers 1500)* (Toulouse: Publications de Toulouse-le-Mirail, 1978); Pierre Charbonnier, *Une Autre France. La Seigneurie Rurale en Basse Auvergne du XIVe au XVIe Siècle* (Clermont-Ferrand: Institut d'Etudes du Massif Central, 1980); Michel Le Mené, *Les Campagnes Angevines à la Fin du Moyen Âge: vers 1350–vers 1530* (Nantes: Éditions Cid, 1982); Jean Gallet, *La Seigneurie Bretonne 1450–1680. L'Exemple du Vannetais* (Paris: Publications de la Sorbonne, 1983); Guy Bois, *The Crisis of Feudalism: Economy and Society in Eastern Normandy c. 1300–1550* (Cambridge: Cambridge University Press, 1984); Jean Tricard, *Les Campagnes Limousines du XIVe au XVIe siècle: Originalité et Limites d'une Reconstruction Rurale* (Paris: Publications de la Sorbonne, 1996).
9. S. R. Epstein, *Freedom and Growth: The Rise of States and Markets in Europe, 1300–1750* (London and New York: Routledge, 2000), 49.
10. Bois, *Crisis.*
11. Marc Bloch, *Les Caractères Originaux de l'Histoire Rurale Française,* Nouvelle Édition (Paris: A. Colin, 1960 [1931]).
12. That is, excluding districts held in *appanage* by princes of the blood and French territories of the Holy Roman Empire. Ferdinand Lot, "L'État des Paroisses et des Feux de 1328," *Bibliothèque de l'École des Chartes* 90 (1929): 51–107, 256–315.
13. Jacques Dupâquier, *Histoire de la Population Française, 1. Des Origines à la Renaissance* (Paris: Presses Universitaires de France 1988), 262–263.
14. "Les célèbres conjectures de F. Lot, d'après l'État des feux de 1328, aboutissent à compter 15 ou 16 million d'âmes en France, d'où une densité rurale de 35 à 38 habitants au km^2, si forte que la survie de cette masse humaine n'aurait pas être assurée." Perroy, "À l'Origine," 168.
15. Goldsmith's contention that "[e]verything we know about the economic and social structures of France in the early fourteenth century suggests not overpopulation, but light population" seems to me untenable in light of the documented specialization of farming districts. James Goldsmith, "The Crisis of the Later Middle Ages: The Case of France," *French History* 9 (1995): 424.
16. Oded Galor and David Weil, "Population, Technology and Growth: From Malthusian Stagnation to the Demographic Transition and Beyond," *American Economic Review* 90 (2000): 806–828.
17. Dupâquier, *Population Française,* 242–260; Tricard, *Campagnes Limousines*, 89. Charbonnier, *Une Autre France*, 286–287.
18. Fourquin, *Campagnes*, 63.
19. To judge from Cassini's map of 1785, which would not have exaggerated the extent of the medieval vineyard, vines probably covered 10 percent of the region's cultivated territory. Fourquin, *Campagnes,* 74–76.

20. "C'est dans l'Élection de Paris qu'on reconnaît surtout le pouvoir de l'art sur la nature; des terres sinon très-mauvaises, chargés de riches productions . . . dont il est facile de rendre raison. Les provisions qui, de tous les points de la France, viennent se consommer dans cette ville, sont rendues en engrais aux terres qui l'avoisinent." Hilaire-François Gilbert, *Traité des Prairies Artificielles . . . dans la Généralité de Paris, et sur la Culture qui lui Convient le Mieux.* (Paris: Imprimerie de la Veuve d'Houry et Debure, 1789). http://gallica.bnf.fr/ark:/12148/bpt6k436 1826 [1790]), 20.
21. Alain Derville, *L'Agriculture du Nord au Moyen Âge. Artois, Cambrésis, Flandre Wallonne* (Lille: Presse Universitaires du Septentrion, 1999), 46–49.
22. Gérard Sivéry, *Structures Agraires et Vie Rurale dans le Hainaut à la Fin du Moyen Âge* (Lille: Presses Universitaire de Lille, 1973), vol. 1, 316–317.
23. Elisabeth Carpentier and Michel Le Mené, *La France du XI*[e] *au XV*[e] *Siècle : Population, Société, Économie* (Paris: Presses Universitaires de France, 1996), 234.
24. Bois, *Crisis*, 150.
25. Carpentier and Le Mené, *La France,* 329.
26. Richard Cantillon judged that a French peasant family living on bread, vegetables, and water could survive on one-and-a-half to two acres. Richard Cantillon, *Essay on the Nature of Commerce in General,* trans. Henry Higgs (New Brunswick: Transaction Publishers, 2001 [c. 1730]), 19.
27. Derville, *Agriculture du Nord*, 54.
28. Fourquin, *Campagnes*, 93–94.
29. Maurice Berthe, "Marché de la Terre et Hiérarchie Paysanne dans le Lauragais Toulousain," *Campagnes Médiévales. L'Homme et son Espace. Études Offertes à Robert Fossier,* ed. Elisabeth Mornet (Paris: Publications de la Sorbonne, 1995): 297–311.
30. Berthe, "Marché," 301–302.
31. Fouquin, *Campagnes,* 185–186.
32. Bois, *Crisis,* 150.
33. Fourquin, *Campagnes*, 96–97; J.-M. Richard, "Thierry d'Hireçon, Agriculteur Artésien, 13. 1328," *Bibliothèque de l'École des Chartes* 53 (1892): 383–416, 571–604.
34. Charles Higounet, *La Grange de Vaulerent: Structure et Exploitation d'un Terroir Cistercien de la Plaine de France XII*[e]*-XV*[e] *Siècle* (Paris: SEVPEN, 1965), 32–37.
35. Berthe, "Marché," 306.
36. Lot, "État des Paroisses," 292–293. In the 1470s Olivier de Beaumer, a peasant holding five to eight hectares of good land in lower Brittany, was assessed at one-third of a fiscal *feu.* His neighbor, a fisherman holding two or three hectares, was rated at one-sixteenth. In the official accounts their holdings would have been grouped with others to make up one *feux.* Gallet, *Seigneurie Bretonne*, 180.
37. Froissart, *Chroniques,* vol. 4, 100.
38. Jean Favier, "Une Ville entre Deux Vocations: La Place d'Affaires de Paris au XVe Siècle," *Annales, Économies, Sociétés, Civilisations* 79 (1974): 60–61.
39. Paul Bairoch, *La Population des Villes Européennes: Banque de Données et Analyse Sommaire des Résultats, 800–1850* (Geneva: Droz, 1988); Boutruche, *Crise.*
40. Carpentier and Le Mené, *La France,* 323.
41. Bairoch, *Population.*
42. Carpentier and Le Mené, *La France,* 372.
43. Carpentier and Le Mené, *La France,* 323, 371.

44. Carpentier and Le Mené, *La France* , 376.
45. Tricard, *Campagnes Limousines*, 91–96.
46. K. Lesins, "Afalfa, Lucerne," *Evolution of Crop Plants*, ed. N. W. Simmonds (New York: Longman, 1976), 165–167.
47. M. Zohary and D. Heller, *The Genus* Trifolium (Jerusalem: Israel Academy of Science and Humanities, 1984), 1.
48. Mauro Ambrosoli, *The Wild and the Sown: Botany and Agriculture in Western Europe: 1350–1850* (Cambridge: Cambridge University Press, 1997), 20–23.
49. Frédéric Audoin-Rouzeau, "Compter et Mesurer les Os Animaux. Pour une Histoire de l'Élevage et de l'Alimentation de l'Antiquité au Temps Modern," *Histoire et Mesure* 10 (1995): 277–312.
50. The older view of a medieval 'agricultural revolution' has been decisively repudiated. See, among others, Georges Raepset, "Les Prémices de la Mécanisation Agricole entre Seine et Rhin de l'Antiquité au 13e Siècle," *Annales, Histoire, Science Sociale* 50 (1995): 911–942; Marie-Claire Amouretti, "L'Attelage dans l'Antiquité: le Prestige d'une Erreur Scientifique," *Annales, Économies, Sociétés, Civilisations* 46 (1991): 219–232.
51. Robert Fossier, *La Terre et les Hommes en Picardie Jusqu'à la fin du XIIIe Siècle,* nouvelle édition (Amiens: Centre Régional de Documentation Pédagogique, 1987), 427–429. Derville argues that the introduction of these fallow legumes was probably the work of small farmers, since large lay and ecclesiastical proprietors were reluctant to have land taken out of fallow for fear it would reduce yields. Derville, *Agriculture,* 51–52.
52. Jean-Pierre Devroey, "Entre Loire et Rhin: Les Fluctuations du Terroir de l'Épeautre au Moyen Age," *L'Épeautre.* (Triticum spelta*). Histoire et Ethnologie,* eds, J.-P. Devroey and Jean-Jacques van Mol (Treignes: Editions Dire, 1989), 89–105; J.-P. Devroey, "La Céréalculture dans le Monde Franc," in *L'Ambiente Vegetale nell'altro Medioevo.* (Spoleto: Centro Italiano di Studi Sull'alto Medioevo, 1990), 221–256
53. Fossier, *Terre et hommes,* 333, 379; Philippe Contamine, "Le Cheval dans l'Économie Rural d'après des Archives de l'Ordre de l'Hôpital," *Campagnes Médiévales*, ed. E. Mornet,163–179. Derville dates the introduction of horses to the eleventh century. Derville, *Agriculture du Nord,* 49–50.
54. Pascal Reigniez, *L'Outil Agricole en France au Moyen Âge* (Paris: Errance, 2002).
55. Georges Comet, "Technology and Agricultural Expansion in the Middle Ages: The Example of France North of the Loire," in *Medieval Farming and Technology: The Impact of Agricultural Change in Northwest Europe*, eds. Grenville Astill and John Langdon (Leiden, New York, Köln: Brill, 1997), 11–40; Georges Raepset, "The Development of Farm Implements between the Seine and the Rhine from the Second to the Twelfth Centuries," in *Medieval Farming*, eds. Astill and Langdon, 41–68.
56. Hélène Olland, "Un Exemple de Reconstruction: Colombey-lès-Choiseul (1485–1550)," in *La Reconstruction après la Guerre de Cent Ans. Actes du 104e Congrès des Sociétés Savantes. Bordeaux, 1980* (Paris: Publications de la Sorbonne, 1981), 74–76.
57. A. C. Zeven and C. J. Stemerdink, "A Cluster Analysis of Eight Medieval Manuscripts Based on Depicted Plant Taxa," *Journal d'Agriculture Tropicale et de Botanique Appliquée* 23 (1986): 225–242; Ambrosoli, *Wild and Sown*, 165–167, 171, 183–184.
58. Georges Comet, "L'Iconographie des 'Plantes Nouvelles' ou une Approche des Débuts de la Botanique Moderne," in *Campagnes Médiévales,* ed. Mornet, 31–57.

59. By the thirteenth century property held in fief was no longer merely a defined territory, but covered ownership of many different income streams. Henri Sée, *Les Classes Rurales et le Régime Domanial en France au Moyen Âge* (Paris: Girard et Frères, 1903), 561.
60. This account is commonly employed by economists to model the early medieval agrarian economy. See Douglass C. North and Robert Paul Thomas, "The Rise and Fall of the Manorial System: A Theoretical Model," *Journal of Economic History* 31 (1971): 777–803.
61. Jean Durliat, *Les Finances Publiques de Dioclétien aux Carolingiens* (Sigmaringen: Jan Thorbeke Verlag, 1990); Elisabeth Magnou-Nortier, "Le Grand Domaine: des Maîtres, des Doctrines, des Questions," *Francia* 15 (1987): 659–700; E. Magnou-Nortier, "La Gestion Publique en Neustrie: les Moyens et les Hommes (VIIe–IXe Siècles)," in *La Neustrie: Les Pays au Nord de la Loire de 650 à 850,* ed. Hartmut Atsma (Sigmaringen: Jan Thorbeke Verlag 1989), 271–318; Karl-Ferdinand Werner, *Naissance de la Noblesse: L'Essor des Élites Politiques en Europe* (Paris: Fayard, 1998); James Lowth Goldsmith, *Lordship in France, 500–1500* (New York: Peter Lang, 2003).
62. On the survival of allodial land to the twelfth century, see Laurent Feller, "Statut de la Terre et Statut des Personnes: L'Alleu Paysan dans l'Historiographie depuis Georges Duby," *Etudes Rurales* 45–46 (1997): 147–164. Guy Bois, *The Transformation of the Year One Thousand: The Village of Lournand from Antiquity to Feudalism*, trans. Jean Birrell (Manchester and New York: Manchester University Press, 1992) gives a Marxist interpretation of that survival.
63. Certain properties originating in Roman imperial estates supported public functions. With the collapse of Roman administration, they fell to rulers of successor states, who managed them directly or delegated their administration to ecclesiastical establishments. The Carolingian capitulary *De villis*, which is usually considered to document a classical manor employing corvée labor on the demesne, is actually a memorandum of rules governing the administration of such an estate. See Elisabeth Magnou-Nortier, "Capitulaire '*De Villis et Curtis Imperialibus*' (vers. 810–813). Texte, Traduction et Commentaire," *Revue Historique* 299 (1998): 643–689.
64. In particular Jean-Pierre Devroey, *Puissants et Misérables: Système Social et Monde Paysan dans l'Europe des Francs (VIIe–IXe siècles)* (Bruxelles: Académie Royale de Belgique, 2006).
65. Late Roman fiscal practice assessed taxes on nominal units to which individuals and lands were attached for the purpose of apportioning tax liability; Durliat, *Finances Publiques.* Goldsmith argues that the system was adapted to lightly settled territories, but that with the colonization (and taxation) of new territories after 900, it became increasingly cumbersome to administer and was replaced in the twelfth century by direct assessments on farmsteads and individuals along lines that had been devised to tax newly cleared land. Goldsmith, *Lordship,* 105–107.
66. Proportional charges on output seem to have been introduced into southern France somewhat earlier than in the north. The earliest examples from Provence and the southwest date to the late tenth century. Louis Stouff, "Redevances à Part de Fruits et de Métayage dans la Provence Médiéval: Tasques et Facherie," in *Les Revenus de la Terre: Complant, Champart, Métayage en Europe Occidentale (IXe–XVIIIe Siècles). Flaran. Septièmes Journées Internationales d'Histoire, 1985.* (Auch: Centre Culturel de l'Abbaye de Flaran, 1987), 43–60; Germain Sicard et Mireille Sicard, "Redevances à Part de Fruits et de Métayage dans le Sud-Ouest de la France au Moyen Âge," in *Revenus de la Terre*, 61–74.

67. Gérard Sivery, "Les Tenures à Part de Fruit et le Métayage dans le Nord de la France et les Pays-Bas jusqu'au Début du XVIe Siècle," in *Revenus de la Terre*, 27–42
68. In 1315 the right to levy an arbitrary *taille* on 50 men and women in the Châtellenie of Romorantin was worth 40 livres a year, a considerable sum. Guérin, *Vie Rurale*, 203.
69. Boutruche, *Crise*, 66–68.
70. Boutruche, *Crise*, 49.
71. Lorcin, *Campagnes*, 290.
72. William A. Weary, "La Maison de la Trémoille pendant la Renaissance: une Seigneurie Agrandie," in *La France de la Fin du XVe Siècle. Renouveau et Apogée, dirs.*, Bernard Chevalier and Philippe Contamine, (Paris: CNRS, 1985), 202.
73. Patrick Karl O'Brien, "Path Dependency: Or Why Britain Became an Industrialized and Urbanized Economy Long before France," *Economic History Review* 49 (1996): 213–249.
74. Marc Bloch, *Seigneurie Française et Manoir Anglais* (Paris: A. Colin, 1967).
75. Robert Brenner, "Agrarian Class Structure in Pre-Industrial Europe," *Past & Present* 70 (1976): 30–75; "The Agrarian Roots of European Capitalism," *Past & Present* 97 (1982): 16–113.
76. Feller, "Statut de la Terre."
77. "It was custom that finally decided the fate of the legal heritage of the preceding age. Custom had become the sole living source of law, and princes, even in their legislation, scarcely claimed to do no more than interpret it." Marc Bloch, *Feudal Society*, trans. L. A. Manyon (Chicago: Phoenix Books, 1964), 111.
78. Fustel de Coulanges, N. D. *L'Alleu et le Domaine rural* Paris: Hachette, 1889.
79. Sée, *Classes Rurales*, 560–563. The right to hypothecate fiefs dates to the 1360s, no doubt owing to the need to raise ransoms following the defeat at Poitiers. Fourquin, *Campagnes*, 123–124.
80. At least 72 hectares in the *grange* of Vaulerent were charged with *cens*, possibly half its original endowment in 1136, at which time the original seigneurie was already divided among several possessors. Higounet, *Vaulerent*, 33–34.
81. O'Brien, "Path Dependency."
82. Wright, *Knights and Peasants*, 69.
83. "But if on both sides war is decided upon and begun by the Councils of the two kings, the soldiery may take spoil from the kingdom at will, and make war freely; and if sometimes the humble and innocent suffer harm and lose their goods, it cannot be otherwise." Honoré Bouvet, *The Tree of Battles* (1387), Part IV, chapter 58. Cited in Wright, *Knights and Peasants*, 1.
84. "When Provisions, Fuel and Horse-meat fell short in one village, they marched away full-speed to the next; wasting it in like manner." Sir John Fortescue, *De Laudibus Legum Angliae: A New Translation*. London: T. Evans (1775), 122. http://find.galegroup.com/ecco/infomark.do?&contentSet=ECCOArticles&type=multipage&tabID=T001&prodId=ECCO&docId=CW125623858&source=gale&userGroupName=crepuq_mcgill&version=1.0&docLevel=FASCIMILE>.
85. Fourquin, *Campagnes*, 226.
86. *Letters from Petrarch*, trans. Morris Bishop (Bloomington: Indiana University Press, 1966), 196.
87. "We have ourselves seen the vast plains of Champagne, Beauce, Brie, the Gâtinais, the countries of Chartres, Dreux, Maine and Perche, the French

as well as the English Vexin, the country of Caux from the Seine almost to Amiens and Abbéville, the district of Senlis from the Soissonais and the Valois to Laon and beyond to the watershed of Hainault totally deserted, uncultivated, abandoned, and emptied of their inhabitants, covered with brush and brambles, and in regions where trees were once scarce the return of thick forests." Basin, *Histoire de Charles VII*. I, 85–89.

88. Isabelle de Botton and Marie Offredo-Sarrot, "Ruines et Reconstruction Agraire dans les Commanderies du Grand Prieuré de France," in *La Reconstruction après la Guerre de Cent Ans,* 79–122.
89. See in particular John Bell Henneman, *Royal Taxation in Fourteenth-Century France: The Development of War Financing 1322–1356* (Princeton: Princeton University Press, 1971); *Royal Taxation in Fourteenth-Century France: the Captivity and Ransom of John II* (Philadelphia: American Philosophical Society, 1976), and Philippe Contamine et al., dirs., *L'Impôt au Moyen Âge : l'Impôt Public et le Prélèvement Seigneurial fin XIIe-début XVIe Siècle* (Paris : Ministère de l'Économie, des Finances et de l'Industrie, Comité pour l'Histoire Économique et Financière de la France, 2002).
90. Martin Wolfe, *The Fiscal System of Renaissance France* (New Haven: Yale University Press, 1972).
91. Philippe Contamine, *Guerre, État et Société à la Fin du Moyen Âge: Études sur les Armées du Roi de France 1337–1494* (Paris and La Haye: Mouton, 1972); Peter S. Lewis, "Les Pensionnaires de Louis XI," in *La France de la Fin du XVe Siècle*, ed. Contamine 167–181.
92. The mechanics of this operation are clearly set out in J. D. Gould, *The Great Debasement* (Oxford: Clarendon, 1970), Chapter 2.
93. John Day, "'Crise du Féodalisme' et Conjoncture des Prix à la Fin du Moyen Âge," *Annales, Économies, Sociétés, Civilisations* 34 (1979): 309–310; Harry A. Miskimin, *Money and Power in Fifteenth-Century France.* (New Haven: Yale University Press, 1984), 58.
94. Carpentier and Le Mée, *La France,* 385.
95. Fourquin, *Campagnes Parisiennes*, 408.
96. Gérard Sivéry, *Saint Louis et Son Siècle* (Paris: Taillandier, 1983), 275.
97. Tricard, *Campagnes Limousines*, 16.
98. Wright, *Knights and Peasants*, 39–40.
99. Philippe Contamine, "Lever l'Impôt en Terre de Guerre: Rançons, Appatis, Souffrances de Guerre dans la France des XIVe et XVe Siècles," in *L'Impôt Public . . . 1. Le Droit d'Imposer*, dirs. P. Contamine et al.,11–39.
100. Guérin, *Vie rurale*, 166–167; Tricard, *Campagnes Limousines,* 31–32.
101. "Afin qu'à leur retour ils ne passent par ledit pays d'Auvergne." Charbonnier, *Une Autre France,* 508–509.
102. Henri Dubois, "Le Commerce de France au Temps de Louis XI," in *La France de la Fin du XVe Siècle,* 18–19.
103. Michel Le Mené, "Métayage et Bail à Cheptel dans l'Ouest de la France (1335–1342)," in *Campagnes Médiévales,* ed. Mornet, 697–707.
104. Marie-Thérèse Lorcin, *Vivre et Mourir en Lyonnais à la Fin du Moyen Âge* (Paris: Editions du CNRS, 1981), 37.
105. Ronald Findlay and Mats Lundahl, "Towards a Factor Proportions Approach to Economic History: Population, Precious Metals and Prices from the Black Death to the Price Revolution," in Ronald Findlay et al., eds. *Bertil Ohlin. A Centennial Celebration* (Cambridge and London: MIT Press, 2002), 495–528.
106. Carpentier and Le Mené, *La France,* 389–397.
107. Carpentier and Le Mené, *La France.* 426.

108. "Of other types of meat they do not so much as taste, unless it be the Inwards and Offals of Sheep and Bullocks, and the like, which are killed for the better sort of People, and the Merchants . . . As for their Poultry, the Soldiers consume them, so that scarce the eggs, slight as they are; are indulged them by way of a Dainty.' Fortescue, *De laudibus legum Anglaie,* 126
109. Guy Fourquin, "Les Débuts du Fermage: l'Exemple de Saint-Denis," *Etudes Rurales* 22–24 (1966): 30.
110. Higounet, *Vaulerent,* 52. The tenants would have required a margin of at least 25 percent to cover the risk and capital cost.
111. Richard, "Thierry d'Hireçon"; Derville, *Agriculture du Nord,* 160–174.
112. Alain Derville, "Dîmes, Rendements du blé et 'Révolution Agricole' dans le Nord de la France au Moyen Âge," *Annales, Économies, Sociétés, Civilisations* 42 (1987): 1411–1432 ; Derville, *Agriculture du Nord,* 57–58; Michel Morineau, *Les Faux-Semblants d'un Démarrage Économique: Agriculture et Démographie en France au XVIIIe Siècle* (Paris: Armand Colin, 1971).
113. E. A. Wrigley, "The Transition to an Advanced Organic Economy: Half a Millennium of English Agriculture," *Economic History Review* 59 (2006), 435–480.
114. Gérard Béaur, "From the North Sea to Berry and Lorraine: Land Productivity in Northern France, 13th–19th Centuries," in *Land Productivity and Agro-Systems in the North Sea Area: Middle Ages—20th Century,* eds. Bas. J. P. van Bavel and Erik Thoen (Turnhout: Brepols, 1999), 136–167.
115. Richard, "Thierry d'Hireçon," 388–389; Derville, *Agriculture,* 102.
116. Richard, "Thierry d'Hireçon," 392–393; Derville, *Agriculture,* 157.
117. An entry for Roquétoire mentions expenditures for 'flotter les prés.' Richard, "Thierry d'Hireçon," 406.
118. Richard, "Thierry d'Hireçon," 403; Derville, *Agriculture,* 103
119. Derville, *Agriculture,* 99–101.
120. In the 1320s a farmer of a 280 hectare farm near Douai paid a 25 percent penalty rate for late payment on a loan resulting from military requisition of his grain stocks. Derville, *Agriculture,* 154.
121. In 1321–22 the merchant handling Thierry d'Hireçon's grain sold 3,288 hectoliters in the town markets of Saint-Omer, Aire, and Douai. At his death in 1328 Thierry d'Hireçon's granaries held enough grain to feed at least 2,400 persons for a year. Derville, *Agriculture,* 64.
122. Morineau, *Faux-Semblants,* 128.
123. Hugues Neveux, *Vie et Déclin d'une Structure Économique: Les Grains du Cambrésis Fin du XIVe-Début du XVIIIe Siècle* (Paris: Mouton, 1980), 61; Derville, *Agriculture,* 210.
124. Carpentier and Le Mené, *La France,* 419.
125. Fourquin, *Campagnes,* 265.
126. Higounet, *Vaulerent,* 59.
127. Fourquin, *Campagnes,* 82.
128. Charbonnier, *Une Autre France,* 291.
129. Arlette Higounet-Nadal, *Histoire du Périgord* (Toulouse: Privat, 1983), 144.
130. Michel Le Mené, "La Conjoncture Économique Angevine sous le Règne de Louis IX," in *La France de la Fin du XVe siècle,* 52.
131. Lartigaut, *Campagnes du Quercy,* 40.
132. Fourquin, *Campagnes,* 265.
133. Stouff, "Redevances à Part," 52.
134. Le Mené, "Redevances à Part," in *Les Revenus de la Terre,* 23.
135. Lartigaut, *Campagnes du Quercy,* 490.
136. Guérin, *Vie Rurale,* 170–172.
137. Fourquin, *Campagnes,* 138–139.

138. Charbonnier (1980), 353.
139. Guérin, *Vie Rurale,* 170.
140. By the late fourteenth century, many of the poorer knights were 'dropping out' because of the expense. Lartigaut, *Campagnes du Quercy,* 436–439.
141. Captal de Buch, Seigneur de Grailly paid for 50,000 obit masses on his behalf. Boutruche, *Crise,* 276. On the social and psychological pressures behind these expenditures, see Jean Favier, *Paris au XVe siècle, 1380–1500* (Paris: Hachette, 1982), 67–82.
142. Boutruche, *Crise*, 239–240.
143. Lorcin, *Campagnes de la Région Lyonaise.*
144. Jean Tricard, "Livres de Raison et Présence de la Bourgeoisie dans les Campagnes Limousines (XIVe–XVe Siècle)," in *Campagnes Médiévales*, ed. Mornet 118–119.
145. Lartigaut, *Campagnes du Quercy,* 61–65.
146. Lartigaut, *Campagnes,* 137 ; Charbonnier, *Une Autre France,* 44–45.
147. "Jehan Culin moyennant le rendage pour les masures et censives de 5 sols et 60 sols pour les terres et en oultre a la charge de faire réédifier maisons de deux travées d'estable dedans quatre ans et de dessayer mettre en culture dix arpents en dedans 6 ans," De Botton and Offredo-Sarrat, "Ruines et Reconstruction," 96.
148. See Yvonne Bézard, *La Vie Rurale dans le Sud de la Région Parisienne de 1450 à 1560* (Paris: Firmin-Didot, 1929) and Fourquin, *Campagnes.*
149. Lartigaut, *Campagnes du Quercy,* 147.
150. "Ledit Crespières marioit ses enfans masles, incontinant sera tenu de les pourveoir et mettres dehors d'avecque luy avecques leurs femmes et ne pourront demourer avecques luy oudit hostel sans le congé desdits Célestins et par escript," Bézard, *Vie Rurale,* 113–114.
151. Moriceau, *Fermiers.*
152. Lartigaut, *Campagnes du Quercy,* 196.
153. Le Mené, "Métayage et Bail à Cheptel"; Tricard, *Campagnes Limousines,* 149–152.
154. A contract from Quercy in the fifteenth century shows an implicit return of 75 percent on the capital advanced. There is no indication that the rate was unusual, though the high proportion of sheep at risk of murrain and other maladies probably accounts for the high rate; Lartigaut, *Campagnes du Quercy,* 440.
155. Tricard, *Campagnes Limousines,* 160–164
156. Lartigaut, *Campagnes du Quercy,* 311.
157. Lartigaut, *Campagnes du Quercy,* 140–141.
158. "Quand le peuple est retourné audit pais, les terres estoient au si grand ruyne et désolation que n'estoit homme ne femme qui osast aller au pais recuillir ses revenues ne autres choses." Cited in Bézard, *Vie Rurale,* 49.
159. "Pour doubte que quand ceulx à qui'l les auroit baillé ou bailleroit, les aurez essartez et mis en labeur et revenue, aucuns se apparaissent qui y demandassent ou reclamassent aucun droit." Bézard, *Vie Rurale,* 52.
160. Boutruche, *Crise*, 297–298.
161. "Touchant les rentes constituées sur les maisons et héritages à Paris." Letter issued by Henry VI. 1428. *Recueil Général des Anciennes Lois Françaises Depuis l'An 420 jusqu'à la Révolution de 1789* (Paris (1821–1833), vol. 8, 50.
162. Charbonnier, *Une Autre France,* 18–19.
163. Lorcin, *Campagnes,* 256–258.
164. René Verdier, "Les Terriers en Dauphiné. Instruments de Résistance Seigneuriale," in *Terriers et Plans-Terriers du XIIIi[e] au XVIIIi[e] Siècle,* eds. Ghislain Brunel et al. (Paris: École des Chartes. Bibliothèque de l'Histoire Rurale, 2002), 207–16; Denise Angers, "Terriers et Livres-Terriers en Normandie (XIIIe au XVIIIe Siècle)," in *Terriers et Plans-Terries,* 19–35.

BIBLIOGRAPHY

Ambrosoli, M. *The Wild and the Sown: Botany and Agriculture in Western Europe: 1350–1850,* trans. by M. McCann Salvatorelli. Cambridge: Cambridge University Press, 1997.

Amouretti, M.-C. "L'Attelage dans l'Antiquité: le Prestige d'une Erreur Scientifique." *Annales, Économies, Sociétés, Civilisations* 46 (1991): 219–232.

Angers, D. "Terriers et Livres-Terriers en Normandie (XIIIe au XVIIIe Siècle)," in *Terriers et Plans-Terriers du XIIIi[e] au XVIIIi[e] Siècle,* edited by G. Brunel, O. Guyotjean, and J.-M. Moriceau, 19–35. Paris: École des Chartes. Bibliothèque de l'Histoire Rurale, 2002.

Audoin-Rouzeau, F. "Compter et Mesurer les Os Animaux. Pour une Histoire de l'Élevage et de l'Alimentation de l'Antiquité au Temps Modern." *Histoire et Mesure* 10 (1995): 277–312

Bairoch, P. *La Population des Villes Européennes: Banque de Données et Analyse Sommaire des Résultats, 800–1850.* Geneva: Droz, 1988.

Basin, T. *Histoire de Charles VII,* edited by C. Samaran. Paris: Les Belles Lettres, 1933.

Béaur, G. "From the North Sea to Berry and Lorraine: Land Productivity in Northern France, 13th–19th Centuries," in *Land Productivity and Agro-Systems in the North Sea Area: Middle Ages–20th Century,* edited by B. J. P. van Bavel and E. Thoen, 136–167. Turnhout: Brepols, 1999.

Berthe, M. "Marché de la Terre et Hiérarchie Paysanne dans le Lauragais Toulousain,"in *Campagnes Médiévales. L'Homme et son Espace. Études Offertes à Robert Fossier,* edited by Elisabeth Mornet, 297–311. Paris: Publications de la Sorbonne, 1995.

Bézard, Y. *La Vie Rurale dans le Sud de la Région Parisienne de 1450 à 1560.* Paris: Firmin-Didot, 1929.

Bloch, M. *Les Caractères Originaux de l'Histoire Rurale Française,* Nouvelle Édition. Paris: A. Colin, 1960 (1931).

Bloch, M. *Feudal Society,* translated by L. A. Manyon. Chicago: Phoenix Books, 1964.

Bloch, M. *Seigneurie Française et Manoir Anglais.* Paris: A. Colin, 1967.

Bois, G. *The Crisis of Feudalism: Economy and Society in Eastern Normandy c. 1300–1550.* Cambridge: Cambridge University Press, 1984.

Bois, G. *The Transformation of the Year One Thousand: The Village of Lournand from Antiquity to Feudalism,* translated by J. Birrell. Manchester and New York: Manchester University Press, 1992.

Boutruche, R. *La Crise d'une Société. Seigneurs et Paysans du Bordelais pendant la Guerre de Cent Ans.* Paris: Les Belles Lettres, 1963.

Brenner, R. "Agrarian Class Structure in Pre-Industrial Europe." *Past & Present* 70 (1976): 30–75.

Brenner, R. "The Agrarian Roots of European Capitalism." *Past & Present* 97 (1982): 16–113.

Cantillon, R. *Essay on the Nature of Commerce in General,* trans. by H. Higgs. New Brunswick: Transaction Publishers, 2001 [c. 1730].

Carpentier E. and M. Le Mené. *La France du XIe au XVe Siècle: Population, Société, Économie.* Paris: Presses Universitaires de France, 1996.

Charbonnier, P. *Une Autre France. La Seigneurie Rurale en Basse Auvergne du XIVe au XVIe Siècle.* Clermont-Ferrand: Institut d'Etudes du Massif Central, 1980.

Comet, G. "L'Iconographie des 'Plantes Nouvelles' ou une Approche des Débuts de la Botanique Moderne," in *Campagnes Médiévales, L'Homme et son Espace. Études Offertes à Robert Fossier,* edited by Elisabeth Mornet, 31–57. Paris: Publications de la Sorbonne, 1995.

Comet, G. "Technology and Agricultural Expansion in the Middle Ages: The Example of France North of the Loire," in *Medieval Farming and Technology: The Impact of Agricultural Change in Northwest Europe,* edited by G. Astill and J. Langdon, 11–40. Leiden, New York, Köln: Brill, 1997.

Contamine, P. *Guerre, État et Société à la Fin du Moyen Âge: Études sur les Armées du Roi de France 1337–1494.* Paris and La Haye: Mouton, 1972.

Contamine, P. "Le Cheval dans l'Économie Rural d'après des Archives de l'Ordre de l'Hôpital," in *Campagnes Médiévales. L'Homme et son Espace. Études Offertes à Robert Fossier,* edited by E. Mornet, 163–179. Paris: Publications de la Sorbonne, 1995.

Contamine, P. "Lever l'Impôt en Terre de Guerre: Rançons, Appatis, Souffrances de Guerre dans la France des XIVe et XVe Siècles," in *L'Impôt Public et le Prélèvement Seigneurial fin XIIe–début XVIe Siècle.1. Le Droit d'Imposer,* directed by P. Contamine, J. Kerhervé and A. Rigaudière, 11–39. Paris: Ministère de l'Économie, des Finances et de l'Industrie, Comité pour l'Histoire Économique et Financière de la France, 2002.

Contamine, P., J. Kerhervé, and A. Rigaudière, directors. *L'Impôt au Moyen Âge : l'Impôt Public. Colloque tenu à Bercy les 14, 15, 16 Juin 2000.* Paris: Ministère de l'Économie, des Finances et de l'Industrie, Comité pour l'Histoire Économique et Financière de la France, 2002.

Day, J. "'Crise du Féodalisme' et Conjoncture des Prix à la Fin du Moyen Âge." *Annales, Économies, Sociétés, Civilisations* 34 (1979): 305–318.

De Botton, I. and M. Offredo-Sarrot. "Ruines et Reconstruction Agraire dans les Commanderies du Grand Prieuré de France," in *La Reconstruction après la Guerre de Cent Ans. Actes du 104e Congrès des Sociétés Savantes. Bordeaux, 1980,* 79–122. Paris: Publications de la Sorbonne, 1981.

Derville, A. "Dîmes, Rendements du blé et 'Révolution Agricole' dans le Nord de la France au Moyen Âge." *Annales, Économies, Sociétés, Civilisations* 42 (1987): 1411–1432.

Derville, A. *L'Agriculture du Nord au Moyen Âge. Artois, Cambrésis, Flandre Wallonne.* Lille: Presse Universitaires du Septentrion, 1999.

Devroey, J.-P. "Entre Loire et Rhin: Les Fluctuations du Terroir de l'Épeautre au Moyen Age," in *L'Épeautre.* (Triticum spelta*). Histoire et Ethnologie,* edited by J.-P. Devroey and Jean-Jacques van Mol, 89–105. Treignes: Editions Dire, 1989.

Devroey, J.-P. "La Céréalculture dans le Monde Franc," in *L'Ambiente Vegetale nell'altro Medioevo,* 221–256. Spoleto: Centro Italiano di Studi Sull'alto Medioevo, 1990.

Devroey, J.-P. *Puissants et Misérables: Système Social et Monde Paysan dans l'Europe des Francs (VIIe–IXe siècles).* Bruxelles: Académie Royale de Belgique, 2006.

Dubois, H. "Le Commerce de France au Temps de Louis XI," in *La France de la Fin du XVe Siècle: Renouveau et Apogée,* directed by B. Chevalier and P. Contamine, 15–29. Paris: CNRS, 1985.

Dupâquier, J. *Histoire de la Population Française, 1. Des Origines à la Renaissance.* Paris: Presses Universitaires de France 1988.

Durliat, J. *Les Finances Publiques de Dioclétien aux Carolingiens.* Sigmaringen: Jan Thorbeke Verlag, 1990.

Epstein, S. R. *Freedom and Growth: The Rise of States and Markets in Europe, 1300–1750.* London and New York: Routledge, 2000.

Estienne, C. and J. Liébaut. *L'Agriculture et la Maison Rustique.* Paris: 1578 [1567]. http://gallica.bnf.fr/ark:/12148/bpt6k52718g.

Favier, J. "Une Ville entre Deux Vocations: La Place d'Affaires de Paris au XVe Siècle." *Annales, Économies, Sociétés, Civilisations* 79 (1974): 1245–1279.

Favier, J. *Paris au XVe siècle, 1380–1500.* Paris: Hachette 1982.

Feller, L. "Statut de la Terre et Statut des Personnes: L'Alleu Paysan dans l'Historiographie depuis Georges Duby." *Etudes Rurales* 45–46 (1997): 147–164.

Findlay, R. and M. Lundahl. "Towards a Factor Proportions Approach to Economic History: Population, Precious Metals and Prices from the Black Death to the Price Revolution," in *Bertil Ohlin: A Centennial Celebration*, edited by R. Findlay, L. Jonung and M. Lundahl, 495–528. Cambridge and London: MIT Press, 2002.

Fortescue, Sir John. *De Laudibus Legum Angliae. A New Translation*. London: T. Evans, 1775. http://find.galegroup.com/ecco/infomark.do?&contentSet=ECCOArticles&type=multipage&tabID=T001&prodId=ECCO&docId=CW125623858&source=gale&userGroupName=crepuq_mcgill&version=1.0&docLevel=FASCIMILE>.

Fossier, R. *La Terre et les Hommes en Picardie jusqu'à la fin du XIIIe Siècle*. Nouvelle Édition. Amiens: Centre Régional de Documentation Pédagogique, 1987.

Fourquin, G. *Les Campagnes de la Région Parisienne à la Fin du Moyen Âge*. Paris: Presses Universitaires de France, 1964.

Fourquin, G. "Les Débuts du Fermage: l'Exemple de Saint-Denis." *Etudes Rurales* 22–24 (1966): 7–81.

Froissart, J. *Chroniques*, edited by S. Luce. Paris: J. Renouard, 1869–1957.

Fustel de Coulanges, N. D. *L'Alleu et le Domaine rural*. Paris: Hachette, 1889.

Gallet, J. *La Seigneurie Bretonne 1450–1680: L'Exemple du Vannetais*. Paris: Publications de la Sorbonne, 1983.

Galor, O. and D. Weil. "Population, Technology and Growth: From Malthusian Stagnation to the Demographic Transition and Beyond." *American Economic Review* 90 (2000): 806–828

Gilbert, H.-F. *Traité des Prairies Artificielles . . . dans la Généralité de Paris, et sur la Culture qui lui Convient le Mieux*. Paris: Imprimerie de la Veuve d'Houry et Debure, 1789. http://gallica.bnf.fr/ark:/12148/bpt6k436.

Goldsmith, J. L. "The Crisis of the Later Middle Ages: The Case of France." *French History* 9 (1995): 417–450.

Goldsmith, J. L. *Lordship in France, 500–1500*. New York: Peter Lang, 2003.

Gould, J. D. *The Great Debasement*. Oxford: Clarendon, 1970.

Guérin, I. *La Vie Rurale en Sologne au XIVe et XVe Siècles*. Paris: SEVPEN, 1960.

Henneman, J. B. *Royal Taxation in Fourteenth-Century France: The Development of War Financing 1322–1356*. Princeton: Princeton University Press, 1971.

Henneman, J. B. *Royal Taxation in Fourteenth-Century France: The Captivity and Ransom of John II*. Philadelphia: American Philosophical Society, 1976.

Higounet, C. *La Grange de Vaulerent: Structure et Exploitation d'un Terroir Cistercien de la Plaine de France XIIe–XVe Siècle*. Paris: SEVPEN, 1965.

Higounet-Nadal, A. *Histoire du Périgord*. Toulouse: Privat, 1983.

Lartigaut, J. *Les Campagnes du Quercy après la Guerre de Cent Ans (vers. 1440–vers. 1500)*. Toulouse: Publications de Toulouse-le-Mirail, 1978.

Le Mené, M. *Les Campagnes Angevines à la Fin du Moyen Âge (vers. 1350–vers. 1530)*. Nantes: Éditions Cid, 1982.

Le Mené, M. "La Conjoncture Économique Angevine sous le Règne de Louis IX," in *La France de la Fin du XVe siècle La France de la Fin du XVe Siècle: Renouveau et Apogée*, directed by B. Chevalier and P. Contamine, 51–60. Paris: CNRS, 1985.

Le Mené, M. "Les Revenus de la Terre dans l'Ouest de la France au Moyen Âge," in *Les Revenus de la Terre: Complant, Champart, Métayage en Europe Occidentale (IXe–XVIIIe Siècles). Flaran. Septièmes Journées Internationales d'Histoire, 1981*, 9–42. Auch: Centre Culturel de l'Abbaye de Flaran, 1987.

Le Mené, M. "Métayage et Bail à Cheptel dans l'Ouest de la France (1335–1342)," in *Campagnes Médiévales: L'Homme et son Espace. Études Offertes à Robert Fossier,* edited by E. Mornet, 697–707. Paris: Publications de la Sorbonne, 1995.

Lesins, K. "Afalfa, Lucerne," in *Evolution of Crop Plants,* edited by N. Simmonds, 165–168. New York: Longman, 1976.

Lewis, P. S. "Les Pensionnaires de Louis XI," in *La France de la Fin du XVe Siècle: Renouveau et Apogée,* directed by B. Chevalier and P. Contamine, 167–181. Paris: CNRS, 1985.

Lorcin, M.-T. *Les Campagnes de la Région Lyonnaise au XIVe et XVe Siècles.* Lyon: Bosc, 1974.

Lorcin, M.-T. *Vivre et Mourir en Lyonnais à la Fin du Moyen Âge.* Paris: Editions du CNRS, 1981.

Lot, F. "L'État des Paroisses et des Feux de 1328," *Bibliothèque de l'École des Chartes* 90 (1929): 51–107, 256–315.

Magnou-Nortier, E. "Le Grand Domaine: des Maîtres, des Doctrines, des Questions," *Francia* 15 (1987): 659–700.

Magnou-Nortier, E. "La Gestion Publique en Neustrie: les Moyens et les Hommes (VIIe–IXe Siècles)," in *La Neustrie: Les Pays au Nord de la Loire de 650 à 850,* edited by H. Atsma, 271–318. Sigmaringen: Jan Thorbeke Verlag 1989.

Magnou-Nortier, E. "Capitulaire '*De Villis et Curtis Imperialibus*' (vers. 810–813) Texte, Traduction et Commentaire." *Revue Historique* 299 (1998): 643–689.

Miskimin, H. A. *Money and Power in Fifteenth-Century France.* New Haven: Yale University Press, 1984.

Moriceau, J.-M. *Les Fermiers de l'Île de France.* Paris: Fayard, 1994.

Morineau, M. *Les Faux-Semblants d'un Démarrage Économique: Agriculture et Démographie en France au XVIIIe Siècle.* Paris: Armand Colin, 1971.

Neveux, H. *Vie et Déclin d'une Structure Économique: Les Grains du Cambrésis Fin du XIVe–Début du XVIIIe Siècle.* Paris: Mouton Neveux 1980.

North D. C. and R. P. Thomas. "The Rise and Fall of the Manorial System: A Theoretical Model." *Journal of Economic History* 31 (1971): 777–803.

O'Brien, P. K. "Path Dependency: Or Why Britain Became an Industrialized and Urbanized Economy Long before France." *Economic History Review* 49 (1996): 213–249.

Olland, H. "Un Exemple de Reconstruction: Colombey-lès-Choiseul (1485–1550)," in *La Reconstruction après la Guerre de Cent Ans: Actes du 104e Congrès des Sociétés Savantes. Bordeaux, 1980,* 63–78. Paris: Publications de la Sorbonne, 1981.

Perroy, É. "À l'Origine d'une Économie Contractée: les Crises du XIVe Siècle." *Annales, Économies, Sociétés, Civilisations* 4 (1949): 167–182.

Perroy, É. *The Hundred Years War,* trans. by W. B. Well. New York: Capricorn Books, 1965.

Petrarch, *Letters from Petrarch,* trans. by M. Bishop. Bloomington: Indiana University Press, 1966.

Potter, D. *A History of France, 1460–1560: The Emergence of a Nation-State.* New York: St. Martin's Press, 1995.

Raepset, G. "Les Prémices de la Mécanisation Agricole entre Seine et Rhin de l'Antiquité au 13e Siècle." *Annales, Histoire, Science Sociale* 50 (1995): 911–942.

Raepset G. "The Development of Farm Implements between the Seine and the Rhine from the Second to the Twelfth Centuries," in *Medieval Farming and Technology: The Impact of Agricultural Change in Northwest Europe,* edited by G. Astill and J. Langdon, 41–68. Leiden, New York, Köln: Brill, 1997.

Recueil Général des Anciennes Lois Françaises De puis l'An 420 jusqu'à la Révolution de 1789. Paris: s.n., 1821–1833.

Reigniez, P. *L'Outil Agricole en France au Moyen Âge.* Paris: Errance, 2002.

Richard, J.-M. "Thierry d'Hireçon, Agriculteur Artésien, 13. 1328," *Bibliothèque de l'École des Chartes* 53 (1892): 383–416, 571–604.

Sée, H. *Les Classes Rurales et le Régime Domanial en France au Moyen Âge.* Paris: Girard et Frères, 1903.

Sicard, G. and M. Sicard, "Redevances à Part de Fruits et de Métayage dans le Sud-Ouest de la France au Moyen Âge," in *Les Revenus de la Terre: Complant, Champart, Métayage en Europe Occidentale (IXe–XVIIIe Siècles). Flaran. Septièmes Journées Internationales d'Histoire, 1981,* 61–74. Auch: Centre Culturel de l'Abbaye de Flaran, 1987.

Sivéry, G. *Saint Louis et son Siècle.* Paris: Taillandier, 1983.

Sivéry, G. *Structures Agraires et Vie Rurale dans le Hainaut à la Fin du Moyen Âge.* Lille: Presses Universitaire de Lille, 1973.

Sivery, G. "Les Tenures à Part de Fruit et le Métayage dans le Nord de la France et les Pays-Bas jusqu'au Début du XVIe Siècle," in *Les Revenus de la Terre: Complant, Champart, Métayage en Europe Occidentale (IXe–XVIIIe Siècles). Flaran. Septièmes Journées Internationales d'Histoire, 1985,* 27–42. Auch: Centre Culturel de l'Abbaye de Flaran, 1987.

Stouff, L. "Redevances à Part de Fruits et de Métayage dans la Provence Médiéval: Tasques et Facherie," in *Les Revenus de la Terre: Complant, Champart, Métayage en Europe Occidentale (IXe–XVIIIe Siècles). Flaran. Septièmes Journées Internationales d'Histoire, 1985,* 43–60. Auch: Centre Culturel de l'Abbaye de Flaran, 1987.

Tuetey, A., ed. *Journal d'un Bourgeois de Paris, 1405–1449.* Genève: Slatkine Reprints, 1975 [1881].

Tricard, J. "Livres de Raison et Présence de la Bourgeoisie dans les Campagnes Limousines (XIVe–XVe Siècle)," in *Campagnes Médiévales. L'Homme et son Espace. Études Offertes à Robert Fossier,* edited by E. Mornet, 109–122. Paris: Publications de la Sorbonne, 1995.

Tricard, J. *Les Campagnes Limousines du XIVe au XVIe siècle: Originalité et Limites d'une Reconstruction Rurale.* Paris: Publications de la Sorbonne, 1996.

Verdier, R. "Les Terriers en Dauphiné. Instruments de Résistance Seigneuriale," in *Terriers et Plans-Terriers du XIIIi^e au XVIIIi^e Siècle,* edited by G. Brunel, O. Guyotjean and J.-M. Moriceau, 207–216. Paris: École des Chartes. Bibliothèque de l'Histoire Rurale, 2002.

Weary, W. A. "La Maison de la Trémoille pendant la Renaissance: une Seigneurie Agrandie," in *La France de la Fin du XVe Siècle: Renouveau et Apogée,* directed by B. Chevalier and P. Contamine, 197–212. Paris: CNRS, 1985.

Werner, K.-F. *Naissance de la Noblesse: L'Essor des Élites Politiques en Europe.* Paris: Fayard, 1998.

Wolfe, M. *The Fiscal System of Renaissance France.* New Haven: Yale University Press, 1972.

Wright, N. *Knights and Peasants: The Hundred Years War in the French Countryside.* Woodbridge, UK: Boydell Press, 1998.

Wrigley, E. A. "The Transition to an Advanced Organic Economy: Half a Millennium of English Agriculture," *Economic History Review* 59 (2006), 435–480.

Zeven A. C., and C. J. Stemerdink. "A Cluster Analysis of Eight Medieval Manuscripts Based on Depicted Plant Taxa," *Journal d'Agriculture Tropicale et de Botanique Appliquée* 23 (1986): 225–242

Zohary M., and D. Heller. *The Genus* Trifolium. Jerusalem: Israel Academy of Science and Humanities, 1984.

4 Italy*

Paolo Malanima

At the beginning of the 1960s, two different views of the Italian Renaissance economy were proposed: the first by Roberto Sabatino Lopez and Harry Miskimin[1] and the second by Carlo Maria Cipolla.[2] According to Lopez and Miskimin, the epoch of growth from the tenth century to 1300 was followed by a period of gloom. Decline in population, and especially urban population, industry and banking, characterized the Italian economy in the century after the Black Death. This "stagnationist"[3] approach was openly criticized by Cipolla. In his view, the Italian Renaissance was not an age of crisis or depression. After the Black Death, the population diminished considerably and, with it, both the agricultural and the non-agricultural product declined in absolute terms. Probably, however, according to Cipolla, population declined much more than output and, as a consequence, per capita product rose.

In the 1960s it was impossible to support the hypothetical suggestion by Cipolla and outline Italian per capita output during the Renaissance. Very little was known at the time about either product or population. Historical research has, however, made progress since then. Nowadays data on population and urban inhabitants are available for the whole of Italy; information on prices and wages is richer; research on agricultural output, the relationships between landowners and workers, and agricultural contracts is much more advanced. Only in the case of finance, commerce, and industry—once the central interest of historians dealing with the Italian economy during the Renaissance—has progress been scantier in the last few decades. On the whole, in the case of Italy, it is possible to collect quantitative information on several economic variables since the end of the thirteenth century.

The focus in the following pages will be on the trend of product (per capita and aggregate) in agriculture, industry, and services. In all branches of activity, I will try to shed light on the production function; that is on output as a function of the level of technology (together with useful human knowledge), labor, capital, and natural resources. Since the efficiency of the economic system is a function not only of the technology, but also of the institutions, I will recall some of the main institutional changes.

From an economic viewpoint, as A. Sapori suggested in 1952, the Italian Renaissance lasted longer than it did from a cultural perspective. According to Sapori, the Renaissance economy spanned the period from the tenth or eleventh century to 1550.[4] Although this proposal is plausible, I will refer to the epoch traditionally defined as the Renaissance: that is from the second half of the thirteenth century to the second half of the sixteenth.

I will try a macroeconomic approach to the Renaissance economy, beginning in with the "Population" section. In the "Agriculture" and "The Non-agricultural Sectors," I will deal with the output of agriculture, followed by industry and services. In the section "The Product of the Renaissance Economy," the product of the three sectors will be combined to provide a complete view of per capita and aggregate product. An explanation of the main changes will be presented in the "Growth and Decline" section.

Since the available quantitative data especially concern the Center and the North, the following reconstruction will refer primarily to this part of Italy.

POPULATION

Trends and Density

Although population censuses for Italy are only available from the sixteenth century onward, fiscal documents on rural and urban inhabitants dating back to the late thirteenth century allow us to outline the demographic trend of the Italian population. Recently population figures for 1300 have been increased by about 10 percent,[5] while later figures have hardly been modified.[6] Research on specific regions more or less confirms the trend proposed in the past by Karl Julius Beloch in a study that is still the major basic reconstruction of the Italian population since the late Middle Ages.[7] Although the series of population for Italy as a whole are usually presented for 50 years intervals, it is possible to interpolate decadal figures (Figure 4.1).[8] A range of uncertainty of 10 percent around our figures on the fourteenth and fifteenth centuries would be considered plausible by most medievalists. The range diminishes from the sixteenth century.[9]

Several distinct periods (similar to the demographic trend of most European regions) can be identified:

- following a period of growth, which probably began in the tenth century, the medieval Italian population reached its peak in the decades after 1300, with about 12–13 million inhabitants;

- the Black Death in 1348–49 started the epoch of demographic decline. Several plague epidemics, after the first outbreak, intensified the fall in the following decades. The lowest level was attained in 1420–40, when the population was scarcely higher than seven million;
- a period of recovery followed. The level of population of the first half of the fourteenth century was reached again, and probably exceeded, at the beginning of the seventeenth century, when the Italian population was about 13.3 million inhabitants. In a region such as Tuscany, whose demographic history is better known, the pre-Black Death level (estimated at about 1.1 million) had not yet been reached in 1620–30 (when the inhabitants were 960,000).

During the Renaissance, the density of population in Italy was, in comparative terms, particularly high. In 1300, when there were in Europe (without Russia) nine inhabitants per km^2, the Italian average was 41.5. If we refer to the Center and North of Italy—the most inhabited part of the country—the density was 48.1, while in England and France it was around 30, and in Germany about 24.[10] Italian demographic density decreased to 25–30 in the fifteenth century and rose again to the 1300 level at the end of the sixteenth century.

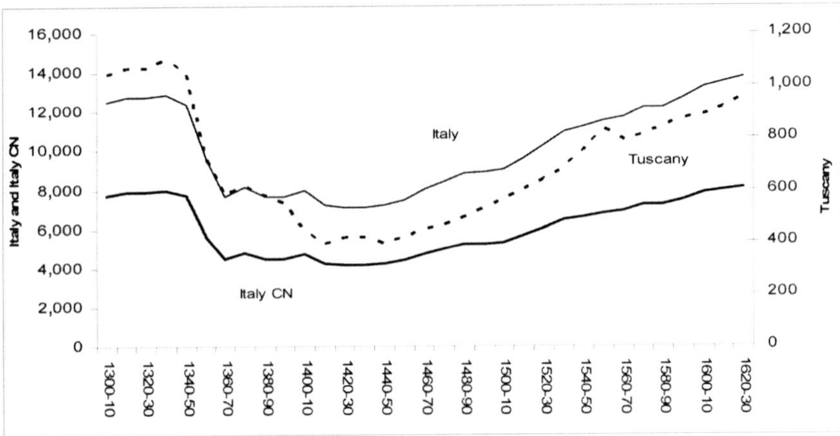

Figure 4.1 Italian population in the Center and North and in Tuscany (1300–1630) (decadal data).

Note: The left vertical axis refers to the population of Italy and Central and North of Italy (000); the axis to the right refers to the population of Tuscany (000).

Sources: Beloch, *Bevölkerungsgeschichte Italiens,* and *La popolazione d'Italia*, Bellettini, *La popolazione italiana*, Del Panta, Livi Bacci, Pinto, Sonnino *La popolazione italiana dal Medioevo a oggi*. For Tuscany: Breschi, Malanima, *Demografia ed economia in Toscana: il lungo periodo (secoli XIV–XIX)*, in M. Breschi, P. Malanima (eds.), *Prezzi, redditi, popolazioni in Italia: 600 anni (dal secolo XIV al secolo XX)* (Udine: Forum, 2002).

Population and Prices

Information on prices is available for several cities from the late Middle Ages onwards, although the best documented area is Tuscany. Both private (account books) and public documents allow the reconstruction of a yearly index from the late thirteenth century. Non-Tuscan data has been used for comparative purposes (Figure 4.2).[11]

It is well-known that, in pre-modern economies, a direct relationship between population and prices exists. Agricultural prices rose from the beginning of the thirteenth century, and, more rapidly, from about 1270, when the population was rising.[12] The upward trend continued for some decades after the Black Death. It is to be noted that Italian prices did not immediately diminish after the fall in population. The wider availability of money in most families and rising demand continued to fuel the upward trend in prices.[13] From about 1390 prices began to diminish, reaching their lowest level in 1420–60. A new rise started from 1470. Sixteenth century demographic growth was accompanied by the upward trend of prices. The end of the period in question is also the end of the so-called 'price revolution' in Italy. From 1600 onwards, the index declines.

AGRICULTURE

Natural Resources and Land Productivity

The dense Italian population inhabited a region of Europe relatively poor in natural resources, in comparative terms. Italy shares its physical

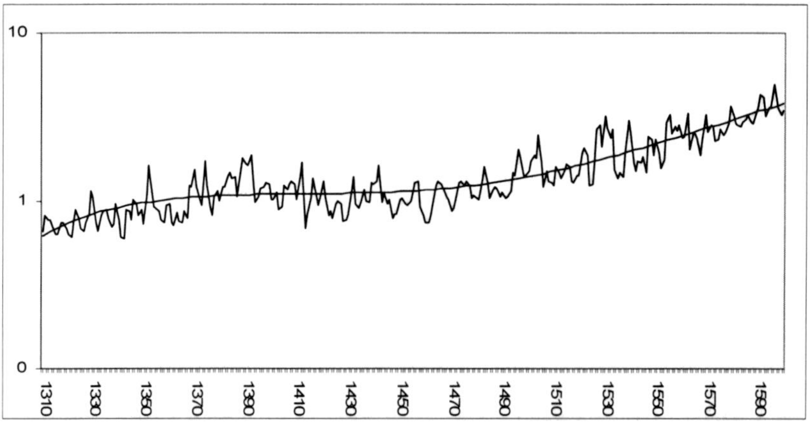

Figure 4.2 Price index 1310–1600 (1420–40=1) (log vertical axis).
Note: Polynomial trend (3rd degree equation).
Source: Appendix (col. 1).

characteristics with the other Mediterranean regions. Plains are scarce; cereal production per hectare is modest. The scarcity of arable land is partially compensated by the availability of soils suitable for the cultivation of trees and particularly vineyards. In Italy, 40 percent of the surface is made up of hills (between 300 and 600–700 meters above sea level); another 40 percent is covered with mountains (more than 700 meters above sea level). A mere 20 percent of the peninsula is flat, the only big plains being located in the Po Valley in the North and Apulia in the South. In the past, traditional arable agriculture covered, on the whole, about 45 percent of Italian territory, that is, all the plains and part of the hills.[14]

As is the case elsewhere in Europe, with the exception of England, data on yields are very scanty until the fourteenth century. For previous centuries we have data from the land inventories of religious institutions. For the late Middle Ages information collected by historians refers only to the Center and the North of the peninsula and is based on farms' accounting books.

On the scarce Italian arable land cereal yields are low, in comparison with Northern European regions, due particularly to soil aridity in spring and summer. We know that from the tenth to the fourteenth century, wheat yields rose in Italy from two quintals per hectare or less, to between 3.5 and five (Table 4.1).[15] The desertion of unproductive soils after the Black Death contributed to the rise in the level of yields from 1350 to about 1550.[16] The level then attained was only to be exceeded at the end of the nineteenth century. In the first half of the nineteenth century yields were in the range five to nine quintals per hectare in the North, four to eight in the Center, and three to seven in the South.[17] Land intensification was higher where the density of population was higher.[18] A comparison with England reveals a deep and increasing difference from the late Middle Ages onwards.[19]

Table 4.1 Wheat Yield in the Center and North of Italy from 1150 to 1650 (Quintals per Hectare)

	Italy CN
1150–1250	3.6
1250–1350	3.6-4.8
1350–1450	4.8-6.0
1450–1550	6.0
1550–1650	5.8

Note: The available data for Italy refer to yields per seed and not per hectare. In order to work out yields per hectare, I have assumed 120 kg per hectare as seed quantity.

Sources: Malanima, *La fine del primato. Crisi e riconversione nell'Italia del Seicento* (Milano: Bruno Mondadori, 1998): 42; Malanima, *L'economia italiana*.

Climate

Often natural resources in a region are considered invariable, but climatic changes can deeply influence resource availability, especially in the fragile Mediterranean landscapes.[20] I have already recalled that, in Italy, 40 percent of the territory is hilly. Now we know that a change of only one degree in the average temperature is likely to displace the altitude of wheat cultivation by about 100 meters above sea level.[21] Of the 31 million hectares that make up the whole of Italy, land between 600 and 700 meters covers more than two million hectares. A fall in the temperature of only one degree implies a drop in cultivation from 700 to 600 meters, and a decline in wheat production by an amount that could feed one to two million people.

Thanks to recent research, we now know the change in temperature in the region of the Alps during late medieval growth and the Renaissance (Figure 4.3).[22] It may be noted that the early medieval rise in population coincided with the so-called *Medieval Climatic Optimum*.[23] Temperature maxima during the Medieval Warm Period, between 800 and 1300, were on average about 1.7°C higher than the minima in the Little Ice Age and similar to present-day values. For a hilly country such as Italy the increase in natural resources, thanks to mild temperatures, contributed to supporting economic progress during the High Middle Ages, allowing the long-term cultivation of many more lands than before. Population rose accordingly and stabilized in the first decades of the fourteenth century, just when the so-called Little Ice Age was beginning.[24] Cultivation could no longer be carried out on parts of the hills. The decline in the average temperature from the late thirteenth century meant a sharp drop in food supply for thousands of people, while famines, unknown for several

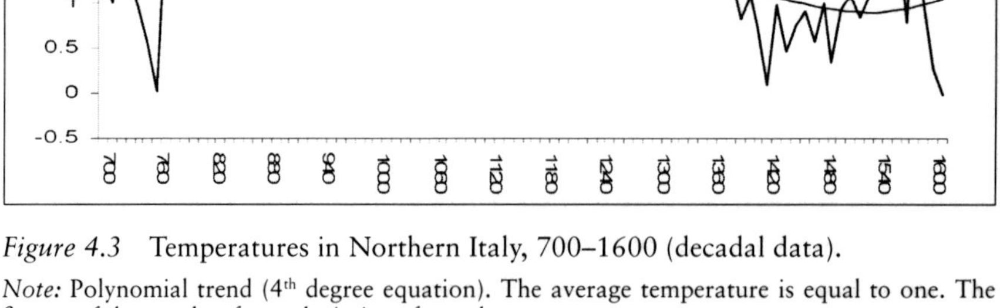

Figure 4.3 Temperatures in Northern Italy, 700–1600 (decadal data).

Note: Polynomial trend (4th degree equation). The average temperature is equal to one. The figures of the graph refer to deviations from the average.

Source: Mangini, Spötl, Verdes, *Reconstruction of Temperature in the Central Alps During the Past 2000 years*, in "Earth and Planetary Science Letters", (2005) 235, 3–4: 741–751.

centuries, began once more to hit the Italian population.[25] The sharp fall in the volume of agricultural output was not compensated by the rise occurring at the same time in per hectare yields, due, as we saw, to the abandonment of the least productive lands and the cultivation of the most productive soils. This change in temperature is likely to have influenced the course of the Italian economy (and others) much more than changes in institutions and techniques so often mentioned by historians.

Resources and Capital

The wealth of the Italian nation in 1861 has been calculated as 46–47 billion lire.[26] Estimates concerning the late nineteenth century and, obviously even more so, those relating to the late Middle Ages suggest nothing more than orders of magnitude and their long-term trend. Lands and dwellings in the countryside represented in 1861 almost half the total wealth: 22 billion lire. Since dwellings were evaluated at 1.6 billion lire, the agricultural wealth of Italy was made up of land transformed by centuries of labour and capital investment. Livestock, not included in the earlier calculation, was 1.5 billion lire.

Richard Goldsmith proposed an estimate of the wealth of the Florentine Republic in 1427, based on the Catasto.[27] The total wealth of about 17.4 million florins, corresponding to six times the annual output, was composed primarily of real estate and residential structures (68 percent). Resources per head of population were then high because of the high mortality resulting from several plagues. The new upward trend of population from the mid-fifteenth century is likely to have provoked a decline in capital and resources per worker. In the Republic of Florence, wealth per capita in 1427 was 30–40 percent higher than in Italy in 1861.[28]

During the phase of medieval growth, which came to an end after 1300, capital formation in the cities flowed towards agriculture.[29] We know that, in the following centuries, as population pressure intensified, sizeable investments were made in land reclamation. Since capital formation is a function of the marginal efficiency of capital, and since marginal efficiency of capital depends on technological progress, for the Renaissance period[30] we cannot but expect a low level of investment in a *mature agrarian economy* such as that of Italy. As will be seen, the indirect evidence, based on wage trends, suggests diminishing marginal labor productivity from the late Middle Ages onwards. A plausible determinant of this decline is the fall in capital and resources per worker, while technological progress was unable to reverse the downward trend.

Labor and Institutions

During the medieval phase of growth, from the tenth to the fourteenth century, important changes occurred in the agricultural labor market and especially in the institutions regulating the supply of labor. Seigneurial power weakened and the feudal dependence of peasant workers on landowners diminished and then vanished.[31] The manor as the institution that regulated peasant agricultural work disappeared during the eleventh and twelfth centuries.[32] Only in some northern mountainous areas, far from the urban agglomerations, and in the South, did seigneurs hold on, at least partly, to their feudal juridical power over rural populations. The causes often referred to, when dealing with the decline of this institution, are the progress of the market economy in the late Middle Ages, on the one hand, and the struggle by the urban communes against the feudal lords in the countryside, on the other. Several documents in which towns decreed the full personal freedom of the serfs are preserved.[33] This institutional change contributed to a more efficient allocation of labor and probably enhanced labor productivity in the countryside and cities, as a consequence of higher labor mobility.

The disappearance of the manorial economy was followed by the proliferation of small landownership. However, from the fourteenth century, which is when land censuses become available for some areas in the Center, small ownership was rapidly diminishing.[34] Rural families were forced to depend more and more on landowners and to work their lands on the basis of rent contracts. For the cultivation of their lands, use of wage labor by landowners was not widespread.

Sources, such as the agrarian contracts, allow for a satisfactory view of agrarian production relationships during the late Middle Ages. The topic has been the subject of abundant literature.[35] The disappearance of the manorial economy was followed by forms of land rent; either the rent was paid in kind (as in the case of the share tenancy, widespread from the fourteenth century, especially in Central Italy) or in money, as was common in the Po Valley. Wage labor was not widespread in the Italian Renaissance countryside. We have no direct information on its importance, although most medievalists would agree on a magnitude of 10–20 percent of the whole labor force being employed in agriculture (but not all the year round). The percentage was higher in Southern Italy than in the North. Advanced banking techniques in the cities co-existed in the North with a countryside where money was almost unknown by the peasant families. This is a feature peculiar to this region of Europe.

Wage rates, usually per day, provide detailed information on labor incomes and labor productivity. Indirect information—especially rent contracts—suggests that, where peasants were not employed as wage laborers, but as farmers whose income was made up of the share of total product after the payment of the rent,[36] the general trend was similar to that of the wage rates: that is, declining after the fifteenth century.[37] Competition among workers, despite labor market constraints, implied the convergence of diverse forms of labor income towards the level of money wages.

Innovations and Techniques

The period in question was not an innovative epoch. From the fifteenth century on, in the Center and North, the only meaningful change was the spread of the mulberry tree providing raw material for the developing silk industry.[38] By contrast, maize and rice only began to spread from the second half of the sixteenth century, at the end of the period we are dealing with, and their influence on land productivity was modest until a century later. Changes in the density of population were therefore followed by extensive growth and intensification in the exploitation of land. During the Renaissance, three-field rotation prevailed on the plains, while on the hills the two-field system and even the swidden, or shifting cultivation, were relatively widespread. In Roman antiquity, in the fertile plains of the Po Valley, convertible husbandry was already practised. It was again to be found during the late Middle Ages especially between Lodi, Milan, and Cremona, over an area where wet agriculture prevailed and where the urban elite and governments had invested in drainage and canal building.[39] Here, as regards the seed, a yield to seed ratio of 8:1 was sometimes reached, while the usual level on Italian arable land was around 4:1 to 6:1.[40]

As far as techniques for raising labor productivity in agriculture are concerned, no change took place during this period. The simple symmetric plow (with the exception of the Po Valley, where the asymmetric wheel-plow was already known in antiquity), the scarcity of draft animals and the widespread use of the spade and hoe continued to characterize this Mediterranean countryside. Italian agriculture between 1300 and 1600 could be defined as a *mature technological system*. During the Renaissance no significant change took place in the use of plows, working animals, or tools.[41] Only from 1800 on, and especially from the end of the nineteenth century, as recent research shows, new engines began to raise the level of labor productivity remarkably.[42]

Capital formation is spurred on by technological progress and then a growing marginal efficiency of capital. When technology and therefore agricultural and industrial growth are stagnating, any surpluses are more advantageously used in conspicuous consumption, such as building villas in the countryside, than in investment in agriculture or industry. Ample evidence on this kind of investment is still noticeable both in the cities and countryside.

Rural Wages

Documents on agricultural wages in the late Middle Ages are scanty. In Tuscany notarial documents and the account books of private and public institutions allow us to build a continuous yearly series of wage rates spanning the long period from 1320 to 1600.[43]

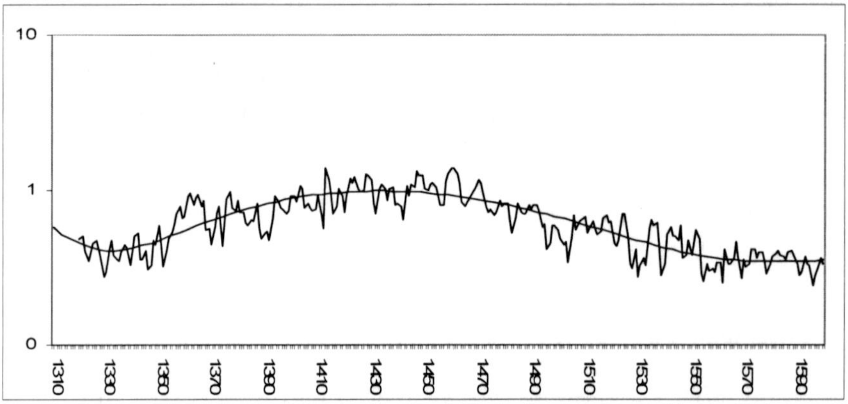

Figure 4.4 Index of real wage rates in agriculture, 1320–1600 (1420–40=1) (log vertical axis).

Note: Polynomial trend (5th degree equation).
Source: Appendix (col. 2).

Real agricultural wage rates show the following trend (Figure 4.4):[44]

- a decline prior to the Black Death;
- a strong increase from 1350 to 1460–70;
- a steep decline from 1460–70 to 1600.

It is, however, important to remember that a wage—per week, per month, or per year—is the result of the wage rate multiplied by the time actually worked. For the period we are dealing with, we know the level of wage rates, but not wages, since we do not know how many hours were worked in a year. It is plausible to suppose that, while wage rates increased and then decreased sharply in the period under examination, peasants worked shorter hours when wage rates were high and vice versa.[45] An intensification of labour—more workers and more hours per year—took place during the sixteenth century.[46]

The wages-population relationship is clearly inverse: decline in population as a consequence of the plague implied a rise in capital and resources per worker and subsequently in productivity and wage rates, whereas population growth from the mid-fifteenth century onwards implied decline in productivity and subsequently in wage rates.

Agricultural Product

Yearly series of population, prices, wages, and temperatures, together with information on technology already make it possible to draw some provisional conclusions on the trend of the rural economy. We saw that in the last phase of medieval growth the pressure of population was increasing. As far as

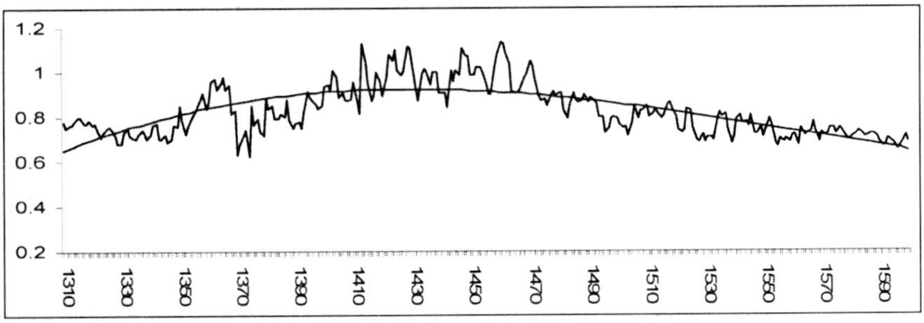

Figure 4.5 Per capita agricultural product, 1310–1600 (1420–40=1).
Note: Polynomial trend (3rd degree equation).
Source: Appendix (col. 5).

agriculture is concerned the unfavorable climatic conditions on the one hand and the technical stagnation on the other, together with the drop in resources and capital per worker were contributing to a decline in rural labor productivity. As a consequence, labor incomes were already diminishing in the decades before the Black Death.[47] However, the arrival of the plague and the subsequent high mortality were able to invert the trend for about a century.

Since direct information on the agricultural product for the epoch in question is scarce and refers, in any case, to small farms and short periods, we can draw a general outline of the trend of agricultural product by combining the information from the series on prices and wages.[48]

The graph (Figure 4.5) can be considered as the synthetic result of multiple events taking place both in prices (agricultural and non-agricultural) and labor incomes. Per capita agricultural output immediately rose following the Black Death; then, after declining for a decade, it rose continuously until 1420–60, to diminish thereafter until the end of the sixteenth century. The hypothesis of agricultural prosperity for about a century after the Black Death seems better supported by the evidence than is the view of decline. However, agricultural output represents only a part, although a large part, of the total product. Our attention must now be turned to the non-agricultural side of the economy.

THE NON-AGRICULTURAL SECTORS

Cities

Data on urban inhabitants have been collected by scholars from different sources such as fiscal documents, chronicles, the number of men able to bear arms, professional groups (such as notaries), and population censuses (in this case only from the sixteenth century).[49] The degree of reliability improves during the period here in question.[50]

Since the late Middle Ages, the Center and North Italy have been characterized by several big cities, without a dominating capital city (such as Paris, London, Constantinople or, in early modern Southern Italy, Naples). The nature of Italian urbanisation, at least from the late Middle Ages until today, could be defined as polycentric (see Map).

In the centuries we are dealing with, between 59 and 96 centers were inhabited by more than 5,000 inhabitants and 21 to 53 by more than 10,000. This polycentric character is clearly revealed by the rank-size distribution (the distribution of towns according to their size), which was quite stable between 1300 and 1600 (Table 2). The number of cities dropped in the fifteenth century. The decline in total population also resulted in a fall in urbanization.[51]

Figure 4.6 Main Italian cities in 1300 (with more than 15,000 inhabitants).

Table 4.2 Number of Italian Cities (with More Than 5,000, 10,000, and 20,000 Inhabitants) and Coefficients of the Rank-Size Distribution, 1300–1600

	Number>5,000	*Number>10,000*	*Number>20,000*	*Coefficientsr-s-d*
1300	193	79	26	0.72
1400	94	26	15	0.72
1500	146	51	18	0.75
1600	208	75	25	0.75

Note: The coefficients of the rank-size distribution are computed through the following regression: $\log S_r = S_1 - u \log r$: where S_r is the size (the population) of a particular city; S_1 the size of the first (main) city; and r the rank (represented by the series of natural numbers from 1, the main city, to n, the smallest city). The coefficient u is represented in column 5. While a result higher than 1 is correlated with the presence of one or more large dominating cities, a less steep slope, as in the case of Italy, suggests a more polycentric distribution.

Source: Malanima, "Urbanisation and the Italian Economy".

Apart from the three main centers with more than 100,000 inhabitants in 1300, Florence, Milan, and Venice, several significant towns were located in the northern half of the peninsula and above all in the Po Valley and in the Center. Naples was already a large city, with more than 30,000 inhabitants, but was not yet in the leading group. Big cities in the South were fewer than the North.

All these towns grew during the medieval expansion, from the tenth to the fourteenth century, thanks to the immigration of people from the countryside, supported by the remarkable progress of industrial activities and services (political, administrative, religious, military, and economic), and the struggle against feudal powers of the communes, whose interest was to allow the mobility of rural inhabitants towards the developing urban industries.[52]

The Urban Sectors

Today economic growth theories have repeatedly emphasized the role of human interchange in the rise of useful knowledge.[53] This interchange or intercommunication is likely to take place primarily, and almost exclusively, in the cities. Between 1300 and 1600, Italian centers of more than 5,000 inhabitants comprised a population between 2.5 and three million (in 1300 and 1600) and 1.1 million (in 1400). The impact of human interaction is likely to have been much stronger within this European region than elsewhere in the continent. Nowhere was the rate of urbanization over a relatively wide area as high as in the Italian peninsula. Only in Flanders, in an area 10 times smaller than Italy, was the rate of urbanization higher. The effects of urban culture on technological progress and innovation have often been emphasized. The Renaissance was, after all, the outcome of urban culture in the most urbanized areas of Europe.[54]

Especially after 1350, the expansionist policy of the major, and financially strong, Italian cities pushed toward the formation of regional states whose main examples are the Republics of Florence, Venice, and Genoa and the State of Milan. Several minor states continued to exist in the interstices of the main regional city-states.[55] The fragmentation of the political scene in the North was the result of the competition and struggle among many strong rival cities.

In the South the situation was different; it was more similar to that taking place north of the Alps, with the formation of a relatively large kingdom with a sizeable capital, Naples, seat of the crown, court, and aristocracy. No other city or center of power was able to shatter in the South the Neapolitan supremacy, with the exception of the Papal State, another important seat of power able to counterbalance other peninsular powers both in the South and the North.

On the basis of indirect information, we know that in the thirteenth century immigration into the cities rose thanks to increasing textile (wool, cotton, and silk) and banking activities, which formed the basis of the economy and were the dominating sectors. Ample literature is available on these urban sectors. For a long time, until the 1970s, urban industries and trade were the central interest of the medieval economic historian.[56]

While there were no meaningful technological innovations in agriculture in the period we are dealing with, by contrast, we know that technological changes and new industrial sectors (such as printing) were spreading within urban economies. Indirect evidence of technological dualism in agriculture and industry is provided by the relative trends of agricultural and industrial prices (Figure 4.7).[57]

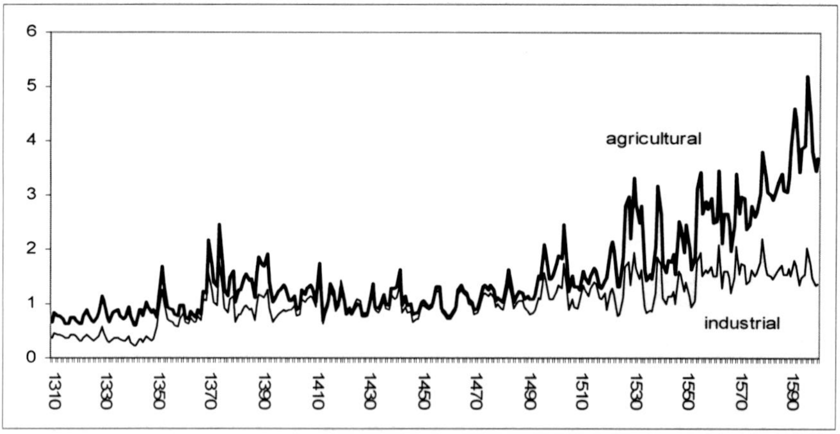

Figure 4.7 Agricultural and industrial price indices, 1310–1600 (1420–40=1).
Source: Malanima, *L'economia italiana*: 405.

We see that, during the sixteenth century, while agricultural prices were rising under the pressure of the population, industrial prices grew much less. A noteworthy example is represented by the prices of silk textiles, where innovative techniques and forms of organization were progressing fast and making labor more efficient.[58]

Labor and Wages

Wages can suggest the trend of labor productivity within the cities. While in agriculture wages were not the ordinary form of income from labor, in the cities the majority of the population depended on wages for subsistence. Wage rates, therefore, provide an important clue to the conditions and standards of living of a considerable percentage of the population. Series of wages in the building industry, usually based on the account books of rich families and institutions, have been elaborated. Once again more data are available for Tuscany than other Italian areas, but we have series of wages for Venice from 1380, Genoa from 1500, and Naples from 1530.[59]

Masons' wage rates suggest a trend shared by many other urban workers (Figure 4.8).[60]

The same three phases already stressed in the case of agricultural laborers are to be found in the movement of masons' wage rates, although with some differences in intensity:

- the decline prior to the Black Death is clear both for urban and rural workers;

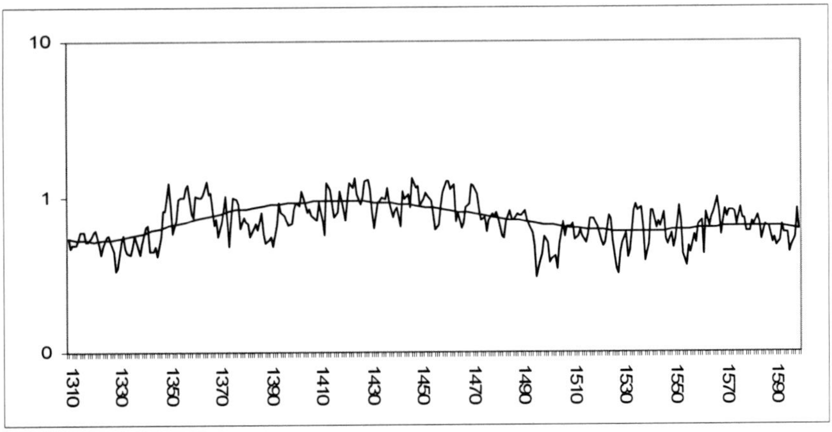

Figure 4.8 Index of real masons' wage rates, 1310–1600 (1420–40=1) (log vertical axis).

Note: Polynomial trend (5th degree equation).

Source: Appendix (col. 3).

- the increase from 1350 to 1460–70 is more modest for urban than rural workers;[61]
- the decline from 1460–70 to 1600 is not so steep and, in any case, not so continuous.

Urbanization

In 1300 Italian urbanization, particularly in the Center and North, was considerably higher than elsewhere in Europe. In the South, together with the islands (Sicily and Sardinia), the level was lower in 1300 and 1400, although still high from a European perspective. It is uncertain if in this epoch some backwardness of the Southern economy relative to the North already characterized the Italian economy. Although the existence of two Italies has been suggested,[62] nothing certain can be said about a North-South disparity in the late Middle Ages (Table 4.3).

The trend of urbanization suggests a decline during the fifteenth century, a recovery in between 1450 and 1550, and another decline thereafter, at least in the Center and North. Urbanization apparently grew in the South and the islands, although it was a consequence of the rising number of large centers inhabited by peasant families, which could be defined as 'agro-towns,' rather than true cities.[63]

A plausible explanation for the decline in the rate of urbanization in the fifteenth century is that, in Euro-Mediterranean cities, depopulated after the Black Death, the customers of luxury Italian industries and services were fewer and more dispersed, pushing up the cost of transportation: the accessible clientele had diminished.

Although in the cities a generally small percentage of the population worked in the primary sector, and in the villages there were always some craftsmen, the rate of urbanization (when centers with more than 5,000 inhabitants are included) provides good information on the relative ratio of non-agricultural employment. Urbanization rates are, however, lower than the percentage of population working outside agriculture. Data on

Table 4.3 Urbanization Rates in Central and Northern Italy (CN), in the South with the Islands (SI), and in the Whole of Italy (Centers with 5,000 inhabitants and More), 1300–1600 (%)

	CN	*SI*	*Italy*
1300	21.4	18.6	20.3
1400	17.6	8.5	13.9
1500	21.0	21.5	21.2
1600	18.4	28.6	22.6

Source: Malanima, *Urbanisation and the Italian Economy.*

urbanization suggest that 15–25 percent of the population were employed in secondary and tertiary jobs. It may be supposed that another 5–10 percent of non-agricultural workers lived in the countryside.

Capital Formation in the Towns

It is a widespread opinion that Italian cities were rich and that in these cities inequality was notable; a fact confirmed by scholarly research on Renaissance Tuscany.[64] We also know that financial institutions existed and were able to channel savings into capital. During the High Middle Ages, the phase of progress up to about 1300, the savings of landowners and especially merchants were invested both in the countryside and towns. From the middle of the fourteenth century to about 1450 the fall in population implied a rise in fixed capital and natural resources per worker, as the high level of labor productivity and wage rates confirm.[65] Probably the need for investment was low, as the decline in the rate of interest also suggests.[66] The wealth of rich urban families was channeled towards buildings, a form of relatively unproductive capital, and art.

The prevailing low rate of interest during the sixteenth century testifies to the fact that, in the mature Italian economy, given technological stability in the primary sector, the low marginal productivity of capital did not attract savings. To the question often asked by historians, whether capital formation was low because the rich Italian families used their incomes on palaces, churches, and art we could answer that, since the productivity of investment was low, rich families spent their incomes in a more socially attractive way.[67] Buildings and art are rather the consequence of the low capital formation than the cause.

Non-agricultural Product

As mentioned earlier, secondary and tertiary sectors were not wholly concentrated in the towns, although the majority were urban. In the period with which we are dealing, no remarkable changes took place in this town-country distribution. As far as we know, the fifteenth century was not an age of proto-industrialization.

For industry and trade, as with agrarian production, direct information on the output of commodities and services refers only to specific firms and banks or companies. On the whole, it is insufficient for trying to define the general movement of non-agricultural product. However, we can trace a trend on the basis of information concerning urbanization. In the Center and North of Italy the level of urbanization after the Unification (1861) and in the following decades was more or less in the same range as in the late Medieval and early Modern Ages. On that basis we can compute the share of the non-agricultural per capita product in previous centuries (Table 4.4).[68]

Table 4.4 The Percentage of the Non-agricultural Sectors in the Gross Product, 1300–1650, in the Center and North of Italy

	%
1300	49.3
1350	42.6
1400	42.4
1450	41.3
1500	48.6
1550	46.7
1600	43.8
1650	38.0

Source: Malanima, "Measuring" and Malanima, "The Long Decline of a Leading Economy: GDP in Central and Northern Italy 1300–1913."

First, it may be seen that the proportion of non-agricultural output in the total GDP is higher in this pre-modern Italian economy than often assumed by scholars dealing with pre-modern agrarian economies. In part, this result depends on the relatively advanced character of the Italian Renaissance economy. It also depends, however, on the underestimation by historians, when dealing with the pre-modern economies, of the non-agricultural product and especially of services. Probably not only in Italy, but elsewhere in Europe, industry and services together represented about 40–50 percent of the gross product in the period in question.[69]

In Italy, the non-agricultural share of product was over 10 percentage points higher in 1300 than in 1650. In the fifteenth century the curve drawn by Italian industries and services diminished sharply, to return to the level of 1300 in the first half of the sixteenth century, and then to fall again, reaching its lowest level since the Middle Ages in 1650. This result concurs with the trend often suggested by past historians on the basis of the fragmentary evidence provided by the production of specific sectors and companies. The increase in the agricultural product contributed to counterbalancing the decline of non-agricultural output during the fifteenth century.

THE PRODUCT OF THE RENAISSANCE ECONOMY

An Index of Wage Rates

We are now able to compose an aggregate view of incomes and product.

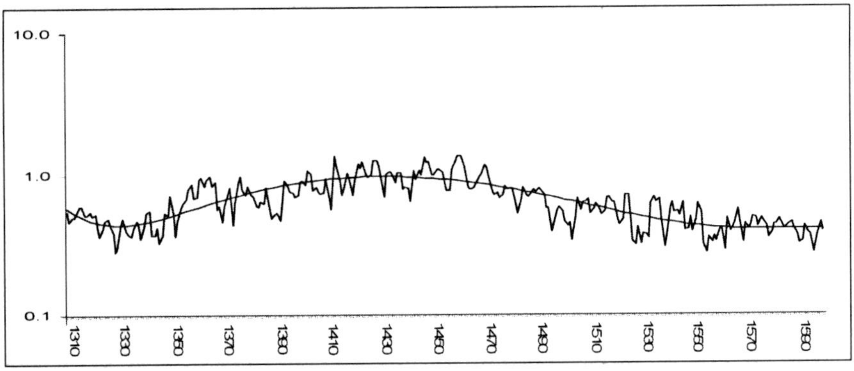

Figure 4.9 Index of wage rates, 1310–1600 (1420–40=1)(log vertical axis).
Note: Polynomial trend (5th degree equation).
Source: Appendix (col. 6).

The index of labor incomes is based on earlier indices of rural and urban wage rates, weighted by the relative importaznce of the rural and urban labor forces,[70] proxied by urbanization rates (Figure 4.9).[71]

Since a higher percentage of the labor force was in the countryside than in the towns, the result corresponds more closely to agricultural than to urban wages. The trend confirms the decline between 1300–50, the increase culminating in 1420–60, and the subsequent fall.

An Index of Per Capita Product

On the basis of agricultural output, and the percentage of non-agricultural, it is now possible to present a view of the Italian product, both per capita and aggregate (Figure 4.10).[72]

We can distinguish three phases in the trend over three centuries:

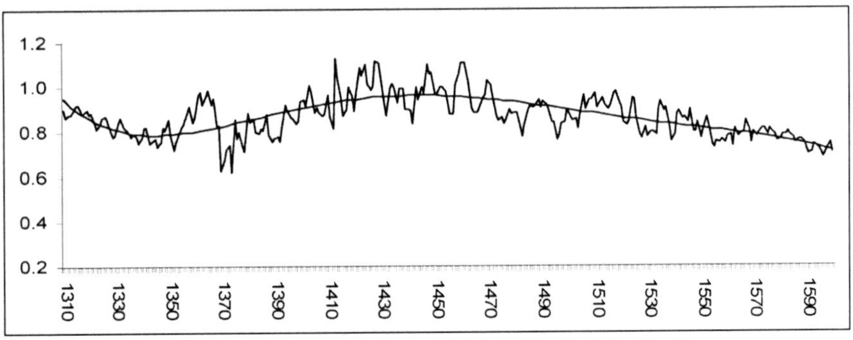

Figure 4.10 Index of per capita product, 1310–1600 (1420–40=1).
Note: Polynomial trend (5th degree equation).
Source: Appendix (col. 6).

1. the decline from a high level during the first half of the 14th century, lasting until 1370;[73]
2. the rise from 1370 to 1470;
3. the fall from 1470 to the end of our series (with some decades of recovery between the 1490s and 1520s).

The relatively high level around 1300 was the result of the urban economy (50 percent of the product); the fifteenth century peak was based, by contrast, on agriculture (urban output per capita was, in fact, diminishing); again, for some decades between 1480–1550, secondary and tertiary sectors partially compensated the agricultural decline. A clearly downward trend was only visible from the second half of the sixteenth century. On the whole, agricultural and non-agricultural sectors counterbalanced themselves and maintained a high level of output and income from 1300 to the middle of the sixteenth century.

International comparisons are difficult for the period we are dealing with. We can only say that in the decades 1420–60 the highest level in Italy is close to that attained by the Netherlands in 1650–1700 and by the United Kingdom in 1820.[74] Between the late Middle Ages and the start of modern growth these three leading economies shared quite similar levels of average product.[75]

Since we have two reliable estimates on per capita product for the Florentine Republic in 1427–40, we can check the previous series through a comparison between the first half of the fifteenth century and the period after the Unification.[76] We discover that both direct data (deflated by means of our price index) and the index of per capita product, suggest a decline of about 25–30 percent between about 1420–40 and 1860–70.[77] From the Renaissance period onwards, the Italian economic trend was more or less downward until the start of relatively recent modern growth, which began in Italy around 1880.

An Index of Gross Product

Since changes in per capita product fluctuated within a narrow range, the trend of the aggregate product between 1300–1600 closely follows that of population (Figure 4.11).[78]

While there was no crisis in per capita product during the Renaissance, gross product diminished sharply just when average incomes were at their highest level.

GROWTH AND DECLINE

The Intensive Production Function

To explain the trend, we can start from a production function, including resources together with capital and labor:

$$Y = TF(L,K,R)$$

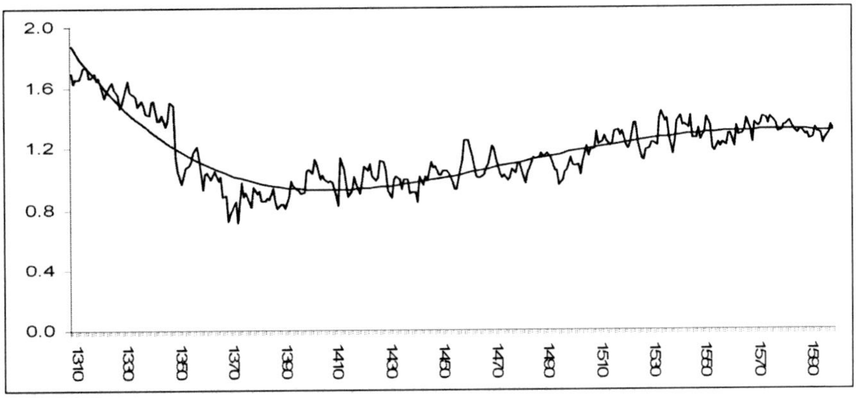

Figure 4.11 Index of gross product in the Center and North of Italy, 1310–1600 (1420–40=1).

Note: Polynomial trend (4th degree equation).
Source: Appendix (col. 7).

where Y is product, T the level of technology together with human useful knowledge, and L, K, and R are the production factors: respectively labor, capital, and natural resources.

A clearer view is given by the so-called intensive form of the production function; here obtained by dividing both the dependent and independent variables by labor (L):

$$\frac{Y}{L} = TF\left(\frac{K}{L}, \frac{R}{L}\right)$$

The dependent variable is now the average labor productivity (Y/L). A direct relationship exists between Y/L, on the one hand, and capital (K/L) and natural resources per worker (R/L), both multiplied by the level of technique (T), on the other.

The Trend: 1300–48

Technological change was unable, in the long run, to counterbalance the declining ratios K/L and R/L and make capital or resources more productive. The ratio R/L diminished as a consequence both of rising population and worsening climatic conditions from the end of the thirteenth century. Capital per worker did not compensate this fall, as the drop in wage rates show. Productivity (Y/L) was declining in the first half of the fourteenth century when population was about 12–13 million. The reasons for this trend lie in the interplay of R, K, and L in the background of a relatively stable level of technology. The high medieval growth was reaching its phase of *maturity*. The favorable epoch of slow progress, supported by good climatic conditions (and subsequently more natural resources), investment in agriculture, and institutional changes was coming to an end. From this viewpoint, Lopez and Miskimin were correct in their analysis.

The Trend: 1348–1470

The arrival of the Black Death in 1348 changed the picture radically. Epidemics are exogenous in relation to the production function. Worsening economic conditions in the previous decades cannot be considered as a determinant of plague. Plague is, after all, a random variable. Its spread, however, was favored by the high density of population (which fostered a higher probability of infection and transmission of disease and a more unhygienic environment, with more rats and fleas). Necessity and chance are connected in the spread of epidemics. Population growth does not cause infection directly, but indirectly fosters the probability of infection. The relationship between economy and epidemics is not deterministic.

Plague caused a sudden change in the production function. It destroyed men, but not resources and capital. The drastic fall in available labor implied a change in the ratios K/L and R/L. Capital and resources per worker rose rapidly because of the fall in the denominator. Both labor productivity and wage rates improved. A favorable epoch began for the survivors of the Black Death and the frequent plagues that followed. The high living standards during the Italian Renaissance, similar to those of the Dutch Golden Age some 200 years later, were supported by the high mortality. It was possible then to work less,[79] to enjoy improved living conditions,[80] to invest surpluses in building palaces and churches, and in art. In a sense, all this was based on the change in relative prices of production factors prompted by the shock of death. Growth in per capita terms was not the result of the increase of the numerator of our ratios (K and R), or the progress of technology (T), as during modern growth, but of the diminution in the denominator. If by growth we mean increasing per capita income, then from about 1350–1550 there was growth in Italy, although a strange kind of growth, supported as it was, not by technical progress or rising capital formation, but by the high mortality during the era of plague.

The Trend: 1470–1600

Improved living standards and, particularly, fewer epidemics[81] favored family formation and a rise in population in the second half of the fifteenth century. With the background of a stable technological level and diminishing natural resources per worker (prompted also by the low temperatures during the Little Ice Age), from 1550–60 onwards labor productivity began to decline again and, with it, per capita product and living conditions. The happy epoch of the Italian Renaissance was reaching its end. While death supported the Renaissance economy, life was, by contrast, the main determinant of its end. After all, Ruggiero Romano was right in his representation of the Renaissance economy as a prosperous age between two crises: the crisis of the first half of the 14th century and the crisis of the 17th century.[82]

A Geometric Representation: Growth

A geometric representation can help clarify the main lines of the trend. The following Figure 4.12 is nothing more than the intensive form of the production function, where, on the vertical axis, we find labor productivity (Y/L) and, on the horizontal, the reciprocal of the ratio of resources plus capital as to labor $L/(K+R)$.[83]

The horizontal line S represents the level of individual subsistence. As soon as the ratio $L/(K+R)$ increases, labor productivity diminishes as a consequence of decreasing returns to labor. The increase can depend on the rise in L, but also on the diminution of $K+R$. In both cases a displacement to the right occurs. While the classical economists looked especially at L, the numerator of our ratio and, in their view, decreasing returns always depended on its rise, foregoing analysis witnesses the importance of non-economic and non-deterministic factors, such as climatic changes and epidemic shocks. Chance plays a major role.

Fifteenth century economic conditions correspond to the point of Y/L in B. Here are the main economic features:

- gross product (the area $ABCD$) is far higher than the subsistence (the area SS_1CD);
- the surplus of the economy ABS_1S, the share of product that exceeds mere economic reproduction, is wide;
- this surplus beyond mere reproduction can allow both consumption over and above subsistence level and investment in building and art.

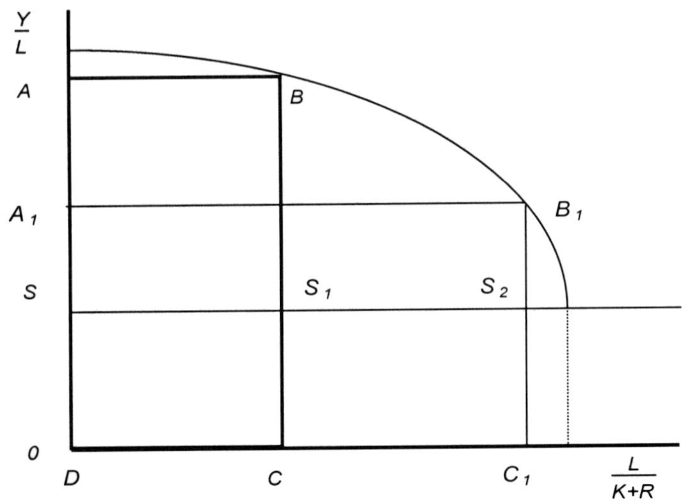

Figure 4.12 The intensive production function.

A Geometric Representation: Decline

From the 1470s to the end of the sixteenth century, labor productivity declined as *L* rose, while resources (because of the drop in temperature) and capital were diminishing, at least in relative terms. The *L/(K+R)* ratio increased and labor productivity moved towards B_1. In that case, the area of gross product was higher than before, primarily because population was 60 percent more than it was in *B*:

$$A_1B_1C_1D > ABCD$$

The volume of surplus was, however, relatively lower:

$$\frac{A_1B_1C_1D}{SS_2C_1D} < \frac{ABCD}{SS_1CD}$$

Here the main differences from the earlier century are summarized:

- in 1550–1600 the surplus as a ratio to subsistence was lower than it was around 1450;
- wage rates were lower, since productivity was lower, and they approached bare subsistence;
- people were forced to work longer hours and more members of the family had to work harder and harder to displace the curve of average product to the right and hence increase their income;
- the volume of investment in building and art was relatively lower, although, in absolute terms, it might have been higher than before.

From the end of the sixteenth century, the long Italian Renaissance was ending.

CONCLUSION

Following Cipolla, if we take per capita product as the main economic indicator, the period we are dealing with was an epoch of wealth and relatively high standard of living. It was the period of the *maturity* of the Italian economy.[84] While urban sectors were prosperous and progressing, the relative technological stability of the agrarian base prevented further advancement. Already in the first phase of our history, before the Black Death, the economy was declining. The arrival of the plague, an external shock, postponed this decline. An epoch of prosperity—albeit based on death—was beginning. The formation of a surplus beyond the immediate need for survival and the scanty opportunities for productive investment allowed this surplus to be channeled towards building churches and palaces. The

Renaissance was supported by flourishing economic conditions. From the second half of the fifteenth century onwards, the revival of demographic expansion in the presence of low capital formation, of unfavorable climatic conditions and diminishing availability of natural resources, started the decline, despite the counterbalancing effect of some prosperous decades for industrial, commercial, and banking activities. The technological constraints that prevented agricultural production from supporting the growth in population resulted, in the end, in rapidly rising agricultural prices, relatively diminishing industrial prices and declining profits.[85] Productivity fell and, as it did so, the Renaissance economy reached its end. The technological constraints of mature, traditional agriculture were, after all, the main obstacle to further expansion.

As in Roman times and subsequently, for some 1,500 years, Italy had been the center of the Western Euro-Mediterranean civilization and also one of the world's most advanced areas, if not the most advanced; from the late Renaissance onwards it slipped from center stage into the background, where it remained for a long time.

NOTES

* The Appendix of the chapter together with the presentation of the statistical procedures and series concerning late medieval to early modern Italian economy (population, prices, urbanisation, etc.) are available at www.paolomalanima.it. Any series used in the present paper is analyzed on the website. See also the Appendix in Paolo Malanima, *L'economia italiana. Dalla crescita medievale alla crescita contemporanea*, Bologna, Il Mulino, 2002 on data and documents concerning the Italian economy from the late Middle Ages until the end of the nineteenth century. The whole series of GDP in Italy from 1300 until 1913, together with the presentation of the statistical methods, is published in Paolo Malanima, "The Long Decline of a Leading Economy. GDP in Central and Northern Italy 1300–1913", in *European Review of Economic History* 15 (2011): 169–219.

1. Roberto S. Lopez, Harry A. Miskimin, "The Economic Depression of the Renaissance," *Economic History Review*, II s., XIV (1962): 408–426.
2. Carlo Maria Cipolla, "Economic Depression of the Renaissance?" *Economic History Review*, II s., XVI (1964): 519–27.
3. The term was already used by Cipolla, "Economic Depression of the Renaissance?".
4. Armando Sapori, *Il Rinascimento economico*, in *Studi di storia economica (secoli XIII-XIV-XV)*, Firenze, Sansoni, 1982 (1st ed. 1952): I, 618–652. See also Richard A. Goldthwaite, *The Economy of Renaissance Florence*, Johns Hopkins University Press, Baltimore, 2009, where the Renaissance economy covers the long period from the eleventh century until the end of the sixteenth.
5. See the chapter by Pinto in Lorenzo Del Panta, Massimo Livi Bacci, Giuliano Pinto, Eugenio Sonnino, *La popolazione italiana dal Medioevo a oggi* (Bari-Roma: Laterza, 1996).
6. See the comments by Guido Alfani, "Population et environnement en Italie du Nord au XVIe siècle, " *Population*, 62, (2007): 667–705.

7. Karl Julius Beloch, *Bevölkerungsgeschichte Italiens* (Berlin-Leipzig: De Gruyter, 1937–1961).
8. Data on population are presented and discussed in Malanima, *L'economia italiana*. App. I, and, from antiquity until 1900, in Elio Lo Cascio, and Paolo Malanima, "Cycles and Stability. Italian Population Before the Demographic Transition (225 B.C.–A.D. 1900)," *Rivista di Storia Economica*, n.s. (2005), XXI, 3: 5–40.
9. See, however, the comments by Giovanni Levi, "L'energia disponibile," in *Storia dell'economia italiana*, R. Romano (ed.) (Torino: Einaudi, II, 1991), 141–168 on Carlo Maria Cipolla, "Four Centuries of Italian Demographic Development," in *Population in History. Essays in Historical Demography*, D. V. Glass, D. E. C. Eversley (eds.) (London: Edward Arnold, 1965: 570–587.
10. These data and their sources are presented in Paolo Malanima, *Pre-modern European Economy. One Thousand Years (10th–19th Centuries)* (Leiden-Boston: Brill, 2009) and Paolo Malanima, "The Long Decline of a Leading Economy", (forthcoming) and Malanima, *L'economia italiana*, App. I.
11. For Tuscany we can use yearly prices for almost all the items in the basket from 1310 on; we have only wheat prices for the second half of the thirteenth century. I discussed the problem of sources for prices in Malanima, *L'economia italiana*, App. 3. The basket used to build the price index is presented and discussed in Malanima, *L'economia italiana*, Paolo Malanima, "Wages, Productivity and Working Time in Italy 1300–1913," *Journal of European Economic History*, 36 (2007): 127–174. A series concerning Naples from 1474 onwards, in Giuseppe Coniglio, "La Rivoluzione dei prezzi nella città di Napoli nei secoli XVI e XVII," in *Atti della IX riunione scientifica della Società Italiana di statistica (Roma, 7–8 gennaio 1950)* (Spoleto, 1952) has also been used for comparisons between North and South. A yearly consumer price index has been built by Robert Allen, "The Great Divergence in European Wages and Prices from the Middle Ages to the First World War," *Explorations in Economic History*, 38, (2001): 411–447. Similarities and differences between these two indices are presented at www.paolomalanima.it.
12. David Herlihy, *Medieval and Renaissance Pistoia: the Social History of an Italian Town, 1200–1430* (New Haven: Yale University Press, 1967).
13. I follow the explanation given by John Munro, *Before and after the Black Death: Money, Prices, and Wages in Fourteenth-Century England*, Department of Economics, University of Toronto, Working Paper n. 24 (2004), on the rising trend in prices for some decades after the Black Death.
14. Svimez, *Un secolo di statistiche italiane. Nord e Sud 1861–1961*. (Roma, Svimez, 1961) Chap. 1. This data refers, however, to the nineteenth century.
15. Massimo Montanari, *La società medievale di fronte alla carestia*, in Id., *Campagne medievali* (Torino: Einaudi, 1984): 191–200.
16. Often yields are higher when population pressure forces farmers to intensify the use of land. During the fifteenth century, however, the abandoning of the less fertile lands implied a rise in yields.
17. Giorgio Porisini, *Produttività e agricoltura: i rendimenti del frumento in Italia dal 1815 al 1922*, in "Archivio dell'Unificazione Italiana", XX, 1971: 24.
18. The meaning of "land intensification" is the same as in Ester Boserup, *The Conditions of Agricultural Growth* (London: Earthscan, 1965).
19. Although the figures proposed for England by Gregory Clark, "Yields per Acre in English Agriculture, 1250–1860: Evidence from Labour Inputs," *Economic History Review*, II s., XLIV (1991): 445–460 and Bruce M. S.

Campbell, *English Seigniorial Agriculture 1250–1450*. (Cambridge: Cambridge University Press, 2000): 306 ff. for the late Middle Ages are different, they are, however, higher than those relating to Italy in the same period.
20. See the classical reconstruction of Mediterranean geography put forward by Fernand Braudel, *La Méditerranée et le monde méditerranéen à l'epoque de Philippe II* (Paris: Colin, 1966) (2nd ed.).
21. Patrick R. Galloway, "Long-Term Fluctuations in Climate and Population in the Preindustrial Era," *Population and Development Review*, 12, (1986): 1–24.
22. Research done by paleo-climatologists in recent years on temperatures in the Northern Hemisphere confirms the series presented in Figure 4.3 relating to the Alps. See, as examples, Michael E. Mann, Raymond S. Bradley, M. K. Hughes, "Northern Hemisphere Temperatures During the Past Millennium: Inferences, Uncertainties, and Limitations," *Geophysical Research Letters*, 26, (1999): 759–762.
23. See Mann's recent work Michael E. Mann, "Medieval Climatic Optimum," in *The Earth System: Physical and Chemical Dimensions of Global Environmental Change*, 1, in, *Encyclopedia of Global Environmental Change*, T. Munn (ed.), (Chichester: Wiley, 2002): 514–516: a brief survey devoted specifically to the period in question.
24. Giuliano Pinto, *Firenze e la carestia del 1346–47*, in Id., *La Toscana nel tardo Medioevo. Ambiente, economia rurale, società* (Firenze: Sansoni, 1982): 333–379 (1st ed. 1972).
25. See especially Massimo Montanari, *L'alimentazione contadina nell'alto Medioevo* (Napoli: Liguori, 1979), and Massimo Montanari, *La società medievale di fronte alla carestia*, in Id., *Campagne medievali* (Torino: Einaudi, 1984): 191–200.
26. See the important work by Raymond W. Goldsmith, and Salvatore Zecchini, "The National Balance Sheet of Italy (1861–1973)." *Rivista di Storia Economica*, n.s., XV (1999): 3–20.
27. See Raymond W. Goldsmith, *Pre-modern Financial Systems. A Historical Comparative Study* (Cambridge: Cambridge Univ. Press, 1987): 145 ff. The ratio of wealth to per capita GDP is confirmed by the following estimate of product, in section 4. The Florentine Catasto is the well-known land and wealth census relating to the Florentine Republic.
28. The comparison is based, for 1427 Tuscany, on Goldsmith, *Pre-modern Financial Systems* and, for 1861 Italy, on Goldsmith, Zecchini, "The National Balance Sheet of Italy (1861–1973)."
29. A wide variety of literature exists on the topic starting with Carlo Cattaneo, *Saggi di economia rurale*, ed. L. Einaudi (Torino: Einaudi, 1975), who wrote at the middle of the nineteenth century.
30. As will be seen in section 2.5. Ruggiero Romano, *Tra due crisi: l'Italia del Rinascimento* (Torino: Einaudi, 1971), and Ruggiero Romano, *Paese Italia. Venti secoli di identità* (Roma: Donzelli, 1997), while mentioning the investments in agriculture, always stressed the backward character of Italian agriculture in his numerous essays.
31. A fine reconstruction of all these changes is proposed by Antonio I. Pini, *Città, comuni e corporazioni nel medioevo italiano* (Bologna: Clueb, 1986). Feudalism represented in Italy as elsewhere a dynamic phase in the building of European civilization. This dynamic phase was reconstructed by Cinzio Violante, *La società milanese nell'età precomunale* (Roma-Bari: Laterza, 1981) (1st ed. 1953), in his great book on Milanese society in the early Middle Ages. A negative view of feudalism in Italian history is presented in several chapters of the *Storia d'Italia*, ed. by R. Romano, C. Vivanti (Torino: Einaudi, 1972–91). See also Romano, *Paese Italia*.

32. Paolo Cammarosano, *Le campagne nell'età comunale (metà sec. XI-metà sec. XIV)* (Torino: Loescher, 1974): 94 ff., where several documents have been collected and presented.
33. See those collected in Pietro Vaccari, *Le affrancazioni collettive dei servi della gleba* (Milano: Istituto per gli studi di politica internazionale, 1939).
34. Giovanni Cherubini, *Signori contadini borghesi. Ricerche sulla società italiana del basso Medioevo* (Firenze: La Nuova Italia, 1974), and Giovanni Cherubini, "La proprietà fondiaria nei secoli XV–XVI nella storiografia italiana," *Società e Storia*, I, 1 (1978): 9–34, presented and discussed the sources concerning landownership.
35. See especially Giorgio Giorgetti, *Contadini e proprietari nell'Italia moderna. Rapporti di produzione e contratti agrari dal XVI secolo a oggi* (Torino: Einaudi, 1974) and Giorgio Giorgetti, *Capitalismo e agricoltura in Italia* (Roma: Editori Riuniti, 1977).
36. Labor incomes are often hidden in pre-modern economies, especially in agriculture, and correspond to a part of the total income available to the rural family after payment of the rent. I assume here that wages also bear witness to the trend of the hidden labor income.
37. See the view of evolution proposed by Giorgetti, *Contadini e proprietari nell'Italia moderna.*
38. See especially Francesco Battistini, "La diffusione della gelsibachicoltura nell'Italia centro-settentrionale: un tentativo di ricostruzione," *Società e Storia*, XV (1992): 393–400; Francesco Battistini, "La produzione e il commercio della seta greggia in Italia alla fine del XVIII secolo," *Società e Storia*, XIX (1997): 889–907; Francesco Battistini, *L'industria della seta in Italia nell'età moderna* (Bologna: Il Mulino, 2003); Francesco Battistini, "La produzione, il commercio e i prezzi della seta grezza nello Stato di Firenze 1480–1860," *Rivista di Storia Economica*, n.s., XXI, (2005): 233–272; Francesco Battistini, "Seta ed economia in Italia. Il prodotto 1500–1930," *Rivista di Storia Economica*, n.s., XXV, (2007): 283–318.
39. Anna M. Rapetti, *Campagne milanesi. Aspetti e metamorfosi di un paesaggio rurale fra X e XII secolo* (Cavallermaggiore: Gribaudo, 1994): 99 ff., refers to canals built in the ninth through tenth centuries. See also Domenico Sella, *Crisis and Continuity. The Economy of Spanish Lombardy in the Seventeenth Century* (Harvard: Harvard University Press, 1979): App. C and especially Mauro Ambrosoli, *Scienziati, contadini e proprietari. Botanica e agricoltura nell'Europa occidentale* (Torino: Einaudi, 1992).
40. The abandonment of the least productive soils was, as already seen, the main reason of these satisfactory or even remarkable yields.
41. Giovanni Cherubini, "Le campagne italiane dall'XI al XV secolo", in *Storia d'Italia*, IV, G. Galasso (ed.) (Torino: Utet, 1981): 267–448 supplies a good synthesis of the techniques in late medieval Italian agriculture.
42. The topic has been widely discussed in Giovanni Federico, and Paolo Malanima, "Progress, Decline, Growth: Product and Productivity in Italian Agriculture, 1000–2000," *Economic History Review*, II. s. (2004): 437–464.
43. Sergio Tognetti, "Prezzi e salari nella Firenze tardomedievale: un profilo," *Archivio Storico Italiano*, CLIII (1995): 263–333 puts together the available Tuscan series.
44. The sources for the construction of series of rural wage rates are presented in Malanima, "Wages, Productivity and Working Time in Italy 1300–1913." See the series in the Appendix.
45. When population was rising, probably the volume of agricultural imports was also rising. It represented, in any case, a modest fraction of total production as shown by Maurice Aymard, *Venise, Raguse et le commerce du*

blé pendant la seconde moitié du XVIe siècle (Paris: SEVPEN, 1966), and Fernand Braudel, *La Méditerranée et le monde méditerranéen à l'epoque de Philippe II*, Paris: Colin, 1966) (2nd ed.).

46. The topic is discussed in Malanima, "Wages, Productivity and Working Time in Italy 1300–1913", and Malanima, "The Long Decline of a Leading Economy."
47. In England, by contrast, a drop in wages characterized the thirteenth century as a whole, while in the 50 years before the Black Death wages fluctuated at around the same low level: Campbell, *English Seigniorial Agriculture 1250–1450*: 4–5.
48. A direct calculation of agricultural output is hard or impossible to do for the period we are dealing with. On the method I followed to elaborate the series of per capita agricultural product, see the Appendix to this paper at www.paolomalanima.it.
49. In all these cases, the share of population (such as armies and professional groups) has to be multiplied by a coefficient, to compute the urban population on the whole.
50. In the book by Maria Ginatempo, and Lucia Sandri, *L'Italia delle città. Il popolamento urbano tra Medioevo e Rinascimento (secoli XIII–XVI)* (Firenze, Le Lettere, 1990), data on urban population are presented and discussed for all of Italy in the late Middle Ages. The complete database of Italian cities from 1300 until 1861 is available at www.paolomalanima.it.
51. I come back to the problem of urbanization in section 3.4.
52. As recalled in section 2.4.
53. See especially Joel Mokyr, *The Gifts of Athena. Historical Origins of the Knowledge Economy* (Princeton: Princeton University Press, 2002), and, from an economic perspective, Oded Galor, "From Stagnation to Growth: Unified Growth Theory", in P. Aghion, S. Durlauf (eds.), *Handbook of economic growth* (North Holland, Elsevier: 2005): 171–293. Oded Galor, and David N. Weil, "Population, Technology and Growth: from the Malthusian Regime to the Demographic Transition," *American Economic Review*, 110 (2000): 806–828.
54. See the fine article by C. Marco Belfanti, "Guilds, Patents, and the Circulation of Technical Knowledge. Northern Italy During the Early Modern Age", in *Technology and Culture* (2004): 569–589.
55. On the topic see the articles collected in Giorgio Chittolini (ed.), *La crisi degli ordinamenti comunali e le origini dello stato del Rinascimento* (Bologna: Il Mulino, 1979).
56. I refer to the Italian medieval economic historian.
57. The sources of the graph are the same as the series in Malanima, *L'economia italiana*: 405 (although in this work only decadal series were presented).
58. Battistini, "La produzione, il commercio e i prezzi della seta grezza nello Stato di Firenze 1480–1860" deals with the evolution of this sector.
59. As discussed in Malanima, *L'economia italiana:* App. IV, which shows both the similarities and differences among the available series of building wages. Goldthwaite's work (Richard A. Goldthwaite, *The Building of the Renaissance Florence* (Baltimore and London: The Johns Hopkins University Press, 1980) on the building industry and wages in Florence is still remarkable.
60. The sources for the construction of series of urban wage rates are presented in Malanima, "Wages, Productivity and Working Time in Italy 1300–1913."
61. See, however, the fall in the 1370s and 1380s. On these post-plague decades see the remarks by Munro, *Before and after the Black Death.*
62. By David Abulafia, *The two Italies. Economic Relations Between the Norman Kingdom of Sicily and the Northern Communes* (Cambridge: Cambridge University Press, 1977).

63. Because in the South of Italy many towns are agro-towns, and from the 16th this specific characteristic is much more widespread than before, I use the series of urbanisation in the Centre and North for the following elaboration of non-agricultural production.
64. See David Herlihy, Christiane Klapisch-Zuber, *Les Toscans et leurs familles. Une étude du catasto florentin de 1427* (Paris : Presses Universitaires de la Fondation Nationale des Sciences Politiques, 1978) : passim.
65. Federico-Malanima, "Progress, Decline, Growth: Product and Productivity in Italian Agriculture, 1000–2000."
66. See the evidence collected by Stephan R. Epstein, *Freedom and Growth. The Rise of States and Markets in Europe, 1300–1750* (London and New York: Routledge, 2000): passim. Still useful is also Sidney Homer, and Richard Sylla, *A History of Interest Rates* (New Brunswick and London, Rutgers University Press, 1991) (1st ed. 1902).
67. On the topic see especially the important works by Richard A. Goldthwaite, "The Empire of Things: Consumer Demand in Renaissance Italy," in *Patronage, Art and Society in Renaissance Italy*, F. W. Kent, P. Simons (eds.) (Oxford: Clarendon Press, 1987): 153–175; Richard A. Goldthwaite, *Wealth and the Demand for Art in Italy 1300–1600* (Baltimore and London: The Johns Hopkins University Press, 1993).
68. The method is fully explained in Malanima, "The Long Decline of a Leading Economy."
69. The topic is discussed by Malanima, *Pre-modern European Economy.*
70. I have used urbanisation rates relating to the Center and North.
71. As we see in the Appendix (col. 2), we have no data on agricultural wages for the decade 1310–20. They are calculated approximately through the rates of increase of the urban wages.
72. The method used to calculate the series is the same as the one already presented by Paolo Malanima, "Measuring the Italian Economy 1300–1861," *Rivista di Storia Economica*, XIX (2003): 265–295, although in the present series (in the Appendix), annual data are elaborated instead of decadal as previously. Data used in Figure 4.10 and the methods used are presented in Malanima, "The Long Decline of a Leading Economy."
73. The fall in the 1370s depends heavily on the Florentine prices and wages used to build the series. On the period, see especially Charles M. De La Roncière, *Prix et salaires à Florence au XIVe siècle* (Roma, Ecole Française de Rome, 1982), and Giuliano Pinto, *Il personale, le balie e i salariati dell'ospedale di San Gallo di Firenze (1395–1406)*, in Id., *Toscana medievale. Paesaggi e realtà sociali* (Firenze: Le Lettere, 1993): 113–149.
74. A comparison is possible on the basis of Angus Maddison, *The World Economy. Historical Statistics* (Paris: OECD, 2003).
75. See especially Jan Luiten Zanden Van, "Una estimacion del crecimiento económico en la Edad Moderna," in *Investigaciones de Historia Economica*, I, (2005): 9–38 both for the comparisons and an alternative (but not so different) reconstruction of the Italian GDP since the Middle Ages. See also Jan Luiten Van Zanden, "Early Modern Economic Growth. A Survey of the European Economy, 1500–1800," in *Early Modern Capitalism*, M. Prak (ed.) (London-New York: Routledge, 2001): 69–87.
76. Goldsmith, *Pre-modern Financial Systems*: Chap. 9; Lodovico Ghetti, *Inventiva d'una imposizione di nuova gravezza*, in G. Roscoe, *Vita di Lorenzo De' Medici detto il Magnifico* (Pisa: N. Capurro, 1816): I, App. 1, written in the 1440s. On Ghetti's data see Goldthwaite, *The Building of the Renaissance Florence*, p. 346, and Victor Rutenburg, *A proposito del prodotto lordo fiorentino, un progetto d'imposta del primo Quattrocento,* in *Prodotto*

lordo e finanza pubblica secoli XIII–XIX, ed. by A. Guarducci (Firenze: Le Monnier, 1988): 865–870.

77. A yearly series of per capita output in the Center and North of Italy in current prices is presented in Malanima, "The Long Decline of a Leading Economy". In the same paper I compare the reconstructed series with direct information relating to the Florentine Republic in 1420–50.
78. In the graph population figures are per decade. Smoothed by means of a mobile average, these are then multiplied for the yearly per capita GDP index.
79. As noticed, for England, by Munro, *Before and after the Black Death.*
80. See, in particular for Tuscany, Maria S. Mazzi, and Sergio Raveggi, *Gli uomini e le cose nelle campagne fiorentine del Quattrocento* (Firenze: Olschki, 1983).
81. Lorenzo Del Panta, *Le epidemie nella storia demografica italiana (secoli XIV–XIX)* (Torino: Loescher: 1986) [1st ed. 1980].
82. Romano, *Tra due crisi: l'Italia del Rinascimento.*
83. The use of the reciprocal allows a clearer representation of the relationships in question.
84. It should be remembered that the subtitle of Carlo Maria Cipolla, "The Decline of Italy: the Case of a Fully Matured Economy," *Economic History Review*, II s., V (1952): 178–187.
85. Giuseppe Parenti, *Prime ricerche sulla rivoluzione dei prezzi a Firenze,* in Id., *Studi di storia dei prezzi* (Paris: Maison des Sciences de l'Homme, 1981) (1st ed. 1939), in his important work on Florentine prices in the sixteenth century already clearly focused on the key factors of the problem.

BIBLIOGRAPHY

Abulafia, David. *The Two Italies: Economic Relations Between the Norman Kingdom of Sicily and the Northern Communes.* Cambridge: Cambridge University Press, 1977.

Alfani, Guido. "Population et environnement en Italie du Nord au XVIe siècle." *Population* 62 (2007): 667–705.

Allen, Robert. "Economic Structure and Agricultural Productivity in Europe, 1300–1800." *European Review of Economic History* 4 (2000): 1–26.

Allen, Robert. "The Great Divergence in European Wages and Prices from the Middle Ages to the First World War." *Explorations in Economic History*, 38, (2001): 411–447.

Ambrosoli, Mauro. *Scienziati, contadini e proprietari. Botanica e agricoltura nell'Europa occidentale.* Torino: Einaudi, 1992.

Aymard, Maurice. *Venise, Raguse et le commerce du blé pendant la seconde moitié du XVIe siècle.* Paris: SEVPEN, 1966.

Battistini, Francesco. "La diffusione della gelsibachicoltura nell'Italia centro-settentrionale: un tentativo di ricostruzione." *Società e Storia*, XV (1992): 393–400.

Battistini, Francesco. "La produzione e il commercio della seta greggia in Italia alla fine del XVIII secolo." *Società e Storia*, XIX, (1997): 889–907.

Battistini, Francesco. *L'industria della seta in Italia nell'età moderna.* Bologna: Il Mulino, 2003.

Battistini, Francesco. "La produzione, il commercio e i prezzi della seta grezza nello Stato di Firenze 1480–1860." *Rivista di Storia Economica*, n.s., XXI, (2005): 233–272.

Battistini, Francesco. "Seta ed economia in Italia. Il prodotto 1500–1930." *Rivista di Storia Economica*, n.s., XXV, (2007): 283–318.
Bellettini, Athos. "La popolazione italiana dall'inizio dell'età volgare ai nostri giorni." In Ruggiero Romano, Corrado Vivanti (eds.), *Storia d'Italia*, 5, 1 Torino: Einaudi, (1973): 487–532.
Belfanti, C. Marco. "Guilds, Patents, and the Circulation of Technical Knowledge. Northern Italy During the Early Modern Age." *Technology and Culture*, 2004 (45.3): 569–589.
Beloch, Karl Julius. *Bevölkerungsgeschichte Italiens*. Berlin-Leipzig, De Gruyter, 1937–1961.
Beloch, Karl Julius. "La popolazione d'Italia nei secoli sedicesimo, diciassettesimo e diciottesimo." In, *Storia dell'economia italiana,* Carlo Maria Cipolla (ed.), I, Torino: Einaudi, 1959: 449–500.
Boserup, Ester. *The Conditions of Agricultural Growth*. London: Earthscan, 1965.
Braudel, Fernand. *La Méditerranée et le monde méditerranéen à l'epoque de Philippe II*. Paris: Colin, 1966 (2nd ed.).
Breschi, Marco and Malanima, Paolo. "Demografia ed economia in Toscana: il lungo periodo (secoli XIV–XIX)." In *Prezzi, redditi, popolazioni in Italia: 600 anni (dal secolo XIV al secolo XX),* Marco Breschi, Paolo Malanima (eds.), Udine, Forum, 2002: 109–142.
Cammarosano, Paolo. *Le campagne nell'età comunale (metà sec. XI-metà sec. XIV)*. Torino: Loescher, 1974.
Campbell, Bruce M.S. *English Seigniorial Agriculture 1250–1450*. Cambridge: Cambridge University Press, 2000.
Cattaneo, Carlo. *Saggi di economia rurale*. L. Einaudi (ed.). Torino: Einaudi, 1975.
Cherubini, Giovanni. *Signori contadini borghesi. Ricerche sulla società italiana del basso Medioevo*. Firenze: La Nuova Italia, 1974.
Cherubini, Giovanni. "La proprietà fondiaria nei secoli XV-XVI nella storiografia italiana." *Società e Storia*, I, 1978, 1: 9–34.
Cherubini, Giovanni. "Le campagne italiane dall'XI al XV secolo", in *Storia d'Italia*, G. Galasso (ed.), IV, Torino: Utet, 1981: 267–448.
Chittolini, Giorgio (ed.). *La crisi degli ordinamenti comunali e le origini dello stato del Rinascimento*. Bologna: Il Mulino, 1979.
Cipolla, Carlo Maria. "The Decline of Italy: the Case of a Fully Matured Economy." *Economic History Review*, II s., V, 1952: 178–187.
Cipolla, Carlo Maria. "Economic Depression of the Renaissance?" *Economic History Review*, II s., XVI, 1964: 519–527.
Cipolla, Carlo Maria. "Four Centuries of Italian Demographic Development," In *Population in History. Essays in Historical Demographie*, D. V. Glass, D. E. C. Eversley (eds.). London: Edward Arnold, 1965: 570–587.
Clark, Gregory. "Yields per Acre in English Agriculture, 1250–1860: Evidence from Labour Inputs." *Economic History Review*, II s., XLIV, 1991: 445–460.
Coniglio, Giuseppe. "La Rivoluzione dei prezzi nella città di Napoli nei secoli XVI e XVII." In *Atti della IX riunione scientifica della Società Italiana di statistica (Roma, 7–8 gennaio 1950)*, Spoleto, 1952: 1–36.
Contadini e proprietari nella Toscana moderna, 1, *Dal Medioevo all'Età Moderna*. Firenze: Olschki, 1979.
De La Roncière, Charles M. *Prix et salaires à Florence au XIVe siècle*. Roma: Ecole Française de Rome, 1982.
Del Panta, Lorenzo. *Le epidemie nella storia demografica italiana (secoli XIV–XIX)*. Torino, Loescher: 1986 [1st ed. 1980].
Del Panta, Lorenzo, Livi Bacci, Massimo, Pinto, Giuliano, Sonnino, Eugenio. *La popolazione italiana dal Medioevo a oggi*. Bari-Roma: Laterza, 1996.

Epstein, Stephan R. *Freedom and Growth. The Rise of States and Markets in Europe, 1300–1750*. London and New York: Routledge, 2000.
Federico, Giovanni and Malanima, Paolo. "Progress, Decline, Growth: Product and Productivity in Italian Agriculture, 1000–2000." *Economic History Review*, II. s., 2004: 437–464.
Galloway, Patrick R. "Long-Term Fluctuations in Climate and Population in the Preindustrial Era." *Population and Development Review*, 12, 1986: 1–24.
Galor, Oded. "From Stagnation to Growth: Unified Growth Theory", in P. Aghion, S. Durlauf (eds.). In *Handbook of economic growth*, North Holland, Elsevier: 2005: 171–293.
Galor, Oded and Weil David, N. "Population, Technology and Growth: from the Malthusian Regime to the Demographic Transition." *American Economic Review*, 110, 2000: 806–828.
Ghetti, Lodovico. *Inventiva d'una imposizione di nuova gravezza*, in G. Roscoe, *Vita di Lorenzo De' Medici detto il Magnifico*. Pisa: N. Capurro, 1816, I, App. 1.
Ginatempo, Maria and Sandri, Lucia. *L'Italia delle città. Il popolamento urbano tra Medioevo e Rinascimento (secoli XIII–XVI)*. Firenze: Le Lettere, 1990.
Giorgetti, Giorgio. *Contadini e proprietari nell'Italia moderna. Rapporti di produzione e contratti agrari dal XVI secolo a oggi*. Torino: Einaudi, 1974.
Giorgetti, Giorgio. *Capitalismo e agricoltura in Italia*. Roma: Editori Riuniti, 1977.
Goldsmith, Raymond W. *Pre-modern Financial Systems. A Historical Comparative Study*. Cambridge: Cambridge University Press, 1987.
Goldsmith, Raymond W. and Zecchini, Salvatore. "The National Balance Sheet of Italy (1861–1973)." *Rivista di Storia Economica*, n.s., XV, 1999: 3–20.
Goldthwaite, Richard A. *The Building of the Renaissance Florence*, Baltimore and London: The Johns Hopkins University Press, 1980.
Goldthwaite, Richard A. "The Empire of Things: Consumer Demand in Renaissance Italy." In *Patronage, Art and Society in Renaissance Italy*, F. W. Kent, P. Simons (eds.), Oxford: Clarendon Press, 1987: 153–175.
Goldthwaite, Richard A. *Wealth and the Demand for Art in Italy 1300–1600*. Baltimore and London: The Johns Hopkins University Press, 1993.
Goldthwaite, Richard A. *The Economy of Renaissance Florence*. Baltimore: Johns Hopkins University Press, 2009.
Herlihy, David. *Medieval and Renaissance Pistoia: the Social History of an Italian Town, 1200–1430*. New Haven: Yale University Press, 1967.
Herlihy, David, Klapisch-Zuber, Christiane. *Les Toscans et leurs familles. Une étude du catasto florentin de 1427*. Paris : Presses Universitaires de la Fondation Nationale des Sciences Politiques, 1978.
Homer, Sidney and Sylla, Richard. *A History of Interest Rates*. New Brunswick and London: Rutgers University Press, 1991 (1st ed. 1902).
Levi, Giovanni. "L'energia disponibile." In *Storia dell'economia italiana*, R. Romano (ed.), Torino: Einaudi, vol. 2, 1991: 141–168.
Livi Bacci, Massimo. *La popolazione nella storia europea*. Roma-Bari: Laterza, 1998.
Lo Cascio, Elio and Malanima, Paolo. "Cycles and Stability. Italian Population Before the Demographic Transition (225 B.C.–A.D. 1900)." *Rivista di Storia Economica*, n.s., 2005, XXI, 3: 5–40.
Lopez, Roberto S., Miskimin, Harry A. "The Economic Depression of the Renaissance." *Economic History Review*, II s., XIV, 1962: 408–426.
Maddison, Angus. *The World Economy. Historical Statistics*. Paris: OECD, 2003.
Malanima, Paolo. *Aspetti di mercato e prezzi del grano e della segale a Pisa dal 1548 al 1818*. In M. Mirri (ed.), *Ricerche di Storia Moderna*, vol. 1, Pisa, Pacini,

1976 (monthly original data of agricultural products on which the article was based are now available at www.iisg.nl).

Malanima, Paolo. *La fine del primato. Crisi e riconversione nell'Italia del Seicento.* Milano: Bruno Mondadori: 1998.

Malanima, Paolo. *Risorse, popolazioni, redditi: 1300–1861*, in *Storia economica d'Italia*, Pierluigi Ciocca, Gianni Toniolo (eds.), Roma-Bari: Laterza, 1999, vol. 1, 43–124.

Malanima, Paolo. *L'economia italiana. Dalla crescita medievale alla crescita contemporanea.* Bologna: Il Mulino, 2002.

Malanima, Paolo. "Measuring the Italian Economy 1300–1861." *Rivista di Storia Economica*, XIX, 2003: 265–295.

Malanima, Paolo. "Urbanisation and the Italian Economy During the Last Millennium." *European Review of Economic History*, 9, 2005: 97–122.

Malanima, Paolo. "Wages, Productivity and Working Time in Italy 1300–1913." *Journal of European Economic History*, 36, 2007: 127–174.

Malanima, Paolo. *Pre-modern European Economy. One Thousand Years (10th–19th Centuries).* Leiden-Boston: Brill, 2009.

Malanima, Paolo. "Decline or Growth? European Cities and Rural Economies 1300–1600." *Jahrbuch für Geschichte des ländlichen Raumes*, 6, 2009: 18–44.

Malanima, Paolo. "The Long Decline of a Leading Economy. GDP in Central and Northern Italy 1300–1913." *European Review of Economic History* 15, 2011: 169–219.

Mangini, A., Spötl, C., Verdes, P. "Reconstruction of Temperature in the Central Alps During the Past 2000 years." *Earth and Planetary Science Letters*, 235, 3–4, 2005: 741–51.

Mann, Michael E. "Medieval Climatic Optimum." In *The Earth System: Physical and Chemical Dimensions of Global Environmental Change*, 1, in, *Encyclopedia of Global Environmental Change*, T. Munn (ed.). Chichester: Wiley, 2002: 514–516.

Mann, Michael E., Bradley R. S., Hughes M. K. "Northern Hemisphere Temperatures During the Past Millennium: Inferences, Uncertainties, and Limitations." *Geophysical Research Letters*, 26, 1999: 759–762.

Mann, Michael E. and Jones P. D. "Global Surface Temperatures over the Past two Millennia." *Geophysical Research Letters*, 30, n. 15, August, 2003.

Mazzi, Maria S. and Raveggi, Sergio. *Gli uomini e le cose nelle campagne fiorentine del Quattrocento.* Firenze: Olschki, 1983.

Mokyr, Joel. *The Gifts of Athena. Historical Origins of the Knowledge Economy.* Princeton: Princeton University Press, 2002.

Montanari, Massimo. *L'alimentazione contadina nell'alto Medioevo.* Napoli: Liguori, 1979.

Montanari, Massimo. *Rese cerealicole e rapporti di produzione.* In Id., *Campagne medievali.* Torino: Einaudi, 1984: 54–85.

Montanari, Massimo. *La società medievale di fronte alla carestia*, in Id., *Campagne medievali.* Torino: Einaudi, 1984: 191–200.

Munro, John. *Before and after the Black Death: Money, Prices, and Wages in Fourteenth-Century England.* Department of Economics, University of Toronto, Working Paper n. 24, 2004.

Parenti, Giuseppe. *Prime ricerche sulla rivoluzione dei prezzi a Firenze*, in idem, *Studi di storia dei prezzi.* Paris: Maison des Sciences de l'Homme, 1981 (1st ed. 1939).

Pini, Antonio I., *Città, comuni e corporazioni nel medioevo italiano*, Bologna, Clueb, 1986.

Pinto, Giuliano. *Firenze e la carestia del 1346–47*, in idem, *La Toscana nel tardo Medioevo. Ambiente, economia rurale, società.* Firenze: Sansoni, 1982: 333–379 (1st ed. 1972).

Pinto, Giuliano. *Il personale, le balie e i salariati dell'ospedale di San Gallo di Firenze (1395–1406)*. In idem, *Toscana medievale. Paesaggi e realtà sociali*, Firenze: Le Lettere, 1993.

Pinto, Giuliano. "Dalla tarda antichità alla metà del XVI secolo", in Lorenzo Del Panta, Massimo Livi Bacci, Giuliano Pinto, Eugenio Sonnino. *La popolazione italiana dal Medioevo a oggi*. Bari-Roma: Laterza, 1996: 15–71.

Porisini, Giorgio. *Produttività e agricoltura: i rendimenti del frumento in Italia dal 1815 al 1922*. In "Archivio dell'Unificazione Italiana", XX, 1971.

Rapetti, Anna M. *Campagne milanesi. Aspetti e metamorfosi di un paesaggio rurale fra X e XII secolo*. Cavallermaggiore: Gribaudo, 1994.

Romano, Ruggiero. *Tra due crisi: l'Italia del Rinascimento*. Torino: Einaudi, 1971.

Romano, Ruggiero. *Paese Italia. Venti secoli di identità*. Roma: Donzelli, 1997.

Rutenburg, Victor. *A proposito del prodotto lordo fiorentino, un progetto d'imposta del primo Quattrocento*. In A. Guarducci (ed.), *Prodotto lordo e finanza pubblica secoli XIII–XIX*. Firenze: Le Monnier, 1988: 865–870.

Sapori, Armando. *Il Rinascimento economico*, in *Studi di storia economica* (*secoli XIII–XIV–XV*). Firenze: Sansoni, 1982: vol. 1, 618–652.

Sella, Domenico. *Crisis and Continuity. The Economy of Spanish Lombardy in the Seventeenth Century*. Harvard: Harvard University Press, 1979.

Storia d'Italia. R. Romano, C. Vivanti (eds.). Torino: Einaudi, 1972 ff.

Svimez. *Un secolo di statistiche italiane. Nord e Sud 1861–1961*. Roma: Svimez, 1961.

Tognetti, Sergio. "Prezzi e salari nella Firenze tardomedievale: un profilo." *Archivio Storico Italiano*, CLIII, 1995: 263–333.

Vaccari, Pietro. *Le affrancazioni collettive dei servi della gleba*. Milano: Istituto per gli studi di politica internazionale, 1939.

Violante, Cinzio. *La società milanese nell'età precomunale*. Roma-Bari: Laterza, 1981 (1st ed. 1953).

Zanden Van, Jan Luiten. "Early Modern Economic Growth. A Survey of the European Economy, 1500–1800." In *Early Modern Capitalism*, M. Prak (ed.). London-New York: Routledge, 2001: 69–87.

Zanden Van, Jan Luiten. "Una estimacion del crecimiento económico en la Edad Moderna." *Investigaciones de Historia Economica*, I, 2005: 9–38.

5 Byzantium

Kostis Smyrlis

To a large extent the evolution of the Byzantine economy runs parallel to that of Western Europe and this includes the fourteenth-century crisis which interrupted a long period of demographic and economic growth.[1] Besides certain more or less important structural differences, what above all distinguishes Byzantium from other countries in the late Middle Ages are the extremely unstable political conditions and almost constant warfare that marked the period extending from the 1340s to the definitive establishment of Ottoman power in the Balkans, more than a century later. The combined effect of these circumstances and the plague are responsible for the severe demographic and economic crisis of the last Byzantine century. But the agrarian economy was apparently experiencing difficulties already before these troubles occurred.

A few words about chronological and geographical limits. The late Byzantine period usually begins in 1204, after the conquest of Constantinople by the Fourth Crusade which resulted in the fragmentation of the Empire into smaller political entities. It ends in 1453, the year of the capital's capture by the Ottomans. After 1204, the Byzantine Empire was at first centered in Nicaea, in Asia Minor, and then, from 1261, in the recaptured capital of Constantinople. This state only achieved a partial recovery of the former Byzantine Empire's territories in Asia Minor and the Balkans (see Figure 5.1). In the 1260s, nevertheless, it comprised some of the wealthiest and most densely populated regions of the pre-1204 Empire, that is the fertile valleys of western Asia Minor and the rich provinces of Bithynia, Thrace, and Macedonia. Byzantium was not able to check the Turkish push in the latter part of the thirteenth century and by the beginning of the fourteenth century it had lost practically all of its territories in Asia Minor. By the middle of the same century, most of the European provinces had been taken over by the Serbs who were succeeded towards the end of the century by the Ottomans. In the last hundred years of its existence the Empire controlled very limited territories. Most of the discussion that follows concerns the period up to the 1340s both because the material is more abundant for this time-span and on account of the fact that conditions were very different in Byzantium's

Figure 5.1 Byzantium, c. 1265. After Dimiter Angelov, *Imperial Ideology and Political Thought in Byzantium, 1204–1330* (Cambridge: Cambridge University Press, 2006). Copyright © 2006 Dimiter Angelov. Reprinted with the permission of Cambridge University Press.

final century. This era of political upheaval and severe economic crisis will be discussed in a separate section.

Political developments influenced the economy's evolution and, in the period extending up to the 1340s, none was more significant than the conquest of 1204. There was large-scale destruction and pillaging both in Constantinople and in the provinces. Armies crossed the countryside causing people to flee; the coastal areas became exposed to piracy. The confusion that followed the temporary collapse of the Byzantine establishment led to a large-scale re-arrangement of the ownership pattern which certainly affected land exploitation.[2] These were short-term developments that were overcome as soon as stability returned. A more lasting consequence of the Fourth Crusade was the political fragmentation of the Byzantine world into relatively weak successor states, which allowed the Italian maritime powers, Venice and Genoa, to dominate commerce. The decline of Constantinople's importance as an urban center and the Byzantine aristocracy's relative impoverishment are also related to the diminished size of the late Empire. As already suggested, the political revival after 1204 was short-lived. Byzantine power in Asia Minor began declining in the late thirteenth century. The disruptive Turkish raids, which seriously affected the population, only ended with the region's complete conquest at the beginning of the fourteenth century.[3] The European provinces enjoyed greater stability in spite of some Serbian invasions in Macedonia towards the end of the thirteenth century. More trouble and destruction came in the first half of the fourteenth century with Catalan mercenaries pillaging parts of Thrace and Macedonia in 1305–08 and Byzantine armies fighting each other during the civil war of 1321–28.[4]

Political history determined the quantity and quality of the surviving sources. Byzantium having been conquered twice, the second time definitively, all state archives were destroyed. Lay archives were also lost as the aristocracy dissolved or joined the Ottomans, who overhauled the land ownership regime. This explains why from a bureaucratic state that had one of the highest literacy levels in medieval Europe only a smattering of documents has survived. Most of these are preserved in the archives of a few monasteries that have lasted to our days. It follows that practically all of the evidence on the countryside concerns monastic estates. These documents, which are about 2,000, cover certain regions of Macedonia, where the powerful monasteries of Mount Athos had their possessions, and, to a lesser extent, the western coast of Asia Minor. Not only do these sources offer limited geographic coverage but are also unequally distributed over time, with the first half of the fourteenth century being the best documented period, at least as far as Macedonia is concerned. The most precious documents for the study of rural economy and demography are the *praktika*, that is inventories drafted by state officials recording a large landowner's properties and dependant peasants, along with the taxes burdening land and people. We possess only a few dozens of *praktika*, the bulk of the remaining documents recording sales or donations in favor of monasteries. Together with the *praktika*, these deeds are a source for studying the fortune of these establishments and their acquisition practices. As far as the management of the estates is concerned, practically no Byzantine estate account has survived. The best source on management techniques and the landowners' mentality are a number of monastic rules (*typika*) that contain regulations on the administration of the estates and their revenues.[5] The Ottoman tax registers (*tahrir defterleri*), beginning in the fifteenth century, also offer valuable information concerning in particular the demography and agriculture. We are, nevertheless, lacking direct evidence or quantitative data on many crucial issues, notably on farming techniques and yields. Information on the urban economy and the exchanges is even more deficient than that regarding the agrarian economy. As far as trade is concerned, the most significant evidence comes from documents preserved in Italian archives, in particular those of Venice, which offer indirect information on the activities of Byzantine merchants.[6] The increasing archaeological data concerning our period have begun to be exploited by economic historians notably in the examination of manufacture and artisanal production, activities on which little is known otherwise.[7]

DEMOGRAPHY

It is now generally accepted that after a low in the seventh or eighth century, there began in Byzantium a period of population growth that lasted up to the fourteenth century. The evidence on population is quite meager. The only quantitative information concerns certain Macedonian villages whose population is known from a number of early fourteenth-century *praktika*. For nine of these villages we also possess data from the early twelfth century, which show a substantial population increase between these two dates, on average 82 percent.[8] This evidence is in agreement with information from other parts of the Empire also suggesting a growth of population.[9] Assuming that the rate of demographic growth seen in Macedonia was replicated in the other parts of Byzantium, in the 1260s the total population of the reconstituted Empire may have been around 4.5 million.[10]

Opinions diverge as to when and why decline began in the course of the fourteenth century. Angeliki Laiou, who analyzed the data for Macedonian villages belonging to Athonite monasteries, observed that population declined in the majority of the settlements of her sample during the first four decades of the fourteenth century. She has concluded that there was a demographic crisis in this region which started in the early years of the century and continued into the 1340s when the plague dealt a catastrophic blow to the population. Laiou has attributed the decline both to political troubles (Catalan raids and civil wars) and to the impoverishment of Macedonian peasants caused by the gradual alienation of their property to their landlords (see below). She has shown that the poorer the peasants were the more mobile they became, that is, the more likely to migrate. Both insecurity and lack of resources made peasants flee their landlords' estates and establish themselves in other localities of Macedonia or beyond its limits.[11] Jacques Lefort has proposed a different scenario.[12] Unlike Laiou, he attributes the economic crisis, which he accepts, to overexpansion and reduced returns from land. His study of certain Macedonian regions (Chalkidike, Strymon River valley, Mount Pangaion) has shown that marginal and unproductive lands were put to cultivation, a phenomenon obviously resulting from the growth of population. Moreover, Lefort has insisted that population in Macedonia continued to expand until the arrival of the plague in 1347, a claim based on the evidence provided by a larger sample of villages than that used by Laiou.[13] Lefort has here retained only the number of households as an indicator for the population's size, not the number of family members recorded by the assessor, which he considers less trustworthy.[14] According to his data, though population diminished in a majority of villages between c. 1300 and c. 1320 and in a significant minority of settlements between c. 1320 and c. 1340, growth in the other villages outweighed this decline so that in both sub-periods there was an overall increase of population of 12 and 11 percent respectively. Lefort explains the relatively negative data for the c. 1300–c. 1320 span as the reflection of a temporary demographic crisis, possibly provoked by the Catalans' passing in 1307, which did not alter the general positive trend that continued up to the coming of the plague.[15] One may note here the information that in the years leading to 1321 the central government in Constantinople managed to significantly increase taxation, something which concords better with a positive rather than with a negative demographic context.[16] Laiou has maintained her thesis in the face of Lefort's arguments. She has accepted, however, that there was a crisis of overexpansion, but only in some areas of Macedonia.[17] Laiou is not alone in thinking that there was still space for expansion. Commenting on the apparent difficulty of state officials to find public estates settled with peasants and the frequent mention of abandoned lands, Nicolas Oikonomides has suggested that in early fourteenth-century Macedonia there was more land than could be exploited by the available manpower.[18] The most compelling evidence that there was room for expansion before the plague hit comes from the Ottoman tax registers of the early sixteenth century, where several villages' population is considerably superior to what it was in the early fourteenth century.[19]

THE ORGANIZATION OF PRODUCTION

Production largely took place within the context of estates, which may have corresponded to the territory of a village or to a part of it. Ideally, estates were continuous land units. But this was rarely true in practice; physically disconnected parcels of arable, vineyard, and pasture land were located more or less near the main estate on which they depended administratively. There were also modest properties that were not attached to any estate but belonged to independent peasants; our data does not allow us to judge their extent.[20] Estate size varied considerably. A modest-sized estate in thirteenth-century Macedonia measured approximately 30 hectares of arable and vineyards.[21] A larger estate in fourteenth-century Thrace contained, before it was divided, more than 600 hectares of land of all qualities.[22] Vaster estates are also attested, such as the one situated near Smyrna in Asia Minor whose surface has been estimated at approximately 1,350 hectares. This land corresponded to the territory of a village and was for the most part mountainous.[23]

There is no way of estimating what percentage of land was controlled by the different types of landowners. The state may have owned the largest share.[24] However, the estates it directly controlled and exploited at this time were relatively few. The usufruct of the greatest part of public land was ceded to individuals in exchange for their providing services, mostly military (under the *pronoia* system). The next two largest portions belonged to the great lay and ecclesiastical landowners, most notably the powerful monasteries. The property controlled by the latter grew in the period under consideration mainly through the acquisition of lands coming from the aristocracy and the peasantry and to a lesser extent the state.[25] Few laymen ever amassed the amount of properties typical for large monasteries. The least important share of the land was in the ownership of peasants, whether these were dependent or not. The dependent peasants (*paroikoi*), that is those living on grounds belonging to a large landowner, are the ones we know best thanks to the *praktika* that contain lists of them and their properties. The wealth of the *paroikoi* varied greatly from one estate to another but also within the same village; many were landless. Generally speaking, dependent peasant properties included small plots of garden, orchards and, quite often, modest vineyards. In early fourteenth-century Macedonia, peasants of monasteries owned on average approximately 0.2 hectares of vineyards.[26] More rarely, the property of *paroikoi* included arable land. Only few of these peasants owned considerable quantities of arable (five hectares or more) while the majority owned very little, meaning that they too, like most other peasants, had to rent land from a landlord.[27] In most estates, the arable land owned by peasants must have corresponded to a fraction of that belonging to the monastery[28]. At least in monastic estates, global peasant property was diminishing in our period. Laiou's analysis of the censuses of certain Macedonian villages belonging to Athonite monasteries has shown a gradual impoverishment, both in lands and animal power, of dependant peasant populations between c. 1300 and c. 1340. The decline of the number of oxen, on average by 35 percent in Laiou's sample, is remarkable. The peasants' lands were absorbed by the estate owners.[29] It is possible that our sources exaggerate the problem: the peasants' condition in lay properties may not have been as bad as it appears in monastic estates (cf. below). Large landowners continued to acquire in this period land from independent peasants. There is plenty of data showing peasants, dependent or not, alienating small parcels of land, arable and vineyard, to monasteries and powerful individuals. The periodic financial problems of the peasants, caused in particular by a bad harvest, and, no doubt, pressure from the landlords, allowed the latter to acquire lands, sometimes at reduced prices.[30] The growth of the population may have contributed to the deterioration of the peasants' economic condition. Expansion into marginal lands would have meant that in some places returns from land were diminishing, thus making the peasants more vulnerable to their lords' expansionist policies.[31] The decrease in the number of oxen is no doubt also related to the peasants' long-term economic problems and to some extent to the effects of war.

Besides monastic properties, there is little data on the exploitation and management of lay and public estates. It is traditionally assumed that exploitation techniques were the same for all types of large property. But there are some, more or less certain, differences that could have influenced land exploitation. Unthreatened by division through inheritance and less affected by political circumstances, monastic fortunes tended to enjoy greater continuity than lay fortunes. In contrast to landowners based in cities and *pronoia* holders, who in most cases would manage their possessions from a distance, rural monasteries were situated relatively near their properties.[32] This proximity may have favored policies that implied a close management of the estates, such as the carrying out of land improvement schemes and the acquisition of the peasants' land in order to rent it or exploit it directly.[33] It is finally also possible that monasteries generally enjoyed greater tax exemptions than lay landowners. This would have allowed monks to offer better terms to peasants wishing to settle or simply work on their estates, making the latter more densely populated.

Great rural monasteries possessed several estates scattered in a more or less narrow zone around the main house, although geography and land availability modified this model. Monasteries with access to the sea could own estates situated at a relatively great distance. These estates were normally close to the coast or to a river, that is, accessible by boat. Monastic fortunes reached a peak in the course of the fourteenth century. In 1376, the monastery of Vatopedi, one of the wealthiest houses of Mount Athos, possessed 46 villages or estates (including some urban dependencies), situated for the most part in eastern Macedonia. Their total surface was certainly much greater than that attested (c. 6,500 hectares); it was probably closer to that calculated for Lavra, another powerful Athonite monastery, which controlled more than 27,000 hectares in 1350. A medium-sized monastery would be more like that of Lembiotissa, near Smyrna, which towards the end of the thirteenth century possessed 10 estates of a total surface of more than 2,000 hectares.[34] Powerful aristocrats, especially those living in

Constantinople, no doubt resembled the large monasteries of the city which owned numerous estates concentrated in the provinces closest to the capital, Thrace and Bithynia, but also further afield. Most of these properties were situated near the sea.[35] The fact that great estates tended to be located near the sea is in part related to the terrain of Asia Minor and Greece, where mountains limit arable land to a narrow zone around the sea; but it also has to do with the large estates' need to transport their agricultural produce, especially cereals.[36] The majority of landowners, lay or monastic, were much more modest than those mentioned above. An often quoted lay fortune, that of Theodosios Skaranos, seems to have consisted of a single estate of less than 30 hectares of land dedicated for the most part to cereal cultivation but including also 2.4 hectares of vineyard.[37] Skaranos was of course well above the bottom of the social and economic ladder, which was occupied by the peasants.

The existing documentation only contains hints as to how the produce of monastic estates might have been commercialized or used in order to provide for the main house. It would seem that estates closest to the latter sent their surplus there while more distant estates sold their produce either locally to merchants or, apparently more often, shipped it to large markets on the monastery's boats. This model is only valid for rural houses, not in the case of monasteries situated in cities, especially Constantinople, the Empire's largest market.[38]

The estates were exploited thanks to the work of the peasants, whether these were settled there or not. As stated above, besides the land they owned, peasants usually had to rent additional plots in order to cultivate cereals but also to plant vineyards and gardens. It seems that the greater proportion of seigneurial land was leased out to peasants. On an estate in early fourteenth-century Thrace directly exploited land corresponded to less than a third of the total domanial land.[39] There are examples of lower proportions of directly exploited land from the pre-1204 period.[40] The amount of arable land peasants cultivated, whether this was theirs or rented, depended on a number of factors:[41] on the peasant's workforce, in particular the number of oxen available to him;[42] on the abundance of arable land which in its turn depended on demographic pressure; and finally, the predominance in some regions of different cultures, such as viticulture, could diminish the land allocated to cereals. The above explain why we see in our sources peasants who own a pair of oxen holding farms of very different sizes, from 4.4 hectares to well over 10 hectares. We have relatively good data on the number of oxen peasants owned. Again, here there is great variation between villages. In 25 villages of the region of Thessalonike belonging to the monastery of Lavra in 1321 more than half of the peasant households did not own any ox, while approximately 29 and 19 percent owned two and one ox respectively (ratio of oxen to households: 0.76:1).[43] Peasants with only one ox obtained the pair of oxen needed for plowing probably by collaborating with other peasants of the same category. As for those who had no draft animals, they may have in some cases been able to use oxen provided by the landlord.[44] But, most likely, the majority of these people tilled the land using hand tools.[45]

Peasants leasing fields had to pay a rent, either a fixed one in cash or, more commonly, a rent in kind, corresponding, in the case of arable land, to one-third of the harvest.[46] Landowners received cash payments for lands rented to individuals who turned them into vineyards; mills were also given out to lessees who paid a rent in cash and/or kind.[47] Besides the rent paid for the lands they cultivated, *paroikoi* also had to perform labor services which went into the exploitation of the demesne.[48] The number of days of labor peasants owed every year varied significantly from one estate to the other: cases of 12, 24, and 52 days of labor are attested; sometimes labor services were commuted to cash payments. The reasons for this variation escape us, but we may attribute it to local custom and, possibly, to agreements between landlords and peasants. Texts of the eleventh and twelfth centuries suggest that landowners or their estate managers sometimes tried to raise the peasants' rents and corvées.[49] Such attitudes no doubt persisted and may have intensified in the thirteenth and early fourteenth centuries, when manpower was more abundant than before. Nevertheless, during the same centuries the number of corvées owed by peasants was registered in the *praktika* established by state officials; this may have made these arrangements fixed offering some protection to the peasants.[50] It seems likely that in many estates corvée labor was sufficient for the exploitation of the greatest part of the demesne.[51] The importance of wage labor for the exploitation of the demesne is hard to estimate given the nature of our sources which tend to record only peasants settled in an estate. The consensus is that its weight was not great. This kind of labor may have been more common for the exploitation of vineyards and the keeping of animals and less significant for the cultivation of the arable.[52]

FORMS OF LAND EXPLOITATION AND FARMING TECHNIQUES

A great variety of husbandry practices reflected the diversity in climate and terrain that characterized the Byzantine Empire, even at its reduced post-1204 size.[53] The effort to achieve self-sufficiency tended to mitigate variation, meaning that grain was produced almost everywhere and wine and olive oil where possible. Some areas, nevertheless, specialized in particular products, either because the soil and climatic conditions favored certain husbandry practices or in response to demand from a nearby market.

The main grain sown was wheat followed by barley, oats, millet, and rye; in certain areas of fifteenth-century Macedonia wheat and barley represented half and one-third of cereal production, respectively. Spring wheat was also sown in February or March. Dry legumes, such as lentils, chick peas, and broad beans were an important element of everyday diet. They were cultivated in gardens but also in fields. Vineyards, whose produce of grapes and above all wine was particularly profitable, were to be found almost everywhere. They were usually cultivated in small plots belonging to, or rented by, peasants, though large vineyards, owned by landlords, were also common. Given its profitability, wine was transported great distances. The wines of several islands and coastal locations of the Aegean and the Black seas were appreciated in Constantinople. At the same time, both the capital and the city of Thessalonike were surrounded by important vineyards.[54] Vineyards were widespread in the Strymon valley and Chalkidike regions of Macedonia, as can be seen in the documentation coming from the Athonite monasteries. In certain parts of Macedonia, vineyards covered as much as 16 percent of the cultivated area.[55] The zone of cultivation of the olive tree is more restricted than that of the vine. Certain areas, such as the Peloponnese, the Aegean islands, Bithynia, and the area around Smyrna specialized in the production of olive oil. In Smyrna, olive trees were a common possession of peasants;[56] but they were also one of the main assets of the monastery of Lembiotissa, for we know that it acquired 570 trees in the last three quarters of the thirteenth century.[57] Fresh vegetables and fruits were produced by peasants, who often owned small gardens and orchards in order to complement their diet but also for the market. The cultivation of fruit trees and gardens was lucrative near towns, most notably in the case of Thessalonike and Constantinople, where large gardens are attested.[58]

Most peasants owned some kind of animals, needed for their products and as workforce. Peasant livestock included poultry; pigs, sheep, and goats; horses, mules, and donkeys; and cows and oxen. Beehives were another common possession of peasants. With the exception of some villages specializing in animal rearing and leaving aside those well-off peasants who had a few dozens of sheep and several other beasts, peasants generally owned very few animals.[59] To a large extent, these animals were geared towards satisfying the subsistence needs of the peasant families. It was different in the case of the livestock owned by powerful individuals or institutions, comprising thousands of sheep and hundreds of cattle, which were reared for the market and for the estates' exploitation.[60] There were significant regional variations, animal husbandry being most important in areas with good pasture and in the less fertile and mountainous zones, such as the interior of Asia Minor and some islands.

There is very limited data on farming techniques. Often there is no direct evidence but simply assumptions based on the knowledge or not of certain practices. Techniques generally remained traditional, unchanged since antiquity. Land lay fallow every second year, at least when there was sufficient supply of it. Manure's fertilizing properties were well-known but it probably played a limited role outside gardens and the fields within the villages (*esochorapha*, *esothyria*) which could be cultivated intensively. There is little evidence for stable manure,[61] but, apparently, after the harvest fields were given over to animals for pasture.[62] The planting of legumes and spring-wheat on fallow land were ancient practices certainly followed by the Byzantines, but to an unknown extent.[63] Selective sowing is also mentioned, something which probably led to an increase of yields over time.[64] In terms of agricultural implements, there was hardly any change since antiquity as far as we can tell from tool depictions in illuminated manuscripts and the archaeological finds. In any case, some of the innovations that appeared in Western Europe, such as the heavy plow with a moldboard and the scythe, were not suited to Byzantine terrain.[65] Maybe the most significant method for improving productivity, both in terms of its effectiveness and its widespread application, was irrigation, sometimes carried out at a large scale by great landowners. It concerned mostly gardens but also vineyards and fruit trees, including olive trees.[66]

Our knowledge of yields is also disappointing. Oil production has been estimated at two to three liters of oil per olive tree; wine production at about 12 hectoliters per hectare. Both estimates are essentially based on what we know about the production of Mediterranean regions in modern times.[67] Cereal yields vary greatly depending on soil and climate, both of which are wildly diverse in the territories under discussion. Here too little is known. Data concerning different areas of the Byzantine world in the Middle Ages range from 1.6 to five grains of wheat or millet for one sown, on average 3.3:1, that is 4.2 quintals per hectare[68]. Scholars have also looked at yields recorded in early twentieth-century Greece and Turkey, Ottoman registers, and modern travelers' accounts. In 1921, wheat yields in Greece ranged from 4.9 to 11.5 quintals per hectare; in certain Ottoman tax registers they averaged between four and six quintals per hectare.[69] Notwithstanding the variation of yields, there have been attempts to establish what would have been the average cereal yield in Byzantium. Until recently most scholars accepted the average yields of 3–3.5 grains for one sown (3.8–4.5 quintals per hectare) proposed by Nicolas Svoronos on the basis of what is known on the land's rent and the data mentioned above.[70] Nikola Kondov has challenged Svoronos' average yield, which he finds too low on the basis of dietary and agronomic arguments; he suggested that a yield of 5.2–4.2:1 (6.7 and 5.4 quintals per hectare) was more likely.[71] In the last years, alongside with the greater optimism regarding the general trend of the economy, scholars have accepted considerably higher yields than Svoronos had, of 5.6 and 4:1 (7.2 and 5.1 q/ha) for the first and the second quality land, respectively.[72] Their estimates are based on the likely composition of peasant budgets[73] and, in one case, the interpretation of data concerning a concrete estate.[74] These calculations are more or less problematic, either because they assign too great a role on cereals, in the case of the budgets,[75] or because they rely on incomplete and insecure evidence.

Agricultural production kept growing in Byzantium up to the middle of the fourteenth century as more land was brought under cultivation and as a result of more intensive farming. Both peasants and landlords contributed to this process, although their aims and way of action differed. There is mostly indirect evidence on the extension of land under cereal cultivation, thanks to clearing or draining, which was carried out both in a piecemeal fashion by peasants or, in larger schemes, at the initiative of landlords. Within the context of a growing population, peasants were forced to bring new land under cultivation in order to feed themselves. This process is relatively well-documented in the case of the village of Radolibos in eastern Macedonia, where soils of poor quality and distant from the settlement were turned into fields between the twelfth and the fourteenth century.[76] Landlords no doubt played an important role in the foundation of the new estates or hamlets that appear in documents from thirteenth- and early fourteenth-century Macedonia.[77] Such schemes would have involved the establishment of peasants on the new settlements. The creation of estates by landlords aimed at creating marketable surpluses.[78]

Contrary to cereal cultivation, there is abundant evidence on investment in high-yield activities such as the planting of vineyards and fruit trees and the creation of gardens and mills. This kind of activities was the most common type of land improvement. They were undertaken by a variety of individuals, including powerful landlords, owners of medium-sized estates and peasants who disposed of some surplus. Especially the planting of vineyards, which were profitable even at a small scale, was essential for peasants who needed to acquire cash in order to pay their taxes. For wealthier investors, these improvements would aim at self-sufficiency but also at creating surpluses for the market.[79] Amelioration projects could include the irrigation of the planted vineyards and trees, something that as we have seen greatly increased yields.

Recent scholarship has underlined the role of large estates in intensifying exploitation thanks to their greater resources.[80] According to certain monastic rules dating from the twelfth to the early fourteenth century, it was among the obligations of estate managers to see that the properties' revenues grow, in particular thanks to improvements and the active supervision of the farmers.[81] These texts do not only reveal their authors' profit-oriented mentality; they also tell us something about the realities of the time: with proper management, returns from land were expected to grow, something which may be taken to suggest that land productivity was generally on the rise. Besides monastic rules, other texts also testify to the landowners' efforts to achieve greater yields as well as to the moral value attached to land improvement in the thirteenth and fourteenth centuries.[82] The resources and efforts that were dedicated to ameliorations should not be exaggerated nevertheless. It seems, in particular, that the greatest portion of the monastic landlords' monetary surplus was used for the purchase of land rather than the improvement of existing properties.[83]

ARTISANAL PRODUCTION

In the course of the eleventh and twelfth centuries secondary production grew significantly.[84] A larger and wealthier population, foreign demand, and technological advances that made products cheaper contributed to this growth. Besides Constantinople, the traditional center of artisanal production, numerous provincial towns appeared or acquired importance in this period as loci of pottery, glass, and silk manufacture. As in the past, luxury products were created for the elite, whose demand certainly grew. But, increasingly in this period, items of lesser quality were produced to satisfy the needs of a larger population of relatively well-off consumers. A part of the production was exported outside the Empire, notably to Italy, southern France, and Egypt. Byzantine techniques were often more advanced and the quality of the products generally superior to those of Western Europe.

This promising situation would change, nevertheless, following Byzantium's conquest and fragmentation in 1204. Sooner or later, secondary production began to decline and some industries eventually ceased altogether. Fewer types of objects were produced and for a geographically reduced market. Byzantine products were increasingly replaced by cheaper Western goods that were imported in large quantities by Italian merchants. As Western manufactured goods flooded the markets, Byzantium's exports of raw materials to the West grew. Pottery continued for a while in the same twelfth-century lines but by the middle of the thirteenth century Constantinople stopped producing the pottery it used to export. After that point there is no more evidence of large organized workshops. Smaller production centers persisted catering to a local or regional market. In Italy, local production replaced Byzantine imports whereas in Byzantium imported ceramics, especially Italian, gradually supplanted local ware. The situation seems to have been very similar in the case of glass, where Venetian imports displaced Byzantine products. The silk industry was a domain where Byzantium was superior to the West before 1204. This too declined rapidly after the Empire's conquest. Besides the capital, the two bigger centers of silk production, Thebes and Corinth, were now outside the Empire. No new production centers came to replace them in Byzantium. But in the areas under Latin rule silk cloth manufacture declined also: production at Corinth ceased immediately after 1204; in other places, it lasted longer and exceptionally in Thebes into the 1320s. Increasingly, Byzantium and the territories under Latin control became exporters of raw silk, importing silk cloth from Venice. Commenting on the secondary production's decline in the pre-plague period, Laiou concludes: "neither manufacturing nor . . . trade came to the rescue of the economy, whose agriculture had already perhaps reached its Malthusian limits."[85] The demographic and economic decline after the middle of the fourteenth century did not make things better. The diminished demand, coming from the few individuals who concentrated wealth in their hands, was mostly satisfied by imported products.

URBANIZATION, AGRICULTURAL MARKETS, AND COMMERCE

In the period preceding the conquest of Constantinople by the Fourth Crusade, the Byzantine Empire possessed a sizeable urban population, higher than most countries in the West. The general growth of population, the development of secondary production and commerce, and other job or client opportunities offered by the government and the wealthy households in the cities helped urban population expand. Growth was greater in the European provinces than in Asia Minor on account of the troubles caused in the latter by the Turkish invasion of the late eleventh century. Towns flourished in Greece. According to some scholars, a few places may have had a population of around 20,000. Thessalonike, the Empire's second largest city, was certainly above that limit.[86] As before, by far the most important city remained Constantinople. A chronicler of the Fourth Crusade claimed that it was home to at least 400,000 inhabitants. In any case, its population greatly outnumbered that of any other city in Europe.[87] No figures are available for the late Byzantine cities until the fifteenth century. It has been suggested that urban population decreased after 1204, even before the arrival of the plague, and this in spite of the continued demographic growth. Constantinople's population in the first half of the fifteenth century has been estimated at 40,000 to 50,000, on the basis of contemporary accounts.[88] Other chronicles give for Thessalonike 25,000 or 40,000 inhabitants for the year 1423.[89] Both cities were at one of their lowest points at the time. Constantinople's population certainly collapsed after 1204, not only on account of the immediate exodus of a part of the population but also because of the city's impoverishment as the capital of a reduced empire. The city's population no doubt picked up after its recovery by the Byzantines in 1261. It was now the capital of a larger empire, housing the imperial court and administration, as well as important aristocratic houses. Monasteries and welfare establishments were restored, though their significance was now smaller than before 1204. Finally, Constantinople continued to benefit from its role as an important commercial center. According to one guess, the capital may have had more than 100,000 inhabitants in the thirteenth century.[90] In spite of the influx of people fleeing the Turks' advance in Asia Minor or the insecurity in the countryside,[91] the population may have already began to decline in the early fourteenth century, as the state and the aristocracy became poorer. In the last century of Byzantium conditions deteriorated. Though trade continued to flourish, the territories Constantinople controlled kept shrinking. The arrival of the plague in 1347, its recurring outbreaks, and one Ottoman blockade at the turn of the fifteenth century further reduced the population. As far as provincial cities are concerned, the archaeological evidence, which is patchy and more or less insecure, presents a mixed image with some places, Pergamon, Sardis, Monembasia, attaining their greatest prosperity or expansion in the thirteenth century and others, like Athens, apparently declining after 1204.[92] At any rate, none of these places seems to have been very important, and it is indeed unlikely that any town's population surpassed 10,000.[93] Even before the arrival of the plague, several regions suffered from wars and its consequences on agriculture and commerce; the downsizing of the administration and the decline or stagnation of secondary production had a negative effect on urban demography.

In all cities, areas within the walls or at a close proximity were given to cultivation, as gardens, vineyards, but also as wheat-fields. The products of these husbandries supplemented the imports from the countryside where from the greater part of the foodstuffs came. In most cases, this countryside coincided with their immediate hinterland. Not for Thessalonike and even less so for Constantinople, the two largest cities both with access to the sea. Besides imports from its fertile neighboring provinces, Bithynia and Thrace, the capital absorbed foodstuffs and other provisions originating from all around the Aegean and Black seas. A part of this produce came from the estates of the city's large landlords, without ever entering the commercial circuit. Large urban monasteries and, no doubt, also lay households, owned boats with which they transported surplus produce from their provincial estates. Nevertheless, the majority of the urban population and to some extent monasteries and lay households relied on the market.[94] The market was provided by merchants who bought agricultural produce in the provinces, often in ports where the sellers congregated. These would have included local landlords and peasants. The latter may have alternatively sold their surpluses to their own landlords.[95] The peasants were obliged to engage in some exchange of this kind in order to obtain the cash they needed every year, mainly in order to pay their taxes. Even at its reduced post-1204 size, the population of Constantinople, and to a lesser degree that of Thessalonike, created a significant attraction for both large-scale producers and merchants of foodstuffs. This pull certainly influenced the landlords' attitudes, especially in the provinces neighboring these cities.

An insight into the interaction between town and countryside is given by the Ottoman tax registers concerning the lower Strymon valley. According to calculations based on the 1454/5 register, approximately 37,000 people lived in the villages in the administrative districts of Serres, Zichna, and Keşişlik, whereas the combined population of the towns in this region, Serres and Zichna, was about 9,000, that is 20 percent of the total population.[96] The inhabitants of Serres exercised a variety of professions. While many were employed in the service sector, most numerous were the artisans who were chiefly involved in the production of cloth, finished garments and footwear. Besides serving as a general market for its province, Serres may have produced clothes for an even larger zone.[97]

After 1204, Byzantium was penetrated, much more than before, by Italian merchants, especially the Venetians and the Genoese. The territories that formed the twelfth-century Empire became part of an international commercial network increasingly dominated by the Italians where the eastern Mediterranean mostly provided raw materials to the West and imported manufactured goods. The greater Western demand and the commercial and financial techniques introduced by Latin merchants and settlers led to an intensification of both long- and short-distance trade and stimulated the production of market-oriented commodities. The main beneficiaries of this growth were the Latins, though Byzantine-held territories were also affected. The domination of the Venetians and the Genoese was based on their strong presence in the Aegean and the Black sea, where they had colonies and trading posts, and on the commercial privileges, in particular tax exemption, which they enjoyed in these territories.[98] Moreover, the Italians had access to larger capital resources and catered for a vaster market than their Byzantine counterparts.[99] Byzantine commerce is largely obscured by the source material available to us but it is clear that it was at a disadvantage, especially because of the unequal competition with the Italians.[100] Byzantine regional and sometimes international trade continued, most notably in the case of the town of Monembasia, whose merchants were active in both the Aegean and Black seas and as far as the Middle East. However, the Byzantines could not rival the Italians. Largely ousted from international markets they were left with local and regional exchanges, often as providers for the large-scale commerce of the Italians. Things seem to have changed somewhat after the middle of the fourteenth century when the sources show an expansion of trade in Greek hands both in terms of volume and space, with a significant engagement in the Black Sea and a presence also in the eastern Mediterranean and Western Europe. At least partly, this greater involvement in trade may be explained by the abandonment of Byzantine conservative attitudes towards it. No doubt influenced by the example of the Italians and with revenues from land and imperial service vanishing, Byzantine society turned to the only alternative left, commerce.[101] The lively commercial activity, either in Italian or Greek hands, certainly contributed to the vitality of certain cities, especially after the crisis set in. This is most notable in the case of Constantinople and Thessalonike, both important consumers but also relay stations of regional and international trade.[102]

STANDARDS OF LIVING AMONG LANDLORDS AND PEASANTS

The revenues of a landlord came from a number of sources. First, from his estates in the countryside where rent would be collected mostly in kind but also in cash. There would also be revenues in kind coming from the demesne land exploited thanks to corvée and wage labor. Landowners often also owned urban real estate, shops and houses, most of which were rented. Of great significance were the peasants' taxes, paid in cash or in kind. Great landowners were in this period often awarded partial or total tax exemption for their properties, including their dependent peasants. This did not mean that the peasants ceased to pay taxes, but that the landlords could keep this money for themselves. Landowners also engaged in commercial and financial activities. Several powerful monasteries, for example, owned boats which they used to buy and sell agricultural products. The monks also lent money for an interest. The extent of these activities certainly varied from case to case. At least until the middle of the fourteenth century the revenues from commercial and financial activities were in most cases of a lesser importance than those obtained from the exploitation of the real estate. Finally, certain renowned monasteries enjoyed a steady flow of cash donations, usually in exchange of prayers.[103]

Practically no document recording the revenues of a landowner or of one of his estates has come down to us.[104] Models, including hypotheses on the importance of certain elements of a landowners' budget (e.g. the yield), suggest a net revenue of around three percent of the land's value, for the pre-1204 period.[105] As tax exemption became common for large landowners after the twelfth century their net revenue rose accordingly. Often they paid little for their lands whereas they had the right to keep for themselves their peasants' taxes. The revenues the monastery of Lavra would derive in 1321 from the arable land it held in the district of Thessalonike have been calculated at 4,320 to 4,860 gold coins, depending on the grain's price, or 13 to 15 percent of the land's value.[106] To a large extent, the great difference in net revenue between the pre-1204 models and Lavra in 1321 is owed to the fact that in the latter case taxes are not subtracted from the income since the monastery is thought to have been tax exempt.[107] At about the same time, Lavra also had the right to collect from its dependant peasants in the district of Thessalonike a total of 1,575 gold coins of tax, an amount which is not hypothetical but known thanks to the *praktika*.[108] Of course, as suggested above, the monastery would have other revenues as well but apparently the peasants' taxes were only second to land exploitation. The same would be valid for public estates, which paid no tax, whether these were directly controlled by the state or, more often, in the hands of *pronoia* beneficiaries. Lay landowners too enjoyed tax exemptions but probably to a lesser extent than great monasteries.

There are some model peasant budgets concerning the pre-1204 period and exclusively cereal revenues that differ mostly with regard to the yield and burden of tax or rent each scholar accepts. They all agree, nevertheless, that the wealthier peasants, those possessing a pair of oxen or more and cultivating land in excess of eight hectares, would be able to achieve a marketable surplus; this would be significantly larger if the peasant were a landlord and not a tenant, that is when he would not have to pay a rent for the land but only tax.[109] Not only were these peasants in the minority, but, as it has been rightly emphasized, it makes little sense to insist on cereal revenues given the importance of polyculture and polyactivity for peasant households.[110] The significance of vineyards and olive trees has already been underlined. Peasants also cultivated gardens and fruit trees, raised a number of different animals producing milk, meat, and wool, kept bees, went fishing, produced silk or linen, exploited forest resources, and could engage in artisanal activity or be employed as agricultural or construction workers.

THE LATE MEDIEVAL CRISIS

Before considering the acute crisis that erupted following the arrival of the plague, it is useful to briefly review the main political developments of this period given their impact on the economy.[111] For reasons of space, I will focus on the better documented regions of Macedonia, Lemnos, and Thrace. I have already mentioned the troubles of the first half of the fourteenth century that were caused by the Catalans and the civil war of 1321–28 and which affected Thrace and Macedonia. The political situation deteriorated dramatically from the 1340s. A new, more catastrophic, civil war in two episodes (1341–47; 1352–57) weakened the Empire and allowed its neighbors to encroach upon its territories. By 1345, the Serbs had conquered the greatest part of Macedonia. Instability in the border regions persisted as fighting with the Serbs continued intermittently in the 1350s and early 1360s.[112] A document of 1362 states that the Serbs were pillaging the villages around Thessalonike.[113] The situation was not better in Thrace which was devastated in the 1340s by Turkish troops participating in the civil war. Turkish raids continued in the 1350s and 1360s, as the Ottomans, by then firmly established in Asia Minor, began their expansion into Europe. After the conquest of Thrace in the 1360s, the Ottomans turned to Macedonia. A period of raids followed their victory at the Maritza River in 1371 up until the 1380s, when they accomplished the conquest of the province. Turkish piracy, which had already begun in the early fourteenth century, continued at this time to ravage the islands and coastal regions of the northern Aegean. Apart from the immediate destruction and pillaging, Turkish raids—whether by land or by sea—often involved the abduction and enslavement of local populations. The first Ottoman conquest of Macedonia meant that there was stability for a while. Constantinople, on the contrary, had to deal with a protracted Ottoman blockade from 1394. The capital was only saved by Timur's defeat of Bayezid at the battle of Ankara in 1402, which ushered in a period of troubles for the Ottomans and allowed the Byzantines to recover some territories in Thrace and Macedonia. Ottoman weakness was short-lived, and from the 1420s there began the reconquest of the lost territories, which ended with the capture of Thessalonike in 1430. Macedonia and Thrace were now firmly in Ottoman hands. Only the Peloponnese, some islands, and Constantinople remained Byzantine. After a new unsuccessful siege in 1422, the capital finally succumbed in 1453.

The economy entered a period of profound crisis after the middle of the fourteenth century. Data on the agrarian economy in the last century of Byzantium are even less plentiful than before. The main tendencies are nevertheless clear: severe underpopulation, abandonment of previously exploited lands, and disruption of communications and commerce. Demographic decline is primarily the result of the plague that hit the Byzantine world in 1347 and kept returning every 10 years or so through the fifteenth century.[114] The frequent warfare and raiding that depleted the population through death and enslavement contributed to the decline. The few data available show a dramatic decrease of the population. But our documentation is biased and may exaggerate the crisis: it has been noted that most of our information comes from regions close to the coast that are likely to have been hit harder by the epidemic and piracy.[115] With regard to Chalkidike, the documents speak of deserted peasant farms and, in the case of Mount Athos, of ruined hermitages.[116] On one occasion, peasants apparently fled their homelands in the Kassandra peninsula, moving several kilometers to the north to settle at a location that was soon after fortified by the monastery of Vatopedi.[117] Villages or estates in western Chalkidike were abandoned at an unprecedented rate in the second half of the fourteenth century. In five known villages that were not deserted the population dropped precipitously in the same period (57 percent).[118] The island of Lemnos also appears to have been seriously depopulated at this time, as is suggested by the frequent mention in documents of abandoned lands and the low numbers of the peasants recorded.[119] Communications and exchanges were seriously affected by the insecurity of the period. Urban demand declined as city populations dwindled and became impoverished. The prices of grain, however, rose in the second part of the fourteenth century. No doubt, this is the result of the disruption of trade but possibly also of a decline in production, which must have suffered from the lack of manpower and insecurity.[120]

These circumstances did not affect everybody in the same way. Those worse hit were no doubt the large lay landowners who lost control of their properties in areas under foreign occupation or who were unable to properly exploit their estates due to the shortage of manpower and the prevailing insecurity.[121] Although the troubles certainly disturbed monasteries as well, causing the decline of some, several of the great houses of the provinces, most notably those of Mount Athos, were able to preserve their properties under different rules.[122] These monasteries were probably also more successful in maintaining, to some extent, the exploitation of their estates, thanks to their greater resources of wealth and peasants. The monks could transfer to depopulated estates peasants coming from other areas, and sometimes from other properties of theirs. We know of four such transfers from Macedonia and elsewhere to the island of Lemnos carried out by the monastery of Vatopedi, two of which took place in the second half of the fourteenth century and two in the first half of the fifteenth. In 1405, the monastery of Lavra also planned to resettle some of its peasants in Lemnos.[123] Other such examples are known from Macedonia where deserted villages were populated thanks to the efforts of monasteries but also lay landowners.[124] There is no doubt, nevertheless, that few laymen had at this time the resources available to great monasteries. In fact, these establishments profited from the aristocracy's troubles to expand their landed possessions, acquiring by donation or at very low cost lay estates that were depopulated or threatened by confiscation.[125] The state participated in the effort to restore land exploitation, sometimes in conjunction with monasteries. On one occasion, in the early fifteenth century, the emperor donated an abandoned village to the Athonite monastery of Dionysiou. The state and the monastery would combine their resources in order to bring the property back to cultivation.[126]

At least in some respects, the peasants who did not fall victim to epidemic, war, and enslavement, must have found themselves in an improved position after the middle of the fourteenth century. Depopulation made manpower sought-after and land abundant. Peasants may have been able to negotiate better terms with their landlords. Indeed, the dues peasants owed to landowners in early fifteenth-century Macedonia seem to be much lower than those known from the pre-plague period.[127] Irrespective of whether this was a result of Ottoman influence, this change represents an evolution in the relations between peasants and landlords, which cannot be unrelated to the crisis. Peasants also seem to have acquired a lot of land. In the early fifteenth-century island of Lemnos peasants of the monastery of Dionysiou owned large amounts of arable (30–40 hectares), much more than it was normal a century earlier and certainly vaster than they could cultivate. Our data are very limited but it appears that the peasants in Lemnos were better off than those in Macedonia in terms of animal power at the beginning of the fifteenth century. Whereas in Lemnos the ratio of oxen per household ranged from 0.8 to 1.5, in Macedonia it was 0.4, half of what it was at the beginning of the fourteenth century.[128]

Though no doubt of a limited scale, the settlement of peasants and the other efforts to bring lands back to cultivation may have helped stabilize the agrarian economy laying the ground for future recovery. As far as population trends are concerned, judging from the few *praktika* available from early fifteenth-century Chalkidike, the population of monastic villages stagnated in the first two decades of that century.

Table 5.1 Number of Peasant Households in Villages of Chalkidike Belonging to the Monasteries of Vatopedi (Va) and Lavra (La), 1404–1420

	1404	*1409*	*1418*	*1420*
Eladiaba (Va)	11	13		
Gomatou (La)		21		18
Drymosyrta (La)	37	35		
Hermeleia (Va)	18	17	17	
Lantzou (Va)	9	13	23	
Prosphorion (Va)	11	11	5	
Hagios Mamas (Va)	28	21	23	

Sources: 1404: Lefort et al., *Actes de Vatopédi III*, nos. 188, 189; Lemerle et al., *Actes de Lavra III*, no. 155. 1409: Lefort et al., *Actes de Vatopédi III*, no. 200; Lemerle et al., *Actes de Lavra III*, no. 161. 1418: Lefort et al., *Actes de Vatopédi III*, no. 211. 1420: Lemerle et al., *Actes de Lavra III,* no. 165.

Signs of improvement can be found towards the middle of the fifteenth century when Macedonia was firmly part of the Ottoman Empire. A tax register dating from 1454/5 shows that in certain villages of Chalkidike populations were beginning to recover from the crisis whereas in the Strymon valley they were sometimes greater than in the early fourteenth century. The re-establishment of security but also in some cases the settlement of Turkish peasants contributed to recovery.[129] However, probably as a result of the recurring plague, the demographic expansion in southeastern Macedonia remained slow and uncertain between 1454/5 and 1478/9, the date of a second tax register that indicates an overall increase of 4.72%. After 1478/9, the pace of growth accelerated and by the beginning of the sixteenth century populations in most documented villages were significantly superior to their medieval maximums.[130] The situation in Lemnos remained unclear until its final conquest by the Ottomans in 1479. The population of about 3,000, calculated on the basis of the 1490 Ottoman tax register, appears very low in comparison to that of about 5,000, suggested by the following register of 1519. Whatever the reason for this phenomenon may be, it seems safe to conclude that the greater stability of the late fifteenth and early sixteenth century allowed the island's population to expand.[131]

CAUSES AND DURATION OF THE CRISIS

Several crucial questions related to the fourteenth-century crisis remain unanswered given the scarcity of information. On the basis of the evidence from Macedonia, it is clear that there was a crisis already before the serious troubles of the 1340s. However, both the causes and importance of this crisis are debatable. At the core of these questions lies the peasantry's impoverishment in the course of the first half of the fourteenth century. This was probably the result of a combination of factors. In some areas of Macedonia, the growth of population meant that resources were becoming scarcer. The policy of the landlords to acquire peasant land was decisive. Either through pressure or simply profiting from the peasants' financial difficulties, the powerful appropriated the peasants' land. Though the impoverishment of the populations is a serious limiting factor for demographic expansion, it seems that overall population kept growing up to the 1340s. This can only mean that the crisis was not very severe yet and that there were available resources. Indeed, there was apparently still space for expansion.

The landlords' acquisition of peasant properties meant a number of things. When acquiring from independent peasants, the landlords were expanding their estates, thus normally increasing their revenues. Moreover, when they absorbed the lands of their own dependent peasants, great landowners could extract more surplus from the peasants who now had to pay a rent instead of a tax. Investment in real estate was the preferred destination of the annual surplus in cash of lay and monastic landowners since at least the eleventh century.[132] Though the amelioration of lands was one of the duties of estate managers it probably absorbed fewer funds than purchase of property, as was no doubt the case with other possible investments, such as commerce and money lending. Land acquisition was motivated by the desire to augment income. It has already been noted that boosting profits through an increase in production and thanks to efficient management was the goal of monastic and other landowners since the twelfth century. The fact that landlords pursued the acquisition of their dependent peasants' land, something which reduced the taxes the latter owed to them, shows that the landlords were more interested in maximizing their rent in kind rather than their tax revenues, which in turn suggests a market-oriented attitude. It seems reasonable to assume that until the plague hit demand for agricultural products remained high thanks to both domestic demand and the growing needs of the West that was now well-connected with the eastern Mediterranean. The question is whether the policy of land acquisition continued to make economic sense in the first half of the fourteenth century, or whether the landlords were simply continuing blindly an earlier model. Were the revenues of large landowners rising in the early fourteenth century or were they pursuing unreasonable policies, as Laiou has suggested? The monasteries' strategy of land acquisition impoverished their peasants and caused some to flee or made their households less viable. Over time, this would have resulted in a stagnating or decreasing peasant population. Most likely, this process is also related to the diminishing animal power in peasant ownership. As far as the peasant populations are concerned, one may assume that their decrease in some villages would not have worried landowners excessively, especially in the context of continued demographic expansion. The decline in the number of oxen is another story. If our data are indeed representative of all types of estates, the drop in the number of draft animals would have seriously affected the landlords' revenues as this would have meant that less land could be cultivated. Only a proportionate increase in the number of oxen provided by the landlord could have offset the problem. We will never know what would have happened if plague and war had not ravaged Byzantium from the 1340s on. In any case, in 1347, the peasantry was certainly weakened and this probably intensified the plague's effects.

Though we do not have the kind of data that would allow us to distinguish short-term fluctuations in the second half of the fourteenth century, it is clear that recovery was very slow as the early fifteenth-century documentation suggests. It is in fact probable that conditions were worsening in the course of the second half of the fourteenth century. The severe decline of population after 1347 must have brought some sort of relief for the peasants who survived, because of the greater abundance of good land. Marginal lands could now be abandoned, meaning that productivity probably rose. Moreover, it is likely that the peasants' dues to their landlords diminished. However, it does not seem that the peasants, and even less so their landlords, profited from any of this in the medium-term. Not only were the peasants still very few at the beginning of the fifteenth century, they were sometimes also poorer than before. The situation that prevailed in the European provinces of the Empire during the second half of the fourteenth century was so unstable that an early recovery was impossible. War and piracy disrupted cultivation and caused the death, enslavement, or impoverishment of the peasantry. Insecurity combined with the recurrence of the plague kept population low. The landowners that managed to keep their estates in a fast changing political climate could not maintain the previous levels of exploitation. Many estates were abandoned. The impoverished Byzantine aristocracy could do little to react to this situation. The most important elements of stability were the great rural monasteries, which assured a degree of continuity in land exploitation and settlement. Conditions became slightly better in the course of the early fifteenth century as the warfare subsided. It was this improvement that allowed for the recovery we witness in the later part of the same century.

NOTES

1. For a comparison between the Byzantine and Western medieval economies, see most recently Angeliki E. Laiou and Cécile Morrisson, *The Byzantine Economy* (Cambridge: Cambridge University Press, 2007), 235–247.
2. See Kostis Smyrlis, *La fortune des grands monastères byzantins, fin du xᵉ-milieu du xivᵉ siècle* (Paris: Centre de Recherche d'Histoire et Civilisation de Byzance-Collège de France, 2006), 176–178; Angeliki E. Laiou, "The Agrarian Economy, Thirteenth–Fifteenth Centuries," in *The Economic History of Byzantium, From the Seventh through the Fifteenth Century*, 3 vols., ed. Angeliki E. Laiou (Washington: Dumbarton Oaks Research Library and Collection, 2002), 1, 313–314.
3. Speros Vryonis, Jr., *The Decline of Medieval Hellenism in Asia Minor and the Process of Islamization from the Eleventh through the Fifteenth Century* (Berkeley: University of California Press, 1971), 250–258.

4. For a brief survey of political developments in this period, see Stephen W. Reinert, "Fragmentation," in *The Oxford History of Byzantium*, ed. Cyril Mango (Oxford: Oxford University Press, 2002), 249–263.
5. On the preserved Byzantine documents in general, see Alexander Beihammer, "Eastern Mediterranean Diplomatics: The Present State of Research," in Diplomatics in the Eastern Mediterranean 1000–1500: *Aspects of Intercultural Communication*, ed. Alexander Beihammer, Maria Parani, and Chris Schabel (Leiden: Brill, 2008), 4–6. For a discussion of monastic archival documents and *typika*, see Smyrlis, *La fortune*, 23–29.
6. On these documents, see Beihammer, "Eastern Mediterranean Diplomatics," 12–15.
7. See most recently Laiou and Morrisson, *The Byzantine Economy*, 115–130, 182–200.
8. Jacques Lefort, "Population et peuplement en Macédoine orientale, IXe-XVe siècle," in *idem*, *Société rurale et histoire du paysage à Byzance* (Paris: Association des amis du centre d'histoire et civilisation de Byzance, 2006), 239–240.
9. For the period up to the thirteenth century, see Alan Harvey, *Economic Expansion in the Byzantine Empire, 900–1200* (Cambridge: Cambridge University Press, 1989), 35–79; Jacques Lefort, "The Rural Economy, Seventh–Twelfth Centuries," in *The Economic History of Byzantium* (as in n. 2), 1, 267–271; and most recently *idem*, "Population et démographie," in *Le monde byzantin II. L'Empire byzantin (641–1204)*, ed. Jean-Claude Cheynet (Paris: Presses universitaires de France, 2006), 215–218. For the late period: Laiou, "The Agrarian Economy," 312–315. While the general demographic trend is clear, little is known about regional variation and temporary fluctuations. On the possibility of a temporary population decline in Macedonia after the Fourth Crusade, see Konstantinos Moustakas, "He demographike krise tou hysterou Mesaiona ston helleniko choro. He periptose tes notioanatolikes Makedonias (14os–15os ai.)," *Mnemon* 25 (2003): 19–20.
10. Based on an estimated average density of 15 people per km^2 for the whole empire whose surface in 1265 was c. 300,000 km^2. Accepting Jacques Lefort's suggestion that before the plague there were 20 people per km^2 in the Macedonian countryside, there would have been about 15 people per km^2 in 1265 (assuming that the 82 percent growth was evenly spread throughout the years between 1100 and 1347): "Les villages de Macédoine orientale au Moyen Âge (X^e^-XIVe siècle)," in *idem*, *Société rurale* (as in n. 8), 499. The lower densities of more mountainous areas than Macedonia are considered to be counterbalanced by the urban population. On a more optimistic figure for the density of population in early fourteenth-century Macedonia (34 people per km^2), see Angeliki E. Laiou-Thomadakis, *Peasant Society in the Late Byzantine Empire: A Social and Demographic Study* (New Jersey: Princeton University Press, 1977), 42–43. Guided by known population densities of the early and late Ottoman period, Johannes Koder has suggested that in 1280 the Byzantine Empire and Latin Greece, with a combined surface of c. 350,000 km^2, would have had between three and 5.5 million inhabitants: *Der Lebensraum der Byzantiner: historisch-geographischer Abriß ihres mittelalterlichen Staates im östlichen Mittelmeerraum* (2nd edition) (Vienna: Fassbänder, 2001), 152–153. Warren Treadgold has guessed that in 1282 the empire's population was five million: *A History of the Byzantine State and Society* (Stanford: Stanford University Press, 1997), 841.
11. Laiou-Thomadakis, *Peasant Society*, Ch. 6.
12. Lefort, "Population et peuplement," 239–242.
13. Compare Lefort, "Population et peuplement," Table 2 (p. 241) to Laiou-Thomadakis, *Peasant Society*, 17.

14. Lefort, "Population et peuplement," 238, 239 and "Radolibos: population et paysage," in *idem*, *Société rurale* (as in n. 8), 167–172.
15. The Catalans' crossing through Thrace and Macedonia provoked what seem to be the only known instances of famine in those provinces during the first decades of the fourteenth century; for Thrace, see Angeliki E. Laiou, "The Provisioning of Constantinople during the Winter of 1306–1307," *Byzantion* 37 (1967); for Macedonia, see the evidence from Chalkidike in Jacques Bompaire et al., eds., *Actes de Vatopédi I, des origines à 1329* (Paris: Lethielleux, 2001), no. 43 (1308–1312), especially p. 242. Also related to warfare is another case of famine that affected Constantinople following the arrival of great numbers of refugees fleeing the Turkish advance in Asia Minor: Georges Pachymérès, *Relations Historiques*, vols. 1–2, ed. Albert Failler, trans. Vitalien Laurent; vols. 3–4, ed. and trans. Albert Failler (Paris: Belles Lettres, 1984, 1999), 4, 453, ll. 19–24. It is not clear whether the famine that hit southern Greece and Crete in 1317 also affected Thrace and Macedonia: Freddy Thiriet, *Délibérations des assemblées vénitiennes concernant la Romanie, Tome I, 1160–1363* (Paris: Mouton, 1966), 174, no. 389.
16. Nicephorus Gregoras, *Byzantina Historia*, 1–2, ed. Ludwig Schopen (Bonn: E. Weber, 1829–1830), 1, 317.
17. Laiou, "The Agrarian Economy," 315–316; as evidence that there was still abundant land in some places, Laiou mentions the example of a village in Chalkidike, where new settlers appear in the 1330s and 1340s, and the fact that the price of land remained stable or even decreased in the early fourteenth century. This last argument would be a strong one if our data on prices were not so limited; cf. Cécile Morrisson and Jean-Claude Cheynet, "Prices and Wages in the Byzantine World," in *The Economic History of Byzantium* (as in n. 2) 2, 815–878. On the question of overexpansion, cf. Laiou and Morrisson, *The Byzantine economy*, 169–170, where the idea of 'a Malthusian impasse' for the late thirteenth century is accepted without qualifications. Laiou's thesis of a decline in the early fourteenth century is accepted, most recently, by Dionysios Stathakopoulos, "Population, Demography and Disease," in *The Oxford Handbook of Byzantine Studies*, ed. Elizabeth Jeffreys, John Haldon, and Robin Cormack (Oxford: Oxford University Press, 2008), 313.
18. Nicolas Oikonomides, "The Role of the Byzantine State in the Economy," in *The Economic History of Byzantium* (as in n. 2) 3, 1,046.
19. See Moustakas, "He demographike krise," 22 and Table 2 (p. 24).
20. Cf. Laiou, "The Agrarian Economy," 318, 326, 328.
21. See below n. 37. Here and in what follows I am using the rough equivalence of 1 hectare = 10 *modioi*.
22. The estate of Mamitzon, one-third of which measured 2,100 *modioi*: Louis Petit, ed., "Actes de Chilandar," *Vizantijskij Vremennik* 17 (1911), Appendix 1, no. 92 (1323).
23. The village of Bare in the thirteenth century: Smyrlis, *La fortune*, map 2 (p. 58).
24. Cf. Oikonomidès, "The Role of the Byzantine State," 1,005.
25. For the period up to the middle of the fourteenth century, see Smyrlis, *La fortune*, 176–182.
26. Laiou-Thomadakis, *Peasant Society*, table V-1 (p. 159); cf. Lefort, "Les villages de Macédoine orientale," 495 n. 34.
27. Laiou, "The Agrarian Economy," 328 ff.
28. Laiou, "The Agrarian Economy," 339–40: in certain estates or groups of estates owned by monasteries peasant land corresponded to one-tenth, one-fifth, and one-half of seigneurial land whereas in one case, that of the village

of Mamitzon near Constantinople, it was almost equal to it. This last case seems exceptional at least as far as monasteries are concerned. An even lower proportion of approximately 1/20 is also attested: Jacques Lefort et al., eds., *Actes de Vatopédi II, de 1330 à 1376* (Paris: Lethielleux, 2006), no. 81, ll. 53–68. It has been suggested that on public estates held under the *pronoia* system *paroikoi* may have owned more arable land: Laiou, "The Agrarian Economy," 339. On the reasons that may explain the variations in the amounts of arable owned by peasants in different estates, see the discussion *ibidem*, 341–345.

29. Laiou-Thomadakis, *Peasant Society*, 182–185, 203 ff.
30. Smyrlis, *La fortune*, 155–156, 243–244.
31. On the cultivation of marginal lands, see Lefort, "Population et peuplement," 242; cf. Laiou, "The Agrarian Economy," 315–316.
32. On lay landowners living in town, see Lefort, "The Rural Economy," 240.
33. On Constantinopolitan landowners and the management of their estates, see Paul Magdalino, *The Empire of Manuel I Komnenos, 1143–1180* (Cambridge: Cambridge University Press, 1993), 169–171; cf. Lefort, "The Rural Economy," 291, who does not think that the great landowners' status influenced their attitude towards investment and land amelioration. On the importance of peasant land in estates held in *pronoia*, cf. above n. 28. On the exploitation of *pronoiai*, see also Oikonomides, "The Role of the Byzantine State," 1,046.
34. On Vatopedi's fortune: Lefort et al., *Actes de Vatopédi II*, table on p. 17. On Lavra and Lembiotissa: Smyrlis, *La fortune*, 52–59.
35. On the location of monastic properties in general: Smyrlis, *La fortune*, 127–132. See, for example, the case of the monastery of Lips in Constantinople, whose fortune closely reflected that of its foundress, Empress Theodora Palaiologina: *ibidem*, 62–63.
36. Cf. Lefort, "The Rural Economy," 250–251. On the location of crown domains in the twelfth century, see Magdalino, *The Empire of Manuel I*, map on p. xxii.
37. See Jacques Lefort, "Une exploitation de taille moyenne au XIIIe siècle en Chalcidique," in *idem*, *Société rurale* (as in n. 8), 203–204 and Laiou, "The Agrarian Economy," 355–357.
38. Alan Harvey, "Land, Taxation and Trade in the Eleventh Century Monastic Economy: The Case of Evergetis," in *The Theotokos Evergetis and Eleventh-Century Monasticism*, ed. Margaret Mullet and Anthony Kirby (Belfast: Belfast Byzantine Enterprises, School of Greek, Roman and Semitic Studies, the Queen's University of Belfast, 1994), 135; Smyrlis, *La fortune*, 319 ff. Cf. *idem*, "The Management of Monastic Estates. The Evidence of the Typika," *Dumbarton Oaks Papers* 56 (2002): 254–256. On the sale of large estates' agricultural produce to merchants, see Klaus-Peter Matschke, "Commerce, Trade, Markets, and Money, Thirteenth–Fifteenth Centuries," in *The Economic History of Byzantium* (as in n. 2), 2, 801–802.
39. The estate of Mamitzon: Laiou, "The Agrarian Economy," 329.
40. Lefort, "The Rural Economy," 242–243.
41. On the size of the peasant farm, see Lefort, "The Rural Economy," 247–248 and Laiou, "The Agrarian Economy," 328–334.
42. Estimates as to the amount of arable a peasant with two oxen could cultivate vary, ranging from eight hectares to more than 20 hectares: Erich Schilbach, *Byzantinische Metrologie* (Munich: C. H. Beck, 1970), 68–70; cf. Nicolas Oikonomides, "Ottoman Influence on Late Byzantine Fiscal Practice," *Südost-Forschungen* 45 (1986): 14–16. Apparently, the Byzantines did not use horses for plowing: Michel Kaplan, *Les hommes et la terre à Byzance*

du VIe au XIe siècle. Propriété et exploitation du sol (Paris: Publications de la Sorbonne, Université de Paris I-Panthéon-Sorbonne, 1992), 51.
43. Laiou, "The Agrarian Economy," 340–341 and Table 3 (p. 342).
44. Lefort, "The Rural Economy," 235, 246. On the livestock of landlords, see below n. 60.
45. Oxless peasants working the land with hand tools are briefly mentioned in Kaplan, *Les hommes et la terre*, 47 and Anthony Bryer, "The Means of Agricultural Production: Muscle and Tools," in *The Economic History of Byzantium* (as in n. 2), 1, 108. Cf. the longer discussion in John W. Nesbitt, *Mechanisms of Agricultural Production on Estates of the Byzantine Praktika* (PhD diss., Univerity of Wisconsin, 1972), 89 ff.
46. Our information on rent is very limited: Laiou, "The Agrarian Economy," 338–339.
47. See Smyrlis, *La fortune*, 184–85, 187.
48. On peasant labor services in general, see Laiou, "The Agrarian Economy," 334–337. On the days of corvée labor, see Smyrlis, *La fortune*, 184 n. 6.
49. Smyrlis, *La fortune*, 206.
50. Nicolas Oikonomides has suggested that in the eleventh century it was probably the landlord who fixed the number of days of labor his peasants owed: *Fiscalité et exemption fiscale à Byzance (IXe–XIe s.)* (Athens: Fondation nationale de la recherche scientifique, Institut de recherches byzantines, 1996), 106 n. 117. There is evidence that already before 1204 the number of labor days owed by the peasants was registered in official documents (*ibidem*, on the Lampsakos *praktikon*).
51. According to one estimate, 20 to 24 percent of the seigneurial land of the monastery of Lavra could be cultivated thanks to corvée labor at the beginning of the fourteenth century: Paul Lemerle et al., eds., *Actes de Lavra IV, études historiques—actes serbes—complements et index* (Paris: P. Lethielleux, 1982), 165–167; accepting that the importance of Lavra's demesne lands was similar to that attested for the estates mentioned above, corresponding to one-third or less of the seigneurial land, corvée labor would suffice for the exploitation of all or most of Lavra's directly exploited land. But, this estimate is too optimistic: it is based in particular on the assumption that a peasant with two oxen could cultivate 15 hectares of land, a figure that seems high; cf. Lefort, "The Rural Economy," 247–248.
52. For the period before the thirteenth century, see Kaplan, *Les hommes et la terre*, 350, 352, 355; Lefort, "The Rural Economy," 237, 241–242 and Smyrlis, *La fortune*, 184, 186, 203; for the late period: Laiou, "The Agrarian Economy," 336–337.
53. For what follows see in general Lefort, "The Rural Economy," 248–267, Harvey, *Economic Expansion*, 120–162, and Laiou, "The Agrarian Economy," 319–328. A map indicating the products of the empire's regions may be found in Michael F. Hendy, *Studies in the Byzantine Monetary Economy, c. 300–1450* (Cambridge: Cambridge University Press, 1985), 70.
54. On Constantinople, see the case of the monastery of Lips which at the turn of the fourteenth century owned almost 24 hectares of vineyards within the city or in its immediate vicinity (Smyrlis, *La fortune*, 62); the monastery of Kecharitomene at the beginning of the fifteenth century owned more than 4.5 hectares of vineyards outside the city's walls (Harvey, *Economic Expansion*, 148). On Thessalonike: Smyrlis, *La fortune*, 185, 223, 226.
55. Lefort, "The Rural Economy," 254.
56. Démétrios Kyritsès and Kostis Smyrlis, "Les villages du littoral égéen de l'Asie Mineure au moyen âge," in *Les villages dans l'empire byzantin*, ed. Jacques Lefort, Cécile Morrisson, and Jean-Pierre Sodini (Paris: Lethielleux, 2005), 446.

57. Smyrlis, *La fortune*, 151. The monastery no doubt owned many more olive trees.
58. For Thessalonike see Lefort, "The Rural Economy," 253–254; for Constantinople, see the case of the monastery of Lips, which owned several plots of garden amounting to almost 10 hectares in or very near the city (see above n. 54). One of these garden plots is said to have measured four hectares.
59. In 1300/1, in certain villages of the district of Thessalonike, peasants owned on average one pig, five sheep or goats, 0.7 cows, and 1.2 beehives: Laiou-Thomadakis, *Peasant Society*, Table v-1 (p. 159). On oxen, see above n. 43.
60. See some examples of large flocks and herds in Smyrlis, *La fortune*, 124–125 and Laiou, "The Agrarian Economy," 354–355.
61. Harvey, *Economic Expansion*, 127–128.
62. Lefort, "The Rural Economy," 257.
63. According to Lefort ("The Rural Economy," 257–258), legumes were not simply a garden produce but had a place in the cereal crop cycle. For a different opinion, see Harvey, *Economic Expansion*, 126, 142.
64. Lefort, "The Rural Economy," 257–258.
65. Harvey, *Economic Expansion*, 122–123; Kaplan, *Les hommes et la terre*, 47–55; Bryer, "The Means of Agricultural Production," 107–108, 109.
66. Harvey, *Economic Expansion*, 134–135, 145–146, 161.
67. Lefort, "The Rural Economy," 253, 256. On olive oil production, see also Laiou "The Agrarian Economy," 359.
68. See Nicolas Svoronos, "Remarques sur les structures économiques de l'empire byzantin au XIe siècle," *Travaux et Mémoires* 6 (1976): 57 n. 32. To the data cited by Svoronos, I have added those given in Jean Richard, "Le casal de Psimolofo et la vie rurale en Chypre au XIVe siècle," in *idem*, *Les relations entre l'Orient et l'Occident au Moyen Âge* (London: Variorum, 1977), art. 4, 140, 141; but, I have not taken into consideration the yield suggested by the text of arithmetic exercises published by Uspenskij (see below n. 70), because this is not a concrete case. In agreement with Jacques Lefort et al., *Géometries du fisc byzantin* (Paris: Lethielleux, 1991), 45 n. 23, I do not think that the metrological text cited by Schilbalch (*Byzantinische Metrologie*, 57) and Svoronos refers to cereal yield. Yield in quintals per hectare: yield per grain sown × 0.128 (quintal sown per *modios*; one *modios* of wheat—12.8 kg—was normally sown over one *modios* of land -c. 1,000 m^2; see Lefort, "The Rural Economy," 258 n. 179) × 10 (number of *modioi* per hectare).
69. Lefort, "The Rural Economy," 259; Kaplan, *Les hommes et la terre*, 80–82; Harvey, *Economic Expansion*, 139.
70. Svoronos, "Remarques," 57 n. 32, modifying his earlier estimate of 3:1. Svoronos' estimate is accepted in Harvey, *Economic Expansion*, 180 and Kaplan, *Les hommes et la terre*, 82. The Byzantine texts that can be taken to reflect average cereal yield do not contradict Svoronos' estimates. In the often quoted example from the sixth-century *The Life of Saint Nicholas of Sion*, concerning mountainous Lycia in southern Asia Minor, a yield of 5:1 was considered exceptionally high: Ihor Ševčenko and Nancy Paterson-Ševčenko, ed. and trans., *The Life of Saint Nicholas of Sion* (Brookline: Hellenic College Press, 1984), 92, 94. A text of arithmetic exercises published by Feodor Uspenskij mentions a yield of 100:24, i.e. approximately 4.2 for 1: "Vizantijskie zemlemery. Nabljudenija po istorii sel'skago hozjajstva," in *Trudy VI arheologičeskago s"ezda v" Odesse (1884 g.)*, 2 (Odessa: A. Šul'ce, 1888), 305 n. 5. The last text is a romance in verse, apparently originating from mid-thirteenth-century western Asia Minor, which includes the description of 12 statues, the personifications of the months of the year. Each month holds a scroll; July's scroll says that he expected to harvest 10 times what he

had sown whereas November's says that the land produced three times what he gave it. In a text of this kind, the lower figure is more significant than the upper: it cannot be worse than what people thought of as a reasonably good yield. Panagiotis Agapitos, ed., *Aphegesis Libistrou kai Rodamnes. Kritike ekdose tes diaskeues 'alpha'* (Athens: Morphotiko Hidryma Ethnikes Trapezes, 2006), ll. 1,140–1,441, 1,169–1,170; on the romance's origin and date: pp. 48–55, 66. I would like to thank Panagiotis Agapitos for his valuable comments on these passages.

71. Nikola Kondov, "Über den wahrscheinlichen Weizenertrag auf der Balkanhalbinsel im Mittelalter," *Études Balkaniques* 10 (1974): 97–109. Kondov's yield of 5.2:1 is based on a misunderstanding of the text of exercises mentioned above which he only knew through Uspenskij's translation: *ibidem*, 97, 108 and Feodor Uspenskij, "Nabljudenija po sel'sko-hozjajstvennoj istorii v" Vizantii," *Žurnal" Ministerstva Narodnago Prosvješenija* 259 (1888): 258–259.
72. Lefort, "The Rural Economy," 259–260, 300–303; Laiou, "The Agrarian Economy," 346–347. Cf. Laiou and Morrisson, *The Byzantine Economy*, 65.
73. Lefort, "Radolibos: population et paysage," 187–188; Nicolas Oikonomidès, "Terres du fisc et revenu de la terre aux xe–xie siècles," in *idem*, *Social and Economic Life in Byzantium*, ed. Elizabeth Zachariadou (Aldershot: Variorum, 2004), art. 11, 335–336. Cf. Lefort, "The Rural Economy," 260 n. 196.
74. Lefort, "Une exploitation de taille moyenne," 204–207.
75. See below on the peasants' living standards.
76. Lefort, "Radolibos: population et paysage," 172–184 and *idem*, "The Rural Economy," 271. Cf. Harvey, *Economic Expansion*, 64, 161.
77. Lefort, "Population et peuplement," 234–238 and *idem*, "The Rural Economy," 273.
78. Laiou "The Agrarian Economy," 353–357.
79. Laiou, "The Agrarian Economy," 357–364.
80. See for the middle period Harvey, *Economic Expansion*, 12, 121, 135, 159–161; cf. Lefort, "The Rural Economy," 291–296.
81. Smyrlis, *La fortune*, 206–207. On domanial accounting and the quest of profit, cf. Lefort, "The Rural Economy," 295–296. On landowners anticipating greater yields following land improvements, see Harvey, *Economic Expansion*, 159.
82. Emperor John III Vatatzes (1221–1254) apparently tried to increase agricultural production on imperial estates and encouraged the aristocracy to do the same on their lands: Gregoras, *Byzantina Historia*, 1, 41–42. Writing in the early fourteenth century, historian George Pachymeres reported that many considered making one's properties more productive instead of acquiring new lands to be a great virtue: Pachymérès, *Relations Historiques*, 1, 287. Of course, in all societies, great virtue tends to be the exception rather than the rule.
83. Smyrlis, *La fortune*, 238–244.
84. For what follows, see Laiou and Morrisson, *The Byzantine Economy*, 115–130, 182–200.
85. Laiou and Morrisson, *The Byzantine Economy*, 195.
86. Laiou and Morrisson, *The Byzantine Economy*, 131. According to Laiou, Thessalonike's population may have reached 150,000 in the twelfth century. All these figures are educated guesses and seem to be more or less optimistic.
87. Geoffrey de Villehardouin, "The Conquest of Constantinople," in Chronicles of the Crusades, trans. Margaret R. B. Shaw (Harmondsworth: Penguin,

1963), 93. This figure is often accepted as the upper limit of the capital's population: Paul Magdalino, *Constantinople médiévale. Études sur l'évolution des structures urbaines* (Paris: De Boccard, 1996), 56–57; Angeliki E. Laiou, "The Human Resources," in *The Economic History of Byzantium* (as in n. 2), 1, 51 (300,000–400,000); Laiou and Morrisson, *The Byzantine Economy*, 131. Cf. David Jacoby, "La population de Constantinople à l'époque byzantine: un problème de démographie urbaine," in *idem*, *Société et démographie à Byzance et en Romanie latine* (London: Variorum, 1975), art. 1, 107–109 (250,000?).

88. Alfons M. Schneider, "Die Bevölkerung Konstantinopels im XV. Jahrhundert," *Nachrichten der Akademie der Wissenschaften in Göttingen, Philologisch-historische Klasse* 9 (1949): 236–237.

89. Cited in Paul Lemerle, "La domination vénitienne à Thessalonique," in *Miscellanea Giovanni Galbiati* (Milano: U. Hoepli, 1951), 3, 222; cf. Peter Charanis, "A Note on the Population and Cities of the Byzantine Empire in the Thirteenth Century," in *The Joshua Starr Memorial Volume* (New York, 1953), 141 n. 33. Anthony Bryer considers the 40,000 figure as improbably high: "The Structure of the Late Byzantine Town: *Diokismos* and the *Mesoi*," in *Continuity and Change in Late Byzantine and Early Ottoman Society*, ed. Anthony Bryer and Heath Lowry (Birmingham: University of Birmingham, Centre for Byzantine Studies; Washington: Dumbarton Oaks Research Library and Collection, 1986), 270 n. 14. Speros Vryonis, Jr. has suggested a more modest 10,000 for 1429–30: "The Ottoman Conquest of Thessaloniki in 1430," in *Continuity and Change* (as above), 320; cf. Nevra Necipoğlu, *Byzantium Between the Ottomans and the Latins: Politics and Society in the Late Empire* (Cambridge: Cambridge University Press, 2009), 109, n. 92.

90. Klaus-Peter Matschke, "The Late Byzantine Urban Economy, Thirteenth–Fifteenth Centuries," in *The Economic History of Byzantium* (as in n. 2), 2, 465.

91. Vryonis, *The Decline of Medieval Hellenism*, 253–255.

92. Klaus Rheidt, "The Urban Economy of Pergamon," in *The Economic History of Byzantium* (as in n. 2), 2, 625–626; Clive Foss and Jane A. Scott, "Sardis," *ibidem*, 2, 620–621; Haris Kalligas, "Monemvasia, Seventh–Fifteenth Centuries," *ibidem*, 2, 883–884; Maria Kazanaki-Lappa, "Medieval Athens," *ibidem*, 2, 642–646. Cf. also Matschke's views on the possible growth of Didymoteichon, Serres, and Ioannina in the thirteenth and early fourteenth centuries, and the sustained growth of Mistra, the capital of Byzantine Peloponnese: "The Late Byzantine Urban Economy," 465.

93. This is the opinion of Matschke, "The Late Byzantine Urban Economy," 465; cf. Laiou and Morrisson, *The Byzantine Economy*, 196.

94. Smyrlis, *La fortune*, 221–222, 226–227. Cf., for the middle period (ninth–twelfth centuries), the diverging views in Harvey, *Economic Expansion*, 206 and Paul Magdalino, "The Grain Supply of Constantinople, Ninth–Twelfth Centuries," in *Constantinople and its Hinterland: Papers from the Twenty-seventh Spring Symposium of Byzantine Studies, Oxford, April 1993*, ed. Cyril Mango and Gilbert Dagron (Aldershot: Variorum, 1995), 35–47; unlike Harvey, Magdalino emphasizes the importance of commerce for the provisioning of Constantinople.

95. Matschke, "Commerce," 800–802; David Jacoby, "Changing Economic Patterns in Latin Romania: The Impact of the West," in *The Crusades from the Perspective of Byzantium and the Muslim World*, ed. Angeliki E. Laiou and Roy Parviz Mottahedeh (Washington: Dumbarton Oaks Research Library and Collection, 2001), 216; cf. Magdalino, "The Grain Supply."

96. Konstantinos Moustakas, *The Transition from Late Byzantine to Early Ottoman Southeastern Macedonia (14th–15th Centuries): A Socioeconomic and Demographic Study* (PhD diss., University of Birmingham, 2001), 190. Moustakas' calculations are based on the assumption that each household (*hane*) comprised five members (*ibidem*, 188–189). The population of Serres and Zichna is calculated at 6,453 and 2,859, respectively. In fact, the urban population had just diminished, probably by a few hundreds, with the forced transfer of the two towns' Jews to newly conquered Constantinople: *ibidem*, 256–257. Apparently more than a hundred Jews lived in Zichna at the beginning of the fourteenth century: Lisa Bénou, ed., *Le Codex B du monastère Saint-Jean-Prodrome (Serrès) (XIIIe–XVe siècles)* (Paris: Association Pierre Belon, 1998), nos. 154 (1328) and 125 (after 1328).
97. Moustakas, *The Transition*, 264–268 and Table 7 (p. 320): 176 cloth and garment artisans out of 290 persons with a known profession.
98. Matschke, "Commerce," 771–772, 789; Laiou and Morrisson, *The Byzantine Economy*, 200–204; and, most recently, David Jacoby, "Thirteenth-century Commercial Exchange in the Aegean: Continuity and Change," in *Change in the Byzantine World in the Twelfth and Thirteenth Centuries, First International Sevgi Gönül Byzantine Studies Symposium, 25–28 June, 2007*, ed. Ayla Ödekan, Engin Akyürek and Nevra Necipoğlu (Istanbul: Vehbi Koç Vakfı, 2010), 187–194.
99. Laiou, "The Byzantine Economy: An Overview," in *The Economic History of Byzantium* (as in n. 2), 3, 1,160.
100. Matschke, "Commerce," 772, 789. See also Angeliki E. Laiou, "The Byzantine Economy in the Mediterranean Trade System, Thirteen-Fifteenth Centuries," in *eadem, Gender, Society, and Economic Life in Byzantium* (Hampshire: Variorum, 1992), art. 7.
101. Matschke, "Commerce," 789–799. On the Byzantine aristocracy's new attitude towards commerce after the middle of the fourteenth century, see Nicolas Oikonomidès, *Hommes d'affaires grecs et latins à Constantinople (XIIIe–XVe siècles)* (Montreal: Institut d'études médiévales Albert-le-Grand; Paris: J. Vrin, 1979), 114–123; and Matschke, "Commerce," 803–805.
102. Matschke, "Commerce," 786, 795–796, and *passim*.
103. For the sources of revenue of great monasteries, see Smyrlis, *La fortune*, 209–211.
104. Two documents of the earlier period record peasant dues: Maria Nystazopoulou-Pelekidou, ed., *Byzantina engrapha tes mones Patmou. II, Demosion leitourgon* (Athens: Ethnikon Hidryma Ereunon, Kentron Byzantinon Ereunon, 1980), no. 50 (1073); and Jacques Lefort et al., *Actes d'Iviron II, du milieu du XIe siècle à 1204* (Paris: P. Lethielleux, 1990), app. 2 (first decade of the twelfth century).
105. Lefort, "The Rural Economy," 302–305 (3 percent); Oikonomides, "The Role of the Byzantine State," 1,002 and *idem*, "Terres du fisc," 329–332 (3.3 percent). Both models assume that all land is arable, cultivated in cereals and rented.
106. Laiou, "The Agrarian Economy," 349–350 modifying the calculations of Svoronos in Lemerle et al., *Actes de Lavra IV*, 170–171. Again, here it is assumed that all land is rented and, as in the other models, calculations are based on a hypothetical land productivity. Laiou has also tried to calculate the revenues of a middle-sized landowner: "The Agrarian Economy," 355–356.

107. Also, compared to Lefort's model, Laiou assumes a lower average land price and a higher rent (one-third as opposed to Lefort's one-fourth) and she does not subtract management expenses.
108. Lemerle et al., *Actes de Lavra IV*, 171.
109. Kaplan, *Les hommes et la terre*, 493–522; Lefort, "The Rural Economy," 299–303. Cf. Harvey, *Economic Expansion*, 138, 180; Oikonomidès, *Fiscalité*, 129–135 and "The Role of the Byzantine State," 1,001–1,004.
110. Laiou, "The Agrarian Economy," 346–348. On the percentage of peasants owning two oxen, see the case of Lavra monastery's estates in 1321, cited above p. 135. Laiou has refrained from trying to estimate the revenues of a peasant household.
111. Cf. the account in Reinert, "Fragmentation," 263–283.
112. See, in particular, the case of Chalkidike: Nicolas Oikonomides, "Hoi dyo Serbikes katakteseis tes Chalkidikes ton ID aiona," *Diptycha* 2 (1980–1981): 294–299; cf. Lefort et al., *Actes de Vatopédi II*, no. 111 (1358).
113. Lefort et al., *Actes de Vatopédi II*, no. 118, ll. 35–36.
114. On the outbreaks of the plague, see Marie-Hélène Congourdeau, "Pour une étude de la peste noire à Byzance," in *Eupsychia. Mélanges offerts à Hélène Ahrweiler*, 2 vols. (Paris: Publications de la Sorbonne, 1998), 1, 149–163; Heath W. Lowry, "Pushing the Stone Uphill: The Impact of Bubonic Plague on Ottoman Urban Society in the Fifteenth and Sixteenth Centuries," *The Journal of Ottoman Studies* 23 (2003): 93–132.
115. Laiou, "The Agrarian Economy," 366.
116. On the raids affecting Chalkidike and eastern Macedonia: Nicolas Oikonomidès, ed., *Actes de Dionysiou* (Paris: P. Lethielleux, 1968), 7–9; Mirjana Živojinović, "Concerning Turkish Assaults on Mount Athos in the 14th Century, based on Byzantine Sources," *Orijentalni Institut u Serajevu, Prilozi za Orijentalnu Filologiju* 30 (1980): 501–516; Lefort et al., *Actes de Vatopédi II*, 204; Jacques Lefort et al., eds., *Actes d'Iviron IV, de 1328 au début du XVIe siècle* (Paris: CNRS Éditions—P. Lethielleux, 1995), no. 87A (1341), ll. 232–236 and p. 81. On Lemnos, see John F. Haldon, "Limnos, Monastic Holdings and the Byzantine State: *ca.* 1261–1453," in *Continuity and Change* (as in n. 89), 181–183.
117. Lefort et al., *Actes de Vatopédi II*, nos. 111 (1358) and 112 (c. 1358), concerning events of the second half of the 1340s.
118. Lefort, "Population et peuplement," 243–246.
119. On the shortage of manpower in Lemnos, see the discussion in Haldon, "Limnos," 183–185 and Laiou, "The Agrarian Economy," 365. The 1348 *praktikon* registering Vatopedi's properties on the island records a remarkable number of abandoned lands or farms (*exaleimmata*): Lefort et al., *Actes de Vatopédi II*, no. 98.
120. Laiou, "The Agrarian Economy," 364–366.
121. See the case of Arsenios Tzamplakon who in 1355 and 1356 donated his vast but depopulated properties in Macedonia to the monastery of Vatopedi in exchange for annual pensions: Lefort et al., *Actes de Vatopédi II*, 23. Some Byzantine landowners apparently found it impossible to exploit the estates they had recovered after the Serbian rule of Macedonia had ended in 1371 and alienated them to Athonite monasteries: Laiou, "The Agrarian Economy," 366–367; Nicolas Oikonomidès, "The Properties of the Deblitzenoi in the Fourteenth and Fifteenth Centuries," in *Charanis Studies: Essays in Honor of Peter Charanis*, ed. Angeliki E. Laiou-Thomadakis (New Brunswick: Rutgers University Press, 1980), 180–186; and Jacques Lefort et al., eds., *Actes de Vatopédi III, de 1377 à 1500* (forthcoming), nos. 162 (1380), 163 (1383).

122. Nicolas Oikonomidès, "Patronage in Palaiologan Mt Athos," in *Mount Athos and Byzantine Monasticism: Papers from the Twenty-eighth Spring Symposium of Byzantine Studies, March 1994*, eds. Anthony Bryer and Mary Cunningham (Aldershot: Ashgate/Variorum, 1996), 99–100; and Lefort et al., *Actes de Vatopédi II*, 21–24. On monastic property in Macedonia after the first Ottoman conquest of the province, see Kostis Smyrlis, "The First Ottoman Occupation of Macedonia (c. 1383–c. 1403): Some Remarks on Land Ownership, Property Transactions and Justice," in Diplomatics in the Eastern Mediterranean (as in n. 5), 327–339.
123. The peasants settled by Vatopedi on an estate in Lemnos before 1368 bore names that sometimes betray a Macedonian or Thracian origin: Lefort et al., *Actes de Vatopédi II*, no. 128, ll. 44–52. Additional peasants from Macedonia had been settled on the same estate before 1387: Lefort et al., *Actes de Vatopédi III*, no. 165, ll. 60–73. Between 1415 and 1442, finally, the monks made two more transfers to Lemnos of peasants coming from Macedonia and Epiros: *ibidem*, no. 227, ll. 75–82. On Lavra: Paul Lemerle et al., eds., *Actes de Lavra III, de 1329 à 1500* (Paris: P. Lethielleux, 1979), no. 157. In the 1490 Ottoman register of Lemnos, 12 percent of the adult male married households can be identified as newcomers to the island on the basis of their names, mostly originating from other islands or the Balkans: Heath W. Lowry, *Fifteenth Century Ottoman Realities: Christian Peasant Life on the Aegean Island of Limnos* (Istanbul: Eren, 2002), 56–62. At least in part, this phenomenon should be ascribed to the efforts of the Athonite monasteries which had extensive properties on the island. Cf. also the foreigners John Haldon has identified in monastic documents concerning Lemnos, which largely date from the second half of the fourteenth century: "Limnos," 184.
124. Lefort, "Population et peuplement," 246. For an additional example of a layman settling peasants on an abandoned estate, see the case of Phronimos Mpogdanos who, some years before 1400, had assured the cultivation of a land situated north of Chalkidike by bringing peasants from "far away": Lefort et al., *Actes de Vatopédi III*, no. 184.
125. Besides the acquisition of lay properties, there was also a wave of new foundations on Athos with seven new monasteries created between the second half of the fourteenth century and the fist half of the fifteenth century: Oikonomides, "Patronage in Palaiologan Mt Athos." See also Laiou, "The Agrarian Economy," 367.
126. Laiou, "The Agrarian Economy," 367–368.
127. According to Oikonomides' calculations, the dues of Macedonian peasants owning two oxen in the early fifteenth century were between 23 and 68 percent lighter than they were a century earlier: "Ottoman Influence," esp. 23–24; cf. *idem*, "The Role of the Byzantine State," 1,039. The mention in 1359 of an agreement between Vatopedi and prospective settlers of an estate in Lemnos concerning the dues they would owe to the monastery might reflect the better bargaining position of the peasants after the plague: Lefort et al., *Actes de Vatopédi II*, no. 114, ll. 44–52, esp. 51–52.
128. Laiou, "The Agrarian Economy," 366 and Table 6 (p. 365). The low ratio of oxen to households in early fifteenth-century Macedonia, in conditions of low demographic density, appears puzzling; it must be noted that it concerns a total of three villages.
129. Lefort, "Population et peuplement," 246 and Table 4 (p. 245). On Turkish settlement in Macedonia since the later fourteenth century, see also Vasilis Dimitriades, "Phorologikes kategories ton chorion tes Thessalonikes kata

ten Tourkokratia," *Makedonika* 20 (1980): 401; Moustakas, "The Transition," 200–202, 248; and Necipoğlu, Byzantium Between the Ottomans and the Latins, 99–100.

130. Moustakas, "He demographike krise," 28–33 and Table 2 (p. 24).
131. These figures, 2,917 and 4,888 for 1490 and 1519 respectively, are proposed by Lowry who accepts that in Lemnos each household (*hane*) had 3.8 members. Lowry attributes the low figure of 1490 to an exodus of a part of the islanders: *Fifteenth Century Ottoman Realities*, 49–62.
132. Smyrlis, *La fortune*, 238–244.

BIBLIOGRAPHY

Agapitos, P. ed. *Aphegesis Libistrou kai Rodamnes. Kritike ekdose tes diaskeues 'alpha'*. Athens: Morphotiko Hidryma Ethnikes Trapezes, 2006.

Angelov, D. *Imperial Ideology and Political Thought in Byzantium, 1204–1330*. Cambridge: Cambridge University Press, 2006.

Beihammer, A. "Eastern Mediterranean Diplomatics: The Present State of Research," in Diplomatics in the Eastern Mediterranean 1000–1500*: Aspects of Intercultural Communication*, edited by A. Beihammer, M. Parani, and C. Schabel, 1–24. Leiden: Brill, 2008.

Bénou, L., ed. *Le Codex B du monastère Saint-Jean-Prodrome (Serrès)* (XIIIe–XVe *siècles)*. Paris: Association Pierre Belon, 1998.

Bompaire, J., J. Lefort, V. Kravari, C. Giros, eds. *Actes de Vatopédi I, des origines à 1329*. Paris: Lethielleux, 2001.

Bryer, A. "The Means of Agricultural Production: Muscle and Tools," in *The Economic History of Byzantium, From the Seventh through the Fifteenth Century*, 3 vols., edited by A. E. Laiou, vol. 1, 101–113. Washington: Dumbarton Oaks Research Library and Collection, 2002.

Bryer, A. "The Structure of the Late Byzantine Town: *Diokismos* and the *Mesoi*," in *Continuity and Change in Late Byzantine and Early Ottoman Society*, edited by A. Bryer and H. Lowry, 263–279. Birmingham: University of Birmingham, Centre for Byzantine Studies; Washington: Dumbarton Oaks Research Library and Collection, 1986.

Charanis, P. "A Note on the Population and Cities of the Byzantine Empire in the Thirteenth Century," in *The Joshua Starr Memorial Volume*, 135–148. New York, 1953.

Congourdeau, M.-H. "Pour une étude de la peste noire à Byzance," In *Eupsychia. Mélanges offerts à Hélène Ahrweiler*, 2 vols., 1, 149–163. Paris: Publications de la Sorbonne, 1998.

Dimitriades, V. "Phorologikes kategories ton chorion tes Thessalonikes kata ten Tourkokratia," *Makedonika* 20 (1980): 375–459.

Foss, C. and J. A. Scott. "Sardis," in *The Economic History of Byzantium, From the Seventh through the Fifteenth Century*, 3 vols., edited by Angeliki E. Laiou, 2, 615–622. Washington: Dumbarton Oaks Research Library and Collection, 2002.

Gregoras, N. *Byzantina Historia*, 2 vols., edited by Ludwig Schopen. Bonn: E. Weber, 1829–1830.

Haldon, J. F. "Limnos, Monastic Holdings and the Byzantine State: *ca.* 1261–1453," in *Continuity and Change in Late Byzantine and Early Ottoman Society*, edited by A. Bryer and H. Lowry, 161–215. Birmingham: University of Birmingham, Centre for Byzantine Studies; Washington: Dumbarton Oaks Research Library and Collection, 1986.

Harvey, A. *Economic Expansion in the Byzantine Empire, 900–1200*. Cambridge: Cambridge University Press, 1989.

Harvey, A. "Land, Taxation and Trade in the Eleventh-century Monastic Economy: The Case of Evergetis," in *The Theotokos Evergetis and Eleventh-Century Monasticism*, edited by M. Mullet and A. Kirby, 124–136. Belfast: Belfast Byzantine Enterprises, School of Greek, Roman and Semitic Studies, the Queen's University of Belfast, 1994.

Hendy, M. F. *Studies in the Byzantine Monetary Economy, c. 300–1450*. Cambridge: Cambridge University Press, 1985.

Jacoby, D. "Changing Economic Patterns in Latin Romania: The Impact of the West," in *The Crusades from the Perspective of Byzantium and the Muslim World*, edited by A. E. Laiou and R. P. Mottahedeh, 197–233. Washington: Dumbarton Oaks Research Library and Collection, 2001.

Jacoby, D. "La population de Constantinople à l'époque byzantine: un problème de démographie urbaine," in *idem*, *Société et démographie à Byzance et en Romanie latine*, article 1. London: Variorum, 1975. Originally published in *Byzantion* 31 (1961): 81–109.

Jacoby, D. "Thirteenth-century Commercial Exchange in the Aegean: Continuity and Change," in *Change in the Byzantine World in the Twelfth and Thirteenth Centuries. First International Sevgi Gönül Byzantine Studies Symposium, 25–28 June, 2007*, edited by A. Ödekan, E. Akyürek, and N. Necipoğlu, 187–194. Istanbul: Vehbi Koç Vakfı, 2010.

Kalligas, H. "Monemvasia, Seventh–Fifteenth Centuries," in *The Economic History of Byzantium, From the Seventh through the Fifteenth Century*, 3 vols., edited by A. E. Laiou, vol. 2, 879–897. Washington: Dumbarton Oaks Research Library and Collection, 2002.

Kaplan, M. *Les hommes et la terre à Byzance du VIe au XIe siècle. Propriété et exploitation du sol*. Paris: Publications de la Sorbonne, Université de Paris I-Panthéon-Sorbonne, 1992.

Kazanaki-Lappa, M. "Medieval Athens," in *The Economic History of Byzantium, From the Seventh through the Fifteenth Century*, 3 vols., edited by A. E. Laiou, vol. 2, 639–646. Washington: Dumbarton Oaks Research Library and Collection, 2002.

Koder, J. *Der Lebensraum der Byzantiner: historisch-geographischer Abriß ihres mittelalterlichen Staates im östlichen Mittelmeerraum*, 2nd edition. Vienna: Fassbänder, 2001.

Kondov, N. "Über den wahrscheinlichen Weizenertrag auf der Balkanhalbinsel im Mittelalter." *Études Balkaniques* 10 (1974): 97–109.

Kyritsès, D. and K. Smyrlis. "Les villages du littoral égéen de l'Asie Mineure au moyen âge," in *Les villages dans l'empire byzantin*, edited by J. Lefort, C. Morrisson, and J.-P. Sodini, 437–451. Paris: Lethielleux, 2005.

Laiou, A. E. "The Agrarian Economy, Thirteenth–Fifteenth Centuries," in *The Economic History of Byzantium, From the Seventh through the Fifteenth Century*, 3 vols., edited by A. E. Laiou, vol. 1, 311–375. Washington: Dumbarton Oaks Research Library and Collection, 2002.

Laiou, A. E. "The Byzantine Economy in the Mediterranean Trade System, Thirteen–Fifteenth Centuries," in *eadem*, *Gender, Society, and Economic Life in Byzantium*, article 7. Hampshire: Variorum, 1992. Originally published in Dumbarton Oaks Papers 34–35 (1980–1981): 177–222.

Laiou, A. E. "The Byzantine Economy: An Overview," in *The Economic History of Byzantium, From the Seventh through the Fifteenth Century*, 3 vols., edited by A. E. Laiou, vol. 3, 1,145–1,164. Washington: Dumbarton Oaks Research Library and Collection, 2002.

Laiou, A. E. "The Human Resources," in *The Economic History of Byzantium, From the Seventh through the Fifteenth Century*, 3 vols., ed. Angeliki E. Laiou, vol. 1, 47–55. Washington: Dumbarton Oaks Research Library and Collection, 2002.

Laiou, A. E. "The Provisioning of Constantinople during the Winter of 1306–1307." *Byzantion* 37 (1967): 91–113.

Laiou, A. E. and C. Morrisson. *The Byzantine Economy*. Cambridge: Cambridge University Press, 2007.

Laiou-Thomadakis, A. E. *Peasant Society in the Late Byzantine Empire: A Social and Demographic Study*. New Jersey: Princeton University Press, 1977.

Lefort, J. "Une exploitation de taille moyenne au XIIIe siècle en Chalcidique," in *idem*. *Société rurale et histoire du paysage à Byzance*, 201–209. Paris: Association des amis du centre d'histoire et civilisation de Byzance, 2006. Originally published in *Aphieroma ston Niko Svorono*, 2 vols., edited by B. Kremmydas, C. A. Maltezou, and N. Panagiotakes, vol. 1, 362–372. Rethymno: Panepistemio Kretes, 1986.

Lefort, J. "Population et démographie," in *Le monde byzantin II. L'Empire byzantin (641–1204)*, edited by Jean-Claude Cheynet, 203–219. Paris: Presses universitaires de France, 2006.

Lefort, J. "Population et peuplement en Macédoine orientale, IXe–XVe siècle." In *idem*. *Société rurale et histoire du paysage à Byzance*, 229–247. Paris: Association des amis du centre d'histoire et civilisation de Byzance, 2006. Originally published in *Hommes et richesses dans l'Empire byzantin, VIIIe–XVe siècle*, edited by Vassiliki Kravari, Jacques Lefort and Cécile Morrisson, 63–82. Paris: Lethielleux, 1991.

Lefort, J. "Radolibos: population et paysage," in *idem*. *Société rurale et histoire du paysage à Byzance*, 161–200. Paris: Association des amis du centre d'histoire et civilisation de Byzance, 2006. Originally published in *Travaux et Mémoires* 9 (1985): 195–234.

Lefort, J. "The Rural Economy, Seventh–Twelfth Centuries," in *The Economic History of Byzantium, From the Seventh through the Fifteenth Century*, 3 vols., edited by A. E. Laiou, vol. 1, 231–310. Washington: Dumbarton Oaks Research Library and Collection, 2002.

Lefort, J. "Les villages de Macédoine orientale au Moyen Âge (X^e–XIVe siècle)." In *idem*. *Société rurale et histoire du paysage à Byzance*, 489–500. Paris: Association des amis du centre d'histoire et civilisation de Byzance, 2006. Originally published in *Les villages dans l'empire byzantin*, edited by J. Lefort, C. Morrisson and J.-P. Sodini, 289–299. Paris: Lethielleux, 2005.

Lefort, J., R.-C. Bondoux, J.-C. Cheynet, J.-P. Grélois, and V. Kravari. Collaboration J.-M. Martin. *Géometries du fisc byzantin*. Paris: Lethielleux, 1991.

Lefort, J., V. Kravari, C. Giros, and K. Smyrlis, eds. *Actes de Vatopédi II, de 1330 à 1376*. Paris: Lethielleux, 2006.

Lefort, J., V. Kravari, C. Giros, K. Smyrlis, and R. Estangüi Gómez, eds. *Actes de Vatopédi III, de 1377 à 1500*. Forthcoming.

Lefort, J., N. Oikonomidès, and D. Papachryssanthou, eds., V. Kravari and H. Métrévéli, collab. *Actes d'Iviron II, du milieu du XIe siècle à 1204*. Paris: P. Lethielleux, 1990.

Lefort, J., N. Oikonomidès, D. Papachryssanthou, and V. Kravari, eds., H. Métrévéli, collab. *Actes d'Iviron IV, de 1328 au début du XVIe siècle*. Paris: CNRS Éditions—P. Lethielleux, 1995.

Lemerle, P. "La domination venitienne à Thessalonique," in *Miscellanea Giovanni Galbiati*, 3 vols., vol. 3, 219–225. Milano: U. Hoepli, 1951.

Lemerle, P., A. Guillou, N. Svoronos, and D. Papachryssanthou, eds. *Actes de Lavra III, de 1329 à 1500*. Paris: P. Lethielleux, 1979.

Lemerle, P. A. Guillou, N. Svoronos, and D. Papachryssanthou, eds. S. Ćirković, collab. *Actes de Lavra IV, études historiques—actes serbes—complements et index*. Paris: P. Lethielleux, 1982.
Lowry, H. W. *Fifteenth Century Ottoman Realities: Christian Peasant Life on the Aegean Island of Limnos*. Istanbul: Eren, 2002.
Lowry, H. W. "Pushing the Stone Uphill: The Impact of Bubonic Plague on Ottoman Urban Society in the Fifteenth and Sixteenth Centuries." *The Journal of Ottoman Studies* 23 (2003): 93–132.
Magdalino, P. *Constantinople médiévale. Études sur l'évolution des structures urbaines*. Paris: De Boccard, 1996.
Magdalino, P. *The Empire of Manuel I Komnenos, 1143–1180*. Cambridge: Cambridge University Press, 1993.
Magdalino, P. "The Grain Supply of Constantinople, Ninth–Twelfth Centuries," in *Constantinople and its Hinterland: Papers from the Twenty-seventh Spring Symposium of Byzantine Studies, Oxford, April 1993*, edited by C. Mango and G. Dagron, with the assistance of G. Greatrex, 35–47. Aldershot: Variorum, 1995.
Matschke, K.-P. "Commerce, Trade, Markets, and Money, Thirteenth–Fifteenth Centuries," in *The Economic History of Byzantium, From the Seventh through the Fifteenth Century*, 3 vols., edited by Angeliki E. Laiou, vol. 2, 771–806. Washington: Dumbarton Oaks Research Library and Collection, 2002.
Matschke, K.-P. "The Late Byzantine Urban Economy, Thirteenth–Fifteenth Centuries," in *The Economic History of Byzantium, From the Seventh through the Fifteenth Century*, 3 vols., edited by A. E. Laiou, vol. 2, 463–495. Washington: Dumbarton Oaks Research Library and Collection, 2002.
Morrisson, C. and J.-C. Cheynet. "Prices and Wages in the Byzantine World," in *The Economic History of Byzantium, From the Seventh through the Fifteenth Century*, 3 vols., edited by Angeliki E. Laiou, vol. 2, 815–878. Washington: Dumbarton Oaks Research Library and Collection, 2002.
Moustakas, K. "He demographike krise tou hysterou Mesaiona ston helleniko choro. He periptose tes notio-anatolikes Makedonias (14os–15os ai.)." *Mnemon* 25 (2003): 9–23.
Moustakas, K. *The Transition from Late Byzantine to Early Ottoman Southeastern Macedonia (14th–15th Centuries): A Socioeconomic and Demographic Study*. PhD diss., University of Birmingham, 2001.
Necipoğlu, N. Byzantium Between the Ottomans and the Latins: Politics and Society in the Late Empire. Cambridge: Cambridge University Press, 2009.
Nesbitt, J. W. *Mechanisms of Agricultural Production on Estates of the Byzantine Praktika*. PhD diss., Univerity of Wisconsin, 1972.
Oikonomidès, N. "Hoi dyo Serbikes katakteseis tes Chalkidikes ton ID aiona." *Diptycha* 2 (1980–1981): 294–299.
Oikonomidès, N. *Fiscalité et exemption fiscale à Byzance (IXe–XIe s.)*. Athens: Fondation nationale de la recherche scientifique, Institut de recherches byzantines, 1996.
Oikonomidès, N. *Hommes d'affaires grecs et latins à Constantinople (XIIIe–XVe siècles)*. Montreal: Institut d'études médiévales Albert-le-Grand; Paris: J. Vrin, 1979.
Oikonomidès, N. "Ottoman Influence on Late Byzantine Fiscal Practice." *Südost-Forschungen* 45 (1986): 1–24.
Oikonomidès, N. "Patronage in Palaiologan Mt Athos," in *Mount Athos and Byzantine Monasticism: Papers from the Twenty-eighth Spring Symposium of Byzantine Studies, March 1994*, edited by A. Bryer and M. Cunningham, 99–111. Aldershot: Ashgate/Variorum, 1996.
Oikonomidès, N. "The Properties of the Deblitzenoi in the Fourteenth and Fifteenth Centuries," in *Charanis Studies: Essays in Honor of Peter Charanis*, edited by A. E. Laiou-Thomadakis, 176–198. New Brunswick: Rutgers University Press, 1980.

Oikonomidès, N. "The Role of the Byzantine State in the Economy," in *The Economic History of Byzantium, From the Seventh through the Fifteenth Century*, 3 vols., edited by Angeliki E. Laiou, 3, 973–1058. Washington: Dumbarton Oaks Research Library and Collection, 2002.

Oikonomidès, N. "Terres du fisc et revenu de la terre aux xe–xie siècles." In *idem*, *Social and Economic Life in Byzantium*, edited by E. Zachariadou, article 11. Aldershot: Ashgate/Variorum, 2004. Originally published in *Hommes et richesses dans l'Empire byzantin, viiie–xve siècle*, edited by V. Kravari, J. Lefort, and C. Morrisson, 321–338. Paris: Lethielleux, 1991.

Oikonomidès, N., ed. *Actes de Dionysiou*. Paris: P. Lethielleux, 1968.

Pachymérès, G. *Relations Historiques*, vols. 1–2, edited by A. Failler, trans. by V. Laurent; vols. 3–4, edited and trans. by A. Failler. Paris: Belles Lettres, 1984, 1999.

Nystazopoulou-Pelekidou, M., ed. *Byzantina engrapha tes mones Patmou. II, Demosion leitourgon*. Athens: Ethnikon Hidryma Ereunon, Kentron Byzantinon Ereunon, 1980.

Petit, L., ed. "Actes de Chilandar." *Vizantijskij Vremennik* 17 (1911), Appendix 1.

Reinert, S. W. "Fragmentation," in *The Oxford History of Byzantium*, edited by C. Mango, 248–283. Oxford: Oxford University Press, 2002.

Rheidt, K. "The Urban Economy of Pergamon," in *The Economic History of Byzantium, From the Seventh through the Fifteenth Century*, 3 vols., edited by A. E. Laiou, vol. 2, 623–629. Washington: Dumbarton Oaks Research Library and Collection, 2002.

Richard, J. "Le casal de Psimolofo et la vie rurale en Chypre au xive siècle," in *idem*, *Les relations entre l'Orient et l'Occident au Moyen Âge*, article 4. London: Variorum, 1977. Originally published in *Mélanges d'Archéologie et d'Histoire publiés par l'École Française de Rome* 54 (1947): 121–153.

Schilbach, E. *Byzantinische Metrologie*. Munich: C. H. Beck, 1970.

Schneider, A. M. "Die Bevölkerung Konstantinopels im XV. Jahrhundert." *Nachrichten der Akademie der Wissenschaften in Göttingen, Philologisch-historische Klasse* 9 (1949): 233–244.

Ševčenko, I. and N. Paterson-Ševčenko, ed. and trans. *The Life of Saint Nicholas of Sion*. Brookline: Hellenic College Press, 1984.

Smyrlis, K. "The First Ottoman Occupation of Macedonia (*c*. 1383–*c*. 1403): Some Remarks on Land Ownership, Property Transactions and Justice," in Diplomatics in the Eastern Mediterranean 1000–1500*: Aspects of Intercultural Communication*, edited by A. Beihammer, M. Parani, and C. Schabel, 327–348. Leiden: Brill, 2008.

Smyrlis, K. *La fortune des grands monastères byzantins, fin du xe–milieu du xive siècle*. Paris: Centre de Recherche d'Histoire et Civilisation de Byzance-Collège de France, 2006.

Smyrlis, K. "The Management of Monastic Estates: The Evidence of the Typika." *Dumbarton Oaks Papers* 56 (2002): 245–261.

Stathakopoulos, D. "Population, Demography and Disease," in *The Oxford Handbook of Byzantine Studies*, edited by E. Jeffreys, J. Haldon, and R. Cormack, 309–316. Oxford: Oxford University Press, 2008.

Svoronos, N. "Remarques sur les structures économiques de l'empire byzantin au xie siècle." *Travaux et Mémoires* 6 (1976): 49–67.

Thiriet, F. *Délibérations des assemblées vénitiennes concernant la Romanie, Tome I, 1160–1363*. Paris: Mouton, 1966.

Treadgold, W. *A History of the Byzantine State and Society*. Stanford: Stanford University Press, 1997.

Uspenskij, F. "Nabljudenija po sel'sko-hozjajstvennoj istorii v" Vizantii." *Žurnal" Ministerstva Narodnago Prosvješenija* 259 (1888): 229–259.

Uspenskij, F. "Vizantijskie zemlemery. Nabljudenija po istorii sel'skago hozjajstva," in *Trudy VI arheologičeskago s"ezda v" Odesse (1884 g.)*, vol. 2, 272–341. Odessa: A. Šul'ce, 1888.

de Villehardouin, G. "The Conquest of Constantinople," in Chronicles of the Crusades, trans. by Margaret R. B. Shaw, 27–162. Harmondsworth: Penguin, 1963.

Vryonis, S., Jr. *The Decline of Medieval Hellenism in Asia Minor and the Process of Islamization from the Eleventh through the Fifteenth Century*. Berkeley: University of California Press, 1971.

Vryonis, S., Jr. "The Ottoman Conquest of Thessaloniki in 1430," in *Continuity and Change in Late Byzantine and Early Ottoman Society*, edited by A. Bryer and H. Lowry, 281–321. Birmingham: University of Birmingham, Centre for Byzantine Studies; Washington: Dumbarton Oaks Research Library and Collection, 1986.

Živojinović, M. "Concerning Turkish Assaults on Mount Athos in the 14th Century, based on Byzantine Sources." *Orijentalni Institut u Serajevu, Prilozi za Orijentalnu Filologiju* 30 (1980): 501–516.

6 Spain

Ana Rodríguez

> *When, in the thirteenth century, a peninsular peasant looked at a flow of water, he would see, were he an Andalusian, an orchard; were he a Christian, a cereal mill. But were the observer a Hispano-Christian lord, what he would see would be a drinking trough for a seasonally migratory flock of sheep. Or might it be possible that the protagonist of our visions was not a peasant or lord of the thirteenth century but a twentieth-century historian? What, for a historian from Andalusia, Valencia or Low Aragon might be a product (wheat, oil, wool) for the market would, for a historian from Old Castile, be an element of manorial dominion that served as an inevitable motive for conflict between lords and peasants, whereas for a researcher of Old Catalonia, it might be data for the study of the development of peasant involvement in the market. Obviously, where one historian sees a patchwork of flourishing orchards, farmed and well-kept by the merry effort of an Andalusian family-linked community, another historian might see a setting of a saltus progressively left aside by a successful dryland farming ager aggressively imposed by feudal lords.*[1]

This quotation summarizes a significant part of the problems we encounter in the study of the medieval economy in the Iberian Peninsula, a territory with great geographical diversity covering an area of almost 500,000 km^2. This diversity stems from factors that might be common to extensive regions, such as climatic and geological differences, particular historical evolutions, agricultural landscapes, property structures, models of farming, peasant rights, and the role of communities or regional nobilities. In the same way, the various peninsular regions have generated distinct regional historiographical approaches, which are rarely overcome by general overviews. There are, however, specific circumstances in the Hispanic kingdoms that constitute a medieval reality apparently very different in character from the other Christian kingdoms, an understanding of which is essential to an analysis of the models of economic growth and crisis in the late Middle Ages.

The lack of sources that would enable the creation of economic and demographic series is one of the reasons for the scarcity of works dealing with these questions in the Hispanic kingdoms. This is obviously a general problem for medievalists working in any geographical domain, but in the

Iberian Peninsula, it becomes particularly pronounced in kingdoms like Castile. The immense abyss that separates the volume and preservation of sources in the various kingdoms cannot be completely explained by accidental loss or destruction during wars and dynastic changes. It is important to stress the existence of a very widespread written culture in the Kingdom of Aragon, across all social groups, compared to the Castilian world, in which written documents—and therefore notarial records—were much less frequently used. The notarial records preserved in regions like Valencia show a significant written activity in the daily life of both rural and urban communities, and they constitute very valuable sources, especially for the fifteenth century.

The lack of direct demographic sources is a general problem for medievalists, who have to resort to other types of evidence. In the case of the Hispanic kingdoms, there is the further problem of inequality between the indirect sources—those of the fiscal kind—among the different kingdoms. For the Kingdom of Castile, no fiscal censuses have been preserved for the fourteenth and fifteenth centuries. Elsewhere, a useful source for these centuries is found in the *fogajes* (hearth tax records) in Catalonia (where they start in 1359), Valencia, and Aragon. The hearth books of the districts of Navarre also constitute a first-rate source. In using the data provided by these kinds of sources, however, we face an insoluble problem: determining the number of inhabitants per household. A figure of four to five inhabitants seems to be accepted as a convention, but it is obvious that this figure varied across space and time. On the other hand, there is no doubt that the number of inhabitants per household was lower after an epidemic, and that the population increase took place within households before becoming apparent in the number of hearths.[2]

In Castile, especially in Andalusia, there are censuses of an exclusively local type; those of the city of Seville are well-known, especially those for the fifteenth century. Nevertheless, the use of these local sources raises numerous problems, since a part of the population is excluded. The fiscal censuses include only the heads of the families who paid taxes and do not include exempt social groups or ethnic and religious minorities. For the Kingdom of Aragon, some particular sources are preserved. Since the beginning of the thirteenth century, the Aragonese monarchy had claimed a tax to redeem the royal right to debase the coinage (the *monedaje*). This tax gave rise to nominal records of the tax collection, where the names of the tax-payers were included.[3]

Finding sources that illustrate the organization of production and agricultural yields is even more difficult before the second half of the fifteenth century. Once again, the Kingdoms of Aragon and Navarre stand out for both the number and quality of the sources, which include property inventories and the fiscal accounts of Navarre. Aragonese ecclesiastical institutions like the *Pía Almoina*, in charge of charity and feeding the poor in the cities, recorded data of great interest, relating to the impact of the Black Death. Despite this relative richness, the sources are in general territorially and chronologically scattered, hindering the establishment of general series. The documentation of land transactions and agricultural agreements establishing relationships between lords and peasants are sometimes almost the only source for most of the Hispanic kingdoms. The analysis of living standards and consumption as a way to assess the effect of the crisis on the medieval peasantry is almost unknown to Spanish historiography, although it has been tackled in the last few years through the study of *post mortem* inventories—very scarce in the medieval period yet fairly abundant for the early modern age.[4]

Chronicles and literary sources have influenced the approach that has been traditionally applied to the analysis of the complex circumstances surrounding the economic and social development of the Hispanic kingdoms in the late Middle Ages, in which special weight has been given to demographic factors. Moreover, the only Christian king who died in the epidemic—which had spread through Europe in 1348—was the king of Castile, Alfonso XI, who died in the spring of 1350 during the siege of Gibraltar. The rapid spread of the Black Death in the Hispanic kingdoms and its devastating results were reflected in the account of the king's death and the significant losses of his armies in the Castilian chronicles of the fourteenth century.[5] The chroniclers' view of a serious demographic crisis, worsened by the war and the widespread political instability, has traditionally been the starting point used by Spanish historiography in discussions of the fourteenth-century crisis. Some aspects of it have been discussed since the 1970s. Special attention was given to demographic subjects including the local and regional impact of the Black Death and changes in patterns of settlement, especially settlement desertion.[6] The crisis of the fourteenth century in Castile was taken up again by historians, who, in the 1980s, considered not only the demographic impact but also the price and wage increases, the reduction of the area of cultivation, the reduction of cereal production, and the increase in production costs.[7] In the Kingdom of Aragon, following the explanatory model of Catalan decadence in the fifteenth century set out by Pierre Vilar,[8] revisionist accounts of the crisis focused on the analysis of the specific case of the city of Barcelona, a commercial center that suffered serious social conflict during the fourteenth and fifteenth centuries.[9] The crisis of the fourteenth century in the Kingdom of Navarre was also studied in the 80s using more abundant and richer documentary fiscal sources than were available for Castile and Aragon.[10] Nevertheless, the crisis of the late Middle Ages in the Iberian Peninsula has, to a large extent, still to be investigated;[11] these gaps in research will be evident throughout the pages of this paper.

PATTERNS OF INTEGRATION: ECONOMIC GROWTH AND THE ORGANIZATION OF PRODUCTION

The *Reconquista* process, the extraordinary territorial expansion of the Christian kingdoms of the North against the Muslims of al-Andalus between the eleventh and fifteenth centuries, marked the course of history in the Iberian Peninsula in the Middle Ages. Politically, the *Reconquista* generated the different peninsular kingdoms, grouped into two important political entities: the Kingdoms of Castile and Aragon; and the three minor kingdoms, Portugal, Navarre, and the Muslim Kingdom of Granada (which was conquered by the Catholic Monarchs in 1492). The expansion of the peninsular Christian kingdoms towards the South proceeded at different rates, which marked the way in which the new territories were progressively integrated into them, creating different social, economic, demographic, and political conditions. Besides the economic and institutional growth of the eleventh–thirteenth centuries, which was very similar to that taking place in the rest of Western Europe, there was also an extraordinary territorial growth, which contributed to the specificity of its political, social, and economic development; this territorial growth was marked out by the

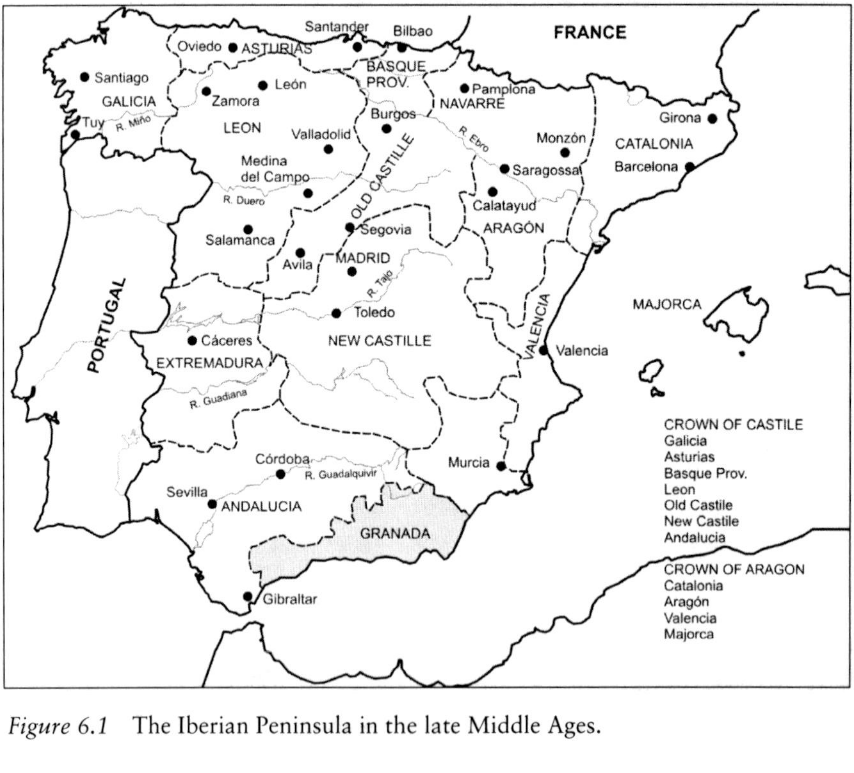

Figure 6.1 The Iberian Peninsula in the late Middle Ages.

Christian conquests of Toledo (1085), Saragossa (1118), Cordoba (1236), Valencia (1238), and Seville (1248). The exploitation and settlement of the conquered territory took different forms according to the differing chronology of conquest, the ways land was granted by the royal authority, and the pre-existing demographic and economic structures.[12]

Facing the dearth of men and the need to defend the border, the region between the Douro and the Tagus was resettled, by means of granting vast territories and great privileges (*fueros*) to both old cities and newly founded towns, in order to draw population from other places. An agricultural structure was consolidated in this area, in which—together with small owners with various legal conditions, noblemen, and churchmen—there were also great areas of land in collective ownership (mountains, communal pastures, wastelands). The resettlement of the areas between the Tagus and Sierra Morena followed different paths. The essential problem faced by the kings of Castile was the occupation of extensive territories, very close to the great Muslim centers, to which it was difficult to attract Christian settlers. The solution adopted was to grant such territories to major military orders and big monasteries. All this led to a settlement strategy with a few widely scattered inhabited centres and vast areas of land destined as pastures for seasonally migratory flocks of sheep. In the Ebro valley, as in Castile, as lands were conquered, cities were granted *fueros*, to attract a Christian population, and huge territories, castles, and even peasants were given to lords, for their exploitation. However, the difference in the resettlement of these areas was that the kings of Navarre and Aragon and the counts of Catalonia faced a numerous Muslim population—the *Mudejar*—who were allowed to stay on their lands under capitulation agreements. The environment continued to be, in broad terms, very similar to that of the Andalusian period, although the deliberate foundation of monasteries led to innovations in patterns of settlement and agricultural techniques.

The Christian victory of Navas de Tolosa in 1212 left vast spaces to be populated by Christian settlers. For instance, the Kingdom of Castile expanded by more than 100,000 km^2 (almost doubling its total extent) over the course of 30 years, culminating in the conquest of Seville in 1248. The Castilian and Aragonese monarchs distributed the conquered lands—in the so-called *Repartimientos* (royal inventories of property granted to settlers in the newly conquered lands)[13]—among lay lords and ecclesiastical institutions, as well as among the peasants who wished to settle there. However, while the Muslim population continued to be very numerous in the Kingdom of Aragon, the *Mudejar* uprising of 1264 in Andalusia and Murcia resulted in their expulsion, which—added to the return of many Christian settlers to their northern homelands—altered the initial structure established by the monarchs. As a result of the new circumstances from the end of the thirteenth century onwards, the big owners increased their economic power by occupying new lands and concentrating those already owned.[14]

The different phases of settlement of the vast areas recovered from the Muslims are also reflected in aspects such as landownership, manorial structures, peasant subjection, and the proportion of land in the hands of the king, noblemen, and peasant communities. Three regions can be distinguished in the Kingdom of Castile depending on the phases of the expansive process. In the North of the kingdom—Galicia, Leon, and the former territory of Castile—landownership was initially characterized not only by a fragmentation of both noble and royal properties but also by the solidarity of peasant communities based on a pattern of nucleated settlement in most of these areas.[15] Conditions changed with time, and social relations in particular were transformed by the establishment of large Benedictine and Cistercian monasteries. Small peasant properties as well as the community organization of a considerable part of the payment of rents to lords are recorded in the documentation preserved. This source also records the progressive takeover of small properties by lords, the territorial concentration of their possessions and the gradual imposition of royal jurisdiction.[16] Lands could be given to peasants either collectively or individually. Conditions varied depending on whether those lands were already in cultivation and whether they were subject to contracts *ad plantandum*, which were collectively bestowed on a group of peasants.

The twelfth and thirteenth centuries saw a period of expansion of the cultivated areas and of population increase throughout the whole kingdom. The abundance of land in the swathes of territory that were progressively added to the kingdom as a result of the Reconquest and the formation of great seigneurial dominions—cultivated by dependent peasants—coincided with a form of land possession in which peasants had a high level of freedom to administer their resources and determine their own exploitation strategies. In broad terms, the overlap between big manorial properties and small peasant possession was one of the most outstanding characteristics of the Castilian system. Moreover, it was a manorial system in which ecclesiastical—as opposed to lay—landownership was predominant, and indirect exploitation of land prevailed over direct exploitation. Exploitation consisted of *corvées*—called *sernas* in Castile—which had to be rendered by tenants in reduced manorial demesnes, and which decreased with time.

The conquest of Andalusia resulted in the implantation of new methods of exploitation. Contrary to what had happened further north, the expulsion from the conquered lands of a significant proportion of the Muslims who lived there facilitated the creation of more homogeneous production structures. The *Repartimientos* of the thirteenth century provided both the high lay nobility of Castile and some ecclesiastical institutions with large manors, but land plots were also distributed among *milites* and other noblemen of lower rank who had taken part in military campaigns. The difficulties of settling these territories led a considerable number of the beneficiaries of land distribution—especially Castilian noblemen of middle rank—to leave their possessions and return to their places of origin.

Throughout the fourteenth century, new *Repartimientos*—of a more local nature this time—of large properties in lowland Andalusia, progressively developed, although peasant property never disappeared.[17] Moreover, it retained its prominence in certain areas: around Seville, in the area of Aljarafe and Ribera, 60–70 percent of the peasant population owned lands in the fifteenth century. It has been argued that access to land by peasants would evolve in parallel with the consolidation of large properties: agricultural contracts in large properties—in the form of long-term leases for the exploitation of cereals, olive, and vines—coexisted with the family exploitation of properties of very small dimensions. In the fifteenth century, the manorial strategy consisted of assigning groups of peasants to overly small plots of land that required them to work for extra income in the lord's estate.[18]

There is also a clear regional differentiation resulting from the different stages of Christian conquest in the Kingdom of Aragon. Catalan historiography traditionally makes the distinction between two forms of subjection. The manorial forms found in Old Catalonia were the result of a long process of resistance to subjection (eleventh and twelfth centuries) and, later, legal recognition of seigneural power (thirteenth century), which had reinforced the subjection of peasants. The peasants paid heavy rents and were subject to servitude—the so-called *remensas*—as well as customary laws (the so-called 'bad customs') such as the *ius maletractandi*. In New Catalonia, on the other hand, the peasants paid lighter tribute and were not subjected to servitude, as a result of the franchise charters granted throughout the twelfth century for the settlement and organization of the territory. In both domains, ecclesiastical property was the most abundant and—although the weight of both the manorial demesne and the *corvées* was higher than in Castile—the *mansi* granted to the peasants for the indirect exploitation of the manorial dominions represented the basic production unit. The degraded legal situation of the *remensas* did not necessarily correspond with a precarious economic situation. The practice of indivisible inheritance in Catalonia, forcing peasants to leave two-thirds or three-quarters of their inheritance to just one descendant (the *hereu*), meant—to the peasants—the solution to the problem of generational change and—to the lords—the simplification of the management of their dominions as well as the consolidation of a lasting exploitation structure.[19]

The devastation of the rural population by plague entailed—as a reaction—a tougher manorial stance, although the situation varied depending on the areas and the lords' need to keep their lands inhabited. Thus, in the same period, peasants were offered a reduction of their rents and allowed to occupy the deserted *mansi* in fertile areas (Plana de Vic, Ampurdá, Maresme, Vallés), whereas in the mountain areas, which would have still been more deserted, servitude was reinforced in order to keep cultivators on the land. Once the difficulties were overcome, the lords tried to re-establish the rights given up during the crisis and re-impose bad customs.

The *remensa* conflict in the fifteenth century broke out as a result of this reaction to better times.

As in Catalonia, the manorial system in Aragon was much more oppressive north of the Ebro than south of it. In the 'old lands,' the decrease in income resulting from the crisis of the fourteenth century prompted the strict subjection of serfs, the full exercise of the civil and criminal jurisdiction that most lords possessed on their manors and which excluded any possibility of appeal to a higher court, and also the exercise of the *ius maletractandi*, which was recognized by the Justice of Aragon as a manorial right in 1332. The legislation derived from the General Courts in the fifteenth century insisted on peasant attachment to the land, but contrary to what happened in Catalonia, acts of resistance to it were isolated.[20] South of the Ebro, on the other hand, the Aragonese peasant situation was different. *Mudejares* predominated there, holding land according to a sharecropping system, enjoying freedom of movement and the direct protection of the royal authority and no ecclesiastical tithes.

In the recently conquered Kingdom of Valencia, the situation was very different from that of the old territories of the kingdom. According to the capitulation agreements and the constant, but weak, trickle of Catalan and Aragonese settlers to the new lands, a significant part of the Valencian cultivated lands continued to be worked by Muslims (*Mudejar*) who, at the end of the thirteenth century, represented the vast majority of the population of the kingdom and who were still predominant in the fourteenth and fifteenth centuries. The level of subjugation and exploitation they suffered was probably significant, higher than that of Christians, who received good lands and paid low perpetual rents subject to long-term leases (*emphyteusis*). In Majorca, more than 40 percent of the population lived in the city, exploitation of manorial domains being subject to *emphyteusis*, according to which peasants were forced to pay rents to lords who lived in the city but who gave their tenants a high level of freedom.

WAYS OF LAND EXPLOITATION AND FARMING TECHNIQUES

The existence of two Spains—dry and humid—is the first distinguishing feature in methods of land exploitation and systems of cultivation. Other features are the variety of social models in the peninsular territories as well as, again, the pace of the conquest against al-Andalus, since the influence of Andalusian cultivation systems based on irrigation techniques accounts for some key aspects of agricultural development in the south and east of the Peninsula. In dry Spain there were fields of wheat and barley—intended for animal consumption—and vineyards and orchards; in the north, which was colder and wetter with poorer quality land, the crops were rye, millet, and spelt—probably the most important cereal for peasant consumption in the region—with an abundance of pastures and communal mountain areas; in

Valencia and Murcia, after the Christian conquest of the thirteenth century, orchards and rice fields predominated; in Andalusia, New Catalonia, and Low Aragon, there were olive and fig trees and, in the late Middle Ages, a large presence of industrial plants such as flax and hemp. This would be, broadly speaking, the regional distribution of crops. Another factor to be added is the importance, throughout the Middle Ages, of stockbreeding, a complementary resource and occasionally a determinant of land exploitation strategies.[21]

In the central plains of Castile, the *tierras de pan llevar* (wheat-growing land) were most representative of Castilian agriculture. They were based on a biennial rotation system, lands being left fallow every other year. The fallow year was forced by slow soil recovery due to climatic conditions, and also by stockbreeding requirements, complementing pasture land. This was the most common system in Castile, although in some areas such as the western plains, which were subject to erosion (Salamanca, Zamora, Extremadura), the need to combine land cultivation with exploitation of livestock led to the organization of production based on fallow periods of two or more years. Crops—generally rye—were only sown every third year, leaving the land at rest the other two years, one as wasteland and the other as fallow land, thereby enabling a more stockbreeding-centered economy[22].

In some regions it seems that more intensive cultivation systems were implemented, thus considerably reducing the area of fallow. In parts of Segovia, from the thirteenth century, the sowing of cereals was alternated with legumes, which, besides enriching the land, meant that crops were harvested two out of every three years.[23] Some authors argue that, in Galicia, different systems had also been implemented since the thirteenth century, which greatly limited the resting period of the soil. This intensification could be achieved either by sowing a winter cereal after the spring harvest (wheat after millet, for instance)—thus limiting the fallow period to six or seven months—or by introducing legumes (which appear regularly in the Galician sources after 1220). These would be cultivated in the spring, following the millet harvest and before the sowing of wheat. This practice resulted in not only the diversification of production but also land fertilization.[24]

In the big towns (*Concejos*) located to the south of the Douro, the lack of labor, the vastness of deserted areas and the proximity of the border all contributed to the development of sheep rearing. The great development of transhumance did not occur until the establishment in 1273 of a regulatory livestock institution—*La Mesta*—linked to the big stock owners, which maintained the monopoly of transhumance and the production and commercialization of wool.[25] The flocks of *La Mesta* spent the summer in the central mountain ranges of Castile and the winter in La Mancha and Extremadura. After the fourteenth century, vast areas had been transformed into pastures, and fields had been enclosed with the aim of leasing the grass for the use of the transhumant livestock. In the fourteenth and fifteenth centuries, favored by the demographic crisis and the crown's support, a great expansion of sheep flocks took place: it is estimated that in 1400 there were three million sheep in Castile and five million in 1480. Castilian wool was almost all used for trade and destined for foreign markets. It was concentrated on Burgos from the mid-thirteenth century, and there it was purchased by Castilian, Flemish, and Italian merchants and exported to the textile mills of Flanders.[26] This market expanded significantly at the end of the fourteenth century. Nevertheless, compared to what happened in other regions in Europe, Castilian wool production did not cause an extensive division of labor, since it only found its way to local weaving mills on rare occasions.

Vine exploitation had been, since the High Middle Ages, complementary to cereal exploitation. Despite widespread references to vineyards in the cereal regions of Castile, significant transformations took place only at the end of the Middle Ages, above all in their distribution and extent. The progress of viticulture in the fifteenth century is apparent even in regions where the conditions for cultivation were poor. The references to lands under vines are very abundant and sharecropping contracts for their exploitation became widespread. In places like Paredes de Nava (Palencia), a basically grain-growing region, vineyards occupied 18 percent of the total cultivated surface at the end of the fifteenth century. The new vineyards did not, in this case, replace cereal production, but were only small plots on the periphery of cultivated fields.[27] This process of vine specialization and progress was not homogeneous in Castile: data from regions like Segovia or Burgos show the decline of the cultivation in the fifteenth century.

The thirteenth century was the period of vineyard expansion in southern Galicia, a tendency reinforced during the fourteenth century, and associated with production for the market. The abundance of references to the vine is remarkable when compared to most cereals. The analysis (as seen in Table 6.1) shows that the area taken up by vineyards increased until 1320 but came to a standstill or slightly decreased between 1320 and 1340. These circumstances—the expansion of the vine and the decrease of the area used for cereals—probably played a role in generating the crisis of the first half of the fourteenth century; the standstill of vineyard expansion between 1320 and 1340 being attributed to the appearance of widespread famines at that time, which revealed the urgent need to produce more bread.[28] In the second half of the 14th century, there was a sharp increase in vineyard exploitation. This, in turn, was probably due to the drop in both cereal production and prices as a result of lower demand following the crisis, coupled with the maintenance of wine prices sustained by export demand through urban centers. Vineyards did not take up new lands in Galicia, but they did replace cereals or became the main cultivation of previously deserted lands that were re-occupied.

Table 6.1 Land Allocation (Percent) in the Region of the Bishopric of Tuy (Galicia) in the Fourteenth Century

Years	*Vine*	*Cereals*
1280–1300	53.4	46.5
1300–1320	60.6	39.3
1320–1340	59.2	40.7
1340–1360	72.3	27.6
1360–1380	75.3	24.6
1380–1400	63.1	36.8
Total	**66.1**	**33.9**

Source: E. Portela, *La región del obispado de Tuy en los siglos XII al XV*, 283.

The vine hardly appears in sources from the period of the Christian conquest of Andalusia, the resettlement documents of the fourteenth century. In the fifteenth century, however, around 70 percent of the rural population in the area of Seville had vineyards, although of very small dimensions. Except in isolated cases, the big Andalusian owners did not get directly involved in wine production, but they handed over to the peasants small plots of land in exchange for rents in money and kind. Landlords, on the other hand, focused on cereals (which had good regional markets and were easier to produce) and olive groves (more expensive to produce but with good export possibilities). A correlation was thus established in Andalusia between the big cereal and olive grove property and the small vineyard holding. Peasant life was divided between the cultivation of their own vine plots, whose yields did not reach subsistence threshold, and salaried work on the big lay property, where they carried out the seasonal tasks of wheat and olive production.[29]

The expansion of the cultivated area devoted to raw materials for the textile industry underwent a commercializing dynamic similar to that of wine in Castile. The proliferation of *rubia tinctorum* and *grana*—plants to dye fabrics—or flax clearly shows the replacement of traditional crops by other, more profitable, competitors to cereals.[30] The existence of an institutional framework that encouraged the commercialization of rural surpluses and the spread of alternative crops is obvious in the late Middle Ages. Since at least the thirteenth century there had been, on a regional scale, a network of weekly markets that were exempt from the payment of transference tax (*alcabala*). There are also records of the acceleration, parallel to the phase of economic growth that took place during the fifteenth century, of the creation of weekly markets exempt from the payment of the *alcabala*, which seems to be a clear indicator of the consumption capacity of the population. However, the involvement of the rural world in Castilian trade has hardly been studied.

A regional distribution of cultivation is also clear in the Kingdom of Aragon. In Low Aragon, dry lands and irrigated lands co-existed and almost the same products were sown in orchards (which were irrigated) and fields (which were not). Presumably, the cultivation system was based on a biennial rotation, although in purely dry areas, fallow cycles were probably longer. The growth of different types of cereals and the exploitation of vines and industrial plants such as flax or hemp, as well as leguminous plants, characterized the agrarian system, although it is impossible to find out how the land was distributed between various types of cultivation. The demographic decline of the first half of the fourteenth century might have entailed a reduction of the agricultural surface in favor of pasture lands, although there is no data to confirm this hypothesis. On the other hand, it is possible to prove the redistribution of production within the totality of cultivated lands. In the second half of the fifteenth century, the documentation of the area of Alcañiz records the almost total predominance of cereal agriculture and a reduction of wine production even to the extent of its becoming marginalized, contrary to the situation in other peninsular areas. Some general characteristics of the solution to the crisis, like the development of sheep rearing and agricultural specialization, are first perceptible in southern Aragon in the 1360s. On the other hand, cereals, saffron, oil, and wool became products aimed at export because they were easily transported along the Ebro waterway.[31]

Between 1350 and 1500, the cultivated area decreased in Catalonia as a result of demographic contraction and rural emigration. Rural labor tended to be concentrated in the most fertile areas or those with a better legal statute for peasants. The organization of markets on a regional scale favored the cultivation of crops that had a higher success rate in the cities, as shown in the fiscal documentation of the tithe collection. There was a growing demand for wine, fruit, rice, vegetables and pulses, sugar, and saffron. The growth of the textile industry demanded vegetal fibers (flax, hemp and cotton), dyes (pastel, *gualda* and *rubia*) and thistles to card the woolen cloths. Some of these cultivations did not thrive. Of those that were consolidated, only the vine, the legumes, saffron, and some fruits coincided with cereals in the dry areas. While legumes could alternate and fruits could co-exist with wheat and barley, the others were exclusive, causing a decrease in the area under cereals.[32] Therefore, the demographic decline did not mean an increase in the relative availability of grain, for its production was also reduced. In fact, after the Black Death, Catalonia became a cereal importer, whose domestic demand, even in normal years, was partially covered by surpluses obtained by traders in other regions of the Kingdom of Aragon, or overseas.

Data related to productivity is very scarce and fragmentary. Evidence reveals intensive agriculture, but work implements were archaic and technological innovation was almost non-existent in the High Middle Ages. Thus, in Castile, the advance of tilled land and the increase in output was not the result of technological progress but of peasant toil. Oxen were not replaced by horses for fieldwork; until the mid-fifteenth century, or even at the beginning of the sixteenth century in some regions, the use of mules in agriculture was not widespread. Land yields are known for some specific years but it is not possible to establish an evolution because there is no continuity in the record. Land yields were very likely to vary significantly depending on the different types of soil, climatic conditions, and crop variation. It is commonly accepted that, in view of the absence of technological innovation in medieval Hispanic agriculture, the increase of production was only possible by means of the increase in the peasant workforce. Nevertheless, yields were probably improved by other factors related to the improvements in the fertilization of fields and the introduction of new cultivation systems. In any case, these changes probably occurred very late.

In the central areas of the Kingdom of Castile, in the twelfth and thirteenth centuries, increasing production is reported, due to the application of more labor inputs in cereal cultivation. This would enable a slight increase in yields, which around 1300 would be 3:1 for wheat and 4.2:1 for barley[33]. Wheat yields would range between 3:1 and 3.5:1 in other areas of Castile. There are other calculations of yields around 1300 which are rather higher: 4:1 to 4.8:1 for wheat, 3.7:1 for rye, and 5.1:1 for barley.[34] Vineyards, in turn, which required less land and more intensive work, produced a crop annually and had yields significantly higher than those obtained with cereals; the yields were also more heterogeneous: depending on area and year, between two and 50 hectolitres per hectare.[35]

There is no specific local data that might clarify the issue of land productivity in the Kingdom of Aragon. In Low Aragon, land yields are reckoned around 8:1 in good fertile lands whereas there are estimates for half that figure in the rest of the kingdom.[36] In the Kingdom of Valencia, agricultural growth was based, before and after the fourteenth-century crisis, on extensive farming practices; intensive farming, however, became more frequent with time by means of the development of irrigation systems and increasingly specialized production, boosted by commercial demand. The increase in productivity in Valencia was not so much related to the use of manure (which was scarce due to the absence of efficient stockbreeding practices) or of nitrogen-rich plants. Rather, it was boosted by the implementation of irrigation systems in the final decades of the Middle Ages. Indeed, water enabled faster soil regeneration and two or three harvests per year.[37]

Besides the general absence of data concerning productivity, there is also the problem of the different ways of calculating land area throughout the different territories, and even within the same kingdom. In Castile, the average size of cereal farms has been reckoned between three and four *cahíces* of sowing (1 *cahíz*=666 litres) probably rather higher than in other European regions, whereas the average extent of a peasant vineyard would be one *aranzada* (0.45 hectares).[38] In Catalonia, it is estimated that the average dimensions of a peasant's holding would range between six and 11 hectares, distributed between 13 and 20 parcels of land in dry areas, with a cultivation system of *año y vez* (biennial rotation). At the end of the fifteenth century, the tax records preserved for Valencia enable us to deduce that five hectares was the limit over which subsistence was guaranteed, both for irrigated and dry lands.[39]

Records from the northern Iberian Peninsula suggest that, in the final decades of the thirteenth century, agricultural yields began to decrease. In Navarre, some documents mention *tierras cansadas de mucho labrar* ('lands exhausted due to overworking'). Since 1270, the abandonment of some vineyards had been recorded by the Cathedral of Segovia; simultaneously, the area of land that produced cereal crops yearly was less extensive than in previous periods and it was probably subject to less intensive farming.[40] It is important to note, however, that the decrease in cultivated land does not necessarily entail a loss of production. It might result from the abandonment of the lands of the estates of the cathedral chapter, or from the adoption of cultivation systems that were more extensive than biennial rotation. This is obviously one of the interpretative problems arising from the characteristics of the available sources. The comparison between the data of the Book of Accounts of 1338 relating to the monastery of Sahagún and the Book of Incomes of Sahagún, made up by the archbishop of Toledo in 1353 at the request of the Papacy, does not enable us to compare land yields but it does permit us to verify the dramatic reduction of monastic incomes–around 53 percent of them—in a period of 15 years.[41]

For the 1358–1366 period the evolution of agricultural production in the possessions of some noblemen of the region of Seville enables us to draw a yield chart. According to the accounts of the lands in Aznalcázar and Santillán, property of Ferrán García de Santillán, the best wheat harvest was in 1359–60, with a yield of 8.8:1 and the worst was in 1361–2, with a yield of 0.9:1. The best barley harvest, with a yield of 6.8:1, was in same year as wheat; the worst year, with a yield of 1.5:1, also coincides with the worst year for wheat, the year the Guadiamar river overflowed, resulting in the loss of crops (Table 6.2).

The fall of manorial income levels seems obvious in the accounting series that have been developed. In the mid-fifteenth century, royal incomes in some Catalan localities had dropped by more than 60 percent, and at the end of the fourteenth century, they were still a third lower than at the beginning of the century.[42] Nevertheless, a more detailed analysis of the different sources of feudal income may moderate most alarmist conclusions. Although there was an undoubted initial fall of the income resulting from rents—a logical consequence of the demographic crisis—other income, such as the entry fines paid by the peasants in Catalonia, probably benefited from higher mobility of tenants.[43] At the same time, other incomes

Table 6.2 Agricultural Yield-to-Seed Ratios in the Possessions of Ferrán García de Santillán (Seville)

	Wheat		*Barley*	
	Aznalcázar	*Santillán*	*Aznalcázar*	*Santillán*
1358–1359	2.7	---	---	4.2
1359–1360	8.8	---	6.8	---
1360–1361	3.5	---	6.2	---
1361–1362	0.9	2.9	1.5	5.1
1362–1363	3	---	---	4.4
1363–1364	---	3.9	---	---
1364–1365	---	---	---	---
1365–1366	6.7	---	5.7	---

Source: Antonio Collantes, "Un modelo andaluz de explotación agraria bajomedieval," *Actas de las I Jornadas de Metodología Aplicada de las Ciencias Históricas*, Santiago, 2, 135–154, 1975.

of a fiscal or jurisdictional nature, besides the manorial monopolies, might have been maintained and even made up for the loss. This has been argued in Valencia, where between 1250 and 1500, in spite of the adverse circumstances, the manorial incomes of its central region would have experienced an upturn.[44] The difficulty of maintaining the income level forced the lords to look for complementary or alternative sources by serving the crown. This could be by direct participation in war, by participating in an increasingly centralized administration or, normally, by performing tax-collecting tasks through leasing (the *alcabala* sales tax) in the Kingdom of Castile, or investing in national debt, of which many examples are known in the Kingdom of Aragon (especially Catalonia and Valencia).

Throughout the fifteenth century, cereal yields in the central regions of Castile were probably very variable. In the Burgos area, the figures range between 2.1:1 and 7.5:1 for wheat and between 2.5:1 and 6:1 for barley and they vary considerably according to year and landowner. These data correspond with those known for Castilian agriculture at the beginning of the early Modern Age.[45] The gradual growth of agricultural productivity in the Kingdom of Aragon at the end of the Middle Ages is verified. This productivity, however, was obtained in many different ways in the different territories. For instance, the reduction in fallow land was not achieved in the same way in Catalonia as in Valencia (by means of the irrigation of the cereal lands), but through greater intensification in terms of fertilizers and labor inputs.

DIFFICULT TIMES? POPULATION DYNAMICS, FOOD SUPPLIES, AND POLITICAL VIOLENCE

In February 1348, the Black Death entered the Iberian Peninsula through Majorca and reached the coast of the Kingdom of Aragon in May. It reached the region of Seville around 1350, the year King Alfonso XI died of it in Gibraltar. A considerable number of measures taken by the Courts of Valladolid of 1351, such as regulation of prices and wages, revision of a significant number of tax contributions, and regulation of the marriage of widows reflect the problems of raised mortality, which can certainly be attributed to the first outbreak of the plague in Castile.[46] In subsequent years, after 1348, the Moorish and Jewish quarters of the Kingdom of Aragon were depopulated. For example, in Saragossa, where the General Courts were adjourned, the kings granted moratoria to the indebted population and the toll lessors were ruined.[47] In the second half of the fourteenth century, new data on epidemics is recorded. The Courts of Burgos of 1367 refer to the plague of 1363, and this date coincides with the so-called 'childrens' plague' in Catalonia. An epidemic broke out once again in the Kingdom of Aragon in 1384.[48] Meanwhile, in the Kingdom of Castile, there were new outbreaks in 1374, 1383, 1399, and 1402 in Andalusia. Between 1412 and 1414, mortality spread across the whole kingdom, and between 1434 and 1438, an epidemic coincided with famine. In 1442–1443, the plague also broke out in some parts of the northern Castile.

The degree of food shortages depended on various circumstances. There is scarce evidence available on the phenomenon of shortages in Castile before the mid-fourteenth century. It is possible, however, to identify periods of great hunger that seem to have affected most parts of the kingdom in the years 1299–1301, 1309–1311, 1331–1334, and 1334–1348.[49] Throughout the first decades of the fourteenth century, there are constant references to the 'bad years' in Castilian local sources, although some of them probably had a wider regional scope than others. The Cantabrian and Andalusian coastal regions suffered, to a lesser extent, the shortages of the first half of the century. One of the shortages best narrated in Castile is the one suffered by the army during the siege of Algeciras between September and November 1343. The description of price dynamics, the causes of the increase in the price of cereals, and the role of other types of food is most interesting. A shortage of grain forced people to turn to products of lower quality, such as chickpeas, broad beans, dried figs, or even horses that had died from starvation. The narrator describes the increase in prices as well. Before July 1343, the king purchased barley in Castile. After being transported to the camp, its price was multiplied by six; after the accidental fire of the grain warehouse and general penury, the prices of both barley and flour were multiplied by 2.5. The interruption of supply in November 1343 caused a new price increase. From before the fire to the time of greatest shortage, prices had been multiplied by 10.[50] The municipal sources and chronicles also enable us to establish a chronology of the famines in Catalonia throughout the fourteenth century. Cereals were very frequently scarce between 1300 and 1304 and from 1382 to 1385: 1333 is referred to in Catalan sources as the *mal any primer*, 'the first bad year'; in Valencia, 1343 is known as the *any de la gran fam* ('the great hunger year').[51] The Books of the Courts of Castile and Aragon have few direct references to shortages—except for 1345 and 1348—but there are indirect references to their effects, levels of debt, and poverty: moratoria on debts, protection of work animals, restriction of exports, and prohibition to block the internal circulation of food products.[52]

Castile's demographic weight among all the Hispanic kingdoms is clear. The Kingdom of Castile represented 76 percent of all the territories ruled by the Catholic Monarchs in the second half of fifteenth century, having 81.7 percent of the inhabitants. The northern Meseta, around the Douro basin, had a relatively abundant population as a result of the early resettlement. The southern Meseta, on the other hand, always had a low population density, except for some centers such as Toledo. Andalusia underwent significant demographic changes in the late Middle Ages. The Kingdom of Aragon had a much lower population, equivalent to roughly a quarter of Castile's, with significant internal variation; it is also noticeable that there was a dramatic fall of the population in Catalonia during the fourteenth and fifteenth centuries. The small Kingdom of Navarre apparently also suffered significant demographic loss as a result of the crisis, although the data provided by the especially rich documentation are at present in the process of being reviewed.[53] As shown in Table 6.3, the Kingdoms of both Castile and Navarre recovered at the end of the Middle Ages from the demographic decline, as did most of the territories of the Kingdom of Aragon apart from Catalonia, the only peninsular region that never recovered its pre-Black Death levels.

Table 6.3 Population Comparison (1300–1480)

	c. 1300	*c. 1480*
Kingdom of Castile	*4,500,000*	*4,500,000 (Ladero 4,300,000 in 1492)*
Kingdom of Aragon	*1,000,000*	*815,000*
Catalonia	550,000	260,000
Aragon	200,000	250,000 (Sesma 200,000)
Valencia	200,000	250,000 (Rubio 400,000)
Majorca	50,000	55,000
Kingdom of Navarre	*100,000*	*100,000*

Source: T. Ruiz, Spain's Centuries of Crisis, 32 (from J. A. García de Cortázar, Historia de España Alfaguara II: La época medieval, Madrid, 1973), with modifications and additional notes by Ana Rodríguez.

Few records have been preserved that might enable us to estimate the population of Castile in the fourteenth century. The most outstanding is the so-called *Libro Becerro de las Behetrías*, a survey of landownership commissioned by King Pedro I at the beginning of his reign, in 1352. The *Becerro de las Behetrías* constitutes an incomparable source about manors in the north of Castile.[54] The *Becerro* survey made an inventory of the manors of most of the villages of Castile in the north of the Douro, slightly more than a thousand villages grouped in fifteen *merindades* or administrative districts, with an area of c. 30,000 km^2. It details the populated and the deserted places or wastelands (*yermos*), the name of the landowner and the incomes and benefits of the peasants. Some historians, like Teófilo Ruiz, have considered the *Libro Becerro de las Behetrías* an exceptional record of the devastating results of the Black Death in the high number of deserted places which would thus prove a significant loss of population. This source, however, presents the sort of problems that exist when trying to use fiscal documentation to estimate population figures.[55] The deserted villages recorded therein are not always devoid of population, only of tax-payers, considering all the people such as noblemen who were tax exempted. The term which is used, *yermo*, may be misleading: it refers both to a deserted place and a wasteland, and it is possible that the latter might be the most common meaning in the *Becerro de las Behetrías*. Finally, thanks to the documentation kept in nearby monasteries, it has been verified that, occasionally, some places appear to be populated although they had been recorded as deserted in the *Becerro*.

As for the fifteenth century, when there are more local sources, regional estimates have been developed.[56] The global figures for population in the Kingdom of Castile suggest a remarkable population increase in the last century of the Middle Ages, recovering from the demographic loss due to the plague.[57] The cities to the south of Castile did, in general, achieve significant demographic strength,[58] though these figures were later revised downwards.[59] From the regional point of view, the population was not distributed uniformly. In the northern coastal region, from Galicia to the Basque Country, population levels were rather stable throughout the Middle Ages, with urban centers less populated than in the South.

The general population of the Kingdom of Aragon amounted to around one million inhabitants; of them, half were more densely concentrated in Catalonia, even though it amounted to less than a third of the territory. It seems clear that Catalonia, starting with a much higher population density, suffered a more dramatic fall in the fourteenth and fifteenth centuries, to the extent of being the only peninsular territory that had not recovered by the end of the Middle Ages to its pre-Black Death levels. Aragon, with a much lower population density, recovered fourteenth-century levels by the end of the fifteenth century, in much the same way as Castile. On the eve of the forced conversion by the Catholic Monarchs in 1492, the Mudejar population was significant (30 percent in Valencia, 11 percent in Aragon, yet only 1.5 percent in Catalonia).

According to the tax records of the courts of the Kingdom of Aragon, compiled since 1364, it is reckoned that, from the second half of the fourteenth century, the population progressively recovered pre-crisis levels, reaching a population of 200,000 inhabitants in slightly less than 50,000 km^2 at the end of the fifteenth century. With such a low population density, Aragon was able to keep its levels of population relatively constant throughout the later Middle Ages.[60] The consequences of the worst catastrophes of the fourteenth century—the recurrent outbreaks of the plague in 1348, 1362, and 1380, and the famine in 1375—were thus minimized. The fall of around 40 percent of population did not prevent stabilization, starting in the fifteenth century, and recovery in the second half of the same century.

On the other hand, in Catalonia, the population suffered a dramatic fall between the fourteenth and the fifteenth centuries, with a reduction of the population by almost half, in contrast to the general recovery of the rest of peninsular territories. The *fogatge* (hearth tax record) of 1365 shows the steep decrease in population that would have occurred at the beginning of the 1360s, an impression reinforced by the *fogatge* ordered by the courts in 1378. But local documentation supports a slow depopulation process, not only the catastrophic outcome of epidemics. Estimates in regions such as the Plana de Vic show that at the beginning of the fifteenth century two-thirds of the *mansi* had disappeared. It is important to bear in mind that mortality is not the only factor behind this reality: emigration to other areas or to urban centers, or a concentration of lands through inheritance and intermarriage must be taken into account.[61] Local studies also show noticeable regional differences. The fall of population in inner Catalonia and in the environs of Barcelona (around 45 percent) is higher than in the coastal area (40 percent).[62]

Barcelona, the most populated city in the Peninsula with a population of around 50,000 inhabitants in 1340, underwent a reduction in numbers to 20,000 by 1477, a decline exceeded by cities such as Valencia and Seville. As evidence of the devastating results of the epidemics in Barcelona, it is usually claimed that the enlargement of the city walls, started in 1359 by King Pedro IV, was pointless, for the city would remain empty until the eighteenth century. Without denying this obvious fact, it seems, however, that the population decline of Barcelona, together with the rest of Catalonia, differed in its chronology from that of the rest of Hispanic territories. The population of Barcelona was relatively high until the second half of the fifteenth century, when it suffered a dramatic fall as a result of inner-city violence and the long civil war of 1464–1472. Catalonia, therefore, had its lowest population levels at the beginning of the fifteenth century, which only started to recover at the beginning of the sixteenth century. This late recovery proves that there were other factors besides the death toll, which was nonetheless high: factors that caused a relative backwardness from which it would be impossible to recover after the wars of the fifteenth century.

The Kingdom of Valencia covered a fairly sparsely populated territory. The conditions imposed on resettlement after the Reconquest, and the mobility of the *Mudejar* population, which preferred urban settlement, also marked their demographic dynamics. The political role played by the city of Valencia contributed to its growth.[63] At the end of the fifteenth century, its walls contained a fifth of all the inhabitants of the kingdom, thanks to—among other things—its growing influence on the control of maritime trade in the Mediterranean, and to the detriment of Barcelona. Nevertheless, it is practically the only city of the Kingdom of Aragon whose population increased throughout the fourteenth century, with the arrival of new settlers, as shown in the so-called books of settling (*avecindamientos*) that were maintained from the end of the century onwards.[64]

In periods of scarcity, Catalan cities had at their disposal the 'city wheat' provided by the council. At the end of the Middle Ages, the tendency in these cities was to open their wheat and other cereal markets to merchants from outside Catalonia to increase the amount on sale and force prices to fall; nevertheless, the freedom to import grain co-existed with a strict public control of exports.[65] Municipal intervention in the supply and commercialization of grain was articulated through the creation of stock regulation and price valuation. Big cities could not always afford their cereal policy and had to resort to borrowing to finance it. With a costly combination of market intervention and regulations, the Catalan town councils managed to mitigate the consequences of poor harvests, eradicate the queues of hungry people and intensify their control over the population. All this was at the expense, however, of incurring debt, which—according to some—was the origin of the decline of the city in the Modern Age.

In Andalusia, documentary series like the ecclesiastical tithes of the richest cereal-bearing areas in Seville, which have a complete record from the fifteenth century, show—despite fluctuations—an expansion of Sevillian agricultural production, which boosted the importance of the growing city.[66] From 1408—the first year of the tithe series—onwards, it has been verified that the causes of bad harvests were not only physical or climatic. Among other reasons were the constant movements of troops along the borders with the Nazarite Kingdom of Granada and the mass grain exports to Portugal and Aragon—to guarantee the supply of Valencia and Barcelona. The control exercised by the Castilian kings over cereal production and movement was to make itself felt progressively more throughout the fifteenth century. The royal policy on cereal exports had consequences that were surely unforeseen: the rise of prices, shortages, and a hindrance to any military campaigns—by land or sea—starting from Andalusia. On the other hand, if grain exports were totally banned, many of the places in Andalusia that regularly imported—on the Atlantic coast and in the borderlands with Granada—suffered famine. The tithe series confirm that the last years of the fifteengh century corresponded with the expansion of Sevillian rural production. Despite some mishaps (natural calamities, the plagues of 1494 and 1497, and the droughts of 1501–1504), prices remained stable and supply never suffered. In 1500, the Catholic Monarchs decreed the free export of grains through the ports. In 1504, at the death of Queen Isabel, the Kingdom of Castile and Andalusia was experiencing the most severe crisis of subsistence of the whole reign.[67]

The fourteenth and fifteenth centuries were indeed times of great political unrest in the Iberian Peninsula, with both regional violence and wars among the different kingdoms. In the fifteenth century, significant episodes of violence were performed by a variety of social groups: peasants, impoverished knights, local nobles, and even lords trying to reinforce their legal position over tenants. According to the rebels themselves, years of bad harvests and plagues were the cause of the *irmandiña* (brotherhood) rioting in Galicia between 1467 and 1469.[68] The Catalan civil war (1462–1472) marked, in turn, the political development of the Kingdom of Aragon in the fifteenth century. At the same time, a riot broke out when the *remensa* peasants—who were subject to payment of the *redimentia* in case they abandoned the land—confronted their lords. This rioting continued until 1486, when the so-called 'bad customs,' which had reinforced the dependence of the peasants and their subjection to the land, were abolished.[69] The urban world—Barcelona in the decade of 1450—was also affected by conflicts. The abundance of local conflicts in Catalonia throughout the fifteenth century is one of the reasons explaining its decay in comparison with the other territories of the Kingdom of Aragon. Another reason is that Barcelona was replaced by Valencia as the major commercial capital of the kingdom, dealing a death blow to Barcelonan prosperity, where there was neither economic nor demographic recovery during the fifteenth century.[70]

The conflicts of that period were not the cause of the crisis but they were an important exogenous factor, as well as a sign of deep social and economic instability.[71] It has been stressed—although it has not been possible to quantify—that military campaigns had an influence on the demographic collapse of the fourteenth century. There are records of the displacement of communities by the war and the death toll during raids and attacks. It is also likely that the references to deserted places and the lower tax demands on the inhabitants of some specific cities are related—at least partly—to the flight or emigration of families who were either threatened or ruined by war. The devastating consequences of the conflicts on the rural world are clearly reflected in the documentation: destruction of small villages and agricultural infrastructures, crop and livestock losses in the raids, the need of the armies to live and get food in the field, deliberate policies of razing and sacking the enemy territory. All these factors contributed to aggravating the crisis.[72] Between 1374 and 1375, the raids by foreign mercenaries throughout Catalonia contributed to worsen the effects of the crisis. These conflicts intensified the shortage of supplies in the cities and rural areas of the Kingdom of Aragon.[73]

The impact of the war on the economic situation was not strictly limited to agriculture. On the one hand, the military successes could alter the circulating money supplies as a consequence of the plunder and of *paria*, money paid by defeated Muslims to Christians; on the other hand, the need to pay the general costs and wages forced the monarchs to make currency devaluations. A general increase of the tax burden in Castile as a result of the war has been noticed. The monarchy had to complement the traditional tax resources allocated to the war with new types of taxes, such as the *alcabala* (taxing trade and all type of transfers); extraordinary services approved by the General Courts ever more regularly; the appropriation of ecclesiastical incomes; and resorting to loans.

Nevertheless, peasant communities were more often unsafe because of violence among nobles. In the Kingdom of Castile, the donation of places and small villages of *realengo* (belonging to the king) to nobles enabled the new lords to impose arbitrary demands. Often, they tried to re-establish the 'bad customs,' or impose short-term leases on the settlers of their lands, in order to stop the lands from falling in value. The sources of that period recall some significant episodes concerning the murder of some lords at the hands of the inhabitants.[74] There are also references to feudal villains who entered the monastery or council domains, destroyed the crops and collected taxes that did not belong to them.[75] Some monasteries of the area of Galicia even had to redo their cartularies because the earlier documents relating to their domain management had disappeared in the violence of the *milites*.[76]

THE INTERPRETATION OF THE EVIDENCE

The interest in the fourteenth century crisis, which emerged comparatively late among Hispanic historians, took place at a moment when it was important to find elements in common with wider European studies, thereby leaving behind the topics of Spanish specificity promoted by the Franco regime. This tendency had been overcome with some implicit assumptions of commonality of processes—plague, famine, poor harvests, climatic changes, demographic decline, agricultural collapse, monetary instability, trade crisis, war, and social conflict, and so on—during the fourteenth century, between Spain and Europe.[77] Most of these factors were obviously present in the Spanish late Middle Ages. The supremacy of some factors over others depends on the chosen approach and the sources analyzed. Thus, the end of agricultural expansion, technological stagnation, and the evidence of declining yields caused by the exploitation of marginal lands at the end of the thirteenth century have been considered as proof of Neo-Malthusian arguments. On the other hand, certain aspects, such as the increase of manorial pressure and the violence of nobles, have incorporated Marxist theory (through the Brenner and Bois theses) into the study of the crisis of feudalism in the Iberian Peninsula.[78]

Nevertheless, attempts to transfer European models to the Hispanic case need to incorporate into their analysis specific aspects that result from the long historical development of Hispanic societies. Among these should be included the enormous weight of the monarchy in the processes of the settlement and organization of Hispanic territories, the low demographic pressure on lands and resources (at least in the regions incorporated after the eleventh century), and the improved conditions of the Castilian peasantry offered by the possibility of emigration to the South (although this excluded the Aragonese, who suffered much higher demands on behalf of their lords). Also important was the permanent 'war economy' that the Spanish kingdoms endured, which generated an enormous yet irregular circulation of currency and riches and determined the relations between kings and noblemen. It is therefore only possible to interpret the process of economic growth and crisis in the Hispanic kingdoms by assessing the impact of these specific factors.

The first and essential difference between the Hispanic and European experience relates to demography. Although the European population figures recorded by Paolo Malanima show similar trends to those of Spain (growth in the thirteenth century, decline in the fourteenth, and recovery in the fifteenth), it is however necessary to consider two aspects. Firstly, the lower density of population in the Hispanic kingdoms: in a territory only slightly smaller than France, the population figures are similar to those of much smaller England and Wales (as shown in Table 6.4). Secondly, there is the huge internal diversity of historical processes and the chronology of demographic change, both of which are only perceptible if these global population figures are broken down to a regional scale, as was shown in Table 6.3.

In the Iberian Peninsula, although a certain degree of local demographic pressure may have been recorded, the excess of population was never a

Table 6.4 Population Comparison in Europe (1300–1500)

	Territory	*Population 1300*	*Population 1400*	*Population 1500*
France	544,000 km2	16 million	12 million	15 million
England & Wales	151,000 km2	5.75 million	3 million	3.5 million
Spain	505,000 km2	5.5 million	4.5 million	5 million

Source: Paolo Malanima, "Decline or Growth? European Cities and Rural Economies 1300–1600," paper presented in the Conference *Economic Town-Country Relations in Europe in the Later Middle Ages and at the Beginning of the Early Modern Period*, University of Vienna June 7th–9th, 2007.

problem. The situation, particularly in the Kingdom of Castile, was the opposite of that in Western Europe. The Neo-Malthusian theory of a 'full world' is inapplicable, considering the incorporation of the rich expanse of lands in the Guadalquivir valley into Castile in the mid-thirteenth century, and the ensuing population redistribution from more populated areas. Paradoxically, however, the rapid process of integration of al-Andalus caused the breakdown and disorganization of production systems in the lands further north after the second half of the thirteenth century. The repopulation of al-Andalus meant a constant migratory flow of peasants, which caused the demographic deterioration in Castile that is evident in the sources, with references to deserted villages as well as the reduction of both royal and manorial incomes. Thus, the depopulation caused by the Black Death of 1348, only a century after the conquest of Seville, was just another contribution to an ongoing problem.[79] Therefore the result would be similar to that derived from overpopulation in other European territories, but sooner: a Castilian route to the fourteenth century crisis started from the demographic decline experienced from the end of the thirteenth century.

In Andalusia, the failure of the repopulation program of the thirteenth century and the fields emptied by the expulsion of the *Mudejar* in 1264 would worsen its demographic weakness and would lead to the economic crisis of the fourteenth century. However, the relationship between the failure of settlement policies and the economic crisis may be more complex. A lower population density need not be negative in a livestock economy—which most of Andalusia was in the later Middle Ages. Also, the high number of deserted villages recorded in the second half of the thirteenth century can be interpreted as a new settlement pattern derived from significant modifications in regional agricultural structures.[80]

A similar revision may be applied to some depopulation data in the north of the Peninsula. Some studies on specific Castilian regions in the fourteenth century show that the depopulation process in some areas actually resulted in the concentration of population in big centers, to the detriment of smaller towns. The depopulation process might also occasionally have been because the peasant community, weakened by exogenous factors (war, epidemics), could not withstand the lord's tax pressure. This would especially be the case in places where taxes were shared between the villagers through joint capitation, because anyone leaving would entail an increase in the contribution of the rest of the villagers. This situation would drive the peasants, overwhelmed by tax regulations, to flee to places offering better exemptions and privileges.[81]

Another factor to be taken into account is the diversity of manorial strategies that were implemented as a solution to the crisis, given the evidence of decreasing population and deterioration of taxable incomes. The duration of contracts and the changes in obligations imposed on peasants for the exploitation of manorial lands—as shown in the Galician *foros*—reveal the different phases of the economic situation between the thirteenth and fifteenth centuries and might account for its evolution over time.[82] Generally, we can state that from 1250 ecclesiastical institutions transferred their lands to peasants for long terms or in perpetuity, as a way to secure their income and maintain agricultural activity on their land, despite the risk of ceding control of them to their peasants.[83] Between 1370 and 1450 there is the highest number of long-term *foros* concessions ever recorded. Nevertheless, from the second half of the fifteenth century onwards, economic recovery resulted in the proliferation of short-term contracts in the Kingdom of Castile, which enabled the update of incomes that had been at a standstill for decades. In northern Galicia, the big monasteries and cathedrals—Meira, Lourenzá, Mondoñedo—dramatically reduced the percentage of perpetual *foros*, thereby hardening peasant conditions (see Figure 6.2).[84]

The general strategy followed in the monastic domains of the northern Iberian Peninsula, of producing wine and exploiting industrial crops for regional markets, has already been mentioned. However, there was also an interest in retaining pastures, despite the risk of conflicts with communities and the nobility, which is clear evidence of the intensification of stockbreeding in the last decades of the Middle Ages.

In an urban framework, the accounting books of the Cathedral of Burgos provide references to prices and wages, working conditions and the fluctuations of agricultural production during the central decades of the fourteenth century.[85] The interpretation of this data shows that the impact of the crisis was hardly perceptible. It is possible that there might have been population stagnation but no demographic crisis: there are no references

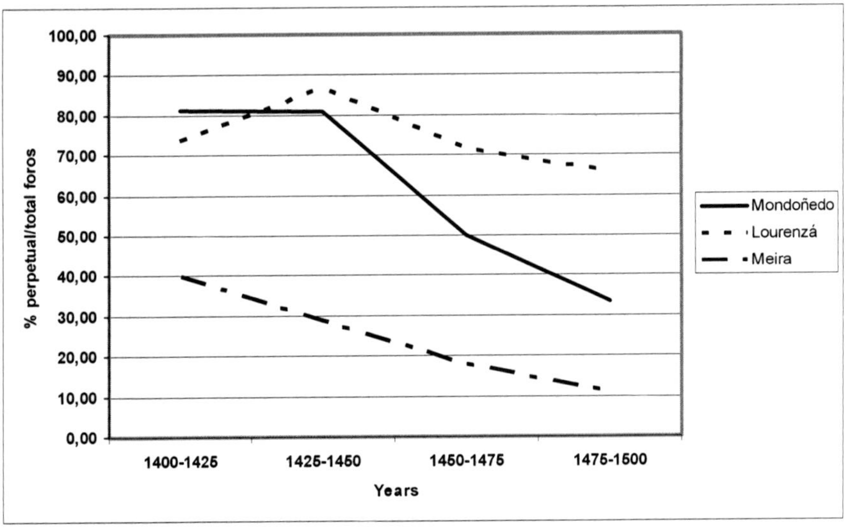

Figure 6.2 Relation of perpetual *foros* over the total *foros* granted by the Cathedral of Mondoñedo, the monastery of Lourenzá and the monastery of Meira in the fifteenth century.

to houses deserted or untenanted. Cities, which were better prepared to provide for their inhabitants in periods of shortage, probably received rural immigrants. The canons of the Cathedral of Burgos consolidated their position in the urban property market. Urban incomes increased steadily from 1370 and there was also an increase of cereal production after 1380. This might be explained if we trace the crisis back to the second half of the thirteenth century and characterize the fourteenth century as one of stagnation rather than recession. In any case, the most successful figures in Burgos were merchants specializing in the sale of cloth, who were socially and politically acclaimed in the fourteenth century. On the other hand, the worst of the crisis would affect monastic income dramatically in rural areas, outside the influence of markets and the city.

In the Kingdom of Aragon and especially in Catalonia, despite the significant impact of the Black Death, which was responsible for a dramatic demographic decline, the crisis–with all its harshness—did not appear until the mid-fifteenth century, proving that it was not caused by exogenous factors, such as the Black Death and food shortages. At about the same time as economic recovery began in Castile, Catalonia showed the first symptoms of imbalance and weakness. It continued to lose population until reaching the minimum marked by the hearth tax record of 1497, by which time the traffic in the port of Barcelona was significantly reduced. Long-distance trade went through a crisis around 1415, and, in parallel, a good part of the Catalan cloth market disappeared. The general financial and monetary crisis that affected the whole of Europe in the last decades of the fourteenth century had huge repercussions for Catalonia because of the insolvency of the crown, in debt as a result of its expansionist policy. The reduction in the size of the population multiplied the pressure of taxation—which had already been increased to pay off royal debts—on those who remained. All this led to the abandonment of many settlements: it is significant that fewer deserted villages are recorded in the years after the Black Death than in the fifteenth century. This can be explained—as in the Kingdom of Castile in the fourteenth century—by the impossibility of collectively meeting payments and debts that became more and more costly. Lords, in turn, reacted to the collapse of agrarian incomes by trying, towards the end of the fourteenth century, to undo pacts agreed with the peasants after the Black Death. This caused social strife such as the *remensa* fight for the *masos ròneçs* (the *mansi* left uninhabited after the Black Death, and joined to neighboring *mansi* in conditions favorable to the peasants).

In this regard, political factors have been considered in Catalan historiography to be a key explanation of the deep crisis that broke much later than elsewhere in Europe. The civil war (1462–1472) and, above all, the outbreak of the aforementioned *remensa* conflict were important factors in the collapse of the Catalan economy of the second half of the fifteenth century. A phase of depression dating back to one century earlier was worsened by the impact of the severe crisis brought on by the war.[86] The overall demographic effect is clear. Catalonia was the only peninsular territory that had not recovered by the end of the Middle Ages to the level of population it had had before the Black Death.

The crisis of the fifteenth century hit the peninsular kingdoms in different ways and at different times. In some territories, the Black Death had devastating results, whereas in others it is even difficult to detect its effects. However, the catastrophes of these decades did not hit a 'full world' because—contrary to elsewhere in Europe—there were not enough people in the Iberian Peninsula in the last decades of the thirteenth century. There were significant regional imbalances that influenced the pace of recovery at the end of the Middle Ages. Political factors had a great impact on the crisis, as proven in the case of Catalonia. While Barcelona fell from the highest splendor to the brink of collapse, Valencia inherited a good part of its commercial traffic, growing significantly more important in the second half of the fourteenth century. There was an early solution to the crisis in Castile, which, since the end of the fourteenth century and more clearly in 1420–1430, had entered a remarkable phase of growth. The demographic recovery, the recommencement of settlement of new lands, with more intensive agriculture, the development of cattle rearing, the progress of urbanization following the Black Death, the increase in craft production and the expansion of the wool trade, placed Castile among the most dynamic areas of Europe in the middle of the fifteenth century.[87]

Trade, agriculture, and the intensification of markets produced changes that led to recovery in the Iberian Peninsula. Changes came about—the intensification of markets, crop diversification, flexibility in making improvements, associations between agriculture and industry—that were capable of mobilizing more peasant effort, and the development of processing activities that did not require a division of labor among workers with different technical skills. These were activities that widened the spectrum of available resources and made the rural economy more resistant to the effects of bad harvests.[88] From the 1460s onwards, general recovery became perceptible. The causes of recovery were mainly endogenous.[89] Patterns of growth were also powerful. At that time, Castilians had already begun expanding into the Canary Islands, which only a few decades later would lead them to America.

NOTES

1. José Ángel García de Cortázar and Pascual Martínez Sopena, "Los estudios sobre historia rural de la sociedad hispanocristiana," *Historia Agraria* 31 (2003): 57–58.
2. In the case of Catalonia, it has been stated that the number of inhabitants per household was higher in the mountain areas than in the lowlands, as well as higher in the countryside than in the cities. Gaspar Feliú, "La demografia

baixmedieval catalana. Estat de la qüestió i propostes de futur," *Revista d'Historia Medieval* 10 (1999): 42.

3. The *monedajes* differ from the hearth tax distributions in how tax-payers are defined, since in this case what is taken into account is the patrimony, rather than the residence, as in the case of the censuses. J. Angel Sesma and Carlos Laliena, eds., *La población en Aragón en la Edad Media (siglos XIII–XV). Estudios de demografía histórica* (Zaragoza: Leyere, 2004) devotes several articles to this subject.
4. Methodology and new lines of research in Jaume Torras and Bartolomé Yun, eds, *Consumo, condiciones de vida y comercialización. Cataluña y Castilla, siglos XVII–XIX* (Valladolid: Junta de Castilla y León, 1999).
5. Pedro López de Ayala, *Crónica del Rey Don Pedro y del Rey Don Enrique, su hermano, hijos del rey don Alfonso Onceno*, ed. Germán Orduna (Buenos Aires: Secrit, 1994), 3–4.
6. Julio Valdeón, "La crisis del siglo XIV en la Corona de Castilla," in *La historia en el contexto de las ciencias humanas y sociales. Homenaje a Marcelo Vigil Pascual*, ed. María José Hidalgo de la Vega (Salamanca: Universidad de Salamanca, 1989); Julio Valdeón, "Datos sobre la población de Castilla en el siglo XIV. El caso de Valbuena de Duero," *Archivos Leoneses* 55–56 (1974); Julio Valdeón, "Un despoblado castellano del siglo XIV: Fuenteungrillo," *En la España Medieval* 3 (1982). This author provides a general description of the crisis.
7. An overall approach in Ángel Vaca, "La Peste Negra en Castilla. Aportación al estudio de algunas de sus consecuencias económicas y sociales," *Studia Historica. Historia Medieval* 2 (1984).
8. Pierre Vilar, *La Catalogne dans l'Espagne Moderne. Recherches sur les fondements économiques des structures nationales* (Paris: S.E.V.P.E.N, 1962), 490–508.
9. Claude Carrère, *Barcelone, centre économique à l'époque des difficultés, 1380–1462* (Paris: Mouton & Co, 1967). A historiographic revision in Gaspar Feliú, "La crisis catalana de la Baja Edad Media: estado de la cuestión," *Hispania* 64/2, 217 (2004): 438–450.
10. A classic approach in Maurice Berthe, *Famines et épidémies dans les campagnes navarraises à la fin du Moyen Âge* (Paris: S.F.I.E.D., 1984).
11. A current revision in Mercedes Borrero, "El mundo rural y la crisis del siglo XIV. Un tema historiográfico en proceso de revisión," *Edad Media* 8 (2007): 44–49.
12. The best synthesis in Hilario Casado, "La economía de las Españas medievales (c.1000–c.1450)," in *Historia económica de España, siglos X–XX*, ed. Francisco Comín et al. (Barcelona: Crítica, 2002), 14–22.
13. The most important Books of *Repartimientos* are published in Julio González, *Repartimiento de Sevilla* (Madrid: C.S.I.C., 1951); Antoni Ferrando, *Llibre del repartiment de Valencia* (Valencia: Vicent García, D. L., 1984); Enric Guinot and Josep Torró, ed., *Repartiments medievals a la corona d'Aragó: segles XII–XIII* (Valencia: Universitat de València, 2007).
14. The consideration of the resettlement of Andalusia as an essential factor in the Castilian crisis in the late Middle Ages has generated an intense debate starting with Teófilo F. Ruiz, "Expansion et changement: la conquête de Seville et la société castillane (1248–1350)," *Annales, Économies, Sociétés, Civilisations* 3 (1979): 554–555. Opposite views in Manuel González, *La repoblación en la zona de Sevilla durante el siglo XIV* (Sevilla: Universidad de Sevilla, 1993), 25–33; Manuel González, *En torno a los orígenes de Andalucía. La repoblación del siglo XIII* (Sevilla: Universidad de Sevilla, 1988), 83–90.

15. The maintenance of community structures prior to feudalization and the degree of freedom of the Castilian peasantry have been essential discussions in Spanish historiography. Reyna Pastor, *Resistencias y luchas campesinas en la época del crecimiento y la consolidación de la formación feudal. Castilla y León, siglos X–XIII* (Madrid: Siglo XXI, 1980), 7–10, 56–60.
16. On the expansion of feudal models, José Ángel García de Cortázar, *La sociedad rural en la España medieval* (Madrid: Siglo XXI, 1988), 55–76.
17. González, *En torno a los orígenes de Andalucía*, 90–97; González, *La repoblación en la zona de Sevilla*, 49–56.
18. Mercedes Borrero, *Mundo rural y vida campesina en la Andalucía medieval* (Granada: Universidad de Granada, 2003), 180–181.
19. Mercè Aventín, "Familia i unitat d'explotació," in *Història agrària dels Països Catalans: Edad Mitjana*, ed. Josep M. Salrach (Barcelona: Fundació Catalana per a la Recerca i la Innovació, 2004), 594–595.
20. Esteban Sarasa, *Sociedad y conflictos sociales en Aragón, siglos XIII–XV: estructuras de poder y conflictos de clase* (Madrid: Siglo XXI, 1981), 140–142.
21. Casado, "La economía de las Españas medievales," 25–28.
22. Because the animals could benefit the land—which was at rest for two years—by providing manure for the next sowing season. Jesús García Fernández, "Champs ouverts et champs clôturés en Vieille-Castille," *Annales, Économies, Sociétés, Civilisations* 20/4 (1965): 693–694.
23. Julio Valdeón, *Los países de la Corona de Castilla. La Baja Edad Media peninsular. Siglos XIII al XV. La población, la economía, la sociedad. Historia de España Menéndez Pidal* (Madrid: Espasa Calpe, 1996), 107.
24. Ermelindo Portela, *La región del obispado de Tuy en los siglos XII al XV* (Santiago de Compostela: Edición local, 1976), 123–128.
25. The classic approach to its origins and development in Julius Klein, *The Mesta: A Study in Spanish Economic History: 1273–1836* (Cambridge, MA: Harvard University Press, 1920).
26. On textile industry, Hilario Casado, *Señores, mercaderes y campesinos. La comarca de Burgos a fines de la Edad Media* (Valladolid: Junta de Castilla y León, 1987), 242–246.
27. Juan Carlos Martín Cea, *El mundo rural castellano a fines de la Edad Media: el ejemplo de Paredes de Nava en el siglo XV* (Valladolid: Junta de Castilla y León, 1991), 80.
28. Portela, *La región del obispado de Tuy*, 282–283.
29. Borrero, *Mundo rural y vida campesina en la Andalucía medieval*, 258, 266.
30. Rafael Oliva, "El mundo rural en la Corona de Castilla en la Baja Edad Media. Dinámicas socio-económicas y nuevas perspectivas de análisis," *Edad Media* 8 (2007): 320.
31. Carlos Laliena, *Sistema social, estructura agraria y organización del poder en el Bajo Aragón en la Edad Media (siglos XII–XV)* (Teruel: Instituto de Estudios Turolenses, 1987), 227–229, 235–238.
32. The boom experienced by saffron should be related to its different uses: a prized condiment, used in the preparation of medicines and cosmetics, a coloring for high quality fabrics, such as silk. Saffron, cultivated in inner Catalonia, first penetrated the domestic market, and was later successful in foreign markets, being exported from 1334 to Germany, Flanders, and the East. In the regions passed through by the route connecting Barcelona to Saragossa, saffron cultivation increased during the fifteenth century at the expense of cereals; Antoni Riera, "Crisis frumentarias y políticas municipales de abastecimiento en las ciudades catalanas durante la Baja Edad Media," in *Crisis*

de subsistencia y crisis agrarias en la Edad Media, ed. Rafael Oliva and Pere Benito. (Sevilla: Universidad de Sevilla, 2007), 131.

33. Angel Barrios, *Estructuras agrarias y de poder en Castilla. El ejemplo de Avila (1085–1320)* (Salamanca: Universidad. Institución Gran Duque de Alba, 1983), 167–170.
34. Julián Clemente, La economía campesina en la Corona de Castilla (1000–1300). (Barcelona: Crítica, 2003), 44, 109 ft.13.
35. The *Libro del Castillo de Sesa* shows the accounts of the agricultural year 1276–1277 in a manor dependent of the bishop of Huesca, in Aragon. From the data contained in the book of accounts, it is possible to establish the yield-to-seed ratio of each product: 4.2:1 for wheat, 5.7:1 for barley, and 2.5:1 for oats. It is not possible to draw any conclusions about yields per hectare. M. Dolores Barrios, *Una explotación agricola en el siglo XIII. Sesa (Huesca)* (Zaragoza: Anubar, 1983), 38–39.
36. Laliena, *Sistema social, estructura agraria y organización del poder*, 239–240.
37. Antoni Furió, *Història del País Valencià* (Valencia: Alfons el Magnànim. Generalitat Valenciana, 1995), 131.
38. Clemente, *La economía campesina en la Corona de Castilla*, 44, 56.
39. Antoni Furió, "Tierra, familia y transmisión de la propiedad en el país valenciano durante la Baja Edad Media," in *Relaciones de poder, de producción y de parentesco en la Edad Media y Moderna: aproximación a su estudio*, ed. Reyna Pastor (Madrid: C.S.I.C., 1990), 309–310.
40. García de Cortázar, *La sociedad rural en la España medieval*, 188.
41. Angel Vaca, "Una manifestación de la crisis castellana del siglo XIV. La caída de las rentas de los señores feudales. El testimonio del monasterio de Sahagún," *Studia Historica* 1, 2 (1983): 159; The edition of the source in Juan José García González, *Vida económica de los monasterios benedictinos en el siglo XIV* (Valladolid: Universidad de Valladolid, 1972), 179–193.
42. Antoni Furió, "Temps de represa i creixement. La recuperació del final de l'Edat Mitjana i l'inici de la Moderna," in *Història agrària dels Països Catalans: Edad Mitjana*, ed. Josep M. Salrach (Barcelona: Fundació Catalana per a la Recerca i la Innovació, 2004), 200.
43. Josep Fernandez Trabal and Antoni Riera, "La crisi econòmica i social al camp," in *Història agrària dels Països Catalans: Edad Mitjana*, ed. Josep M. Salrach (Barcelona: Fundació Catalana per a la Recerca i la Innovació, 2004), 133–134.
44. Ferrán García Oliver, *Terra de feudals. El País Valencià en la tardor de la Edat Mitjana* (Valencia: Alfons el Magnànim. Institució Valenciana d'Estudis i Investigació, 1991), 84–85.
45. Casado, *Señores, mercaderes y campesinos*, 180–181.
46. Jaime Sobrequés, "La peste Negra en la Península Ibérica," *Anuario de Estudios Medievales* 7 (1970–1): 71.
47. Christian Guilleré, "La Peste Noire à Gérone (1348)," *Anales del Instituto de Estudios Gerundenses* 27 (1984): 87–161. In Gerona, 224 men and 160 women died of the epidemic of 1348, as it is recorded in the documentation of the testamentary *Pias Causas*.
48. Christian Guilleré, "Nouvelles recherches sur les épidemies à la fin du XIVe siècle. L'example de Vic (Catalogne). La mortalité de 1372 à 1407," in *Population et démographie au Moyen Âge*, ed. Olivier Guyotjeannin (Paris: Editions du CTHS, 1995), 119–143. The mortality in Vic from 1372 to 1407 has also been studied through the extreme unction and burial registers.

49. The first mention of significant mortality in the Castilian kingdom is found in 1301; the famine of 1333 also caused a significant death toll. Carlos Reglero de la Fuente, "Les disettes dans le Royaume de Castille (entre 1250 et 1348)," (paper presented at the Conference *Les disettes dans la conjoncture de 1300 en Méditerranée occidentale,* Rome, Italy, February 27–28, 2004). My acknowledgements to the author for his kindness in letting me consult this unpublished work.
50. Reglero de la Fuente, "Les disettes dans le Royaume de Castille."
51. Antoni Riera, "Els pròdroms de les crisis agràries de la baixa edad mitjana a la Corona d'Aragó: 1250–1300, " *Miscel.lània en Homenatge al P. Agustí Altisent* (Tarragona: Diputació de Tarragona, 1991), 39–41.
52. Reglero de la Fuente, "Les disettes dans le Royaume de Castille."
53. Juan Carrasco, *La población de Navarra en el siglo XIV* (Pamplona: Universidad de Navarra, 1973); On a new model, Guillermo Castán and Salvador Dueñas, "Revisión de la incidencia de la Peste Negra (1348) en Navarra a través de un modelo matemático de población," *Studia Historica. Historia medieval* 24 (2006): 277–291.
54. A general explanation in Carlos Estepa, *Las behetrías castellanas* (Valladolid: Junta de Castilla y León, 2003); Luis Martínez, "El señorío abadengo en Castilla. Consideraciones sobre su formación y desarrollo (siglos XI-XIV)," *Edad Media* 8 (2007): 245–248; the edition of the source in Gonzalo Martínez, ed., *Libro Becerro de las Behetrías: estudio y texto crítico* (León: Centro de Estudios e Investigación San Isidoro, 1981).
55. Teófilo F. Ruiz, *Crisis and Continuity. Land and Town in Late Medieval Castile* (Philadelphia: University of Pennsylvania, 1994), 319–323. He even considers that the *Libro Becerro* is written to quantify this loss. However, it is important to bear in mind that the intention to clarify the complex manorial situation in the area is clear in the Courts of Valladolid, from where the order to make out the fiscal survey came. My acknowledgements to Carlos Estepa for his comments in this regard.
56. The specific population figures in the different territories of the Kingdom of Castile are detailed in Valdeón, "Los países de la Corona de Castilla," 31–46
57. Jaume Vicens Vives, *Manual de Historia Económica de España* (Barcelona: Teide, 1959), 223–224.
58. As is the case of Andalusian towns: Antonio Collantes de Terán, *Sevilla en la Baja Edad Media. La ciudad y sus hombres* (Sevilla: Ayuntamiento de Sevilla, 1977), 152–171.
59. García de Cortázar estimates that the population in 1450 was around 4.5 million inhabitants, roughly the same as in the beginning of the fourteenth century. Ladero proposes an even lower estimate: 4.3 million inhabitants in 1492, once the Kingdom of Granada had been added to the Kingdom of Castile. José Ángel García de Cortázar, *La época medieval* (Madrid: Alianza Editorial, 1973), 298. Three million in 1300; 2.5 in 1400 and four in 1490, are the estimates of Paulino Iradiel, et al., *Historia medieval de la España cristiana* (Madrid: Cátedra, 1989), 470–473.
60. Studies related to this subject in Sesma and Laliena, *La población en Aragón en la Edad Media.*
61. Feliú, "La demografia baixmedieval catalana," 32–33.
62. On climatic conditions between 1380 and 1450, Jose Antonio López, et al., "Historia de la vegetación en el litoral de Gerona entre los siglos VIII y XX d.C. Cambios climáticos y socioeconómicos desde una perspectiva paleoambiental," *Arqueología y Territorio Medieval* 15 (2008): 18–19.

63. Enrique Cruselles, "La población de la ciudad de Valencia en los siglos XIV y XV," *Revista d'Historia Medieval* 10 (1999): 66–68.
64. Eliseo Vidal, *Valencia en la época de Juan I* (Valencia : Universidad de Valencia, 1974), 85–88.
65. Riera, "Crisis frumentarias y políticas municipales de abastecimiento," 137, 156–159.
66. Isabel Montes, "Crisis de subsistencias y comercio exterior de cereales en la Sevilla del siglo XV," in *Crisis de subsistencia y crisis agrarias en la Edad Media*, ed. Rafael Oliva and Pere Benito (Sevilla: Universidad de Sevilla, 2007), 161.
67. Montes, "Crisis de subsistencias y comercio exterior," 191.
68. On this general subject: Angel Rodríguez González, *Las fortalezas de la mitra compostelana y los Irmandiños. Pleito Tabera-Fonseca* (Pontevedra: Fundación Pedro Barrié de la Maza, 1984).
69. The classic general approach in Jaime Vicens Vives, *Historia de los remensas en el siglo XV* (Barcelona: C.S.I.C., 1945).
70. Feliú, "La crisis catalana de la Baja Edad Media," 455–456.
71. Francisco García Fiz, "'Las guerras de cada día'. En la Castilla del siglo XIV," *Edad Media* 8 (2007): 173–179.
72. Valdeón, "La crisis del siglo XIV en la Corona de Castilla," 222–225.
73. Documented records show that, ruined by the high prices of food and the new taxes, many rural and urban families were forced to sell their lands in order to acquire some grain. Riera, "Crisis frumentarias y políticas municipales de abastecimiento": 152–153.
74. Julio Valdeón, *Conflictos sociales en el reino de Castilla en los siglos XIV y XV* (Madrid: Siglo XXI, 1975): 107–110.
75. Salustiano Moreta, *Malhechores-feudales: violencia, antagonismos y alianzas de clases en Castilla siglos XIII–XIV* (Madrid: Cátedra, 1978), 61–69.
76. Miguel Romaní, ed., *Libro Tumbo de Pergamino. Un códice medieval del monasterio de Oseira* (Santiago de Compostela: Universidad de Santiago, 2003), 3–4.
77. Hilario Casado, "¿Existió la crisis del siglo XIV? Consideraciones a partir de los datos de la contabilidad de la Catedral de Burgos," in *Castilla y el mundo feudal : Homenaje al profesor Julio Valdeón*, ed. M. Isabel del Val Valdivieso, et al. (Valladolid: Junta de Castilla y León, 2009), 10–11. My acknowledgements to professor Casado for his kindness in letting me consult this still unpublished work.
78. On interpretation of the crisis, García de Cortázar, *La sociedad rural en la España medieval*, 187–200.
79. Ruiz, *Crisis and Continuity*, 291–313; Teófilo F. Ruiz, *Las crisis medievales (1300–1474)* (Barcelona: Crítica, 2007), 48–51. From this point of view, the Reconquest had a pernicious effect on Castilian society, since the incorporation of Andalusia did not only entail the crisis of the 14th century in the North—by causing a demographic collapse—but also gave rise to a historical gulf between the peninsula and the rest of Europe which lasted until, and characterized, the modern period.
80. Borrero, "El mundo rural y la crisis del siglo XIV," 52–55. It is not easy to estimate the Islamic population before the Christian conquest. Arabic place names (toponymy) cannot always be considered as centers of population.
81. Angel Vaca, "La estructura socioeconómica de la Tierra de Campos a mediados del siglo XIV," *Publicaciones de la Institución Tello Téllez de Meneses* 39 (1977): 396–398.
82. As in the years of famine and poor harvests. On this subject, Ana Rodríguez, "'Foyse da terra no ano das chuvias. . .' Carestías y subsistencia en el noroeste

peninsular en los siglos XII yXIII", in *Crisis de subsistencia y crisis agrarias en la Edad Media*, ed. Rafael Oliva and Pere Benito (Sevilla: Universidad de Sevilla, 2007), 213–218.

83. "Es más provechoso para el monasterio darla asi en censo enfitéutico y contrato perpetuo que no tener la tierra como la teníamos" ("It is more beneficial to the monastery to give the land in emphyteusis and perpetual lease than to have it as we used to do"), stated in a document of the first half of the fifteenth century of the monastery of Matallana. Julio Valdeón, "Citeaux en Castille au Bas Moyen Âge : l'exemple de Matallana" in *Les Espagnes médiévales. Aspects économiques et sociaux. Mélanges offerts à Jean Gautier Dalché* (Paris: Les Belles Lettres, 1983), 48. It is verified in many other monastic domains, such as that of the monastery of Sandoval. Refer to Juan Antonio Sebastián Amarilla, "Del 'fuero' al arrendamiento. Tenencia y explotación de la tierra en León entre la Edad Media y la Edad Moderna," *Revista de Historia Económica* 17, 2 (1999): 316–317.
84. Maria Xose Rodríguez Galdo, *Señores y campesinos en Galicia, siglos XIV–XVI* (Santiago de Compostela: Pico Sacro, 1976), 38–39.
85. Casado, "¿Existió la crisis del siglo XIV?," 16–18.
86. Feliú, "La crisis catalana de la Baja Edad Media", 451–452.
87. José Antonio Sebastián Amarilla, "La Edad Media (c. 100–c. 1450). Configuración y primer despegue de la economía europea," in *Historia económica mundial. Siglos X–XX*, ed. Francisco Comín et al. (Barcelona: Crítica, 2005), 64–65.
88. Bartolomé Yun, "Economic cycles and structural changes," in *Handbook of European History. 1400–1600: Late Middle Ages, Renaissance and Reformation*, ed. Thomas A. Brady et al. (Leyden: E.J. Brill, 1994), 71–72
89. Chris Dyer, *Making a Living in the Middle Ages: The People of Britain 850–1520* (New Haven and London: Yale University Press, 2002). Economic recovery from the late medieval depression depended fundamentally on an improvement in living standards among the survivors of the disasters of the 14th century, on their easier access to resources, on their capacity to escape the pressures of seigneurial rents that were too inelastic to follow the rapid pace of change in peasant economies, and on the effects of the crisis on income distribution.

BIBLIOGRAPHY

Aventín, M. "Familia i unitat d'explotació," in *Història agrària dels Països Catalans: Edad Mitjana*, edited by J. M. Salrach, 467–504. Barcelona: Fundació Catalana per a la Recerca i la Innovació, 2004

Barrios, A. *Estructuras agrarias y de poder en Castilla. El ejemplo de Avila (1085–1320)*. Salamanca: Universidad. Institución Gran Duque de Alba, 1983.

Barrios, M. D. *Una explotación agricola en el siglo XIII. Sesa (Huesca)*. Zaragoza: Anubar, 1983.

Barros, C. *Mentalidad justiciera de los irmandiños. Siglo XV*. Madrid: Siglo XXI, 1990.

Berthe, M. *Famines et épidémies dans les campagnes navarraises à la fin du Moyen Âge*. Paris: S.F.I.E.D.,1984.

Borrero, M. *Mundo rural y vida campesina en la Andalucía medieval*. Granada: Universidad de Granada, 2003.

Borrero, M. "El mundo rural y la crisis del siglo XIV. Un tema historiográfico en proceso de revisión." *Edad Media* 8 (2007): 37–58.

Carrasco, J. *La población de Navarra en el siglo XIV*. Pamplona: Universidad de Navarra, 1973.

Carrère, C. *Barcelone, centre économique à l'époque des difficultés, 1380–1462*. Paris: Mouton & Co., 1967.

Casado, H. *Señores, mercaderes y campesinos. La comarca de Burgos a fines de la Edad Media*. Valladolid: Junta de Castilla y León, 1987.

Casado, H. "La economía de las Españas medievales (c. 1000–c. 1450)," in *Historia económica de España, siglos X–XX*, edited by F. Comín, M. Hernández, and E. Llopis, 13–49. Barcelona: Crítica, 2002.

Casado, H. "¿Existió la crisis del siglo XIV? Consideraciones a partir de los datos de la contabilidad de la Catedral de Burgos," in *Castilla y el mundo feudal: Homenaje al profesor Julio Valdeón*, vol. 1, edited by M. del Val Valdivieso, and P. Martínez Sopena, 9–26. Valladolid: Junta de Castilla y León, 2009.

Castán, G. and S. Dueñas. "Revisión de la incidencia de la Peste Negra (1348) en Navarra a través de un modelo matemático de población." *Studia Historica. Historia medieval* 24 (2006): 275–314.

Clemente, J. *La economía campesina en la Corona de Castilla (1000–1300)*. Barcelona: Crítica, 2003.

Collantes de Terán, A. *Sevilla en la Baja Edad Media. La ciudad y sus hombres*. Sevilla: Ayuntamiento de Sevilla, 1977.

Cruselles, E. "La población de la ciudad de Valencia en los siglos XIV y XV." *Revista d'Historia Medieval* 10 (1999): 45–84.

Dyer, C. C. *Making a Living in the Middle Ages: The People of Britain 850–1520*. New Haven and London: Yale University Press, 2002.

Estepa, C. *Las behetrías castellanas*. Valladolid: Junta de Castilla y León, 2003.

Feliú, G. "La demografia baixmedieval catalana. Estat de la qüestió i propostes de futur." *Revista d'Historia Medieval* 10 (1999): 13–43.

Feliú, G. "La crisis catalana de la Baja Edad Media: estado de la cuestión." *Hispania* 64/2, 217 (2004): 435–466.

Fernandez T., J. and A. Riera. "La crisi econòmica i social al camp," in *Història agrària dels Països Catalans: Edad Mitjana*, edited by J. M. Salrach, 119–180. Barcelona: Fundació Catalana per a la Recerca i la Innovació, 2004.

Ferrando, A. *Llibre del repartiment de Valencia*.Valencia: Vicent García, D. L., 1984.

Furió, A. "Tierra, familia y transmisión de la propiedad en el país valenciano durante la Baja Edad Media," in *Relaciones de poder, de producción y de parentesco en la Edad Media y Moderna: aproximación a su estudio*, edited by R. Pastor, 305–328. Madrid: C.S.I.C., 1990.

Furió, A. *Història del País Valencià*. Valencia: Alfons el Magnànim. Generalitat Valenciana, 1995.

Furió, A. "Temps de represa i creixement. La recuperació del final de l'Edat Mitjana i l'inici de la Moderna," in *Història agrària dels Països Catalans: Edad Mitjana*, edited by J. M. Salrach, 181–245. Barcelona: Fundació Catalana per a la Recerca i la Innovació, 2004.

García de Cortázar, J. Á. *La época medieval*. Madrid: Alianza Editorial, 1973.

García de Cortázar, J. Á. *La sociedad rural en la España medieval*. Madrid: Siglo XXI, 1988.

García de Cortázar, J. Á. and P. Martínez. Sopena. "Los estudios sobre historia rural de la sociedad hispanocristiana." *Historia Agraria* 31 (2003): 57–83.

García Fernández, J. "Champs ouverts et champs clôturés en Vieille-Castille." *Annales, Économies, Sociétés, Civilisations* 20/4 (1965): 693–700.

García Fiz, F. "'Las guerras de cada día'. En la Castilla del siglo XIV." *Edad Media* 8 (2007): 145–181.

García González, J. J. *Vida económica de los monasterios benedictinos en el siglo XIV*. Valladolid: Universidad de Valladolid, 1972.

García Oliver, F. *Terra de feudals. El País Valencià en la tardor de la Edat Mitjana*. Valencia: Alfons el Magnànim. Institució Valenciana d'Estudis i Investigació, 1991.

Guinot, E. and J. Torró, eds. *Repartiments medievals a la corona d'Aragó: segles XII–XIII*. Valencia: Universitat de València, 2007.

González, J. *Repartimiento de Sevilla*. Madrid: C.S.I.C., 1951.

González, M. *La repoblación de la zona de Sevilla durante el siglo XIV. Estudio y documentación*. Sevilla: Universidad de Sevilla, 1975.

González, M. *En torno a los orígenes de Andalucía. La repoblación del siglo XIII*. Sevilla: Universidad de Sevilla, 1988.

González, M. *La repoblación en la zona de Sevilla durante el siglo XIV*. Sevilla: Universidad de Sevilla, 1993.

Guilleré, C. "La Peste Noire à Gérone (1348)." *Anales del Instituto de Estudios Gerundenses* 27 (1984) : 87–161.

Guilleré, C. "Nouvelles recherches sur les épidemies à la fin du XIVe siècle. L'example de Vic (Catalogne). La mortalité de 1372 à 1407," in *Population et démographie au Moyen Âge*, edited by Olivier Guyotjeannin, 119–143. Paris: Editions du CTHS, 1995.

Iradiel, P., S. Moreta, and E. Sarasa. *Historia medieval de la España cristiana*. Madrid: Cátedra, 1989.

Klein, J. *The Mesta: A Study in Spanish Economic History: 1273–1836*. Cambridge, MA: Harvard University Press, 1920.

Laliena, C. *Sistema social, estructura agraria y organización del poder en el Bajo Aragón en la Edad Media (siglos XII–XV)*. Teruel: Instituto de Estudios Turolenses, 1987.

López, J. A., L. López Merino, S. Pérez Díaz and Á. Mateo Mínguez "Historia de la vegetación en el litoral de Gerona entre los siglos VIII y XX d.C. Cambios climáticos y socioeconómicos desde una perspectiva paleoambiental." *Arqueología y Territorio Medieval* 15 (2008): 13–28.

López de Ayala, P. *Crónica del Rey Don Pedro y del Rey Don Enrique, su hermano, hijos del rey don Alfonso Onceno*, edited by G. Orduna. Buenos Aires: Secrit, 1994.

Martín Cea, J. C. *El mundo rural castellano a fines de la Edad Media: el ejemplo de Paredes de Nava en el siglo XV*. Valladolid: Junta de Castilla y León, 1991.

Martínez, G, ed. *Libro Becerro de las Behetrías: estudio y texto crítico*. León: Centro de Estudios e Investigación San Isidoro, 1981.

Martínez, L. "El señorío abadengo en Castilla. Consideraciones sobre su formación y desarrollo (siglos XI–XIV)." *Edad Media* 8 (2007): 243–277.

Martínez C, and J. Miguel, eds. *El nivel de vida en la España rural, siglos XVIII–XX*. Alicante: Universidad de Alicante, 2002.

Montes, I. "Crisis de subsistencias y comercio exterior de cereales en la Sevilla del siglo XV," in *Crisis de subsistencia y crisis agrarias en la Edad Media*, edited by R. Oliva and P. Benito: 161–198. Sevilla: Universidad de Sevilla, 2007.

Moreta, S. *Malhechores-feudales: violencia, antagonismos y alianzas de clases en Castilla siglos XIII–XIV*. Madrid: Cátedra, 1978.

Oliva, R. "El mundo rural en la Corona de Castilla en la Baja Edad Media. Dinámicas socio-económicas y nuevas perspectivas de análisis." *Edad Media* 8 (2007): 95–328.

Pastor, R. *Resistencias y luchas campesinas en la época del crecimiento y la consolidación de la formación feudal. Castilla y León, siglos X–XIII*. Madrid: Siglo XXI, 1980.

Portela, E. *La región del obispado de Tuy en los siglos XII al XV*. Santiago de Compostela: Edición local, 1976.

Reglero de la Fuente, C. "Les disettes dans le Royaume de Castille (entre 1250 et 1348)." Paper presented at the Conference *Les disettes dans la conjoncture de 1300 en Méditerranée occidentale,* Rome, Italy, February 27–28, 2004.

Riera, A. "Els pròdroms de les crisis agràries de la baixa edad mitjana a la Corona d'Aragó: 1250–1300. " *Miscel.lània en Homenatge al P. Agustí Altisent*: 35–72. Tarragona: Diputació de Tarragona, 1991.

Riera, A. "Crisis frumentarias y políticas municipales de abastecimiento en las ciudades catalanas durante la Baja Edad Media," in *Crisis de subsistencia y crisis agrarias en la Edad Media*, edited by R. Oliva and P. Benito: 125–160. Sevilla: Universidad de Sevilla, 2007.

Rodríguez, A. "'Foyse da terra no ano das chuvias . . . ' Carestías y subsistencia en el noroeste peninsular en los siglos XII y XIII," in *Crisis de subsistencia y crisis agrarias en la Edad Media*, edited by R. Oliva and P. Benito: 199–220. Sevilla: Universidad de Sevilla, 2007.

Rodríguez Galdo, M. X. *Señores y campesinos en Galicia, siglos XIV–XVI.* Santiago de Compostela: Pico Sacro, 1976.

Rodríguez González, A. *Las fortalezas de la mitra compostelana y los Irmandiños. Pleito Tabera-Fonseca.* Pontevedra: Fundación Pedro Barrié de la Maza, 1984.

Romaní, M, ed. *Libro Tumbo de Pergamino. Un códice medieval del monasterio de Oseira.* Santiago de Compostela: Universidad de Santiago, 2003.

Ruiz, T. F. "Expansion et changement: la conquête de Seville et la société castillane (1248–1350)." *Annales, Économies, Sociétés, Civilisations* 3 (1979): 548–565.

Ruiz, T. F. *Crisis and Continuity. Land and Town in Late Medieval Castile.* Philadelphia: University of Pennsylvania Press, 1994.

Ruiz, T. F. *Las crisis medievales (1300–1474).* Barcelona: Crítica, 2007.

Sarasa, E. *Sociedad y conflictos sociales en Aragón, siglos XIII–XV: estructuras de poder y conflictos de clase.* Madrid: Siglo XXI, 1981.

Sebastián Amarilla, J. A. "Del 'fuero' al arrendamiento. Tenencia y explotación de la tierra en León entre la Edad Media y la Edad Moderna." *Revista de Historia Económica* 17, 2 (1999): 305–338.

Sebastián Amarilla, J. A. "La Edad Media (c. 100–c. 1450). Configuración y primer despegue de la economía europea," in *Historia económica mundial. Siglos X–XX*, edited by F. Comín, M. Hernández, and E. Llopis: 15–66. Barcelona: Crítica, 2005.

Sesma, J. A. and C. Laliena, eds. *La población en Aragón en la Edad Media (siglos XIII–XV). Estudios de demografía histórica.* Zaragoza: Leyere, 2004.

Sobrequés, J. "La peste Negra en la Península Ibérica." *Anuario de Estudios Medievales* 7 (1970–1): 67–97.

Torras, J. and B. Yun, eds. *Consumo, condiciones de vida y comercialización. Cataluña y Castilla, siglos XVII–XIX.* Valladolid: Junta de Castilla y León, 1999.

Vaca, Á. "La estructura socioeconómica de la Tierra de Campos a mediados del siglo XIV." *Publicaciones de la Institución Tello Téllez de Meneses* 39 (1977): 229–398.

Vaca, Á. "Una manifestación de la crisis castellana del siglo XIV. La caída de las rentas de los señores feudales. El testimonio del monasterio de Sahagún." *Studia Historica* 1, 2 (1983): 157–166.

Vaca, Á. "La Peste Negra en Castilla. Aportación al estudio de algunas de sus consecuencias económicas y sociales." *Studia Historica. Historia Medieval* 2 (1984): 89–107.

Valdeón, J. "La crisis del siglo XIV en Castilla: Revisión del problema." *Revista de la Universidad de Madrid* 20 (1972): 161–182.

Valdeón, J. "Datos sobre la población de Castilla en el siglo XIV. El caso de Valbuena de Duero." *Archivos Leoneses* 55–56 (1974): 309–316.

Valdeón, J. *Conflictos sociales en el reino de Castilla en los siglos XIV y XV.* Madrid: Siglo XXI, 1975.
Valdeón, J. "Un despoblado castellano del siglo XIV: Fuenteungrillo." *En la España Medieval* 3 (1982): 705–716.
Valdeón, J. "Citeaux en Castille au Bas Moyen Âge: l'exemple de Matallana," in *Les Espagnes médiévales. Aspects économiques et sociaux. Mélanges offerts à Jean Gautier Dalché*, 45–52. Paris: Les Belles Lettres, 1983.
Valdeón, J. "La crisis del siglo XIV en la Corona de Castilla," in *La historia en el contexto de las ciencias humanas y sociales. Homenaje a Marcelo Vigil Pascual,* edited by M. J. Hidalgo de la Vega: 217–236. Salamanca: Universidad de Salamanca, 1989.
Valdeón, J. *Los países de la Corona de Castilla. La Baja Edad Media peninsular. Siglos XIII al XV. La población, la economía, la sociedad. Historia de España Menéndez Pidal.* Madrid: Espasa Calpe, 1996.
Vicens Vives, J. *Historia de los remensas en el siglo XV.* Barcelona: C.S.I.C., 1945.
Vicens Vives, J. *Manual de Historia Económica de España.* Barcelona: Teide, 1959.
Vidal, E. *Valencia en la época de Juan I.* Valencia: Universidad de Valencia, 1974.
Vilar, P. *La Catalogne dans l'Espagne Moderne. Recherches sur les fondements économiques des structures nationales.* París: S.E.V.P.E.N, 1962.
Yun, B. "Economic cycles and structural changes," in *Handbook of European History: 1400–1600: Late Middle Ages, Renaissance and Reformation*, edited by T. A. Brady, H. A. Oberman, and J. D. Tracy: 113–145. Leyden: E. J. Brill, 1994.
Yun, B. "El siglo de la hegemonía castellana (1450–1590)," in *Historia económica de España, siglos X-XX*, edited by F. Comín, M. Hernández, and E. Llopis: 51–84. Barcelona: Crítica, 2002.

7 Scandinavia

Janken Myrdal

INTRODUCTION

What drives progress? The case this chapter seeks to make is that a famine or an epidemic, which is generally seen as 'catastrophic' or 'disastrous' for the structure of society, may in the longer term have a positive outcome. A 'major crisis' is in an ordinary dictionary defined as "a stage in a sequence of events at which the trend of all future events, especially *for better* or worse, is determined" (my italics), and in this chapter, more specifically, a 'major crisis' is defined as a structural crisis, a challenge to the social structure.[1] The theory presented here is that crisis and expansion could go hand in hand. An upward trend, whether in population or production, tends to reach crisis point and the crisis could pave the way for the next step forward.

The tenth to the twelfth centuries were a time of technological breakthroughs and economic expansion. But the expansion gradually came to a stop, making society more vulnerable to the challenges of famines and epidemics. When the Black Death struck, a vicious circle began. The reaction of the upper classes was to try to defend their incomes, throwing society into a deeper recession. Later this resulted in societal change and reconstruction, which in the long-term was important for renewed economic expansion. To examine this theory, different phases within the period of crisis have to be distinguished.

This chapter begins by describing the ecology and climate of the Nordic countries and political events of relevance.[2] Then we discuss the source materials underlying the discussion. The social structure, including indications of class struggle, plays a specific role in explaining the course of events. Technological change around 1000–1200 is of vital importance, and the approach to technology focuses on the 'technological complex,' and the many small changes involved.[3]

Plague has its place in demographic change, and one should not underestimate the role of the recurring epidemics in the late medieval crisis. But I argue that the crisis is not only about the disease but a decline in the standard of living and security, followed by the restructuring of society, which later resulted in a higher standard of living (including an increase in non-agrarian consumption).

In recent years, all of the Nordic countries, fired by internal competition and mutual inspiration, have produced multi-volume works on agrarian history—in total, thirteen volumes for Denmark-Sweden-Norway, and three for Southern Jutland—which facilitate synthesis.[4] I refer to these generally as background for the research presented below.

PHYSICAL GEOGRAPHY AND POLITICS

The physical geography of Scandinavia can be roughly described as follows. The plains of Denmark run into the vast North European Plain stretching from Russia to southern England; the boreal forests of Sweden adjoin the taiga of northern Eurasia; and the Norwegian coast is formed by the steep western flank of the north-south Scandinavian mountain ranges. Also found are the natural resources that provided a foundation for early trade: fish along the Norwegian coast and in the Öresund Sound, and iron and copper in central Sweden. Mining and pre-industrial iron and copper production were highly dependent on an abundance of wood.

Much of Europe can be characterized as an agricultural frontier in the period c. 800–1300 but, especially in the Nordic countries, mountain districts, moorlands, and woodland areas were opened up for more intensive use. Chris Wickham has described this as a European pattern, showing that it reflected a growing regional diversification of labor.[5] There are some examples from archeology: Ingvild Öye has described rural iron production in Norway in the High Middle Ages. In the woodlands along the border between medieval Sweden and Denmark, small-scale iron production developed. One example is a farm, in southern Sweden (Småland), established during the thirteenth century and abandoned around 1400, where a small plot of arable land was surrounded by many heaps of slag from the production of bog-iron.[6] In the mining districts of central Sweden, large-scale production started in the tenth and eleventh centuries, and, during the Middle Ages, 900 blast furnaces were established in this region (and around 5,500 bloomeries in all of Sweden).[7] It became a dynamic economic center, especially from the late Middle Ages, exporting iron to much of Northern Europe. This large-scale production eventually killed the widespread small-scale production.

Scandinavia has been politically unified only during brief interludes, but forms a distinct region, in large part due to the common language. Even today, the differences between Norwegian, Danish, and Swedish are no greater than what in other language areas would be called dialects. These three countries have also been politically related to each other, for simple geopolitical reasons, as the two peninsulas west of the Baltic Sea.

Denmark, Sweden, and Norway emerged as three different states in the ninth to the eleventh centuries. They all reached out to neighboring regions during the period of economic expansion: during the Viking age, Norway dominated the northern Atlantic, including Iceland, the Faroe Islands, and Shetland. For a time in the thirteenth century, Denmark established a small empire in the southern Baltic, at the same time as Sweden conquered Finland. In the fourteenth century the economic expansion imploded and, confronted by the threat of German expansionism, Scandinavia became politically united, only to break apart again in the fifteenth century.

Denmark had already undergone a political collapse in the 1330s. In a civil war, German princes took control of the country and raised taxes dramatically. The same thing occurred in Sweden after the 1360s. The three countries were drawn into a witches' cauldron of war and civil war, a dimension of the larger European crisis. German princes, who had already lost revenue in their homelands, turned to the Nordic countries for compensation. Political and dynastic considerations had a role in these civil wars, but sometimes the documents openly reveal that the driving force behind the actions was economic. Many documents also describe the plunder-based economy that was then introduced via military invasions and temporary taxes. There are many parallels in the rest of Europe at the time, but the most famous is the Hundred Years' War.[8]

Eventually, in the 1390s, the entire Nordic region was brought under a single ruler, Queen Margaret, whose father was a king of Denmark, husband was a king of Norway, and father-in-law was a king of Sweden. German noblemen who chose to stay were assimilated as Scandinavians and, along with the Danish nobility, came to dominate the United Kingdoms of Scandinavia, the 'Union.' But taxes were not lowered. Instead, in about 1400, the tax system was restructured, ostensibly to phase out the numerous unregulated and temporary taxes. In practice, however, the restructuring merely served to stabilize taxes at a high level. New, additional taxes were introduced when the united Nordic state ventured into war in northern Germany. The collapse of the Union is described below, in the section about popular rebellions, but it was partly the result of raised taxes and an increasing level of class struggle.

The most important change of frontiers between the three Scandinavian countries came in the seventeenth century, when the southern part of the peninsula, Scania (Skåne) and the surrounding areas (Skåneland), which were Danish in the Middle Ages, became Swedish. Some Norwegian districts were also conquered by Sweden during this period, and have been Swedish ever since.

SOURCE MATERIALS

Documentary source material for Scandinavia is scarce before the end of the Middle Ages. Much more so than elsewhere, the economic historian must rely on non-documentary evidence and the circumstantial evidence found in written sources. This is not an unmitigated drawback, as it allows non-documentary sources to prompt additional questions. Scholars in countries with abundant documentary material can become prisoners of these riches.

Hence, archeology has played an important role in the historiography of medieval Scandinavia. The archeological evidence includes excavations of agrarian settlements, analytical pollen studies, and wood material from urban middens. The lack of written sources leads to differences in the naming of periods, as Scandinavian scholars count the 'Middle Ages' as extending from c. 1000 to 1500 and refer to the preceding period as the 'late Iron Age.' In this chapter, I will, however, use the normal European terminology.

The documentary sources derive from various periods. The 20 or so surviving regional laws, c. 1000–1300, are the earliest documentary records. The written codification of regional and, later, national laws was a part of a process of state formation. Hence, no new law codices were drafted in the late Middle Ages, although statutes on specific subjects continued to be issued.

Charters and letters (collectively referred to by Scandinavian historians as 'diplomas') are another important group of sources. Such documents were often composed at the district-court, by professional scribes, and were read aloud before being attested. They primarily concern land transactions, but also deal with other aspects of government. They were preserved on farms and manors and, from the seventeenth century onwards, nearly all of them were collected by historians for the national archives. There are altogether about 100,000 of them from Denmark, Sweden, and Norway. While twelfth-century diplomas are rare, they become more common in the thirteenth century and, by the mid-fourteenth century, they reach a plateau that lasts until the end of the Middle Ages.

A number of land registers have been preserved, most of them from the fourteenth and fifteenth centuries. Toward the end of the Middle Ages, we see more variety in the sources, with the appearance of town archives (including council minutes). Manorial accounts containing details about sowing, harvests, and so on, survive from the end of the fifteenth century.

Pictorial material exists from two periods. The oldest dates from the twelfth to the fourteenth centuries and includes sculptures in churches and a few wall paintings. The second tranche consists of hundreds of fifteenth-century churches adorned with wall paintings that have been preserved. It is not unusual for these religious images to have agrarian allusions, for instance, in depictions of Adam and Eve at work. There are few domestic illuminated manuscripts.

The sixteenth century sees a veritable explosion of material. The establishment of a strong state produced a flood of documents. In Sweden, which benefited from a stable government and was never conquered, most have survived. This material extends to millions of pages. Sweden, from the sixteenth century, and Denmark, from the seventeenth, required the annual registration of essentially all farms in tithe rolls and tax rolls, and individual royal estates at a level of detail down to which crops were planted in specific fields and how much butter was produced per cow.

SOCIAL STRUCTURE

Although the Nordic region was on the outer edge of Europe, it was undoubtedly involved in the more general European social processes. Here, I look at three aspects of agrarian social structure: the estate system, the villages, and the distribution of land ownership.[9]

Estates: It was once assumed that, from the early Iron Age and during the European early Middle Ages, most Nordic farmers had been mainly freeholders, with a few slaves and chieftains. A picture of a rather more stratified society now emerges, with many thralls (slaves). This society was not as stratified as it was in other parts of Europe at the time, but it was far from egalitarian. The stratification was probably, in many parts of Scandinavia, raised to a new level between the Viking age (eighth to tenth centuries) and the eleventh and twelfth centuries, when the system started to change, in a process of feudalization. Private ownership of land (in the more precise and juridical sense), and a system of manors and tenants were established at this time. The regional law codes, and later the national law codes underpinned this system. Slavery had been abolished by the thirteenth century, a process that probably started earlier. The former thralls often remained attached to the estate, but as crofters.

When we first see the manorial system in the thirteenth century, the estate structure in southern and central Scandinavia consisted of centrally located manors (with demesnes), often fairly small, surrounded by subordinate units. The central unit was managed by a *villicus* (steward) who also had a sharecropping farm, which might be the demesne; sharecropping meant that his livestock, seed, and implements were owned by the landowner. The *villicus* paid a very high rent for this land, often as much as half the net harvest. Some of the smaller farms surrounding the main farmstead were tenant farms, but many were extremely small units (crofts), which contributed labor to the manorial demesne. Some of these crofters also had specialized roles, such as fishermen, smiths, or herders. In a number of inventories of landowners' livestock and implements in the steward's keeping, we find that cattle numbers were relatively small on some manors, with a basic herd consisting of perhaps as few as two oxen and four cows. Doubtless most of the surrounding crofts had no draft animals at all, relying on spades and mattocks. As much of the production was directed to stock farming, this implies mainly that these 'manors' were relatively small.

Northern Sweden was different. Here, earlier chieftainships—evident from their large burial mounds and the high-quality goods buried with them—were dissolved and replaced by a more egalitarian agrarian society of free peasants. In the thirteenth century these peasants had been incorporated into a feudal structure and were required by both the state and the church to pay taxes and tithes, although there was an absence of nobility and very few large estates in this area from the thirteenth century onwards. How this change occurred is unclear, but it is probably related to the region's incorporation into the Swedish state.

Early in the fourteenth century, the entire manorial system throughout Scandinavia was in flux. Once both a sharecropper and a steward, the *villicus* increasingly took on the status and function of steward or bailiff. The manors, by the same token, tended to become centers of administration for a large number of tenant farms. Some of the earlier estates would later develop into villages and hamlets, with tenant farms.

After the huge epidemics from 1350 to the late fourteenth century (see pp. 223–224), this became the normal Scandinavian pattern. The small crofters surrounding the manor became tenants. With plenty of vacant farmsteads, no one wanted to be a crofter. The number of relatively small manors declined, many being subdivided into tenant farms. This left a few large manors with demesne agriculture and fairly large stocks of animals. Starting in the second half of the fifteenth century, these emerged as the manorial farms of the nobility. This structure—of tenant farms generally equivalent in size and a smaller number of larger manors—remained the dominant manorial system in southern and central Scandinavia until the eighteenth century.

Free peasants, owning their own land but paying taxes to the Crown, constituted a large or a major part of the peasantry in many regions. This also influenced the manorial structure, and the tenants often had a legal position superior to those in many other parts of Europe. Serfdom proper did not exist in Scandinavia during the High Middle Ages.

Villages: A system of villages and family farms existed as early as the eleventh and twelfth centuries. The relationship between the estate system and the villages is still not clear. Many villages on the plains consisted of one or two manors, others consisted entirely of tenant farms or freeholders.

Three systems, primarily regionally based, can be identified. The first is of large villages, mainly found on the plains of Denmark, similar in form to those found all over the continent; second, hamlets of two to four farms, found predominantly in Swedish forest districts; and third, isolated farms, common in the narrow valleys of Norway, but also scattered throughout the Scandinavian periphery. The regional distribution of these systems was not as clear-cut as the foregoing list implies. For example, there were also large villages in the river valleys of northern Sweden, which were entitled to use vast areas of woodland. In times of population growth, isolated farms, or 'homesteads,' such as those along the Norwegian coasts, were often subdivided to form hamlets and, later, in periods of population decline, re-amalgamated.

The village, in the sense of a cluster of several farms, had existed for a long time, but the village as a socio-economic system took on a new role in the Nordic countries in the eleventh and twelfth centuries. A large proportion of the regional and national laws focused on the village community, and the legislation provided protection that strengthened such communities and regulated several new phenomena. Fences and ditches were two innovations and larger common fields another. Previously, farms had had individual fields ('lots') but, with new cultivation, larger, contiguous fields shared by the whole village or hamlet were now being created. At the same time, farming systems were regulated according to two-field or three-field crop rotation cycles in the now larger common fields.

Another change was the appearance of a new type of enclosure. In the plains, the field systems bordered each other but, in many regions, every hamlet was surrounded by its own fields, enclosed with a common fence, and maintained by the peasants in the village, where every farm had its specific sections of the fence. A prerequisite for this abundance of fencing, around every village, was a specific type of fence. In most of the Nordic region (excluding Denmark, which lacked extensive forests) withy fences were being introduced. This was an impenetrable fence consisting of pairs of stakes, held together with withies, and many rails laid in between. This fence was effective but required a lot of timber of a specific size. Withy fences were built around the common fields and meadows of the village and could encircle dozens of kilometers, giving structure to the landscape. Pasture was normally outside these fences. The term 'inland-outland' applies to this landscape (not to be confused with the 'infield-outfield' of medieval England, where the border between the two categories often changed).

When two villages had fields bordering each other no fence was needed and, on the plains, whole systems of contiguous villages could be established, similar to the common fields in England.

Land ownership: The distribution of land ownership cannot be ascertained before the sixteenth century (Table 7.1).[10] Around 1500, freeholders were not at all evenly distributed, but were instead concentrated in three large areas: northern Sweden, southern Norway, and south-western Denmark (see Figure 7.1). From a European perspective, these regions are unique for their large proportion of free peasants (often nearly 100%). This is partly because of the geography and ecology of this peripheral area, and partly due to successful class struggle. It is likely that much of this landowning structure has its roots in the period of change around 1000, although the late Middle Ages saw some changes.

Table 7.1 The Distribution of Land Ownership, by Percentage, in Scandinavia c. 1500–1520

	Denmark	*Norway*	*Sweden*	*Finland*
Nobility	39	15	24	3
Church	36	48	25	3
Crown	10	7	6	-
Peasants	15	30	45	95

Sources: See endnote 10.

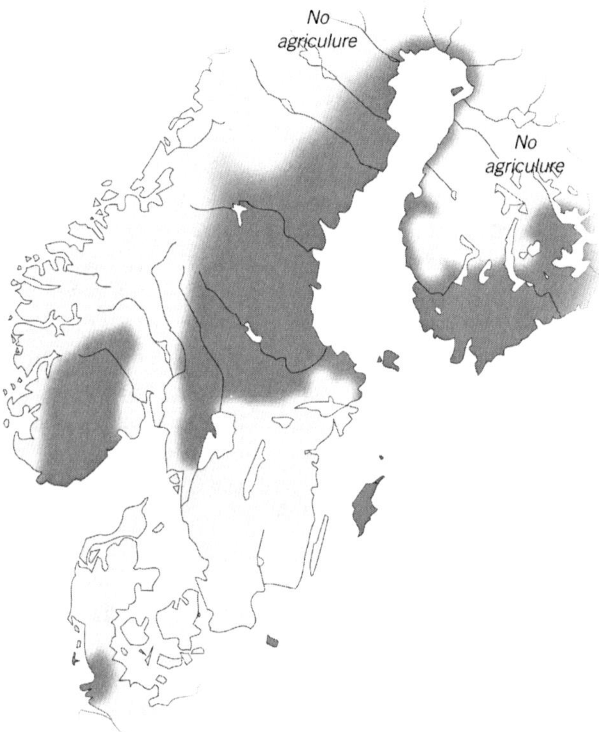

Figure 7.1 Areas where more than approximately 60 percent of the land was owned by peasant freeholders in the sixteenth and seventeenth centuries.

During the late Middle Ages the shifts in landownership between the major groups were not dramatic, but some trends can be commented upon. After the Black Death, the share owned by the church generally increased in all three countries, one reason being the donations of abandoned farms to the church. The share of the nobility declined, while that of the Crown remained unchanged in Norway and Sweden, and increased in Denmark. The tendencies diverge with respect to the share held by peasant freeholders, which declined in Denmark, did not change in Norway, and increased in Sweden. This was largely a result of different outcomes of the class struggles in the three countries. In Denmark, for example, a significant number of farmers in northern Jutland had lost their right of ownership to the Crown as a result of the unsuccessful peasant revolt of the 1440s.

INTER-CLASS POWER RELATIONS

Rents: The population decline and the abandonment of farmsteads after the Black Death left tenant farmers and crofters in a better negotiating position, but did not lead automatically to lower rents. A survey of the evidence for 'minor class struggle,' mainly in charters and letters but also in statutes, shows a general increase in conflict between lords and tenants after 1350, with disputes between tenant farmers and landowners becoming particularly common. Farmers refused to pay some rents or to perform day labor. Another common conflict concerned buildings that tenants had neglected to repair on the farms they had taken over.[11]

The most common form of protest was, however, that the peasants simply left their holdings. In the 1370s, Danish landowners attempted to introduce compulsory statutes to keep the tenant farmers on their estates, but were unsuccessful. In Sweden, similar attempts were made in the 1440s, again unsuccessfully.[12] Swedish and Norwegian peasants never became bound to the land but, in the 1490s, landowners on the Danish islands (Sjælland, Møn, Lolland, Falster) succeeded in establishing a new legal practice, which meant that no tenant was allowed to move from the farm without the landowner's consent.[13] Thus, the most populous areas of Denmark essentially began to conform to the pattern of consolidated serfdom in Eastern Europe, although Danish serfdom never took the harsh form that eventually came into existence in Poland and Russia.[14]

Land rents fell sharply all over Scandinavia but are difficult to calculate for several reasons. One is that the estate system changed. Most of the small crofters disappeared and the small manors were dissolved, so the farmsteads whose rents might be compared were often not the same. Many farms came to include lands belonging to abandoned farms, now often turned to pasture and meadow. The rent was also negotiable and the amount shown in the land registers was not always what was paid. In addition, there were small, temporary rents that could vary from year to year and were not recorded. Tenants close to the manor often paid in products that could not be transported far (such as eggs) or with labor services. During the late Middle Ages most tenants paid their main rent in kind: grain on the fertile plains, butter in the woodlands, skins and hides in mountain regions, fish along the Norwegian coast, and, around the

Swedish mining districts, iron, which the farmers bartered in exchange for their agrarian products. Money rent was common in Denmark and Sweden but not in Norway.[15]

The post-1350 decline was mostly over before 1400. A number of calculations point at a reduction of the rent of about one-third to two-thirds for farms in cultivation throughout the whole period. Reduction for farms on the plains could be severe, but generally the decline in the Norwegian mountain districts went even deeper.[16] Combined with the abandonment of farms, this brought about a dramatic reduction in rental income for the nobility, the church and the Crown. The higher and more powerful parts of the nobility tried to find other ways with which to maintain their incomes, typically with taxes or plundering.

Taxes and popular rebellions: Robber barons, new taxes, and war were a general European phenomenon, the so-called 'feudal reaction.' This in turn triggered a counter-reaction of popular resistance, and local peasants' revolts became regional and sometimes even national in scope. These large national rebellions had shifting backgrounds and causes. I will restrict myself here to Nordic examples.

Nordic rebellions had one power center in the marshlands in south-western Jutland, which is a special case because of the partly self-governing 'peasant republic,' Dithmarschen. This region was dominated by rich farmers or, rather, clans of rich farmers. The Danish kings vainly tried to subdue the region during the Middle Ages, but only succeeded in the sixteenth century.

The other center of rebellion was Sweden, particularly the mining districts. The pivotal issue in Scandinavia, outside Dithmarschen, was the struggle against the heavy burden of taxes. In Denmark and Norway, major peasant uprisings occurred from the later part of the 1430s and into the 1440s, directly inspired by the earlier major rebellion in Sweden. These uprisings were almost entirely peasant movements, with little support from the nobility. The Danish rebellion in northern Jutland (1438–41) was brutally suppressed.

The armed peasants' movement in Sweden and Finland is distinctive in that it combined with elements within the Swedish nobility to gain control over the government and oust the Danish nobility dominating the Union. The peasants' armies became increasingly well-organized and well-equipped (for example, the more expensive crossbow came into general use, replacing the longbow). Noble armies of knights, squires, and their mercenary soldiers were defeated several times in the Swedish forests.

The first major uprising occurred during 1434–39 (lasting longest in Finland), and resulted in national taxes being reduced by a third. It was followed by civil war, with peasant armies in 1457, 1463–71, 1497, and 1501–02 (the last also involving Norway). From a formal point of view these peasant armies often fought for what they considered as the legal 'regent' (Swedish: *riksföreståndare*), and thus they were not rebels but protectors of the state. But they had a price for their engagement, and those from the nobility that wanted support from the gradually more powerful peasant armies had to negotiate.

The result was a partial breakdown of the state tax system, which allowed tax-paying peasants in different regions to negotiate local settlements. On average, the state taxes dropped to approximately half or less of what they had been in the early fifteenth century.

This shift of power in class relations also had an impact on other areas. The peasants gained greater influence over church administration and appointed the board that managed the finances of their local church. In the justice system, the peasant assemblies at the district court gained greater influence over the appointment of judges and juries. Many peasant assemblies even had their own copies of the national law made, which gave them an advantage in negotiating.

The position of the nobility weakened. The decline continued in Norway as an aspect of Norway's integration into the Danish state. In Sweden, the gradual weakening of the nobility in the late middle ages instead paved the way for the strong state, as the nobility allowed themselves to be integrated into this form of government. In Denmark, there was a marked concentration of power and landownership in the hands of the upper level of the nobility.

CROPS AND CULTIVATION SYSTEMS

In the damp North Atlantic region, oats were the dominant crop. They were the most important grain in much of Norway but, in eastern Scandinavia, they were not cultivated in large quantities until after the Middle Ages, so cavalry horses were instead given barley as their concentrated feed.

Barley had a prominent position throughout the Nordic region, and was completely dominant in Sweden. Barley was used for unleavened flatbread, porridge, gruel, and beer. Barley was malted and then brewed into beer, which may be considered as more a source of nourishment than an inebriant. The beer was initially brewed with bog-myrtle. Hops were introduced on the Continent in the thirteenth century and somewhat later in Scandinavia. In the fifteenth century, the State went so far as to order all farmsteads in Denmark and Sweden to cultivate hops, which continued to be imported throughout the Middle Ages. German hopped beer was always considered better than the domestic equivalent.

Rye cultivation can be traced far back in time, but as a dominant crop it was introduced in two waves. The first came in the eleventh to the thirteenth centuries, from the south. It was associated with black bread and the oven, and paralleled the transition to three-field crop rotations across large parts of the Danish plains. The second wave of rye cultivation came mainly after the Middle Ages, but had already begun in the fifteenth century. It came from the east—from Finland and the Baltic region—and the whole of eastern Sweden became a rye-cultivating area in the sixteenth century. This wave of rye cultivation is not associated with black bread, but rather with leavened crispbread—of the kind visitors to Sweden encounter today.

Cultivation of peas and other legumes did occur, but not to such an extent that it affected the cultivation system. Marling was not practiced until after the Middle Ages, and then as part of a more intensive labor investment in agriculture.

Two-field and three-field crop rotations were introduced in a transformation that took place between the eleventh and thirteenth centuries. The technological precondition was the appearance of improved plowing implements that could break large areas of overgrown fallow. It must be emphasized that different crop rotation systems often shaded into each other, with parts of the cultivated field laid in fallow, or parts of the fallow cultivated with a temporary fence around the plot.[17]

Three-field crop rotation became the predominant method in the plains of central Denmark (barley-rye-fallow), and two-field crop rotation in the plains settlements of eastern Sweden (barley-fallow). In the sixteenth century, rye was incorporated in a two-field system (rye/barley-fallow). In Norway, western Denmark, and Sweden's forest settlements, single-field crop rotation was the norm, often involving smaller fallow areas. These crop rotation systems could develop into more regular four- or five-field systems. In most of Jutland, a specific system called the field-grass system developed, without much need for fencing, but with fallow every fourth year or less. Convertible husbandry, as it was developed on the British Isles, first appeared in the seventeenth and eighteenth centuries.

The land was laid out in strips in the field, and every farmer had to cooperate with the other farmers over matters such as the proper time for harvesting and the arrangement of strips in the fields (often from east to west, in the same order as the farms along the village street—the 'sun division,' Swedish: *solskifte*). In addition, if a farmer became sick during the harvest, his neighbors were obliged to help him.

The most important issue for the village community was the management of the common fence around the fields. The common fence was divided into sections, and every farm had to manage a specific section. To understand this, we have to go back to the inland-outland system explained above, with a strict border between pastures (outland) on the one hand and fenced arable land and meadows (inland) on the other. Withy fences of wood were rebuilt again and again over the centuries following the same field boundaries. Keeping up these fences became a major task for the village community. If any farmer mismanaged his section of the common fence around the fields, livestock (and wild animals) could break through and cause much loss of crops and hay. In both regional and national laws, whole sections, covering many paragraphs, deal with when and how maintenance of fences was to be done; how fences should be constructed; how anyone catching an animal in the fields should handle the situation (the animal must not be killed, instead the guilty farmer had to be tracked down); and fines for non-compliance.

STOCK FARMING

In Northern European stock farming, animals were housed during the winter. Cattle were kept indoors for about half the year, longer in the far north, and for a shorter period in southern Scandinavia. Without this, it would have been impossible to keep domesticated cattle in northern Scandinavia (wild oxen were never—even in prehistory—found north of central Sweden). Sheds protected milk cows in particular against the cold and the damp, and this improved milk production. The use of cow houses (byres) also facilitated the efficient collection of manure. Animals kept outdoors in severe winters (when pastures were covered with frost or snow) always suffered severely, but a cattle-housing system allowed farmers to maintain a herd of consistent size. The greatest difficulty was collecting fodder, and meadowlands and hay gathering were crucial aspects of farming throughout Scandinavia.[18]

The regular use of byres was introduced in the Nordic countries between 100 BCE and 100 CE, along with the scythe, rake, and other elements of the technological complex. (This was later than in the Netherlands and along the southern North Sea coast up to Jutland.) In northern Scandinavia with harsh winters, this package of technology became important for the efficient combination of stock breeding with arable farming, in which animals are used for manure and traction.

A key change in Scandinavia was that production was drawn into the feudal economy, through taxes and rent. From an early date, butter became a commodity for trade and tax in kind. The explanation is that butter—the fat of the fat—has a high calorie density in relation to its weight, and therefore has a high value, making profitable transport possible.

A prerequisite for the storage of butter was access to salt, which was initially imported from northern Germany. Toward the end of the Middle Ages, cheaper salt was increasingly imported from France, with some limited domestic production along the Danish coast supplying a small part of the demand. Technological change was a further prerequisite. The plunge churn appears in both pictures and archeological material in north-western Europe, from the ninth century onwards, becoming ubiquitous throughout the area by the eleventh century. (The components of the plunge churn are unique, so the presence or absence of butter churns is easy to identify in major archeological finds of wooden material.) This butter churn, with its stave and plunger for agitating the cream to turn it into butter, made it possible to process large quantities of cream (compared with the earlier shake churn).[19]

From the end of the Middle Ages, with the shifting of agricultural production toward stock farming, butter exports increased, as may be seen, for instance, in customs records from Lübeck. Butter became an important export commodity, but less important than Norwegian cod or Swedish iron and copper. Later in the fifteenth century, a long-distance trade in live animals developed, especially in oxen from Denmark (and southern Sweden). The animals were driven long distances to the places where they would be consumed, often to urban centers in Flanders and northern Germany, as part of the increasingly extensive trade in oxen throughout Europe at that time. During the late Middle Ages and the sixteenth century, farmers in southern Sweden started to sell their oxen for use—as food, traction, and ropes—in the expanding mining district in Sweden.

Another change discovered through archeological research is the gradual decline in the size of cows throughout the Middle Ages. A survey of more than 200 measurable skeletons from Sweden shows that the average height of a cow at the withers decreased from about 110 centimeters to just over 100 centimeters. Cows began increasing in size again in the sixteenth century (a trend confirmed by documentary sources), particularly in areas where the ox trade flourished. The cattle breeds were small to begin with and one possible explanation for the continuing decrease in size could be the strong focus on butter production, which led to calves being weaned quickly, which, in turn, stunted their growth. The ox trade preferred bigger animals because it was aimed at producing meat instead of butter.

Prices give a further clue to the change. The Swedish prices have recently been thoroughly researched, showing that prices for butter and oxen fell about 10–15 percent during the fifteenth century relative to the price of grain. The price of butter fell continuously from the middle of the fourteenth century, whereas the price of oxen fell steeply in the late fifteenth century. The explanation is probably that the production of butter started to grow with the shift towards animal husbandry after the Black Death, but the long-distance trade in oxen was not organized on a large scale until 100 years later.[20]

Stock farming practices changed too, with herding practices a key example. In the early Middle Ages, the herder was usually an adult male. In large parts of Europe, a gradual transition took place during the late and High Middle Ages, from the private herder, often a slave, to the village herder.[21] This development can be seen in Denmark, but in the other Scandinavian countries, mainly due to the shortage of male labor in the wake of the Black Death, there was a transition from male herders to women and children watching over the animals.[22] The hamlets in central Scandinavia were so small that a system of village herders was impossible.

TILLING

There is a tendency to underestimate technological changes in traditional societies because they appear insignificant from our own 'high-tech' perspective. Another obstacle to the investigation of technological change is that it is rarely recorded in documentary sources. Consequently, the history of technology is dependent on preserved artifacts and pictorial material. The following description may seem overly detailed but, taken as a whole, the technical changes it describes had a critical impact on development.[23] This new technological package is the fundamental explanation for a whole social leap forward, including population increase, new and larger towns, and the building of thousands of churches.

The essential characteristic of the technological shift that took place in the Nordic countries in the eleventh and twelfth centuries is the increased use of iron. In his work on medieval agriculture, Georges Duby has pointed to an increase in the number of iron implements as a crucial improvement.[24] The key agricultural change was the increased use of iron for tilling tools rather than merely for cutting tools; because tilling caused dramatically more wear on tools, it stimulated a correspondingly dramatic increase in iron consumption. Another pervasive change was the appearance of specialized tools for specific tasks. Axes are one example, with some axes specially for timber cutting and 'bearded' axes for producing a plane surface.

In an initial phase, c .600–1000, cutting tools became larger, especially scythes, where blade length almost doubled and the actual blade type changed. The first small iron plowshares were also introduced during this period. Ard shares made of hard wood were in use up to about the ninth century, but not after that.

The use of iron increased in the eleventh and twelfth centuries and became pervasive in Scandinavia throughout the agrarian sector. One of the most important changes was the increase in the size of the iron plowshare (or ard share). This working part at the tip of the plowing tool became heavier. Iron shares had been introduced from around 400–600 in northern Europe and, until c. 1000, the normal iron share in Northern Europe weighed around 0.3–0.4 kg. From c. 1000–1200, some shares in Sweden increased to 1–1.5 kg, although smaller shares were still used for light tasks. This heavier plowshare (or ard share) was longer, resulting in not only deeper but more stable tilling. This meant that grassland could be tilled better, favoring the introduction of systems of regular crop rotation (either two-field or three-field as discussed before). The documents of that time also talk about two types of shares, a light one for sowing and a heavier one for breaking the fallow. (The iron share was the most expensive part of the plow or the ard, and the laws and documents often talk specifically about it.) In the Danish area, the heavy wheeled plow prevailed and the customary share became even heavier, up to around 1.5–4 kg—and these plows also had coulters.[25] In Germany the changeover to a heavier share may have already started before 1000. In Norway, too, heavier shares were introduced before or around 1000.[26] For Russia, dating poses a problem and shares have to be analyzed as types. One type, from about the eleventh century, normally weighed 0.8–0.9 kg, and a later type from about the twelfth to fourteenth centuries weighed about 2.0–3.5 kg.[27]

Grith Lerche performed a long series of experimental plowings with a replica of a medieval Danish wheeled plow. She used five different shares and plowed altogether 8.5 hectares over three years. The experiment showed that, with better iron, the wear was around 0.15 kg per hectare but, with cheap and bad iron, it could be as much as 0.4 kg per hectare.[28] When one of the larger shares had worn down to 30–40 percent of the original size, the whole share had to be replaced. Smaller shares could only be allowed to wear down to 15–20 percent before being replaced. The same coulter was used throughout the experiment and, though heavy (6.5 kg), the wear was only 0.07 kg per hectare.

The increase of the weights of iron shares, together with more numerous heavy plowings caused by the regular fallow introduced with the two- or three-field systems, led to an increase of iron consumption in agriculture, and farming became dependent on metal production and trade. Thus, increased agrarian production not only gave the impetus for the growth of towns, but was also promoted by urbanization and non-agrarian production.

Another change that agrarian historians more typically emphasize is the transition from the ard to the moldboard plow. The plow type that was introduced to Scandinavia from Germany was the moldboard plow with a wheeled fore-carriage, which made the whole implement very stable. The introduction of the wheeled plow had begun in the ninth century in southern Jutland but gained momentum in the eleventh to thirteenth centuries in most of Denmark, including Scania. At the same time, light wheel-less plows were being introduced in southern Norway and were thus part of a dissemination zone for light plows around the northern part of the North Sea, from Norway to Scotland. In the rest of Scandinavia, people continued to use ards, but they were often of the improved type with a longer share.

The iron-shod spade was yet another key change. It had existed since Roman times in southern Europe and was found in the British Isles thereafter, but was not introduced into northern Europe until c. 900–1100. It brought a radical improvement in digging. At the same time, an extensive system of ditches to divert water was introduced, making it possible to cultivate wetter areas. Along the southern North Sea coast, large dikes were built around coastal areas, which also promoted the development of more efficient digging tools. Both changes—the laying of ditch systems around the fields and the building of dams against the sea—required more thoroughgoing cooperation between the farms, and thus form a component of social transformation.

One further innovative tool used in arable farming forms part of this technological complex: the harrow. Before the harrow, large rakes had been used. The harrow is often linked to the introduction of the moldboard plow, because the latter increases the need for further tillage after plowing, but harrows were also used together with the ard. Improvement of the efficiency of the horse as a draft animal was an essential precondition for the development of the harrow, because only horses could provide sufficient speed to till the soil. This had been accomplished around the same time, with better harnesses and horseshoes.

It is impossible to describe precisely the distribution of draft animals (horses and oxen) in Scandinavia, as we can for England, because we must rely on fragmentary evidence. The horse was the dominant draft animal in northern Scandinavia from the Viking era onwards, owing to its versatility in the context of small-scale farming. The ox was the dominant draft animal in most of southern Scandinavia although horses were common in large tracts of Denmark. In the late Middle Ages, a transition to using the horse as a draft animal occurred in areas towards the north, such as the Swedish province of Uppland. Here, as in England, the causes are more likely to have been social and economic than technical.

Although I have not discussed all the known technical innovations, omitting the flail, the watermill, and the windmill, we can safely say that they were extensive and interrelated: plowing methods with cultivation systems, harnesses with harrows, and so on. These integrated innovations can be considered as 'agrarian technological complexes' with mutually related elements, which would explain their simultaneous introduction. Parallel to these innovations, technical systems with some differences in individual elements were introduced throughout Europe, in a massive shift of agrarian technology (involving common trends such as the increased use of iron and improved cultivation systems) and rising land production of cereals.

This parallelism indicates that the general shift occurring in social structures throughout much of Europe played a crucial role, along with the burgeoning market and a state power that provided a measure of stability. That exploitation changed is another part of the process.

The process of new cultivation began early in Scandinavia, in the eighth and ninth centuries. In the later phase of the expansion, cultivation spread to the large forests and other peripheral areas. This outward expansion into previously almost uninhabited regions lasted from the twelfth to the fourteenth century. In Scandinavia, it can be traced mainly through pollen analysis and the archeological excavation of settlements.[29] There is also documentary evidence from the end of the process and, in the early fourteenth century, we find new cultivation projects in northern Sweden, with the country's rulers (whether the bishop or the king) providing funding for such projects along the most northerly river valleys, organized in roughly the same way as the contemporaneous expansion into eastern Germany, Poland, and the Baltic region.

Land continued to be brought into cultivation in the peripheral areas until the Black Death, but even before then, there were signs of recession and some of the old plains settlements of southern Scandinavia began to be abandoned. It was in these peripheral areas, toward the end of the Middle Ages, that cultivation started to expand again.

PRODUCTIVITY

The yield of a few late medieval manors can be calculated, but only as the yield:seed ratio.[30] The figures from three manors in eastern central Sweden reveal yield:seed ratios between 1481 and 1512 of 3:1–3.5:1 for rye and barley and, from one manor in Schleswig between 1518 and 1537, of 4:1–5:1 for barley and 7:1 for rye.[31] In the sixteenth century the yield:seed ratio was generally increasing to about 5:1–6:1 on the fertile plains of eastern central Sweden, an increase that was well under way in the 1530s and 1540s.[32] The population grew and production was increasingly labor-intensive.

The documents give no direct evidence about the yields in the High Middle Ages. The level of rents during the thirteenth and fourteenth centuries in eastern central Sweden could give hints about the productivity, as the unit for land assessment was linked to an assumed standard both for the seed and the harvest. These estimates are very uncertain, but point to a yield:seed ratio of around 3:1–6:1.[33] The late Middle Ages could, if these calculations are correct, have seen a period of falling land productivity because of scarcity of labor, as is found in other parts of Europe.[34]

Where labor productivity is concerned, we must rely entirely on indirect sources and focus primarily on technical change. For the High Middle Ages, we can assume that increased crop cultivation (and a new level of intensification) did not lead to any substantial increase in labor productivity. One detail that could provide a clue is that many of the small farmers (crofters, often former thralls) living around the large farmsteads had no draft animals, and were forced to work the soil with spade and mattock. This is familiar from Continental sources, but there is only indirect evidence of it for Scandinavia, where images of the toiling Adam and Eve dating from the twelfth to the thirteenth centuries clearly depict the use of spades and mattocks. They show several identifiable details, such as sod-turning. Another typical feature of these early illustrations is that sowing and digging were being done simultaneously. With a draft animal, the fields are first broken up with an ard or a plow; after that, the fields are sown; and finally the seed is covered using an ard or a harrow. In these images of hand cultivation, the sowing is done by the male (Adam) and the heavy work with the spade or mattock by the female (Eve). This motif disappears completely in the late Middle Ages, when we have only Adam, leaning on his spade. These rather realistic images, coupled with evidence that there were many crofters who lacked draft animals, indicate some kind of spade tilling instead of plowing.

During the post-plague period, we see a general tendency toward labor-saving innovations. One was the transition from arable farming to stock farming, and land records show how abandoned farms were used by neighboring farmers as pasture land or meadow land. But there was also a purely technical change in harvesting and mowing, the busiest time of the year on the farm, when all available labor was put to use. The sickles used for harvesting grain acquired longer blades. The scythes used for the hay harvest also took on a longer, more efficient form with longer blades and improved shafts. These technical innovations made it possible for a shrinking population to keep large areas of the landscape under cultivation. (The scythe, however, was not used in Scandinavia to harvest grain until after the Middle Ages.)

These late medieval technological innovations did not generally raise land productivity, and it is likely that more extensive cultivation, with less weeding and so on, instead tended to lower the yields.

DEMOGRAPHICS: FROM GROWTH TO FARM ABANDONMENT

Population up to 1350: Population data for Scandinavia, prior to the sixteenth century, are unreliable, even when we combine several sources. Nonetheless, based mainly on archeological investigations (number of sites, pollen analysis), we can say that during the expansion period from the eleventh to the thirteenth centuries, the population increased at least twofold, and probably more.

National estimates can be made for the middle of the fourteenth century but, first, border changes must be considered. The most important of them is that the southern part of the Scandinavian peninsula, Scania (Skåne) and the surrounding areas (Skåneland) were Danish in the Middle Ages, but have been Swedish since the seventeenth century. These accounted for slightly under one-fifth of the Danish population. Along the Norwegian-Swedish border three provinces were turned Swedish in the seventeenth century, and they accounted for about one-tenth of the Norwegian population.

The most important source is a few local and regional registers of households. A further source of data is the number of churches in the period: there were approximately 1,350 in Norway, 2,350 in Denmark, and 1,750 in Sweden (in the medieval realms of these three countries, but excluding Southern Jutland). These figures do not reveal temporal trends, rather they represent the 'medieval maximum' in the middle of the fourteenth century. A third source is 'Peter's Pence,' a papal tax to which every household in the same region was supposed to pay the same amount.[35] In Scandinavia, households in some peripheral regions were exempted from payment. For Sweden and Norway, sums are reported for all dioceses around 1330, and 30–40 percent more was paid from Sweden than from Norway. From the sixteenth and seventeenth centuries, we have fairly good population estimates, which can be used in combination with the medieval sources to reconstruct a population change. All of these different sources are beset with interpretation problems and must be weighed against each other.[36]

A cautious estimate would give a total population at this time of just above two million, distributed as follows: Norway, approximately 0.55 million; Sweden, approximately 0.7 million; and Denmark (including Scania but not Southern Jutland), approximately 0.95 million. Population levels had probably begun to stagnate in Denmark after the middle of the thirteenth century, but growth continued in Norway and Sweden until the middle of the fourteenth century.

Signs of stagnation—such as abandoned farmsteads—began to appear in the early fourteenth century in central areas, mainly the plains in Denmark, but cultivation continued, at the same time, to be extended at the periphery.

The crop failure, famine, and cattle disease of 1315–17 are described by only a few sources—but at this time the total documentary source material is still so thin that even major developments could go unrecorded.

The plague: The real shock came with the Black Death. The type of disease that struck during the Black Death and the following pandemics was probably some form of plague.[37] In recent years, progress in research has been achieved by combining several different source materials: wills, gravestones bearing dates, death rolls, tax rolls, chronicles, etc. This has made it possible to establish a sequence for the entire period of the plague in northern Europe.

Most of the studies in Table 7.2 use the number of wills per year as their basic data.[38] Norway is the only country in Scandinavia which lacks

Table 7.2 Significant Recorded Outbreaks of the Plague or Other Major Epidemics 1348–1499 in Northern Europe

N. Germany/ Lübeck	*Denmark*	*Sweden*	*Norway*	*Iceland*	*England*
1350	**1350**	**1350**	1349–50		1348–49
1358	**1360**	**1359–60**	1360		1360–62
1367	**1368**	**1368–69**	1370–71		1368–69
1376	**1377**	*1374–77*			
			1379	1379	1379–83
1387–88	**1387–89**	*1389*	1391–92		1389–93
1396	**1396**				
	1400			**1402–04**	1400
1406	1405	1405			1405–07
	1415	**1413**			1413
1420	*1418–19*	**1420–21**	1420?	1420–21	1420
					1427
1433					1433–34
1438–39	**1440-42**	**1439–40**	**1438–39?**		1438-39
1451	1454–55	1455	**1452**		
	1460		1459		1457–58
1464	*1464*	**1464–65**	1465–72?		1463–64
					1467
	1472–74	*1472–74*		1472	1471
	1481		1479–80?		1479–80
1483–84	*1484–87*	*1484*			1485
	1494–96	**1495**		**1494**	

Note: Epidemics recorded in wills in bold (and for Iceland years with an abundance of contemporary documents), and those not recorded in wills in italics. Will statistics in Norway have not been studied for the whole period.

Sources: See endnote 38.

a detailed study of late medieval epidemics. For Iceland the plagues of 1402–04 and 1494 are well-documented in contemporary sources. England is included as a comparison to Scandinavia.

Not all of these epidemics were the same disease as that which struck 1348–1350, the 'plague.' For instance, Icelandic scholars assume that Iceland only was struck by two outbreaks of the plague, 1402–04 and 1494, both with an enormous mortality. The other epidemics in Table 7.2 were less devastating, and at least two (1379, 1472) were possibly smallpox.[39]

The consistency among the countries in northern Europe is striking. Jean-Noël Biraben in the 1970s made a catalogue of 'places' hit by the plague in Europe, using a rather miscellaneous collection of data. His results can only be analyzed on a general level. I have summarized his results for all of northwestern, northern, and central Europe, and the similarity to Table 7.2, which gives better and more firm data, is noticeable.[40]

Judging by the increase in the number of wills, the first three epidemics were the most severe. A period of less severe epidemics followed. There was a succession of serious epidemics in the decades from 1410 to 1430, after which the mortality rate seems to have gradually declined. The occurrences of the plague can be identified as follows: c. 1350–71: extremely severe; c. 1371–1401: somewhat less severe; c. 1405–21: again severe; after 1421: gradually becoming less severe.

As regards mortality, it is not until the end of the Middle Ages that Scandinavia has rolls that allow us to track the number of households in detail, e.g. for Stockholm 1464–65, when excess mortality was about 10–15 percent. This is about the same mortality as other European epidemics at this time.

For the first three epidemics, however, there is one source that gives us some idea of the magnitude of the decline: 'Peter's Pence.' This tax was levied as a fixed sum per household. For Norway and Sweden, payments were reported throughout the first half of the fourteenth century. There are a number of problems with the interpretation of the source—for example, arrears remaining from one year to the next—and the figures are therefore approximate. To make any statement concerning average changes, we need a series of years.

There are uninterrupted accounts for six Swedish dioceses covering 1319–1353/56. A gradual increase is reported during this period up to the outbreak of the plague, which may be partly due to population growth. In the 1351–53 account, the total sum had decreased by around 35–40 percent. The two largest dioceses have accounts preserved for a few years thereafter: there was a further 20 percent decline after the second plague epidemic in 1360, and another fall of a similar size after the third epidemic in 1369. According to this source, between 1350 and 1370, the total population had been cut by half.

Subsequently, Peter's Pence for the archdiocese is recorded intermittently up to the middle of the fifteenth century. The total indicates a degree of recovery or, at least, stagnation, up to the 1410s, followed by a new decline as a result of the epidemics up to the beginning of the 1420s. By the 1430s, payments had recovered to the level they had been after the three major epidemics of 1350–69. While there is some uncertainty regarding the interpretation of this series, it shows what we might expect to find.

For Norway, there are records for all five dioceses for the years before and after 1330, and then for the middle of the 1350s. If we assume that the rate of increase in the 1340s corresponded to the Swedish rate, the drop after 1349–50 was approximately one-third. There are, however, no later records of Peter's Pence for Norway.

The increases in the number of wills in 1349–50, 1360, and 1369 are comparable for all three countries. The best individual records are from Gotland, the large island in the Baltic Sea, which has extant death records from 1350. These indicate a fifteen-fold increase in mortality, which is in line with the rest of Europe.

For the nobility and higher clergy, it is possible to reconstruct mortality with the help of prosopographic studies. For Denmark and Sweden, elite groups (bishops and royal councilors) appear to have had a considerably lower mortality (approximately 10–20 percent during the first outbreak of the plague) than the general population. In Norway, mortality was surprisingly high even among the elite. The explanation for this is uncertain: perhaps they lived in closer proximity to the common people than did their counterparts in the other countries. But the distinction may also be partly due to the collapse of the Norwegian state apparatus after the Black Death. The numbers of charters and letters, indicating activity among the upper strata of society in Scandinavia, continued to grow in Sweden and Denmark (due to conflicts over land and testaments) but, in Norway, the number declined sharply in the wake of the plague. This may be interpreted as the collapse of the relatively small elite in the country.[41]

Farm abandonment: The identification of abandoned farmsteads is a classic focus of research on the crisis of the late Middle Ages. We must be aware, however, that abandonment is not directly connected to the population decline that resulted from the plague, but rather reflects a restructuring of the settlement pattern, when people migrate to regions with better conditions for agriculture, leaving poor farms in the periphery.

During the crisis, three main periods can be identified: 1350/70 to 1420/50, which was marked by general farm abandonment and migration toward the more fertile plains in central Sweden and Denmark; 1420/50 to 1500/20, characterized by a burgeoning recultivation process; and 1500/20 continuing into the seventeenth century, an age of rapid new cultivation and expansion throughout the region, particularly in Sweden and Finland.

Land records are the main source, but charters and letters can also be used. From Denmark, there are some comprehensive land records from the fourteenth century, but fewer from the fifteenth century. From Norway and Sweden, there are a few early records, but some quite important ones from the fifteenth century. During the great upheaval after the Black Death, knowledge about many farmsteads fell away, and there is thus significant underreporting of abandoned farmsteads, even in detailed land registers.

Extensive research was done in all the Nordic countries in the 1970s, but it was compromised by the historians' inability to agree on a common method.[42] In Figure 7.2, a new compilation is presented. The Nordic countries have been divided into three main regions, showing different degrees of farm abandonment from 1350 to the lowest point in population decline, around 1450. In the plains, primarily in Denmark, as well as Sweden, up to one-third of farmsteads were abandoned; throughout most of the Nordic region, between one- and two-thirds of the farmsteads were abandoned; but in the Norwegian mountain regions and Swedish forest settlements, over two-thirds of the farmsteads were abandoned.

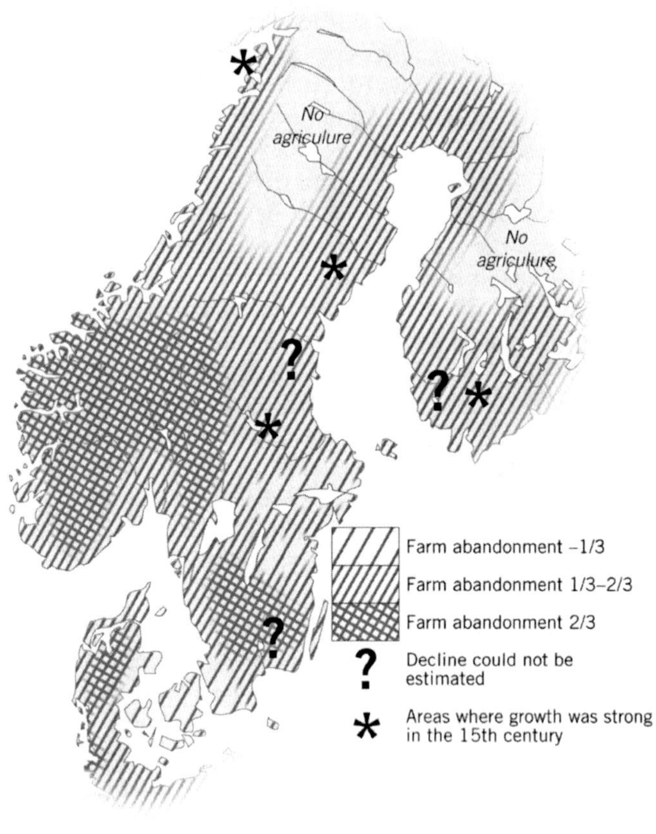

Figure 7.2 The approximate extent of farm abandonment in Scandinavia from 1349/1350 to the middle of the fifteenth century, in three levels.

Widespread farm abandonment did not begin until the 1360s and 1370s. The explanation for the delay has to be that until then there were many landless and poor people who could take over the vacant farmsteads. While farm abandonment continued for a long period and was most severe in the late fourteenth century, the nadir was not reached on the plains until around the 1420s, and in peripheral areas somewhat later. Thus, it was not only linked to the plague epidemics, but must also be explained by socio-economic factors, to which I will return.

The most exhaustive studies, which involve a battery of methods and materials, have been carried out in Norway. The mapped zones in Norway are the most reliable. A number of local investigations have been undertaken for Sweden, but much of the country has yet to be studied. Denmark presents the most difficult case. Not only does the lack of good land records from the fifteenth century create difficulties, but also much of the abandonment of individual farmsteads took place in large villages. The number of farms in a village could decrease considerably but, judging from written or archeological sources, the whole village still seems to be full of activity. The assumption of extensive abandonment in Jutland is primarily based on the abandonment of many medieval churches during the later Middle Ages. This is accompanied by the total abandonment of the seaboard of south-western Jutland after storm flooding in January 1362 wiped out 30 parishes in one fell swoop, and later on 44 parishes were recorded as swallowed by the sea. One important cause of the disaster (or this sequence of disasters) was that the reduced population was incapable of maintaining the sea defenses.

Population, 1450–1500: The extent of farm abandonment can be estimated by using a regressive method, extrapolating backward from well-supported population data for the sixteenth and seventeenth centuries. The total population, at its nadir around 1450, can be estimated at one million for all of Scandinavia, distributed as follows: Norway slightly under 0.2 million; Sweden approximately 0.4 million; Denmark 0.55 million or slightly more.[43] The decrease in Norway is thus around two-thirds of the population and in Sweden and Denmark around 40 percent.

The uncertainty of the figures makes it difficult to draw any extensive conclusions, other than that Norway was probably harder hit by depopulation. The peasants fled the mountain areas and went to more fertile areas or to the coast where they became fishermen-peasants. A redistribution occurred in all the countries from the peripheral areas to the more central plains and perhaps also from Norway to the other countries. This can also be substantiated by sources from the latter fourteenth century. For example, the Uppsala Cathedral land register from the 1370s states that a number of farms in the plain settlement around Uppsala, in eastern Sweden, had been taken back into cultivation, but at lower rent.

The recovery generally began in the second quarter of the fifteenth century, but especially in areas focused on production of fish, iron, and other commodities for sale and the areas situated on the agricultural frontier. The increased activity was manifested not only economically, but also by the erection of the first stone churches in these peripheral areas. In Finland, there was actually an increase in the population in the hundred years after 1350, even though the plague probably had reaped its victims in this region, too. By around 1500, the population had reached 0.2–0.3 million, perhaps having been half that in 1350.

Urbanization: The towns were affected relatively less than rural settlements. Here, again, Scandinavia cannot provide figures before the end of the Middle Ages, when the number of town dwellers in Denmark was around 10 percent; in Sweden, around 5 percent; in Norway, probably somewhat lower; and in Finland perhaps only 1–2 percent. Here 'towns' are counted as those with a privileged legal status. Most of them were extremely small in a European context, with a few hundred inhabitants. The larger towns, Bergen, Stockholm, Malmö, and Copenhagen, had only around 5,000 inhabitants each in the late Middle Ages.

Even though there are no data on the total urban populations throughout the Middle Ages, we can take the number of foundations of towns as a rough measure. In Denmark and Sweden, towns were founded in a rising wave from the eleventh to the early fourteenth century. This was followed by a break of about half a century, after the Black Death, before a new but lesser wave of towns started to be founded in the early fifteenth century; that is, before recultivation began. The sequence was somewhat different for Norway: towns were founded at an equally early stage, but the tide had already ebbed by the thirteenth century and no more new towns were founded until the end of the fifteenth century.[44] During the late Middle Ages, town dwellers in the two largest Scandinavian countries also emerged as a political power: in Sweden, an economically and politically significant axis was established between mining interests in central Sweden and the merchants around Lake Mälaren, particularly in Stockholm. In Denmark, the merchants in the towns around the Öresund Sound (Malmö and Copenhagen) emerged as significant power brokers.

STANDARD OF LIVING AND SOCIAL CONSUMPTION

Food: It would be reasonable to assume that the standard of living improved in the late Middle Ages. The size of farm fields and meadows increased and technical innovations boosted labor productivity. The advantages of rising production per household may initially have been offset by the feudal reaction, war, plunder, and increased taxes. But from the 1430s and 1440s onwards, taxes decreased and rents were at their lowest point. This, combined with the assured rise in labor productivity (production per capita), must have resulted in greater surpluses for the common people.

For the sixteenth century, the documentary material indicates that the majority of the population enjoyed a degree of prosperity. The source material from this period is abundant and there are many lists of the food and drink provided to hospital patients, soldiers, laborers on large farms, etc. It is also possible to make detailed budget calculations. People consumed a lot, including a great deal of meat and beer.

With respect to the Middle Ages, the documentary sources provide almost no opportunities to study how much people ate and drank and one must rely on indirect evidence. One such example is physical stature, which can be measured from skeletal remains.

A number of rural and urban cemeteries in Denmark and Sweden have been excavated and the results for thousands of individuals presented. Burial sites were often used over long periods, so the skeletons can only be roughly divided into two main periods: 1000–1350, and 1350–1500. Consequently, it is impossible to trace the changes during the hundred years before 1350, for instance. The interesting thing is that, between the High Middle Ages and the late Middle Ages, there is no difference in people's height.[45] The mean height for males was 172–173 cm. and for females 159–160 cm., but there was some regional variation. Men in northern Sweden were taller (173–174 cm.) than men in Scania and eastern Denmark (with a mean height of 170–172 cm.) while, in central Sweden and western Denmark, measurements were in between. There is a tendency for urban populations to be taller.

Several factors influence physical stature, including genetics (which may have determined the regional differences), but diet is the crux. Although there may have been a higher standard of living in the late Middle Ages, it seems that this did not mean better nutrition and a higher calorie intake, which would have promoted growth in stature; instead, perhaps, people were drinking more beer instead of milk and eating more fatty meat.[46] This is comparable to the situation in the seventeenth century through the early eighteenth, for which the documentary material clearly shows that the diet of most of the population steadily declined both in quality and quantity, and preserved skeletons show a corresponding diminution in stature.

Non-agrarian products: The late Middle Ages generally witnessed an increase in craft-based production. People bought more tools and other goods made of iron, and iron production in central Sweden increased. The price of iron and copper in Sweden fell, in the late Middle Ages, by as much as about 40 percent relative to the price of grain, mainly due to technological change and rising production.[47] Textile production in Flanders also found increased markets in Scandinavia. A general tendency, which has been studied with reference to Denmark, is that, in the towns, the number of crafts mentioned in documentary sources increases sharply after the middle of the fourteenth century. This increased consumption of non-agrarian products can also be substantiated by archeological material, such as combs made of bone, which become increasingly common in late medieval excavations. They are less worn and plainer than those of the High Middle Ages, which had been richly ornamented. This first period of 'mass consumption' also explains why towns recovered faster: the rising standard of living was accompanied by a relative shift from agrarian to non-agrarian production.[48]

Increased popular consumption can also be seen in developments such as the culture of carnival, which was embraced in the fifteenth century even in the north, and in the formation of parish guilds to organize festivities. The number of holidays increased, particularly because more local saints were now venerated and, by the end of the Middle Ages, total holidays—Sundays included—amounted to about 100 days a year.

Building activity: Another area in which non-agrarian consumption was manifested was building construction.[49] Because buildings, or their ruins, still remain, we can construct time series from the eleventh century onwards. Buildings can be dated in different ways, often through a combination of architectural history, archeology, dendrochronology, and also, in some cases, written documentation of building activity.

In general, construction followed the upswing in the eleventh to the thirteenth centuries. Scandinavia was filled with parish churches, wooden at first and later, starting in the twelfth century in southern and central Scandinavia, of stone. In Norway, wooden churches remained the most common type. Churches were followed by abbeys and cathedrals, in a rising wave of construction that began in the middle of the twelfth century. At this time, the towns also constituted major construction projects. Starting in the thirteenth century, an increasing number of castles were built of stone and wood throughout Scandinavia. Then came the plague, which put an end to most building projects.

Data on farmsteads in northern Scandinavia is an interesting supplementary source. These wooden buildings, with dovetailed corners (block buildings), were built so they could be disassembled and rebuilt, and the timber was such that they could stand for hundreds of years. The advent of dendrochronology allowed researchers to date old wooden buildings in rural Norway and Sweden, and it turned out that many were medieval, including some from the thirteenth century. A curve showing building construction would rise before the middle of the fourteenth century and suddenly plummet in the 1360s. For many years, there was no need to cut down trees for construction, as buildings and timber were available in abandoned farmsteads. From the mid-fifteenth century, the felling of timber for buildings started again.

There is one category that does not conform to the pattern, however, and it provides the key to the crisis of the late Middle Ages. Castles and fortifications have been inventoried and dated throughout much of Scandinavia, and they consistently reveal an upswing directly after the Black Death. Even though the population dropped by half, investments in strongholds and castle construction rose. The number of noble castles rose first,

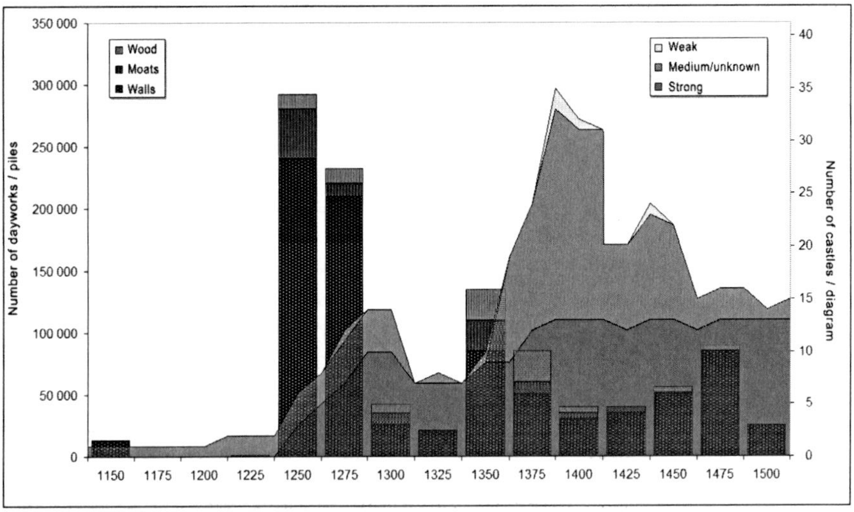

Figure 7.3 Royal castles in Sweden 1150–1525. Based on data by Christian Lovén, *Borgar och befästningar i det medeltida Sverige* (Stockholm: Kungl. Vitterhets-, historie- och antikvitetsakademien, 1996).

with royal castles following. Even though many of the new castles were relatively small, the result was a sharp increase in burdens placed on the people. The turnaround began in the 1430s with the major peasant revolts, whose object was frequently to burn and raze the castles, and the number of functioning castles fell sharply toward the end of the fifteenth century.

Other types of construction followed demographic and economic trends. Toward the end of the Middle Ages, once again trees were felled to construct dovetail-jointed buildings. Parish churches were expanded and given new vaulting, often beautifully painted. But it was not until well into the sixteenth century that the extensive construction of fortifications and castles began again, now under the aegis of the strong state.

CRISIS THEORY

At the outset I defined a 'major crisis' as a structural crisis, a challenge to the social structure. In this, the last section of this chapter, expansion, stagnation, catastrophe, dysfunctional reaction, and reconstruction will be placed along a timeline and illustrated by data from the survey above. Of these phases the last three can be counted as parts of a 'major crisis': catastrophe, reaction, reconstruction.

In my interpretation, every phase has an intrinsic dynamic that tends to carry over into the next phase. It will be argued that technological change can be seen as a process with an inner dynamic, and the same is valid for social change. Technological and social change also interact, favoring and hindering each other. To understand how, one has to separate the different phases in the long wave of expansion and contraction before new expansion.

At the beginning of our period, feudal institutions allowed the establishment of a new technological complex, though different in its components in different regions. For instance, instead of the wheeled plow and three-field rotation, as in northern France, the ard with a longer share and two-field rotation were, in much of Scandinavia, essential elements in a larger technical complex. Through a feedback mechanism, the new technological complexes allowed the development of a more sophisticated and encompassing social and institutional structure. But, by c. 1300, once this process had exhausted its possibilities, the first signs of stagnation became evident—although in some regions more than in others.

The middle of the fourteenth century saw the onset of the epidemics that hit a society where margins were narrower than before, starting a vicious circle of infighting and destruction. This turned into a major crisis, as defined earlier, and the whole social web was torn apart. Further economic expansion was contingent upon social and institutional transformations that were not to happen until the mid-fifteenth century. These new transformations were to pave the way for the next technological leap forward in the sixteenth century.

The Nordic historiography of the late medieval crisis was for a long time bogged down in the question of whether there had been a population decrease at all, but—when the reality of the crisis came to be accepted—the explanations adopted generally followed along the same lines as the European discussion. Causes such as population pressure and soil exhaustion, or the limitations imposed by social structures, have been widely discussed. The recurring epidemics are commonly used to explain the crisis.[50] I will refer to some of the European discussion that has inspired my interpretation of medieval Scandinavia. Many factors, for instance, technological change in non-agrarian sectors and the organization and lifestyle of the nobility, have been left out of the detailed survey above.

Expansion from c. 800/1000 to 1250/1350: This period of expansion consisted of several linked major transformations. My account draws on the multifaceted descriptions of this period presented by Georges Duby.[51]

One transformation was the new agrarian technological complex. I have pointed to several important elements, though none of them can be identified as the single most important. Heavier plowshares were combined with new crop-rotation systems. Iron-shod spades were of importance for ditching. New and more efficient axes facilitated clearances and assarting.

A second major transformation was the virtuous cycle that evolved between the increasing agrarian production, which allowed the expansion of trade and markets, and increasing non-agrarian output such as iron, which in turn was a crucial raw material for many of the new agrarian technologies.

A third transformation was a new social and legal structure that came to partly underpin a more complicated agrarian production. For instance, ditching, fencing, and the common field system were protected by regional and national laws. This new social structure also demanded a greater surplus production, to be paid over as regular taxes or land rent, otherwise it would not have been possible to erect castles, or maintain a heavy cavalry with its expensive war horses. The nobility began to enjoy a European lifestyle, which is livelily portrayed in contemporary chronicles and letters.

Of these three principal and interconnected transformations I consider the first to be the most important, as it affected the overwhelming majority of the population and production. Most of the evidence presented in the overview relates to this change of agrarian technology.

Partial stagnation from c. 1300 to c. 1350: The southern parts of Scandinavia witnessed a period with patches of stagnation, whereas in the north and the woodlands assarting and clearances continued right up to the Black Death. In the literature of technological change, distinctions are often made between invention, innovation (the first application of inventions), and the process of diffusion that brings about the widespread adoption of new techniques. The different elements of the technological complex seem to have been firmly in place by the thirteenth century and therefore the ability of this society to increase the productivity of the land must by then have reached a peak.[52]

But aside from purely technological factors, stagnation can also result from the presence of a rigid social structure that, in itself, became a hindrance to further technological development. We do not have sufficient sources to analyze the economic and technological viability of peasant farms but it is likely that the institutional characteristics of feudalism imposed constraints (even in the case of free peasants—in the form of taxes), which probably contributed to stagnation. In other words, stagnation was caused by reaching the limit imposed by current technology, on which there were institutional limitations, which themselves became a more important factor as the process of stagnation went on.

Nitrogen deficiency was one of the greatest problems in pre-industrial agriculture and has been much debated among agricultural historians.[53] For medieval Scandinavia, the sources do not show whether there was a tendency to overuse land resources. The process of expansion seems to have come to a halt by 1300 in the plains of southern Scandinavia, as in the Danish islands, and the abandonment of farms shows that it may even have gone into reverse. This was also enhanced by the crop failures of the 1310s, which hit much of north-western Europe, including Denmark. Land clearance continued in northern Scandinavia (northern Sweden and parts of Finland), the importance of which would appear later, when these areas were among the first to recover from the catastrophe of the epidemics.

It is difficult to tell how this stagnation affected the living standards of the population before the Black Death. The archeological material, mainly human skeletons from excavated graveyards, cannot be dated to a single century, and the written sources do not help us until the late fifteenth century.

The catastrophe from c. 1350 to c. 1370: In this chapter, we have shown how the epidemics attacked in two major waves. The first and worst came with three epidemics, 1348–50, 1358–61 and 1367–71. The total population was at least halved. Then followed three decades with less devastating epidemics and then, again, from c. 1400 to c. 1420, a further series of exceptionally severe epidemics followed, after which epidemics struck every decade, but with decreasing mortality.

The second epidemic, of around 1360, was throughout Europe (including Scandinavia), called 'the death of the children,' suggesting that it was possible for adults who survived the first epidemic to develop a degree of immunity. This can also explain why there was a periodicity, at least in Northern Europe, with an initial peak during the 20 years after the first epidemic and a second peak that began 20–30 years after that, when there were sufficient adults in the population who had not been exposed to the plague.

If the plague had been the sole cause of demographic and economic depression, then population ought to have started to increase after c. 1370, after the plague lost its initial virulence. The initial reduction of population—by creating vacant farms—offered those who survived, and the next generation, opportunities for marriage and rearing more children, which should, in turn, have led to a rapid increase in population. That this did not occur, and that the abandonment of farms and progressive depopulation continued into the second quarter of the next century, suggests that we have to identify other factors to explain a prolonged period of stagnation.

Dysfunctional societal reaction from c. 1350/1360 to c. 1430/1440: The disasters—the crop failures in the 1310s and the plague epidemics in 1349–71 in Scandinavia—were historical accidents, but they struck a stagnant society that showed its cultural ambitions through investment in forms of conspicuous consumption. Many of these, for example the building of parish churches and town houses, were abandoned immediately, at the beginning of the demographic crisis, while others, such as the noble lifestyle, came to play a part in the dysfunctional phase of the crisis. My interpretation of this period is influenced by the theory of Guy Bois concerning the 'feudal reaction.'[54] As Bois explains, the nobility, especially in their role as elite soldiers, had to maintain a high level of conspicuous consumption because it was through this that they defined themselves.[55]

The type of disease that struck during the Black Death caused an extremely high mortality rate among the common people, but the elite often escaped relatively lightly. A consequence of the plague was that it immediately created a relatively large surviving elite class, which was not inclined to reduce the costs of its lifestyle. Although the nobility in Scandinavia led a much simpler life than their counterparts in England and northern

France, their high level of consumption, and also the way they tried to defend it, tended to cause disruption to the economy.[56]

The problem the nobility faced was that of maintaining their income at a time of falling rents and an increasing abandonment of land. As the elite class, they were armed, organized, relatively more numerous than before the disaster and, by shifting towards a plunder-based economy, were able to pursue this dysfunctional process for some time. The establishment of a plunder-based economy can be seen in qualitative analyses of contemporary sources (chronicles, letters, poetry). But there are also quantitative measures, of which one of the most important is the number of castles. After the Black Death, the building of both royal and noble castles increased all over Scandinavia and served as a drag on economic recovery.

The dysfunctional phase in Scandinavia was exacerbated by the diffusion of the crisis from Germany to Scandinavia, as the nobility in politically stronger parts of Europe tried to compensate for their loss of income at home by attacking politically and militarily weak Scandinavia. This started as early as the 1330s in Denmark, after the famine, and spread to the rest of Scandinavia in the 1360s. Robber barons from Germany as well as Scandinavia were intent on defending their own high levels of consumption well-beyond what the depopulated land could now support. Once the German robber barons had been ousted from Scandinavia, with the establishment of the Union in the 1390s, the crown and nobility continued to maintain high levels of taxation.

Social and economic recovery and reconstruction from c. 1440/50 to c. 1520/30: The restructuring phase in Scandinavia was marked by peasant resistance and armed struggle that led to a redistribution of the wealth of society. My interpretation of this period is not inspired by any specific scholar, but similar analyses can be found in the literature. Even if the economy and the population were recovering, this phase was still a part of the 'major crisis' as I have defined it, as it was the outcome of the challenge to the pre-existing structures, and thus the dysfunctional phase continues into the phase of reconstruction that followed.

In documents from the early fifteenth century, peasants are found to claim that heavy taxes are forcing them to abandon their farms; we also have letters of complaint from peasant communities. Their protests soon developed into forms of resistance even as the growing depths of the crisis undermined the economic base of the elite. A shift of balance in the class struggle occurred, most marked in Sweden with its many free peasants.

The successful revolts, or rather armed struggle over state control, together with a number of minor actions and negotiations, marked the transition of the dysfunctional phase into a reconstruction phase, which entailed a change in production, consumption, and social structure. Redistribution of surplus production was crucial. Rents had already declined in the late fourteenth century, but the full effect of this had been counteracted by the plunder-based economy. When this feudal reaction came to a halt and taxes fell to a much lower level, the relative share of production that stayed with the peasant household tended to increase. Farmers could thus invest in agriculture, but also spend more on non-agrarian products. Mass consumption normally tends to have an impact on the development of industry and trades.

The first result was that agrarian production was rationalized by means of more effective tools and more extensive utilization of acreage. Many of these innovations, such as the scythe with a longer blade, demanded more iron, and the change went hand-in-hand with falling iron prices, because of technological improvements and a tremendous expansion in the Swedish mining districts in the late Middle Ages. The period was also characterized by technological changes in transport, printing, and military technology such as gunpowder, etc. The new advances of the sixteenth century thus occurred on a higher plane, in a process that started during the late medieval reconstruction of production.

Another important result was the changed pattern of consumption. Diets probably began to include more expensive products in Scandinavia, as they did elsewhere, even if we only have hints of the increased consumption of meat, beer, salt, butter, and other such products. The ox trade, which developed in Denmark and southern Sweden in the late fifteenth century, can be seen as a part of such a European change of food habits, and this trade became of utmost importance for Danish agriculture in the sixteenth century.

Large groups of the population also started to consume more non-agrarian products, which became a powerful incentive for increased trade and pre-industrial development during the later Middle Ages. These changed patterns of consumption were both an expression of a new distribution of the surplus production, which favored the broader masses, and at the same time a lever for a new and expanding economy.

Another important process was the gradually changing role of the state. Social structures and ideologies were created to counterbalance the social strife that grew out of the dysfunctional phase, which threatened to upset the stability of the social structure. A stronger state eventually developed, especially in Sweden. The king and the crown increasingly came to be looked upon as an institution that should support and protect the people. This transformation of the state was not concluded until the early sixteenth century, but it had its roots in the unruly but formative fifteenth century. In Denmark, with a strong high nobility, a similar new state and a new kingdom evolved during the late Middle Ages.

In addition, the changed power relationships between the classes brought other changes, such as a more important role for one segment of the local population, namely the peasants (or more precisely: the older male peasants), who came to control their local communities through their church economy and the local court, and even the regional district court. Together, these changes, on the state level, but also on the local level, can be described as a renegotiation of the social contract.

Late medieval society in Scandinavia was still a feudal society, in many respects brutal and oppressive, but of a different kind to the less organized feudalism of the High Middle Ages. This new organized feudalism was better adapted to the European economy that came to dominate the sixteenth century. The state could protect trade, and encourage clearances, by allowing tax reduction, but also by opening up the woodlands, declaring them to be state property and giving them over to colonists.

The economic expansion of the High Middle Ages eventually led to stagnation, at least in some economically important and well-populated regions. At the same time, a buoyant expansionary economy raised expectations. Among these we can see cathedral building as a prime example of the ambitions not only of the nobility but of society as a whole. When the population was reduced by half and overall production shrank drastically, the nobility could not easily reduce their consumption in line with their reduced incomes. For a time this caused a deepening of the crisis, which provoked a struggle that challenged the very structure of society and which resulted, in time, in the reconstruction of the social order. This 'new deal' could form the basis for a new expansion.

NOTES

1. *Webster's Unabridged Dictionary of the English Language* (New York: Random House, 2001), 477. For the intellectual history and etymology of the concept of 'crisis' in the West from the centuries B.C.E. until today, see Reinhart Koselleck, "Krise," in *Geschichtliche Grundbegriffe: Historisches Lexikon zur politisch-sozialen Sprache in Deutschland*, vol. 3 (Klett-Cotta, Stuttgart, 1982), who also discusses the 'inflation' of the concept during the last hundred years, when the term 'crisis' has been used for every possible negative change.
2. The Nordic region includes Finland and Iceland, but I do not discuss them to any great extent here.
3. Grenville Astill et al., "Introduction," in *Medieval Farming and Technology: The Impact of Agricultural Change in Northwest Europe*, eds. Grenville Astill and John Langdon (Leiden: Brill, 1997).
4. The volumes on the Middle Ages are: Denmark: Erland Porsmose, "Middelalder 1000–1536," *Det danske landbrugs historie*, vol. 1, ed. Claus Bjørn. (Odense: Landbohistorisk selskab, 1988). Norway: Ingvild Øye, "Landbruk under press 800–1350," in *Norges landbrukshistorie,* vol. 1, ed. Reidar Almås (Oslo: Det Norske Samlaget, 2002); Kåre Lunden, *Norges landbrukshistorie, 1350–1814, vol. 2, Frå svartedauden til 17. mai* (Oslo: Det Norske Samlaget, 2002). Norway in English: Ingvild Øye, "Farming Systems and Rural Societies ca. 800–1350," in *Norwegian Agricultural History*, ed. Reidar Almås (Trondheim: Tapir Academic, 2004); Kåre Lunden, "Recession and New Expansion 1350–1814," in *Norwegian Agricultural History*, ed. Reidar Almås (Trondheim: Tapir Academic, 2004). Sweden: Myrdal, J. *Det svenska jordbrukets Historia*, vol. 2, *Jordbruket under Feodalismen 1000–1700*. Stockholm: Natur och kultur/LT, 1999. For Southern Jutland: Bjørn Poulsen, "Middelalderens landbrug," in *Det sønderjyske landbrugs historie,* vol. 2, *Jernalder, vikingetid & middelalder*, ed. Per Ethelberg et al. (Haderslev: Haderslev Museum, 2003). However, I have drawn primarily from my own book from 1999, and Öye's and Poulsen's interpretations

are similar. For a synthesis of Danish economic history in English, see Nils Hybel and Bjørn Poulsen, *The Danish Resources c. 1000–1550: Growth and Recession* (Leiden: Brill, 2007). Indispensable for every survey of Scandinavian medieval history is the encyclopedia: *Kulturhistoriskt lexikon för nordisk medeltid*, vol. 1–22 (Allhem: Malmö 1956–1978).

5. Chris Wickham, *Framing the Early Middle Ages: Europe and the Mediterranean 400–800* (Oxford: Oxford University Press, 2005), 292–293.
6. Øye "Landbruk," 384; Johan Åstrand, *En medeltida skogsgård vid Markaryd* (Växjö: Smålands museum, 2007).
7. Gert Magnusson, "Lapphyttan: An Example of Medieval Iron Production," in *Medieval Iron in Society*, ed. Gert Magnusson (Stockholm: Jernkontoret and Riksantikvarieämbetet, 1985); Gert Magnusson, "Bergslagen," in *Sveriges nationalatlas: Stockholm—Mälarregionen*, ed. Ulf Sporrong (Bromma: Sveriges nationalatlas (SNA), 2008), 63 and personal comment from Gert Magnusson. It is interesting that Sweden, together with Germany, was in the forefront of iron technology in the High Middle Ages.
8. *Scandinavia*: Myrdal, *svenska*, 146–149 and Poulsen "Middelalderens landbrug," 501–507. Detailed presentation of the argument, e.g. Guy Bois, *The Crisis of Feudalism: Economy and Society in Eastern Normandy c. 1300–1550* (Cambridge: Cambridge University Press, 1984) for Normandy, and for Germany: Werner Rösener, *Agrarwirtschaft, Agrarverfassung und ländliche Gesselschaft im Mittelalter* (München: R. Oldenbourg, 1992), 107–109 on *Raubrittertum*/'the robber barons.'
9. On social structure in general see references in note 4, specifically on the decline of slavery and manorial structure see Erik Ulsig, "Højmiddelalderens danske godssystem set i et europæisk sammenhang," *Bol og by* 1996: 2 and articles in Thomas Lindkvist and Janken Myrdal, eds., *Trälar: Ofria i agrarsamhället från vikingatid till medeltid* (Stockholm: Nordiska museet, 2003) and on villages/farms see for Norway: Ingvild Øye, "Norway in the Middle Ages: Farms or Hamlets and Villages too?" *Ruralia* 3 (2000) and for Denmark: Erland Porsmose, *De fynske landsbyers historie* (Odense: Odense University, 1987).
10. Table 7.1 and Figure 7.1 are based on: General: Eva Österberg, "Social aspects," in *Desertion and Land Colonization in the Nordic Countries c. 1300–1600*, ed. Svend Gissel (Stockholm: Almqvist & Wiksell International, 1981), 210–212. Denmark: Carsten Porskrog Rasmussen "Kronens gods," in *Danmark i senmiddelalderen*, eds. Per Ingesman and Jens Villiam Jensen (Aarhus: Aarhus universitetsforl., 1994); Carsten Porskrog Rasmussen, "Adelens godsrigedom 1490–1660," in *Riget, magten og æren: Den danske adel 1350–1660*, eds. Per Ingesman and Jens Villiam Jensen (Aarhus: Aarhus universitetsforl., 2001); Anders Bøgh "Bundones Regis," in *Konge, kirke og samfund: De to øvrighedsmagter i dansk senmiddelalder*, ed. Agnes S. Arnórsdóttir et al. (Århus: Aarhus Universitetsforlag, 2007); Hybel and Poulsen, *Danish Resources*, 400. Sweden: Lars-Olof Larsson "Jordägofördelningen i Sverige under Gustav Vasas regering," *Scandia* 51 (1985); Lars-Olof Larsson, *Kalmarunionens tid från drottning Margareta till Kristian II* (Stockholm: Rabén Prisma: 1997), 123–124. Norway: Rolf M. Hagen et al., *Norsk historisk atlas* (Oslo: Cappelen, 1980), map 65 A–E; Bjørkvik, H. *Aschehougs Norgeshistorie*, vol. 4, *Folketap og sammenbrudd 1350–1520*, Oslo: Aschehoug, 1996, 63, 83, 228. Finland: Rainer Fagerlund "Den äldre Vasatiden 1523–1617," in *Finlands historia*, vol. 2, ed. Märtha Norrback (Esbo: Schildt, 1993), 14.
11. Myrdal, J. "Den folkliga klasskampen före Engelbrektsupproret," *Folkets historia* (1993/2), and also Myrdal, *svenska*, 173–180.

12. Concerning these attempts to tie the peasants to the land, see Erik Ulsig "Befolkningsfald, landgildefald og jordpriser i det 14. Århundrede," *Historisk Tidsskrift* 101 (2001): 13, and Janken Myrdal "Fritagningen i Skånings-Åsaka 1445," *Folkets historia* (1985/1).
13. Dahlerup, T. *Gyldendal og Politikens Danmarkshistorie* vol 6, *De fire stænder 1400–1500*. Copenhagen: Gyldendalske boghandel, 1989, 90–99; Jeppe Büchert Netterstrøm, "Feud, Protection, and Serfdom in Late Medieval and Early Modern Denmark (c. 1400–1600)," in *Forms of Servitude in Northern and Central Europe: Decline, Resistance and Expansion*, eds. Paul Freedman and Monique Bourin, (Turnhout: Brepols, 2005), 369–370.
14. Perry Anderson, *Lineages of the Absolutist State* (London: NLB, 1975), 196–197 points at the difference between Western Europe with a strong state and the disappearance of serfdom, and Eastern Europe with a weaker state and an increased serfdom in the late Middle Ages and sixteenth century. This is also true for Denmark where the state for a long time was much weaker than in Sweden. Not until the late seventeenth century did a strong and absolutist state come to be established in Denmark.
15. Svend Gissel, "Rents and Other Indicators," in *Desertion and Land Colonization in the Nordic Countries c. 1300–1600*, ed. Svend Gissel (Stockholm: Almqvist & Wiksell International, 1981), 151 map over main rent in different products in Scandinavia around 1500.
16. Rent reduction: Norway: Lunden, *Norges*, 47–48; Denmark: Ulsig, "Befolkningsfald," 2–5; Ulsig, *Århusundersøgelsen—under Det nordiske Ødegårdsprojekt* (Aarhus: Aarhus Universitetsforl. 2004), 53–57; Hybel and Poulsen, *Danish Resources*, 192, 312. Sweden: Myrdal, *svenska,* 144–145 and Myrdal, *Digerdöden, pestvågor och ödeläggelse* (Stockholm: Sällsk. Runica et mediævalia, 2003), 193–194; Alf Ericsson, *Attungen—ett medeltida fastighetsmått* (Uppsala: Swedish University of Agricultural Sciences, 2007), 37–38.
17. For an overview of Scandinavian field systems in a European context, with a map over field systems in all of Europe in the seventeenth century, see Karl-Erik Frandsen, "Studies of Field Systems and Agrarian Structures in some European Regions," in *Agrarian Systems in Early Modern Europe*, ed. Britt Liljewall (Stockholm: Nordiska museet, 1999).
18. Generally on stock farming see references in note 4, and also Janken Myrdal, *Boskapsskötseln under medeltiden*, (manuscript).
19. Regarding the plunge churn as a technological innovation, see Janken Myrdal, "The Plunge Churn from Ireland to Tibet," in *Food and Drink and Travelling Accessories*, eds. Alexander Fenton and Janken Myrdal (Edinburgh: John Donald, 1988).
20. Johan Söderberg, "Prices and Economic change in Medieval Sweden," *Scandinavian Economic History Review* 55 (2007): 143–146, 148. The price curve has since been slightly reworked in a project with Johan Söderberg and collaborators.
21. Warren Ault, *Open-Field Farming in Medieval England: A Study of Village By-Laws* (London: Allen & Unwin, 1972), 46–48. Regarding village herders as a consequence of the dissolution of slavery, see Guy Bois, *The Transformation of the Year One Thousand: The Village of Lournand from Antiquity to Feudalism* (Manchester and New York: Manchester University Press, 1992), 120.
22. Janken Myrdal, "Source Pluralism and a Package of Methods," in *Methods and the Medievalist: Current Approaches in Medieval Studies*, ed. Marko Lamberg et al. (Newcastle: Cambridge Scholars, 2008), 145–155.
23. In addition to the syntheses in agrarian history mentioned in note 4, this sequence of events has been described in Janken Myrdal, *Medeltidens*

åkerbruk: agrarteknik i Sverige ca 1000 till 1520 (Stockholm: Nordiska museet, 1985); Janken Myrdal, "The Agricultural Transformation of Sweden, 1000–1300," in *Medieval Farming and Technology: The Impact of Agricultural Change in Northwest Europe*, eds. Grenville Astill and John Langdon, 147–172 (Leiden: Brill, 1997); Bjørn Poulsen, "Agricultural Technology in Medieval Denmark," in *Medieval Farming and TechnologyL The Impact of Agricultural Change in Northwest Europe*, eds. Grenville Astill and John Langdon (Leiden: Brill, 1997); Annette Hoff, *Recht und Landschaft: der Beitrag der Landschaftsrechte zum Verständnis der Landwirtschafts- und Landschaftsentwicklung in Dänemark ca. 900–1250* (Berlin: De Gruyter, 2006), published in Danish 1997.

24. Georges Duby, *Rural Economy and Country Life in the Medieval West* (London: Edward Arnold, 1968), 20, 107–108, 112, and 349 about a growing stratification caused by expensive investments in iron implements; Georges Duby, *The Early Growth of the European Economy: Warriors and Peasants from the Seventh to the Twelfth Century* (London: Weidenfeld, 1974), 14–16 about increased use of iron in northern Europe; 194–198 about iron used first for cutting tools and then for plows. Other historians, especially in France, have also emphasized this change, e.g. Bois, *Transformation*, 97.
25. Sweden and Scania: a diagram in Myrdal, *svenska*, 56 and an incomplete list in Janken Myrdal, "Swedish Plough Shares 500–1800," in *Tools and Traditions: Studies in European Ethnology Presented to Alexander Fenton*, ed. Hugh Cheape (Edinburgh: National Museums of Scotland, 1993). Denmark, Germany, and Czechia: Grith Lerche, *Ploughing Implements and Tillage Practices in Denmark from the Viking Period to About 1800: Experimentally Substantiated* (Herning: Kristensen, 1994), 208–220. Czechia 800–900: Jan Klápště and Anne Nissen Jaubert, "The Diffusion of the Plough," in *Archaeology of Medieval Europe*, vol. 1, *Eight to twelfth centuries AD*, ed. James Graham-Campbell (Aarhus: Aarhus University Press, 2007), 99. Shares from Sweden: c. 400–600: 0.35; c. 500–600: 0.3; c. 600: 0.4; c. 800–1000: 0.25; c. 800–1000: 0.3; c. 1000–1400: 0.4; c. 1100–1300: 0.6; c. 1100–1300: 0.25; c. 1100–1300: 0.3; c. 1100–1300: 1.0; c. 1200–1400: 1.4; c. 1200–1500: 1.2; c. 1300–1500: 0.6; c. 1300–1500; 0.9 and c. 1300–1500: 1.1 (two rusty shares attached to each other); c. 1450–1500: 0.5; c. 1450–1500: 1.75. Scania: c. 1100–1200: 0.3; c. 1100–1350: 0.5; c. 1100–1350: 0.45; c. 1100–1350: 0.95. Denmark: c. 800–900: 0.25; c. 1200–1300: 2.1; c. 1200–1500: 1.5; c. 1360: 4.0; c. 1400–1500: 1.3; c. 1400–1500: 3.0; c. 1500–1600: 1.0. Germany: c. 800–900: 0.3; c. 800–1000: 1.3; c. 1430: 1.5; c. 1430: 1.4. Czechia: c. 800–900: 0.2–0.5; c. 1400–1500: 2.0.
26. Öye, "Landbruk," 332–333; Öye, "Farming Systems," 121.
27. R. E. F. Smith, "Some Tillage Implement Parts in the Zausailov Collection, National Museum of Finland," *Tools & Tillage* 4, 4 (1983): 206–207, 212–214 table with weights; cf Jean-Marie Pesez, "Outils et techniques agricoles du monde medieval," in *Pour une archéologie agraire*, ed. Jean Guilai (Paris: A. Colin, 1991), 134–140 with archeological examples of this change to larger shares from Russia, the Baltic, and Germany, but without presenting weights.
28. Lerche, *Ploughing Implements*, 187–192. For two large shares, with an original weight of around 2.5 kg, the wear was respectively 0.4 kg and 0.16 kg per hectare; for three smaller shares, with an original weight around 1.2 to 1.6 kg, the wear was 0.14 to 0.15 kg per hectare.
29. E.g. Per Lagerås, *The Ecology of Expansion and Abandonment: Medieval and Post-medieval Agriculture and Settlement in a Landscape Perspective* (Stockholm: National Heritage Board, 2007) develops a new method for

analyzing pollen diagrams, sorting those of high quality and measuring significant change. With this method he can also identify the late medieval crisis, when the new farms on clearances in the woodland are again abandoned after the plagues.

30. Transforming this to hectoliters per hectare is not possible for Sweden and Denmark, because we do not know the area of the land sown. (In the sixteenth century such calculations could be made, but still without precision.) The seed was often the scarce resource rather than the available land area, and thus the medieval farmer (and also the early modern farmer) looked to the yield:seed ratio as the return on investment. Estimates of yield:seed ratio can often be found already in the accounts; calculations made by the bailiff or his accountant.
31. For Sweden: Myrdal, *åkerbruk*, 261. For Schleswig: Poulsen, "landbrug," 675. For Norway: Lunden, "Recession," 165 writes that the yield:seed ratio in medieval Norway was around 4:1, but this is a sheer guess not at all based on the sources.
32. From c. 1540–1680 there are a large number of detailed manorial accounts in Sweden, and estimates can be made for yield, amount of fallow, etc. See Lotta Leijonhufvud, *Grain Tithes and Manorial Yields in Early Modern Sweden: Trends and Patterns of Production and Productivity c. 1540–1680* (Uppsala: Swedish University of Agricultural Sciences, 2001) for three manors on the plains in eastern central Sweden, covering about 25 years per manor, with yield:seed ratios of around 5:1–6:1, and for eight manors in other parts of Sweden covering about 35 years per manor, but on these the yield:seed ratios were only around 3.5:1–4.5:1.
33. A total registration of documents on the medieval rent and land assessment in central parts of Sweden in Ericsson, *Attungen*, 22–23, 38–40. He has also identified a possible decrease in the yield:seed ratio from late thirteenth century.
34. This has been noted from other parts of Europe; e.g. for England, see John Hatcher and Mark Bailey, *Modelling the Middle Ages: The History and Theory of England's Economic Development* (Oxford: Oxford Univeristy Press, 2001), 58.
35. Joseph R. Strayer, ed., *Dictionary of the Middle Ages*, vol. 1–13 (New York: Scribner, 1982–1989) s.v. 'Peter's Pence'; *Lexikon des Mittelalters*, vol. 1–9 (München: Deutscher Taschenbuch, 2002), s.v. 'Peterspfennig.' Peter's Pence in the Nordic countries, see note 36.
36. Estimates of the population and the decline that occurred in the late Middle Ages are a central topic of discussion in medieval history research, and Scandinavia is no exception. For Denmark: Hybel and Poulsen, *Danish Resources*, 382 cite a high figure—2 million in 1350—but that presupposes a late medieval decline for which there is scant evidence, cf. Jørgen Elsøe Jensen, *Gensidig afhængighed—en arv fra fortiden: Danmarks middelaldebyer—et vidnesbyrd om spredning av vestlig civilization* (Odense: Syddansk Universitetsforlag, 2010), 168 who gives figures for Denmark closer to my estimates: 1.1 million 1350 and 0.7 million 1400. Otherwise, the figures relating to population and farm abandonment are based on the agricultural syntheses I mentioned at the outset (especially Lunden, and Poulsen), as well as, for Denmark: Svend Gissel, "Forskning i den senmiddelalderlige agrarkrise," in *Danmark i senmiddelalderen*, eds. Per Ingesman and Jens Villiam Jensen (Aarhus: Aarhus universitetsforl., 1994). For Sweden: Lennart Andersson Palm, *Livet, kärleken och döden: Fyra uppsatser om svensk befolkningsutveckling 1300–1850* (Göteborg: L. Palm, 2001) and Myrdal, *Digerdöden*. For Norway: Liv Marthinsen, "Maksimum og minimum.

Norsk busetnadshistorieetter DNØ," in *Innsikt og utsyn: festskrift til Jørn Sandnes, Kjell Haarstad et al. eds.* (Trondheim: Historisk institutt, NTNU, 1996); Bjørkvik, Folketap, 35. For Finland: Eljas Orrman, "Ett försök att beräkna bebyggelsens omfattning i Finland vid utgången av högmedeltiden," in *Innsikt og utsyn : festskrift til Jørn Sandnes,* Kjell Haarstad et al. eds., (Trondheim: Historisk institutt, NTNU, 1996). Regarding the number of churches in Denmark: Anders Andrén, *Den urbana scenen: Städer och samhälle i det medeltida Danmark* (Malmö: Liber Förlag, 1985) 72, 87, 134. In Norway: Knut Helle, K. *Aschehougs Norges historie,* vol. 3, *Under kirke og kongemakt 1130–1350,* Oslo: Aschehoug 1995, 55. In Sweden: Palm, *Livet,* 50. Regarding Peter's Pence and the Black Death: Myrdal, *Digerdöden,* 32–38, and Janken Myrdal, "The Black Death in the North," in *Living with the Black Death,* ed. Lars Bisgaard and Leif Søndergaard (Odense: University Press of Southern Denmark, 2009), 75–77.

37. A rather fierce discussion has been going on between the heretics who believe the disease during the Black Death and also during the Justinian pandemic in the sixth century to be some other pathogen, and the orthodox view identifying it as *Yersinia pestis.*
38. Table 7.2 is based on: N. Germany/Lübeck: Jürgen Hartwig Ibs, *Die Pest in Schleswig-Holstein von 1350 bis 1547/48: eine sozialgeschichtliche Studie über eine wiederkehrende Katastrophe* (Frankfurt am Main: Lang, 1994). (Ibs, *Pest,* 206–207 also presents a table of plagues in all of Northern Germany, including Hamburg, etc.) Denmark: Lars Bisgaard, "Plague in Denmark," in *Living with the Black Death,* ed. Lars Bisgaard and Leif Søndergaard (Odense: University Press of Southern Denmark, 2009). Sweden: Janken Myrdal, "The Forgotten Plague: The Black Death in Sweden," in *When Disease Makes History: Epidemics and Great Historical Turning Points,* ed. Pekka Hämäläinen (Helsinki: Yliopistopaino, 2006), 155. Norway: Ole Jørgen Benedictow, *Svartedauen og senere pestepidemier i Norge: Pestepidemiens historie i Norge 1348–1645* (Oslo: Unipub, 2002), 103; *Kulturhistoriskt lexikon för nordisk medeltid,* vol. 13, s.v. 'Pest', col. 238–246. Iceland: Árni Daníel Júliusson, *Bønder i pestens tid: Landbrug, godsdrift og social konflikt i senmiddelalderens islandske bondesamfund* (Copenhagen: Københavns Universitet, 1996), 111–122. England: John Hatcher, *Plague, Population and the English Economy 1348–1530* (London: Macmillan, 1977), 32, 57.
39. Júliusson, *Bønder, 122.*
40. Jean-Noël Biraben, *Les hommes et la peste en France et dans les pays européens et méditerranéens,* vol. 1–2 (Paris: Mouton, 1975–1976), and analyzed in Myrdal, "Forgotten Plague," 156–157. I have used data from Biraben's five regions in northwestern, Northern and Central Europe; 1/ England/ Scotland/ Ireland; 2/ Belgium/ The Netherlands/ Luxembourg; 3/ Germany/ Austria/ Bohemia/ Switzerland; 4/ Poland/ The Baltic countries; 5/ Scandinavia. To identify major epidemics the following criteria have been used: those that were recorded in at least three of these regions and in more than six 'places.' The major epidemics for this part of Europe, and according to Biraben's catalogue, are: 1348–50, 1359–61, 1363–65, 1370–72, 1401–02, 1419–21, 1427; 1437–39, 1450–52, 1464–65, 1472–74, 1482, 1484, 1487; 1493–96. On the regional and local level his dataset cannot be used without firmer investigations.
41. Myrdal, "Black Death," 78–81. The numbers of charters and letters per annum in Norway fell from around 50–60 to around 20–30 after 1350 until the end of the century. In Sweden and Denmark, on the other hand, they rose from around 100 to 150–200 in the decades after the Black Death.
42. Svend Gissel et al. ed., *Desertion and Land Colonization in the Nordic countries c. 1300–1600* (Stockholm: Almqvist & Wiksell international,

1981) and criticism of this project in Myrdal, *Digerdöden*, 168–183. Swedish scholars counted only deserted farms firmly documented among the scarce sources, whereas Norwegian scholars tried to reconstruct a 'medieval population maximum' by combining a number of sources including place names, archeological remains, etc. as well as written documents. Thus the Swedish investigations tended to give many fewer deserted farms than the real number, while the Norwegians ran the risk of giving numbers that were too high. Since the 1980s, methods have been further developed, both in Norway and Sweden, and often pointed at numbers closer to the Norwegian investigations than to the Swedish. Danish scholars took an intermediate position.

43. Cf note 35. Colin McEvedy and Richard Jones, *Atlas of World Population History* (London: Lane, 1978), 51 give for Scandinavia a decrease from 1.75 to 1.25 million between 1350–1450. This is an underestimation of the growth before 1350, and the decrease thereafter. There are also estimates of a steeper decline in Sweden, for instance Palm, *Livet*, 28 with an estimated Norwegian decline for Sweden, about 70 percent. A more conservative estimate in Myrdal, *Digerdöden*, 245, with an estimated decline of 40 percent or slightly more.
44. Andrén, *urbana scenen*, 32 and Sven Lilja, *Städernas folkmängd och tillväxt: Sverige (med Finland) ca 1570-tal till 1810-tal* (Stockholm: Stads- och kommunhistoriska institutet, 1996), 25–26.
45. See Jesper Boldsen, "Height Variation in Denmark A.D. 1100–1988," in *Populations of the Nordic Countries: Human Population Biology from the Present to the Mesolithic*, ed. Elisabeth Iregren and Rune Liljekvist (Lund: Institute of Archaeology, 1993); Caroline Arcini, *Health and Disease in Early Lund: Osteo-pathologic Studies of 3,305 Individuals Buried in the First Cemetery Area of Lund 990–1536* (Lund: Lund University, 1999) and Lars Werdelin, Janken Myrdal, and Sabine Sten, "Patterns of Stature Variation in Medieval Sweden," *Hikuin* 27 (2000). In Denmark and Scania the material is from six rural and four urban places, from Sweden three rural and three urban—and the most extensive material is from the town Lund in Scania. Only cemeteries and layers with a dating closer than 200–300 years have been included and only those with more than 10 individuals. Nikola Koepke and Joerg Baten, "Biological Standard of Living in Europe During the Last Two Millennia," *European Review of Economic History* 9 (2005) have made a survey of all of Europe, and of the above mentioned they only refer to Arcini, *Health*. They have split up the material into centuries, but I do not understand how they have managed to do this. They show a serious dip in the thirteenth century, which I cannot reconstruct from the data. Neither of the articles from Scandinavia quoted here has any indication of this, quite the contrary: "no chronological trends with regard to bone length in the material from Lund," Arcini, *Health*, 70, is a typical statement. The real fall in stature—especially among men—in Scandinavia came in the seventeenth century, but that is another story; see A. Gustafsson, L. Werdelin, B. Tullberg, and P. Lindenfors, "Stature and Sexual Stature Dimorphism in Sweden, From the 10th to the End of the 20th Century," *American Journal of Human Biology* 19 (2007).
46. Cf. for England Christopher Dyer, *Everyday Life in Medieval England* (London: Hambledon, 1994), 98.
47. Söderberg, "Prices," 131–134, 148.
48. For a discussion of this process, see Johan Söderberg, *Sveriges ekonomiska och sociala historia: Medeltiden* (Malmö: Liber-Hermod, 1996), 121–135;

Myrdal, *svenska*, 153–166; Poulsen, "landbrug," 567–569, 578–579; and Hybel and Poulsen, *Danish Resources*, 264–265.

49. For all building categories, including wooden houses, see Myrdal, *svenska*, 160, 393, where also evidence from Finland and Eastern Denmark has been included. Christian Lovén, *Borgar och befästningar i det medeltida Sverige* (Stockholm: Kungl. Vitterhets-, historie- och antikvitetsakademien, 1996) is the main source for castles in medieval Sweden. There are some European parallels, see Christopher Dyer, *Standards of Living in the Later Middle Ages: Social Change in England c. 1200–1520* (Cambridge: Cambridge University Press, 1989), 102 for England.
50. Cf. for England Hatcher and Bailey, *Modelling*, for the older discussion Nils Hybel, *Crisis or Change: The Concept of Crisis in the Light of Agrarian Structural Reorganization in Late Medieval England* (Aarhus: Aarhus University Press, 1989). Nordic discussion see e.g. Porsmose, "Middelalder" who points out population increase together with high taxes as main causes; Lundén, *Norges* emphasizes recurring epidemics as the decisive factor for population decrease. Myrdal, *svenska* and also Poulsen, "landbrug" are close to the theory advanced in this article.
51. Duby, *Rural Economy* and Duby, *Early Growth*.
52. It was only in the sixteenth century that a new phase of intensification in land use and a new complex of different 'small' interconnected innovations took place, see Janken Myrdal, "The Agrarian Revolution Restrained: Swedish Agrarian Technology in the 16th Century in a European Perspective," in *Agrarian Systems in Early Modern Europe*, ed. Britt Liljewall (Stockholm: Nordiska museet, 1999).
53. Robert Allen, "The Nitrogen Hypothesis and the English Agricultural Revolution: A Biological Analysis," *Journal of Economic History* 68 (2008) who emphasizes biology; Harry Kitsikopoulos, "Convertible Husbandry vs. Regular Common Fields: A Model on the Relative Efficiency of Medieval Field Systems," *Journal of Economic History* 64 (2004) is more inclined to point at managerial practice as a decisive factor.
54. The interpretation given in Bois, *Crisis* as well as by his revisiting of the subject in Guy Bois, *La grande dépression médiévale XIVe et XVe siècles: La precedent d'une crise systémique* (Paris: Presses universitaires de France, 2000) where he ascribes a larger role to the plague.
55. Bois, *Crisis*, 299.
56. The lifestyle of the nobility has not been my main topic, but it can be studied through many excellent excavations of castles, for instance the military stronghold Boringholm erected in the 1360s in Jutland, Denmark where a number of high status objects were found, such as imported pottery from France, bronze spur, drinking glass, see Jan Kock and Else Roesdahl, *Boringholm–en østjysk træborg fra 1300-årene* (Højbjerg: Jysk Arkæologisk Selskab, 2005). This was a typical after-the-plague castle, and the lifestyle of those living at the castle shows no definite signs of restrained conspicuous consumption.

BIBLIOGRAPHY

Allen, R. "The Nitrogen Hypothesis and the English Agricultural Revolution: A Biological Analysis." *Journal of Economic History* 68 (2008): 182–210.

Anderson, P. *Lineages of the Absolutist State*. London: NLB, 1975.

Andrén, A. *Den urbana scenen: Städer och samhälle i det medeltida Danmark*. Malmö: Liber Förlag, 1985.

Arcini, C. *Health and Disease in Early Lund: Osteo-pathologic Studies of 3,305 Individuals Buried in the First Cemetery Area of Lund 990–1536*. Lund: Lund University, 1999.
Astill, G., J. Langdon, and J. Myrdal. "Introduction," in *Medieval Farming and Technology: The Impact of Agricultural Change in Northwest Europe*, edited by G. Astill and J. Langdon, 1–10. Leiden: Brill, 1997.
Åstrand, J. *En medeltida skogsgård vid Markaryd*. Växjö: Smålands Museum, 2007.
Ault, W. *Open-Field Farming in Medieval England: A Study of Village By-Laws*. London: Allen & Unwin, 1972.
Benedictow, O. J. *Svartedauen og senere pestepidemier i Norge: Pestepidemiens historie i Norge 1348–1645*. Oslo: Unipub, 2002.
Biraben, J.-N. *Les hommes et la peste en France et dans les pays européens et méditerranéens*, vol. 1–2. Paris: Mouton, 1975–1976.
Bisgaard, L. "Plague in Denmark," in *Living with the Black Death*, edited by L. Bisgaard and L. Søndergaard, 85–112. Odense: University Press of Southern Denmark, 2009.
Bjørkvik, H. *Aschehougs Norgeshistorie*, vol. 4, *Folketap og sammenbrudd 1350–1520*. Oslo: Aschehoug, 1996.
Bøgh, A. "Bundones Regis," in *Konge, kirke og samfund: De to øvrighedsmagter i dansk senmiddelalder*, edited by A. S. Arnórsdóttir, P. Ingesman and B. Poulsen, 117–150. Århus: Aarhus Universitetsforlag, 2007.
Bois, G. *The Crisis of Feudalism: Economy and Society in Eastern Normandy c. 1300–1550*. Cambridge: Cambridge University Press, 1984.
Bois, G. *The Transformation of the Year One Thousand: The Village of Lournand from Antiquity to Feudalism*. Manchester and New York: Manchester University Press, 1992.
Bois, G. *La grande dépression médiévale XIVe et XVe siècles: La precedent d'une crise systémique*. Paris: Presses universitaires de France, 2000.
Boldsen, J. "Height Variation in Denmark A.D. 1100–1988," in *Populations of the Nordic Countries: Human Population Biology from the Present to the Mesolithic*, edited by E. Iregren and R. Liljekvist, 52–60. Lund: Institute of Archaeology, 1993.
Dahlerup, T. *Gyldendal og Politikens Danmarkshistorie* vol 6, *De fire stænder 1400–1500*. Copenhagen: Gyldendalske boghandel, 1989.
Duby, G. *Rural Economy and Country Life in the Medieval West*. London: Edward Arnold, 1968.
Duby, G. *The Early Growth of the European Economy: Warriors and Peasants from the Seventh to the Twelfth Century*. London: Weidenfeld, 1974.
Dyer, C. *Everyday Life in Medieval England*. London: Hambledon, 1994.
Dyer, C. *Standards of Living in the Later Middle Ages: Social Change in England c. 1200–1520*. Cambridge: Cambridge University Press, 1989.
Ericsson, A. *Attungen—ett medeltida fastighetsmått*. Uppsala: Swedish University of Agricultural Sciences, 2007.
Fagerlund, R. "Den äldre Vasatiden 1523–1617." In *Finlands historia*, vol. 2, edited by M. Norrback, 11–124. Esbo: Schildt, 1993.
Frandsen, K.-E. "Studies of Field Systems and Agrarian Structures in some European Regions," in *Agrarian Systems in Early Modern Europe*, edited by B. Liljewall, 146–196. Stockholm: Nordiska museet, 1999.
Gissel, S. "Rents and Other Indicators," in *Desertion and Land Colonization in the Nordic Countries c. 1300–1600*, edited by S. Gissel, 143–171. Stockholm: Almqvist & Wiksell International, 1981.
Gissel, S, "Forskning i den senmiddelalderlige agrarkrise," in *Danmark i senmiddelalderen*, edited by P. Ingesman and J. Villiam Jensen, 25–39. Aarhus: Aarhus universitetsforl, 1994.

Gissel, S. et al., eds. *Desertion and Land Colonization in the Nordic countries c. 1300–1600*. Stockholm: Almqvist & Wiksell international, 1981.

Gustafsson, A., L. Werdelin, B. Tullberg, and P. Lindenfors. "Stature and Sexual Stature Dimorphism in Sweden, From the 10th to the End of the 20th Century." *American Journal of Human Biology* 19 (2007): 861–870.

Hagen, R. M. , et al. *Norsk historisk atlas*. Oslo: Cappelen, 1980.

Hatcher, J. *Plague, Population and the English Economy 1348–1530*. London: Macmillan, 1977.

Hatcher, J. and M. Bailey. *Modelling the Middle Ages: The History and Theory of England's Economic Development*. Oxford: Oxford University Press, 2001.

Helle, K. *Aschehougs Norges historie, vol. 3, Under kirke og kongemakt 1130–1350*. Oslo: Aschehoug 1995.

Hoff, A. *Recht und Landschaft: der Beitrag der Landschaftsrechte zum Verständnis der Landwirtschafts- und Landschaftsentwicklung in Dänemark ca.900–1250*. Berlin: De Gruyter, 2006.

Hybel, N. *Crisis or Change: The Concept of Crisis in the Light of Agrarian Structural Reorganization in Late Medieval England*. Aarhus: Aarhus University Press, 1989.

Hybel, N. and B. Poulsen. *The Danish Resources c. 1000–1550: Growth and Recession*. Leiden: Brill, 2007.

Ibs, J. H. *Die Pest in Schleswig-Holstein von 1350 bis 1547/48: eine sozialgeschichtliche Studie über eine wiederkehrende Katastrophe*. Frankfurt am Main: Lang, 1994.

Jensen, J. E. *Gensidig afhængighed—en arv fra fortiden: Danmarks middelaldebyer—et vidnesbyrd om spredning av vestlig civilization*. Odense, Syddansk Universitetsforlag, 2010.

Júliusson, Á. D. *Bønder i pestens tid: Landbrug, godsdrift og social konflikt i senmiddelalderens islandske bondesamfund*. Copenhagen: Københavns Universitet, 1996.

Kitsikopoulos, H. "Convertible Husbandry vs. Regular Common fields: A Model on the Relative Efficiency of Medieval Field Systems." *Journal of Economic History* 64 (2004): 462–499.

Klápště, J. and A. Nissen Jaubert. "The Diffusion of the Plough," in *Archaeology of Medieval Europe. 1, Eight to twelfth centuries AD*, edited by J. Graham-Campbell, 98–99. Aarhus: Aarhus University Press, 2007.

Kock, J. and E. Roesdahl. *Boringholm—en østjysk træborg fra 1300-årene*. Højbjerg: Jysk Arkæologisk Selskab, 2005.

Koepke, N. and J. Baten. "Biological Standard of Living in Europe During the Last Two Millennia." *European Review of Economic History* 9 (2005): 61–95.

Koselleck, R. "Krise," in *Geschichtliche Grundbegriffe: Historisches Lexikon zur politisch-sozialen Sprache in Deutschland*, vol. 3, 617–650. Klett-Cotta, Stuttgart, 1982.

Kulturhistoriskt lexikon för nordisk medeltid, vol. 1–22. Allhem: Malmö, 1956–1978.

Lagerås, P. *The Ecology of Expansion and Abandonment: Medieval and Post-medieval Agriculture and Settlement in a Landscape Perspective*. Stockholm: National Heritage Board, 2007.

Larsson, L.-O. "Jordägofördelningen i Sverige under Gustav Vasas regering." *Scandia* 51 (1985): 61–90.

Larsson, L.-O. *Kalmarunionens tid från drottning Margareta till Kristian II*. Stockholm: Rabén Prisma, 1997.

Leijonhufvud, L. *Grain Tithes and Manorial Yields in Early Modern Sweden: Trends and Patterns of Production and Productivity c. 1540–1680*. Uppsala: Swedish University of Agricultural Sciences, 2001.

Lerche, G. *Ploughing Implements and Tillage Practices in Denmark from the Viking Period to About 1800: Experimentally Substantiated.* Herning: Kristensen, 1994.

Lexikon des Mittelalters, vol. 1–9. München: Deutscher Taschenbuch, 2002.

Lilja, S. *Städernas folkmängd och tillväxt: Sverige (med Finland) ca 1570-tal till 1810-tal.* Stockholm: Stads- och kommunhistoriska institutet, 1996.

Lindkvist, T. and J. Myrdal, eds. *Trälar: Ofria i agrarsamhället från vikingatid till medeltid.* Stockholm: Nordiska museets förl., 2003.

Lovén, C. *Borgar och befästningar i det medeltida Sverige.* Stockholm: Kungl. Vitterhets-, historie- och antikvitetsakad, 1996.

Lunden, K. *Norges landbrukshistorie, 1350–1814, vol. 2, Frå svartedauden til 17. mai.* Oslo: Det Norske Samlaget, 2002.

Lunden, K. "Recession and New Expansion 1350–1814," in *Norwegian Agricultural History,* edited by R. Almås, 144–232. Trondheim: Tapir Academic, 2004.

Magnusson, G. "Lapphyttan: An Example of Medieval Iron Production," in *Medieval Iron in Society,* edited by G. Magnusson, 21–60. Stockholm: Jernkontoret and Riksantikvarieämbetet, 1985.

Magnusson, G. "Bergslagen," in *Sveriges nationalatlas: Stockholm—Mälarregionen,* edited by U. Sporrong, 61–66, Bromma: Sveriges nationalatlas (SNA), 2008.

Marthinsen, L. "Maksimum og minimum: Norsk busetnadshistorieetter DNØ," in *Innsikt og utsyn: festskrift til Jørn Sandnes,* edited by K. Haarstad, et al., 144–182. Trondheim: Historisk institutt, NTNU, 1996.

McEvedy, C. and R. Jones. *Atlas of World Population History.* London: Lane, 1978.

Myrdal, J. *Boskapsskötseln under medeltiden,* (manuscript).

Myrdal, J. "Fritagningen i Skånings-Åsaka 1445." *Folkets historia* (1985/1): 2–7.

Myrdal, J. *Medeltidens åkerbruk: agrarteknik i Sverige ca 1000 till 1520,* Stockholm: Nordiska museet, 1985.

Myrdal, J. "The Plunge Churn from Ireland to Tibet," in *Food and Drink and Travelling Accessories,* edited by A. Fenton and J. Myrdal, 111–137. Edinburgh: John Donald, 1988.

Myrdal, J. "Den folkliga klasskampen före Engelbrektsupproret." *Folkets historia* (1993/2): 14–28.

Myrdal, J. "Swedish Plough Shares 500–1800," in *Tools and Traditions: Studies in European Ethnology Presented to Alexander Fenton,* edited by H. Cheape, 72–75. Edinburgh: National Museums of Scotland, 1993.

Myrdal, J. "The Agricultural Transformation of Sweden, 1000–1300," in *Medieval Farming and Technology: The Impact of Agricultural Change in Northwest Europe,* edited by G. Astill and J. Langdon, 147–172, Leiden: Brill, 1997.

Myrdal, J. *Det svenska jordbrukets historia.* vol. 2, *Jordbruket under Feodalismen 1000–1700.* Stockholm: Natur och kultur/LT, 1999.

Myrdal, J. "The Agrarian Revolution Restrained: Swedish Agrarian Technology in the 16th Century in a European Perspective," in *Agrarian Systems in Early Modern Europe,* edited by B. Liljewall, 96–145. Stockholm: Nordiska museet, 1999.

Myrdal, J. *Digerdöden, pestvågor och ödeläggelse.* Stockholm: Sällsk. Runica et mediævalia, 2003.

Myrdal, J. "The Forgotten Plague: The Black Death in Sweden," in *When Disease Makes History: Epidemics and Great Historical Turning Points,* edited by Pekka Hämäläinen, 141–186. Helsinki: Yliopistopaino, 2006.

Myrdal, J. "Source Pluralism and a Package of Methods," in *Methods and the Medievalist: Current Approaches in Medieval Studies,* edited by M. Lamberg, J. Keskiaho, E. Räsänen, and O. Timofeeva, 134–158. Newcastle: Cambridge Scholars, 2008.

Myrdal, J. "The Black Death in the North," in *Living with the Black Death*, edited by L. Bisgaard and L. Søndergaard, 47–62. Odense: University Press of Southern Denmark, 2009.

Netterstrøm, J. B. "Feud, Protection, and Serfdom in Late Medieval and Early Modern Denmark (c. 1400–1600)," in *Forms of Servitude in Northern and Central Europe: Decline, Resistance and Expansion*, edited by P. Freedman and M. Bourin, 369–384. Turnhout: Brepols, 2005.

Orrman, E. "Ett försök att beräkna bebyggelsens omfattning i Finland vid utgången av högmedeltiden," in *Innsikt og utsyn: festskrift til Jørn Sandnes*, edited by K. Haarstad, et al., 125–143. Trondheim: Historisk institutt, NTNU, 1996.

Österberg, E. "Social Aspects," in *Desertion and Land Colonization in the Nordic Countries c. 1300–1600*, edited by S. Gissel, 205–229. Stockholm: Almqvist & Wiksell International, 1981.

Øye, I. "Norway in the Middle Ages: Farms or Hamlets and Villages Too?" *Ruralia* 3 (2000): 12–23

Øye, I. "Landbruk Under Press 800–1350," in *Norges landbrukshistorie*, vol. 1, *4000 f.Kr—1350 e.Kr*, edited by R. Almås, 215–408. Oslo: Det Norske Samlaget, 2002.

Øye, I. "Farming Systems and Rural Societies ca. 800–1350," in *Norwegian Agricultural History*, edited by R. Almås, 80–140, Trondheim: Tapir Academic, 2004.

Palm, L. A. *Livet, kärleken och döden: Fyra uppsatser om svensk befolkningsutveckling 1300–1850*. Göteborg: L. Palm, 2001.

Pesez, J.-M. "Outils et techniques agricoles du monde medieval," in *Pour une archéologie agraire*, edited by J. Guilai, 131–164. Paris: A. Colin, 1991.

Porskrog Rasmussen, C. "Kronens gods," in *Danmark i senmiddelalderen*, edited by P. Ingesman and J. Villiam Jensen, 69–87. Aarhus: Aarhus universitetsforl., 1994.

Porskrog Rasmussen, C. "Adelens godsrigedom 1490–1660," in *Riget, magten og æren: Den danske adel 1350–1660*, edited by P. Ingesman and J. Villiam Jensen, 497–523. Aarhus: Aarhus universitetsforl., 2001.

Porsmose, E. 1987. *De fynske landsbyers historie*. Odense: Odense University, 1987.

Porsmose, E. "Middelalder 1000–1536." In *Det danske landbrugs historie 1: 4000 f.Kr—1536*, edited by C. Bjørn, 205–406. Odense: Landbohistorisk selskab, 1988.

Poulsen, B. "Agricultural Ttechnology in Mmedieval Denmark," in *Medieval Farming and Technology: The Impact of Agricultural Change in Northwest Europe*, edited by G. Astill and J. Langdon, 115–146. Leiden: Brill, 1997.

Poulsen, B. "Middelalderens landbrug," in *Det sønderjyske landbrugs historie*, vol. 2, *Jernalder, vikingetid & middelalder*, edited by P. Ethelberg, N. Hardt, B. Poulsen, and B. Sørensen, 375–433, 458–712, Haderslev: Haderslev Museum, 2003.

Rösener, W. *Agrarwirtschaft, Agrarverfassung und ländliche Gesselschaft im Mittelalter*. München: R. Oldenbourg, 1992.

Smith, R. E. F. "Some Tillage Implement Parts in the Zausailov Collection, National Museum of Finland." *Tools & Tillage* 4, 4 (1983): 205–215.

Söderberg, J. *Sveriges ekonomiska och sociala historia: Medeltiden*. Malmö: Liber-Hermod, 1996.

Söderberg, J. "Prices and Economic Change in Medieval Sweden." *Scandinavian Economic History Review* 55 (2007): 129–152.

Strayer, J. R., ed. *Dictionary of the Middle Ages*, vol. 1–13. New York: Scribner, 1982–1989.

Ulsig, E. "Højmiddelalderens danske godssystem set i et europæisk sammenhang." *Bol og by* 2 (1996): 8–26.
Ulsig, E. "Befolkningsfald, landgildefald og jordpriser i det 14. Århundrede." *Historisk Tidsskrift* 101 (2001): 1–16.
Ulsig, E. *Århusundersøgelsen—under Det nordiske Ødegårdsprojekt*. Aarhus: Aarhus Universitetsforl, 2004.
Webster's Unabridged Dictionary of the English Language. New York: Random House, 2001.
Werdelin, L. J. Myrdal, and S. Sten. "Patterns of Stature Variation in Medieval Sweden." *Hikuin* 27 (2000): 293–306.
Wickham, C. *Framing the Early Middle Ages: Europe and the Mediterranean 400–800*. Oxford: Oxford University Press, 2005.

8 Central Europe

Grzegorz Myśliwski

INTRODUCTORY REMARKS

The Concept

The fourteenth century was a time of dramatic demographic and economic crisis in Western Europe. Did an economic crisis, parallel or comparable to the circumstances that affected fourteenth-century Western Europe, occur in Central Europe? Or, more broadly, what were the directions of development in this region of Europe at the time of intense crisis in the West? Answering these questions is the aim of the present article. Before we can do so, it is necessary to outline the general economic trends in the region under study between about 1200 and about 1500 in order to set these trends in the context of one another, and then to reach definitive conclusions. This study begins with a basic sketch of the political and geographic circumstances of the economic history of Central Europe. Thereafter, it characterizes the source material that has shaped the work of economic historians concerned with the region, and discusses the most important views on the later medieval economic conditions in this region produced by these historians. Part 2, "Population," depicts the broad contours of demographic transition, with particular focus on the rural population of Central Europe. Part 3, "Agriculture," deals with agriculture—the most important economic sector before the Industrial Revolution. Part 4, "Towns and the Urban Branches of Economic Activity," includes some basic data on urbanization, as well as on the most important branches of the urban economy. Finally, in part 5, "Was there an Economic Crisis in Later Medieval Central Europe?," I present the main historiographical views concerning the state of the Central European economies during the later Middle Ages, and I offer my own comments about those views.

Territory, Climate, and Natural Environment

During the later Middle Ages, Central Europe encompassed the territories of three monarchies: Bohemia, Poland, and Hungary. Between 1200

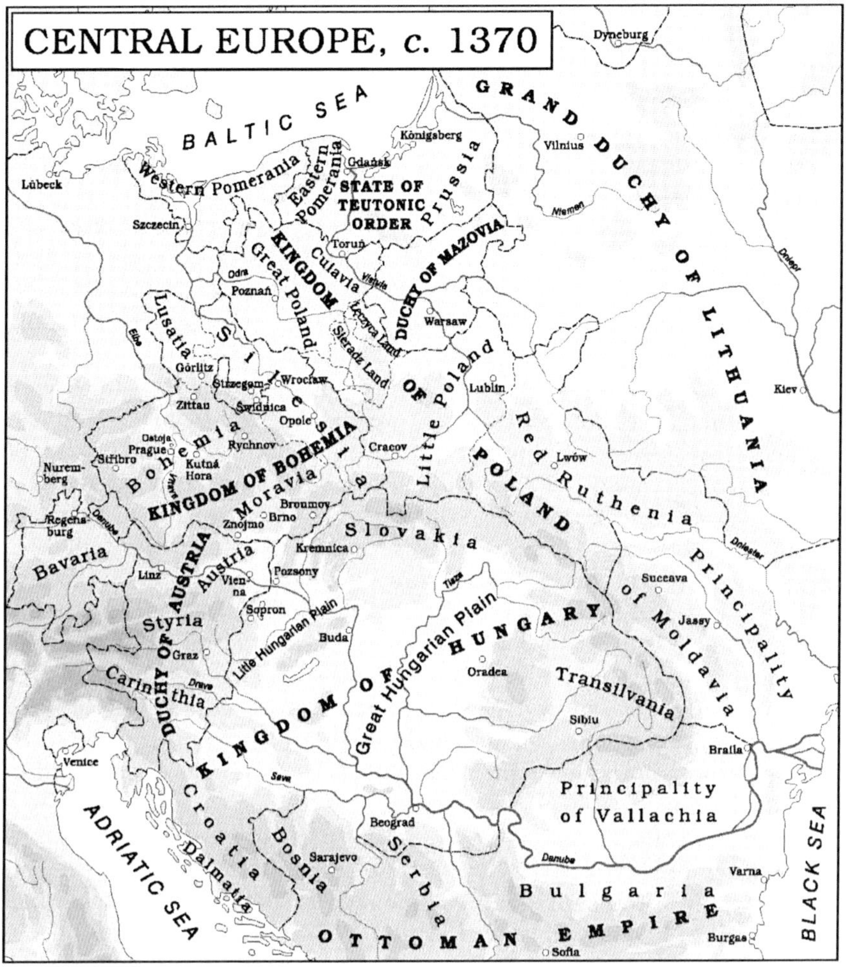

Figure 8.1 Central Europe c. 1370.

and 1500, the political boundaries of these three kingdoms changed many times.[1] In the course of the fourteenth century, the rulers of the Kingdom of Bohemia—which consisted of two core regions, Bohemia and Moravia—annexed two other territories, Lusatia and Silesia, acquired in the period 1319–68, and 1327–35, respectively. Silesia remained part of the Czech Kingdom almost continuously, that is to say, from about 1335 to 1469, and again from 1490 to 1526, with a 21-year interruption (1469–90), when this border region became part of the Hungarian monarchy.

In contrast to the Czech and Hungarian kings, the rulers of Poland had to overcome the long-lasting political disintegration of the country. Until 1320, one Polish duke, Władysław the Short, managed to re-unite several

Piast regions—Great Poland, Little Poland, Cuiavia, and central Poland; but other territories—Silesia, the backward Masovia, and the maritime Eastern Pomerania (which had been subjugated by the Teutonic Order in 1309)—remained outside the reunited Polish Kingdom. Soon thereafter (culminating in 1366), the restored Polish monarchy annexed Red Ruthenia. Eastern Pomerania, densely populated and economically developed, was regained only in 1466.

The Hungarian state embraced the largest territory among all these three monarchies. It encompassed not only Pannonia (the Little and the Great Hungarian Plains), and the economically important Slovakia and Transylvania, but also some Adriatic countries: Croatia, a part of Serbia (including Belgrade), and, for a time, Dalmatia (between 1358 and 1409).

The **climate** of Central Europe is typical for a frontier zone between a mild, maritime zone (Poland, Bohemia, western Hungary), and a continental zone, with its substantial temperature swings causing frost and draught (Hungary to the east of the Danube, including the Great Hungarian Plain and Transylvania). The relatively large territory of medieval Hungary was also influenced by the Mediterranean climate, above all in its Adriatic borderlands. During the period under study, the **climatic conditions** underwent a transition.[2] Between 950 and 1250, the Medieval Climate Optimum (that is to say, a warm and a wet climate) prevailed. From 1250 onwards, the climate deteriorated with the onset of the Little Ice Age, which lasted until mid-nineteenth century. The temperatures dropped, the weather was characterized by frequent changes, and long-lasting heavy rains alternated with droughts, which led to the crop failures and famines—for example, the Great Famine of 1315–22.

In terms of **soils**, Central Europe varied widely, though soil conditions for the development of agriculture were better in the Czech and the Polish areas than in the Kingdom of Hungary.[3] Bohemia and Moravia had loess (a kind of loamy soil) as well as chalky and marly soils—specifically in the north-central Bohemia region, in some parts of southern Bohemia, around the city of Olomouc, and in southern Moravia. In Silesia we find black earths around the city of Wrocław (Breslau in German), and loess soils, to the west of the Odra River. Mediocre sandy and clay soils prevailed throughout the rest of Polish territories. Only in some parts of Poland were there humus soils, black earths, and loess. Apart from Cuiavia, and some sites in Great Poland—in both cases, provinces and sites bordering on Pomerania—those relatively good soils were situated in the southeastern and southern region of Little Poland. With regard to the Kingdom of Hungary, fertile soils (loess and black earths) prevailed in Transdanubia, that is, the region west of the Danube. The Great Hungarian Plain had mainly pastures and meadows. Slovakia and Transylvania were hilly and mountainous, and were sparsely inhabited apart from the valleys. Certainly, all the countries had also alluvial soils, because of a dense network of rivers.

Central Europe has always been a heavily irrigated region, a fact that encouraged settlement and facilitated communication and transportation. Its geographically differentiated territory includes numerous watersheds of very large and large rivers, such as the Danube, the Tisza, the Vltava (in part the same as the Elbe), the Odra, and the Vistula, as well as the watersheds of their tributaries and of numerous smaller rivers.

The Sources

Between 1200 and 1500, literacy and the written culture proliferated throughout Central Europe.[4] The overall quantity of written documentation increased, reaching its peak during the fourteenth and the fifteenth centuries. The Czech royal chancery of the Luxemburg dynasty issued over 10,000 charters and documents between 1310 and 1437.[5] In Hungary a similar number survives from the thirteenth century, and as many as 300,000 were issued between 1301 and 1526.[6] We do not have equivalent estimates of the written output in the Polish territories, but the quantity of documents here must have been lower. However, the edited sources relating to the individual regions of late medieval Poland indicate—though presumably at lower quantities of output—the same direction of development as we can observe in the Bohemian and Hungarian Kingdoms.[7] What complicates our picture is the fact that many of the late-medieval sources have not been inventoried thus far.

The Central European written culture has left behind a variety of types of primary sources.[8] All the countries of the region—especially their natural environment and their economies—were described succinctly by a French friar, around 1308, in the *Anonymi descriptio Europae Orientalis*.[9] Numerous charters and deeds record grants of land, rents in kind, and judicial and economic immunities (i.e. "exemptions of a geographic area, a natural resource, a person, or a group from customary access by rulers and their agents, and from the exercise of power which that access makes possible").[10] Demographic research needs to rely on these uncertain sources, because censuses were first taken in the Central European countries very late, during the second half of the eighteenth century.[11] In the absence of census data, sources very useful for demographic aggregates include the ecclesiastical registers of Church taxes—Peter's Pence in Poland, and the tithe in Hungary, both compiled in the fourteenth century—and the tax register of the Hungarian royal treasury, produced in 1494.[12] Also useful are the collections of customary laws and statutes.[13] The medieval judicial system has given us many valuable sources, such as, in Bohemia, the royal courts books (*registra regalia*);[14] and, in other countries, the numerous books of noble courts (*libri terrestres*) and of village courts, as well as books of town councils and of court assessors (*libri scabinalia*).

The economic historian should also take into consideration books of conveyances, such as, for example, the famous Silesian *Henryków Book*, produced between 1268 and shortly after 1310, and the land register (*Landbuch*) of the Duchy of Wrocław issued in 1353[15]; and manorial surveys from, among others, the Kingdoms of Bohemia and of Hungary (and known in those two contexts under the names *Urbar* or *urbář*).[16] The oldest such register dates from 1338. We must especially note two surveys of the estates belonging to the most eminent Czech family, the Rožemberk, one from the fourteenth, the other from the sixteenth century; and to add fragments of a few merchant accounting books, mostly belonging to the merchants of Czech cities.[17]

Most of these types of sources are pertinent to the medieval countryside but they vary in their information. Some shed light on the legal framework of economic activity; others, on the size of arable fields; yet others, on the number of inhabitants, or on the collected rents in kind and money. In sum, they offer us random samples that enable to carry out case studies in the future. In the meantime, the historian is forced to reach conclusions according to the principle *pars pro toto*. However, what is typical for the majority of the Central European primary sources dating from the later Middle Ages is an almost total absence of data usable for general statistical analysis.

Development or Crisis in Central Europe: State of Research

Two main points of view on the economic situation of Central Europe in the later Middle Ages have dominated in the historiography. Most historians have been of the opinion that the Central European countries underwent a major economic transition and modernization between the twelfth and the fifteenth centuries.[18] Consequently, in contrast to fourteenth-century Western Europe, there was no serious crisis on the scale of the entire region. In order to prove this viewpoint, Marian Małowist, one of its foremost exponents, has considered all the main branches of the society and economy. He outlined a trend of population growth in rural and urban colonization, in the mining industry, and in long-distance trade. Małowist has emphasized the integration of the Central European economy with the Western economy from the fourteenth century onwards. That integration resulted both from the commercial activity of the Polish, Czech, and Hungarian merchants, and from the socio-economic crisis in the West which made Central Europe an attractive area for expansion. The affluent merchants and entrepreneurs began to immigrate into Bohemia, Poland, and Hungary, and to invest large sums of money in trade and in mining. This immigration and investment accelerated the economic development of all these countries during the late Middle Ages.

However, not all historians have shared this optimistic point of view. In the 1950s, František Graus, then the chief Marxist historian in Czech Republic, considered the proliferation of money rent in the European countryside (including the Czech countryside, to which he paid special attention) as a main reason for the outbreak of so-called 'crisis of the fourteenth century.[19] In other words, it was the monetization and the commercialization of socioeconomic relations that led to the deepening of social inequality, to the intensification of class struggle at many levels, and to religious ferment. Despite the fact that each of these phenomena occasionally appeared earlier, their greater territorial extent and intensity during the fourteenth century caused a crisis of the feudal world, including the Bohemian lands.

On the other hand, a different historiographical current, one not limited to Czech historians, has emphasized the economic deceleration and the 'turbulence' of the Czech economy at the time of the 'Hussite revolution,' between 1419 and 1436.[20] Despite some differences between the individual researchers—some of whom argued that the political and religious isolation of the country was temporary and partial—there has been no doubt that the anti-Hussite 'crusades' must have been damaging to the Czech economy. Despite that economy's partial recovery after 1436, it turned out to be impossible to make up for wasted time. The 'Golden Age' of the Czech economy was in the past. Recently, some doubts have also been expressed concerning economic growth in the Kingdom of Poland. Marian Dygo has pointed out that economic development slowed down in the fifteenth century.[21] According to him disequilibrium between labor and land emerged between 1400 and 1500. The disequilibrium was caused principally by the end of technological progress in the course of the fourteenth century. This disproportion between labor and land was increased in some regions by a simultaneous abandonment of arable fields. As a consequence, a labor deficit in many areas occurred. Moreover, some non-agricultural branches of the economy, such as lead mining, metallurgy, the glass industry, and construction, stagnated, or, worse, were affected by several kinds of specific adverse changes. Quite recently Dygo has made an ambitious attempt to assess the economic situation in Central Europe in its entirety, while also taking into account the transitions in the Western European economy during the late Middle Ages.[22] He maintained his critical views on the fifteenth-century Polish economy, pointing out that it had failed to adapt to the more demanding needs of the Western European consumers (for beef, freshwater fish, wheat, and wine). On the other hand, Dygo maintains, the Czech and the Hungarian economies underwent transition, and became able to export more expensive, even luxury-type, commodities to the West, in response to Western demand.

To answer the question whether the Central European economy was in crisis, or whether Central Europe experienced prosperity during the later Middle Ages, one must investigate the history of the main factors of production, and of those main branches of the economy which could enhance economic growth and development.

POPULATION

Aggregate Figures and Population Densities

Due to the randomness of the data, demographic calculations, especially concerning aggregates, can only be carried out with great approximation and uncertainty. And, needless to say, demographic research and its results have always resulted in much controversy. To avoid misunderstandings and distortions resulting from territorial changes of the three major political units with which we are principally concerned, some historians have focused not on entire countries, but on their core regions. Following this methodology, I have decided to treat Silesia as a separate entity. Because of the absence of data concerning the individual regions of medieval Hungary (except for Slovakia[23]), I am constrained to cite demographic figures on the scale of the kingdom as a whole (save for its Adriatic territories).

To proceed, let me begin by comparing the overall land areas of the major political units in the region. The surface of Bohemia and Moravia was 79,000 square kilometers; of Upper and Lower Silesia (together), about 40,000 square kilometers; of the two main regions of Poland (Great and Little Poland) and Masovia (again, together), about 146,000 square kilometers; but of Hungary, in its entirety, 330,000 square kilometers.[24] Next, I turn to overall estimated population levels for these major political units—noting here that, unavoidably, some of the figures derive from slightly different periods. The results are presented in Table 8.1. Data in this table are compiled from various secondary works, in some of which the hypothetical population levels seem to be overstated. However, it is difficult to give a correct global population level with absolute certainty. The only solution seems to be to cite all the current assessments.

Regarding Silesia, there are gaps in our knowledge about the period spanning the entire fifteenth century, apart from a random sample from the archdeaconry of Opole.[25] Due to the fact that during that century the historical circumstances of this region were similar to the developments in the core Czech areas, we may suppose the same demographic trends in Silesia as in the Czech Kingdom in general. Assuming that in the course of the fourteenth century the population of Bohemia and Moravia increased by 40 percent, one can estimate the maximum population of Silesia around 1400 at around 690,000. Because of the dramatic events of the fifteenth century,[26] one may further infer that Silesia's population fell down by a degree similar to the decrease throughout Bohemia-Moravia. Mindful of the possible differences in the demographic dynamics of Bohemia-Moravia, one can nevertheless estimate the population of Silesia around the year 1500 at between 300,000 and 580,000.

Table 8.1 Population in Central Europe (millions)

Years and centuries	*Bohemia and Moravia*[1]	*Silesia*[2]	*Great Poland, Little Poland, Masovia*[3]	*Hungary*[4]	*All the territories*
10–11th century	0.68	0.25–0.26	0.69	0.6	2.22–2.23
c. 1200	1.28	0.32–0.34	(above 0.69)	1.5	above 3.79–above 3.81
the 1st half of the 14th century	above 2.0 (c. 1300)	0.49 (c. 1340)	1.25 (c. 1340)	2.0 (c. 1300)	above 5.74
c. 1400	2.0–2.8	0.49–0.69 (?)	below 1.5[5]	3–3.5 (c. 1430)	6.99–8. 49
c. 1500	1.7	0.30 (?)–0.58 (?)	2.64	3.5–5.0	8.14–9.92

[1] Apart from the data concerning the Czech regions in and around the fourteenth century, see Eduard Maur, "Obyvatelstvo českých zemí ve středověku," in *Dějiny obyvatelstva českých zemí* (Praha : Mladá Fronta, 1996), 52; Eduard Maur, "Les pays tchèques," in *Histoire des populations de l'Europe*, ed. Jean Pierre Bardet and Jacques Dupâquier (Paris: Fayard, 1997), 542. Regarding the fourteenth century, E. Fügedi observed that "The demographic situation at the starting point [around 1300] seems to be fairly clear, though not free of contradictions. The population in the provinces of the Crown of Bohemia [that is, excluding Silesia] ranged from between two and three million, but certainly did not reach three million"; Fügedi, "The Demographic Landscape," 48. This is why I have decided to use the statement "above two million".

[2] Karol Maleczyński, ed., *Historia Śląska*, vol. 1, part 1, 159; Karol Maleczyński, ed., *Historia Śląska*, vol. 1, part 2 (Wrocław: Zakład Narodowy im. Ossolińskich, 1961), 250.

[3] See Gieysztor, "La Pologne," 566–67; for the figures roundabout 1500, see Bogucka and Samsonowicz, Dzieje, 120.

[4] The data presented here follows: Andorka, "La Hongrie," 548 (levels in the tenth century, and around 1200), 550 (levels around 1500); Fügedi, "The Demographic Landscape," 49 (fourteenth-century levels); Engel, *The Realm*, 269 (levels around 1430), 330 (levels around 1500).

[5] Henryk Samsonowicz, "Społeczeństwo w Polsce ok. 1400 roku," in *Polska około roku 1400*, ed. Wojciech Fałkowski (Warszawa: Neriton, 2000) 11. I use the term "below," because Samsonowicz includes Cuiavia in his estimate of the population of Masovia.

In conjunction, these two sets of data—surface areas and the aggregate population levels of the major political units of Central Europe—bring us to the subject of population densities. Estimates of this subject have led to serious discrepancies in the literature. Taking these discrepancies as a point of departure, I decided to calculate the population densities on my own. The results are presented in Table 8.2.

As we can see from these figures, the demographic history of Central Europe has its own course and particularity. These region-wide differences stemmed from several factors: migrations that occurred later than in the West; a partially distinct chronology of natural disasters; and several

Table 8.2 Population Density (Persons per Square Kilometer)

Years or centuries	*Bohemia and Moravia*[1]	*Silesia*[2]	*Great Poland, Little Poland, Masovia*[3]	*Hungary*[4]
10th–11th century	8.7 (c. 1050)	6.2 (c. 1000)	4.7 (c. 1000)	1.8
ca. 1200	13	8–8.5	above 4.7	4–5
the 1st half of the 14th century	25.3 (c. 1300)	10.8 (c. 1340)	8.5 (c. 1340)	5–7 (c. 1300)
c. 1400	25.3–35.4	10.8–17	below 10.2	9.1–15
15th century	22.8 (c. 1500)	7.5–14.5	18 (c. 1500)	10.6–12.1

[1] The high numbers relating to late medieval Bohemia and Moravia have elicited some controversy, for which see Maur, "Obyvatelstvo," 52–53. In other secondary works—which are, however, not specifically concerned with demography—I have found lower estimates, for example 15 persons per square kilometer around 1350 (Małowist, "Z problematyki," 656), and 14 persons per square kilometer by the end of the fourteenth century (Jerzy Kłoczowski, *Młodsza Europa. Europa Środkowo-Wschodnia w kręgu cywilizacji chrześcijańskiej średniowiecza* (Warszawa: Państwowy Instytut Wydawniczy, 2003) 139. A similar estimate, of 15.4 persons per square kilometer, was made by F. Šmahel—a figure Maur considers low; Maur, "Obyvatelstvo," 53). Despite the fact the slightly lower figures appear to be more plausible than the figures quoted in the table, they do not correspond with the calculations of the total population.

[2] For the data concerning the years 1000 and 1340, see Gieysztor, "La Pologne," 567. Concerning the level around 1200, see footnote 34 below. The data from around the years 1400 and 1500 are drawn from the literature, and from the figures presented in Table 8.1.

[3] For the data concerning around 1200, and, in part, the period around 1400 (more precisely, before 1430) see Engel, *The Realm*, 59, 268–269. The remainder is a consequence of the figures presented in Table 8.1.

[4] All assessments regarding population densities c. 1200 result from the division of the figures presented in Table 8.1 by surface (except for Hungary, for which see footnote 32 above).

demographic catastrophes resulting from war. Despite the fact that the population density figures relating to Bohemia and Moravia cited above seem to be too high, there is no doubt that the two Czech regions were the most densely populated area of Central Europe, while the Kingdom of Hungary was the most sparsely settled. These levels resulted from two reasons. First, the economic development of the Czech Kingdom began much earlier than did its counterparts in Poland and Hungary. Second, the territory of the Czech Kingdom was the smallest among these countries, and easiest to populate quickly and densely, whilst Hungary's territory was the largest. On the other hand, in the long-run, the demographic dynamics were consistently expansionary in the three core Polish regions and in Hungary, but regressed in Bohemia, Moravia, and Silesia. That regression must have been the result of the Hussite wars (1419–36), and it was due to the resulting economic slowdown.

The large difference between the demographic history of Hungary and of the rest of Europe was one of the consequences of the Mongol invasion of 1241–42. The war was demographically disastrous for the Arpad monarchy. Current estimations of losses fluctuate between 15 and as much as 50 percent of the total population.[27] The invisibility of this dramatic effect in Table 8.2 appears to confirm Hungary's quite rapid socioeconomic recovery during the second half of the thirteenth century.

THE BLACK DEATH: EVIDENCE AND THEORETICAL CONTROVERSIES

The Great Famine of 1315–22 did not seriously affect the entire territory of Central Europe, the two exceptions being Bohemia between 1316 and 1318, and Silesia.[28] Epidemics, on the other hand, occurred quite frequently in all three countries during the late Middle Ages. That last phenomenon is illustrated in Table 8.3.

Table 8.3 Epidemics in Central European Regions and Countries in the Late Middle Ages

Years	*Bohemia*	*Silesia*	*Poland*	*Hungary*
1349	+	+		+
1350	+	+	+	
1351–1352			+	
1356		+		
1357	+			
1358	+	+		
1359	+		+	+
1360	+		+	+
1361			+	
1362	+			
1363	+		+	
1364			+	
1365			+	
1369–1370	+			
1371	+	+	+	
1374		+		+
1380	+			+
1381				+
1382			+	+

(continued)

Table 8.3 (continued)

Years	*Bohemia*	*Silesia*	*Poland*	*Hungary*
1383–1384			+	
1390	+			
1400				+
1403–1406	+			
1412				+
1413	+	+		
1414–1415	+			
1421	+			
1424			+	
1425	+		+	
1426–1427			+	
1430				+
1434		+		
1438		+		+
1439	+	+		
1440		+		
1441				+
1450			+	
1451	+		+	
1452		+	+	+
1453–1457				+
1461				+
1463	+		+	
1464	+		+	
1465			+	
1466			+	
1467			+	
1468				+
1472				+
1473	+			
1474		+		
1475				+
1479				+

(continued)

Table 8.3 (continued)

Years	*Bohemia*	*Silesia*	*Poland*	*Hungary*
1480			+	+
1481			+	
1482	+		+	+
1483	+	+	+	
1484			+	
1494			+	+
1495	+	+	+	+
1496			+	+
1497		+	+	+
1498			+	
1499			+	
1500			+	

Sources: Maur, "Le pays tchèques," 537; Andorka, "La Hongrie," 549; Gieysztor, "La Pologne," 567; Marek L. Wójcik, "Klęski elementarne w średniowiecznym Wrocławiu. I. Pożary i zarazy", *Rocznik Wrocławski*, 6 (2000): 34–36.

We can see from the table that the epidemics did not occur in these countries simultaneously. Some outbreaks were merely regional. For instance, the Black Death appeared in 1351 and 1352 exclusively in the cities of Gdańsk and Toruń; and in 1356, throughout Silesia, but not elsewhere.[29] Only in the year 1495 did the epidemic occur simultaneously in Poland, Hungary, and the Czech Kingdom.

It is a well-known truth that in Central Europe "the Black Death did not take a heavy toll of the population."[30] Erik Fügedi has explained this regional specificity in terms of a variety of factors. One was a relative sparseness of the population. Another was a stable equilibrium—specifically in Hungary and in Poland—between grain production, animal husbandry, and fishing, a conjunction which made famines relatively rare, and which enhanced human biological immunity to epidemic illness.[31] In his view, specifically in eastern Hungary, epidemic was hindered by a dry continental climate (its low humidity hinders the growth of microbes). Finally, Fügedi referred also to medical research by János Nemeskéri showing that populations with a preponderance of B-type blood—such as exists in Hungary—are relatively immune to microbe-born diseases. Generally speaking, these views have, as of today, been widely accepted.

The Great Plague did emerge on the fringes of Poland (in Pomerania), and in isolated towns of the Kingdoms of Hungary (Oradea, Sopron) and of Bohemia (Brno, Znojmo, Wrocław).[32] Jaroslav Čechura has observed that the pandemic of 1349–50 did not affect Czech regions at all.[33] The subsequent waves of the plague proved to be more destructive. They seem to have emerged in Hungary in the years 1359–60, and in the Czech territories, with particular force, in 1380.[34] For example, after 1380, the population of the Czech town, Stříbro, diminished by 14 percent.[35] Almost the same percentage died in the city of Wrocław in Silesia, when it was struck by the plague much later, in 1496.[36] Yet it seems risky to accept this data as the average level of losses in the Kingdom of Bohemia during the late Middle Ages. The Hussite wars, with their multi-layered consequences, led to a far more severe and long-lasting demographic decline than the epidemics did. That decline occurred, in part, by losses in the anti-Hussite military campaigns, in part by emigration, and in part by the general deterioration in living conditions. As far as we know, this trend was not reversed until the sixteenth century.[37]

In addition, as we also know well, medieval Central Europe was "much more rural than the West."[38] This opinion relates especially to Poland and Hungary, in spite of the slight variation among historians in the estimates of this phenomenon.[39] During the second half of the fifteenth century, in Hungary, the peasantry appears to have comprised between around 81 and 97 percent of the population (with the lower figure more probable), whereas the proportion of the nobility ranged between about 1 and 5 percent. In Poland, the nobility and the peasantry comprised, respectively, 7 or 8 percent, and about 80 percent, of the population. Czech evidence poses a sharp contrast with Poland in terms of the percentage of the nobility, which was 2 percent, whilst the proportion of peasantry was roundabout 78 percent.[40] These figures suggest that the figures concerning the urban inhabitants of the three kingdoms differed sharply. Moreover, there were regional variations, on a level beneath each kingdom, that surprise. For example, at the turn of the sixteenth century, in the backward Duchy of Masovia, the nobility (a very poor social group here) made up as much as 20 percent of the population.[41]

The views on the absence of the Black Death in two Central European countries, Poland and Bohemia, have been disputed recently by the Norwegian historian Ole J. Benedictow.[42] His principal thesis is that the plague epidemic encompassed and decimated both countries, approximately between 1349 and 1351. This view is contrary to the opinion long-held and current among Polish and Czech historians, who either fully deny the presence of the plague in these countries, or consider it to have had a far more limited, less catastrophic impact than was the case in the west of Europe.

Benedictow bases his argumentation on primary source evidence, and on ideological and historiographic considerations. He thinks that after the Second World War the communist regime pressured historians away from an inquiry into the crisis of the late Middle Ages, because that direction of inquiry would have subverted what he thinks was the regime's bias in favor of a dynamic development of the Polish lands during this period.[43]

The Norwegian historian thinks that the appearance of the Black Death in Eastern Pomerania, near Gdańsk, and in Toruń—a fact which is not questioned in Central European scholarship—was bound to result in its diffusion to the south, along the Vistula, to Warsaw.[44] He draws similar conclusions from the records of the eruption of the epidemic in the commercial center, Frankfurt on the Oder, which was situated close to Great Poland and Silesia. Benedictow also relies on the fragment of the Czech source, the *Chronicon Pragense*, which mentions a group of Czech students returning to their homeland from Bologna. As translated by Benedictow, the chronicle's last sentence states that "[o]f the foresaid students . . . only one returned to Bohemia, and his companions all died on the journey." Contrary to the plain meaning of the source, Benedictow attempts to persuade the reader that this closing sentence proves that the students died in Bohemia itself—where, therefore, the plague must have been present—and not while they were on their way to Bohemia: "[T]he last sentence," he notes, "must be taken to mean that only one of the students survived the journey in Bohemia, and succeeded in returning home."

Benedictow couples these arguments with disputing the views and arguments put forward by the Czech historian, Eduard Maur, in 1987.[45] Maur thinks that only southern Moravia was encompassed by the Black Death, because during the relevant period the Czech Kingdom was not closely tied into networks of long-distance trade. To be sure, epidemics did break out in Bohemia, but some time later. The logic of Maur's argument relies on two propositions: the weakness of Bohemia's connections with the plague-affected West, and thus the low likelihood of transmission of the disease; and the conjunction of recurring, though later, epidemics with the country's development during the fourteenth century. Benedictow strongly criticizes these three propositions, and the inferences Maur bases on them.

Benedictow's attempt to establish the presence of the Black Death in Poland and Bohemia is intriguing and interesting. However, it is, in my view, unsuccessful, and reads like an exercise in preconception, indeed a bit of an *idée fixe*. Let us begin with his conjecture regarding the high probability of transmission from the plague-infested Prussia to Warsaw. The presence of the epidemic in the towns of the state of the Teutonic Order is well-known and fully acknowledged in the literature. Thus, the hypothesis of a transmission from Toruń to Warsaw and the neighboring Masovia is not improbable. But historians of the towns situated along the Vistula, and of Masovia, have discerned in the primary sources no evidence of the epidemic whatsoever.

To this resounding documentary silence, let me add that, in Masovia—a region of a relatively late social and economic development—the process of intensive colonization, and generally of the closure of the developmental delay, began during the second half of the fourteenth century—a process that would have been impossible right after a demographic cataclysm of a degree inflicted by the Black Death, had that been present.[46]

Benedictow's arguments in favor of a pandemic in the Czech Kingdom are also doubtful. His interpretation of the *Chronicon Pragense* is tendentious, and completely unsupported by the text itself. The chronicle explicitly states that most of the Czech students died on their return journey to Bohemia, that is to say, before re-entering Czech territory; only one survived the journey. Furthermore, it would be odd if the countries situated between Italy and Bohemia, namely Germany and Austria, had been free of the plague, and if—in contrast to the supposedly plague-infested Bohemia itself—travel through them had not posed a risk of infection.

On the other hand, Benedictow is quite correct in his skepticism toward Maur's views regarding the weakness of the commercial ties between Bohemia and other countries. But what he, in turn, does not take into account is that during the first half of the fourteenth century, the imports brought to Prague by south German merchants were principally luxury goods, and that the distribution of such goods throughout Bohemia was quite limited. Thus, importation of luxury commodities by (possibly) infected merchants was not bound to provoke epidemic in other towns, let alone in the Czech countryside. Benedictow is simply wrong when he criticizes Maur's view concerning the enormously dynamic development of the Czech Kingdom between the recurring phases of the epidemic in later decades. Despite brief periods of regression, and despite regression in certain specific sectors (for example, the flooding of a certain proportion of mines), Bohemia developed dynamically.

Most problematic and flawed, however, are Benedictow's arguments turning on the supposed intersection between politics and historiography. These arguments appear to reflect a very limited knowledge of the Polish and the Czech historiographies, both in the interwar and the postwar period—an impression confirmed by the virtual invisibility of that historiography in the author's footnotes. Even though *The Black Death* was published in 2004, Benedictow is unfamiliar with the Polish or the Czech literature I cite in the present article, including the English-language contribution by Erik Fügedi. It is truly regrettable that Benedictow seeks to compensate for this historiographic ignorance by schematic, simplistic preconceptions concerning the state of historical knowledge in Poland and Czechoslovakia after the Second World War.

His belief in a pressure, supposedly exerted upon historians by the Communist authorities, to avoid the question of a great crisis in the late Middle Ages, so as to present the late medieval period in this region as an age of prosperity, is entirely groundless. First of all, let us recall the article by František Graus on the crisis of the fourteenth century in Europe (including Bohemia; see section titled Development or Crisis in Central Europe: State of Research). Moreover, as early as during the interwar period—before 1938 for Czechoslovakia and 1939 for Poland—it had been obvious to the historians of Poland and of Bohemia that, in its entirety, the fourteenth century was a period of a dynamic economic and civilizational development in both kingdoms. Neither the expansion of rural and urban settlement, nor the development of mining (technological difficulties notwithstanding), or the expansion of long-distance trade, would have been possible had the Black Death occurred in the two countries in their entirety.[47]

Thus, there are no grounds whatsoever for conjuring up the Black Death pandemic, and its catastrophic demographic and economic consequences, within the Polish and the Czech Kingdoms. Outbreaks of the disease occurred only in isolated towns, and did not, in either case, spread throughout the country.

AGRICULTURE

Land

According to the classical idea of David Ricardo, agricultural development depends above all on bringing new areas under cultivation under a regime of demographic growth. In traditional societies, a scarcity of acreage hampered not only the development of farming, but also economic development in general. Following this line of thought, Archibald Lewis discerned, in his famous article published in 1958, a contraction of the rural colonization in the West between 1250 and 1350, caused by a shortage of new land that could be brought under cultivation.[48] Did the same situation occur in Central Europe?

In this region, expansion of arable resulted from two kinds of activity. One was territorial annexation of adjacent localities or regions that often included areas already under cultivation. The other was internal colonization, that is to say, reclamation of forest and turning previously uncultivated land into cultivated arable. Because we have addressed questions of territorial annexations and changes above, let us focus on internal colonization, in the major sub-regions of Central Europe.

Throughout Central Europe, rural colonization accelerated from the twelfth century onward as a consequence of top-down orders issued by rulers and by great landowners (lay and ecclesiastical), and of spontaneous migrations, both domestic and from abroad. Peasants, petty nobles, Cistercians, members of the underclass (including criminals), and, on the other hand, not only Czechs, Poles, Hungarians, Slovaks, but also—and, in the long-term, most importantly—Germans (Saxons, among others), as well as Austrians, Romanians, Ruthenians, Walachians, and, in modest numbers, Walloons—for all these social milieus and ethnic groups, the territories of Central Europe seemed to be 'the Promised Land.[49] The dynamics of these processes differed considerably between, and within, these three countries. Despite the fact that the first country visited by rural colonists, during the eleventh century, seems to have been the Kingdom of Hungary, the most intensive and the speediest colonization occurred within the core Czech regions. The process began here during the twelfth century, reached its peak in the thirteenth (as expressed in the Czech scholarly recognition of the 'agrarian revolution of the thirteenth century'), and ended during the following century. Over the first half of the fourteenth century, its dynamics began to slow down, and from the 1360s onward stagnation ensued.[50] The relatively short period over which this complex process occurred, in comparison with its counterpart in Hungary and in Poland, must have been the result of the relatively small surface of Czech territory—a surface which could be populated with relative ease.

The history of colonization in Hungary was longer. The climax occurred during the thirteenth and fourteenth centuries (apart, to be sure, from the break caused by the Mongol invasion and its demographic aftermath; see section title Aggregate Figures and Population Densities). By the mid-fifteenth century, the entire territory of the kingdom was settled.[51] In the Polish areas, the process began somewhat later than in Bohemia, though also in the course of the twelfth century.[52] It reached its apogee at the same time as did its Hungarian counterpart—that is to say, in the thirteenth and fourteenth centuries—though it lasted longer. A good example is the region of Masovia, densely forested, and characterized by poor soils, where a major leap settlement occurred as late as the fifteenth century, and where colonization continued into the beginnings of the early modern period.[53]

Rural colonization brought about an immense enlargement of acreage. It caused a crucial transition from forestry to farming within many areas, especially in Bohemia and in Poland. Agriculture became the dominant branch of the Czech and the Polish economy of the Middle Ages—displacing, to a certain degree, animal husbandry.

However, medieval migrations had their other side—namely, abandonment of villages, prompted by various causes.[54] Apart from Silesia and Slovakia, it is difficult to reconstruct the chronology of this process, because the evidence is very late, dating as it does only since the start of the sixteenth century. Historians have pointed out that in Bohemia and Moravia abandonment of villages originated as early as the fourteenth century, and that, by the end of the Middle Ages, it affected between 15 and 22 percent of all villages and hamlets, at least in some regions. In the vicinity of the city of Brno, in Moravia, the acreage diminished by 5.5 percent. In Silesia, the analogous process began after around 1420, in connection with the Hussite raids. As a result, in the long-term, as much as between one-quarter and one-half of the arable land was deserted. Regarding Poland, the data attest to the abandonment of approximately between 25 and 30 percent of the arable areas at the beginning of the sixteenth century—a trend that must have begun earlier. In Slovakia, deserted villages appear during the second third of the fifteenth century.

Concerning the remaining territories of the Hungarian Kingdom, I have at my disposal only general assessments of fifteenth-century colonization, without any actual data.[55] The process appears to have intensified there during the early modern period, as a consequence of Turkish expansion. Apart from Slovakia and Silesia, after the troubles associated with the Hussites came to an end—around the 1460s and the 1480s, respectively—abandonment of villages, which of course entailed an abandonment of arable land, must have contributed, in specific localities and regions, to a diminution of acreage. In Bohemia and Moravia this trend does not appear to have been counterbalanced by simultaneous settlement, which, as noted above, had already come to an end. On the other hand, in Poland the presence of an offsetting trend of this kind is quite possible, because of continued settlement in some regions—notably Masovia and Red Ruthenia—into the beginnings of the early modern period.

Techniques: Field Systems and Tools

The period under study witnessed a steady development of farming techniques. A variety of field systems coexisted within the same country, region, and settlement. The two-field system emerged locally during the early Middle Ages while, at the same time, the tradition-based slash-and-burn method was long used alongside the infield-outfield system and the "continuous cultivation (*Einfeld*) of a small portion of ground in proximity to human habitation."[56] The breakthrough consisted in the introduction and the proliferation of the two- and three-field system. Of these two systems, the first fostered animal husbandry, because it left a relatively large amount of fallow field for cattle, whereas the second stimulated the production of cereals.[57] The triennial crop rotation increased the output of crops by 50 percent.[58] The diffusion of the two-field system and, later, the emergence of the three-field system were, in Central Europe, closely connected to the increased settlement, and to the expansion of colonization. Bohemia seems to have been most advanced in this regard—František Graus has found a reference to the three-field system in a source dating from as early as 1125–40 (in the village of Ostoja, 10 km north of Prague).[59] During the late Middle Ages, this innovative system spread throughout the entire Czech Kingdom, including Silesia.[60] In most Polish regions, the three-field system proliferated in the course of the fourteenth and the first half of the fifteenth centuries. In the most backward Mazovia this technique of cultivation was diffused as late as the fifteenth century and thereafter.[61] However, even at the beginning of the early modern period some traditional field systems continued to be in use in Red Ruthenia—above all the slash-and-burn method and the two-field system.[62] The traditional and the innovative field systems also coexisted in Hungary.[63] Likewise in Hungary, between the thirteenth and the mid-fourteenth centuries, a transition took place from the continuous cultivation in one-field to the two- and three-field systems. However, the two newer field systems were supplemented by infield-outfield systems, which proved to be especially useful in some areas of newly assarted fields.[64] At the turn of the sixteenth century, on the scale of the country in its entirety, the two-field system predominated until the eighteenth century.[65]

The evolution of field systems was closely linked with the history of **farm implements.**[66] The breakthrough consisted in the replacement of the ard (the scratch plow, known under its Latin names, *aratrum parvum, uncus*) by the heavy plow (the *aratrum magnum*) and its wheeled version. The heavy instrument allowed a plowing that was faster, more precise, and deeper. The result was expansion of cultivation to the heavier soils. In contrast to the scratch plow, its heavy counterpart corresponded to the needs of the three-field system, that is, the ard was useless in this new field system.[67] Consequently, the application and proliferation of this new implement must have contributed to an increase in the area of land under cultivation, in the crops harvested, and, ultimately, in economic growth in general. Until the thirteenth century, the use of the ard prevailed in the Polish and Bohemian territories as well as in Hungarian Slovakia. Generally speaking, in the course of the settlement expansion and the proliferation of the three-field system, the ard was replaced by the heavy plow. Although this technological change acquired momentum during the second half of the thirteenth century, adoption of the new implement was simultaneous with settlement expansion. This is why (apart from Bohemia), the transition lasted until the fifteenth century, and even longer. On the other hand, in (for example) the hilly and mountainous regions of the Hungarian Kingdom (Transdanubia and Transylvania), the ard was never replaced, throughout the rest of the Middle Ages.[68] Sometimes even in territories where the heavy plow prevailed—such as fourteenth- and fifteenth-century Poland—the ard was still in use as an auxiliary implement.

Organization of Production and Productivity

Despite the apparent preponderance of large feudal estates, especially in late-medieval Hungary and Bohemia, the peasant households played a basic role in Central European agriculture.[69] From the legal point of view, peasants were subordinated to lords. They were tenants, with hereditary rights to their plots of land. In practice, in the villages established under German law the peasants ruled over their arable fields and pastures. Lords retained small areas—demesne farms (*praedia antiqua, ad proprium aratrum*), intended to satisfy their own private needs—and otherwise became rentiers, who owed their standard of living to peasant rents.

During the fifteenth century, the content and kind of rent—in labor, in kind, and in money—differed, in relative importance, in each of these three countries. In the Czech regions money rent seems to have dominated in almost every village, whereas in the Hungarian territories money rent also prevailed, though not to the same high extent as in the Czech Kingdom.[70] The Polish territories (including Masovia) differed from the other two countries in terms of the importance of rent paid in labor. A rent obligation assessed in coin was sometimes actually paid in kind.[71] In the Kingdom of Hungary the peasants were under obligation to work on their lords' arable fields for as little as a few days a year, while in Bohemia that obligation entailed only between 14 and 24 days annually, between the thirteenth and the fifteenth centuries.[72] In theory, the same principle was supposed to be observed in the Kingdom of Poland; the Statute of Warka (1423) subjected the peasants to a labor obligation of 14 days a year on their lord's demesne.[73] However, the Polish practice differed both from Poland's own legal regulations and from the practice in the Czech and Hungarian Kingdoms. As early as 1421, an obligation of serf labor—at the level of one day per week from one *mansus* (c. 17 hectares)—was imposed in the Duchy of Mazovia.[74] One may assume that this change occurred at the initiative of the duke, the more so because we have only a single earlier example of serf labor at this level of frequency, known from a private manor, also in Masovia, and recorded in 1420.[75] From 1477 onward, similar regulations were imposed in the Polish Kingdom itself.[76]

Also in the course of the fifteenth century, in the Polish territories, the relatively small manors of the nobility evolved into large manorial estates, ultimately based on serf labor. The subject of their origins has recently become a contested question. Formerly, the emergence of the serf labor-based great landed property was explained by a variety of factors.[77] Generally, the great estate has been understood as a result of the attempts by the nobility to offset some phenomena that entailed a fall of its revenues, and of the attempts by the nobility to gain new profits. In concrete terms, rural settlement desertion, resulting from large-scale peasant migration, pressed the nobility to keep the labor force required to cultivate the deserted areas anew. In addition, the devaluation of money caused a big slump in the value of money rent paid by lords' tenants. Consequently, the nobles had to look for the new sources of income. Demand for grain in Western Europe increased greatly, hence its production and export became profitable.

Two additional circumstances may have influenced the above changes. First, after the mid-fifteenth century, the nobility was replaced by hired mercenaries in the Polish army. This change supposedly turned the nobility's principal interest toward their landed estates and grain production. Second, in the course of the fifteenth century, as a result of its numerous privileges, the Polish nobility gained hegemony over the other social groups. This fact helped it enserf peasants, and prompted them toward adoption of serf labor.

All these explanations have recently been questioned by Jan Wroniszewski and Krzysztof Mikulski.[78] The two scholars put forward the view that the increasing importance of serf labor resulted from scarcity in the money market in fifteenth-century Poland, and from the growing difficulties the peasants faced in selling their product (grain). The peasants limited themselves to subsistence farming, and to the rendering of labor in place of a money rent. Some moved out of farms subjected to money rent, to the manors on which they assumed the obligation to perform serf labor. Mikulski and Wroniszewski reinterpreted the regulations noted above, including the duty of serf labor, as attempts to establish the maximum range of the serf labor obligation, and not to increase that range. Both authors have noted that it had been lords who decided on the form of rent.

At the outset of the sixteenth century, manors embraced (depending on the region) between 17 and 33 percent of all the arable land in the Kingdom of Poland.[79]

As already noted, similar processes did not occur in the Czech and the Hungarian states in the period under study. In Hungary serf labor-based manors began to emerge in the 1530s, and in its Slovak part—two decades later.[80] In the better-developed Czech territories, this process was still continuing, slowly, as late as the seventeenth century.[81] Consequently, manorial estates encompassed only a small proportion of arable land in the two monarchies: between 5 and 30 percent at the mid-sixteenth century in Hungary, and around 20 percent in the Czech Kingdom about 50 years later.[82] One may assume that in the fifteenth century these percentages must have been much lower.

These three countries also differed in terms of their basic, **primary products.**[83] Rural colonization led to a crucial transition in Poland and Bohemia from the preponderance of forestry and animal husbandry to a preponderance of agriculture, whereas in Hungary, despite its development, farming was secondary to animal husbandry and viticulture. On the other hand, Moravian viticulture managed to export some of its brands of wine, though not of the same reputation abroad as their Hungarian counterparts. In Poland, cattle rearing gained in importance after the annexation of Red Ruthenia in 1366—a region characterized by a highly developed animal husbandry, and a notable source of export of oxen to the West from the fourteenth century onward. Two peculiar features of Czech and Silesian primary production were highly developed beer production and fish farming.[84]

A comparison of the proportions in the production of different grains in these countries points us to a basic difference between Poland and the two other kingdoms. In Bohemia and Hungary a restructuring of production took place in the late Middle Ages. As a result, 'more expensive' cereals began to dominate farming there. In Bohemia, wheat and barley comprised 36 percent of production, rye made up around thirty percent, and millet reached the level of 34 percent.[85] In Hungary, the peasants preferred to grow wheat, which cultivation covered between 50 and 90 percent of the arable.[86] On the other hand, in fourteenth-century Poland, the so-called 'cheap' cereals, millet and rye, dominated—at 42, and at between 39 and 43 percent of the overall production, respectively[87]—while wheat and barley comprised a small part of the total grain production, at 5 percent, and between 3 and 5 percent, respectively.[88] During the next century, these proportions did not change appreciably. Rye and barley remained preponderant (at 40 and 38 percent of total output, respectively), over the other grains: wheat at 9 percent, millet at 6.[89] The proportion of grains cultivated depended on soil quality. The better the soils, the higher the percentage of the "more expensive" cereals. For example, in the village of Chorążyce, near Cracow, wheat cultivation, at thirty percent of total output, prevailed over the cultivation of rye, millet, and barley (at 27, 14, and 14 percent, respectively).[90]

The aforesaid technological and organizational changes contributed to **the growth of the yield ratio**. One needs to recall that productivity usually varied even within a very local area.[91] It also varied with the species of grain.[92] One may assume that, during the twelfth and thirteenth centuries, the primary yield ratio per seed was about 2:1, or even lower.[93] In the later Middle Ages, the ratio generally increased. In Hungary it rose from 2:1, in the thirteenth century, to between 2:1 and 4:1 a century later, and to between 4:1 and 5:1 in the fifteenth century.[94] In Poland as in Hungary, the change was from 4:1 in the fourteenth century, to 5:1 in the fifteenth.[95] In Bohemia, the average yield ratio reached 3.3:1, and a bit higher in the large estates. Some historians think that this ratio remained essentially constant until the eighteenth century, but this opinion seems incorrect, because in the sixteenth century the ratio was between 5:1 and 6:1.[96] Likewise, in the neighboring fourteenth-century Silesia, the yield ratio seems to have reached a level between 4:1 and 5:1.[97]

TOWNS AND THE URBAN BRANCHES OF ECONOMIC ACTIVITY

Urbanization

Needles to say, urbanization contributed to economic growth and development. This process intensified sharply during the thirteenth century, and continued over the subsequent centuries.[98] Bohemia and Moravia became the most urbanized regions of Central Europe, second only to Prussia. Here, around the year 1400 inhabitants of towns and boroughs constituted twenty percent of the entire population.[99] Concerning the Polish and Hungarian Kingdoms, comparable data exist for the year 1500. In the Polish territories (including the part of Prussia incorporated into the kingdom) townspeople are estimated as having reached approximately 16 percent of the total population.[100] When we limit our perspective to Poland's three core regions, noted above—Great Poland, Little Poland, Mazovia—the proportion of this social group falls slightly, to 15 percent. As for Hungary, most historians recognize it as the least urbanized country, where the townspeople comprised as little as between 2 and 3 percent of the total population.[101] Another, considerably higher, estimate of 11 percent, even though it is plausible, still attests to a lower degree of urbanization than obtained either in Bohemia or in Poland.

One must also bear in mind that most Central European towns were small—comprising, usually, less than 1,000 persons. Many of these *oppida* were semi-agrarian or agrarian. Only a handful of cities were large and populous. In the late Middle Ages, Prague and Gdańsk reached no less than 30,000 inhabitants each. A few more—Buda, Wrocław, and Cracow—attained approximately 20,000, or, in the case of Toruń and Lwów/Lemberg, 10,000.[102] Even important economic centers such as Kutná Hora, Cheb, Sibiu/Hermannstadt, Pozsony/Bratislava/Pressburg, Braila/Kronstadt, Lublin, and Brno, were inhabited by only a few thousand townspeople each.

Among the town-based branches of economic activity, only a few exerted a significant impact upon the economic growth of a country to a considerable degree. These included, above all, the textile industry, mining (including metallurgy), and long-distance trade. The important role of these branches resulted from a mass output of production, or, in the case of commerce, from trade in a mass volume of goods.

Urban Industries and their Production

Czech, Silesian, and Polish craft underwent rapid development in the thirteenth and the fourteenth centuries.[103] The earliest craft guilds seem to have been established in Wrocław in 1273.[104] In contrast, Hungarian manufacture is acknowledged to have been underdeveloped and poor[105] because of a small number of craft guilds and of professions practiced, and because of the insignificance of craft in Hungarian exports. Despite some controversies on the role of craft guilds for economic development, they do seem to have stimulated it in the first decades of their existence.[106] Craft guilds concentrated the local labor force, maintained quality control, and, up to a certain moment, satisfied all the needs of local consumers.

Stimulation of economic growth and development resulted from the activity of those craft guilds whose members produced cloth and garments (the textile industry); processed metal, fur, leather, and timber; and worked in construction. These areas of economic activity mattered beyond a local scale. The crafts noted here relied on raw materials imported from other regions or countries, or from abroad (the processing of leather, metal crafts, furriery). The productive needs of urban guilds created an outlet for forestry, mining, and metallurgy. On the other hand, some of their products were exported abroad. The Czech textile industry of Bohemia—Silesia included—produced cloth that was in demand both in Central and in Western Europe. Not only Prague, Wrocław, and Brno, but also smaller towns—Broumov, Rychnov, Świdnica, Strzegom, among others—focused on cloth production for export.[107] Likewise, the textile industry of Great Poland produced cloth for export during the fourteenth and fifteenth centuries.[108]

Mining

Because of the large deposits of precious and base metals, and of salt, in the region, mining played an important role in the economy of Central Europe. According to Marian Małowist, apart from agriculture, it was the mass exploitation of minerals that proved to be the most important reason for an economic development of this region.[109] There were large deposits of gold in Slovakia, Transylvania, and Silesia, of silver in Bohemia and the same three other regions, of copper in Transylvania, of lead in Southern Poland and Upper Silesia, and of salt in Southern Poland. On this basis, approximately 200 mining towns were established.[110] The exploitation of metals and minerals intensified in the thirteenth century, especially in Bohemia and Silesia, and during the subsequent century, above all in the Kingdom of Hungary.[111]

The Hungarian—that is to say, Slovak and Transylvanian—gold output amounted to as much as about 1.5 tons per year, and comprised 75 percent of the total European gold production.[112] Czech silver mining was concentrated in Kutná Hora, where exploitation experienced great development between 1300 and 1350, and the annual output reached around 20 tons. This was equal to around 42 percent of the total European silver mining production.[113] After the mid-fourteenth century, production declined to 10 tons per year, and ended altogether with the Hussite wars.[114] Moreover, intense development of Central European mining was partly, though temporarily, hampered by frequent flooding of the mines, and by the absence of technological ability to drain the flooding. In Silesia these problems arose between about 1270 and the mid-fifteenth century, but they certainly did not affect every mine.[115] Eventually, technological innovations improved draining.[116] In post-Hussite Bohemia, c. 1450, exploitation of silver deposits was resumed thanks to the Czech king Jiři of Poděbrady and the entrepreneurs of Nuremberg. Yet its volume, at around 4.5 tons yearly, never matched the earlier level. As regards the output of lead, in Silesia and Little Poland it reached between about 300 and about 600 tons per year during the late Middle Ages[117]—a level that probably represents between 39 and 43 percent of overall European production in the 1470s.

Long-distance Trade

Before the Mongol invasion and the destruction of the biggest East-Central European emporium, Kiev, in 1240, the cities of Central Europe do not seem to have played an important role in the circulation of international goods. The second half of the thirteenth century was crucial for the subsequent history of Central European commerce. Merchants from all countries of the region established cooperation with the Italian city-states (Venice and Florence),[118] with the German emporia (Cologne, Regensburg, and Nuremberg), as well as with Bruges. Apart from the import of luxury goods—luxury cloth and garments, first-rate wines, metal wares, spices—Central European merchants began to export, and re-export, mass goods (furs, wax, gold, silver, copper, and tin) in those new places of contact. All these contacts enabled Central European cities to be integrated into the pan-European economic system.[119] Moreover, the new domestically produced commodities created by the primary production sector—Hungarian oxen and wines; the Polish cochineal dye called *czerwiec*; and grain, salt, lead, and mercury, not to mention the precious metals noted above, whose export continued during the Late Middle Ages—began to be sent abroad. The role of the Czech (including the Silesian) textile industry has already been stressed.

WAS THERE AN ECONOMIC CRISIS IN LATER MEDIEVAL CENTRAL EUROPE?

Before moving on to my final conclusions, let me address a few outstanding questions. As is well-known, economists define growth in two ways: either as increase in the aggregate level of output (in today's terms, the Gross Domestic Product), or increase in output per capita. To the best of my knowledge, the heretofore explored source materials, and the resulting scholarship, do not allow us to calculate economic growth, or decline, in terms of reliable aggregate numbers, either for Bohemia or for Hungary; and I shall discuss an attempt by Marian Dygo to do so for Poland momentarily. On the other hand, it is possible to say with certainty, though in qualitative terms, that growth, or decline, occurred—though this also only as an approximation, and sometimes even as a hypothesis.

There is no doubt about the rapidity of the expansion of the Central European economies in the thirteenth and the fourteenth centuries. As has already been noted, dynamic development took place in every sector. Rural colonization, technical innovation, a general growth in the yield ratio, progress in urbanization, an emergence of urban crafts, a rapid development of mining, and an equally rapid expansion of long-distance trade—all in the course of these two centuries—attest to the accuracy of this view. Factors such as the devastation of Hungary, and the decimation of its population by the Mongol army, or the flooding of the mines, do not seem to have hampered this expansionary process for a significant length of time. In the absence of as heavy a death toll as elsewhere, Central European economies were more capable of sustaining a trajectory of economic development. That development was also not halted by frequent epidemics and famines, which were, in this region, much smaller in scale and in range than were the Great Famine of 1315–1322 and the mid-fourteenth-century plague in the West. In the course of these two centuries, Poland, Bohemia, and Hungary experienced a great economic leap from a forest-based economy to an economy dominated by agriculture—a major step toward better organization, modernization, and commercialization.

However, the earliest key developments that began, over the long-term, to alter this dynamism occurred in the Kingdom of Bohemia, especially in its two core regions.[120] First, although the debasement in 1340 of the reputable Czech silver coinage did not cause a crisis, it must have influenced the economy to some degree, because it created an inflationary pressure. In addition, the debasement must have worsened the economic situation. More serious problems emerged from the mid-fourteenth century onward. Silver exploitation and production began to decline after around 1350, at the latest. Moreover, rural colonization came to a halt, despite the fact that even today one-third of the territory remains covered by forest.[121] On the other hand, the annexation of Lower Lusatia in 1368 may have tended to counterbalance the decline in the growth of the Czech Kingdom. We do not know whether the same stagnation appeared in the long-distance trade, as has been suspected.[122] For example, during the fifteenth century, Wrocław merchants intensified their commercial links, with Venice and the South German cities, for example.[123] Yet such activities do not seem to have offset the stagnation in agriculture, which occurred in Silesia from 1425 onward,[124] or the deep crisis in Czech silver mining and in the other branches of the economy during the first half of the fifteenth century, and thus at the time of the 'Hussite revolution.' However, from about 1450 onward, the crisis began to subside. Several branches of the economy—viticulture, brewing, fish farming—were untouched by the crisis. Others—silver mining, long-distance trade, the textile industry, and other crafts—began to recover,[125] though they never recovered to pre-Hussite levels of production.

In contrast to the Czech Kingdom, the economies of the Polish and Hungarian Kingdoms experienced efflorescence throughout the entire fourteenth century. The expansion was further stimulated by the subsequent support from rulers. Apart from the dynamic phenomena noted above, let us add the economic advantages to Poland of the annexation of Red Ruthenia, and to Hungary of the annexation of Dalmatia (1358). Setbacks such as the limited impact of the monetary reform in Poland and the political turbulences in Hungary, following the extinction of the Angevin dynasty between 1382 and 1403[126] and the accession of Sigismund of Luxembourg to the throne, were not able to halt the expansion of the economy.

For an economic historian interested in Poland, Hungary, and post-Hussite Bohemia, the fifteenth century represents the biggest puzzle. Marian Dygo's thesis, mentioned above, on the fifteenth-century decline in production per capita in Poland, because original and well-supported, merits discussion. As the same author has noted, new settlement and cultivation were directed toward several new regions. Colonization in the eastern part of the Kingdom of Poland, and in the Duchy of Masovia, continued in the course of the fifteenth century. Consequently, the author's principal argument for a decrease in economic activity—the completion of the diffusion of new tools and techniques of cultivation by the end of the fourteenth century—does not appear to be correct. These innovations continued to proliferate in the newly colonized areas throughout the fifteenth century. Moreover, in contrast to Masovia, high-quality soils were available in other territories, especially the Lublin district and Red Ruthenia. Hence, on the scale of Poland in its entirety, average productivity of agriculture was able to expand (see section titled Organization of Production and Productivity). Let us add to these possibilities and sources of economic expansion the re-annexation of the highly developed and urbanized Prussia in 1466. Despite some problematic developments in a few branches of the economy, it is highly plausible that aggregate production in Poland increased in the course of the fifteenth century.

With regard to the problem of the economic growth and development in the Kingdom of Hungary, the fact of that growth and development seems clear. Despite some economic difficulties, the Hungarian economy developed almost continuously. The period from the first years of the fourteenth century until the death of Sigismund of Luxemburg in 1437 is recognized as a time of Hungary's most rapid economic modernization until the eighteenth century.[127] In other words, economic expansion must have been rapid. Some negative phenomena in the countryside which occurred after 1437 appear to have been of a regional and short-lasting importance (peasant uprising in Transylvania, a devastation of this region by Turkish army). Towns continued to be supported by Sigismund's successors; urbanization continued into the last quarter of the fifteenth century in the 'industrial' Transylvania.[128] The subjugation of the city of Vienna and of Austria in the years 1485–1490 must have been a major source of financial relief for Hungarian merchants, who ceased to be limited by the very burdensome staple right enjoyed by Vienna. Export of oxen to the West blossomed. Let us add the annexation of Silesia, between 1469 and 1490, whose countryside began to recover anew from around 1480 onwards. Investments of large sums of money in Hungarian copper mining, and receiving the resulting enterprises on lease by the most prominent great entrepreneurs of the Early Modern period, the Fugger family (together with Johann Thurzo of Cracow), contributed to a recovery, and to a further development of the Hungarian mining.

We may discern, in the period between 1470 and the outset of the sixteenth century, the peak civilizational—and therefore, among other things, economic–development in Hungary's history.[129] However, it is necessary to raise the question on the negative economic consequences of such events as the loss of the rich territory of Dalmatia in 1409, and the Turkish expansion. In the record state budget expended during the reign of Matthias Corvinus, ranging between 800,000 and a million florins, large sums of money had to be spent on war. On the other hand, war could have stimulated such branches of the economy as cattle and horse rearing, and the production of, and trade in, foodstuffs and weaponry.

In reaching a definitive answer regarding the emergence of an economic crisis in later medieval Central Europe, one must bear in mind that the notion of 'crisis' has referred to a variety of phenomena.[130] I share the view of Jerzy Topolski, who recognized a long-lasting economic recession as the equivalent of 'crisis. Following this definition one may conclude that crises emerged only in the individual countries of Central Europe at different times, or in the individual branches of the economy. To judge from the aforementioned data, and from the general trends of development within each branch, no general crisis arose in late-medieval Central Europe as a whole, of the type and scale that occurred in the West.

ACKNOWLEDGMENTS

I would like to thank Professor Piotr Górecki (University of California, Riverside, US) for his kind criticism, helpful comments and suggestions to this article.

NOTES

1. Among numerous secondary works on late medieval territorial annexations, see: Jörg Hoensch, *Geschichte Böhmens. Von der slavischen Landnahme bis zur Gegenwart* (München: Verlag C. H. Beck, 1997), 117–18, 122; Pál Engel, *The Realm of St. Stephen: A History of Medieval Hungary,* trans. Tamás Pálosfalvi (London and New York: I. B. Tauris, 2001), 35, 110, 134, 162, 164–65, 232–34, 237, 304–05; Paul W. Knoll, *The Rise of the Polish Monarchy: Piast Poland in East Central Europe 1320–1370* (Chicago: The University of Chicago Press, 1972), 121–77, 201–06; Marian Małowist, "Bases économiques du retour de la Poméranie de Dantzig à la Pologne au XVe siècle," in *Croissance et regressions en Europe XIVe–XVIIe siècles,* ed. Marian Małowist (Paris 1972: Colin, 1972), 63–90.
2. Jan Tyszkiewicz, *Ludzie i przyroda w Polsce średniowiecznej* (Warszawa: Państwowe Wydawnictwo Naukowe, 1983), 23–24.
3. Hoensch, *Geschichte Böhmens,* 17–18; Tyszkiewicz, *Ludzie*, 20; Engel, *The Realm,* xiii–xiv; Karol Maleczyński, ed., *Historia Śląska,* vol. 1, part 1 (Wrocław: Zakład Narodowy im. Ossolińskich, 1960), 146–51.
4. See generally Jerzy Kłoczowski, "Le développement de la civilisation en Europe Centrale et Orientale au XIVe et XVe siècles," *Quaestiones Medii Aevi*' 1 (1977): 119–20.
5. Jan Čechura, *České zemé w letech 1310–1378. Lucemburkové na českém trůne* (Praha: Nakladatelství Libri, 1999), 116.
6. Engel, *The Realm,* xvi.
7. Reflecting the expansion in the amount of written material, the editors of the most thoroughly completed series of documents issued in Poland, the *Codex diplomaticus Maioris Poloniae*—specifically documenting the province of Great Poland—ceased publication with documents dated after 1444, because of the enormous increase in the quantity of the sources by the mid-fifteenth century (Antoni Gąsiorowski, "Wstęp," in *Codex diplomaticus Maioris Poloniae*, ed. Antoni Gąsiorowski, Tomasz Jasiński, Tomasz Jurek

and Izabela Skierska, Poznań: Wydawnictwo Poznańskiego Towarzystwa Przyjaciół Nauk, 1999 vol. 11, vi). The eleven volumes include a total of 4,811 documents.

8. Generally, see Jerzy Wyrozumski, *Dzieje Polski do roku 1505* (Warszawa: Państwowe Wydawnictwo Naukowe, 1984), 12–37; Piotr Górecki, *Economy, Society, and Lordship in Medieval Poland* (New York and London: Holmes & Meier, 1992), 17–26; Kazimierz Pacuski, "Przegląd źródeł," in *Dzieje Mazowsza*, vol. 1, ed. Henryk Samsonowicz (Pułtusk: Akademia Humanistyczna im. A. Gieysztora, 2006), 19–42. Engel, *The Realm,* xvi–xvii; Čechura, *České zemé w letech 1310–1378*, 152.
9. Olgierd Górka, ed., *Anonymi descriptio Europae Orientalis Imperium Constantinopolitanum, Albania, Serbia, Bulgaria, Ruthenia, Ungaria, Polonia, Bohemia Anno MCCCVIII exarata* (Cracoviae: Gebethner, 1916), 43–60. For an English translation of the fragment on Hungarian economy, and comment, see László Mákkai, "Economic Landscapes: Historical Hungary from the Fourteenth to the Seventeenth century," in *East-Central Europe in Transition: From the Fourteenth to the Seventeenth Century,* ed. Antoni Mączak, Henryk Samsonowicz, and Peter Burke (Cambridge: Cambridge University Press, 1985): 28–29.
10. Definition by Górecki, *Economy,* 10.
11. In Bohemia, the first census was carried out in 1754, in Hungary in 1784, and in Poland in 1789. Eric Fügedi, "The Demographic Landscape of East-Central Europe," in *East-Cental Europe in Transition: From the Fourteenth to the Seventeenth Century,* ed. Antoni Mączak, Henryk Samsonowicz, and Peter Burke (Cambridge: Cambridge University Press, 1985), 46.
12. Benedykt Zientara et al., *Dzieje gospodarcze Polski do 1939 roku* (Warszawa: Wiedza Powszechna, 1979), 88; Fügedi, "The Demographic Landscape," 48; Leonid Żytkowicz, "Trends of Agrarian economy in Poland, Bohemia and Hungary from the Middle of the Fifteenth to the Middle of the Seventeenth Century," in *East-Cental Europe in Transition: From the Fourteenth to the Seventeenth Century,* ed. Antoni Mączak, Henryk Samsonowicz, and Peter Burke (Cambridge: Cambridge University Press, 1985), 74; Rudolf Andorka, "La Hongrie," in *Histoire des populations de l'Europe*, ed. Jean Pierre Bardet and Jacques Dupâquier (Paris: Fayard, 1997), 545–547.
13. Wyrozumski, *Dzieje Polski*, 29–32; Čechura, *České zemé w letech 1310–1378*, 111; Jan Čechura, *České zemé w letech 1378–1437. Lucemburkové na českým trůne* (Praha: Nakladatelství Libri, 2000), 192; Engel, *The Realm,* 17; Martyn Rady, *Medieval Buda: A Study of Municipal Government and Jurisdiction in the Kingdom of Hungary* (New York: Columbia University Press, 1985), 43–47, 55–66, 122. On the collections of laws in the various countries, see: Hoensch, *Geschichte Böhmens*, 95; Čechura, *České zemé w letech 1310–1378*, 12; Józef Matuszewski, and Jacek Matuszewski, "Einleitung," in *Najstarszy Zwód Prawa Polskiego* (Łódź: Wydawnictwo Uniwersytetu Łódzkiego 1995), 26–49; András Kubinyi, "István Werbőczy als Politiker in der Zeit vor Mohács (1526)," in . . . *The Man of Many Devices, Who Wandered Full Many Ways . . . Festschrift in Honor of János M. Bak,* ed. Balázs Nagy and Marcell Sebők (Budapest: Central European University Press, 1999), 558, 565; Engel, *The Realm*, 350–52.
14. Čechura, *České zemé w letech 1310–1378*, 111.
15. Piotr Górecki, ed., *A Local Society in Transition. The 'Henryków Book' and Related Documents,* (Toronto: Pontifical Institute of Mediaeval Studies, 2007). This is an exceptional, hybrid 'cartulary-chronicle,' written by Cistercian monks of German origin who settled down in Silesia at the time of the intense colonization of this region. For another important source, Gustav A. Stenzel, ed.,

Das Landbuch des Fürstentums Breslau, in *Berichte der Gesellschaft fuer Schlesische Vaterländische Cultur und Geschichte* 1842, 48–141.

16. Čechura, *České zemé w letech 1310–1378*, 143, 197; Čechura, *České zemé w letech 1378–1437*, 186, 198, 214; Jan Čechura, "Rolnictvo v Čechách w pozdním středověku," *Český Časopis Historičky*, 88/4 (1990): 486; Zsigmond Pach, "The Development of Feudal Rent in Hungary in the Fifteenth Century," *Economic History Review* 19 (1966/1): 3.
17. For example: Otto Stobbe, ed., "Mittheilungen aus Breslauer Signaturbüchern," *Zeitschrift für Geschichte und Alterthum Schlesiens*, 8/2 (1867/2): 446–49; František Graus, ed., "Tři zlomky Českých kupeckých knih z doby předhusitské," *Československý Časopis Historický*, 4 (1956), 645–46.
18. Marian Małowist, "The Problem of the Inequality of Economic Development in Europe in the Later Middle Ages," *Economic History Review*, 19 (1966/1): 15–28; Marian Małowist, "Z problematyki wzrostu gospodarczego Europy Środkowo-Wschodniej w późnym średniowieczu i na początku XVI wieku," *Przegląd Historyczny*, 64 (1973): 655–80; Jerzy Topolski, *Narodziny kapitalizmu w Europie*, 3rd edition (Poznań: Wydawnictwo Poznańskiego Towarzystwa Przyjaciół Nauk, 2003) 47; Henryk Samsonowicz and Antoni Mączak, "Feudalism and Capitalism: A Balance of Changes in East-Central Europe," in *East-Central Europe in Transition: From the Fourteenth to the Seventeenth Century*, ed. Antoni Mączak, Henryk Samsonowicz, and Peter Burke (Cambridge: Cambridge University Press, 1985), 10–11. See also: Engel, *The Realm*, 244, 323; Jerzy Wyrozumski, "Was Poland Affected by the Late-medieval Crisis of Feudalism ?," *Acta Poloniae Historica*, 78 (1998): 5.
19. František Graus, "Die erste Krise des Feudalismus," *Zeitschrift für Geschichtswissenschaft* 3 (1955): 565, 583–84, 588–89.
20. Georg Juritsch, *Handel und Handelsrecht in Böhmen bis zur husitischen Revolution. Ein Beitrag zur Kulturgeschichte der österreichischen Länder* (Leipzig–Wien: F. Deuticke, 1907), 114–16; Josef Janáček, "Der böhmische Aussenhandel in der Hälfte des 15. Jahrhunderts," *Historica*, 4 (1962): 43; Čechura, *České zemé w letech 1378–1437*, 176; Richard C. Hoffmann, *Land, Liberties and Lordship in a Late Medieval Countryside: Agrarian Structures and Change in the Duchy of Wrocław* (Philadelphia: University of Pennsylvania Press,1988), 28, 274–75, 284.
21. Marian Dygo, "Was There an Economic Crisis in Late Medieval Poland?," *Vierteljahresschrift für Sozial und Wirtschaftsgeschichte*, 77 (1990): 305–22.
22. Marian Dygo, "Wschód i Zachód: gospodarka Europy w XIV–XV wieku," in *Ziemie polskie wobec Zachodu. Studia nad rozwojem Europy*, ed. Sławomir Gawlas (Warszawa: Wydawnictwo DiG, 2006), 170, 181.
23. Eduard Maur, "La Slovaquie," in *Histoire des populations de l'Europe*, ed. Jean Pierre Bardet and Jacques Dupâquier (Paris: Fayard, 1997): 542–44.
24. Hoensch, *Geschichte Böhmens*, 17; Maria Bogucka and Henryk Samsonowicz, *Dzieje miast i mieszczaństwa w Polsce przedrozbiorowej* (Wrocław: Zakład Narodowy im. Ossolińskich, 1986), 120; Irena Gieysztor, "La Pologne," in *Histoire des populations de l'Europe*, ed. Jean Pierre Bardet and Jacques Dupâquier (Paris: Fayard, 1997): 567; Engel, *The Realm*, 333.
25. K. Maleczyński, ed., *Historia Śląska*, vol. 1, part 2, 16.
26. Let us enumerate the Hussite raids (1428–34), the war with a Czech king Jiři of Poděbrady (1459–1469), combined with the desolation of the Silesian countryside, the growing criminality, natural disasters, disadvantageous climatic change, and debasement of silver coins (Hoffmann, *Land*, 247, 284, 319–20, 326). All of these events affected population figures in Silesia by determining the number of births and deaths as well as migration patterns.

27. Andorka, "La Hongrie," 548; Engel, *The Realm*, 102; Balázs Nagy, "Some Characteristics of Urban Development in Hungary in the Period of the Establishment of Kraków under Magdeburg Law in 1257," in *European Cities of Magdeburg Law: Tradition, Heritage, Identity*, ed. Anna Biedrzycka (Kraków: Muzeum Historyczne Miasta Krakowa, 2007), 116.
28. Marian Małowist, *Wschód a Zachód Europy w XIII–XVI wieku. Konfrontacja struktur społeczno-gospodarczych* (Warszawa: Państwowe Wydawnictwo Naukowe, 1973), 35; Dygo, "Wschód," 166; Marek L. Wójcik, "Klęski elementarne w średniowiecznym Wrocławiu. III. Głód, trzęsienia ziemi i zjawiska astronomiczne," *Rocznik Wrocławski*, 8 (2002): 10.
29. See Gieysztor, "La Pologne," 567; Wójcik, "Klęski . . . I. Pożary i zarazy," 34–36.
30. Ibid., 58.
31. Fügedi, "The Demographic Landscape," 50–51. Władysław Rusiński, "Wüstungen. Ein Agrarproblem des feudalen Europas," *Acta Poloniae Historica*, 5 (1962): 73.
32. Fügedi, "The Demographic Landscape," 50; Engel, *The Realm*, 161; Zientara et al., *Dzieje*, 89.
33. Čechura, *České zemé w letech 1310–1378*, 106.
34. Engel, *The Realm*, 161; Čechura, *České zemé w letech 1378–1437,* 184; Dygo, "Wschód," 167.
35. Čechura, *České zemé w letech 1378–1437*, 185; compare Maur, "Le pays tchèques," 537–538.
36. Wójcik, "Klęski . . . . I. Pożary i zarazy," 36 (3,000 victims of the 20,000–22,000 population of Wrocław at that time).
37. Maur, "Le pays tchèques," 538.
38. Samsonowicz and Mączak, "Feudalism and Capitalism," 10.
39. See: Fügedi, "The Demographic Landscape," 52; Jenö Szücs, *Die drei historischen Regionen Europas* (Frankfurt am Main: Verlag Neue Kritik, 1994), 51; Kłoczowski, *Młodsza Europa*, 177 (according to Molnár).
40. Kłoczowski, *Młodsza Europa*, 177.
41. Henryk Samsonowicz, "Gospodarka i społeczeństwo (XIII–początek XVI w.)," in *Dzieje Mazowsza*, vol. 1, ed. Henryk Samsonowicz (Pułtusk: Akademia Humanistyczna im. A. Gieysztora, 2006), 375–76.
42. Ole J. Benedictow, *The Black Death 1346–1353: The Complete History* (Woodbridge: Boydell Press, 2004), 216, 218–24.
43. This, in Benedictow's view, was why no one has inquired into the prices that obtained in Cracow, capital of the Polish Kingdom, gathered by J. Pelc in his study published before the war. In Benedictow's view, the price fluctuations noted by Pelc attest to some kind of cataclysm, which may have been the Black Death (ibid., 219–20).
44. Ibid., 218–19, 222–23
45. Ibid. 223.
46. As for J. Pelc's compilation of the prices obtaining in Cracow, Poland's medieval capital, this evidence does not justify Benedictow's inference of the presence of the plague in that city at the mid-fourteenth century. For example, Pelc offers very little information about grain prices. In any event, his price survey concerns only one town, though a very important one.
47. Postwar historiography—of which, by the way, only a part was dogmatically Marxist, especially in Poland—did not question this view, because it had no reason to do so. On the contrary, after the Second World War inquiry into economic history—especially commerce, crafts, and mining—became more intensive, and (apart from the exceptions mentioned in the present article)

their dynamic development was emphasized. In the first two decades after the war, in addition to political purges of the universities, pressure by communist authorities consisted in compelling historians to adopt the Marxist view of history, and a revolutionary Marxist value system for evaluating historical events. What became mandatory was inquiry into economic history, and the detection in all historical phenomena of exploitation and class struggle as history's fundamental driving force. This emphasis clouded and distorted the prewar, robustly optimistic view of the dynamic development in Poland and Bohemia, but did not undermine or question the fact of that development. In addition, many outstanding works concerning the expansion of crafts, mining, and commerce were published in those two early decades, and afterwards. Consequently, Benedictow's image of an official prohibition of inquiry into the crisis in the late Middle Ages is entirely inaccurate—squarely contradicted by (to mention but a few examples) the oeuvres of F. Graus, M. Małowist, J. Topolski, or A. Rutkowska-Płachcińska—a body of output about which Benedictow is utterly unaware.

48. Archibald Lewis, "The Closing of the Medieval Frontier (1250–1350)," *Speculum* 33 (1958/4): 480.
49. Jan Klápšte, "Studies of structural change in medieval settlement in Bohemia," *Antiquity*, 65 (1991): 396–97, 400, 405; Hoensch, *Geschichte Böhmens,* 98; Jan Rutkowski, "Poland, Lithuania and Hungary," in *The Cambridge Economic History of Europe,* v. 1, ed. Michael M. Postan (Cambridge: Cambridge University Press, 1986), 494; Mákkai, "Economic landscapes," 27; Samsonowicz and Mączak, "Feudalism," 11; Hoffmann, *Land*, 135; Górecki, *Economy,* 203–04; József Laszlovszky, "Fields system in medieval Hungary," in . . . *The Man of Many Devices, Who Wandered Full Many Ways . . . Festschrift in Honor of János Bak*, ed. Balázs Nagy and Marcel Sebők (Budapest: Central European University Press, 1999), 436; Adrienne Körmendy, *Melioratio terrae. Vergleichende Untersuchungen über die Siedlungsbewegung im östlichen Mitteleuropa im 13.–14. Jahrhundert* (Poznań: Wydawnictwo Poznańskiego Towarzystwa Przyjaciół Nauk, 1995), passim.
50. Luboš Nový, ed., *Dějiny techniky v Československu do konce 18. století,* (Praha: Academia, 1974), 162; Maur, "Les pays tchèques," 536; Hoensch, *Geschichte Böhmens,* 98–99; Čechura, "Rolnictvo," 468; Čechura, *České zemé w letech 1310–1378*, 103.
51. Engel, *The Realm,* 60–61, 101, 112, 114, 262, 267–68; Körmendy, *Melioratio terrae,* passim; Maur, "La Slovaquie," 542–43.
52. Benedykt Zientara, *Heinrich der Bärtige und seine Zeit. Politik und Gesellschaft im mittelalterlichen Schlesien*, trans. Peter O. Loew (München: Oldenbourg, 2002), 185–88; Górecki, *Economy,* 193–284; Wyrozumski, "Was Poland Affected," 8–9.
53. Samsonowicz, "Gospodarka," 277.
54. Generally speaking, historians have pointed out a couple of plausible reasons for peasant migration and the resulting abandonment of fields: a) a gradual depletion of heretofore cultivated soils; b) a rise in population density, and the resulting overpopulation; c) natural disasters: floods, droughts, fires, epidemics; d) a deepening of personal servitude, from which the peasants escaped to other, distant villages; e) a decrease in grain prices, which caused migration by the peasants to towns in search of different sources of sustenance; f) wars. For the leading views on this issue, see Rusiński, "Wüstungen," 56, 61–71; Benedykt Zientara, *Die Agrarkrise in der Uckermark im 14. Jahrhundert,* in *Feudalstruktur, Lehnbürgertum und Fernhandel im Spätmittelalterlichen Brandenburg*, eds. Evamaria Engel and Benedykt Zientara (Weimar: Böhlau,

1967), 325–45; Vasko Simoniti, "Die Wüstungen im 14. und 15. Jahrhundert mit besonderer Berücksichtigung des slowenischen Gebietes," *Mitteilungen des Institut für Österreichische Geschichte,* 103 (1995), 44–49; on deserted villages in Bohemia, see Maur, "Les pays tchèques," 538; in Slovakia—Maur, "La Slovaquie," 543; in Silesia—K. Maleczyński, ed., *Historia Śląska,* vol. 1, part 2, 11, and Hoffmann, *Land*, 145; in Poland—Dygo, "Was There an Economic Crisis," 309; Wyrozumski, "Was Poland Affected," 9.

55. Engel, *The Realm*, 273.
56. On the origins of two-field system in Central Europe see: Henryk Łowmiański, *Początki Polski. Z dziejów Słowian w I tysiącleciu,* vol. 3 (Warszawa: Państwowe Wydawnictwo Naukowe, 1967), 238–41. On the characteristics of other agricultural techniques see Charles Parrain, "The Evolution of Agricultural Technique," in *The Cambridge Economic History of Europe,* vol. 1, ed. Michael M. Postan (Cambridge: Cambridge University Press, 1986), 136–38. On the relevant scholarship and the research methods applied by Hungarian historians and archaeologists, see Laszlovsky, "Fields System," 432–44.
57. Márta Belényesi, "La culture permanente et l'évolution du système biennal et triennal en Hongrie médiévale," *Ergon*, 2 (1960), 324.
58. Rondo Cameron, *A Concise Economic History of the World: From Paleolithic Times to the Present*, (Oxford: Oxford University Press, 1989), 63.
59. Nový, *Dějiny techniky*, 77; Aleksander Gieysztor, "W sprawie początków trójpolówki w Polsce i w krajach sąsiednich," in *Prace z dziejów Polski feudalnej ofiarowane Romanowi Grodeckiemu w 70 rocznicę urodzin,* ed. Z. Kozłowska-Budkowa (Warszawa : Państwowe Wydawnictwo Naukowe, 1960), 75.
60. Nový, *Dějiny techniky,* 161; Čechura, *České zemé w letech 1378–1437,* 252; Maleczyński, *Historia Śląska,* vol. 1, part 2, 38.
61. On the fourteenth-century diffusion of the triennial crop rotation, see Dygo, "Was There an Economic Crisis," 311. The fifteenth-century diffusion of this field-system occurred in Masovia. This innovation was imposed by the Masovian duke, Janusz I; see Jakub Sawicki, ed., *Iura Mazoviae Terrestria,* vol. 1 (Warszawa: Państwowe Wydawnictwo Naukowe, 1972), no. 37, § 3 (*In libertate residens iugera extirpabit*), 55.
62. Antoni Mączak, ed., *Encyklopedia historii gospodarczej Polski do roku 1945*, vol. 1, (Warszawa: Wiedza Powszechna, 1980), 150.
63. Engel, *The Realm*, 272.
64. Belényesi, "La culture permanente," 323.
65. Engel, *The Realm,* 272. In eighteenth-century Hungary, 47 percent of the arable fields were cultivated under the two-field system, 26 percent under the three-field system, 16 percent as shifting cultivation, and 9 percent under the one-field system, that is to say, as continuous cultivation—leaving aside some other patterns of cultivation; Imre Wellmann, "Systemy uprawy roli na Węgrzech w XVIII w.," *Kwartalnik Historii Kultury Materialnej*, 8 (1960/4): 492. However, we need to remember that the Turkish occupation led to a depopulation of the central Hungarian countryside in the sixteenth and seventeenth centuries (Laszlovszky, "Fields system," 438). In many cases the continuous legacy of medieval settlement was broken, and central Hungary was repopulated no earlier than in the eighteenth century.
66. Zofia Podwińska, *Technika uprawy roli w Polsce średniowiecznej* (Wrocław: Zakład Narodowy im. Ossolińskich, 1962), 203, 255, 358; eadem, "Origines et propagation de la charrue sur les territoires polonais," *Ergon*, 2 (1960): 300, 307; Nový, ed., *Dějiny techniky*, 162, 165; Engel, *The Realm*, 272.
67. Podwińska, "Origines," 306.

68. Márta Belényesi, "Der Ackerbau und seine Produkte in Ungarn im 14. Jahrhundert," *Acta Ethnographica Academiae Scientiarum Hungaricae*, 6 (1958/3–4), 269.
69. See Pach, "The Development," 1, 4; Čechura, "Rolnictvo," 480, 483; Leonid Żytkowicz, "Trends of Agrarian Economy in Poland, Bohemia and Hungary from the Middle of the Fifteenth to the Middle of the Seventeenth Century," in *East-Central Europe in Transition: From the Fourteenth to the Seventeenth Century*, ed. Antoni Mączak, Henryk Samsonowicz, and Peter Burke (Cambridge: Cambridge University Press, 1985), 69, 74, 79.
70. Čechura, "Rolnictvo," 495; Pach, "The Development," 9.
71. Górecki, *Economy*, 243–58; Hoffmann, *Land*, 125–32, 203–05; Grzegorz Myśliwski, *Człowiek średniowiecza wobec czasu i przestrzeni (Mazowsze od XII do poł. XVI wieku)* (Warszawa: Krupski i Ska, 1999), 233–38; Piotr Guzowski, *Chłopi i pieniądze na przełomie średniowiecza i czasów nowożytnych* (Kraków: Avalon, 2008), 40.
72. Żytkowicz, *Trends*, 74; Čechura, *České zemé w letech 1310–1378*, 155; idem, *České zemé w letech 1378–1437*, 216, 259.
73. Benedykt Zientara et al., *Społeczeństwo polskie od X do XX wieku* (Warszawa: Książka i Wiedza, 1979), 116. The same rule was practiced in some ecclesiastical manors in fourteenth-century Masovia and in fifteenth-century Little Poland; Hubert Wajs, *Powinności feudalne chłopów na Mazowszu od XIV do początku XVI wieku (w dobrach monarszych i kościelnych)*, (Wrocław: Zakład Narodowy im. Ossolińskich, 1986), 105; Guzowski, *Chłopi*, 38.
74. Wyrozumski, "Was Poland Affected," 16.
75. Wajs, *Powinności*, 104.
76. Stefan Inglot, ed., *Historia chłopów polskich,* vol. 1, (Warszawa: Ludowa Spółdzielnia Wydawnicza, 1970), 192.
77. Zientara et al., *Dzieje*, 157; Maleczyński, ed., *Historia Śląska*, vol. 1, part 2, 49–51; Krzysztof Mikulski and Jan Wroniszewski, "Das Vorwerk und die Wandlungen der wirtschaftlichen Konjunktur in den polnischen Ländern im 14.–17. Jahrhundert," *Bulletin der Polnischen Historischen Mission*, 3 (2005), 45–46.
78. Mikulski and Wroniszewski, "Das Vorwerk," 49–55.
79. Mączak, ed., *Encyklopedia,* vol. 1, 173.
80. Żytkowicz, "Trends", 78.
81. Ibid., 71.
82. Mákkai, "Economic landscapes," 34; Żytkowicz, "Trends," 70, 79.
83. Friedrich Lütge, *Strukturwandlungen im ostdeutschen und osteuropäischen Fernhandel des 14. bis 16. Jahrhunderts*, (München: Verlag der Bayerischen Akademie der Wissenschaften, 1964), 41; Nový, ed., *Dějiny techniky*, 170–172; Istvan M. Kiss, "Agricultural and Livestock Production: Wine and Oxen: The case of Hungary," in *East-Central Europe in Transition: From the Fourteenth to the Seventeenth Century,* ed. Antoni Mączak, Henryk Samsonowicz, and Peter Burke (Cambridge: Cambridge University Press, 1985), 88; Mákkai, "Economic landscapes," 26, 30; Zientara et al., *Dzieje*, 101–02.
84. On fish farming, see *Dějiny techniky,* 173; Hoffmann, *Land,* 364; Hoensch, *Geschichte Böhmens,* 177; Čechura, *České zemé w letech 1378–1437,* 216–17.
85. Dygo, "Wschód," 163, 166.
86. Mákkai, "Economic landscapes," 31.
87. Dygo, "Wschód," 163.
88. Ibid., 163.

89. Andrzej Wyrobisz, "Economic Landscapes: Poland from the Fourteenth to the Seventeenth Century," in *East-Central Europe in Transition: From the Fourteenth to the Seventeenth Century,* ed. Antoni Mączak, Henryk Samsonowicz, and Peter Burke (Cambridge: Cambridge University Press, 1985), 38.
90. Inglot, ed., *Historia*, vol. 1, 176.
91. Georges Duby, "Medieval Agriculture 900–1500," in *The Fontana Economic History of Europe,* vol. 1, ed. Carlo M. Cipolla (London: Collins/ Fontana, 1972), 195.
92. Inglot, ed., *Historia*, vol. 1, 177.
93. Ibid.; Małowist, "Z problematyki," 655. According to Z. Podwińska, ratios ranging between 2:1 and 3:1 for the eleventh century are highly hypothetical (*Technika*, 172).
94. Mákkai, "Economic landscapes," 31; Engel, *The Realm,* 272.
95. Anna Rutkowska-Płachcińska, ed., *Historia kultury materialnej Polski w zarysie,* vol. 2 (Wrocław: Zakład Narodowy im. Ossolińskich, 1978), 55; Guzowski, *Chłopi*, 113; yet in some late medieval Polish villages, the ratio could fluctuate, and attain around 2:3 or 3:8 (Inglot, ed., *Historia,* v. 1, 177).
96. Żytkowicz, "Trends," 69; Nový, ed., *Dějiny techniky*, 344.
97. Maleczyński, ed., *Historia Śląska,* vol. 1, part 1, 380.
98. For lists of newly established ("located") towns, see: Hoensch, *Geschichte Böhmens,* 100–101; Čechura, *České zemé w letech 1310–1378,* 126; Bogucka and Samsonowicz, *Dzieje,* 85–88; Engel, *The Realm,* 111–114; see also László Gerevich, "The Rise of Hungarian Town along the Danube," in *Towns in Medieval Hungary,* ed. L. Gerevich (Boulder–Highland Lakes: Akad Kiádo, 1990), 26–50; András Kubinyi, "Urbanisation in the East-Central Part of Medieval Hungary," in *Towns in Medieval Hungary,* ed. László Gerevich (Boulder–Highland Lakes: Akad Kiádo, 1990), 103–49; Nagy, "Some Characteristics," 116–17; Wyrozumski, "Was Poland affected," 10.
99. Čechura, *České zemé w letech 1310–1378*, 147.
100. Bogucka and Samsonowicz, *Dzieje*, 121.
101. Fügedi, *The Demographic Landscape,* 52; Richard Marsina, "O kształtowaniu się pozycji społeczno-gospodarczej miast średniowiecznych na Słowacji," *Kwartalnik Historii Kultury Materialnej,* 23 (1975), 583; Kłoczowski, *Młodsza Europa*, 177.
102. On the most populous cities, see Samsonowicz and Mączak, "Feudalism," 9–10; the authors of the *Dějiny Prahy* are of the opinion that Prague attained 40,000 inhabitants (125). See, on Buda, Rady, *Medieval Buda*, 41–42; on Wrocław, Mateusz Goliński, "Wrocław od połowy XIII do początków XVI wieku," in C. Buśko, M. Goliński, M. Kaczmarek, L. Ziątkowski, *Historia Wrocławia. Od pradziejów do końca czasów habsburskich* (Wrocław: Wydawnictwo Dolnośląskie, 2001), 207; on Cracow, Wyrozumski, Jerzy Wyrozumski, *Dzieje Krakowa*, vol. 1 (Kraków: Wydawnictwo Literackie, 1992), 315–317.
103. Čechura, *České zemé w letech 1310–1378*, 128–129; Helena Březinová, *Textilní výroba v českých, zemích ve 13.–15. století. Poznání textilní produkce na základě archeologických nălezů* (Praha–Brno: Univerzita Karlova, 2007) 62–63, 103; Wyrozumski, "Was Poland Affected," 11.
104. On the origins of craft guilds in Wrocław, see Goliński, "Wrocław," 110. In Prague guilds seem to have arisen and had their economic impact somewhat later, supposedly at the end of the thirteenth century; the first certain reference to craft guilds occurs as late as 1318; *Dějiny Prahy*, 107, 121.

105. Małowist, *Wschód*, 199, 249; Engel, *The Realm*, 259–260. In the Kingdom of Hungary the first craft guilds were established only from the reign of Louis the Great (1342–82) onward; in one of the more important towns, Sopron, they appeared as late as 1425; Engel, *The Realm*, 259–60.
106. For a brief summary of the pros and cons, see Norman J. G. Pounds, *An Economic History of Medieval Europe* (New York: Longman, 1994), 289, 299.
107. Čechura, *České zemé w letech 1310–1378*, 177; Březinová, *Textilní výroba*, 63, 127; Zientara *et al*, *Dzieje*, 118; Danuta Poppe, "*Pannus polonicalis.* Z dziejów sukiennictwa polskiego w średniowieczu," *Kwartalnik Historii Kultury Materialnej*, 36 (1988): 618.
108. Hektor Ammann, "Wirtschaftsbeziehungen zwischen Oberdeutschland und Polen im Mittelalter," *Vierteljahresschrift für Sozial und Wirtschaftsgeschichte*, 38 (1961): 442–443; Antoni Mączak, *Sukiennictwo wielkopolskie XIV–XVII wiek* (Warszawa: Państwowe Wydawnictwo Naukowe, 1955), 222–226.
109. Marian Małowist, "The Problem of the Inequality of Economic Development in Europe in the Later Middle Ages," *Economic History Review*, 19 (1966/1): 20–21.
110. Danuta Molenda, "Powstawanie miast górniczych w Europie Środkowej w XIII–XVIII w.," in *Czas, przestrzeń, praca w dawnych miastach. Studia ofiarowane Henrykowi Samsonowiczowi w sześćdziesiątą rocznicę urodzin* (Warszawa: Wydawnictwo Naukowe PWN, 1991), 157–176.
111. Karol Maleczyński, "Aus der Geschichte des schlesischen Bergbaus in der Epoche des Feudalismus," in *Beiträge zur Geschichte Schlesiens*, ed. Ewa Maleczyńska (Berlin: Rütten & Loening, 1958), 236–283; Josef Janáček, "L'argent tchèque et la Méditerranèe (XIVe et XVe siècles)," in *Histoire économique du monde méditerranéen 1450–1650. Mélanges en l'honneur de Fernand Braudel*, vol. 1 (Touluse: Privat, 1973), 245–247; Hoensch, *Geschichte Böhmens*, 95; Engel, *The Realm*, 155–156.
112. For these estimations, made by Balint Homan, see Engel, *The Realm*, 156, 247.
113. Janįček, "L'argent," 248. According to this historian, the output could have been even higher, at between 25 and 30 tons, and thus comprising over 50 percent of the entire European output.
114. Ibid., 255.
115. Maleczyński, "Aus der Geschichte," 251–252.
116. See: John U. Neff, "Mining and Metallurgy in Medieval Civilisation," in *The Cambridge Economic History of Europe*, vol. 2, ed. Michael M. Postan and Edward Miller (Cambridge: Cambridge University Press, 1986), 724; Maleczyński, "Aus der Geschichte," 251–252; Peter Ratkoš, "Das Kupferwesen in der Slowakei vor der Enstehung der Thurzo-Fuggerschen Handelsgesellschaft," in *Der Aussenhandel Ostmitteleuropas (1450–1650). Die ostmitteleuropäischen Volkswirtschaften in ihren Beziehungen zu Mitteleuropa*, ed. Ingomar Bog (Köln–Wien: Böhlau Verlag, 1971), 598.
117. Danuta Molenda, *Polski ołów na rynkach Europy środkowej w XIII—XVII wieku* (Warszawa: Wydawnictwo Instytutu Archeologii i Etnologii PAN, 2001), 14–16.
118. František Graus, "Die Handelsbeziehungen Böhmen zu Deutschland und Österreich im 14. und zu Beginn des 15. Jahrhunderts," *Historica* 2 (1960): 93; Engel, *The Realm*, 111; Henryk Samsonowicz, "Relations commerciales Polono-Italiennes dans le bas Moyen Age," in *Studi in memoria di Federigo Melis*, Luigi de Rosa, ed. vol. 2 (Napoli: Giannini, 1978), 287–301.

119. Samsonowicz and Mączak, "Feudalism," 10; Čechura, *České zemé w letech 1310–1378*, 105.
120. Jaroslav Purš and Miroslav Kropilák, ed. *Přehled dějin Československa,* vol. 1, part 1 (Praha: Academia, 1980), 353–356.
121. Hoensch, *Geschichte Böhmens,* 18.
122. Purš and M. Kropilák, ed., *Přehled*, 356.
123. Heinrich Wendt, *Schlesien und der Orient. Ein geschichtlicher Überblick* (Breslau: Hirt, 1916), 45–46, 48–51; Wolfgang von Stromer, "Nürnberg-Breslauer Wirtschaftsbeziehungen im Spätmittelalter," *Jahrbuch für fränkische Landesforschung*, 34–35 (1974–1975): 1091–1092.
124. Hoffmann, *Land,* 319–320, 326.
125. Hoensch, *Geschichte Böhmens,* 151, 177, 179.
126. Engel, *The Realm,* 195–208.
127. Ibid., 244–245.
128. Marsina, 581; Engel, *The Realm,* 323.
129. Engel, *The Realm*, 323.
130. Randolph Starn, "Historians and 'Crisis'," *Past and Present*, 52 (1971): 3–22; Topolski, *Narodziny kapitalizmu*, s. 36; Dygo, "Wschód," 129.

BIBLIOGRAPHY

Ammann, H. "Wirtschaftsbeziehungen zwischen Oberdeutschland und Polen im Mittelalter," *Vierteljahresschrift für Sozial und Wirtschaftsgeschichte*, 38 (1961): 433–443.

Andorka, R. "La Hongrie," in *Histoire des populations de l'Europe*, edited by J. P. Bardet and J. Dupâquier, 545–553. Paris: Fayard, 1997.

Belényesi, M. "Der Ackerbau und seine Produkte in Ungarn im 14. Jahrhundert." *Acta Ethnographica Academiae Scientiarum Hungaricae*, 6 (1958/3–4): 265–321.

Belényesi, M, "La culture permanente et l'évolution du système biennal et triennal en Hongrie médiévale" *Ergon*, 2 (1960): 311–326.

Benedictow, O. J. *The Black Death 1346–1353: The Complete History.* Woodbridge: Boydell Press, 2004.

Bogucka M. and H. Samsonowicz. *Dzieje miast i mieszczaństwa w Polsce przedrozbiorowej.* Wrocław: Ossolineum, 1986.

Březinová, H. *Textilní výroba v českých, zemích ve 13.–15. století. Poznání textilní produkce na základě archeologických nălezū.* Praha–Brno: Univerzita Karlova, 2007.

Cameron, R. *A Concise Economic History of the World: From Paleolithic Times to the Present.* Oxford: Oxford University Press, 1989.

Čechura, J. "Rolnictvo v Čechách w pozdním středověku." *Český Časopis Historičky,* 88 (1990/4): 465–98.

Čechura, J. *České zemé w letech 1310–1378. Lucemburkové na českém trůne.* Praha: Nakladatelství Libri, 1999.

Čechura, J. *České zemé w letech 1378–1437. Lucemburkové na českém trůne.* Praha: Nakladatelství Libri, 2000.

Dějiny Prahy, vol. 1. Paseka–Praha–Litomyšl: Paseka, 1997.

Duby, G. "Medieval Agriculture 900–1500," in *The Fontana Economic History of Europe,* vol. 1, edited by C. M. Cipolla, 175–220. London: Collins/Fontana, 1972.

Dygo, M. "Was There an Economic Crisis in Late Medieval Poland?." *Vierteljahresschrift für Sozial und Wirtschaftsgeschichte* , 77 (1990): 305–22.

Dygo, M. "Wschód i Zachód: gospodarka Europy w XIV–XV wieku," in *Ziemie polskie wobec Zachodu. Studia nad rozwojem Europy,* edited by S. Gawlas, 117–194. Warszawa: Wydawnictwo DiG, 2006.

Engel, P. *The Realm of St. Stephen: A History of Medieval Hungary,* trans. by T. Pálosfalvi. London and New York: I. B. Tauris, 2001.

Fügedi, E. "The Demographic Landscape of East-Central Europe." In *East-Central Europe in Transition: From the Fourteenth to the Seventeenth Century,* edited by A. Mączak, H. Samsonowicz, and P. Burke, 47–58. Cambridge: Cambridge University Press, 1985.

Gąsiorowski, A. "Wstęp," in *Codex diplomaticus Maioris Poloniae,* vol. 11, edited by A. Gąsiorowski, T. Jasiński, T. Jurek, and I. Skierska, 5–6. Poznań: Wydawnictwo Poznańskiego Towarzystwa Przyjaciół Nauk, 1999.

Gerevich, L. "The Rise of Hungarian Town along the Danube." In *Towns in Medieval Hungary,* edited by L. Gerevich, 26–50. Boulder–Highland Lakes: Akad Kiádo, 1990.

Gieysztor, A. "W sprawie początków trójpolówki w Polsce i w krajach sąsiednich," in *Prace z dziejów Polski feudalnej ofiarowane Romanowi Grodeckiemu w 70 rocznicę urodzin,* edited by Z. Kozłowska-Budkowa, 71–79. Warszawa: Państwowe Wydawnictwo Naukowe, 1960.

Gieysztor, I. "La Pologne." In *Histoire des populations de l'Europe,* edited by Jean Pierre Bardet and Jacques Dupâquier, 563–73. Paris: Fayard, 1997.

Goliński, M. "Wrocław od połowy XIII do początków XVI wieku," in C. Buśko, M. Goliński, M. Kaczmarek, L. Ziątkowski, *Historia Wrocławia. Od pradziejów do końca czasów habsburskich,* 96–222. Wrocław: Wydawnictwo Dolnośląskie, 2001.

Górecki, P. *Economy, Society, and Lordship in Medieval Poland.* New York and London: Holmes & Meier, 1992.

Górecki, P., ed. *A Local Society in Transition. The 'Henryków Book' and Related Documents.* Toronto: Pontifical Institute of Mediaeval Studies, 2007.

Górka, O. ed. *Anonymi descriptio Europae Orientalis Imperium Constantinopolitanum, Albania, Serbia, Bulgaria, Ruthenia, Ungaria, Polonia, Bohemia Anno MCCCVIII exarata.* Cracoviae: Gebethner, 1916.

Graus, F. "Die erste Krise des Feudalismus." *Zeitschrift für Geschichtswissenschaft 3* (1955): 552–592.

Graus, F., ed. "Tři zlomky českých kupeckých knih z doby předhusitské." *Československý Časopis Historický* 4 (1956): 645–646.

Graus, F. "Die Handelsbeziehungen Böhmen zu Deutschland und Österreich im 14. und zu Beginn des 15. Jahrhunderts," *Historica* 2 (1960): 77–110.

Guzowski, P. *Chłopi i pieniądze na przełomie średniowiecza i czasów nowożytnych.* Kraków: Avalon, 2008.

Hoensch, J. *Geschichte Böhmens. Von der slavischen Landnahme bis zur Gegenwart.* München: Verlag C. H. Beck, 1997.

Hoffmann, R. C., *Land, Liberties and Lordship in a Late Medieval Countryside. Agrarian Structures and Change in the Duchy of Wrocław.* Philadelphia: University of Pennsylvania Press, 1988.

Ihnatowicz, I., A. Mączak, B. Zientara. *Społeczeństwo polskie od X do XX wieku.* Warszawa: Książka i Wiedza, 1997.

Inglot, S., ed. *Historia chłopów polskich,* vol. 1. Warszawa: Ludowa Spółdzielnia Wydawnicza, 1970.

Janáček, J. "Der böhmische Aussenhandel in der Hälfte des 15. Jahrhunderts." *Historica,* 4 (1962): 39–58.

Janáček, J. "L'argent tchèque et la Méditerranèe (XIVe et XVe siècles)," in *Histoire économique du monde méditerranéen 1450–1650. Mélanges en l'honneur de Fernand Braudel,* vol. 1, 245–262. Touluse: Privat, 1973.

Juritsch, G. *Handel und Handelsrecht in Böhmen bis zur husitischen Revolution. Ein Beitrag zur Kulturgeschichte der österreichischen Länder.* Leipzig–Wien: F. Deuticke, 1907.

Kiss, I. M. "Agricultural and Livestock Production: Wine and Oxen: The Case of Hungary," in *East-Central Europe in Transition: From the Fourteenth to the Seventeenth Century,* edited by A. Mączak, H. Samsonowicz, and P. Burke, 59–83. Cambridge: Cambridge University Press, 1985.

Klápšte, J. "Studies of structural change in medieval settlement in Bohemia." *Antiquity,* 65 (1991): 396–405.

Kłoczowski, J. "Le développement de la civilisation en Europe Centrale et Orientale au XIVe et XVe siècles." *Quaestiones Medii Aevi'* 1 (1977): 111–38.

Kłoczowski, J. *Młodsza Europa. Europa Środkowo-Wschodnia w kręgu cywilizacji chrześcijańskiej średniowiecza.* Warszawa: Państwowy Instytut Wydawniczy, 2003.

Knoll, P. W. *The Rise of the Polish Monarchy: Piast Poland in East Central Europe 1320–1370.* Chicago: The University of Chicago Press, 1972.

Körmendy, A. *Melioratio terrae. Vergleichende Untersuchungen über die Siedlungsbewegung im östlichen Mitteleuropa im 13.–14. Jahrhundert.* Poznań: Wydawnictwo Poznańskiego Towarzystwa Przyjaciół Nauk, 1995.

Kubinyi, A. "Urbanisation in the East-Central Part of Medieval Hungary," in *Towns in Medieval Hungary,* edited by L. Gerevich, 103–149. Boulder–Highland Lakes: Akad Kiádo, 1990.

Kubinyi, A. "István Werbőczy als Politiker in der Zeit vor Mohács (1526)," in . . . *The Man of Many Devices, Who Wandered Full Many Ways . . . Festschrift in Honor of János M. Bak,* edited by B. Nagy and M. Sebők, 558–582. Budapest: Central European University Press, 1999.

Laszlovszky, J. "Fields system in medieval Hungary," in . . . *The Man of Many Devices, Who Wandered Full Many Ways . . . Festschrift in Honor of János Bak,* edited by B. Nagy and M. Sebők, 432–44. Budapest: Central European University Press, 1999.

Lewis, A. "The Closing of the Medieval Frontier (1250–1350)." *Speculum* 33 (1958/4): 475–83.

Lütge, F. *Strukturwandlungen im ostdeutschen und osteuropäischen Fernhandel des 14. bis 16. Jahrhunderts.* München: Verlag der Bayerischen Akademie der Wissenschaften, 1964.

Łowmiański, H. *Początki Polski. Z dziejów Słowian w I tysiącleciu,* vol. 3. Warszawa: Państwowe Wydawnictwo Naukowe, 1967.

Mákkai, L. "Economic Landscapes: Historical Hungary from the Fourteenth to the Seventeenth Century." In *East-Central Europe in transition. From the fourteenth to the seventeenth century,* ed. A. Mączak, H. Samsonowicz and P. Burke, 24–35. Cambridge: Cambridge University Press, 1985.

Maleczyński, K. "Aus der Geschichte des schlesischen Bergbaus in der Epoche des Feudalismus," in *Beiträge zur Geschichte Schlesiens,* edited by E. Maleczyńska, 236–283. Berlin: Rütten & Loening, 1958.

Maleczyński, K., ed. *Historia Śląska,* vol. 1, part 1. Wrocław: Zakład Narodowy im. Ossolińskich, 1960.

Maleczyński, K., ed. *Historia Śląska,* vol. 1, part 2. Wrocław: Zakład Narodowy im. Ossolińskich, 1961.

Małowist, M. *Le développement des rapports économiques entre la Flandre la Pologne et les pays limitrophes du XIIIe au XIVe siècle." Revue belge de Philologie et d'Histoire* 10 (1931/4): 1,013–1,065.

Małowist, M. "The Problem of the Inequality of Economic Development in Europe in the Later Middle Ages." *Economic History Review* 19 (1966/1): 15–28.

Małowist, M. "Bases économiques du retour de la Poméranie de Dantzig à la Pologne au XVe siècle," in M. Małowist, *Croissance et regressions en Europe XIVe–XVIIe siècles*, 63–90. Paris: Colin, 1972.

Małowist, M. *Wschód a Zachód Europy w XIII–XVI wieku. Konfrontacja struktur społeczno–gospodarczych.* Warszawa: Państwowe Wydawnictwo Naukowe, 1973.

Małowist, M. "Z problematyki wzrostu gospodarczego Europy Środkowo-Wschodniej w późnym średniowieczu i na początku XVI wieku." *Przegląd Historyczny* 64 (1973): 655–680.

Marsina, R. "O kształtowaniu się pozycji społeczno-gospodarczej miast średniowiecznych na Słowacji." *Kwartalnik Historii Kultury Materialnej* 23 (1975): 567–586.

Matuszewski, J. and J. Matuszewski. "Einleitung." In *Najstarszy Zwód Prawa Polskiego*, 26–49. Łódź: Wydawnictwo Uniwersytetu Łódzkiego 1995.

Maur, E. "Obyvatelstvo českých zemí ve středověku," in *Dějiny obyvatelstva českých zemí*, 35–73. Praha : Mladá Fronta, 1996.

Maur, E. "La Slovaquie," in *Histoire des populations de l'Europe*, edited by J. P. Bardet and J. Dupâquier, 542–544. Paris: Fayard, 1997.

Maur, E. "Les pays tchèques," in *Histoire des populations de l'Europe*, edited by J. P. Bardet and J. Dupâquier, 536–542. Paris: Fayard, 1997.

Mączak, A. *Sukiennictwo wielkopolskie XIV–XVII wiek.* Warszawa: Państwowe Wydawnictwo Naukowe, 1955.

Mączak, A., ed. *Encyklopedia historii gospodarczej Polski do roku 1945,* vol. 2. Warszawa: Wiedza Powszechna, 1980.

Mikulski, K. and J. Wroniszewski. "Das Vorwerk und die Wandlungen der wirtschaftlichen Konjunktur in den polnischen Ländern im 14.–17. Jahrhundert." *Bulletin der Polnischen Historischen Mission*, 3 (2005): 141–154.

Molenda, D. "Powstawanie miast górniczych w Europie Środkowej w XIII–XVIII w," in *Czas, przestrzeń, praca w dawnych miastach. Studia ofiarowane Henrykowi Samsonowiczowi w sześćdziesiątą rocznicę urodzin*, edited by A. Wyrobisz and M. Tymowski, 157–176. Warszawa: Wydawnictwo Naukowe PWN, 1991.

Molenda, D. *Polski ołów na rynkach Europy środkowej w XIII—XVII wieku.* Warszawa: Wydawnictwo Instytutu Archeologii i Etnologii PAN, 2001.

Myśliwski, G. *Człowiek średniowiecza wobec czasu i przestrzeni (Mazowsze od XII do poł. XVI wieku).* Warszawa: Krupski i Ska, 1999.

Nagy, B. "Some Characteristics of Urban Development in Hungary in the Period of the Establishment of Kraków under Magdeburg Law in 1257," in *European Cities of Magdeburg Law: Tradition, Heritage, Identity*, edited by A. Biedrzycka, 113–117. Kraków: Muzeum Historyczne Miasta Krakowa, 2007.

Neff, J. U. "Mining and Metallurgy in Medieval Civilisation," in *The Cambridge Economic History of Europe,* vol. 2, ed. M. M. Postan and E. Miller, 693–761. Cambridge: Cambridge University Press, 1986.

Nový, L. ed. *Dějiny techniky v Československu do konce 18. století.* Praha: Academia, 1974.

Pach, Z. "The Development of Feudal Rent in Hungary in the Fifteenth Century," *Economic History Review* 19 (1966/1): 1–13.

Pacuski, K. "Przegląd źródeł," in *Dzieje Mazowsza*, vol. 1, edited by H. Samsonowicz, 19–42. Pułtusk: Akademia Humanistyczna im. A. Gieysztora, 2006.

Parrain, C. "The Evolution of Agricultural Technique," in *The Cambridge Economic History of Europe,* vol. 1, edited by M. M. Postan, 126–179. Cambridge: Cambridge University Press, 1986.

Podwińska, Z. "Origines et propagation de la charrue sur les territoires polonais." *Ergon* 2 (1960): 300–310.

Podwińska, Z. *Technika uprawy roli w Polsce średniowiecznej*. Wrocław: Zakład Narodowy im. Ossolińskich, 1962.

Poppe, D. "*Pannus polonicalis*. Z dziejów sukiennictwa polskiego w średniowieczu." *Kwartalnik Historii Kultury Materialnej*, 36 (1988): 617–36.

Pounds, N. J. G. *An Economic History of Medieval Europe*. New York: Longman, 1994.

Purš, J. and M. Kropilák, ed. *Přehled dějin Československa*, vol. 1, part 1. Praha: Academia, 1980.

Rady, M. *Medieval Buda: A Study of Municipal Government and Jurisdiction in the Kingdom of Hungary*. New York: Columbia University Press, 1985.

Ratkoš, P. "Das Kupferwesen in der Slowakei vor der Enstehung der Thurzo-Fuggerschen Handelsgesellschaft," in *Der Aussenhandel Ostmitteleuropas (1450–1650). Die ostmitteleuropäischen Volkswirtschaften in ihren Beziehungen zu Mitteleuropa*, edited by I. Bog, 584–599. Köln–Wien: Böhlau Verlag, 1971.

Rusiński, W. "Wüstungen. Ein Agrarproblem des feudalen Europas." *Acta Poloniae Historica*, 5 (1962): 48–78.

Rutkowska-Płachcińska, A., ed. *Historia kultury materialnej Polski w zarysie*, vol. 2. Wrocław: Zakład Narodowy im. Ossolińskich, 1978.

Rutkowski, J. "Poland, Lithuania and Hungary," in *The Cambridge Economic History of Europe*, vol. 1, edited by M. M. Postan, 487–506. Cambridge: Cambridge University Press, 1986.

Samsonowicz, H. "Relations commerciales Polono-Italiennes dans le bas Moyen Age," in *Studi in memoria di Federigo Melis*, vol. 2, edited by L. de Rosa, 287–301. Napoli: Giannini, 1978.

Samsonowicz, H. "Społeczeństwo w Polsce ok. 1400 roku," in *Polska około roku 1400*, edited by W. Fałkowski, 9–40. Warszawa: Neriton, 2000.

Samsonowicz, H. "L'économie de l'Europe du Centre-Est du Haut Moyen Âge au XVIe siècle," in *Histoire de l'Europe du Centre-Est*, 621–641. Paris: Presses Universitaires de France, 2004.

Samsonowicz, H. "Gospodarka i społeczeństwo (XIII–początek XVI w.)," in *Dzieje Mazowsza*, vol. 1, edited by H. Samsonowicz, 339–393. Pułtusk: Akademia Humanistyczna im. A. Gieysztora, 2006.

Samsonowicz, H. and A. Mączak. "Feudalism and Capitalism: A Balance of Changes in East-Central Europe," In *East-Central Europe in Transition: From the Fourteenth to the Seventeenth Century*, edited by A. Mączak, H. Samsonowicz, and P. Burke, 6–23. Cambridge: Cambridge University Press, 1985.

Sawicki, J., ed. *Iura Masoviae Terrestria*, vol. 1. Warszawa: Państwowe Wydawnictwo Naukowe, 1972.

Simoniti, V. "Die Wüstungen im 14. und 15. Jahrhundert mit besonderer Berücksichtigung des slowenischen Gebietes." *Mitteilungen des Institut für Österreichische Geschichte* 103 (1995): 44–55.

Starn, R. "Historians and 'Crisis'." *Past and Present* 52 (1971): 3–22.

Stenzel, G. A., ed. "Das Landbuch des Fürstentums Breslau," in *Berichte der Gesellschaft fuer Schlesische Vaterländische Cultur und Geschichte* 1842, 48–141.

Stobbe, O., ed. "Mittheilungen aus Breslauer Signaturbüchern." *Zeitschrift für Geschichte und Alterthum Schlesiens*, (1867/2): 446–449.

von Stromer, W. "Nürnberg-Breslauer Wirtschaftsbeziehungen im Spätmittelalter." *Jahrbuch für fränkische Landesforschung*, 34–35 (1974–1975): 1,079–1,100.

Szücs, J. *Die drei historischen Regionen Europas*, 2nd edition. Frankfurt am Main: Verlag Neue Kritik, 1994.

Topolski, J. *Narodziny kapitalizmu w Europie*, 3rd edition. Poznań: Wydawnictwo Poznańskiego Towarzystwa Przyjaciół Nauk, 2003.

Tyszkiewicz, J. *Ludzie i przyroda w Polsce średniowiecznej*. Warszawa: Państwowe Wydawnictwo Naukowe, 1983.

Wajs, H. *Powinności feudalne chłopów na Mazowszu od XIV do początku XVI wieku (w dobrach monarszych i kościelnych)*. Wrocław: Zakład Narodowy im. Ossolińskich, 1986.
Wellmann, I. "Systemy uprawy roli na Węgrzech w XVIII w." *Kwartalnik Historii Kultury Materialnej* 8 (1960/4): 479–99.
Wendt, H. *Schlesien und der Orient. Ein geschichtlicher Überblick*. Breslau: Hirt, 1916.
Wójcik, M. L. "Klęski elementarne w średniowiecznym Wrocławiu. I. Pożary i zarazy." *Rocznik Wrocławski* 6 (2000): 27–40.
Wójcik, M. L. "Klęski elementarne w średniowiecznym Wrocławiu. III. Głód, trzęsienia ziemi i zjawiska astronomiczne." *Rocznik Wrocławski* 8 (2002): 9–22.
Wyrobisz, A. "Economic Landscapes: Poland from the Fourteenth to the Seventeenth Century," in *East-Central Europe in Transition: From the Fourteenth to the Seventeenth Century*, edited by A. Mączak, H. Samsonowicz, and P. Burke, 36–45. Cambridge: Cambridge University Press, 1985.
Wyrozumski, J. *Dzieje Polski do roku 1505*. Warszawa: Państwowe Wydawnictwo Naukowe, 1984.
Wyrozumski, J. "Was Poland Affected by the Late-medieval Crisis of Feudalism?." *Acta Poloniae Historica* 78 (1998): 5–17.
Wyrozumski, J. *Dzieje Krakowa*, vol. 1. Kraków: Wydawnictwo Literackie, 1992.
Zientara, B. *Die Agrarkrise in der Uckermark im 14. Jahrhundert,* in Evamaria Engel and Benedykt Zientara, *Feudalstruktur, Lehnbürgertum und Fernhandel im Spätmittelalterlichen Brandenburg*, 223–396. Weimar: Böhlau, 1967.
Zientara, B. *Heinrich der Bärtige und seine Zeit. Politik und Gesellschaft im mittelalterlichen Schlesien*, trans. by Peter O. Loew. München: Oldenbourg, 2002.
Zientara, B., Mączak, A. Ihnatowicz, I. and Landau, Z. *Dzieje gospodarcze Polski do 1939 roku*. Warszawa: Wiedza Powszechna, 1979.
Zientara, B., Mączak, A., Ihnatowicz, I. *Społeczeństwo polskie od X do XX wieku*. Warszawa: Książka i Wiedza, 1979.
Żytkowicz, L. "Trends of Agrarian Economy in Poland, Bohemia and Hungary from the Middle of the Fifteenth to the Middle of the Seventeenth Century," in *East-Central Europe in Transition: From the Fourteenth to the Seventeenth Century*, edited by A. Mączak, H. Samsonowicz, and P.Burke, 59–83. Cambridge: Cambridge University Press, 1985.

9 Russia

Janet Martin

In Russia the period 1200–1500 was transformative. At the beginning of the thirteenth century, the loose federation of principalities, known as Kievan Rus', was experiencing severe political strains. As princes of the ruling Riurikid dynasty vied for dominance and control over the central capital of Kiev, the bonds among their individual principalities were weakening. Those bonds were severed in the aftermath of the Mongol invasion (1237–40), which resulted in the subjugation of the Rus' principalities to the Mongols' Kipchak Khanate, commonly known as the Golden Horde. For the next century the Rus' principalities functioned as separate polities, each ruled by its own Riurikid prince, who was confirmed in office by his suzerain, the Mongol khan. During the fourteenth century those principalities that had formed the southwestern and western portions of Kievan Rus' and comprise modern Ukraine and Belarus' were absorbed into Poland and Lithuania. The northern Russian principalities, from Novgorod in the west to Vladimir-Suzdal' and Riazan' in the east, gradually from the fourteenth century through the early sixteenth century fell under the domination of the princes of Moscow. As the Golden Horde itself declined under combined political, military, and economic pressures stemming from the disintegration of the Mongol Empire and ultimately fragmented during the fifteenth century into several Tatar khanates, another new realm, Muscovy, also formed. The northern Russian principalities that comprised that realm will be the regions considered in the following discussion.

The development of the Russian agrarian economy was also influenced by the Mongol invasions, which caused massive, if uneven, destruction, and stimulated population flight and resettlement. The capital city of Kiev and Vladimir, the major princely seat of northeastern Rus', were among the towns badly damaged by the Mongol armies. Novgorod, the commercial center in northwestern Russia, however, avoided attack. Following the initial invasion the Rus' princes, as part of their obligations to their new overlords, collected and paid tribute to the Mongol khans, who oversaw their subordinates' activities from the steppe and their new capital Sarai on the lower Volga River. The tribute payments, extracted

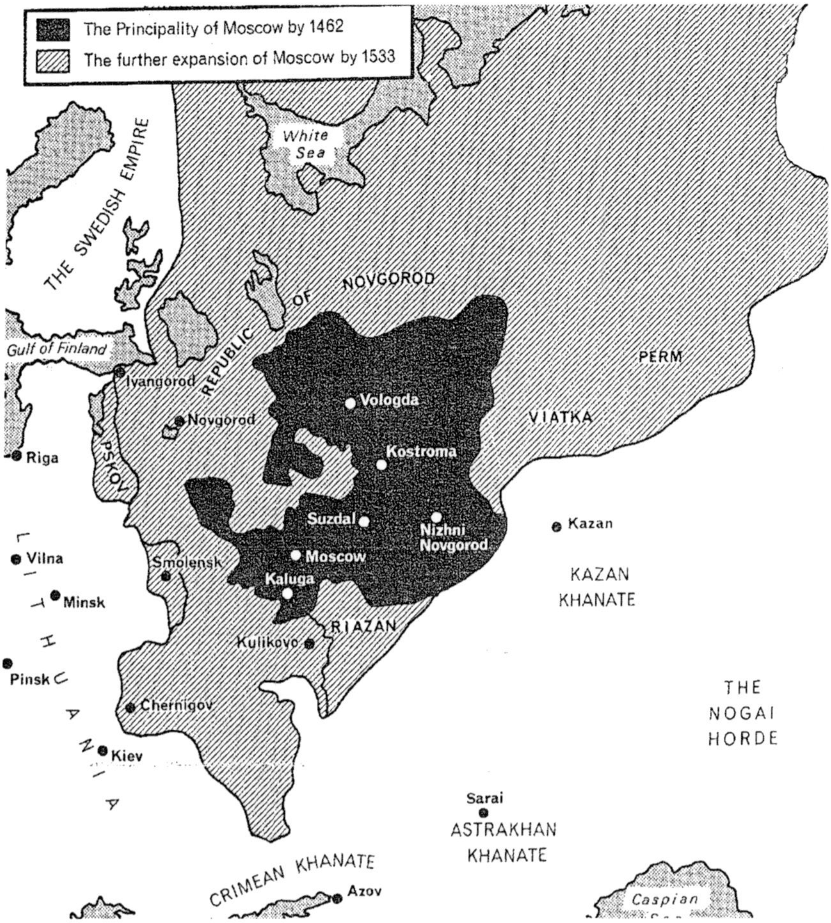

Figure 9.1 The Lands of Rus', 1261–1533. Taken from *The Routledge Atlas of Russian History*, 3rd ed. by Martin Gilbert, copyright 2002 (London and New York). Used by permission of the author.

through extraordinary collections, fees on commercial transactions, and regular taxes on peasants and townsmen, especially in Novgorod, constituted an outflow of large amounts of wealth. As the Russian lands, responding to these new conditions, recovered during the next centuries, Novgorod's relative economic strength receded. Moscow superseded not only Novgorod, but Kiev and Vladimir as well, to become the primary political, ecclesiastical, and economic center of Russia. In the context of these upheavals and political reconfigurations, complicated further by the effects of the Black Death as well as other epidemics, famines, floods, and droughts, the Russian peasantry also experienced a significant transformation. At the beginning of the thirteenth century, the Russian peasant was a free member of his society. At the end of the period, in 1497, a law code, adopted by Grand Prince Ivan III of Moscow, for the first time placed limits on the mobility of peasants throughout his realm.[1] This was the beginning of the process, which was not completed until 1649, that legally enserfed Russia's peasants.[2]

The Mongol invasion not only affected the political, economic, and demographic developments of the lands of Rus', but also scholarly studies of those developments. The initial invasion and subsequent military campaigns conducted against the Rus' principalities involved looting and burning that destroyed written records. The Mongol practice of taking skilled laborers as captives removed scribes from princely and ecclesiastical courts. Scholars, consequently, have limited written sources for this period, particularly for issues relating to agrarian history.

The best sources are land registers compiled at the turn of the fifteenth–sixteenth centuries for the Novgorod lands in northwestern Russia, a couple of decades after Moscow gained political control over the region and altered its land tenure system. The books contain data on recently distributed landed estates; in some cases they include data on the sizes and operations of landed estates before the grand prince of Moscow transformed the system. These books, which are not complete, are the only sources containing quantitative data that yield anything even approaching a comprehensive overview of a significant portion of the Russian lands before 1500. For the other regions and periods the understanding of Russia's rural economy must be patched together from scattered documentary sources, e.g., testaments, land deeds, charters and land grants, records of donations to monasteries, entries in chronicles, references in birchbark documents, and data from archeological studies. In some instances, such as the land tenure of some large monasteries, these sources are abundant enough to allow the formulation of a relatively good view of the accumulation and exploitation of landed estates during the fourteenth and fifteenth centuries. In other instances, there are huge gaps in the source base, hence gaps in the understanding of economic development.

PHYSICAL FEATURES OF NORTHERN RUSSIA

The northern Russian principalities were located above the 55th parallel, i.e., further north than the entire European continent except Scandinavia. The relatively low (100–200 meters above sea level), flat landscape was interrupted by the Valdai hills, which reached heights of over 300 meters and contained the headwaters of four main rivers, the Volga, the Dnieper, the Western Dvina, and the Msta, stretching east, south, west, and north and partitioning the lands of Rus'. In the taiga with its cold temperatures and high humidity, pine, spruce, and birch trees were supported by a podzol soil, consisting of a thin, black, acidy surface layer over a layer of grey soil, leached of most of its nutrients. Soils moderately improved as deciduous trees mixed with the coniferous forests. With the exception of an area in the so-called Volga-Oka mesopotamia, which included the area near Vladimir where the soil was a richer grey forest variety, the soils were, thus, not particularly fertile. A short growing season (c. 120 days of frost-free weather), the extreme temperatures of the northern continental climate, a long period during which snow covered the ground (almost half of the year), and marshy conditions in some areas combined to create a region with low capacity for agricultural production.[3]

CROPS AND FARMING TECHNIQUES

Agriculture on these lands was conducted by peasants. They typically congregated in villages and hamlets, ranging in size from multi-household villages, which were more common in the central region south of the Volga river, to just one to three households in some areas north of the Volga river and in northwestern Russia.[4] Precise information for the sizes of peasant villages and households exists only for the late fifteenth century. Surviving land records from that period for northwestern Russia register over 35,000 peasant settlements; most consisted of between one and five households.[5] In some areas, especially those that contained the oldest settlements or had become parish centers, hamlets and villages were larger. In regions near the Gulf of Finland (in the vicinities of Kopor'e and Iama), for example, settlements contained an average of closer to 17 households, but only rarely exceeded 30. Elsewhere along the Luga River, which flowed past Iama into the Gulf of Finland, seven households per settlement was the norm.[6] An example from central Russia is contained in an excerpt from a land register from the same period for landholdings of the Trinity-St. Sergius monastery. It recorded 37 villages and hamlets in the Radonezh region, located just north of Moscow; they contained a total of 470 peasant and non-agricultural households, dwelled in by 473 male adults. Although some of the larger villages contained dozens of households, some hamlets consisted of just one or two.[7]

Households generally consisted of nuclear families,[8] whose members farmed their plots or fields together. A typical household physically consisted of a hut and outbuildings and a threshing floor within a yard, enclosed by a fence. The family's livestock could be kept within the fenced area; gardens might be within it or outside the enclosure.[9] Households and villages also formed larger units, referred to as the *obshchina* or *mir*, which held some resources, e.g., meadows, fishing rights, and forests, in common possession. The leaders of these communal units managed administrative responsibilities and interactions with princely officials and large, private landowners. Little is known of how these collective units operated. Documents from the late fifteenth century, however, highlight some aspects of their functions. The peasants, acting in concert through their community structures, participated in legal proceedings, including land disputes.[10] Other documentary records indicate that the communes, whose members worked land belonging to a major landowner, had joint responsibility for paying rents and other fees as well as performing labor duties for their landlord.

Variation among crops produced by the peasants of northern Russia was minimal and depended upon geographic location and climate. The most common crops raised by peasants throughout the northern Russian lands were rye and oats. In some regions barley and wheat were also grown. Although less frequently mentioned in documentary sources, millet, which had been more commonly produced in earlier centuries, and buckwheat are attested by archeological evidence. Grains were supplemented by peas, lentils, turnips. In gardens and orchards peasants also grew cabbages, onions, garlic, cucumbers, radishes, beets, and poppy seeds, apples, and cherries. Forest products, such as mushrooms, berries, nuts, honey, and meat obtained by hunting wild animals, supplemented cultivated crops, as did fish obtained from lakes and rivers that watered the region.[11] Flax, hemp, and hops were the most common non-edible crops produced.[12] Hay was widely produced and used, along with oats, as a feed for livestock.

Although the range of crops was relatively stable throughout the Russian lands during the period 1200–1500, farming techniques underwent gradual change. This factor has been the subject of scholarly debate, which revolves around the systems of agriculture employed by peasants. A variety of systems have been observed. The slash-and-burn method survived throughout the period. It was used particularly in times when and locations where the forested lands were not densely populated. Peasants cleared plots in the forest by chopping down trees or slashing the bark, thus killing them, and then chopping them down. They either hauled the logs away or burned them along with surrounding brush. The soil, enriched by the ashes, supported crops for about three years. When it was depleted, peasants shifted their cultivation to other patches, which they cleared in a similar manner. This process could be repeated until the peasants encountered lands cultivated or owned by others, a condition occurring with more frequency as the area under cultivation expanded. Abandoned patches regained their fertility after approximately 40 years.

By the fifteenth century a three-field rotation crop rotation system was being adopted. The mature system involved the division of arable land into three equally sized fields. Peasants typically sowed a winter crop, usually rye, in one field, a spring crop in the second, and left the third fallow. Each year they would rotate the fields. Evidence for the use of this system is both circumstantial and documentary. The appearance of specialized terms for cereal grain crops, such as winter rye and spring-sown oats, imply that two crops were being produced and a method of farming incorporating at least two plots or fields was employed. Evidence of balanced production among the crops has been considered as an indication that fields of approximately equal size had been created.[13] But written records that state the size of crops produced in one field and refer to equal amounts in two other fields, which have been interpreted as evidence of a three-field rotation system, appear only in the late fifteenth century.[14]

While there is general agreement concerning the early use of the slash-and-burn method of farming and the tendency to continue to employ it when conditions encouraged its use throughout the period and similar agreement that the three-field rotation system was becoming the favored system by the end of the period, there has been considerable debate over intermediary forms of production as well as the timing of the introduction of the three-field system. Various forms, including a long fallow system, a two-field system, and a three-field system that did not involve fields of equal size, have been proposed.[15] When using the forest-long fallow system, which developed from the slash-and-burn method, peasants would return to an abandoned plot in the forest after it had lain fallow for an extended period, long enough for scrub and secondary growth to have grown back in the plot. They would then burn that growth, and return the plot to cultivation for a few years until the soil was once again depleted.[16] A variant of this system was an infield-outfield arrangement. According to this arrangement an infield would be continuously cultivated and kept productive by using all available fertilizer, produced by livestock. The more distant, long fallow plot in the forest became the outfield.[17] Others have postulated that forms of a two-field rotation system were adopted to replace the slash-and-burn method of clearing plots.[18] It has been suggested, furthermore, that the addition of a third field to this system, possibly an outfield, became the foundation for the development of the three-field rotation system.[19] An alternative proposal for the evolution of the three-field system focuses on adoption of a method of a three-year rotation in the cultivation of several irregularly shaped, unequally sized, scattered plots.[20]

Despite these debates and some dissenting voices, scholars tend to agree that a three-field rotation system had been adopted in the north-western part of Russia (the Novgorod area) by the last decades of the fifteenth century, although it had probably been introduced earlier.[21] It was also well-known in central Russia, although other practices including slash-and-burn as well as some form of the transition to the three-field system were also in use, and the three-field system may not have become uniformly established until the sixteenth century.[22] Some scholars have concluded that in central Russia the three-field system was adopted earlier on estates belonging to large-scale landowners than on smaller estates; others see little evidence for this conclusion.[23]

The debate over agricultural methods has been closely linked to farm implements that were in use. Evidence for farm tools is drawn from archeological artifacts, illustrations of farming activity, and terms derived from tools and used for agriculturally-based taxes. Combined, these sources indicate that in both northwestern and central Russia an instrument known as the *sokha* was the main tool used for working the soil for planting.[24] The *sokha* was a scratch plow, also described as a forked hoe. It was typically constructed of wood with two closely set 'teeth' or tines that could be equipped with metal plowshares and were set at a relatively steep angle with reference to the soil. This light implement, which required use of only a single horse, was well-suited to forest clearings with their shallow, often stony soils and irregular shapes.[25]

True plows, designed to turn over the soil, would have been suitable only for the heavier soils around Vladimir and areas further south; they were far less common in the northern Russian lands during this period. Some references to plow and plow land appear in documents dated from the mid-fifteenth century. The term for plow (*plug*) was used as a unit of measure. The implement was probably used only on larger estates, if at all.[26]

In addition to the *sokha*, peasants used a harrow to break up clods of earth and smooth the soil, a sickle for harvesting grain and a scythe to cut hay. The short-handled style of scythe was well-suited for cutting grasses that grew around trees, stumps, or boulders or in otherwise confined areas.[27] The horse was the preferred animal for use with the *sokha*. Peasants also raised cattle, pigs, sheep, and poultry. Oxen were known, but relatively rare. Livestock were relatively small in size. In addition to oats and hay, livestock grazed in forests and in fields after the harvests.[28] Although the livestock produced manure which would have fertilized the soil, there is little direct evidence concerning it. Scholars who postulate the use of an infield-outfield method of farming assume it would have been necessary to keep the infield productive on a continuous basis. It is similarly assumed that manure would have been employed in a three-field system. Nevertheless, written sources do not confirm the assumption. In contrast to sixteenth-century documents that specify peasant obligations to their landlords, those from the fourteenth and fifteenth, while mentioning tasks such as mowing hay, do not mention carting or spreading manure.[29]

Despite the adaptation of farming methods to the northern forest zone and its light soils, agricultural yields were low. Figures, determined for the end of the sixteenth century, are reported to have averaged 3–4:1 for rye;

for oats the yield was closer to 3:1. In the richer regions around Vladimir results were better; in northern areas, they were poorer, falling to as low as 1.5–2:1. These results came from soils that had been cultivated for lengthy periods. It is considered probable that in earlier periods, especially when new plots created by the slash-and-burn method were cultivated, their initial yields were significantly higher.[30]

LAND TENURE AND ORGANIZATION OF PRODUCTION

Little is known of land ownership in the thirteenth century. It has been broadly accepted, however, that during the Kievan Rus' era peasants were proprietors of their own lands. Living in family units, they owned their equipment and livestock, cultivated their own plots of the land, and disposed of their crops.[31] But by the eleventh and twelfth centuries, princes, who claimed control over all the territory within their realms, had assumed some lands within them for personal use and granted others to their courtiers or nobles as well as to ecclesiastical institutions. The earliest surviving land grant charters refer to gifts made by Prince Mstislav Vladimirovich of Kiev (ruled 1125–32) and Prince Vsevolod Mstislavich of Novgorod (ruled 1117–36) to the Iur'ev (St. George) monastery in Novgorod. The charters make no mention of agricultural activities undertaken by villagers dwelling on the transferred lands. Vsevolod's gift includes a parish with its land, people, forests, and beehives. Mstislav's grant identifies various fees collected from the rural district that he authorized his son, Vsevolod, to give to the monastery.[32] Some scholars, e.g., Igor' Iakovlevich Froianov, have surmised that princes and their courtiers operated their personal estates not for the cultivation of crops, but for other specialized types of production such as raising livestock, most significantly horses used for military activity, and for the exploitation of other natural resources.[33] This observation is consistent with provisions in the Kievan law codes, which, although specifying punishment for stealing grain from a threshing floor or storage pit, pay less attention to grain cultivation, farming equipment, and even landed property than to animal husbandry.[34] This imbalance has been interpreted to mean that the princes, who issued the codes, placed a relatively low priority on agricultural crops. Elite landowners may also have used slaves and indentured laborers to perform the activities on their estates, not free peasants who pursued their agricultural activities on their own lands.[35] It thus appears that at the outset of the thirteenth century, peasants along with princes, princely courtiers or nobles, ecclesiastical hierarchs, and monasteries were landowners.

The practice of transferring agrarian lands, referred to in documents as villages and hamlets or as rural districts, to private ownership continued in northern Russia during the period 1200–1500. As princes and their boyars, other high-ranking members of the princely courts, ecclesiastical offices, and monasteries gained control over increasing amounts of land, peasants dwelling in villages and hamlets on them were required to pay rent for the use of their fields and the other resources on the land.

The paucity of documentation before the late fourteenth century has made the process of land acquisition during the thirteenth and fourteenth centuries difficult to discern.[36] Surviving records, dated from the last decades of the fourteenth and the fifteenth centuries, reveal, however, that it had been taking place. Grand Prince Dmitry Donskoi (ruled 1359–89) figures in some of the earliest. In c. 1380–82, for example, he participated in a land exchange with a monk. Dmitry took possession of a village with its associated hamlets and gave the monk a retreat that had previously been established on his lands. The chief asset of the lands given to the monk was beehives, not agricultural products.[37] A document recording a sale of land by a princess Feodos'ia, the daughter of the Moscow prince Ivan I Kalita (ruled 1328–40) and widow of Prince Feodor Romanovich of Beloozero, dates from approximately the same time (1380s–90s). The document records the sale of a wasteland with associated lands, waters, and meadows.[38] Feodos'ia also sold other, more extensive landed property in Beloozero to the grandmother of Aleksandr Monastyrev; those properties were passed on to Aleksandr and his descendants, who retained ownership of them through the fifteenth century.[39] Ivan Andreevich Khromyi, who also lived in the fourteenth century, came into possession of a rural district in Beloozero when he married the daughter of Dmitrii Aleksandrovich Monastyrev; that district was his wife's dowry.[40] One of Khromyi's brothers, Fedor Andreevich Sviblo, had also become a major landowner in this period. The wills of Grand Prince Vasily I (ruled 1389–1425) include references to Sviblo's properties, which had been confiscated when he fell into disgrace. The portion of his landholdings mentioned in the wills consisted of 15 villages with associated hamlets that were located in nine different districts.[41] Khromyi's other three brothers were also major landowners in the fourteenth century.[42] The evidence of the confiscation of Sviblo's landed property as well as the cited land transfers all testify to private landownership by members of the political elite earlier in the fourteenth century.

Documents from the fifteenth century also reflect gifts of lands with villages made by princes to their courtiers;[43] a variety of land transactions undertaken by members of landowning families;[44] and exemptions issued by princes to landowners, releasing the peasants on their lands from specified taxes and fees and, in some cases, from the jurisdiction of the prince's officials and courts of law.[45] Although such documents confirm private ownership of allodial lands, few scholars have attempted to analyze them to produce a comprehensive overview of this form of land tenure; it thus remains difficult to gauge its scale or its development during the fourteenth and fifteenth centuries.[46]

More is known about ecclesiastical landowning in central Russia. Churches and, to an even greater degree, monasteries throughout northern

Russia had also become major landowners by the end of the fifteenth century. They acquired lands primarily through purchases and donations, normally given to ensure monks would pray for the souls of the donor and/or specified family members after their deaths. Monasteries also acquired lands by engaging in exchanges and encroaching upon peasant holdings.

Although monasteries were present in central Russia in the thirteenth century, they became major landowners in conjunction with an intensive movement, which began in the second half of the fourteenth century and involved the establishment of monasteries throughout rural northern Russia. A major figure in this movement was St. Sergius of Radonezh (d. 1392), who founded the Trinity monastery by the mid-1370s. Already by the early fifteenth century the wealth of the Trinity monastery had become so great that it constructed two, or possibly three, masonry structures, the only monastic community to have done so without financial assistance from patrons.[47]

The Trinity monastery suffered serious damage in 1408, when Tatar (Mongol) armies staged a punitive campaign into Muscovy, but it recovered and increased its landed possessions through the fifteenth century. It benefited materially in periods of more pervasive disasters, e.g., a series of bouts with the plague (1417–27) and the wars between Grand Prince Vasily II (ruled 1425–62) and his uncle and cousins, who challenged him for the Muscovite throne during the second quarter of the fifteenth century.[48] According to one analysis, the Trinity monastery received 59 lands grants between 1423 and 1445, and thus acquired 83 properties. The study identified another 46 land grants for 65 land parcels that were made to the monastery between the 1445 and 1461.[49] Another analysis indicated that the monastery acquired 63 villages, 81 hamlets, and 160 abandoned settlements during the period 1427–1462; this represented a substantial increase from the 16 villages, 12 hamlets, and 20 abandoned settlements it had acquired between 1392 and 1427. In addition to donations the monastery increased its properties through purchases, exchanges of lands, and encroachments upon lands traditionally cultivated but abandoned by 'black' peasants, i.e., those who worked their own land and whose sole obligation was to pay taxes to their prince. As a result of all these methods, by 1462 the Trinity monastery owned properties in 15 districts; they included not only agricultural lands, but salt works and other non-agricultural enterprises. Although its rate of land acquisition slowed for the rest of the century, it had become one of the largest landowning institutions in Muscovy, with lands clustered in districts along the upper Volga River and outposts, albeit fewer in number, in other locations as well.[50]

The Trinity monastery benefited particularly, but not exclusively, from gifts and donations made by Russian princes. Among the most generous in the early fifteenth century was Prince Iurii Dmitrievich of Zvenigorod and Galich, the uncle and rival of Grand Prince Vasily II, who sponsored the construction of a stone Church of the Trinity after the 1408 attack.[51] Moscow princes joined the list of land donors to the monastery after 1422.[52] Prior to that time the Moscow princes had been more closely associated with other monasteries, including the Simonov monastery, which was founded c. 1370 near Moscow by Fedor, a nephew of Sergei of Radonezh.[53] Kirill, one of the monks at Simonov, eventually left and founded another monastery (1397), which came to be known as the Kirillo-Belozerskii monastery, at Beloozero.[54] Both of these monasteries were among the dozens established in the fourteenth century. Both, in manners similar to those described for the Trinity monastery, became major landowners.[55] They too benefited from disruptions occasioned by the plague and civil wars, purchasing wastelands and receiving landed property as donations.[56]

In northwestern Russia the process of acquiring landed estates followed a somewhat different pattern. Before Muscovy annexed the region of Novgorod in 1478, landed estates in northwestern Russia were owned by slightly fewer than 2,200 proprietors, including Novgorodian boyars, i.e., the political elite of the city, as well as wealthy merchants, the Archbishop and monasteries, and small-scale proprietors.[57] Valentin Lavrent'evich Ianin has reconstructed the landowning patterns of some of the Novgorod boyar families. Starting from the will of Ostaf'ia Onan'inich, dated between 1397 and 1410, he traced the family's ownership of its extensive landholdings back to the testator's grandfather. Other prominent Novgorod boyar families similarly were in possession of large tracts of land during the first half of the fourteenth century. The Mishinich clan owned their lands from the turn of the thirteenth–fourteenth century.[58] Lay landowners in this region acquired their properties through purchases from each other and from peasants, through inheritance, and at times through forceful seizures from peasant communities.[59] From the late thirteenth century Novgorodian boyars founded monasteries and transferred large amounts of landed property to them.[60] Rather than receive lands as princely gifts, Novgorod's officials and boyars made, as early as the 1260s, ongoing efforts to limit ownership of landed property in their region by princes and their officials.[61]

By the third quarter of the fifteenth century Bogdan Esipov was, perhaps, the largest Novgorodian boyar landowner. Data from surviving portions of land registers compiled at the end of that century indicate he possessed at least 700 villages and hamlets, located in all five of the main sectors or 'fifths' of the Novgorod lands. The villagers on his lands engaged not only in raising edible grains and livestock. Some specialized in ironworks, others in producing flax and textiles, in fishing, and in bee-keeping.[62]

In contrast to Esipov and the c. 40 other very large Novgorodian landowners, most of the landowners possessed relatively small estates. Their sizes were due, in some cases to the practice of partible inheritance, which over generations had left individual members of families with reduced shares of what had originally been sizable estates. In other instances small estates were established when 'black' peasants managed to separate from their communities and become smallholders.[63]

Monasteries also became major landowners in northwestern Russia. The Iur'ev monastery, which had received princely gifts early in the twelfth century, became a large monastic landowner by the third quarter of the fifteenth.[64] By this time the estate donated by Prince Mstislav Vladimirovich contained 96 villages and hamlets with 220 adult male peasants.[65] Vsevolod's gift had developed to include 26 hamlets and 191 men.[66] By the late fifteenth century the monastery's landed possessions were extensive. It owned lands and villages throughout the Novgorodian lands, and in some cases was the only landowner of all or almost all the land in entire parishes.[67]

By the end of the era of Novgorodian autonomy peasants had lost possession of most of the arable land and had become rent-payers on privately owned landed estates. In one of Novgorod's five sectors, Derevskaia, which was located to the southeast of the city, virtually all the land (over 90 percent) was possessed by lay or ecclesiastic landowners. Monasteries owned approximately 20 percent; the archbishop owned about 13 percent; less than 9 percent was in the direct possession of peasants.[68] In the recorded area of the Bezhetskaia 'fifth,' the neighboring sector to the east, members of 21 Novgorod boyar families owned 59 percent of the land. The Archbishop owned 23 percent; monasteries possessed 3 percent. The remaining 15 percent was divided among hundreds of smallholders.[69] In all five sectors combined the archbishop, churches, and monasteries owned estates comprising about 25 percent of the land. Of that total the Archbishop possessed about one-fifth or 5 percent of Novgorod's lands, making him the largest single landowner in Novgorod. The archiepiscopate owned over 2000 villages and hamlets containing almost 7000 households, in which over 8000 adult male peasants dwelled. Almost two-thirds of the Novgorod lands belonged to approximately 2000 lay landowners. Data from the surviving land registers indicate that only 43 proprietors (2.2 percent) owned very large estates, which accounted for over 40 percent of the region's grain production. 'Black' peasants possessed just over 9 percent of the land in the Novgorod region.[70]

After the grand prince of Moscow annexed Novgorod in 1478, he arrested or exiled the Novgorodian magnates and confiscated all the landed estates of the lay landowners as well as a major portion of the ecclesiastical properties. He then introduced a new system of land tenure into the region. He transferred men in his service from other portions of his realm to the Novgorod lands, where he distributed portions of the confiscated estates to them. The new estates were held conditionally. The landholders, while having the right to collect rents from peasants dwelling in villages or portions of villages assigned to them, could not dispose of their properties as private landowners. They could not sell or mortgage the property. Exchanges required permission of the grand prince's officials. Although over the course of the next century the estates were frequently retained within families, estate holders could not simply leave their lands as bequests to their heirs; administrative officials formally distributed lands to each new recipient.

Within this new arrangement the grand prince retained a significant portion of the confiscated property as court lands. Peasants also continued to hold some land as taxable or 'black' land.

PEASANT OBLIGATIONS AND INCOMES

Large landed estates in both central and northwestern Russia (before the land redistributions) consisted, as the previous examples illustrate, of multiple villages with their cultivated lands, forests, meadows, and other assets, often scattered over several districts located at some distance from one another.[71] The landowners, whether lay or ecclesiastical, had the right to sell, mortgage, exchange, or give their property as gifts or dowries. Lay landowners rarely dwelled on their rural estates, but remained in towns. Their estates were managed by stewards or overseers, usually indentured bondsmen, who oversaw the collection of rents for their lords as well as additional fees for themselves.[72] For lay landowners in the fourteenth and fifteenth centuries rents constituted only a portion of their incomes. These magnates, who were also members of the political and military elites of their principalities, served as officers in armies and as administrative officials. When serving in the former capacity, they derived incomes from booty captured on military campaigns. When functioning as administrators, they collected special fees, known as 'feeding' (*kormlenie*), from the populations of their jurisdictions, which provided their maintenance and a salary.[73]

Land ownership, nevertheless, gave proprietors the right to collect rents from peasants who dwelled in villages located on their lands. The status of the peasants, the nature and amount of their obligations to the landowners varied, however. Those factors depended upon the landowner, custom, and specifications in charters issued to landowners by their princes.[74]

Peasants paid a variety of taxes to their princes. Those who dwelled on privately owned lands were, in addition, required to pay various fees and rents to their landlords. It has been observed that some of the fees, which are mentioned in early birchbark documents, may have merged into regular rents over time.[75] Before the end of the fifteenth century, however, it is possible to snatch only incidental glimpses of the form and quantities of goods and money peasants paid in taxes and in rents. One birchbark document from Novgorod (1360–80), for example, contains a partial agreement made by a certain Trufan and his brothers to pay rent in the amount of six bushels or baskets (*korobeï*) of rye and one *korob'ia* of wheat. They also committed to pay other fees in the form of malt, martens, squirrel, honey, flax, and a sheep.[76] Approximately a century later peasants in a rural district in the Novgorod lands agreed to pay the Iur'ev monastery 30 *korobei* of rye and an equal amount of oats and to bring them to the monastery. Other fees, including special provisions for the archimandrite, who was based at the Iur'ev monastery, and his entourage should they visit this district, were also specified. They included beer, fish, meat, and bread.[77] While documents such as these provide some insight into the nature of rents, they do not offer sufficient corresponding information to determine rates of payment based either on units of cultivated land or on numbers of peasants or households.

Peasant obligations were influenced also by immunity charters issued by princes to favored landowners and confirmed by their successors. These charters exempted peasants living in named villages or districts belonging to lay or ecclesiastic landowners from specified taxes, trade duties, or from the jurisdiction of princely officials. Thus, the prince of Beloozero, Andrei Dmitrievich, issued an immunity charter (dated between 1397 and 1427) to Kirill, the hegumen of the Beloozerskii monastery, for a particular wasteland and a new settlement, which the monastery had just purchased from another monastery. In the charter the prince released any persons who settled in these two places from paying his tribute (*dan'*) and other fees.[78] Such charters were not uncommon. In the period 1423–1445, the Trinity monastery received a total of 35 immunity charters, most of which were issued by Grand Prince Vasily II or his mother. Over the next 17 years Vasily II issued another 34 immunity charters to Trinity monastery.[79] For the first two-thirds of the fifteenth century princes issued such charters, granting generous tax exemptions, mainly but not exclusively to ecclesiastical institutions; almost all of the lands belonging to ecclesiastical institutions enjoyed some form of immunity.[80] After Ivan III became grand prince (1462), however, the trend began to reverse. Whereas charters he issued in the first decades of his reign released recipients from paying over half of his direct taxes and 30–44 percent of his commercial duties, by the end of the century his immunity charters exempted them from only about one-quarter of the direct taxes and less than 5 percent of trade duties. It has been argued that the curtailment of these tax-free privileges was intended to expand the grand prince's tax base and increase his revenues.[81] The parallel limits on judicial immunities transferred legal jurisdiction and fees to the grand prince.[82] Peasants dwelling on lands that had previously enjoyed fiscal exemptions were subject to greater tax burdens by 1500. Those charged with criminal activity gradually fell under the jurisdiction of grand princely officials and courts.

The most detailed information about peasant obligations relates to northwestern Russia in the late fifteenth century. It derives from the land registers that were compiled at the turn of the fifteenth–sixteenth centuries, after the Muscovite grand prince confiscated and redistributed Novgorod's landed estates. Although they are not all complete, these registers provide the only extensive set of data on landownership, peasant population, and rents before 1500.[83] They describe the new landholders, the villages on their estates, their peasant residents, and the rents paid by the peasants. Some also contain data from the preceding years (c. 1478–1490s), when the confiscations were being undertaken and initial land distributions were being made. In one register, that for the most northerly sector (*Obonezhskaia piatina*), and in some fragments pertaining to lands retained by the grand princely court the scribes included accounts of even earlier rents, those collected by the Novgorodian landowners before their estates had been seized by the Muscovite grand prince.

One such fragment contains data on Degzha, a rural district that had been part of Bogdan Esipov's extensive holdings. It reveals that when Esipov had owned it, the district had contained 72 hamlets. The peasants in the district had paid rent in the form of money, grain (rye, oats, and wheat), and miscellaneous products including flax, sheep, chickens, eggs, butter or oil, hempseed, and hops. It has been calculated that the monetary portion constituted 30 percent of the value of the rent; the other goods combined accounted for 70 percent.[84] Liudmila Valerianovna Danilova, who examined the data for all the documented portions of Esipov's holdings, has summarized his incomes, which derived exclusively from peasant farming and other enterprises. As in the Degzha example, his combined holdings yielded money, grain, and goods in kind. The grains included rye, oats, barley, and wheat. Some peasants were assessed set quantities of grain; others paid shares of their crops. Danilova has estimated that the total amount of grain of all kinds collected by Esipov was 28,000–35,000 puds. In addition, he collected hay, malt, hops, hempseed, peas, sheep, chickens, eggs, butter or oil, cheese, beer, and wood.[85]

The rent mix of the peasants on the estates of another large-scale Novgorodian landowner, Marfa Boretskaia, was somewhat different. Peasants who dwelled on some of her northern holdings paid rents in squirrel pelts. Others who occupied a choice location on the trade and transport route linking Novgorod with the upper Volga River paid exclusively in coin. Yet others paid rents mainly in flax, which was used by peasants of two neighboring hamlets in the production of linen cloth; their rents consisted of lengths of linen and grain or money. Rents, consisting of a variety of commodities and coin, made up the bulk of Marfa Boretskaia's income from her extensive landed estates; a negligible portion was derived from demesnial enterprises. Her monetary rents have been estimated to have accounted for just over half of the total.[86]

The situation of peasants was altered when the grand prince of Moscow redistributed the landed estates he had confiscated from the Novogorodian landowners. But not all peasants were affected in the same manner. The rural district of Degzha, mentioned above, became a possession of the grand princely court. The number of hamlets increased to 90; the monetary portion of rents increased and was supplemented only with grains.[87] In the Vodskaia sector, which was located to the northwest and north of the city of Novgorod and extended to the Gulf of Finland, virtually all of the peasant villages had been possessed by lay or ecclesiastical landowners. After the confiscations and redistributions, almost one-third of the land, like Degzha, became court lands; the peasants on those lands paid their dues to the grand prince and his officials, not private landlords. For those peasants whose villages were assigned to new landholders, rents rose on average by 20 percent. A larger portion of the rent mix, furthermore, tended to be collected in monetary form.[88] Peasants in the Derevskaia sector had similar experiences. In that region too approximately one-third of the land, confiscated from the Archbishop and monasteries, was redesignated as court lands. Rents paid by the peasants dwelling in the villages on those lands were converted into money; the value of their payments typically declined. Those on the privately held estates, in contrast, were generally required to pay higher rents to their new landlords. They also had to pay specified amounts of grain rather than or in addition to portions of their crops.[89] In the Bezhetskaia sector the grand prince kept almost 30 percent of the confiscated ecclesiastical and boyar lands as court lands. He left the status of 'black' or tax-paying peasants unchanged. Fees paid by peasants in three of the recorded rural districts in that 'fifth' rose precipitously in comparison to payments prior to the confiscations; in one they remained approximately the same; and in another they declined.[90]

The new landholders, like those who preceded them in the Novgorod lands, derived most of their estate incomes from peasant rents. The portion of demesnial production was, however, changing in some regions. In the Vodskaia 'fifth' the new landholders introduced more demesnial production, which was, however, carried out by slaves or indentured labor rather than peasants. In Shelonskaia, located south of Novgorod, it appeared rarely. In Derevskaia about 11 percent of the land was cultivated as demesne.[91]

Little is known of how successfully peasants supported themselves or how their situations were affected by their geographic locations within the Muscovite realm or by their status as a 'black,' court, monastery peasant, or a peasant on a hereditary estate or a new conditional tenure, service estate. One attempt to analyze the budget of peasants in the Derevskaia 'fifth' of Novgorod around 1500 calculated that only 3 percent of the peasant households, despite the relatively widespread adoption of the three-field system, grew sufficient grain to sustain the members of the household and their livestock, pay their rents, and also pay taxes and fees to the prince. It pointed out that peasants on court lands, whose fees were generally lower, were more easily able to meet their personal needs and their obligations. The study concluded that livestock production and supplemental products obtained from gardens, orchards, forests, rivers, and lakes were absolutely vital for peasant survival.[92]

These calculations are based, however, on average or normal rates of production. In reality, agricultural output varied considerably due to fluctuations in climatic factors such as rainfall and temperatures as well as to major disruptions associated with wars or disease. Famines, causing the deaths of people, horses, and other livestock, were reported throughout Russia in 1309–10; they were related to unusually warm, snow-free winters and dry summers. Just a few years later, in 1314–16, the Novgorod lands experienced unusually severe winter conditions, causing another famine that killed many and drove up the price of grain. Famine caused by several years of drought occurred throughout Russia in 1332, 1364–66, and 1374. Drought and famine persisted locally in central Russia in 1367–68 and re-occurred in 1371. Similar episodes were reported through the fifteenth century as well with weather-related crop failures and famine afflicting all of Russia in 1421–23, 1430–31, and 1471–72.[93] To offset the risk of poor harvest, peasants would have had to store some portion of their crops, thus reducing the amounts they had available for immediate consumption, seed, and for payment of their rents and other dues.

Peasants did, however, also have the option to move and seek better conditions. Before 1497, when, as noted above, a Muscovite law code limited peasants' rights of departure to a two-week period each year, there were no generalized restrictions on peasant mobility. With rare exceptions that were initiated during the end of the reign of Vasily II, Russian peasants were bound neither to their land nor their landlords. Regardless of debt or other obligations, peasants could thus leave their villages.[94] A birchbark document dated between 1420 and 1430 contained a note to a landowner reporting that half of his rural district had been vacated and the remaining peasants appealed to him to reduce their dues.[95] In some cases peasants took advantage of lower fees and security tendered by large-scale landed proprietors who had received immunity charters and enjoyed tax exemptions, but sought scarce peasant labor to cultivate their lands. Such was the situation in previously cited examples of monasteries, which had acquired wastelands but needed labor to make them productive. Another example is contained in a charter issued in 1447 by Vasily II to the Trinity-St. Sergius monastery for certain lands it possessed in Uglich. It exempted a certain category of peasants, known as long-time residents (*starozhil'tsy*), on those properties from taxes for five years, but offered a seven-year exemption to any former long-time residents who had left, but chose to return.[96] That peasants responded to the variations in their obligations may also be inferred from data in the Novgorod land registers. The 'black' peasants of one Bezhetskaia rural district found their tax obligations rising after the Muscovite prince annexed the Novgorod lands; their fees, however, remained relatively low in comparison to neighboring rural districts. An increase in the number of adult male peasants and in the area of land under cultivation in this district suggests that resident peasants tended to remain there while others, perhaps, moved into the area. Peasants on court lands in a nearby district were required to pay rents and fees totaling about twice the amount paid by their neighbors in the first district. The number of adult males in that district declined, as did the amount of cultivated land per household.[97] Although the evidence is circumstantial, it suggests that at least a portion of the peasant population took advantage of the few options available to them to increase their levels of economic security.

TOWNS AND URBAN CENTERS

Although peasants constituted the vast majority of the northern Russian population and agriculture was their basic occupation, urban populations contributed significantly to the Russian economy and their towns provided more visible indicators of the economic vitality of the Russian principalities than did the peasant villages. Kievan Rus' had been known for its numerous towns, the most famous of which had been Kiev itself. As the capital of the grand prince and the seat of the metropolitan of the Russian Orthodox Church, Kiev was the foremost political and ecclesiastic center of the Russian lands. It functioned as a commercial and craft production center as well. Novgorod, which was the main urban center in the northwest, and Vladimir in the northeastern portion of Kievan Rus' were prominent regional centers. Definitions of what constituted a town vary; consequently scholars have presented different figures for the number of towns in late Kievan Rus' as well as in the post-invasion period. While some emphasize fortifications and military functions and estimate as many as 300 towns in the Russian lands in the pre-Mongol era, others have argued that many of those centers were minor fortresses or large agricultural villages, and that only about one-third to one-half of that number were true towns defined as non-agricultural settlements that provided administrative services for areas surrounding them and had populations and economies based on trade and manufacturing.[98]

By the early thirteenth century, however, Kiev had been sacked three times (1169, 1203, 1235) as a result of warfare among the Rus' princes. In 1240, it was besieged and sacked once again, this time by Mongol forces that had been conducting victorious campaigns in the Russian lands and adjacent areas since 1237. Although reports of the Mongol attack on the city, which describe it as completely destroyed, may be somewhat exaggerated, Kiev certainly lost its prominence. Vladimir, which was also a target of direct assault, remained the nominal seat of the grand prince of Vladimir, the most important prince in the northern Russian lands, but the city never recovered its vitality. Many of the other towns of Russia were similarly devastated by the Mongol onslaught. Archeological studies of 74 towns that had existed in the early thirteenth century have revealed that two-thirds of them (49) had been damaged and burned at the time of the Mongol invasions. Of those, 14 disappeared; another 15 experienced only moderate recovery.[99] It has been estimated that in the fourteenth and fifteenth centuries, in addition to Novgorod, Vladimir, Moscow, and Tver', there were about 130 towns in northern Russia, of which 73 were located in the northeast. Anatolii Mikhailovich Sakharov has contended that of those, only 29 might be considered true urban centers.[100]

Unlike most of the major towns of Kievan Rus', Novgorod escaped the Mongol onslaught. But it, like all the other Russian towns, experienced an economic decline following the Mongol invasion and recovered slowly. One indicator of the patterns of recovery is masonry building construction. David Miller, who has studied the frequency of these projects, which were more expensive than more common wooden construction, has interpreted them not only as reflections of wealth in society, but as signs that individuals within society were able to accumulate and focus sufficient amounts of that wealth to underwrite the projects and also to mobilize the skilled and unskilled labor to complete them. His studies show that in contrast to construction activity before the invasions, during the first 50 years after the invasions virtually no stone or brick structures, such as churches or fortifications, were built. Only one small masonry church near Vladimir and two in Novgorod were erected before 1287. Construction activity began to be undertaken at a faster pace in Novgorod from the beginning of the fourteenth century; in central Russia, it was almost another quarter century before princes and other patrons could mobilize sufficient resources to undertake similar projects. During the next 150 years Novgorod's construction activity outpaced all other northern Russian towns.[101] Nevertheless, other towns, such as Tver' and Moscow, the seats of junior princes of the Vladimir dynastic line at the time of the Mongol invasion, showed signs of slow recovery. Moscow, whose princes gained power at the expense of their Tver' counterparts, eventually replaced Vladimir as the political, ecclesiastic, and commercial capital of central Russia.

The economic element of Moscow's political ascendancy was reflected in its physical development. In 1326, Prince Ivan I Kalita and Metropolitan Petr collaborated in the construction of the Cathedral of the Dormition. Thereafter, Moscow's construction activity outstripped all the other towns of central Russia.[102] While no masonry construction projects were undertaken in Tver' during the second half of the fourteenth century, Grand Prince Dmitry Donskoi built stone-walled fortifications (the Moscow Kremlin) in 1367–68.[103] It has been calculated that the walls required 54,000 cubic meters of limestone and rubble, which had to be transported during the winter over ice from a quarry located 50 kilometers from the building site. The project required a labor force of several thousand men, including masons and other skilled artisans as well as unskilled laborers. The task of gathering a labor force of this scale, which was complicated by the fact that the region had experienced bouts of plague as well as famine in 1364–66, probably involved drafting peasants from the surrounding countryside.[104] Moscow's development proceeded despite devastating Tatar attacks in 1382 and 1408, and culminated in the second half of the fifteenth century, when Grand Prince Ivan III, following a fire in 1476 that destroyed almost two dozen stone and wooden churches in the Kremlin, employed Italian architects to reconstruct the complex of churches and palaces within the fortress.[105]

There are no documented records of the sizes of the populations of Moscow, Novgorod, or the other main Russian cities during the period 1200–1500. Estimates for individual towns have been based on archeological excavations that provide information on the approximate size of the inhabited urban areas and the number of households within those areas. Scholars, using assumptions for the number of persons per household, have then calculated widely ranging figures for the urban populations. Kiev's population in the early thirteenth century has been estimated as high as 50,000 and as low as 25,000. One estimate for the city of Novgorod at the same time is between 20,000 and 30,000. By comparison, estimates for Moscow in the fifteenth century have ranged from 50,000 to 100,000.[106] George Vernadsky, however, asserted the total urban population of Muscovy was less than 13 percent of the entire population, a figure he estimated for the Kievan Rus' urban population.[107]

Urban populations included princes, their courtiers, Church hierarchs and other clergy, merchants, artisans and petty tradesmen, unskilled laborers, and slaves. Merchants engaged in local, intercity, and foreign trade. Novgorod had, perhaps, the most developed commercial activities throughout the period, 1200–1500. By the late twelfth century it had well-established commercial ties with Scandinavian merchants who arrived from Visby on the island of Gotland as well as with German merchants from towns of the Hanseatic League.[108] Each group of foreign merchants initially had its own enclave on the 'trading side' of the city of Novgorod; by the fourteenth century the Gotland court of St. Olaf had merged with the Germans' Peterhof. During the 1260s Novgorodian officials together with princes from central Russia concluded treaties with Lübeck, Riga, and Gotland; the agreements governed the terms of trade, including the foreign merchants' travel to the city, the length of their stays, the regulation of weights and measures, and processes for settling disputes. Typically, foreign merchants made two trips per year; the Germans particularly came by land and by sea, one group in the winter and the second group in the summer. Hanseatic merchants as well as representatives of the Teutonic Knights brought copper, tin, lead, and iron as well as textiles and dyes, metal products, amber and glass, and beer and wine. The most significant import, however, was silver, which became a vital component of the tribute demanded made by the Russians' Tatar (Mongol) overlords. In return for these items Novgorodian merchants exported honey, wax, and fur pelts, primarily squirrel pelts. These items were among the non-agricultural goods collected by the Novgorodian boyars as rents from their peasants, particularly on their more northerly estates. Those peasants who were required to pay portions of their rents in coin may also have marketed these goods. The precise level of involvement of boyars and peasants in the market is, however, not known.[109]

The foreign trade conducted by the merchants of Moscow and other central Russian towns focused more on the Golden Horde to the south and the commercial exchanges that developed at Sarai, the Mongol capital on the lower Volga, which became a market in the vast trade network linked by the Silk Road connecting Europe and Asia. At Sarai Russian merchants purchased luxury goods and everyday items, finished goods and raw materials brought along the Mongol Silk Road from the orient.[110] There they also met and traded with Italian merchants from Black Sea colonies. A group of merchants, which acquired the name *gosti surozhane* or Surozh (Sudak) merchants, were engaged in this trade. From the last decades of the fourteenth century, when the Golden Horde lost its cohesiveness as well as its ability to control commercial traffic, Russian merchants no longer traded exclusively at Sarai. They opened new routes across the steppe to trade directly at the Italian colonies. Neither the disintegration of the Golden Horde nor the capture of the northern Black Sea coast by the Ottoman Turks in 1475 curtailed that trade. Caravans consisting of Russian merchants based at Moscow, Tver', and other central Russian towns as well as Novgorod, continued to travel southward to trade at Caffa and Azov (Azak) with Greek, Armenian, and other merchants from the Ottoman Empire. Some ventured further to trade their wares, mainly fur pelts, leather, hides, and ivory (walrus tusks) at Tokat, Bursa, and even Istanbul. They purchased silks, satins, brocades, gems, spices, dyes, incense, and other luxury items.[111] Moscow also became a hub for trade with Europe. In the 1470s, merchants from Germany and Poland were observed arriving during the winter to purchase luxury fur pelts.[112]

Novgorod participated in the southern trade as well, often through the intermediary of other markets that were developing in towns throughout Russia. Nizhnii Novgorod emerged as a center on the route between Sarai and Moscow.[113] Velikii Ustiug became an important provincial center on the route connecting both Novgorod and Moscow to northern fur tributaries.[114] Merchants from Novgorod and other northern Russian towns imported items, such as oriental glass and glazed pottery. Walnuts, boxtree wood, which was used to fashion combs, textiles, and other oriental goods were among the imports from the Golden Horde that appeared throughout northern Russia.[115]

The intercity trade, particularly between Novgorod and the central Russian towns was encouraged by both Mongol and Russian rulers. Within decades of the Mongol conquest of the Russian lands, the Mongol khan had ordered the Russian princes to safeguard Novgorodian trade with the rest of the Russian principalities, and in 1270 the Grand Prince of Vladimir correspondingly concluded an agreement with Novgorod, providing for Novgorodian merchants to have full access to all the towns of central Russia.[116] Novgorod sold items it received from Baltic merchants as well as its own products, such as fur pelts, to Russian and Tatar trading partners. Among the items it imported from central Russia was grain, which supplemented the relatively poor production in the Novgorod lands. It was particularly necessary in periods when poor harvests in the Novgorod area persisted for several successive years. During periods of political contention the grand princes of Vladimir took advantage of Novgorod's vulnerability and blockaded commercial traffic into the city to exact concessions from it.[117] Merchants from the central Russian towns also contributed to the stocks of wax and honey exported to the Baltic.

Local trade also took place in Russian towns. Ambrogio Contarini, a Venetian ambassador who was obliged to take a detour through Moscow in 1475–76 on his return from a journey to Persia, described the commercial activities in Moscow:

> *The climate is so excessively cold, that the people stay nine months of the year indoors. As it is difficult to travel in the summer time, on account of the thick forests and the great quantity of mud caused by the melting of the ice, they are obliged to get in all their provisions in the spring, for which purpose they use their sani or sledges on which they stow everything, and are easily drawn by one horse. By the end of October the river which passes through the city is frozen over, and the shops and bazaars for the sale of all sorts of things are erected on it, scarcely anything being sold in the town. They do this, as the river, from being surrounded on all sides by the city, and so protected from the wind, is less cold than anywhere else. On this frozen river may be seen, daily, numbers of cows and pigs, great quantities of corn, wood, hay, and every other necessity, nor does the supply fail during the whole winter. At the end of November, all those who have cows or pigs, kill and bring them, from time to time, to the city market. They are frozen whole, and it is curious to see so many skinned cows standing upright on their feet. The meat that you eat has sometimes been killed three months or more.*[118]

Towns were also centers for a wide range of handicraft production. Although the Mongol invasions left some of the finer arts in long-term decline, others revived. The construction projects, noted above, testify to the presence of skilled masters in masonry and carpentry. Military campaigns conducted by the Russian princes similarly reflect the contributions of blacksmiths, armorsmiths, and tanners, among others; Moscow and Tver' became centers for artillery production. More common daily activities required potters and weavers while consumers of luxury goods used the services of silversmiths, coppersmiths, and jewelers. Scribes, icon-painters, and other specialists produced goods for lay and ecclesiastical clients.[119]

Although Russian merchants were categorized by wealth and by the focus of their trade (foreign or domestic), neither they nor artisans were organized well enough to control participation in their occupational activities. Men in the service of Church hierarchs and monasteries, protected from taxation, conducted business in towns on behalf of those institutions.[120] Urban households maintained some livestock in their courtyards, thus reducing the need to purchase some food supplies.[121] Large-scale landowners, who dwelled in towns, had access to an even wider range of food supplies produced on their landed estates, while their slaves or bondsmen produced crafted items for their households.[122] Thus, while town craftsmen and traders performed their activities in their workshops and sold their wares in stalls and markets on the outskirts of towns, often under the shadow of town walls, they competed with representatives of great monasteries and with slaves and bondsmen working directly for their lay masters.

DEMOGRAPHY

The size of the Russian population during the period 1200–1500 is unknown. Scholars, using a variety of methodologies, have offered estimates ranging from three to 10 million during the last half of the fifteenth century. George Vernadsky, who offered the higher figure, judged that the population of nine to 10 million in the late fifteenth century was only moderately higher than the population of Kievan Rus' had been early in the thirteenth century.[123] Although the estimates of the size of the population vary widely, there are fewer disputes over the pattern of change. It is thus acknowledged that the initial Mongol invasions and their subsequent military campaigns into northern Russia had severe demographic and economic consequences for the Russians. About a century later, before the Russians had completely recovered from that demographic calamity, the Black Death entered the northern Russian lands, producing another demographic setback. It was only in the second half of the fifteenth century after domestic warfare had ceased and the plague had subsided that population growth began to take place. It is thought that the size of the population reached pre-plague levels by the end of the fifteenth century.[124]

There is debate among scholars about the extent of the death and destruction occasioned by the onslaught of the Mongol armies in 1237–40, but there is little doubt that large numbers of people were killed and taken captive and destruction was severe. During the three-month campaign in the winter of 1237–38, the city of Vladimir, capital of the main northeastern principality, was besieged and burned. Suzdal', another town of the region, was sacked; Rostov as well as the more minor towns of Tver' and Moscow were also identified among those subjected to direct attack.[125] The countryside was also adversely affected. Although the evidence does not provide quantitative measures of the destruction, anecdotal evidence contained in written sources of the burning and looting of villages as well as of the killing local inhabitants or seizing them as captives is corroborated by archeological evidence of the widespread abandonment of villages in the same areas and at approximately the same time that the Mongol invasions occurred.[126]

The demographic effects of the invasion were uneven. In contrast to some cities, such as Vladimir, which was sacked and burned, Novgorod was initially unaffected. Some towns, such as Tver', which was the subject of a punitive attack in 1327, were seriously affected in subsequent encounters with the Tatars. Some rural areas, too, such as those around Vladimir and Riazan', were more seriously damaged than others. Some of the less vulnerable regions, including those around Moscow and Tver', may have received infusions of refugees from the more devastated locales.[127]

Scholars have estimated that the initial invasions of 1237–40 alone resulted in the loss of 10 percent of the Russian population. This figure covers the full social spectrum, from princes to peasants and slaves, and includes losses due to both death and capture.[128] The drain on the Russian population persisted. The initial invasion was followed by repeated raids and punitive campaigns conducted by the Mongols against the Russians. In just the quarter century following the initial invasion the Mongols from their base in the steppe mounted fourteen more campaigns against northeastern Russia. Mongol military expeditions against the Russian lands tapered off after the 1320s. Tatar forces continued, nevertheless, to take part in disputes between Russian princes, and they launched occasional, but major campaigns against the Russians throughout the period.[129] In addition to casualties resulting from those hostilities, the numbers of Russian princes and commoners alike were reduced as the Mongol khans demanded their participation in military campaigns against other enemies. The Mongols also conscripted skilled artisans and unskilled laborers to construct their capital city of Sarai and, later in the 1340s, its replacement, New Sarai. Russian craftsmen were relocated from Russia to these towns, while others were sent to Mongol centers as distant as Karakorum and China. Captives and conscripts were also sold through the thriving slave trade that became a component of the Mongols' commercial network.[130]

Over the century following the invasions, the Russian population experienced some recovery as reflected, among other factors, by the slowly developing trends of urban growth and construction activity. But then the plague reached Russia. It approached the western frontier of Russia in 1349–51, then appeared in the town of Pskov, located west and south of Novgorod, in 1352 and spread to the rural areas surrounding the city as townsmen fled to monasteries, gave away their property, and took Holy Orders before succumbing to the disease. The chroniclers recorded grim details of bodies piling up at churches and then being buried in common graves due to the lack of plots in cemeteries. When the plague did not abate, the Pskovians called upon the Archbishop of Novgorod for assistance. He arrived and led the town in ceremonial prayers, but succumbed to the disease while returning to Novgorod. The plague, however, reached that city, where, as the chroniclers reported, there were countless casualties.[131] From Novgorod and Pskov the plague spread eastward reaching Beloozero and Suzdal' and, in 1353, Moscow, where the Grand Prince, his two sons, and a brother as well as the metropolitan were among its victims.[132]

The plague returned frequently until the 1420s, then reappeared occasionally. The Black Death or some other epidemic occurred on average once every five years from the time of the first appearance of the Black Death to the end of the fifteenth century.[133] Some attacks, such as the one that occurred in the mid-1360s, which affected towns from Beloozero to Nizhnii Novgorod, were more virulent than others; on that occasion the plague lasted several years and was accompanied by drought and famine. The Black Death was reported again in Novgorod and Pskov in 1389 and 1390. It was reported in seven of the years during the period 1417–1427; famine once again accompanied disease and continued to be reported through the 1430s. It has been estimated, based on comparisons with Western Europe, that the plague cost Russia 25 percent of its population.[134] The comparison does not take into account, however, the effect of other debilitating factors, the most severe of which were the Tatar attacks of 1382 and 1408 and inter-princely wars that raged between 1430 and 1456.

THEORETICAL DISCUSSION

During the twentieth century most of the scholarly inquiry into the socio-economic organization of Russia and its development between 1200 and 1500 revolved around the issue of feudalism. Soviet scholars considered Russia in this period to have been feudal. By this they meant, generally, that Russia was a politically divided, agrarian society, in which large-scale proprietors appropriated land previously possessed by a free peasant population. Having placed peasants under their seigniorial jurisdiction, landlords also appropriated a portion of the output from peasant labor, i.e., they compelled their peasants to pay them monetary fees, payments in kind, and/or labor services.[135] As the small principalities were absorbed into Muscovy during the fourteenth and fifteenth centuries, a centralized 'feudal state' formed. Serving the interests of the elite, feudal lords, it reinforced rather than loosened the bondage of the peasant laborers.[136]

Debates among Soviet scholars as well as between them and Western scholars, who have tended to interpret the sparse documentary evidence differently, have highlighted various factors that challenge the applicability of the feudal model or aspects of it for Russia in the period 1200–1500. They include, as has been noted in the previous discussion, the view that peasants were not serfs, bound to their land and subject to their landlords. Laborers on at least some of the privately owned estates, particularly in the early years of this period, were slaves or indentured bondsmen who managed bee-keeping, horse raising, hunting, or other enterprises for their masters, not peasants cultivating arable lands. Even when their villages and fields became the possessions of private landowners and 'feudal obligations' were imposed on them, peasants retained rights to negotiate their dues and to leave. The small peasant population relative to the area of available land, combined with a universal need for scarce labor and weak princely authority in multiple principalities, enabled peasants to exercise those rights. Another factor that emerges from these debates and challenges the utility of the feudal model is the observation that the burdens placed upon the peasants had not inhibited innovation or their ability to adopt more productive techniques, as their adoption of the three-field system by 1500 illustrates. Although monasteries may have relied heavily on incomes they received from peasants, lay magnates, who derived incomes from a variety of sources, including administrative fees, commerce, and military booty, were not exclusively dependent upon peasant rents and dues and did not share the monasteries' interest in maximizing rents and depriving peasants of their mobility. These observations have supported conclusions that legal restrictions on peasant mobility were introduced in the late fifteenth century and the serf system emerged in the late sixteenth century.

None of these overviews of the Russian socioeconomic organization points to the fourteenth century and the demographic consequences of the Black Death as the stimulus either for the end of serfdom, as it has been argued occurred in many parts of Western Europe, or for its establishment in conjunction with the creation of large grain-exporting landed estates, as has been argued for Eastern Europe. They all present images of overall continuity, either of persistent feudal relations or of a nominally free peasantry, during this period.

The arguments for the establishment of serfdom through a process beginning in the late sixteenth century raise additional questions about the factors influencing this development. Most of the discussion surrounding it highlights an economic crisis that stimulated peasant flight from landed estates during the last few decades of the sixteenth century. Domestic policies and prolonged warfare led to inflation and tax increases, which in combination with disease, famine, and military attacks, provided heavily burdened peasants with compelling incentive to abandon their villages, fields, and obligations. Their mass flight left their masters without incomes necessary to provide military service to the Muscovite tsar. Government decrees beginning in 1580 or 1581, benefiting state military and fiscal interests as well as those of the landholders, cancelled rights of departure for peasants, initially for a year at a time; the restrictions quickly became permanent.[137] The process of enserfment was completed in 1649, as mentioned above.

Interestingly, in contrast to population declines occasioned by the Mongol invasions of the thirteenth century and the plague in the fourteenth century, depopulation in the late sixteenth century is regarded as a factor stimulating the process of enserfment. The pertinent question becomes what factors permitted Russian peasants to maintain their free status before 1500, but prevented them from consolidating that status firmly enough to preserve it through the next century.

Some factors may be raised for consideration. The first is the Mongol invasion and the subsequent subjugation of the northern Russian lands to Tatar hegemony for most of the period. The invasion, as noted, had serious and ongoing demographic consequences for the Russians. The Mongols, having established their hegemony over the northern Russian principalities, also demanded tribute from them. Peasants as well as urban tax-payers contributed to the tribute payments made by princes to the Mongol khan. Failure to pay resulted in Mongol retribution against the princes and their subjects. Lay landowners were thus not the sole beneficiaries of the extraction of wealth from peasant production. The limitation on the incomes they could derive from their peasants contributed to their focus on other sources of revenue and to their relative disinterest in increasing rents and tightening controls over their peasant populations.[138] Rather than impose greater obligations on the peasantry, some landowners, especially those landowners who were recipients of immunity charters granted by princes, were able to attract peasant labor by offering relatively low rents and dues.

In conditions when the size of the population was low, labor was scarce, and political authority was too weak to enforce restrictions on mobility, if they had been issued, peasants were not only legally free, but could exercise that freedom of mobility. The risks associated with climatic and other natural disasters as well as uncontrollable events, such as wars, however, placed a premium on security. Although there were cases of land disputes and claims of misappropriation of peasant lands by those landowners, some peasants, possibly responding to advantages offered in the form of reduced obligations as well as security afforded by large proprietors, found it to be in their interest to negotiate arrangements with those landowners and provide their labor, at least temporarily, on their estates. Within this context peasants were able, without adopting new farming techniques, to raise sufficient crops to maintain themselves and meet their obligations. When their forest plots began to lose fertility, they could clear new ones. If conditions deteriorated, they could exercise their rights of departure.

The Mongol demand for tribute influenced developments in Russia in yet another manner. Mongol political and military support eventually shifted in favor of the princes of Moscow, who were consistently confirmed by the Mongol khans as the grand princes of Vladimir from the late 1320s and charged with responsibility for collecting and delivering tribute. When Tatar power over the Russian lands diminished in the fifteenth century, the Moscow princes used their authority to collect taxes for their own benefit, to subordinate other princes, and to construct the Muscovite state. As the power and administrative capability of the state increased, the grand prince's officials and courts became more involved in settling disputes over land ownership and enforcing agreements between peasants and other landowners.[139] By the late fifteenth century, as discussed above, the Muscovite grand prince was issuing landed estates in the Novgorod lands to men in his service. This form of conditional land tenure, which would become more common throughout the Muscovite realm during the course of the sixteenth century, provided incomes to cavalrymen in the Muscovite army. By the middle of the sixteenth century the Muscovite tsar was exacting military service from all landholders, regardless of the type of land tenure. When the population declined in the late sixteenth century, it was not great landowners, but the state that curtailed peasant mobility. Its actions reflected a convergence of interests of the Muscovite government and those of landholders; both benefited from ensuring that peasants remained on those landed estates. This observation is, in a sense, consistent with the view expressed by advocates of the 'feudal state' model that the centralized Muscovite state acted in the interests of the landowning class at the expense of the peasantry. But, contrary to that model, the Muscovite central authorities were not acting as instruments of the ruling landowning class when they adopted those policies; they were motivated by the need to maintain the state's military and fiscal power. The presence of a relatively strong state with the power to issue and at least partially enforce decrees throughout the entire realm was, thus, a factor that had been absent in the thirteenth and fourteenth centuries, but had a decisive effect on the status of the peasantry in the late sixteenth century.

NOTES

1. In the *Sudebnik* of 1497 peasants were permitted to leave their places of residence once per year, specifically during the week before and the week after St. George's Day in the autumn. The article in the code also specified fees that peasants had to pay their landlords upon departure. H. W. Dewey, compiler, ed., and trans., *Muscovite Judicial Texts 1488–1556* (Ann Arbor, MI: University of Michigan, Dept. of Slavic Languages and Literatures, 1966), 19.
2. For a thorough discussion of the process of enserfment, see Richard Hellie, *Enserfment and Military Change in Muscovy* (Chicago and London: University of Chicago Press, 1971), 77–147.
3. R. E. F. Smith, *Peasant Farming in Muscovy* (Cambridge: Cambridge University Press, 1977), 111; Robert O. Crummey, *The Formation of Muscovy 1304–1613* (London and New York: Longman, 1987), 1–2; R. A. French, "The Early and Medieval Russian Town," in *Studies in Russian Historical Geography*, 2 vols. (London and New York: Academic Press, 1983), vol. 2, 249; Richard Hellie, "The Peasantry," in *The Cambridge History of Russia*, vol. 1, *From Early Rus' to 1689*, ed. Maureen Perrie (Cambridge: Cambridge University Press, 2006), 187.
4. N. A. Gorskaia, *Istoricheskaia demografiia Rossii epokhi feodalizma (Itogi i problemy izucheniia)* (Moscow: Nauka, 1994), 55.
5. A. Ia. Degtiarev, *Russkaia derevnia v XV–XVII vekakh. Ocherki istorii sel'skogo rasseleniia* (Leningrad: Leningradskii gosudarstvennyi universitet, 1980), 23.
6. Degtiarev, *Russkaia derevnia*, 23–27.
7. Institut istorii (Akademiia nauk SSSR), *Akty sotsial'no-ekonomicheskoi istorii severo-vostochnoi Rusi* (ASEI), 3 vols. (Moscow: AN SSSR, 1952–64), 1: 565–571 (No. 649); M. S. Cherkasova, *Zemlevladenie Troitse-Sergieva monastryria v XV–XVI vv.* (Moscow: Arkheograficheskii tsentr, 1996), 102–103.
8. For discussion of arguments that family units in households in single-household hamlets were larger, see Degtiarev, *Russkaia derevnia*, 18.

9. Hellie, "The Peasantry," 288.
10. An example is a complaint made by the Pekhora rural district to Grand Prince Ivan III against the Simonov monastery in the 1460s; ASEI, vol. 2, 377 (No. 381); Smith, *Peasant Farming*, 116; A. I. Kopanev, M. B. Sverdlov, and M. I. Bobovich, eds., *Istoriia krest'ianstva severo-zapada Rossii. Period feodalizma* (St. Petersburg: Nauka, 1994), 51–52.
11. A. D. Gorskii, *Ocherki ekonomicheskogo polozheniia krest'ian severo-vostochnoi Rusi XIV–XV vv.* (Moscow: Moskovskii universitet, 1960), 23–28; Kopanev, *Istoriia krest'ianstva*, 55–57; G. E. Kochin, *Sel'skoe khoziaistvo na Rusi v period obrazovaniia Russkogo tsentralizovannogo gosudarstva, konets XIII–nachalo XVI v.* (Moscow and Leningrad: Nauka, 1965), 223; Smith, *Peasant Farming*, 33–40, 86–87; Pierre Gonneau, *La Maison de la Sainte Trinité. Un Grande-Monastère Russe du Moyen-Âge Tardif (1345–1533)* (Paris: Klincksieck, 1993), 393.
12. The long-stemmed variety of flax, which was particularly well-suited to the climate and soil of northern and northwestern Russia, provided edible fats in the form of oil as well as fibers used to produce clothing, bedding, fishing nets, rope, and candle wicks. Hemp and nettle served similar functions. Heidi M. Sherman, "From Flax to Linen in the Medieval Rus Lands," in *Medieval Clothing and Textiles*, vol. 4, eds. Robin Netherton and Gale R. Owen-Crocker (Woodbridge: Boydell Press, 2008), 2. See also, Gorskii, *Ocherki*, 28, 58–59; Gonneau, *La Maison de la Sainte Trinité,* 402.
13. A. L. Shapiro, ed., *Agrarnia istoriia severo-zapada Rossii: vtoraia polovina XV-nachalo XVI v.* (Leningrad: Nauka, 1971), 345; R. A. French, "The Introduction of the Three-field System," in *Studies in Historical Geography*, vol. 1, 70; Kochin, *Sel'skoe khoziaistvo*, 78–79; A. D. Gorskii, "Iz istorii zemlevladeniia v severo-vostochnoi Rusi XIV–XV vekov," in *Materialy po istorii sel'skogo khoziaistva i krest'ianstva SSSR*, sb. 3 (Moscow: AN SSSR, 1959), 17. It has been pointed, however, that winter and spring crops could also have been cultivated using other systems; e.g., Kochin, *Sel'skoe khoziaistvo*, 79.
14. French, "The Introduction of the Three-field System," 71; A. L. Shapiro, *Problemy sotsial'no-ekonomicheskoi istorii Rusi XIV–XVI vv.* (Leningrad: Leningradskii universitet, 1977), 53; L. V. Danilova, *Ocherki po istorii zemlevladeniia i khoziaistva v Novgorodskoi zemle v XIV–XV vv.* (Moscow: AN SSSR, 1955), 26; Gorskii, *Ocherki*, 32; Gorskii found 17 references to a third field in documents dated between 1454 and 1505; "Iz istorii," 18–19; Gonneau, *La Maison de la Sainte Trinité*, 396–397.
15. R. A. French, "Russians and the Forest," in *Studies in Historical Geography*, vol. 1, 27; idem, "The Introduction of the Three-field System," 65; Smith, *Peasant Farming*, 27.
16. French, "The Introduction of the Three-field System," 67; Shapiro, *Problemy*, 38.
17. French, "The Introduction of the Three-field System," 69.
18. Smith, *Peasant Farming*, 29.
19. French, "The Introduction of the Three-field System," 68, 70–71; Shapiro, *Problemy*, 1977, 51; Gorskii, "Iz istorii," 17–20. One of the villages belonging to the St. Sergius-Trinity monastery was described in the land register, noted above, as having two fields in the Pereiaslavl' district and a third field in Radonezh, which was located to the south of Pereiaslavl'; ASEI, vol. 1, 567 (No. 649). In another example a man left his lands to his grandson, but in the bequest differentiated the third field from the other two and specified its particular location. Gorskii, "Iz istorii," 17, 20; French, "The Introduction of the Three-field System," 71.

20. French, "The Introduction of the Three-field System," 67; Shapiro, *Problemy*, 38.
21. French, "The Introduction of the Three-field System," 72; Shapiro, *Problemy*, 50; Danilova, *Ocherki*, 26.
22. Gorskii, "Iz istorii," 17, 20–21; Gorskii , *Ocherki*, 32–33; Smith, *Peasant Farming*, 28–30, 243–249; Gonneau, *La Maison de la Sainte Trinité*, 396–397. Kochin argues for an earlier date, as early as the fourteenth century and prevailing by the first half of the fifteenth century; *Sel'skoe khoziaistvo*, 158.
23. Smith, *Peasant Farming*, 27; Kochin, *Sel'skoe khoziaistvo*, 79–80; Gonneau, 396–397.
24. Smith, *Peasant Farming*, 16; Kochin, *Sel'skoe khoziaistvo*, 62; Hellie, "The Peasantry," 291.
25. Gorskii, *Ocherki*, 46–47; Shapiro, *Problemy*, 27–28; Smith, *Peasant Farming* 11–21; Jerome Blum, *Lord and Peasant in Russia from the Ninth to the Nineteenth Century* (New York: Atheneum, 1964), 23; Peter I. Lyashchenko, *History of the National Economy of Russia to the 1917 Revolution* (New York: Macmillan, 1949), 180–181.
26. Smith, *Peasant Farming*, 24, 25; Danilova, *Ocherki*, 32–33; Gorskii, "Iz istorii," 26.
27. Smith, *Peasant Farming*, 35, 41; Kopanev, *Istoriia krest'ianstva*, 55; Hellie, "The Peasantry," 291.
28. Gorskii, *Ocherki*, 48; Kopanev, *Istoriia krest'ianstva*, 58; French, "Russians and the Forest," 25: Smith, *Peasant Farming*, 43–45, 94.
29. Gorskii, *Ocherki*, 39; Shapiro, *Problemy*, 58; for use of manure in the sixteenth century, see Lyashchenko, *History of the National Economy*, 181.
30. Crummey, *The Formation of Muscovy*, 4–5; Shapiro, *Problemy*, 65–67; Smith, *Peasant Farming*, 86–87; Gonneau, *La Maison de la Sainte Trinité*, 410. Richard Hellie has considered a 3:1 ratio for rye was the maximum; "The Peasantry," 287.
31. Daniel H. Kaiser, "The Economy of Kievan Rus': Evidence from the *Pravda Rus'skaia*," in *Ukrainian Economic History: Interpretive Essays*, ed. I. S. Koropeckyj (Cambridge, MA: Harvard University Press, 1991), 41; Blum, *Lord and Peasant*, 25, 27
32. S. N. Valk, ed., *Gramoty Velikogo Novgoroda i Pskova* (GVNP), (Moscow and Leningrad: AN SSSR, 1949; reprint ed., Düsseldorg: Brücken-Verlag, 1970), 139–141 (Nos. 80, 81); V. L. Ianin, *Novgorodskaia feodal'naia votchina* (Moscow: Nauka, 1981), 231, 239–240; a translation of Mstislav's grant into English is published in R. E. F. Smith, ed. and trans., *The Enserfment of the Russian Peasantry* (Cambridge: Cambridge University Press, 1968), 28–29 (No. 1). V. L. Ianin, who dates this document c. 1130, also explains that the property, identified as Buets, was not simply a village as the editors of GVNP and Smith described it, but a relatively large rural district (*volost'*) that by the late 15th century contained 96 hamlets with a total of 238 men; *Novgorodskie akty XII-XV vv. Khronologicheskii kommentarii* (Moscow: Nauka, 1991), 135–136 (No. 62); Danilova, *Ocherki*, 43. Vsevolod's grant, according to Ianin, was a large tract encompassing 800 sq. km; Ianin, *Novgorodskaia feodal'naia votchina*, 231–238.
33. I. Ia. Froianov, *Kievskaia Rus'. Ocherki sotsial'no-ekonomichskoi istorii* (Leningrad: Leningradskii universitet, 1974), 56. M. N. Tikhomirov has noted that princes in the fourteenth century continued to use their private lands for non-agricultural purposes, e.g., bee-keeping, hunting, and raising hay, presumably for livestock; M. N. Tikhomirov, *Srednevekovaia Moskva v XIV–XV vekakh* (Moscow: Moskovskii universitet, 1957), 26.

34. Daniel H. Kaiser, trans. and ed., *The Laws of Rus'—Tenth to Fifteenth Centuries* (Salt Lake City, UT: Charles Schlacks, Jr., 1992), 25; idem, "The Economy of Kievan Rus'," 38–43.
35. Kaiser, "The Economy of Kievan Rus'," 51–55. Individuals became slaves through purchase; marriage to a female slave without a stipulation to the man's freedom; or serving as an estate steward without stipulating the person's freedom. Individuals who defaulted on contractual or debt obligations could also become slaves. See also Richard Hellie, *Slavery in Russia 1450–1725* (Chicago: University of Chicago Press, 1982), 49–56.
36. Nancy Shields Kollmann, *Kinship and Politics: The Making of the Muscovite Political System, 1345–1547* (Stanford: Stanford University Press, 1987), 37.
37. ASEI, vol. 2, 338–339, 377–378 (Nos. 340, 381); Smith, *Peasant Farming*, 116.
38. ASEI, vol. 2, 15 (No.1).
39. A. I. Kopanev, *Istoriia zemlevladeniia Belozerskogo kraia XV–XVI vv.* (Moscow and Leningrad: AN SSSR, 1951), 24–25, 30–37; Ianin, *Novgorodskaia feodal'naia votchina*, 224–225.
40. S. B. Veselovskii, *Issledovaniia po istorii klassa sluzhilykh zemlevladel'tsev* (Moscow: Nauka, 1969), 60–61.
41. Kollmann, *Kinship and Politics*, 39; Kochin, *Sel'skoe khoziaistvo*, 314; Veselovskii, *Issledovaniia*, 60; idem., *Feodal'noe zemlevladenie v severo-vostochnoi Rusi*, vol. 1 (Moscow and Leningrad: AN SSSR, 1947), 146–147.
42. Veselovskii, *Issledovaniia*, 60–61.
43. As an example, Grand Prince Vasily II issued a charter bestowing two villages in the Rostov district with their associated hamlets to his boyar Il'ya Borisovich. V. Antonov and K. V. Baranov, compilers, *Akty sluzhilykh zemlevladel'tsev XV-nachala XVII veka* (ASZ), 3 vols. (Moscow: Arkheograficheskii tsentr, Pamiatniki istoricheskoi mysli, Drevlekhranilishche, 1997–2002), vol. 1, 56–57 (No. 67).
44. The documents include records of land sales, wills, and other types of transactions; see, for example, ASZ, vol. 1, 129, 263–65, 293–94 (Nos. 157, 278, 301).
45. For a brief discussion of immunity charters and samples of them, see Marc D. Zlotnik, "Muscovite Fiscal Policy: 1462–1584," *Russian History* 6 (1979): 256 and ASZ, vol. 1, 55–56, 94, 107, 230, 302–303 (Nos. 66, 118, 137, 254, 312).
46. Kollmann, *Kinship and Politics*, 37; for one discussion of this form of landownership, see Veselovskii, *Feodal'noe zemlevladenie*, chapters 7 and 8.
47. David B. Miller, "Monumental Building as an Indicator of Economic Trends in Northern Rus' in the Late Kievan and Mongol Periods, 1138–1462," *American Historical Review* 94 (1989): 389.
48. David B. Miller, "Donors to the Trinity-Sergius Monastery as a Community of Venerators, 1360s–1462," in *Moskovskaia Rus' (1359–1584): kul'tura i istoricheskoe samosoznanie/Culture and Identity in Muscovy, 1359–1584*, eds. A. M. Kleimola and G. D. Lenhoff (Moscow: ITZ-Garant, 1997), 457, 465; Lawrence N. Langer, "The Black Death in Russia: Its Effects Upon Urban Labor," *Russian History* 2 (1975): 58, 60–61.
49. Miller, "Donors," 457, 459–460, 462.
50. After 1462, the monastery acquired only 32 more villages, but it obtained 139 more hamlets; Cherkasova, 60–90, 104; Miller, "Donors," 462, 467; Gonneau, *La Maison de la Sainte Trinité*, 322–338, 397–398.
51. Miller, "Donors," 455–456.
52. Miller, "Donors," 457.

53. L. I. Ivina, *Krupnaia votchina severo-vostochnoi Rusi kontsa XIV-pervoi poloviny XVI v.* (Leningrad: Nauka, 1979), 35.
54. Ivina, *Krupnaia votchina*, 37; Kopanev, *Istoriia zemlevladeniia*, 46–47.
55. Gorskaia, *Istoricheskaia demografiia*, 60. On land disputes between Simonov monastery and 'black' peasants, see Ivina, *Krupnaia votchina*, 52–53.
56. Langer, "The Black Death in Russia," 65; ASEI, vol. 2, 405–408 (No. 400); Ivina, *Krupnaia votchina*, 52.
57. Kopanev, *Istoriia krest'ianstva*, 65–66.
58. Ianin, *Novgorodskaia feodal'naia votchina*, 55, 63–65, 91, 110; V. N. Bernadskii, *Novgorod i Novgorodskaia zemlia v XV veke* (Moscow and Leningrad: AN SSSR, 1961), 52–53. GVNP, 166–168 (No. 110); Kopanev, *Istoriia krest'ianstva*, 68.
59. E,g, GVNP, 279–280 (No. 279); Kopanev, *Istoriia krest'ianstva*, 49, 69.
60. V. L. Ianin, "Medieval Novgorod," in *The Cambridge History of Russia*, vol. 1, *From Early Rus' to 1689*, ed. Maureen Perrie (Cambridge: Cambridge University Press, 2006), 200.
61. GVNP, 9–13, 15–20, 22–24, 26–28 (Nos. 1–3, 6–7, 9, 11, 14); Kopanev, *Istoriia krest'ianstva*, 49–51.
62. Danilova, *Ocherki*, 99–135, 301–304, 328–389.
63. Kopanev, *Istoriia krest'ianstva*, 69; Crummey, *The Formation of Muscovy*, 11.
64. Kopanev, *Istoriia krest'ianstva*, 69.
65. Danilova, *Ocherki*, 163
66. Ianin, *Novgorodskaia feodal'naia votchina*, 238.
67. Ianin, *Novgorodskaia feodal'naia votchina*, 230; A. M. Andriiashev, *Materialy po istoricheskoi geografii Novgorodskoi zemli. Shelonskaia piatina po pistsovym knigam 1498–1576 gg.* (Moscow: Imperatorskoe obshchestvo istorii i drevnostei Rossiiskikh pri Moskovskom universitete, 1914), 44, 183
68. Shapiro, *Agrarnaia istoriia*, 85.
69. Shapiro, *Agrarnaia istoriia*, 230.
70. Kopanev, *Istoriia krest'ianstva*, 65–67; Danilova, *Ocherki*, 44–47, 146–147.
71. Kopanev, *Istoriia krest'ianstva*, 68; Crummey, *The Formation of Muscovy*, 12; Veselovskii, *Feodal'noe zemlevladenie*, 146.
72. Danilova discusses Bogdan Esipov's management of his estates through stewards, who were either selected peasants or slaves; *Ocherki*, 133.
73. Veselovskii, *Feodal'noe zemlevladenie*, 76; Hellie, *Enserfment and Military Change*, 80. For examples of mid-fifteenth century *kormlenie* charters, see ASZ, vol. 1, 57–58 (Nos. 68–69).
74. Gonneau, *La Maison de la Sainte Trinité*, 406.
75. Kopanev, *Istoriia krest'ianstva*, 72.
76. Drevnerusskie berestanye gramoty, Rukopisnye pamiatniki drevnei Rusi, Gramota, No. 136. http://www.gramoty.ru. Accessed October 16, 2010; Kopanev, *Istoriia krest'ianstva*, 72. One *korob'ia* is estimated to have been equal to about seven puds or 252 pounds; Gonneau, *La Maison de la Sainte Trinité*, 67.
77. GVNP, 174 (No. 115); Kopanev, *Istoriia krest'ianstva*, 72.
78. ASEI, vol. 2, 18–19 (No. 9); Kopanev, *Istoriia zemlevladeniia*, 41.
79. Miller, "Donors," 457, 460.
80. Zlotnik, "Muscovite Fiscal Policy," 255.
81. Zlotnik, "Muscovite Fiscal Policy," 255–256.
82. Hellie, *Enserfment and Military Change*, 89. For one example of legal jurisdiction being assigned to the Trinity-Sergius monastery with the exception of murder cases, see Smith, *Enserfment*, 50–51 (No. 14).
83. The main books have been published as *Novgorodskiia pistsovyia knigi*, 6 vols. (St. Petersburg: Arkheograficheskaia kommissiia, 1859–1910; reprint

ed. vols. 1–3, The Hague and Paris: Mouton, 1969); *Pistsovye knigi Obonezhskoi piatiny 1496 i 1563 gg.*, ed. M. N. Pokrovskii (Leningrad: AN SSSR, 1930).

84. NPK, vol. 5, columns 359–365; D. Ia. Samokvasov, *Arkhivnyi material*, 2 vols. (Moscow: Universitetskaia tip., 1905, 1908), 1: 91–93; Danilova, *Ocherki*, 121–122, 363–367.
85. Danilova, *Ocherki*, 128. One pud equals 36 pounds.
86. Danilova, *Ocherki*, 145–146; Shapiro, *Agrarnaia istoriia*, 232; NPK, vol. 6, cols. 23–33; Janet Martin, *Treasure of the Land of Darkness: The Fur Trade and its Significance for Medieval Russia* (Cambridge: Cambridge University Press, 1986), 72–74.
87. NPK, vol. 5: 365.
88. Shapiro, *Agrarnaia istoriia*, 187, 195.
89. Shapiro, *Agrarnaia istoriia*, 100, 103, 105.
90. Shapiro, *Agrarnaia istoriia*, 235, 239–241.
91. Shapiro, *Agrarnaia istoriia*, 114, 134, 136, 197–199.
92. Shapiro, *Agrarnaia istoriia*, 92, 109–112.
93. Arcadius Kahan, "Natural Calamities and Their Effect upon the Food Supply in Russia (An Introduction to a Calalogue)," *Jahrbücher für Geschichte Osteuropas* 16 (1968): 368–370.
94. Hellie, *Enserfment and Military Change*, 5, 81; cf. Gonneau, *La Maison de la Sainte Trinité*, 406.
95. Smith, *Enserfment*, 53 (No. 16); Drevnerusskie berestanye gramoty (No. 301).
96. Hellie, *Enserfment and Military Change*, 81.
97. Shapiro, *Agrarnaia istoriia*, 240–241.
98. Lawrence N. Langer, "The Medieval Russian Town," in *The City in Russian History*, ed. Michael Hamm (Lexington, KY: University of Kentucky, 1976), 12–13; Gorskaia, *Istoricheskaia demografiia*, 52; A. M. Sakharov, *Goroda severo-vostochnoi Rusi XIV–XV vekov* (Moscow: Moskovskii universitet, 1959), 18–23; R. A. French, "The Early and Medieval Russian Town," in *Studies in Historical Geography*, 2: 264.
99. Gorskaia, *Istoricheskaia demografiia*, 52; Lawrence N. Langer, "Muscovite Taxation and the Problem of Mongol Rule in Rus'," *Russian History* 34 (2007): 112.
100. Sakharov, *Goroda*, 128; Langer, "Medieval Russian Town," 13.
101. Miller, "Monumental Building," 367–370, 373.
102. Miller, "Monumental Building," 387; Tikhomirov, *Srednevekovaia Moskva*, 19–21.
103. Miller, "Monumental Building," 370, 376, 377
104. Miller, "Monumental Building," 379–380; Langer, "Black Death," 62, 59–60; Sakharov, *Goroda*, 132.
105. Tikhomirov, *Srednevekovaia Moskva*, 36, 41–42.
106. Gorskaia, *Istoricheskaia demografiia*, 50–51; Langer, "Medieval Town," 13.
107. George Vernadsky, *A History of Russia*, vol. 2, *Kievan Russia* (New Haven: Yale University Press, 1948), 104–105.
108. GVNP, 55–56 (No. 28).
109. Martin, *Treasure*, 61–75, 77–79; Ianin, "Medieval Novgorod," 201, 208; Langer, "Medieval Town," 16–18; GVNP, 56–62 (Nos. 29–32).
110. Thomas S. Noonan, "Russia's Eastern Trade, 1150–1350: The Archeological Evidence," *Archivum Eurasiae Medii Aevii* 3 (1983): 259.
111. Janet Martin, "Muscovite Travelling Merchants: The Trade with the Muslim East (15th and 16th Centuries)," *Central Asian Survey* 4 (1985): 23.

112. Josafa Barbaro and Ambrogio Contarini, *Travels to Tana and Persia*. Works issued by the Hakluyt Society, vol. 49 (London, 1873; reprint ed., New York: Burt Franklin, n.d.), 162.
113. Langer, "Medieval Towns," 21.
114. Martin, *Treasure*, 88–89.
115. Noonan, "Russia's Eastern Trade," 212, 213, 215–217, 259; Langer, "Medieval Towns," 21.
116. GVNP, 11–13 (No. 3).
117. Langer, "Medieval Town," 18.
118. Contarini in *Travels to Tana and Persia*, 161–162.
119. Langer, "Medieval Town," 23–24; Tikhomirov, *Srednevekovaia Moskva*, 69–90.
120. Sakharov, *Goroda*, 147–149.
121. Shapiro, *Problemy*, 74.
122. Peasants who c. 1460 agreed to supply the Iur'ev monastery with rye and oats, as noted above, also committed to transporting the grain to the monastery, thus bringing provisions directly to the monks. GVNP, 174 (No. 115).
123. For a discussion of various population estimates and methods of calculating them, see Gorskaia, *Istoricheskaia demografiia*, 48–52. For Vernadsky's estimate, see *Kievan Russia*, 104; see also idem, *A History of Russia*, vol. 3, *The Mongols and Russia* (New Haven: Yale University Press and London: Oxford University Press, 1953), 219. A. I. Kopanev suggested a figure of six million at the end of the fifteenth century; "Naselenie russkogo gosudarstva v XVI v.," *Istoricheskii zapiski*, no. 64 (1959): 244.
124. Langer, "Black Death," 61–62; Hellie, "The Peasantry," 292.
125. *Polnoe sobranie russkikh letopisei*, vol. 10 (St. Petersburg: Arkheograficheskaia kommissiia, 1885; Moscow: Iazyki russkoi kul'tury, 2000), 106–109 (hereafter PSRL); John Fennell, *The Crisis of Medieval Russia 1200–1304* (London and New York: Longman, 1983), 79–80; idem, *The Emergence of Moscow 1304–1359* (Berkeley and Los Angeles: University of California Press, 1968), 12; Langer, "The Medieval Russian Town," 15.
126. V. V. Kargalov, "Posledstviia mongolo-tatarskogo nashestviia XIII v. dlia sel'skikh mestnostei severo-vostochnoi Rusi," *Voprosy istorii*, no. 3 (1965): 55–57; Gorskaia, *Istoricheskaia demografiia*, 52–53.
127. Kargalov, "Posledstviia," 53, 57; P. D. Malygin, "Sud'by Torzhka i Tveri v XIII veke," in *Rus' v XIII veke. Drevnosti temnogo vremeni*, eds. N. A. Makarov and A. V. Chernetsov (Moscow: Nauka, 2003) 94, 391.
128. E.g., Vernadsky, *The Mongols and Russia*, 338.
129. Langer, "The Medieval Russian Town," 15; Crummey, *The Formation of Muscovy*, 30–31; Kargalov, "Posledstviia," 53, 57; Fennell, *Crisis*, 129. A chronicle account of a campaign into central Russia in 1322, for example, describes an attack on the town of Iaroslavl', which was burned, and the capture of 'innumerable' prisoners; PSRL, 10: 188.
130. Langer, "The Medieval Russian Town," 23; Thomas T. Allsen, "Ever Closer Encounters: The Appropriation of Culture and the Apportionment of Peoples in the Mongol Empire," *Journal of Early Modern History* 1 (1997): 2–4; Donald Ostrowski, *Muscovy and the Mongols: Cross-cultural Influences on the Steppe Frontier, 1304–1589* (Cambridge: Cambridge University Press, 1998), 113–114; Vernadsky, *The Mongols and Russia*, 88, 123, 201, 213, 227, 338–339.
131. Langer, "Black Death," 55–56; PSRL, 10: 222–223.
132. PSRL, 10: 224, 226; Langer, "Black Death," 56.
133. Langer, "Black Death," 61,
134. Langer, "Black Death," 62.

135. For English-language summaries of the Soviet overview, see Blum, *Lord and Peasant*, 90–91; Lyashchenko, *History of the National Economy*, 139–146.
136. L. V. Cherepnin, *Obrazovanie russkogo tsentralizovannogo gosudarstva v XIV–XV vekakh* (Moscow: Sotsial'no-ekonomicheskaia literatura, 1960), 178.
137. On conditions that prompted them and on the decrees, see Hellie, *Enserfment and Military Change*, 95–97.
138. On tribute to the Mongols, see Michel Roublev, "Le tribute aux Mongols d'après les Testaments et Accords des Princes Russes," *Cahiers du monde russe et soviétique* 7 (1966): 487–530, trans. as "The Mongol Tribute According to the Wills and Agreements of the Russian Princes" and republished in *The Structure of Russian History: Interpretive Essays*, ed. Michael Cherniavsky (New York: Random House, 1970), 29–64; idem, "The Periodicity of the Mongol Tribute as Paid by the Russian Princes during the Fourteenth and Fifteenth Centuries," *Forschungen zur Osteuropäischen Geschichte* 15 (1970): 7–13.
139. An example is contained in the c. 1460 agreement between a group of peasants and the Iur'ev monastery, cited above. The document concludes with the monastery invoking princely charters as well as custom to justify measures that would be taken if the peasants did not deliver the grain, as specified in the agreement. GVNP, 174 (No. 115).

BIBLIOGRAPHY

Allsen, T. T. "Ever Closer Encounters: The Appropriation of Culture and the Apportionment of Peoples in the Mongol Empire." *Journal of Early Modern History* 1 (1997): 2–23.

Andriiashev, A. M. *Materialy po istoricheskoi geografii Novgorodskoi zemli. Shelonskaia piatina po pistsovym knigam 1498–1576 gg.* Moscow: Imperatorskoe obshchestvo istorii i drevnostei Rossiiskikh pri Moskovskom universitete, 1914.

Antonov, A. V. and K. V. Baranov, compilers. *Akty sluzhilykh zemlevladel'tsev XV-nachala XVII veka*, 3 vols. Moscow: Arkheograficheskii tsentr, Pamiatniki istoricheskoi mysli, Drevlekhranilishche, 1997–2002.

Barbaro, Josafa and Ambrogio Contarini. *Travels to Tana and Persia.* Works issued by the Hakluyt Society, vol. 49. London, 1873; reprint ed., New York: Burt Franklin, n.d.

Bernadskii, V. N. *Novgorod i Novgorodskaia zemlia v XV veke.* Moscow and Leningrad: AN SSSR, 1961

Blum, J. *Lord and Peasant in Russia from the Ninth to the Nineteenth century.* New York: Atheneum, 1964.

Cherepnin, L. V. *Obrazovanie russkogo tsentralizovannogo gosudarstva v XIV–XV vekakh.* Moscow: Sotsial'no-ekonomicheskaia literatura, 1960.

Cherkasova, M. S. *Zemlevladenie Troitse-Sergieva Monastyria v XV–XVI vv.* Moscow: Arkheograficheskii tsentr, 1996.

Crummey R. O. *The Formation of Muscovy 1304–1613.* London and New York: Longman, 1987.

Danilova, L. V. *Ocherki po istorii zemlevladeniia i khoziaistva v Novgorodskoi zemle v XIV–XV vv.* Moscow: AN SSSR, 1955.

Degtiarev, A. Ia. *Russkaia derevnia v XV–XVII vekakh. Ocherki istorii sel'skogo rasseleniia.* Leningrad: Leningradskii gosudarstvennyi universitet, 1980.

Dewey, H. W., ed. and trans. *Muscovite Judicial Texts 1488–1556.* Ann Arbor, MI: University of Michigan, Dept. of Slavic Languages and Literature, 1966.

Fennell, J. L. I. *The Emergence of Moscow 1304–1359*. Berkeley and Los Angeles: University of California Press, 1968.
Fennell, J. L. I. *The Crisis of Medieval Russia 1200–1304*. London and New York: Longman, 1983.
French, R. A. "The Early and Medieval Russian Town," in *Studies in Historical Geography*, vol. 2, edited by J. H. Bater and R. A. French, 249–277. London and New York: Academic Press, 1983.
French, R. A. "The Introduction of the Three-field System," in *Studies in Historical Geography*, vol. 1, edited by James H. Bater and R. A. French, 65–81. London and New York: Academic Press, 1983.
French, R. A. "Russians and the Forest," in *Studies in Historical Geography*, vol. 1, edited by James H. Bater and R. A. French, 23–44. London and New York: Academic Press, 1983.
Froianov, I. Ia. *Kievskaia Rus'. Ocherki sotsial'no-ekonomichskoi istorii*. Leningrad: Leningradskii universitet, 1974.
Gonneau, P. *La Maison de la Sainte Trinité. Un Grande-Monastère Russe du Moyen-Âge Tardif (1345–1533)*. Paris: Klincksieck, 1993.
Gorskaia, N. A. *Istoricheskaia demografiia Rossii epokhi feodalizma (Itogi i problemy izucheniia)*. Moscow: Nauka, 1994.
Gorskii, A. D. "Iz istorii zemlevladeniia v severo-vostochnoi Rusi XIV–XV vekov," in *Materialy po istorii sel'skogo khoziaistva i krest'ianstva SSSR*, sb. 3, 5–40. Moscow: AN SSSR, 1959.
Gorskii, A. D. *Ocherki ekonomicheskogo polozheniia krest'ian severo-vostochnoi Rusi XIV–XV vv*. Moscow: Moskovskii universitet, 1960.
Hellie R. *Enserfment and Military Change in Muscovy*. Chicago and London: University of Chicago Press, 1971.
Hellie R. *Slavery in Russia 1450–1725*. Chicago: University of Chicago Press, 1982.
Hellie R. "The Peasantry," in *The Cambridge History of Russia*, vol. 1, *From Early Rus' to 1689*, . edited by Maureen Perrie, 286–297. Cambridge: Cambridge University Press, 2006.
Ianin, V. L. *Novgorodskaia feodal'naia votchina (Istoriko-genealogicheskoe issledovanie)*. Moscow: Nauka, 1981.
Ianin, V. L. *Novgorodskie akty XII–XV vv. Khronologicheskii kommentarii*. Moscow: Nauka, 1991.
Ianin, V. L. "Medieval Novgorod," in *The Cambridge History of Russia*, vol. 1, *From Early Rus' to 1689*, edited by Maureen Perrie, 188–210. Cambridge: Cambridge University Press, 2006.
Institut istorii (Akademiia nauk SSSR). *Akty sotsial'no-ekonomicheskoi istorii severo-vostochnoi Rusi*, 3 vols. Moscow: AN SSSR, 1952–64.
Ivina, L. I. *Krupnaia votchina severo-vostochnoi Rusi kontsa XIV-pervoi poloviny XVI v*. Leningrad: Nauka, 1979.
Kahan, A. "Natural Calamities and Their Effect upon the Food Supply in Russia (An Introduction to a Calalogue)." *Jahrbücher für Geschichte Osteuropas* 16 (1968): 353–377.
Kaiser, D. H. "The Economy of Kievan Rus': Evidence from the Pravda Rus'skaia," in *Ukrainian Economic History: Interpretive Essays*, edited by I. S. Koropeckyj, 37–57. Cambridge, MA: Harvard University Press, 1991.
Kaiser, D. H., trans. and ed., *The Laws of Rus': Tenth to Fifteenth Centuries*. Salt Lake City, UT: Charles Schlacks, Jr., 1992.
Kargalov, V. V. "Posledstviia mongolo-tatarskogo nashestviia XIII v. dlia sel'skikh mestnostei severo-vostochnoi Rusi," *Voprosy istorii*, no. 3 (1965): 53–58.
Kochin, G. E. *Sel'skoe khoziaistvo na Rusi v period obrazovaniia Russkogo tsentralizovannogo gosudarstva, konets XIII–nachalo XVI v*. Moscow and Leningrad: Nauka, 1965.

Kollmann, N. S. *Kinship and Politics: The Making of the Muscovite Political System, 1345–1547.* Stanford: Stanford University Press, 1987.

Kopanev, A. I. *Istoriia zemlevladeniia Belozerskogo kraia XV–XVI v.* Moscow and Leningrad: AN SSSR, 1951.

Kopanev, A. I. "Naselenie russkogo gosudarstva v XVI v.," *Istoricheskii zapiski*, 1959, no. 64 (1959): 233-254.

Kopanev, A. I., M. B. Sverdlov, and I. M. Bobovich, eds. *Istoriia krest'ianstva severo-zapada Rossii. Period feodalizma.* St. Petersburg: Nauka, 1994.

Langer, L. N. "The Black Death in Russia: Its Effects Upon Urban Labor," *Russian History* 2 (1975): 53–67.

Langer, L. N. "The Medieval Russian Town," in *The City in Russian History*, edited by Michael Hamm, 11–33. Lexington, KY: University of Kentucky, 1976.

Langer, L. N. "Muscovite Taxation and the Problem of Mongol Rule in Rus'," *Russian History* 34 (2007): 101–129.

Lyashchenko, P. I. *History of the National Economy of Russia to the 1917 Revolution.* New York: Macmillan, 1949.

Malygin, P. D. "Sud'by Torzhka i Tveri v XIII veke," in *Rus' v XIII veke. Drevnosti temnogo vremeni*, edited by N. A. Makarov and A. V. Chernetsov, 92–96, 390–392. Moscow: Nauka, 2003.

Martin, J. "Muscovite Travelling Merchants: The Trade with the Muslim East (15th and 16th Centuries)," *Central Asian Survey* 4 (1985): 21–38.

Martin, J. *Treasure of the Land of Darkness: The Fur Trade and its Significance for Medieval Russia.* Cambridge: Cambridge University Press, 1986.

Miller, D. B. "Monumental Building as an Indicator of Economic Trends in Northern Rus' in the Late Kievan and Mongol Periods, 1138–1462," *American Historical Review* 94 (1989): 360–390.

Miller, D. B. "Donors to the Trinity-Sergius Monastery as a Community of Venerators, 1360s–1462," in *Moskovskaia Rus' (1359–1584): kul'tura i istoricheskoe samosoznanie/ Culture and Identity in Muscovy, 1359–1584*, edited by A. M. Kleimola and G. D. Lenhoff, 450–474. Moscow: ITZ-Garant, 1997.

Milov, L. V., ed. *Agrarnye tekhnologii v Rossii IX–XX vv. XXV sessiia simposiuma po agrarnoi istorii Vostochnoi Evropy. Tezisy dokladov i soobshchenii.* Moscow: Institut Rossiiskoi istorii RAN, 1996.

Noonan, T. S. "Russia's Eastern Trade, 1150–1350: The Archeological Evidence." *Archivum Eurasiae Medii Aevii* 3 (1983): 201–264.

Novgorodskiia pistsovyia knigi, 6 vols. St. Petersburg: Arkheograficheskaia kommissiia, 1859–1910; reprint ed. vols. 1–3, The Hague and Paris: Mouton, 1969.

Ostrowski, D. *Muscovy and the Mongols: Cross-cultural Influences on the Steppe Frontier, 1304–1589.* Cambridge: Cambridge University Press, 1998.

Pokrovskii, M. N., ed. *Pistsovye knigi Obonezhkoi piatiny 1496 i 1563 gg.* Leningrad: AN SSSR, 1930.

Polnoe sobranie russkikh letopisei, vol. 10. St. Petersburg; Arkheograficheskaia kommissiia, 1885; reprint ed. edited by A. Koshelev. Moscow: Iazyki russkoi kul'tury, 2000.

Roublev, M. "The Periodicity of the Mongol Tribute as Paid by the Russian Princes during the Fourteenth and Fifteenth Centuries." *Forschungen zur Osteuropäischen Geschichte* 15 (1970): 7–13

Roublev, M. "Le tribute aux Mongols d'après les Testaments et Accords des Princes Russes," *Cahiers du monde russe et soviétique*, 7 (1966): 487–530. Trans. ed., "The Mongol Tribute According to the Wills and Agreements of the Russian Princes," in *The Structure of Russian History: Interpretive Essays*, edited by M. Cherniavsky, 29–64. New York: Random House, 1970.

Sakharov, A. M. *Goroda severo-vostochnoi Rusi XIV–XV vekov*. Moscow: Moskovskii universitet, 1959.
Samokvasov, D. Ia. *Arkhivnyi material*, 2. vols. Moscow: Universitetskaia tip, 1905, 1908.
Shapiro, A. L. *Problemy sotsial'no-ekonomicheskoi istorii Rusi XIV–XVI vv.* Leningrad: Leningradskii universitet, 1977.
Shapiro, A. L., ed. *Agrarnaia istoriia severo-zapada Rossii: vtoraia polovina XV-nachalo XVI v.* Leningrad: Nauka, 1971.
Sherman, H. M. "From Flax to Linen in the Medieval Rus Lands," in *Medieval Clothing and Textiles*, vol. 4, edited by R. Netherton and G. R. Owen-Crocker, 1–20. Woodbridge: Boydell Press, 2008.
Smith, R. E. F., ed. and trans. *The Enserfment of the Russian Peasantry*. Cambridge: Cambridge University Press, 1968.
Smith, R. E. F. *Peasant Farming in Muscovy*. Cambridge: Cambridge University Press, 1977.
Tikhomirov, M. N. *Srednevekovaia Moskva v XIV–XV vekakh*. Moscow: Moskovskii universitet, 1957.
Valk, S. N. ed. *Gramoty Velikogo Novgoroda i Pskova*. Moscow and Leningrad: AN SSSR, 1949; reprint ed., Düsseldorg: Brücken-Verlag, 1970.
Vernadsky, G. *A History of Russia*, vol. 2, *Kievan Russia*. New Haven: Yale University Press, 1948.
Vernadsky, G. *A History of Russia*, vol. 3: *The Mongols and Russia*. New Haven: Yale University Press and London: Oxford University Press, 1953.
Veselovskii, S. B. *Feodal'noe zemlevladenie v severo-vostochnoi Rusi*, vol. 1. Moscow and Leningrad: AN SSSR, 1947.
Veselovskii, S. B. *Issledovaniia po istorii klassa sluzhilykh zemlevladel'tsev*. Moscow: Nauka, 1969.
Zlotnik, M. D. "Muscovite Fiscal Policy: 1462–1584," *Russian History* 6 (1979): 243–258.

10 Epilogue

Harry Kitsikopoulos

Europe in the year 1200 was a continent in a state of political and economic equilibrium: no major wars tormented its people and there were still sufficient natural resources to accommodate its growing population. Prosperity and security, relative to medieval standards, was the norm. In the next three centuries its economic and social landscape would witness challenges of monumental proportions: widespread poverty, military invasions, civil strife, adverse climatic changes, and a devastating health crisis, such events producing dramatic swings in the standards of living of its people. By the year 1500 the continent found itself at the threshold of a trajectory that eventually led parts of it to the doorstep of modernity while others witnessed the beginning of institutional transformations which compromised their economic growth for centuries to come.

Synthesizing the events of these three centuries is not an easy task; the documentary bounty of England is not duplicated elsewhere, the scarcity of records being particularly extreme along Europe's eastern frontier (Russia and Byzantium). Moreover, making sense of this story at an aggregate level is challenging given the diversity of experiences. Commonalities do exist, however, with demographic trends offering the most convenient starting point for reviewing the evidence.[1]

THE PRE-PLAGUE PERIOD

Historians have made some daring attempts trying to estimate the population of individual European countries but more often than not have come up with wildly different results. While producing exact figures has proven an elusive enterprise, overall trends are, in most cases, beyond dispute. Europe went through a veritable population boom during the thirteenth century forming the tail end of an expansion phase whose origins date back to the eighth or ninth centuries. But it is important to stress that by 1300 there were noticeable regional differences.

On one side there was a territory stretching from England, France, and the Low Countries and extending across the southern flanks of the continent encompassing the Byzantine Empire and Italy (but excluding Spain). This densely populated and highly urbanized part of the continent we will call **Group A**. Italy was placed at the top of the pyramid with 41.5 people/km^2 on average rising to 48.1 in the center and north of the country.[2] England and France trailed close behind with densities in the range of 30–40 people/km^2 but with some noticeable variations within their boundaries; the respective figure in Flanders, Artois, lower Normandy, and the districts surrounding Paris reached up to 90–100, falling down to barely 20 inhabitants in Provence and the Savoie alpine districts.[3] The paucity of records in the case of Byzantium does not allow us to come up with reliable figures but, despite the destruction brought by the Fourth Crusade (1204) which compromised the empire's ability to sustain a growing population, it is fairly certain that Byzantium was placed overall at above the European average of population densities. The more populated parts in Group A were prime candidates (though not necessarily victims) of a classic Malthusian scenario and they may have witnessed a slowdown of demographic growth by the second half of the thirteenth century.

The demographic upswing was accompanied by a swelling in the size of urban populations, the two processes running parallel to each other. By any standards, Italy was at the peak of the ranking scale (along with Flanders), particularly in the central and northern regions where a polycentric urban network was formed with three cities (Florence, Milan, and Venice) exceeding the threshold of 100,000 inhabitants.[4] Holland, England, France, and Byzantium followed with close to a fifth of their populations living in urban environments.[5] Constantinople, with a population which may have reached 400,000 inhabitants in the twelfth century but certainly declined after 1204, deserves special mention. The great metropolis, along with Thessalonike (the second largest city of the empire), exerted a powerful influence through its demand for foodstuffs both to its hinterland but also, given its coastal location, to remote places across the Aegean and the Black Sea.

The most dramatic manifestation of what appears so far to have been a classic overpopulation scenario comes from data regarding sizes of peasant holdings. Half of peasants in England held plots whose size was inadequate in rendering them self-sufficient. The situation in France was even more dramatic. In the most populated parts of the country *minifundia* were quite common, ranging in size between one and three hectares (2.47–7.41 acres) and the price of land skyrocketed in many regions during the thirteenth century: in Normandy it jumped from 2 to 20 livres per acre and in Picardy the price of a *journal* (0.4 hectares) went from 1–3 livres to reaching the range of 6–10 livres; equally dramatic trends have been documented for the evolution of rents (e.g., towards the end of the thirteenth century rents around Lille increased fivefold).[6] It has been estimated that the minimum subsistence size of holding in France was six hectares (14.82 acres), which, if correct, would place 80 percent of the French population below this threshold.[7] This is a staggering statistic and it has been cited as a major reason for the creation of a rural proletariat which fled to towns, hence fueling the frenetic pace of urban growth which characterized the second part of the thirteenth century and resulted in depressing urban real wages. The degree of fragmentation of holdings was equally pronounced in inland Flanders and Holland with most farmers holding 0.5 to 4 hectares (1.23–9.88 acres); similarities with England have also been claimed for Italy in terms of its land distribution pattern, while the absorption of smallholdings by large estates in Byzantium suggests similar developments.[8]

It is truly puzzling how such large numbers of peasants kept body and soul together. The practice of polyculture generating cash crops (e.g., vineyards) which found market outlets in wider interregional networks; proximity to towns offering the opportunity of selling not only grains but also milk and garden produce as well as providing employment opportunities; and raising yields through intensive labor practices are some of the remedies which have been suggested by individual authors in this volume. In the well-documented case of Flanders Thoen pointed out the large number of holdings falling below the threshold of five hectares (12.35 acres) which, according to his estimates, defined a subsistence minimum. But local farmers, despite the prevalence of mediocre sandy-loamy soils, were able to survive through a policy of intensification based largely on the injection of heavy labor inputs resulting in low levels of labor productivity but high land productivity, reaching by the fourteenth century wheat and rye yields of 16–20 hectoliters/hectare (c. 18–23 bushels/acre). Employment in larger farms and the presence of a flourishing cottage industry based on woolens (expanded by the addition of linen production after the epidemics) also offered valuable opportunities for raising household incomes.[9]

Population growth necessitates a proportional increase of food supplies. This maxim raises a major issue of crucial importance to the crisis debate: what methods were used to meet this challenge and how effective were they? The most obvious option was to expand output through land reclamation, a process sometimes initiated by peasants but more often by landlords. But in the territories included in Group A this process started reaching its limits by 1300, to one degree or another. In France, for instance, "the reclamation of land ceased between 1230 and 1280 in most provinces."[10] A second option, which either ran parallel or followed land reclamation with a time lag, was to make more intensive use of arable land with a concomitant reduction of the fallow. The typical course of action was to move from slash-and-burn methods and infield-outfield arrangements to two- and eventually three-course rotations; the higher the population, the more likely it was to find the presence of field systems farther along this continuum of options.[11] By 1300, while less intensive systems were still practiced in less fertile regions of Group A, the three-course rotation was the dominant system.

Land reclamation and greater intensification in the context of common fields, comprising the Ricardian extensive margin of cultivation, would augment aggregate output but sooner or later would also lead to diminishing returns either due to the encroachment upon marginal lands or due to the limitations imposed on manure supplies. Injections of more labor and capital inputs (e.g., thorough weeding, marling), defining the intensive margin of cultivation, can postpone the inevitable decline of productivity; but, most importantly, the regions of Europe that found themselves at the peak of the demographic cycle had to innovate by adopting field systems which could generate more nitrogen (through the accommodation of more animal resources and the cultivation of legumes) and recycle it more efficiently (e.g., convertible husbandry).

To what extent the intensive margin of cultivation and organizational innovations were explored as mechanisms of escape from the Malthusian trap? The evidence presented in this volume makes it clear that there was a dualism within Group A in this regard. On the one hand, there was a broad region defined by a triangle stretching from the Low Countries to Paris' northern hinterland, and extending up to a couple of counties along the southeastern coastline of England (Norfolk, Kent, Sussex) and with a few outliers elsewhere (e.g., in Northern Italy); these parts of Europe rose to the occasion by exemplifying the best of medieval agrarian practices. In Norfolk, Kent, and parts of France and Flanders common practices included multiple plowings, thorough weeding, legumes sown in the place of fallow, the purchase of manure and stall-feeding of cattle, and the purchase of seed as well as high seeding rates.

These elements were combined in the context of very innovative field systems, exemplified in the case of the Low Countries. While communal forms of open-field agriculture were practiced, the system came in variants exhibiting considerable degrees of flexibility and, in fact, was in a process of decay as the thirteenth century progressed. On the other hand, individualized forms of farming were practiced widely, as in the peatlands of Holland. According to van Bavel, the dominant determinant of these regional variations was the degree of seigneurial power, with communal forms of cultivation often associated with the presence of strong lordship. Such flexible arrangements allowed flexible cultivation practices. In fertile coastal parts of Flanders convertible husbandry was widely practiced while variations of infields-outfields were prevalent in the inland parts of the county where poorer soils were prevalent. The progressive nature of these systems is evident by the fact that as population increased and greater intensification became necessary the demarcation lines between infields-outfields became blurry, as well as by the introduction of turnips and legumes in the place of fallows; most importantly, new experimental methods of cultivation were introduced during this period. Similarly, three-course rotations were abandoned in the pre-plague period, opting for more flexible rotations incorporating elements of convertible husbandry along with a prominent cultivation of legumes and the extensive application of marling and urban waste.[12] Flexible field systems, most notably convertible husbandry, were also practiced in an area defined by the triangle Lodi-Milan-Cremona where urban elites also invested in drainage and canal building. These regions, the most progressive in pre-plague Europe, will be called henceforward **Group A-PROGS**.

One is struck, however, by the sporadic appearance of so few instances of innovation and deep capital formation. Part of the explanation may lie in the lack of documentation as in the case of Byzantium where little is known about technical choices. But in instances in which documentation is abundant, allowing us glimpses on such matters, the picture that emerges is clearly disappointing. The preeminent example are the counties surrounding London, one of the most densely populated and urbanized parts of Europe; field systems retained, by and large, a rigid structure and cultivation practices remained extensive, both features reflected on land values that were below the national average. The overall assessment conveyed by several authors in this volume is that by this time (1300) the medieval technological paradigm reached a level of maturity by not generating any major innovations; but the stagnation across the western and southern European economic landscape did not have to be an inevitable outcome if the productive and technological choices within Group A-PROGS were more widely diffused. There was certainly a great differentiation of implements from region to region and a slow shift from oxen to horses but in terms of technological choices capable of boosting land productivity (convertible husbandry, legumes, animal resources) the record was one of stagnation and under performance.[13] The rest of the territories within Group A, comprising the majority, will be called henceforward **Group A-LAGS** (laggards).

The cited data on crop yields also project an impression of dualism similar to that of technological choices, with considerable differentiation across regions but, overall, a mediocre norm. Of the two methods used to measure productivity, yields per unit of land (acre or hectare) provide a better indicator of performance.[14] No other region of Europe seems to have matched the superb record of Flanders and its adjacent counties where yields in the range of 18–37 hectoliters/hectare (over 20.52–42.18 bushels/acre) were recorded, with the highest peaks in Lille, Saint-Omer, Valenciennes, Hainault, and Artois; yield data from the Netherlands are sparse but existing figures reveal figures averaging c. 25 hectoliters/hectare (28.5 bushels/acre). Farms near Paris, in Auvergne, Sologne, Norfolk, Kent, and Sussex (and very few others in the Thames valley and northern Northamptonshire) trailed behind with yields in the range of 20–25 bushels/acre. But since the regions within A-PROGS were exceptional, the norm was defined by A-LAGS. France's typical gross yields did not exceed 10 hectoliters/hectare (11.48 bushels/acre) and the overall English record was virtually identical. The norm in Italy and Byzantium, where poorer soils prevailed, was in the range of 3.9–4.2 quintals/hectare (6.0–6.4 bushels/acre); despite the fact that Byzantium's figures have been challenged as being too pessimistic and Malanima's estimates allow for somewhat higher levels, even the more optimistic scenarios would bring the norm up to 7–8 bushels/acre.[15] This is a remarkable contrast that needs to be stressed in the strongest possible terms: the productivity norm in Group A was in the range of 20–40 percent of the highest recorded yields within the group. That is a truly astonishing gap! It is also worth stressing, as van Bavel has done, that while the norm in most of western and southern Europe between population and yields was inverse, in the Low Countries this relationship was positive.[16]

This economic dualism overlapped with an institutional one defined by virtually identical geographical boundaries. Large parts of Group A were characterized by the most advanced forms of feudalization and the most extensive seigneurial prerogatives. The majority of the English agrarian population bore the label of serfs and despite a multitude of regional differences, it seems reasonable to state that one-third of peasants' annual revenues were transferred to seigneurial authorities, the figure being the center of gravity of a fairly wide range. French peasants enjoyed more personal freedom and tenurial rights but, given the list of obligations cited by Grantham, their burden was fairly similar to their English counterparts, though a higher proportion of their obligations was siphoned towards the state, as opposed to landlords.[17] In Byzantium seigneurial burdens were at least as heavy, peasants having to pay either fixed cash rents or, in most cases, a proportion of their harvest corresponding to a third of total output as well as provide a fair amount of labor services.

In contrast, institutional arrangements within A-PROGS were stunningly different. The personal freedom and light obligations enjoyed by peasants along the southeastern English coastline are too well-documented to need repetition. Seigneurial power was also weakened considerably in Italy by the twelfth century, preserved only in some mountainous areas of the North and South, one important cause of this transformation being the issuing of decrees by towns guaranteeing the personal freedom of serfs. The contractual nature of agrarian tenures was reflected on the prevalence of leaseholds, which took the form of either sharecropping arrangements or the form of money rent prevailing in the Po valley. Another important development, especially in Northern Italy, was the creation of compact farms through the consolidation of properties. It has to be stressed, however, that the prevalence of market forces and of contractual arrangements, elements often identified with capitalist structures, did not translate necessarily to light burdens; sharecropping tenures often specified the payment of half the crop, though other proportions also formed the basis of tenures.[18]

But it was in the Low Countries where one would encounter the most liberal institutional environment within Group A, although the nature of the reclamation movement produced some noticeable regional distinctions. In inland Flanders this movement, being well under way by the twelfth century, reaching its limit by the next one, was mainly undertaken by peasants resulting in two-thirds of the land (maybe more) being controlled by free peasants who paid fairly low rents until the end of the thirteenth century.

Free Dutch peasants controlled a similar proportion of the land, especially in the coastal areas (e.g., in the peatlands), having succeeded in establishing local institutions, which thwarted attempts towards seigneurial domination. In contrast, in some other areas land reclamation was undertaken by lords, resulting in a pronounced polarization of land ownership under a system of leaseholds producing high rents. This phenomenon was noticeable in the Guelders river area and coastal Flanders where reclamation took place through the initiative of the count of Flanders along with members of the nobility and ecclesiastical institutions introducing high rents in the context of short-term leases to large farmers in an effort to recoup their expenses; wealth inequality was particularly pronounced in these areas. It is remarkable that despite the presence of a robust land market throughout the Low Countries which brought a sense of dynamism at the micro level, land ownership distribution remained very stable at the regional level both before and after the Black Death. Overall, there were limited instances of serfdom in the Low Countries with seigneurial power being considerably weakened by the twelfth century and practically coming to an end, in the case of Flanders, with the large scale revolts of 1323–27. The presence of contractual tenures shaped by market forces meant that rents were sometimes high; and labor markets, despite being nominally free, still produced relations of inequality and dependence (e.g., through indebtedness by peasants to lords) resulting sometimes in wages below market value. But institutional rigidities and burdens in the Low Countries, and generally the A-PROGS, were far more limited compared to the A-LAGS.[19]

The rest of Europe (the northeastern quadrant of the continent including Scandinavia, Russia, and Central Europe, joined by Spain) has been excluded from this review up until now because it stands in fairly sharp contrast, at least to the extent we can tell on the basis of more limited evidence.[20] Population densities which comprised the bottom of the ranking order in western and (large parts of) southern Europe, formed the top group in these territories, henceforward called **Group B.** Bohemia and Moravia (and most likely Denmark) had the highest population densities with c. 25 people/km^2, whereas Hungary, the Polish territories, Silesia, Spain, Norway, and Sweden formed the bottom of the pyramid with only 5–10 people/km^2.[21]

Urbanization rates were equally unimpressive. Considerable uncertainty surrounds the respective rate in Kievan Rus' but extrapolating from some post-plague estimates and taking into account the widespread devastations of towns by Mongol attacks, this rate was probably around 10 percent. Central Europe's rate stood at similar levels, with Bohemia and Moravia being the most urbanized territories, followed by Poland, but with Hungary far behind. Towns in these regions achieved a fairly modest size, the most populous ones reaching around 30,000 inhabitants (e.g., Kiev, Novgorod, Prague, Gdańsk). Scandinavia's degree of urbanization was probably the lowest in Europe, hovering around 4–10 percent (the latter figure referring to Denmark) with the largest towns (e.g., Bergen, Stockholm, Copenhagen) having around 5,000 inhabitants each.

Judging solely on these figures, the territories in Group B comprised a world that gazed the Malthusian dead end well into the future. There is no doubt that Iberia and most of Central Europe were still in a state capable of absorbing populations larger than the ones they had by 1300. If the estimate that the typical size of holdings in Catalonia ranged between 6 and 11 hectares (14.82–27.18 acres) is accurate and reflects conditions elsewhere in Iberia, and assuming the subsistence size of holding was around five hectares, it follows that the grand peninsula was still a semi-full world. In the absence of estimates on the size of holding that was economically viable and data on land distribution, it becomes difficult to say how far Russia and Scandinavia were from reaching their Malthusian limits. But some reasonable speculations for the case of Russia project a similar impression. We do know that c. 1500 the typical size of holding in central Russia was 15 desyatins (16.4 hectares or 40.5 acres), though lower in districts with higher population densities (e.g., in parts of the Novgorod region where the figure was seven desyatins). If, as Martin suggests, population levels were similar in 1300 and 1500 it follows that the typical size of holdings may also have been about the same in these two dates. [22]

Evidence on land reclamation and field systems corroborate the assessment that Malthusian positive checks were not imminent in Group B. Land reclamation was ongoing during the thirteenth century in the Polish and Hungarian territories, this phenomenon reaching a peak level by the next century. The process of Reconquista in Spain, involving the expulsion of local Muslim populations, started in the eleventh century and was still going strong by 1300, especially in Andalusia and Murcia in the aftermath of the 1264 uprising, followed by the granting of territories to major military orders as well as to monasteries and lay lords. It is only in the Czech Kingdom, the plains of southern Scandinavia, and the Danish islands that started having some signs of land scarcity by the end of the thirteenth century.

Russian peasants could still afford to use slash-and-burn methods and it was likely that an infield-outfield arrangement was also in place. It is not clear when and to what extent a two-course rotation evolved and at what point it led to the establishment of a three-course rotation; but it is only in the second half of the fifteenth century that the latter appears to have been firmly in place in northwestern (Novgorod region) and central Russia. In the central plains of Castile the two-course rotation was the dominant form (partly due to its unfavorable climate), whereas in the poor soils of the western plains (Salamanca, Zamora, Extremadura) periods of fallow were even longer; the three-course rotation started making significant strides only in parts of Segovia and Galicia. The transition from a two- to a three-course rotation became evident in Poland only by the beginning of the fifteenth century. Scandinavia was a bit more advanced in this transition with the two-course rotation prevailing in eastern Sweden and its more intensive counterpart in central Denmark.

The equivalent of A-PROGS (technological and organizational innovations and injections of heavy labor and capital inputs) is virtually absent in Group B.[23] The amount of data on productivity yields is very limited but it seems to reinforce the notion of low to mediocre levels, particularly in areas with poor ecological endowments.[24] Definitive declarations are not warranted in light of data limitations but it appears that the least productive parts of Europe scored yields that stood at only between 10–20 percent of the Flemish record.

A striking feature of Group B is the slow progress made in the feudalization of these territories; this element, along with differences in terms of demographic and urbanization rates, place it in sharp contrast with the norm in the rest of Europe (particularly with A-LAGS).[25] The feudalization of Scandinavia took place between the eighth and twelfth centuries and was particularly successful in central and southern regions. The presence of labor services has been documented but peasants succeeded in retaining their freedom in some parts of these regions, particularly in southern Norway and southwestern Denmark. In the northern flanks of Scandinavia an egalitarian society was the norm, though by the thirteenth century peasants were obliged to pay tithes and taxes to the state and the Church. All in all, Scandinavian peasants enjoyed a superior legal position than in many other parts of Europe.

Seugneurial authority in Russia progressed along similar lines. Peasants owned their plots and were free to manage them and dispose their outputs. But the eleventh and twelfth centuries mark the beginning of a process during which princes took firm control of their territories and started granting lands to their courtiers, nobles, and monasteries which resulted in peasants having to pay rents and other dues such as labor services; these obligations were collectively owed since the small Russian settlements were organized as communal units. The patchiness of records does not allow us to generalize but Russian experts seem to be broadly in agreement that since the combined weight of taxes and rents were still quite low by the end of the fifteenth century (when records become more abundant), they were likely to also have been low in previous centuries. Peasants were bound neither to their lands nor to their lords and often migrated, seeking plots controlled by lords who had charters of immunity and were in need for labor resources in order to exploit newly acquired lands. Conditions in Central Europe were strikingly similar. States and local aristocracies succeeded in driving peasants into serfdom by the twelfth century but seigneurial obligations were fairly light because peasants could flee the territories of over demanding lords. By the thirteenth century labor services went through a process of commutation to money rents in Bohemia and Poland and there were even reductions in the payment of state taxes.[26]

The process of incomplete feudalization was particularly in a state of flux in Spain. The expulsion of Muslim peasants went to great lengths in southern Castile, Andalusia, and Murcia, giving the opportunity to lords to capture new lands and consolidate their power on those they already controlled; these developments led to the prevalence of large ecclesiastical properties but also to a fair amount of freedom for peasants, something that was deemed necessary in order to attract them to the newly settled areas. On the other hand, seigneurial power remained strong in Old Catalonia where peasants were subject to servitude and paid heavy rents, in Aragon north of the Ebro, and among Muslim peasants (*Mudejar*) who comprised the vast majority of the population in the newly conquered kingdom of Valencia.

In the end, Europe crossed the threshold of the fourteenth century by projecting the impression of a twofold dualism in regional terms. On the one hand, there were the northern and eastern territories (plus Spain), the so-called Group B, which resembled frontier regions with low population densities, internal population shifts due to conflicts, low urbanization rates, a (by and large) weak development of market networks, a level of feudalization which still had an incomplete and immature form, extensive forms of cultivation, limited instances of technological and organizational innovations and, based on a limited record, modest to very low productivity levels. In contrast, most regions in Western and Southern Europe (A-LAGS) were operating at the peak of the Malthusian cycle, achieved high levels of urbanization, strong seigneurial institutions, fairly well-developed commercial networks, less extensive forms of cultivation but technological choices, and productivity levels that were only marginally superior. But within Western and Southern Europe there was also an internal dualism since a limited number of regions (A-PROGS) deviated from the norm in three important respects: by having weak feudal institutions, utilizing the best medieval technology and field systems had to offer, and achieving superb levels of productivity. This neat typology comes at the expense of extreme realism since certain regions in Group B (e.g., Bohemia, parts of Spain and Denmark) were on their way to forming characteristics that would have classified them in Group A; and there were isolated pockets in the latter (e.g., some parts of northern and western England) which had features more akin to regions in Group B. Nevertheless, the benefits that derive from this regional typology in terms of helping us formulate some theoretical abstractions outweigh the drawbacks.

THE FOURTEENTH CENTURY CRISIS: ITS CAUSES AND THE THEORETICAL DISPUTES

There is a broad agreement among historians that the Black Death was a seminal event in European history compromising aggregate economic growth throughout the continent, notwithstanding regional differences. But the theoretical disputes that have evolved over the past several decades, summarized in the introductory essay of this volume, have revolved around the question as to whether the productive performance of the continent matched the demographic growth rate; if so, it justifies pointing to germs and climatic changes as the culprit of the crisis, as opposed to the view of production lagging behind population growth by the early fourteenth century in which case it is obvious we are dealing with a systemic, endogenous crisis and the only pertinent question is what were its causes. The regional typology we outlined will be used to address this issue.

There is little, if any, doubt that the majority of regions in England and France (being part of the A-LAGS) were in a state of deep structural crisis by the second half of the thirteenth century with the extreme fragmentation of holdings being one of the most glaring manifestations of this assertion. There are certainly gaps in our knowledge of medieval peasant budgets resulting in somewhat different estimates on the size of holding capable of ensuring subsistence. But the fairly extensive record on land distribution patterns makes it clear that the majority of peasants in England and France came to possessing plots which ceased ensuring subsistence by 1300. If the laws of supply and demand had any applicability in this period, the movement of prices in product and resource markets projects an equally strong perception of severe strains; in both countries the prices of grains increased and the level of real wages declined from the second half of the thirteenth through the first quarter of the fourteenth century indicating a decline of both labor and land productivity.[27] Despite the fact that monetary factors may have contributed to the trend of product prices, it is far more likely that it was a symptom of lagging production. Further circumstantial evidence is provided by the growing alienation of peasant parcels and a rising crime wave, mostly against property. But perhaps the most dramatic sign of the crisis were the 1315–17 famines eliminating, in the case of England, an estimated 10–15 percent of the population. Harvest failures may stem from non-economic causes but they impacted a population a large part of which was treading at the threshold of subsistence. This fact renders it a structural crisis. In the words of a study referring to the French experience, "at some point during the second half of the thirteenth century, the rate of growth of agricultural production started to lag behind that of population . . . By the early fourteenth century, France, as well as most of Western Europe, was literally crammed with people. The 'ecosystem' (to use Le Roy Ladurie's term) was strained to the breaking point and on the verge of collapse."[28]

Byzantium's crisis was more complex and less well-documented but Smyrlis' account leaves no doubt that economic conditions were worsening. Many peasants sought to escape such conditions, compounded by excessive seigneurial demands, by fleeing. Many of those who decided to stay found themselves having to alienate parcels of their holdings and unable to afford basic resources; a fairly large sample comprising villages in the Macedonian region shows that in 1321 more than half of peasants did not own a single ox. The negative feedback mechanism that developed between the structural failures on the production side and the continuous dominance of its commercial network by Italian merchants reached such a critical point giving the impression that the empire was placed at that point, once and for all, at the economic periphery of Europe.[29]

What were the causes of this systemic crisis? In a recent publication dealing with long-run historical cycles, Turchin and Nefedov stressed the need for coming up with "a synthetic theory that encompasses both demographic mechanisms (with the associated economic consequences) and power relations (surplus-extraction mechanisms). In the dynamic systems framework, it does not make sense to speak of one or the other as 'the primary factor.' The two factors interact dynamically, each affecting and being affected by the other." Historical phenomena may progress in a predictable cyclical form having a periodic character. But in societies with complex characteristics the dynamic may incorporate elements of sensitive dependence and non-linear feedback loops which lead to outcomes envisioned by chaos theory. The latter scenario is particularly plausible in the event of exogenous disturbances relating to geopolitical factors and the ecological environment as well as through the reaction of individual actors which can be portrayed "as a stochastic process, a kind of Brownian motion that also results in erratic, unpredictable changes in the macrosocial trajectory."[30]

I believe that this theoretical framework sets the right tone in terms of how the issue we address should be approached. My explanation places the relationship between the forces and relations of production, the core element of the theory of historical materialism, at the center of this account but, given the abstract nature of this theory, it integrates into it the descriptive power of the Ricardian theory of rent to explain concrete events of this period; in other words, I believe that the two theories can be incorporated within a synthetic framework despite the acrimony developed between their proponents. On the other hand, I feel that the Commercialist approach is relevant and useful in a limited number of cases.

The starting point of my explanation in terms of the developments that took place within the A-LAGS is the unfolding of a strong demographic growth. The dynamics of population growth can only be explicated by studying the socio-economic variables which determined the reproduction patterns of nuclear families. Unfortunately, we know very little about the size of families and how it correlated with material endowments such as holding sizes and thus the demographic factor appears to have progressed with a fair degree of independence, although NIE arguments have offered a plausible hypothesis of how demography tied to other socioeconomic variables (see below).[31] But while the determinants of population growth are still a matter of debate, its impact on the regional strength of feudal institutions appears to be fairly clear. As resources started becoming scarce within A-LAGS, the tension that developed between ruling elites and peasants was resolved to the benefit of the former.[32] It follows that the strong seigneurial institutions which developed within the A-LAGS were the outcome of the interplay between two factors: demography and class conflict.

Once these particular 'relations of production' became entrenched they promoted the expansion of the 'forces of production' in the context of a narrowly defined trajectory. The fact that a large number of estates secured the bulk of their revenues through political compulsion, as opposed from the production and disposal of goods, meant that they focused on securing their property rights on increasingly scarce land.[33] This led to conservative and inflexible field systems as well as reproducing these patterns through land colonization and/or extending the margin of arable at the expense of pastoral husbandry. Moreover, such estates chose to use their extractions to support their military monopoly and extravagant levels of consumption, as opposed to raising productivity through capital formation, because the latter option demanded entrepreneurial attitudes towards innovation which seem to have been absent since they did not have to function as production units vying for market share.[34]

In the context of this explanation the process of land colonization (the Ricardian extensive margin of cultivation), which was often fostered by the ruling elite, does permit a horizontal diffusion of techniques across space consistent with Marx's contention that the relations of production do allow the development of the forces of production up to a point. But this process is finite, and thus teleological, restricted by the availability of land to the point marginal cost becomes equal to marginal revenue. Along this process, the utilization of increasingly marginal plots of land translates to slowly declining labor productivity either due to complacency on the part of manorial estates or the inability of peasants to engage in high levels of capital formation, given the presence of high rates of extraction; in other words, technological diffusion does take place but because it is not optimal it fails to slow down the declining productivity of labor. The record on land productivity indicates a stagnant or declining trend among manorial estates consistent with my thesis; on the other hand, there is no evidence on how land productivity behaved among peasant holdings within the A-LAGS but it is possible that yields may have exceeded those of manorial estates through heavy injections of labor inputs at the expense of labor productivity. Non-Marxist scholars have shown an aversion towards accepting elements of this argument but I feel that one does not have to revert to normative aspects of the Marxist thesis (e.g., the belief on the notion of peasant exploitation), although I do, in order to accept the validity of such statements since, in the end, they are empirically verifiable.[35]

The way my explanation has been formulated so far leaves out of consideration certain political and military events which are an integral part of the crisis debate. This point is particularly relevant in the case of Byzantium, whose internal stability was dealt a powerful blow by the Fourth Crusade (1204) and its plight continued with the raids and final occupation of western Asia Minor by the Ottomans in the late thirteenth century, the Catalan raids at the beginning of the next century, the series of civil wars in 1321–28, 1341–47 (and another one in 1352–57), these conflicts overlapping with Serbian intrusions in Macedonia and the continuing advancement of the Ottoman armies. How do we account for these seemingly non-economic events? While economic historians of different ideological predispositions have often been guilty of ignoring such events, I do believe that economic configurations play the dominant role in driving historical processes and outcomes. I am particularly intrigued in this regard by Myrdal's suggestion that the cross border invasions we witness during this period may have been prompted by dynastic infighting but they may also have been caused by economic crises in the lands of invaders who found in the occupation of foreign lands a way out of their fiscal predicament. Limitations of space did not allow the authors of the various essays in this volume to deal with this question either in the case of Byzantium or the Anglo-French conflict which was initiated in the 1340s, at a time the economic crisis of these two countries reached a crescendo, and raged through the 1470s. But this topic comprises fertile ground for further research.

It is time now to turn to the regions comprising the A-PROGS and discuss their different experience despite the presence of a similar demographic context. The crucial difference between the A-PROGS and A-LAGS lies in the fact that as the population curve got to the point of exerting pressure on their natural resources the balance of power between ruling elites and peasants was such as to create liberal institutional environments characterized by high degrees of personal freedom and rental obligations which were often, though not always, less onerous compared to the A-LAGS. The formation of such institutions shaped the trajectory of their subsequent growth. While producers did push the extensive margin of cultivation, they also had the incentive to raise output and wealth by exploiting the intensive margin since market disposal was the main instrument of revenue creation in the case of landlords.[36] Weak manorialism forced estates to act in a proto-capitalist fashion, attempting to raise revenues through capital formation, which became the vehicle of an impressive process of technological diffusion. Lords were clearly better placed to take advantage of rising demand compared to peasants, whose extreme subdivision of holdings projects, in the words of Slichter van Bath, "not a picture of wealth, but of scarcely controlled poverty."[37] Let us not forget, however, that these peasants were less likely to be victims of heavy seigneurial extractions compared to their counterparts in the A-LAGS and to face less rigid controls over the utilization of land allowing them to develop innovative field systems (e.g., forms of convertible husbandry) boosting yields.[38] It follows that while it would a be a stretch to argue that peasants in the A-PROGS were thriving, it would be equally a mistake not to acknowledge their greater ability to cope with the specter of the Malthusian trap. A strong clue supporting this assessment is the fact that Flemish towns lost 5–10 percent of their population during the Great Famine, with figures being even lower in the countryside, developments which compared very favorably with England and indicate that the population of the Low Countries had a greater ability to deal with temporary but serious famines.[39]

To state the case in more abstract terms using Malanima's notation, while the numerator of the expression L/K+R (L=labor, K=capital, R=natural resources) was increasing during the pre-plague period and R was fairly constant (prior to climatic changes), K, most likely, was increasing faster compared to the A-LAGS. The implication is that the higher capital per worker led to an increase of land productivity (as pre-plague yields from the Low Countries and Italy show); while this increase did not negate the law of diminishing returns in terms of labor productivity (see Figure 4.12 in Malanima's chapter), the decline of the latter started from higher levels.[40] In the end, population growth did create strains but strains do not amount to a crisis; in other words, the A-PROGS did not project the image of an imminent systemic implosion which appears to have been the case in the A-LAGS.

But the relative weakness of seigneurial institutions in A-PROGS did much more than bring their agrarian productivity levels close to their medieval potential. Equally important was the fact that it allowed labor mobility between town and country, fostered increased division of labor, led to the flourishing of secondary (e.g., cottage industries) and tertiary sectors (e.g., financial and banking services), and in the end, resulted in the creation of high levels of non-agricultural wealth. The creation of such wealth was particularly important in regions with ecological profiles that offered limited possibilities since they could use this wealth to buy food supplies in the context of interregional trade flows; this is precisely what the Italian city-states achieved through the expansion of their trade networks. To use Malanima's reasoning, the low marginal efficiency of capital of Italian agriculture channeled investment into the construction of majestic buildings and art as well as into banking and manufacturing whose output was boosted by technological and organizational innovations in key sectors (e.g., textiles) and the emergence of new ones (e.g., printing). The prosperity created by these sectors boosted wealth, counting for half of total output according to Malanima, which was diffused across the population.[41] Agricultural productivity probably benefited from the increase in purchasing power, at least to the extent the limited natural endowment of the region would allow, with trade playing an instrumental role in closing endemic gaps in the supply and demand for foodstuffs. But, as noted earlier, trade in the region during the pre-plague period proved to be a zero-sum game with gains made by Italian merchants coming at the expense of their Byzantine counterparts.

The notion of a systemic crisis seems to be clearly inapplicable in the case of the territories comprising Group B. Granted the more severe limitations imposed by climatic and edaphic conditions on the productive capacity of large expanses in these territories, it appears that population densities remained at levels that could be supported by available resources, although some isolated pockets may have witnessed the first signs of scarcity. Most importantly, again with very few exceptions, seigneurial institutions were not powerful enough to stunt growth. That is not to say that economic conditions were ideal for growth; in fact, far from it given the multiple instances of war activities which plagued these territories during this period. Some of these conflicts were clearly the result of economic crises in the lands the invading armies originated from, such as the invasion of Denmark by German princes in the 1330s. But in areas where peace prevailed and resources were still not fully exploited, such as Bohemia, these areas must have seemed as the Promised Land.

The argument that has been laid out so far distances itself from dogmatic versions of the Neo-Malthusian and Marxist schools by claiming that demographic growth and the outcomes of class conflicts at the local level converged in shaping a mosaic of institutional arrangements across the European landscape and that it was the latter which set the parameters of long-term growth. But liberal institutions were the necessary precondition for growth, not the engine which drove such growth. After all, Eastern and Northern Europe, as well as parts of Spain, had the weakest manifestations of seigneurial institutions but, overall, the lowest levels of productivity. The missing elements in Group B were high population densities and urbanization rates along with extensive market networks. From this point of view, these elements of the Commercialist approach have to be incorporated into the analysis. But it is important to get the order of causation right. Markets were not the first piece of a domino effect which, once it got under way, led eventually to technological innovations and productivity growth eroding in the process seigneurial institutions. The presumed expansion of markets in thirteenth-century England neither led to revolutionizing production methods in the most urbanized part of the country (i.e., the London region) nor did it act as a corrosive agent at the expense of seigneurial institutions; in fact, quite the contrary, it coincided with a hardening of seigneurial obligations, particularly of labor services.[42] The evidence shows that the formation of liberal environments predated increased specialization and economic growth with the expansion of urban centers and market networks compounding growth in a later stage.[43] From my perspective markets boosted growth in A-PROGS, had the potential of doing so in Group B (a potential still largely unrealized by c. 1300 in light of low urbanization and population densities), but had little impact in preventing or reversing the systemic crisis within A-LAGS. It follows that the first of these groups offers the most promising material for testing the applicability of refined tools of the Commercialist approach (e.g., von Thunen's model of economic rent) once the order of causation that would lead to economic expansion is specified as: 1) population growth + successful peasant resistance → 2) weak feudal institutions → 3) division of labor and increased specialization both within and across sectors → 4) market expansion → 5) optimal diffusion of techniques → 6) productivity growth; with the second element in this chain functioning as a necessary precondition and elements 3, 4, and 5 being the mechanisms of growth.

The argument laid here is strikingly similar to those of scholars sympathetic to the perspective of NIE. The crucial conditioning factor of economic growth was the nature of institutions, according to van Bavel, who notes that "those regions where banal lords were weak, such as coastal and inland Flanders and Holland, were the ones which experienced the greatest growth from the 11th century on."[44] In these regions the strong ownership of land on the part of peasants (coupled with inheritance patterns which favored partible inheritance) led to fragmentation of holdings but also the achievement of high levels of productivity, and the presence of labor markets with minimal constraints allowed the flourishing of cottage industries; this virtuous cycle boosted, in turn, the growth of urban centers. It follows that institutional arrangements conditioned the process of urbanization, not the other way around.[45] Van Bavel's argument is even more assertive by stressing that variations in the rates of demographic growth were directly conditioned by institutions. Widespread land ownership by peasants, coupled with relatively high real wages, led to early marriage; in contrast, in areas where large capitalist farms prevailed (e.g., Gelderland river area) driving up the levels of rent and thus blocking access to land for a large number of peasants, population densities were lower.[46] From this perspective, population levels is not an absolute but a relative concept. "The relative mildness of the crisis in Holland and Flanders, which were the most densely populated parts of the Low Countries and had poor soil conditions can only be understood by the balanced distribution of property, freedom, and the high degree of self-determination the ordinary population enjoyed, combined with the convenient organization of exchange and the economic opportunities."[47]

There is one last issue that needs to be addressed which has been associated with the latest version of the Commercialist argument (Campbell's version), although it also finds a strong advocate in Malanima's chapter, that is, the impact of climatic changes. According to this argument, after reaching a climatic optimum by the eleventh century, temperatures started a gradual descent reaching a critical mass by c. 1300; yields were affected everywhere, culminating in the famines of 1315–17, but especially along hillsides where cultivation dropped to lower altitudes due to the decline of temperatures. According to Malanima, this was the single most important factor explaining the European predicament, more so than "changes in institutions and techniques." This argument has caused a fair amount of excitement among economic historians, particularly among experts of the Middle Ages following a publication by Campbell which ties together price data in product and labor markets as well as grain harvests with climatic variations by taking into account dendrochronology.[48] There is still a fair amount of agnosticism, and thus skepticism, on the impact of this factor although, with further research, it may very well prove to have been of decisive importance in destabilizing the European economies prior to the visitation of epidemics. But while Malanima is justified in underplaying the importance of changes in techniques in an age which lacked major technological innovations and the role of institutions in a country where institutions played a minimal role in stunting growth, it is doubtful whether this factor will ultimately distract from the fact that A-LAGS were already facing a deep structural crisis. Climatic changes may have rendered a bad situation worse in A-LAGS and caused strains in the rest of Europe but it was the nature of social institutions which prevented producers in large parts of Western Europe from resolving successfully the pressure imposed by a large population on existing resources.

THE BLACK DEATH AND ITS AFTERMATH

Estimating the human toll taken by the successive visitations of the bubonic plague has proven to be particularly frustrating, especially because it is difficult to disentangle the added impact of migration movements and war activities. The task is less fraught with problems in reference to the most populated parts of Europe (e.g., England, France, Italy) for which there seems to be a broad agreement that they lost approximately half of their population by the early fifteenth century; the similarities of the cited figures suggest they are likely to be in the right order of magnitude. In contrast to these countries, the epidemics had a limited impact both in Flanders and Holland. The limited population decline in the former lasted until c. 1380, causing a recession but was followed by a reversal of the demographic curve and strong growth through the fifteenth century. Population decline was equally mild in Holland, leading van Zanden to estimate that overall population may have increased by 15–25 percent in the period 1350–1500. These demographic trajectories are reflected on real wages, which in both regions increased through the 1380s but remained stable afterwards.[49]

But while common intuition would raise the expectation that low population densities and urbanization rates were bound to translate to lower mortality, the authors of four papers in this volume propose very different figures. Myrdal acknowledges that Swedish data are limited to 'Peter's Pence' payments and that the Norwegian record refers only to the first major epidemic but in the end, he estimates that the decline in Sweden and Denmark was in the order of 40–45 percent, reaching 70 percent in Norway by the time Scandinavia reached its demographic nadir c. 1450. Rodriguez's figures are very similar (40–50 percent), the range determined by regional population densities (e.g., Aragon vs. Catalonia). The plague entered Russian lands in 1349 and kept recurring with fairly high frequency through the 1420s, then reappearing only occasionally, finally allowing demographic recovery towards the end of the fifteenth century at a time when numerous government documents clearly indicate the expansion of land under cultivation;[50] Martin's estimate of an overall one-quarter decline would satisfy conventional wisdom. But the most intriguing assertion is the one made by Myśliwski, who argues that the wave of epidemics appeared only in isolated pockets in Central Europe, as opposed to taking the form of a universal and simultaneous blow rising to the level of a major catastrophe as elsewhere; according to him, mortality was fairly low, in the end simply slowing down demographic and economic growth but allowing population to stand in 1400 at a higher level compared to a century earlier. Population decline was witnessed in the fifteenth century in Bohemia, Moravia, and Silesia but it was the outcome of adverse economic conditions and outward migration caused by the Hussite wars (1419–36), not due to epidemics.

Given the fact that the various chapters in this volume attempt to summarize the current state of research, the citation of figures that go contrary to expectations reflects our agnosticism on the issue of precise demographic levels rather than an attempt on the part of some authors to make statements for the sake of their shock value. The overarching point of importance is that the overall impact of the epidemics was such that the European population may have approached, but not quite reached by 1500, the population levels of c. 1300. The impact on urbanization rates parallels these developments, though with notable differences between countries; for instance, the respective rate in France was reduced by half compared to pre-plague levels, whereas the decline in the Center-North of Italy, Flanders, and Holland was surprisingly less dramatic and thus able to recover their 1300 level by 1500.[51] The decline of urbanization is noteworthy both because cities generated concentrated levels of demand for agricultural products and also because non-agricultural output could be exchanged for other goods through regional trade networks. Malanima, the only author who ventures into precise estimates, argues that both the share of industry and services in total output and urban output per capita in the Center-North of Italy held on until c. 1370 but then both declined for a century but, in the end, reached their pre-plague levels by 1500.[52]

But this was, first and foremost, an agrarian crisis, particularly for the seigneurial sector. The excellent English record on demesnial holdings, presumably mirroring developments elsewhere, shows a precipitous decline both in the injection of labor and capital inputs per unit of land and a considerable scaling down of the proportion of cropping areas to the benefit of fallows and grazing grounds. The development of a flourishing ox trade in Denmark and southern Sweden reflects not only an improvement of living standards among the general population but also the shifting cost structures encountered by demesnes due to the rising cost of labor and the concomitant squeeze of their profit margins. Unfortunately the documentary evidence becomes less abundant during this period, making it even harder to outline the impact of these adjustments within the demesnial sector in terms of its productivity. On purely theoretical grounds, yields may have moved either way. A retreat of cultivation from marginal lands would suggest improvement; on the other hand, the lower degrees of intensification and the lack of major innovations, particularly in terms of field systems would suggest the reverse. The English record shows a very slight increase in the level of yields per acre whereas the Italian evidence points towards improvement to the point of narrowing the gap in relation to mediocre performers (e.g., England) but not eliminating it;[53] on the other hand, Grantham sounds fairly confident in arguing his case of a declining trend. Yield data from the Low Countries become more abundant during this period but still warrant a degree of caution in terms of overall trends. It does seem, however, that Dutch yields remained fairly stable but witnessed a declining trend in areas that used to be at the very peak of land productivity during the pre-plague period (e.g., Lille and Hainault).[54] In the end, however, whatever was the direction of change in terms of yields, the viability of the demesnial sector was largely determined by the collapse of demand leading to its gradual shrinkage in most of Europe.

In the midst of such adverse economic conditions, the continuation of wars whose origins date prior to the epidemics and the initiation of new ones turned a situation from difficult to dramatic in the parts of Europe affected by them. The German involvement in Scandinavia engulfed large parts of this region by 1360; conflict broke out among nobles and between the various kingdoms in Spain leading to currency devaluation and imposition of new taxes; the ongoing Anglo-French conflict brought widespread destruction which reached its apogee during the first four decades of the fourteenth century when a civil war erupted between the Burgundians and the Orleanists; and it was around that time that parts of Central Europe were destabilized by the Hussite wars. But while these conflicts were often protracted but in the end temporary disruptions, the history of Byzantium was about to come to a close. The Ottoman armies invaded Thrace and Macedonia by the second half of the fourteenth century and despite a partial and short-lived recapturing of these territories, the Ottomans took firm control of them by 1430, turning their attacks to Constantinople, which succumbed in 1453. These events, coupled with the recurrent epidemics, caused a demographic collapse, disruption of production, and a severe decline of commerce.

Viewing European feudalism in a broad context, many of these conflicts were not exogenous destabilizing forces but systemic features of it caused by the inability or ruling elites to sustain their previous levels of wealth. German princes, having witnessed a decline of revenues back home, sought to compensate by raising taxes once they took control of parts of Scandinavia. But even when the Scandinavian nobility recaptured and unified the Nordic region in the 1390s it asserted its prerogatives by sustaining taxes at high levels.

While the manifestations of the feudal fiscal crisis are difficult to expound at the level of clashing elites since they often appear to be mere dynastic rivalries, this is not so in the multiple cases of class conflict between lords and peasants that flared up during this period. Putting aside for now the eastern frontier of Europe, in the rest of the continent peasants scored gains compared to the pre-plague period due, among other reasons, to the weakening of seigneurial prerogatives. In Scandinavia peasants fought over the right to abandon their holdings, the level of rents, and the performance of labor services. There were setbacks such as the imposition of serfdom in some Danish islands and the confiscation of their lands by the crown following an unsuccessful revolt in northern Jutland in the 1440s. But, overall, rents declined by the late fourteenth century anywhere from one-third to two-thirds of their pre-plague levels. These were significant gains but they were counterbalanced by the high level of state taxation which lasted until the second half of the fifteenth century, when a number of peasant rebellions succeeded in reducing this burden by half. Overall, the greatest success in reducing seigneurial power was scored in Sweden where the share of land controlled by free peasants increased, remained unchanged in Norway, and declined in Denmark.

Rioting and violence erupted also in Catalonia following the lords' attempt to impose or retain the 'bad customs' of villeinage in order to counteract the shrinking base of paying subjects. Peasants resorted to resistance or fleeing their holdings and, in the end, such attempts proved largely unsuccessful, giving way to liberal tenurial policies. However, when economic conditions improved slowly in the fifteenth century new attempts were made in places like Castile and Catalonia but, in most cases, were again met by resistance; the civil strife which erupted in Catalonia was so widespread that, judging from the extent of the depopulation of villages, it may have had worse impact than the epidemics.

Developments in England had similar outcomes through more peaceful means. The ability of peasants to flee and the willingness of lords to take them strengthened their negotiating power, leading to a gradual abandonment of labor services, the negation of various miscellaneous payments tied to serfdom, and the reduction of rent obligations by as much as 20 percent. A similar situation evolved in France where lords offered rebates on rents, *cens,* and *tailles* (whose real value was already reduced due to repeated debasements of the coin) for a number of years in exchange for having tenants bringing land back to cultivation and restoring production; when it comes to leaseholds, the duration of these tenancies was often extended. These concessions turned to the benefit of peasants who found themselves at the peak of their prosperity by the end of the fifteenth century after a long period of hardships particularly in regions affected by the war. But once economic conditions improved enough, around 1475, the terms of leaseholds and sharecropping were revised upwards. Finally, tenurial arrangements in Northern Italy followed a strikingly similar trajectory resulting in substantial benefits for peasants.

In all of these cases the so-called 'feudal reaction' was fierce, often translating to violence and the expenditure of large sums to support it. The most interesting evidence in this regard is Myrdal's graph (Figure 7.3) on the building activity of castles in Sweden which reached a sharp peak in the second half of the fourteenth century and, despite a decline in the next half century, still remained at fairly high levels. Lords lost many battles in the process but investments in the infrastructure of war were not in vain since by the end of our period they succeeded in retaining landownership and, in most cases, the *seigneurie* remained the dominant institution of agrarian relations. Grantham's conclusion that the "*droit eminent* survived in a chrysalis of parchment, ready to burst once more into life with the restoration of peace and population" may refer to the French case but it echoes the situation in most of the above countries.[55]

On the other hand, the cases of Russia and Central Europe present a sharp contrast. In the former case the princes of Moscow started consolidating their power during the fourteenth century in a territory spanning from Novgorod in the west to Vladimir-Suzdal in the east. During this process monasteries, in particular, went through a spectacular phase of land expansion through the donations of princes, those of peasants in exchange for pray for their souls, or as a result of purchases at times of peasant economic distress. By the next century Mongol control was eliminated and a new realm was established. As this process unfolded we pass from a regime of free peasants to one under which seigneurial control was affirmed through the payment of rents and other dues, though they remained fairly modest until the reign of Ivan III (1462–1505) but by that time the new centralized state and its introduction of major new expenditures started turning the tide. The seminal event was the imposition of a Muscovite law code in 1497 which limited the movement of peasants to only two weeks of the year, thus initiating a process which led to the enserfment of peasants by the middle of the seventeenth century. In Central Europe the process of enserfment began in Poland in the course of the fifteenth century and was followed by similar developments in Hungary and the Czech territories later on. In the end, the contrast between Central Europe/Russia and other territories in the continent lies not so much in the extent of seigneurial obligations since they were fairly similar for most of this period, instead, it lies in the initiation of events towards the end of our period that would bring a sharp institutional dichotomy between them during the sixteenth century and beyond.

In the end, the dynamic interplay between Ricardian and institutional configurations produced radical shifts in virtually every major macroeconomic variable but in ways that led the various regions of Europe into different trajectories. The demographic decline or collapse allowed retreat from marginal lands and a more optimal balance between the arable and pastoral sectors thus offering the potential to peasants of better and more diversified diets, land accumulation, and more capital resources per farm. At the same time, however, these very same developments impacted labor markets in ways that rendered virtually impossible the direct management of demesnes relying heavily on wage labor. Hence, Ricardian forces strengthened the negotiating power of peasants who were faced with the prospect of deeper and more permanent gains by challenging the institutional structure of feudalism; as a result, the agrarian 'relations of production,' the interactions between urban centers and agrarian producers, and the relationships between states *vis-à-vis* aristocratic elites and peasants, all came into question. Multiple instances of the so-called feudal reaction, dynastic infighting, and civil wars were the inevitable outcomes. The balance of power at the regional level ultimately determined how these conflicts played out. In some parts of Europe (e.g., Central Europe and Russia) ruling elites were successful in defending (and eventually augmenting) their prerogatives, while in others the conflict was either protracted but eventually unsuccessful for the elite class (e.g., Catalonia) or fairly minimal (e.g., England) leading to a decline of overall extractions and tenurial arrangements moving away from customary towards contractual forms.[56] In the long-run these transformations highlighted two radically different paths to modernity.

NOTES

1. The choice of topics in terms of presenting a synthesis of the evidence and, even more so, the interpretation of it, reflects exclusively normative preferences of the editor and is in no way binding to the authors of individual papers. The review of the evidence draws from material cited in the chapters of this volume; citations are provided whenever extra sources are utilized.
2. According to Epstein, the Florentine state had a population density of 60–66 persons/km^2; see S. R. Epstein, "Cities, Regions and the Late Medieval Crisis: Sicily and Tuscany Compared," *Past and Present* 130:1 (1991): 16.
3. It is remarkable, however, that even this low figure compared favorably with population densities in parts of Europe not included in Group A (see below).
4. Many others formed substantial urban conglomerations right below them. By using the threshold of over 10,000 inhabitants, Britnell estimated that there were 32–39 of them in 1300. In contrast, only 13 towns achieved this status in England, whereas London's population was only c. 70,000 souls. R. Britnell, "England and Italy in the Early Fourteenth Century: The Economic Contrasts," *Transactions of the Royal Historical Society*, 5th series, 39 (1989) 168–169; idem, "Markets and Incentives: Common Themes and Regional Variations," in *Agriculture and Rural Society after the Black Death: Common Themes and Regional Variations,* eds. C. Dodds and R. Britnell. (Hartfield, UK: University of Hertfordshire Press, 2008) 5.
5. A. Laiou, "The Byzantine Economy: An Overview," in *The Economic History of Byzantium, from the Seventh Through the Fifteenth Century,* vol. 3, ed. idem. (Washington DC: Dumbarton Oaks, 2002) 1,155; R. Brenner, "The

Low Countries in the Transition to Capitalism," in *Peasants into Farmers? The Transformation of Rural Society in the Low Countries (Middle Ages–19th century) in Light of the Brenner Debate,* eds. P. Hoppenbrowers and Jan Luiten van Zanden. (Turnhout: Brepols, 2001) 313; Bas van Bavel, *Manors and Markets: Economy and Society in the Low Countries, 500–1600.* (Oxford: Oxford University Press, 2010) 101, 281–282.

6. In Dauphine 75 percent of the tenants held less than two hectares of land; in Hainault, 60 percent held less than one hectare. Most of the French data cited in this paragraph come from the work of Carpentier and Le Mene (see Grantham's chapter) and are summarized in Peter Turchin and Sergey A. Nefedov, *Secular Cycles* (Princeton and Oxford: Princeton University Press, 2009), 118–119.
7. Bois' work on Normandy concluded that half of the peasantry held plots below the subsistence threshold; G. Bois, *The Crisis of Feudalism: Economy and Society in Eastern Normandy c. 1300–1550* (Cambridge and New York: Cambridge University Press, 1984), 162–163. Note, however, that Grantham believes that two hectares (c. 5 acres) may have been sufficient in feeding a family (see his chapter in this book).
8. For Italy, see Britnell, "England and Italy in the Early Fourteenth Century"; for the Low Countries, see van Bavel, *Manors and Markets*, 244.
9. J. van Zanden "A Third Road to Capitalism? Proto-industrialization and the Moderate Nature of the Late Medieval Crisis in Flanders and Holland, 1350–1550," in *Peasants into Farmers? The Transformation of Rural Society in the Low Countries (Middle Ages–19th century) in Light of the Brenner Debate,* eds. P. Hoppenbrowers, and Jan Luiten van Zanden. (Turnhout: Brepols, 2001); Erik Thoen, "A 'Commercial Survival Economy' in Evolution. The Flemish Countryside and the Transition to Capitalism (Middle Ages–19th Century)." In *Peasants into Farmers? The Transformation of Rural Society in the Low Countries (Middle Ages–19th Century) in Light of the Brenner Debate*, eds. P. Hoppenbrowers and Jan Luiten van Zanden. (Turnhout: Brepols, 2001), 111–119; van Bavel, *Manors and Markets*, 247, 331.
10. Turchin and Nefedov, *Secular Cycles*, 117.
11. It is important to stress, however, that edaphic and climatic conditions also played a major role in this regard.
12. Erik Thoen, "The Birth of 'the Flemish Husbandry': Agricultural Technology in Medieval Flanders," in *Medieval Farming and Technology: The Impact of Agricultural Change in North-west Europe in the Middle Ages*, eds. G. Astil and J. L. Langdon. (Leiden and New York: Brill, 1997); idem, "A 'Commercial-Survival Economy' in Evolution," 105–106; van Bavel, *Manors and Markets*, 136–141; idem, "Arable Yields and Total Arable Output in the Netherlands from the Late Middle Ages to the Mid-19th Century," in *Land Productivity and Agro-systems in the North Sea Area (Middle Ages–20th century), Elements for Comparison*, eds. Bas J. P. van Bavel and Erik Thoen. (Turnhout: Brepols, 1999) 106; Guy DeJongh and Erik Thoen, "Arable Productivity in Flanders and the Former Territory of Belgium in a Long-run Perspective (from the Middle Ages to the End of the Ancien Regime)," in *Land Productivity and Agro-systems in the North Sea Area (Middle Ages–20th century), Elements for Comparison*, eds. Bas J. P. van Bavel and Erik Thoen. (Turnhout: Brepols, 1999) 34–38.
13. In terms of the diversification of implements, being closely linked elements of an interrelated technological matrix, Myrdal's paper provides a particularly detailed account. His account refers to Scandinavia but similar variations existed throughout the continent.

14. Yield per seed data are less reliable despite their greater frequency. If a farmer, for instance, increases the quantity of his seed in equal increments, the law of diminishing returns will result in total yields increasing at a diminishing rate which will translate to declining yields per seed but increasing yields per acre (or hectare). But, whatever their value, yields per seed of 4–5:1, depending on the crop, was the norm in England and Italy, whereas there is some debate as to whether Byzantium reached these levels. For evidence on yields in the Low Countries, see DeJongh and Thoen, "Arable productivity in Flanders," 39–45; Gérard Béaur, "From the North Sea to Berry and Lorraine: Land Productivity in Northern France, 13th–19th Centuries," in *Land Productivity and Agro-systems in the North Sea Area (Middle Ages–20th century), Elements for Comparison*, eds. Bas J. P. van Bavel and Erik Thoen. (Turnhout: Brepols, 1999), 140–141; van Bavel, "Arable yields," 89–90, 102.
15. Epstein has noted significant variations within Italy with wheat yields in Sicily giving a ratio of 10:1 whereas in Tuscany they stood at 4–5:1; see his "Cities, Regions and the Late Medieval Crisis," 35, 39. It should also be borne in mind that the economies of Italy and Byzantium could achieve diversification through the planting of vineyards, olive trees, and fruit trees. But the lack of adequate grain supplies from the hinterland of urban centers did force cities such as Florence, Genoa, and Venice (Milan was an exception) to rely on long-distance trade for such supplies; see Britnell, "England and Italy in the Early Fourteenth Century," 173–176.
16. van Bavel, *Manors and Markets*, 330.
17. See also P. Hoppenbrowers and Jan Luiten van Zanden, "Restyling the Transition from Feudalism to Capitalism: Some Critical Reflections on the Brenner Thesis," in *Peasants into Farmers? The Transformation of Rural Society in the Low Countries (Middle Ages–19th century) in Light of the Brenner Debate,* eds. idem. (Turnhout: Brepols, 2001) 33.
18. Britnell, "England and Italy in the Early Fourteenth Century," 171–172.
19. Thoen, "The Birth of 'the Flemish Husbandry'"; idem, "A 'Commercial Survival Economy' in Evolution," 108, 113, 124–136, 141–142; Brenner, "The Low Countries in the Transition to Capitalism," 308–310, 320–321; van Bavel, *Manors and Markets*, 86–93, 205–213, 242–243.
20. Spain is an odd member of this group in the sense that if it was not for the expulsion of Muslim peasants it may have been classified in Group A. The forced exodus of Muslims created an extraordinary migratory flow towards its southern territories, causing an economic disequilibrium in parts of the north, evident by the depopulation of villages.
21. Population density in Kievan Rus is hard to quantify but it was the only European territory that might have witnessed an absolute decline of its population. At the beginning of the thirteenth century it was subdivided into a number of loosely connected principalities, each vying for domination of the capital Kiev. This political fragmentation of political power was a decisive factor for the defeat by the Mongol armies (1237–40) which led to eliminating 10 percent of the population with further loses in the next quarter century due to subsequent warfare episodes; relative peace returned only after the 1320s when population started showing signs of recovery.
22. It is certain that poor climatic and edaphic conditions played a decisive role and thus the size of holding necessary to ensure subsistence was certainly larger than elsewhere. Martin notes the infertility of Russian lands (with the exception of a stretch in the Volga-Oka region) compounded by the fact that frost-free days were only four months during the year. But the figures on holding sizes, cited in Turchin and Nefedov, *Secular Cycles*, 242–243, are

so high that is virtually certain that Russian peasants did not face yet the specter of land scarcity.

23. In the case of Scandinavia, marling appeared only after the Black Death whereas the earliest we can date the practice of convertible husbandry is the seventeenth century.
24. The bulk of the evidence comes from yields per seed. The norm was 4–5:1, depending on the crop, in Spain and Scandinavia. Russian rates which somewhat exceeded the 3:1 mark have been suggested on the basis of the earliest possible evidence coming from the sixteenth century; given the fact that there were recorded in lands plowed for centuries, such rates may have been higher in the pre-plague period, particularly with the use of the slash-and-burn method which gave a short lived boost in yields. Places like Hungary trailed far behind with rates in the range of 2:1.
25. One may be tempted to put in the same basket Group B with the A-PROGS in terms of the lightness of seigneurial obligations. While that would be correct, there is an important distinction that should be kept in mind. In the case of A-PROGS the lightness of obligations was the result of successfully thwarting, often through violent conflicts (e.g., Flanders), the attempts of ruling elites to advance their prerogatives towards extractions. In contrast, by and large, such attempts were limited and more timid by this time (1300) in Group B.
26. M. Malowist, "The Problem of the Inequality of Economic Development in Europe in the Later Middle Ages," *Economic History Review* 19 (1966): 18–19.
27. The same result on product prices would have ensued even with a stagnant level of land productivity. In the case of medieval France there is a lack of systematic data on wages but there is information on the nominal wages of soldiers; despite their increase there is clearly a decline in real terms. See Turchin and Nefedov, *Secular Cycles*, 117.
28. Ibid., 117, 121.
29. Byzantine merchants (and bankers) were a powerful group prior to 1204, especially in Constantinople, extending their activities both to interregional and international markets; they were both in open competition with their Italian counterparts who practiced their trades on an equal footing in Byzantine territories due to a very liberal institutional environment towards foreign economic agents. But the Fourth Crusade (1204) changed all that. During the political fragmentation of the thirteenth century, interregional trade continued to play an integrative role but it became an activity increasingly under the control of Italian merchants whose dominance became even more apparent during the next century. The output of previously thriving industries (e.g., glass, pottery, and silk) either diminished (e.g., the glass industry decayed due to Venetian imports) or became integrated to the Italian commercial network. Byzantium was increasingly turning into an exporter of raw materials and an importer of finished goods and hence, if (according to one estimate) its non-agricultural output was a quarter of its total wealth during the twelfth century, most likely it declined after the Fourth Crusade. In summarizing these developments, Laiou notes that "a vigorous economy of exchange was important in integrating the Byzantine economy. However, the integration took place into a larger system, which by its very nature limited and circumscribed the role of the Byzantines, since the initiative and the important mechanism lay outside their control. As a result, the Byzantine economy of the second half of the thirteenth century and the first half of the fourteenth was vulnerable not only to its own, internal dynamic, but also to the limitations, crises, and inefficiencies of other states and economies";

"The Byzantine Economy," 1,160. For comments on the evolution of prices and other symptoms of the crisis, see pp. 1,152–1,159.

30. Turchin and Nefedov, *Secular Cycles*; the two quotes in this paragraph are from pages 4 and 22 respectively.
31. Brenner has argued that the propensity to have many children, thereby leading to population growth, was the result of the desire to achieve social insurance (i.e., parents being taken care of at old age) and in order to augment the family labor force. I am highly skeptical of the latter reason in light of my own analysis of peasants' budgets and their annual routine, which reveals that the size of families tended to overshoot beyond the point that would match familial labor supply with the labor needs of peasant holdings. Most importantly, I fail to appreciate how the aforementioned reasons tie to his overarching statement that socio-property relations functioned as the prism which other variables refracted through. See Brenner, "The Low Countries in the Transition to Capitalism," 282, 285.
32. The chapters of this volume referring to the A-LAGS do not focus on this tension because, among other reasons, it relates to events that fall largely prior to the period we examine. But, in the form of some tentative hypotheses, one may argue that regional variations in the degrees of feudalization across Europe were shaped by the following factors: soil fertility played a role with more fertile regions tending to attract a stronger manorial element; whether land reclamation was undertaken through the initiative of lords or peasants; local population densities during the reclamation process, with low population densities leading usually to liberal tenurial conditions as a result of efforts on the part of lords to attract new settlers; and the forms of peasant resistance to the imposition of seigneurial obligations manifesting in disobedience, flight from manors, and (mostly minor) rebellions.
33. The proportion of dues channeled towards feudal states vs. local landlords varied within this group and despite the fact that the functional characteristics of states were different, in the end the effect of such extractions on unproductive forms of disposal and on limiting technological diffusion was the same.
34. The explanation of the Neo-Malthusian argument on the issue of limited technological diffusion based on the lack of investment opportunities and the cultural values of the ruling class is inadequate. We neither have to revert to non-economic explanations nor is it accurate that investment opportunities were limited since the most productive estates achieved this status by investing heavily on labor and capital inputs.
35. I do believe, however, that Marxist historiography has failed to produce a strong empirical record in this regard. It has largely relied on unsystematic references drawn from secondary literature as opposed to engaging in primary research and the use of a quantitative methodology in order to establish the correlation (and causation) between differences in seigneurial revenue sources and their record on investment, technological choices, and productivity levels.
36. While the Ricardian framework points towards the option of raising output both through the intensive and extensive margins of cultivation, it fails to spell out the conditions under which one option is chosen over another. Regional differences on these choices, on the other hand, become clear once the institutional factor is taken into account.
37. Cited by Brenner, "The Low Countries in the Transition to Capitalism," 308; see also Thoen, "A 'Commercial Survival Economy' in Evolution."
38. High yields among peasant holdings in the Low Countries are often attributed to high labor inputs. While this was certainly a contributory factor,

the fact that such high yields were not duplicated in other densely populated areas (e.g., the immediate vicinity of London) implies that field systems played a prominent role and thus the nature of institutions was crucial.

39. Skeletal remains from Maastricht burial sites reveal that class status made a difference in heights, which reflect nutritional levels, high status men averaging 1.75–1.80m vs. 1.69–1.71m for those of low status. Despite these differences, the figures suggest a high calorific intake even for the low strata of the population; see van Bavel, *Manors and Markets*, 142–143, 279.
40. My references to land and labor productivity are meant in a relative sense, i.e., relative to the natural fertility of soils defined by ecological endowments. Northern Italian yields were low compared to northern European regions of A-PROGS but the former had to deal with a much more challenging terrain compared to the latter's soils of exceptional fertility.
41. R. Britnell, "The Towns of England and Italy in the Early Fourteenth Century," *Economic History Review*, 2nd series, 44 (1991).
42. This is a thesis that finds adherents even among non-Marxist historians. Hoppenbrowers and van Zanden, for instance, point out that "where commercialization did not make headway, as in large parts of Western Europe during the late medieval and early modern periods, this was probably due to the increased existence of inefficient institutions . . . related to 'feudal' surplus-extraction based on extra-economic coercion"; see their "Restyling the Transition from Feudalism to Capitalism," 36.
43. Thoen, "The Birth of 'the Flemish Husbandry"'; P. Hoppenbrowers, "Mapping an Unexplored Field: The Brenner Debate and the Case of Holland," in *Peasants into Farmers? The Transformation of Rural Society in the Low Countries (Middle Ages–19th century) in Light of the Brenner Debate,* eds. P. Hoppenbrowers, and Jan Luiten van Zanden. (Turnhout: Brepols, 2001): 42–43.
44. Van Bavel, *Manors and Markets*, 67.
45. Ibid. 384. This point is echoed by Epstein: "The evidence appears to contradict the common hypothesis that more urbanized societies will perform faster thanks to economies of scale and higher concentrations of human capital"; see S. R. Epstein, Introduction to *Town and Country in Europe, 1300–1800*, by idem. (Cambridge and New York: Cambridge University Press, 2001), 10.
46. van Bavel, *Manors and Markets*, 285; idem. "People and Land: Rural Population Developments and Property Structures in the Low Countries, c. 1300–c. 1600," *Continuity and Change* 17 (2002).
47. van Bavel, *Manors and Markets,* 384.
48. See B. M. S. Campbell, "Nature as a Historical Protagonist: Environment and Society in Pre-industrial England," *Economic History Review* 63, 2 (2010).
49. van Zanden, "A Third Road to Capitalism?"; Thoen, "A 'Commercial Survival Economy' in Evolution," 113–115; van Bavel, *Manors and Markets*, 279–280.
50. Turchin and Nefedov, *Secular Cycles*, 242–243.
51. The population of Ypres witnessed a significant decline but the overall urbanization rate in the Low Countries was not affected much. The respective rate in Holland was 40 percent during the fifteenth century at a time when a strong cottage industry was also flourishing. See J. De Vries, "The Transition to Capitalism in a Land Without Feudalism," in *Peasants into Farmers? The Transformation of Rural Society in the Low Countries (Middle Ages–19th Century) in Light of the Brenner Debate*, eds. P. Hoppenbrowers and Jan Luiten van Zanden. (Turnhout: Brepols, 2001), 80–81; and van Zanden, "A

Third Road to Capitalism?". Differences in the decline of urbanization rates brought about some mild, as opposed to radical, realignments in terms of how regions ranked in the respective scale: by 1500 the Low Countries surpassed Italy at the top, followed by Spain, England, and France; in contrast, Central Europe and Scandinavia were at the bottom of the list. See Epstein, "Introduction," 10 (Table 1.1).

52. Malanima attributes the absolute and relative decline in the productivity of the urban sector during the period 1370–1470 mainly to a fall in the demand for luxury goods. While he acknowledges a rising demand per capita for mid-quality goods (especially textiles) on the part of the lower classes, the demand for luxury goods diminished significantly both because the number of wealthy buyers and their incomes declined; but also because transaction costs increased due to the lower volume of sales and the growing geographical sparseness of this clientele. These elaborations were made through personal communication.
53. More drastic improvement has been documented for English manors following convertible husbandry but this group remained a distinct minority during the post-plague period.
54. The reader should be reminded that raw figures on yields per acre/hectare do not always correspond with arable productivity. As an illustration, yields in the vicinity of Bruges were about half of those in the Brussels area and, especially, Lille; but the higher yields were often recorded in farms with longer fallows and thus the productivity gap was narrower. See DeJongh and Thoen, "Arable Productivity in Flanders," 39–45; van Bavel, "Arable yields", 89–90, 102; idem. "A Valuation of Arable Productivity in the Central Part of the Dutch River Area, c. 1360–c. 1570," in *Land Productivity and Agro-systems in the North Sea Area (Middle Ages–20th century), Elements for Comparison*, eds. Bas J. P. Van Bavel and Erik Thoen. (Turnhout: Brepols, 1999) 303; Béaur, "From the North Sea to Berry and Lorraine," 140–141. In terms of other countries, the record is very limited (or non-existent) and it refers to yields per seed which, as was noted previously, are defective indicators of productivity. Most importantly, whatever records do exist they fail to form uniform patterns; for instance, Mysliwski's figures show improvement in the cases of Hungary and Poland; the few surviving data cited by Rodriguez indicate stationary levels of yields per seed, whereas Myrdal speculates that productivity may have declined.
55. The phrase is taken from an earlier draft of his chapter.
56. Even in these latter cases, however, the pattern of land ownership remained fairly stable.

BIBLIOGRAPHY

Astill, G. and J. L. Langdon, eds. *Medieval Farming and Technology: The Impact of Agricultural Change in North-west Europe in the Middle Ages*. Leiden and New York: Brill, 1997.

Béaur, G. "From the North Sea to Berry and Lorraine: Land Productivity in Northern France, 13th–19th Centuries," in *Land Productivity and Agro-systems in the North Sea Area (Middle Ages-20th century), Elements for Comparison*, edited by B. J. P. van Bavel and E. Thoen, 136–167. Turnhout: Brepols, 1999.

Bois, G. *The Crisis of Feudalism: Economy and Society in Eastern Normandy c. 1300–1550*. Cambridge and New York: Cambridge University Press, 1984.

Brenner, R. "The Low Countries in the Transition to Capitalism," in *Peasants into Farmers? The Transformation of Rural Society in the Low Countries (Middle Ages-19th century) in Light of the Brenner Debate*, edited by P. Hoppenbrowers, and J. van Zanden, 275–338. Turnhout: Brepols, 2001.

Britnell, R. "England and Italy in the Early Fourteenth Century: The Economic Contrasts." *Transactions of the Royal Historical Society*, 5th series, 39 (1989): 167–183.

Britnell, R. "The Towns of England and Italy in the Early Fourteenth Century." *Economic History Review*, 2nd series, 44 (1991): 21–35.

Britnell, R. "Markets and Incentives: Common Themes and Regional Variations," in *Agriculture and Rural Society after the Black Death: Common Themes and Regional Variations*, edited by C. Dodds and R. Britnell, 3–19. Hartfield, UK: University of Hertfordshire Press, 2008.

Campbell, B. M. S. "Nature as a Historical Protagonist: Environment and Society in Pre-industrial England." *Economic History Review* 63, 2 (2010): 281–314.

DeJongh, G. and E. Thoen. "Arable Productivity in Flanders and the Former Territory of Belgium in a Long-run Perspective (from the Middle Ages to the End of the Ancien Regime)," in *Land Productivity and Agro-systems in the North Sea Area (Middle Ages–20th century), Elements for Comparison*, edited by B. J. P. van Bavel and E. Thoen, 30–64. Turnhout: Brepols, 1999.

De Vries, J. "The Transition to Capitalism in a Land Without Feudalism," in *Peasants into Farmers? The Transformation of Rural Society in the Low Countries (Middle Ages–19th Century) in Light of the Brenner Debate*, edited by P. Hoppenbrowers and J. van Zanden, 67–84. Turnhout: Brepols, 2001.

Dodds, C. and R. Britnell, eds. *Agriculture and Rural Society After the Black Death: Common Themes and Regional Variations*. Hartfield, UK: University of Hertfordshire Press, 2008.

Epstein, S. R. "Cities, Regions and the Late Medieval Crisis: Sicily and Tuscany Compared." *Past and Present* 130, 1 (1991): 3–50.

Epstein, S. R. Introduction to *Town and Country in Europe, 1300–1800*, by idem, 1–29. Cambridge and New York: Cambridge University Press, 2001.

Hoppenbrowers, P. "Mapping an Unexplored Field: The Brenner Debate and the Case of Holland," in *Peasants into Farmers? The Transformation of Rural Society in the Low Countries (Middle Ages–19th century) in Light of the Brenner Debate*, edited by P. Hoppenbrowers and J. van Zanden, 41–66. Turnhout: Brepols, 2001.

Hoppenbrowers, P. and J. van Zanden. "Restyling the Transition from Feudalism to Capitalism: Some Critical Reflections on the Brenner Thesis," in *Peasants into Farmers? The Transformation of Rural Society in the Low Countries (Middle Ages–19th century) in Light of the Brenner Debate*, edited by P. Hoppenbrowers and J. van Zanden, 19–40. Turnhout: Brepols, 2001.

Hoppenbrowers, P., and J. van Zanden. *Peasants into Farmers? The Transformation of Rural Society in the Low Countries (Middle Ages–19th Century) in Light of the Brenner Debate*. Turnhout: Brepols, 2001.

Laiou, A. "The Byzantine Economy: An Overview," in *The Economic History of Byzantium, from the Seventh through the Fifteenth Century*, vol. 3, edited by A. Laiou, 1,145–1,164. Washington, DC: Dumbarton Oaks, 2002.

Laiou A., ed. *The Economic History of Byzantium, from the Seventh Through the Fifteenth Century*, 3 vols. Washington DC: Dumbarton Oaks, 2002.

Malowist, M. "The Problem of the Inequality of Economic Development in Europe in the Later Middle Ages." *Economic History Review* 19 (1966): 15–28.

Thoen, E. "The Birth of 'the Flemish Husbandry': Agricultural Technology in Medieval Flanders," in *Medieval Farming and Technology: The Impact of Agricultural Change in North-west Europe in the Middle Ages*, edited by G. Astil and J. L. Langdon, 69–88. Leiden and New York: Brill, 1997.

Thoen, E. "A 'Commercial Survival Economy' in Evolution. The Flemish Countryside and the Transition to Capitalism (Middle Ages–19th century)," in *Peasants into Farmers? The Transformation of Rural Society in the Low Countries (Middle Ages–19th Century) in Light of the Brenner Debate*, edited by P. Hoppenbrowers and J. van Zanden, 102–157. Turnhout: Brepols, 2001.

Turchin, P. and S. A. Nefedov, *Secular Cycles*. Princeton and Oxford: Princeton University Press, 2009.

van Bavel, B. J. P. "Arable Yields and Total Arable Output in the Netherlands from the Late Middle Ages to the Mid–19th Century," in *Land Productivity and Agro-systems in the North Sea Area (Middle Ages–20th century), Elements for Comparison*, edited by B. J. P. van Bavel and E. Thoen, 85–112. Turnhout: Brepols, 1999.

van Bavel, B. J. P. "A Valuation of Arable Productivity in the Central Part of the Dutch River Area, c. 1360–c. 1570," in *Land Productivity and Agro-systems in the North Sea Area (Middle Ages–20th century), Elements for Comparison*, edited by B. J. P. Van Bavel and E. Thoen, 297–309. Turnhout: Brepols, 1999.

van Bavel, B. J. P. "People and Land: Rural Population Developments and Property Structures in the Low Countries, c. 1300-c. 1600." *Continuity and Change*, 17 (2002): 9–37.

van Bavel, B. J. P. *Manors and Markets: Economy and Society in the Low Countries, 500–1600*. Oxford: Oxford University Press, 2010.

van Bavel, B. J. P., and E. Thoen, eds. *Land Productivity and Agro-systems in the North Sea Area (Middle Ages–20th Century), Elements for Comparison*. Turnhout: Brepols, 1999.

van Zanden, J. "A Third Road to Capitalism? Proto-industrialization and the Moderate Nature of the Late Medieval Crisis in Flanders and Holland, 1350–1550," in *Peasants into Farmers? The Transformation of Rural Society in the Low Countries (Middle Ages–19th century) in Light of the Brenner Debate*, 85–101. Turnhout: Brepols, 2001.

Contributors

George Grantham, Professor Emeritus, Department of Economics, McGill University. Grantham is studying the development of the French economy from the Middle Ages to the nineteenth century, particularly the nature of agricultural change and the interactions between agricultural and industrial growth. He is the co-editor of two books and over 30 articles published, among others, in the *European Review of Economic History*, *Annales*, *Economic History Review*, and *Journal of Economic History*. He has received prizes and awards both from the American Economic History Association and Cliometrics Society, among others.

Harry Kitsikopoulos, Clinical Professor, Department of Economics, NYU. Kitsikopoulos has published about a dozen articles on the economy of medieval England, among others, in the *Journal of Economic History*, *Economic History Review*, and *Agricultural History Review*. He has held fellowships from the NEH and the Smithsonian.

Paolo Malanima, Professor of Economic History in Magna Graecia University, Catanzaro, and currently Director of the Institute of Studies on Mediterranean Societies (National Research Council, Italy) in Naples. He is the author of several books and articles both in collections of essays and academic journals such as the *Economic History Review* and the *European Review of Economic History*. His main fields of research are: urbanization, prices and incomes, pre-modern GDP growth, income distribution, energy consumption, Italian economic history, and global history.

Janet Martin, Professor, Department of History, University of Miami. Martin has written dozens of articles on medieval and early modern Russian history as well as two books: Treasure of the Land of Darkness: The Fur Trade and its Significance for Medieval Russia, (Cambridge 1986; paperback edition, 2004), and Medieval Russia, 988–1584 (Cambridge 1995; 2nd ed., Cambridge 2007). Dr. Martin is currently conducting research on landholding and the centralization of power in sixteenth century Russia.

Janken Myrdal, Professor of Economic and Agrarian History, Swedish University of Agricultural Sciences, Uppsala, Sweden. Myrdal has written several books and articles, specializing in the medieval history of Scandinavia and the agricultural history of Sweden. He was the main editor of the five-volume *The Agrarian History of Sweden* (in Swedish), and wrote the volume on the Middle Ages and the early modern period.

Grzegorz Myśliwski, Assistant Professor at the Institute of History, Department of History, Warsaw University, Poland. Mysliwski has several publications (in Polish, English, and German) focusing on medieval mentality, society, and long-distance trade, especially between the twelfth and the mid-sixteenth centuries. He has written on Poland and other central European countries and their relations with the Holy Roman Empire, North Italy, and Flanders.

Ana Rodríguez, Scientific Researcher in Medieval History at the Spanish High Council for Scientific Research (CCHS-CSIC). Rodriguez is interested in power structures in the Hispanic Kingdoms, dealing in particular with the socialization and legitimization of political power and the interaction between royal and ecclesiastical groups and local communities in Castile and Leon. She is the author (or co-author) of four books, and has published about 30 articles in Spanish and international journals.

Kostis Smyrlis, Assistant Professor, Department of History, NYU. Smyrlis is the author of a book and several articles dealing with the middle and late Byzantine economy and institutions. He is co-editor of the series *Archives de l'Athos,* which publishes the medieval documents kept in the monasteries of Mount Athos in Greece.

Index